COLLABORATIVE NETWORKS AND THEIR BREEDING ENVIRONMENTS

IFIP – The International Federation for Information Processing

IFIP was founded in 1960 under the auspices of UNESCO, following the First World Computer Congress held in Paris the previous year. An umbrella organization for societies working in information processing, IFIP's aim is two-fold: to support information processing within its member countries and to encourage technology transfer to developing nations. As its mission statement clearly states,

> *IFIP's mission is to be the leading, truly international, apolitical organization which encourages and assists in the development, exploitation and application of information technology for the benefit of all people.*

IFIP is a non-profitmaking organization, run almost solely by 2500 volunteers. It operates through a number of technical committees, which organize events and publications. IFIP's events range from an international congress to local seminars, but the most important are:

- The IFIP World Computer Congress, held every second year;
- Open conferences;
- Working conferences.

The flagship event is the IFIP World Computer Congress, at which both invited and contributed papers are presented. Contributed papers are rigorously refereed and the rejection rate is high.

As with the Congress, participation in the open conferences is open to all and papers may be invited or submitted. Again, submitted papers are stringently refereed.

The working conferences are structured differently. They are usually run by a working group and attendance is small and by invitation only. Their purpose is to create an atmosphere conducive to innovation and development. Refereeing is less rigorous and papers are subjected to extensive group discussion.

Publications arising from IFIP events vary. The papers presented at the IFIP World Computer Congress and at open conferences are published as conference proceedings, while the results of the working conferences are often published as collections of selected and edited papers.

Any national society whose primary activity is in information may apply to become a full member of IFIP, although full membership is restricted to one society per country. Full members are entitled to vote at the annual General Assembly, National societies preferring a less committed involvement may apply for associate or corresponding membership. Associate members enjoy the same benefits as full members, but without voting rights. Corresponding members are not represented in IFIP bodies. Affiliated membership is open to non-national societies, and individual and honorary membership schemes are also offered.

COLLABORATIVE NETWORKS AND THEIR BREEDING ENVIRONMENTS

IFIP TC5 WG 5.5 Sixth IFIP Working Conference on VIRTUAL ENTERPRISES, 26-28 September, 2005, Valencia, Spain

Edited by

Luis M. Camarinha-Matos
New University of Lisbon
Portugal

Hamideh Afsarmanesh
University of Amsterdam
The Netherlands

Angel Ortiz
Polytechnic University of Valencia
Spain

Springer

Library of Congress Cataloging-in-Publication Data

A C.I.P. Catalogue record for this book is available from the Library of Congress.

Collaborative Networks and Their Breeding Environments, Edited by Luis M. Camarinha-Matos, Hamideh Afsarmanesh and Angel Ortiz

p.cm. (The International Federation for Information Processing)

ISBN-10: (HB) 0-387-28259-9
ISBN-13: (HB) 978-0387-28259-6
Printed on acid-free paper.

Printed in the United States of America.

9 8 7 6 5 4 3 2 1 SPIN 11539094 (HC)
springeronline.com

TABLE OF CONTENTS

TECHNICAL SPONSORS:

ifip

IFIP WG 5.5 COVE
Co-Operation infrastructure for Virtual Enterprises and electronic business

ECOLEAD
European Collaborative Networked Organizations Leadership Initiative
IST IP 506958 project

ORGANIZATIONAL CO-SPONSORS

UNIVERSITAT POLITÈCNICA DE VALÈNCIA

New University of Lisbon

UNINOVA

UNIVERSITEIT VAN AMSTERDAM

This work has been partially funded by The Ministerio de Educación y Ciencia of Spanish Govern under grant DPI2004-22263-E and the Polytechnic University of Valencia under grant PPI-04-05."

PRO-VE'05 – 6th IFIP Working Conference on VIRTUAL ENTERPRISES

Valencia, Spain, 26-28 September 2005

Conference Chair: Dr. Hamideh Afsarmanesh (NL)
Program Chair: Prof. Luis M. Camarinha-Matos (PT)
Organization Chair: Prof. Angel Ortiz (ES)
Associated events Chair: Prof. Ricardo Rabelo (BR)

REFEREES FROM THE PROGRAMME COMMITTEE

Hamideh Afsarmanesh (NL)
Dimitris Assimakopoulos (FR)
Américo Azevedo (PT)
Eoin Banahan (UK)
José Barata (PT)
Peter Bernus (AU)
Peter Bertok (AU)
Kirsimarja Blomqvist (FI)
Luis M. Camarinha-Matos (P)
Wojciech Cellary (PL)
Prasun Dewan (US)
Frans M. van Eijnatten (NL)
Jens Eschenbaecher (DE)
João Pinto Ferreira (PT)
Joaquim Filipe (PT)
Myrna Flores (CH)
Cesar Garita (CR)
Ted Goranson (US)
Fernando Guerrero (ES)
Angappa Gunasekaran (US)
Tarek Hassan (UK)
Tomasz Janowski (PL)
Toshiya Kaihara (JP)
Alexandra Klen (BR)
Ned Kock (US)
Adamantios Koumpis (GR)
George Kovacs (HU)
Nada Lavrac (SI)
Geleyn Meijer (NL)
José M. Mendonça (PT)
Arturo Molina (MX)
Ugo Negretto (DE)
Laszlo Nemes (AU)
Shimon Y Nof (US)
Ovidiu Noran (AU)
Gus Olling (US)
Martin Ollus (FI)
Angel Ortiz (ES)
Luis Osório (PT)
Sofia Pinto (PT)
Michel Pouly (CH)
Kenneth Preiss (IL)
Goran Putnik (PT)
Ricardo Rabelo (BR)
Bob Roberts (UK)
Rainer Ruggaber (DE)
Roberto Santoro (IT)
Hans Schaffers (NL)
Weiming Shen (CA)
Amit Sheth (US)
António L. Soares (PT)
Jorge P. Sousa (PT)
Klaus-Dieter Thoben (DE)
Alain Zarli (FR)

FOREWORD

Collaborative networks – towards consolidation

Progress in collaborative networks continues showing a growing number of manifestations including virtual organizations, virtual enterprises, dynamic supply chains, professional virtual communities, collaborative virtual laboratories, etc. with a wide spectrum of application domains. The realization that all these collaborative forms represent variations of a more general paradigm has lead to their consolidation into ***Collaborative Networks*** *(CN) as a new scientific discipline.*

Contributions to CN coming from multiple reference disciplines have been extensively investigated. In fact developments in CN have benefited from contributions of multiple areas, namely computer science, computer engineering, communications and networking, management, economy, social sciences, law and ethics, etc. Furthermore, some theories and paradigms defined elsewhere have been suggested by several research groups as promising tools to help define and characterize emerging collaborative organizational forms. Although still at the beginning of a long way to go, there is a growing awareness in the research and academic world, for the need to establish a stronger ***theoretical foundation*** *for this new discipline and a number of recent works are contributing to this goal.*

From a utilitarian perspective, agility has been pointed out as one of the most appealing characteristics of collaborative networks to face the challenges of a fast changing socio-economic context. However, during last years it became more evident that finding the right partners and establishing the necessary preconditions for starting an effective collaboration process are both costly and time consuming activities, and therefore an inhibitor of the aimed agility. Among others, obstacles include lack of information (e.g. non-availability of catalogs with normalized profiles of organizations) and lack of preparedness of organizations to join the collaborative process. Overcoming the mismatches resulted from the heterogeneity of potential partners (e.g. differences in infrastructures, corporate culture, methods of work, and business practices) requires considerable investment. Building trust, a pre-requisite for any effective collaboration, is not straight forward and requires time. Therefore the effective creation of truly dynamic collaborative networks requires a proper context in which potential members are prepared to rapidly get engaged in collaborative processes. The concept of ***breeding environment*** *has thus emerged as an important facilitator for wider dissemination of collaborative networks and their practical materialization.*

PRO-VE represents a good synthesis of the work in this area, and plays an active role in the promotion of these activities. Being recognized as the most focused scientific /

technical conference on Collaborative Networks, PRO-VE continues offering the opportunity for the presentation and discussion of both the latest research developments and practical application case studies. Following the IFIP vision, PRO-VE offers a forum for collaboration and knowledge exchange among experts from different regions of the world.

This book includes the selected papers for the PRO-VE'05 conference, representing a comprehensive overview of recent advances in various domains and lines of development of collaborative networks. Of particular relevance are the topics of holistic approaches and breeding environments management, creation and management of virtual organizations and professional virtual communities, performance measurement and management, benefit analysis, trust management, process modeling and meta-modeling, ICT infrastructures and support services, legal issues, and case studies.

The PRO-VE'05 held in Valencia, Spain, continues the 6th event in a series of successful conferences of PRO-VE'99 (held in Porto, Portugal), PRO-VE 2000 (held in Florianopolis, Brazil), PRO-VE'02 (held in Sesimbra, Portugal), PRO-VE'03 (held in Lugano, Switzerland), and PRO-VE'04 (held in Toulouse, France).

We would like to thank all authors both from academia/research and industry for their contributions, as well as the dedication of the program committee members and other reviewers that helped with the selection of articles and contributed with valuable comments to improve the quality of the various chapters. As a result of this cooperative and highly distributed work we hope that the PRO-VE'05 book will become a valuable tool to all of those interested in advances and challenges of the collaborative networks.

The editors,

Luís M. Camarinha-Matos
Faculty of Sciences and Technology
New University of Lisbon, Portugal

Hamideh Afsarmanesh
Faculty of Sciences
University of Amsterdam, The Netherlands

Angel Ortiz
Research Centre for Production Engineering and Management
Polytechnic University of Valencia, Spain

PART 1

HOLISTIC APPROACHES TO COLLABORATIVE NETWORKS

1 ECOLEAD: A HOLISTIC APPROACH TO CREATION AND MANAGEMENT OF DYNAMIC VIRTUAL ORGANIZATIONS

Luis M. Camarinha-Matos [1], Hamideh Afsarmanesh [2], Martin Ollus [3]
[1] *New University of Lisbon / Uninova, PORTUGAL, cam@uninova.pt*
[2] *University of Amsterdam, THE NETHERLANDS, hamideh@science.uva.nl*
[3] *VTT Industrial Systems, FINLAND, martin.ollus@vtt.fi*

The wide dissemination and effective materialization of the foreseen benefits of dynamic virtual organizations require a holistic approach to understand, model, and develop the needed infrastructures and tools to support the full life cycle of this organizational paradigm. Under this scope, the ECOLEAD integrated project was launched with the aim of creating the necessary foundations and mechanisms for establishing an advanced network-based industry society. The main underlying concepts, approach and preliminary results of this ongoing initiative are briefly summarized.

1. INTRODUCTION

The notion of dynamic virtual organizations (VO) has raised high expectations in various application domains. Among the potential benefits of these collaborative networks, a number of possibilities have been vastly mentioned in the literature, including increased access to market opportunities, sharing risks, reducing costs, achieving business goals not achievable by a single organization, etc. The rapid formation of a VO, triggered by a business opportunity and specifically tailored to the requirements of that opportunity, is also pointed out as an expression of agility, a survival element in turbulent market scenarios.

Pursuing these expectations, during the last 10~15 years a large number of R&D projects tried to establish technological foundations as well as operating practices for the support of Virtual Enterprises /Virtual Organizations. This effort is particularly visible in Europe through the European Commission funded programs (e.g. ESPRIT, IST, INCO), but also in the USA and other geographical regions (Australia, Brazil, Mexico, Japan, to name a few). Programs such as IMS (Intelligent Manufacturing Systems) also supported various projects in this area involving organizations from various continents.

This trend has so far led to an extensive amount of empirical base knowledge that now needs to be leveraged. In addition to the identification of many required components, tools, and the base infrastructure functionalities, awareness is being built and partially studied, even in the traditional collaborative organizations, regarding the fundamental configuration and operational rules, as well as the behavioral patterns that emerge. Nevertheless we are still far from a wide dissemination and adoption of this paradigm. It is now urgent to consolidate and synthesize the existing knowledge, setting a sound foundation for the future research and development in this area.

In fact, these initiatives, together with practical realizations of many variations of virtual organizations, have generated a large amount of empiric knowledge that is however still disperse and fragmented. The IST VOSTER project represented an attempt to consolidate some of this existing knowledge [6]. More recently, in part as a result of initiatives such as the THINKcreative [4] and VOmap [3, 5] projects among others, it became evident that there is a need for investing on more fundamental research towards the creation of a sound theoretical foundation for VOs as well as a more holistic understanding of this paradigm. The ECOLEAD integrated project is an initiative in this direction which aims at creating the necessary foundations and mechanisms for establishing an advanced and network-based industry society.

2. ECOLEAD AND COLLABORATIVE NETWORKS

A large variety of organizational forms of collaboration have emerged during the last years as a result of the many socio-economic challenges faced by society and enabled by the new ICT developments. Advanced and highly integrated supply chains, virtual enterprises, virtual organizations, professional virtual communities, value constellations, virtual institutes, and collaborative virtual laboratories, represent only the tip of a major trend in which enterprises and professionals seek complementarities and joint activities to allow them participate in competitive business opportunities, in new markets and / or reaching scientific excellence for innovative developments. Similar trends can be found in the none-profit / social-oriented contexts, e.g. in incident management, time bank, elderly care networks, etc.) [4]. All these examples are manifestations of the more general concept of collaborative network.

A collaborative network (CN) is constituted by a variety of entities (e.g. organizations and individuals) that are largely autonomous, geographically distributed, and heterogeneous in terms of their: operating environment, culture, social capital and goals. Nevertheless these entities collaborate to better achieve common or compatible goals, and their interactions are supported by computer networks. Unlike other networks, in CN collaboration is an intentional property that derives from the shared belief that together the network members can achieve goals that would not be possible or would have a higher cost if attempted by them individually.

Collaborative networks of organizations provide a basis for competitiveness, world-excellence, and agility in turbulent market conditions. They have the potential to support SMEs in identifying and exploiting new business potential, boosting innovation, and increasing their knowledge. Networking of SMEs with large-scale enterprises also contributes to the success of the big companies in the global market. Reinforcing the effectiveness of collaborative networks, mostly based on SMEs, and creating the necessary conditions for making them an endogenous reality in the European industrial landscape, are key survival factors.

A key question is however, how to guarantee the basic requirements to enable such dynamism and agility for collaborative networks. Among others, the formation of any collaborative coalition depends on some base commonality among its members, including: sharing of common or compatible goals, possessing some level of mutual trust, having established some common or interoperable computer infrastructures, and having agreed on some common policies, codes for practice and value systems, e.g. common policies for business practices in industry-based collaborative networks. Achieving these challenging base conditions is a pre-requisite for agility in collaborative networks.

Related to the need for agility, another discussion point is whether collaborative networks shall be temporary or long-term establishments. While temporary organizations seem to better fit the dynamics of the market and the variable duration of business opportunities, long-term organizations better cope with trust building processes, and the investment on common infrastructures and code of practice. Some existing interesting and successful experiments have combined both types of organizations in a hybrid network, namely a long-term (growing and permanent) club or cluster of organizations that are willing and somewhat prepared to cooperate, and shorter-term coalitions involving subsets of these organizations that are dynamically assembled in order to respond to business opportunities. In this context, the ECOLEAD vision is that in ten years, in response to fast changing market conditions, most enterprises and specially the SMEs will be part of some sustainable collaborative networks that will act as breeding environments for the formation of dynamic virtual organizations.

The fundamental assumption in ECOLEAD is that a substantial increase in materializing networked collaborative business ecosystems requires a comprehensive holistic approach. Given the complexity of the area and the multiple inter-dependencies among the involved business entities, social actors, and technologic approaches, the substantial breakthroughs cannot be achieved with only incremental innovation in isolated areas. Therefore, ECOLEAD addresses three most fundamental and inter-related focus areas - constituting ECOLEAD pillars - as the basis for dynamic and sustainable networked organizations including: Breeding Environments, Dynamic Virtual Organizations, and Professional Virtual Communities.

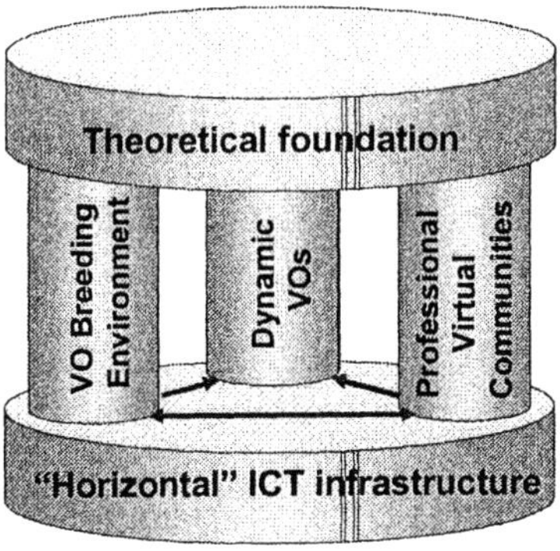

Figure 1 – ECOLEAD components

A **VO Breeding Environment** (VBE) represents an association or pool of organizations and their related supporting institutions that have both the potential and the interest to cooperate with each other, through the establishment of a "base" long-term cooperation agreement. When a business opportunity is identified by one member (acting as a broker), a subset of the VBE members can be rapidly selected to form a virtual organization. Long standing relationships - regional clustering being an example – when driven by the willingness to cooperate and anchored on common business practices, form a natural business ecosystem where trust is incrementally built and where ad hoc collaborations can be established. Therefore VBE represents a group of organizational entities that have developed advanced preparedness for cooperation, for the cases when specific opportunities arise.

Dynamic Virtual Organization are temporary alliances of organizations that come together to share skills or core competencies and resources in order to better respond to business opportunities and produce value-added services and products, and whose cooperation is supported by computer networks. Within a VBE context the VO is rapidly assembled into a business entity enabling the actual collaboration of enterprises and individuals to respond to a specific collaboration opportunity (business oriented or other). The temporary nature of VOs, the needed inter-organizational processes, and the potentially diverging objectives of the partners, require the development of a VO management system, which is based on the preparedness created in the VBE and covering the full life cycle of the VO, namely its creation, operation, and dissolution phases.

Professional Virtual Community (PVC) represents the combination of concepts of virtual community and professional community. Virtual communities are defined as social systems of networks of individuals, who use computer technologies to mediate their relationships. Professional communities provide environments for professionals to share the body of knowledge of their professions such as similar working cultures, problem perceptions, problem-solving techniques, professional values, and professional behavior. PVCs cannot be dissociated from the underlying business ecosystem of the society, due to their contractual links (social-bounds) with all the consequences at the intellectual property and life maintenance levels. PVCs are one of the most relevant elements for keeping the business ecosystem "alive" and for launching and operating dynamic VOs of the future.

The ECOLEAD pillars are supported and reinforced by two horizontal developments:

Theoretical foundation. Sustainable development of collaborative networked organizations needs to be supported by strong fundamental research leading to the establishment of Collaborative Networks as a new scientific discipline. Ad-hoc approaches and poor understanding of the behavior of the collaborative structures and processes mainly characterize the past developments in the area of collaborative networked organizations. There is not even a commonly agreed definition for the virtual organization concept. ECOLEAD includes the establishment of a sound theoretical foundation, and a reference architecture at all levels, as a pre-condition for the next generation of collaborative networks.

Horizontal ICT infrastructure. Implantation of any form of collaborative network depends on the existence of an ICT infrastructure. In order to leverage the potential benefits of the collaborative networked organization paradigm, more flexible and generic infrastructures need to be designed and implemented. The lack of common reference architectures and generic interoperable infrastructures, together with the rapid evolution of the underlying technologies, represents a major obstacle to the practical evolution of the area. As part of the ECOLEAD foundation, a generic, transparent, easy to use and affordable horizontal infrastructure for collaboration is being designed.

3. VO BREEDING ENVIRONMENTS

3.1 Aims

Traditionally, clusters/associations of organizations are established in a geographic region [1], with the advantage of having common business culture, and sense of community, and typically focused on one of the specialty sectors of the region. What is challenging today is to tackle this restriction, and at best replace it by a new "support-environment" called a breeding environment, that applies effective Information/communication infrastructures to provide common grounds for interaction/collaboration, facilitates the configuration and establishment of VOs, assists with the operation of VOs, introduces new approaches and mechanisms to build trust, defines a collaboration business culture, and the common value systems and working/sharing principles among independent organizations, even from different geographical regions. Cultural ties and particular human relationships are important motivating factors to start up and form such associations representing the VBE, as the support environment for dynamic formation of VOs.

VBE is a regulated open but controlled-border association of its members. It aims at improving the preparedness of its member organizations for joining the potential future VOs, hence providing a cradle for dynamic and agile establishment of opportunity-driven collaborative networks. Proper management of the VBE during its entire life cycle is at the heart of this support environment. Some of the main aims of the VBE can be formulated as follows:

- Establish the base trust for organizations to collaborate in VOs, by gathering/preparing the credibility records of organizations, as well as the definition of proper credit-assignment principles.
- Reduce the cost/time to find suitable partners for configuration of the VOs.
- Assist with the creation, reaching agreements, and contract negotiation for establishment of VOs.
- Assist with the dynamic re-configuration of the VOs, thus reducing the risk of big losses due to some organization failures.
- Provide some commonality for interaction and "accepted business culture", by offering:
  - Base ICT infrastructure (for collaboration), thus reducing the set up times during the VO formation.
  - Cooperative business rules (measured by the developed common metrics to evaluate member's credibility & performance).
  - Template contracts for involvement in VOs (samples are provided for VOs).
  - Base ontology for the sector (to be incrementally developed within the VBE).

VBE can also serve as the basis for some support institutions (e.g. insurance companies, education organizations, etc.) to provide the so called "life maintenance" facilities to its members.

3.2 Actors and roles in a VBE

Organizations or actors in a VBE can include:

- **Business entities** providing products and services to the market that get involved in the VOs to gain quantitative profit.
- **Non-profit institutions** that get involved in the VOs to gain qualitative profit.

- **VO Support institutions**, for example: legal and contractual service providers, companies supporting life maintenance to individuals (e.g. insurance and training companies), ministries, sector associations, chamber of commerce, environmental organizations, etc.

Participants in a VBE can play several roles. The following main roles are considered:

- **VBE member** – this is the basic role played by those organizations that are registered at the VBE and are ready to participate in the VBE activities.
- **VBE administrator** – performed by the organization responsible for the VBE operation and evolution, promotion of cooperation among the VBE members, filling the skill/competency gaps in the VBE by searching and recruiting/inviting new organizations into the VBE, daily management of the VBE general processes, e.g. assignment/reassignment of rights to different actors in the VBE based in their responsibilities, conflict resolution, preparation of bag of assets, making common VBE policies, among others.
- **Opportunity Broker** or simply **Broker** – performed by a VBE actor (a VBE member organization or an individual representing a VBE member) that identifies and acquires new collaboration opportunities (business opportunities or others), by marketing VBE competencies and assets and negotiating with (potential) customers. There is the also the possibility of this brokerage function being played by an outside entity as a service to the VBE.
- **VO Planner** or business integrator – performed by a VBE actor that, in face of a new collaboration opportunity (designed by an opportunity broker), identifies the necessary competencies and capacities, selects an appropriate set of partners (VBE members and even outsiders in case there is not enough competencies and/or capacities inside the VBE), and structures the new VO. In many cases the roles of opportunity Broker and VO planer are performed by the same actor.
- **VO coordinator** – performed by a VBE actor that will coordinate a VO during its life cycle in order to fulfill the goals set for the collaboration opportunity that triggered the VO.

Additional roles that might be useful considering in a VBE are: VBE advisor (or an advisory board), VBE Service provider, VBE Ontology provider, etc.

In general it is possible that several roles are performed by the same actor. The access rights to the information and support tools available in the VBE management system will depend on the specific role played by an actor.

3.3 VBE life cycle

The life cycle of the VBE represents all the stages that a VBE may go through, from its creation stage, to its operation, and possible dissolution. In fact VBE, being a long-term alliance, and considering its valuable bag of assets gradually collected in the VBE, its dissolution is a very unusual situation. Instead, it is much more probable that the VBE goes through another stage, a so called metamorphosis stage, where it can evolve and change its form and purpose. On the other hand, it is the case that only during the operation stage of the VBE, the VO can be created. VBEs by nature are self organizing and can be modeled and represented following the principles of the Chaordic system thinking [7]. Fig.2 represents the five stages of the VBE life cycles in a chaordic diagram.

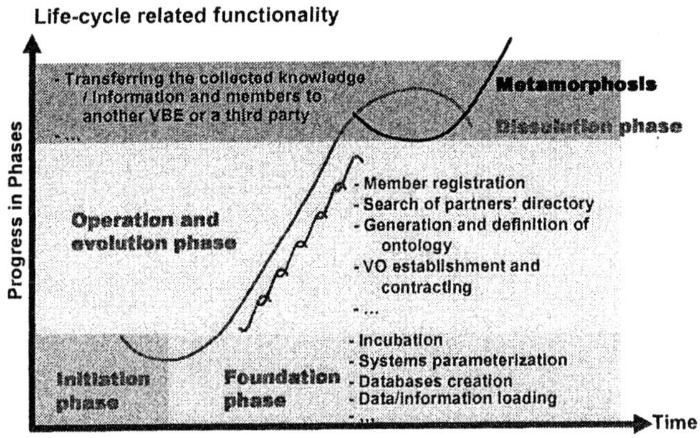

Figure 2 – VBE life cycle in terms of chaordic systems thinking

Considering that typically VBEs serve specific sectors/domain and have specific aims, there will be many different sector/domain-dependent VBEs needed to be established in future in order to support the creation of different forthcoming VOs. Therefore, it is important to provide support for all stages of the VBE's life cycle and not only focus on its operation stage.

3.4 VBE Management

Management of the VBE during its life cycle is at the heart of the VBE research and development. Due to the fact that there are so far no defined "reference models" for the VBEs, to address their different aspects including their behavior, structure, topology, cultural/legal framework, etc., there are no clear definitions of what exact activities are associated with the VBEs, that need to be supported by their management system. However, several examples of the traditional industry-based VBEs can already be found in practice that can be used as a source of inspiration for our work, e.g. the cases represented by Virtuelle Fabrik [10] and ITESM [8, 9]. Defining a comprehensive and generic "reference model" for VBEs very challenging. Nevertheless, with basis on the initial empiric knowledge that can be gathered from existing cases, it is realistic to gradually define a "reference framework for VBEs", addressing some of the aspects of the reference model for VBEs, such as its behavior, topology, and structure.

Furthermore, simultaneous to the definition of this reference framework, our approach is to design a *system architecture* for the VBEs management, defining models of its components as well as methodologies and mechanisms to support its behavior. Earlier studies performed by several members of the ECOLEAD consortium in some other VO related projects, including: THINKcreative [4], VOmap [5], VOSTER [6], PRODNET [2], etc., are used as the starting point. So far, with the initial studies in ECOLEAD, the following general base *required functionality* are identified for different stages of the VBE life cycle:

Base functionality supporting the VBE creation – This phase includes two main steps: (1) initiation / recruiting, which requires the establishment and setup of a common base infrastructure, recruiting potential organizations to join the VB, and establish some base ontology / thesaurus of the domain, to establish the vision and strategic objectives of the VBE are defined; (2) VBE foundation, requiring support for parameterization of the used systems, setting up the necessary links, creation of the necessary databases (with initial meta-data / ontology), and populating these information structures.

Base functionality supporting the VBE operation and evolution – This phase requires support for: (i) Management of competencies and assets, (ii) Registration of new members (including profiling, characterization of competencies, products, services, etc.), (iii) Assisting VO creation, (iv) Incremental generation / evolution of meta-data / ontologies for the domain / sector, (v) Keeping records of past performance and collaboration processes, (vi) Assessment and assistance tools, (vii) Collaboration support (e.g. newsgroups, discussion forum, common information repositories, etc.), (viii) Management and evolution of working and sharing principles and rules, (ix) Acquisition and management of common knowledge and assets.

Base functionality supporting the VBE metamorphosis – This phase will require assistance for the design of the aimed new organizational structure, selection and reorganization of the information and knowledge collected during the VBE operation and that might be transferred to the new organization, analysis and adjustment to the new context, etc. In the case of *VBE dissolution* there is a need to plan the transfer of its collected knowledge, information, bag of assets to its members or another organization based on defined agreements.

4. VO CREATION

4.1 VO creation and VBE

One important issue in collaborative networks is the formation of dynamic VOs/VEs. How can we quickly plan, find partners, and organize them in a collaborative network once a business or collaboration opportunity shows up?

Early works assumed that partners could be easily selected from the wide open universe of available enterprises / organizations. This assumption however ignores a number of difficulties:

- How to know about the mere existence of potential partners in the open universe and deal with incompatible sources of information?
- How to acquire basic profile information about organizations, when there is no common template or standard format?
- How to quickly establish an inter-operable collaboration infrastructure, given the heterogeneity of organizations at multi-levels, and the diversity of their information systems?
- How to build trust among organizations, which is the base for any collaboration?
- How to develop and agree on the common principles of working and sharing?
- How to quickly define the agreements on the role and responsibilities of each partner, to reflect sharing of tasks and the rights on the produced results?

Perhaps influenced by the developments in the e-commerce area, lately some authors started to consider markets of enterprises / organizations as a source for potential partners. The notion of market would provide means to find organizations (market directory) and perhaps some normalized profile and even some (minimal) references about those organizations. This is a concept frequently adopted by simple multi-agent based systems for partners' selection.

However, when the goal is to find partners for *collaboration*, the notion of market does not satisfy all necessary features. In order to support rapid formation of consortia it is necessary that potential partners are *ready to participate* in a collaborative network. This readiness includes common (interoperable) infrastructure, common operating rules, cooperation agreement, etc. Collaboration also requires a level of trust among organizations that is not a typical requirement in a simple market. Therefore, ECOLEAD considers the existence of a breeding environment [2] as a necessary context for the effective creation of virtual organizations. VO creation is the first step of the VO life cycle with the VBE operation phase (Fig. 3).

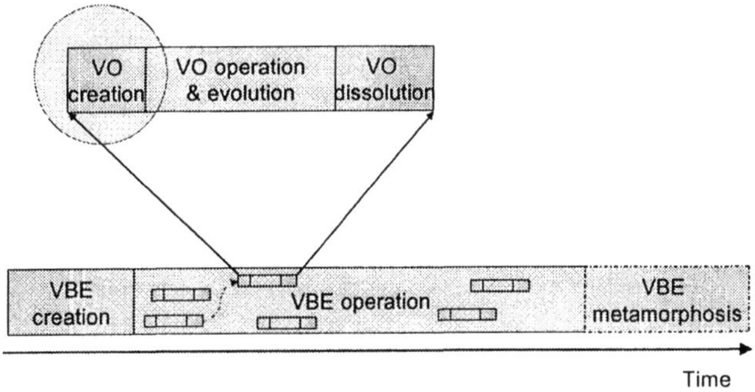

Figure 3 – VO creation within the life cycle of a VO and a VBE

4.2 VO creation process

The following main steps (Fig. 4) have been identified for the VO creation process:

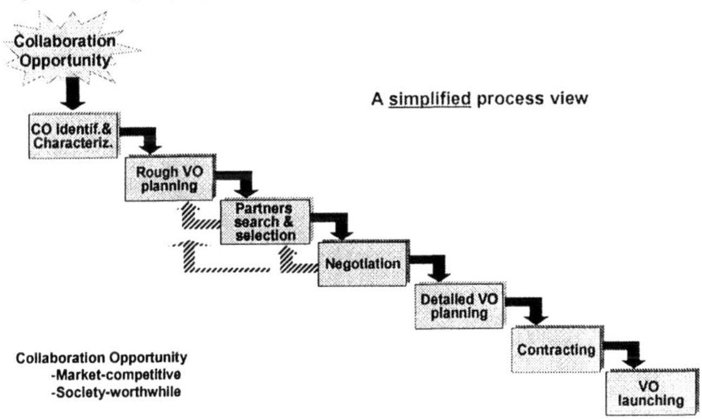

Figure 4 – Simplified VO creation process

♦ *Collaboration Opportunity Characterization*: this step involves the identification and characterization of a new Collaboration Opportunity (CO) that will trigger the formation of a new VO. Collaboration opportunities might be external, originated by a (potential) customer and detected by a VBE member acting as a broker. Some opportunities might also be generated internally, as part of the development strategy of the VBE. Support tools for CO representation and feasibility analysis are important at this stage. The main actors involved in this step are the broker and the customer).

♦ *Draft VO planning*: determination of a rough structure of the potential VO, identifying the required competencies and capacities, as well as the organizational form of the VO and corresponding roles. Functionalities to support the structural and topological design of the VO architecture, model the (macro) collaborative process, and assess (simulation) different options are necessary. The main roles involved in this step are the broker and the VO planner.

♦ *Partners search and selection*: perhaps one of the most addressed topics in past research, this step is devoted to the identification of potential partners, and their assessment and selection. Search mechanisms, assessment criteria, analysis of past performance record and level of preparedness, etc., are among the necessary support functions. This phase requires mainly the VO planer and VBE member roles.

♦ *Negotiation*: is an iterative process to reach agreements and align needs with offers. It can be seen as complementary to the partners' selection process. Negotiation protocols and mechanisms, decision making process, and forms of representation of agreements are important requirements here. The VO planner and VBE member are the main roles involved here.

♦ *Detailed VO planning*: once partners have been selected and collaboration agreements are reached, this step addresses the refinement of the VO plan and its governance principles. Assignment of roles and responsibilities, definition of operating rules and further refinement of the (macro) collaboration process are included in this phase. The VO planner and VBE member are the main roles required in this step. Interactions with the broker might also be necessary.

♦ *Contracting*: involves modeling of contracts and agreements as well as the contracting process itself, before the VO can effectively be launched. Semi-automatic or even automatic mechanisms can be considered for some application domains. This step might be considered in close interaction with the negotiation phase. Main roles involved in this step are the VO planner, the VBE member, the VO coordinator and possibly the broker and the customer.

♦ *VO launching*: the last phase of the VO creation process, i.e. putting the VO into operation, is responsible for tasks such as configuration of the ICT infrastructure, instantiation of the collaboration spaces, assignment and set up of resources, notification of the involved members, and manifestation of the new VO in the VBE. Main roles required here are the VO coordinator, the VBE member, and possibly the VBE administrator.

5. VO MANAGEMENT

The definitions of a VO often assume that a virtual organization behaves and can be managed in some way like a single organization. However, major challenges for VO management come from two characteristics: the temporary nature of a VO and the distribution of operations in independent but interdependent organizations with their own aim, behavior and culture.

To achieve an efficient management of VOs, ECOLEAD takes a broad approach towards VO Management by defining that *VO Management denotes the organization, allocation and co-ordination of resources and their activities as well as their inter-organizational dependencies to achieve the objectives of the VO within the required time, costs and quality frame.*

VO management applies knowledge, skills and/or tools in order to achieve the VO goals. The management of Virtual Organizations to a large extent deals with humans and it is performed by humans. In most cases the human aspect is considerable as the last decisions about management actions usually are done by the VO managers, who also may imply different management styles. However, it is not always possible to rely on management experience and thus systematic means and tools are needed.

The required dynamic management implies that needs of management actions are identified in real time. Consequently, an efficient performance measurement system should also be in place to give reliable, real-time indicators about the performance of the VO. The basic challenge is to *develop real time-time performance measurement based management approaches* fulfilling the requirements and features of the definition above. The behavior of such a management approach is illustrated in Fig. 5, where the management is considered as a real-time control loop.

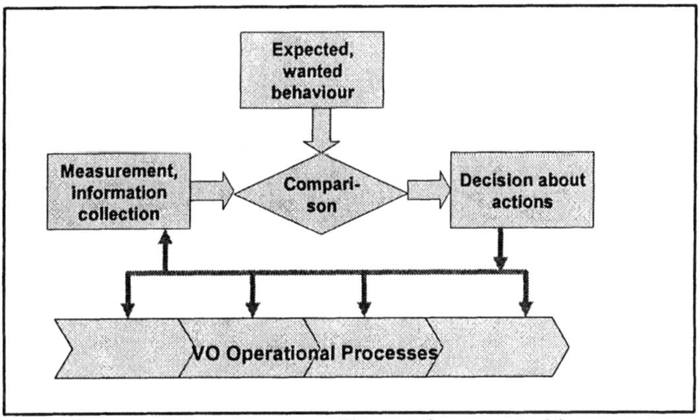

Figure 5 – VO management illustrated as a control loop

The efficiency of a VO can be judged from three different viewpoints:

1. The fulfillment of the task, i.e. keeping expected costs, time and quality
2. The efficiency of the VO and the collaboration
3. The efficiency of the management approach and management methods

Most of the VO management actions are devoted to ensure an efficient task fulfillment. The indicators for getting this performance are also mostly related to obvious measurements, mentioned above. Actions to maintain or enhance this performance are usually devoted to coordination of activities among the partners in the VO taking into account the challenges coming from the features of the VO.

The efficiency of virtual organizations depends heavily on the performance of the partners and their collaboration. This performance may, in addition to the task, depend on the configuration of the VO. The relationship between partner performance and the task fulfillment is not easy to model, nor are there obvious measurements available. Some of them are also qualitative and perhaps even subjective. However, the virtual breeding environment (VBE) would benefit from information about some indicators or measurements. Such information is essential in the creation of new VOs and is assumed to be collected as parameters in the value system of the VBE. One of the challenges in is to create models for judging and managing partners' performance based on the concrete measurements available and the processes established for the task fulfillment.

The aim of the work on VO Management is to develop efficient approaches for this Management. Consequently, also the efficiency of the management itself needs to be understood. Issues like task distribution, coordination principles, incentive systems, information flows, etc have an impact on the performance of a VO. Like for the partner performance, the challenge here is to develop a better understanding of the relationship between management approach and the fulfillment of the tasks given to the VO. This relationship should give the basis for the measurement of the management performance and also support possible actions for enhancement of the management.

The approach requires an appropriate monitoring and measurement system. Consequently, the development of a *performance measurement system* supporting the VO Management is a key activity. This system has to rely on models of the processes to be managed in order to help in identifying the relevant management actions in different situation. The aim of the ECOLEAD project is to integrate the performance measurement and VO Management and demonstrate the performance based VO Management approach.

In the dissolution phase of a VO, all valuable outcome from the VO need to be handled in a proper way and given to sustainable entities within the VBE (and PVC if individuals from a PVC are involved). In addition to the outcome of the task fulfillment, which can contain product documents, warranties, IPR rights, etc, the VBE may need information about experiences and the performance of the VO to be considered in the creation of future VOs. Also knowledge about customers and markets, collected during the VO operation, are important in future activities. The experience may be used by future VOs. In order to support such a support such actions, ECOLEAD will focus also on the *management of the inheritance* of the achievements of VOs.

Based on the aimed developments described above, a collection of *e-support functions* for the management of VOs are being designed and developed.

6. INTERACTIONS WITH PVC

Part of the ECOLEAD holistic approach includes the investigation of the inter-relationships between the VBE/VO and the PVC. In fact the importance of the "human component" in the formation and promotion of new organizational forms is becoming a more relevant research issue.

Analogy is one of the perspectives to exploit. A PVC can be seen as the counterpart of a VBE when the focus is on collaborative networks of professionals. A Virtual Team (VT) is analogous to a VO in the sense that it is a temporary group of people, members of the PVC that get engaged in jointly taking over a business opportunity. Therefore, at a conceptual level, most logical components of the

VBE/VO framework can apply to PVC/VT. Some issues, however, require a different focus in the case of PVC/VT. That is, for instance, the "life maintenance institutions" that seem fundamental for a sustainable PVC, or some support services (e.g. life long training) addressing the needs of humans.

Another perspective is related to the interactions between the two classes of organizations when they co-exist in the same business ecosystem. PVC members might be members (employees) of organizations involved in a VBE. This can happen either when the VBE promotes the existence of the PVC or when the PVC exploits additional skills that are not relevant to the core business of the employers. In the first case the VBE might use the PVC as a mechanism to leverage its participation in dynamic markets and boosting innovation, by creating new motivation to their members. In the second case, the competencies exploited by the PVC might be outside the contractual bounds between professionals and their employers, but nevertheless contribute to generate new business opportunities with benefits for all.

It is therefore important to better understand:

- The role of PVCs in launching / triggering new VOs;
- The formation of hybrid organizations VO-VT;
- The limits and opportunities of the contractual bounds between PVC members and their counterparts in the VBE;
- The possibilities of VTs formed to solve problems of the VBE, VO, or a single VBE member.

These are important research issues requiring further work in order to design appropriate support tools and policies.

7. CONCLUSIONS

Collaborative networks are already recognized in the society as a very important instrument for survival of organizations in a period of turbulent socio-economic changes. A growing number of collaborative-networked organization forms are emerging as a result of the advances in the information and communication technologies, the market and societal needs, and the progress achieved in a large number of international projects.

Nevertheless most of the past initiatives have addressed only partial aspects, failing to understand and properly support the various business entities and their inter-relationships in complex and fast evolving business ecosystems. The ECOLEAD project is pursuing a more holistic approach considering both long-term and temporary organizations as well as networks of organizations and networks of people. A new framework for advance collaborative networked organizations is expected from this integrated project.

Complementarily the ECOLEAD project is also addressing the need for establishing a more sound theoretical foundation for collaborative networks in order to turn this growing research area into a recognized new scientific discipline.

This paper introduced the approach and current developments towards the stated goals.

Acknowledgments. This work was supported in part by the ECOLEAD project funded by the European Commission. The authors thank the valuable contributions of their partners in the ECOLEAD consortium.

8. REFERENCES

1. Bremer, C.; Mundim, A.; Michilini, F.; Siqueira, J.; Ortega, L. - A Brazilian case of VE coordination, in *Infrastructures for Virtual Enterprises*, Kluwer Academic Publishers, Boston, Oct 1999.
2. Camarinha-Matos, L.M.; Afsarmanesh, H. - Elements of a base VE infrastructure, L.M. Camarinha-Matos, H. Afsarmanesh, *J. Computers in Industry*, Vol. 51, Issue 2, Jun 2003, pp. 139-163.
3. Camarinha-Matos, L.M.; Afsarmanesh, H. - A roadmap for strategic research on virtual organizations. In *Processes and Foundations for Virtual Organizations*, Kluwer Academic Publishers, Boston, 2003.
4. Camarinha-Matos, L.M.; Afsarmanesh, H. (Ed.s) - *Collaborative networked organizations – A research agenda for emerging business models*, Kluwer Academic Publishers, Boston, 2004.
5. Camarinha-Matos, L.M.; Afsarmanesh, H.; Loeh, H.; Sturm, F.; Ollus, M. - A strategic roadmap for advanced virtual organizations. In *Collaborative Networked Organizations: A research agenda for emerging business models*, Kluwer Academic Publishers, Boston, 2004.
6. Camarinha-Matos, L. M.; Afsarmanesh, H., Ollus, M. – Virtual Organizations: Systems and Practices, Springer, Boston, 2005.
7. van Eijnatten, F. M. – Chaordic systems thinking chaos and complexity to explain human performance management, in *Proceedings of Business Excellence I* (G. Putnik, A. Gunasekaran, Ed.s), ISBN 972-8692-08-0, University of Minho, Portugal, 2003.
8. Mejia, R.; Molina, A. - Virtual enterprise broker: Processes, methods and tools, in *Collaborative business ecosystems and virtual enterprises*, Kluwer Academic Publishers, Boston, May 2002.
9. Molina, A. and Flores M. - Exploitation of Business Opportunities: The role of the virtual enterprise broker, in *E-Business and Virtual Enterprises. Managing Business to Business Cooperation* (Camarinha-Matos, Afsarmanesh and Rabelo, Ed.s), Kluwer Academic Publishers, Boston, Dec. 2000.
10. Plüss, A.; Huber, C. – Virtuellefabric.CH – A source network for VE in mechatronics, in *Virtual Organizations – Systems and Practices*, Springer, Boston, 2005.

2 REQUEST BASED VIRTUAL ORGANISATIONS (RBVO): AN IMPLEMENTATION SCENARIO

Bob Roberts
Centre for Applied Research in Information Systems
Kingston University, UK
R.Roberts@kingston.ac.uk

Adomas Svirskas, Brian Matthews
Business and Information Technology Department
CCLRC Rutherford Appleton Laboratory, UK
{A.Svirskas, B.M.Matthews}@rl.ac.uk

Evolving e-commerce technologies increasingly enable organisations to participate in different types of network forms or in electronic markets with previously unidentified trading partners. Virtual organisations (VO) take different forms, have varying lifecycles and involve different scope and depth of relationships. This paper examines the literature in terms of the terminology of virtual organisations, the business drivers, the common theoretical concepts and models as well as the enabling technologies. A specific form of VO, Request Based Virtual Organisation (RBVO), is then considered in relation to these VO variants, particularly as realised through the practical work done within the framework of the EU sponsored LAURA project that facilitates interregional zones of adaptive electronic commerce.

1. INTRODUCTION

The literature presents a common theme of increasing competitive pressures on companies exacerbating the need for greater flexibility, efficiency, responsiveness and innovation. The common theme is one of traditional external boundaries of organisations beginning to blur, often with e-commerce as a key enabler of such change. Such links may take different forms, have varying lifecycles and involve different scope and depth of relationships. The separation between internal and external processes becomes less clear as inter-organisational systems facilitate more co-ordinated exchange and sharing of information and this may involve the innovative use of e-commerce technologies for new organisational arrangements, value acceleration and new value added processes.

Request based Virtual organisations (RBVOs) are a special kind of Virtual Organizations, and comprise a cluster of partnering organizations that have totally replaced their vertical integration into a virtual one. By their nature, RBVOs are short-lived entities that are formed with the identification of a business opportunity offered by electronic commerce. This introduction is followed by Section 2 which examines the business drivers, the common theoretical concepts and models as well as the enabling technologies for VOs. In section 3, the RBVO concept as realised through the EU sponsored LAURA project is introduced and compared to the VO characteristics identified in section 2. Section 4 then expands on the technical architecture chosen to support the RBVO concept in the LAURA context while section 5 concludes with the outcomes of the LAURA project, the realisation of the benefits and the future research ideas. These ideas include trust and security aspect in VO management related areas and are based on choreographed B2B interaction models.

2. A REVIEW OF VIRTUAL ORGANISATIONS (VOs)

2.1 The Business Drivers

A recurring theme in the earlier inter -organisational system (IOS) literature is the role of IT as a key enabler for competitive advantage through cementing relationships with customers and by enabling integration forwards or backwards in the industry value chain (Cash and Konsynski 1985, Cash 1985, Johnston & Vitale 1988). Benjamin and Malone (1986) also noted that through electronic networks firms may achieve an integration effect by tightly coupling processes at the interface between stages of the value chain.

More recent literature suggests that the broad concept of the virtual organisation has accelerated with the emergence of Internet / Web based communities of common interest and that enterprises are aligning within a series of 'value networks' against other groups of enterprises (Bovet & Martha 2000, Bressler & Grantham 2000). The evolution of the B2B Internet environment will increasingly provide the means to integrate supply chain practices and inter-organisational trading processes. Shorter product life cycles, more intensive competition, faster technological change and more specialised markets have led to various kinds of inter-organisation agreements, collaborations and partnerships as firms join together to create partnerships and also incorporate small firms in recognition of their capability for flexibility, responsiveness and innovation (Davidow & Malone 1992, Rhodes & Carter 1994, Hagel & Armstrong 1997, Aldrich 1999).

2.2 Virtual Organisation Terminology

A virtual organisation (VO) is described in many cases as a network among organisations while others argue that VOs should not be viewed solely as networks among organisations but as a radical approach to management, or a strategic approach that leads to dynamically re-configurable enterprises (Sieber & Griese 1999, Saabeel et al 2002). Lethbridge (2001) observes that while a member may exercise more power than others within the VO, each member operates as both a member of a VO and as an independent organisation. Lethbridge also notes that each member of a VO may also be a member of one or more other VOs.

There is, however, a lack of consistent terminology in the various discussions of organisational networks in the literature, with terms such as virtual networks, strategic networks, dynamic networks, extended networks and value networks.

These different terms are often used as synonyms but sometimes also indicate different characteristics related to longevity, purpose and culture. Nikoleris and Johansson (2003), for example, differentiate between virtual and extended enterprises as two emerging forms of dynamic networked organisations. Virtual enterprises are described as temporary consortiums of independent member companies who come together to exploit a particular market opportunity while the focus of extended enterprises is on longer term collaborative alliances. However, the success of both relies heavily on the seamless and effectively facilitated information flow between the participating enterprises and the ability to analyse, measure and improve communication.

Timmers (1999) also differentiates between value networks and dynamic markets where the former is characterised by a limited number of long term relationships while the latter involves many relationships over shorter time scales in order to maximise product, price or delivery configurations by selecting appropriate business partners. Marjanovic (2002, p.713), on the other hand, coins the term 'dynamic virtual enterprises' that involves rapid teaming of business partners (in particular small and medium sized enterprises) in pursuit of specific business objectives. *"Business partners are linked dynamically (on demand) according to the requirements made by the customer. Thus, partners collaborate on a short term basis (during the VE lifecycle) to solve a particular business problem. Once the problem is solved cooperation ends and the virtual enterprise ceases to exist."*

2.3 Technologies for Enabling Virtual Organisations

Silva et al (2003), in reference to the implementation of what they refer to as the agile/virtual enterprise (A/VE) model, argue that two main inter related aspects must be met; dynamic reconfigurability and business alignment of the A/VE with the market requirements. In reviewing the offerings of key e-marketplace makers they noted that while all of them still supported EDI, Web Services and ebXML are the most promising technologies for the creation of dynamic collaborative environments and business process integration.

Choudhury (1997) examined the evolving issue of inter-organizational information systems from the standpoint of a firm making strategic decisions about inter-organisational (IOS) development. Choudhury addressed the questions of what types of IOS might be useful, and how those IOS might be developed. Three types of IOS are described: electronic monopolies (e.g. supporting a sole source relationship for a product), multilateral IOS (e.g. communicating with a large number of trading partners over a single logical inter-organisational link and electronic dyads (e.g. EDI links between buyers / sellers). However, the increasing feasibility of adopting a peer to peer (P2P) approach for B2B e-commerce offers a new IOS option. Lee (2004), for example, argues that the need for centralised exchanges decreases through P2P networks and that a P2P architecture offers advantages over exchange based models including avoidance of fees charged by exchanges, reduction in the complexity and expense of networking and the scalability of P2P networks. Lee goes on to suggest that P2P e-commerce can be viewed as a 'dynamic electronic dyad' from the IOS perspective where the buyer/seller dynamically establishes individual logical links with each of a dynamically selected number of sellers/buyers.

3. RBVO IN RELATION TO THE LITERATURE

The RBVO concept encapsulates many of the characteristics described in the broad range of VO literature i.e. the flexible and dynamic reconfigurability of independent companies who come together to leverage on the complementarity of their competencies, products and services to meet market needs. However, while e-commerce may mean that asking for quotes from an increasing number of sellers can mitigate ignorance of the price of a very well defined product, overcoming ignorance of product quality and other supplier capabilities may be more difficult. The RBVO is coupled with the concept of sector specific Service Level Agreements (SLA) to address this issue. Furthermore, organisations participating in RBVO formations can reduce the costs of market search, and benefit from more effective monitoring schemes thus lowering transaction costs. Improved information flows can also facilitate improved planning and more co-ordinated actions to reduce uncertainty.

The authors of this paper were engaged in a project co-funded by the European Commission entitled "LAURA – Adaptive Zones for Interregional Electronic Commerce based on the concepts of Request-Based Virtual Organizations and sector-specific Service Level Agreements" (LAURA Project 2004). The LAURA project aims to increase the competitiveness and business efficiency of Small and Medium Enterprises (SMEs) from the Less Favoured Regions (LFRs) of Europe, by introducing state-of-the-art electronic commerce in those companies. This project innovates in introducing the concept of Request-Based Virtual Organizations (RBVOs) that are formed using the concept of sector-specific Service Level Agreements between trading partners.

The architecture and technology approach of the LAURA project supports the RBVO concept, builds on opportunities offered by the peer to peer (P2P) approach and utilises the latest e-business standards, such as ebXML. The discovery phase, for example, is implemented using a P2P approach, as a natural form of discovery behaviour. Subsequent phases of search for particular products and potential partners within the identified domains (matchmaking) as well as business conversations use a more conventional approach that innovate by building on aspects of ebXML such as BPSS and ebXML messaging.

The distinctive characteristics of RBVO as encapsulated in the LAURA project can be summarised as:

- A cluster of geographically dispersed organisations either within regions or inter regionally (typically SMEs).
- Organisations are independent and may belong to different RBVOs simultaneously and at different times.
- A possibility for an enterprise to discover potential business partners upon demand and advertise itself in a standard way.
- A range of relationships from transactional to collaborative that vary dynamically over time in response to market opportunities.
- The P2P architecture provides a flexible topology for virtual formations (JXTA 2004).
- The ebXML standard provides the foundation for messaging and business process management (EBXML 2003)
- Business documents are modelled according to the Open Applications

Group Integration Specification – OAGIS (Rowell 2002; Flebowitz 2002, Dubray 2001).

- Support Centres provide a low cost and trust oriented environment conducive to SME involvement and thus improve their competitiveness and business efficiency.
- Sector specific SLAs provide a means to analyse and measure the performance of participants.
- Lower transaction costs for geographically dispersed transactions.

4. THE ARCHITECTURE TO SUPPORT RBVO CONCEPTS IN THE LAURA CONTEXT

The concept of Virtual Organisation (VO) must be supported by appropriate architectural and technical implementation solutions, as well as suitable operational services, in order to provide its expected value for business partners. In addressing this particular task certain general B2B collaboration aspects were identified which led to the development of a generic architectural framework. Three areas of particular importance were singled out for end-to-end business collaboration; discovery and matchmaking of the business partners, secure and reliable business data transmission and business process specification and enactment.

The discovery and matchmaking aspect of the overall B2B problem becomes especially important in the SME e-business context, mainly due to the potential for a great number of collaborative participants, the diversity of their capabilities, the lack of standardisation for product and service description, as well as the absence of mechanisms to harmonise the latter. In order to fully reveal the potential of RBVOs as highly dynamic virtual business formations an innovative approach is taken, which is based on natural trading behaviour pattern, expressing direct interaction between partners. Recent developments in the peer-to-peer (P2P) computing field allow this pattern to be implemented. This approach results in a more flexible topology for virtual formations and bridges the gap between the isolated 'islands' thus forming a business to business grid that widens the possibilities for collaboration and increases their availability to business partners.

In the LAURA network context there are two types of peers:

- Domain Hubs, acting on behalf of SMEs, which are not capable of using LAURA business collaboration service themselves
- Advanced SMEs, using the LAURA collaboration service connected to their back-office and/or ERP systems

Project JXTA provides a simple and generic framework for P2P networking and provides a base P2P infrastructure over which other P2P applications can be built. The JXTA Protocols document describes six XML-based protocols that standardise the methods used by peers to discover each other and interact to form peer groups (JXTA 2004).

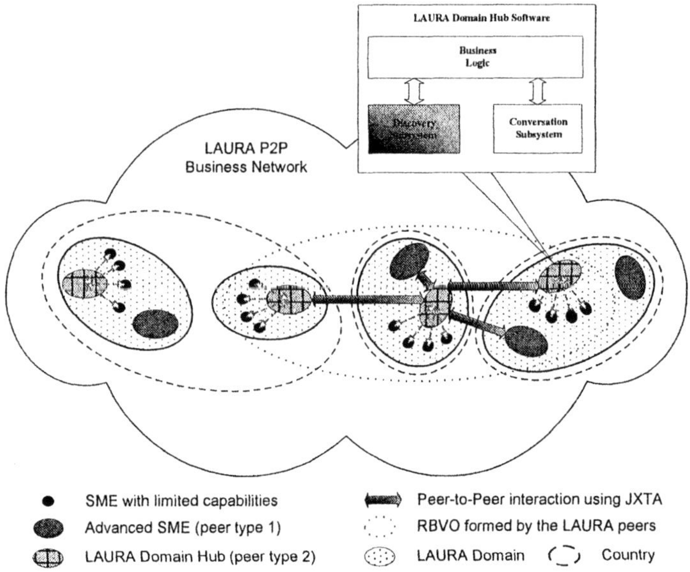

Figure 1. LAURA Virtual Network based of the concept of peer-to-peer interaction builds on JXTA virtual network (JXTA 2004) conceptual structure

The JXTA technology is particularly applicable from the RBVO point of view and especially with regard to the multi-domain nature of the solution. The JXTA Virtual Network, which allows flexible mapping between the physical resources and the logical entities, required for a multi-domain e-business network such as LAURA is shown in Figure 1.

5. CONCLUSIONS AND FUTURE WORK

As well as implementing a fully functional software prototype in the five European regions, the Laura Project has successfully carried out the establishment and operation of Support Centres enabling regional SMEs to conduct on-line B2B transactions on an intra and interregional level. This reflects the adoption of innovative notions such as the RBVO concept enabled by technology approaches such as EBXML and P2P to meet SME business requirements. The main objective of the deployment partners was the introduction of the LAURA proposed e-commerce solution in the participating regions, at both the operational and technology level. More specifically, they co-ordinated the introduction of e-commerce zones into selected pilot SMEs and, based on their experience of regional business environment, they evaluated the operation of LAURA proposed e-commerce zones.

The consortium has also provided a concrete dissemination and exploitation strategy for the project results and the commercialization of concepts, methodologies and prototypes developed in the project. The German LAURA partners have set up a spin-off “e-commerce-express.de GmbH I.G” for the exploitation of the LAURA solution in Germany, which will offer LAURA services and additional back-end support to already running support initiatives relating to e-commerce (www.ecommerceexpress.de). This LAURA based system is marketed as an adaptable solution and an online collaborative commerce system for SMEs with production to order characteristics. The system automates administrative processes with stakeholders in the supply chain and adds eCommerce functions to extend the boundaries and benefit of an SME's ERP system.

Some of the ideas and experience gained in the LAURA project will be applied in another EU sponsored project related to dynamic VOs - TrustCoM (Dimitrakos 2004), as two of the authors are working now in the TrustCoM project. The main objective of TrustCoM is to provide a trust and contract management framework enabling the definition and secure enactment of collaborative business processes within Virtual Organisations that are formed on-demand, are self-managed and evolve dynamically, sharing computation, data, information and knowledge across enterprise boundaries, in order to tackle collaborative projects that their participants could not undertake individually, or collectively offer services to customers that could not be provided by the individual enterprises.

A novel trust and contract management reference architecture that will enable collaborative work within VOs leveraging the emerging convergence of Web Services and Grid technologies will be constructed. A realisation of the TrustCoM framework will be delivered by means of open-standards Web Services based specifications and a reference implementation. Validation will take place within industrial strength test-beds in the areas of collaborative engineering and provision of ad hoc, aggregate electronic services. Despite the differences of technologies used in the two projects, the set of issues is largely the same in both cases - location of the partners and services, selection of the appropriate services, secure collaboration, business rules enactment, etc. This similarity helps to transfer the knowledge and apply it in a new context.

The architecture described in this paper does not explicitly address RBVO management by assuming the overall information about VO to be a sum of the knowledge shared by involved participants and the operation of such community is governed only by business collaborations. While this approach simplifies the architecture and its instantiation considerably, there might be cases when a virtual community needs to be managed more explicitly and the participants need to commit to the policies of such virtual formation as a whole before they can enter bi-lateral or multi-lateral collaborations. The drivers for such approach may include: higher security and trust requirements, more sensitive business area, stronger audit requirements, etc.

6. ACKNOWLEDGEMENTS

The results presented here are partially funded by the European Commission under contract IST-2001-33251 through the project LAURA. The future research ideas arise from the work in TrustCoM project, funded by the European Commission under contract IST-2003-01945. The authors would like to thank members of respective partner organisations of both projects for their valuable input and help.

7. REFERENCES

1. Aldrich, D.F. (1999), *Mastering The Digital Marketplace*, John Wiley, Chichester
2. Benjamin, R.I., Malone,W.T. & Yates, J. (1986), Electronic Markets And Electronic Hierarchies. *CISR Working Paper No 137*. Centre For Information Systems Research, Sloane School of Management, Massachusetts Institute Of Technology.
3. Bovet, D. & Martha, J., (2000), *Value Nets: Breaking the Supply Chain To Unlock Hidden Profits*, John Wiley, Chichester
4. Bressler, S. E. & Grantham, C.E., (2000) *Communities of Commerce*, McGraw Hill, new York
5. Cash,J.I. Jr, (1985), Interorganisational Systems: An Information Society Opportunity Or Threat? *The Information Society*, 3(3), 199-228.
6. Cash, J.I. & Konsynski, B.R. (1985), IS Redraws Competitive Boundaries, *Harvard Business Review*, March-April, 134-142
7. Choudhury, V. (1997), Strategic Choices in the Development of Inter-Organizational Information Systems, *Information Systems Research*, Vol 8, No 1
8. Davidow, W.H & Malone, S.M. (1992), *The Virtual Corporation - Structuring And Revitalizing The Corporation For The 21st Century*, Harper Collins, New York
9. Dimitrakos, T. et al (2004), *TrustCoM - A Trust and Contract Management Framework enabling Secure Collaborations in Dynamic Virtual Organisations*. ERCIM News No. 59, pp 59-60, Sophia Antipolis, France. http://www.ercim.org/publication/Ercim_News/enw59/dimitrakos2.html (accessed December 2004).
10. Dubray, J.J. (2001). OAGIS Implementation Using the ebXML CPP, CPA and BPSS specifications v1.0. http://www.openapplications.org/downloads/whitepapers/frameworks (accessed December 2004)
11. EbXML. (2003). The ebXML Framework, http://www.ebxml.org (accessed November 2004)
12. Flebowitz, M. (2002). OAGIS 8.0: Practical Integration meets XML Schema. XML Journal, Volume 03, Issue 09. http://www.openapplications.org/news/articles/XMLJ-Sept02-OAGIS8PracticalIntegrationMeetsXMLSchema.pdf (accessed November 2003)
13. Hagel, J. & Armstrong, A. (1997), *Net.Gain: Expanding Markets Through Virtual Communities*, Harvard Business School Press, Harvard
14. JXTA (2004). JXTA Technology: Creating Connected Communities. http://www.jxta.org/project/www/docs/JXTA-Exec-Brief.pdf (accessed February 2005)
15. LAURA (2003). EU IST-2001-33251 project. http://www.lauraproject.org
16. Lee, K.J. , Peer-to-Peer Electronic Commerce and Intelligent Systems, http://space.postech.ac.kr/vod/s011204/ppt1204/ppt1204.pdf. (Accessed August 2004)
17. Lethbridge, N., (2001), An I-Based Taxonomy of Virtual Organisations and the Implications for Effective Management, *Developing Effective Organisations*, Vol 4, No 1, pp.16-24
18. Marjanovic, O. (2002), Supporting Co-ordination in Dynamic Virtual Enterprises, *Proceedings of 15th Bled Electronic Commerce Conference, e-Reality: Constructing the e-Economy*, Bled, Slovenia, June 17-19, pp. 712-726,
19. Nikoleris, G. & Johansson, N. (2003), Managing the Exchange of Data in the Extended Enterprise, *Proceedings of 10th ISPE International Conference*, Madeira, 28-30 July, pp. 317-321
20. OFBiz. (2003). The Open For Business Project, http://www.ofbiz.org (accessed November 2003)
21. Rayport J.F. & Sviolka J.H. (1994) Managing in the Marketspace, *Harvard Business Review*, 72(6) (Nov-Dec) pp. 140-150
22. Rhodes, E. & Carter, R. (1994), Engineering The Virtual Enterprise, Paper presented at *Research Forum, 5th World Congress Of EDI Users*, Brighton, June 14-15
23. Rowell, M. (2002). OAGIS: A Canonical Business Language. XML Journal, Volume 03, Issue 09.
24. Saabeel, W. et al. (2002), A Model Of Virtual Orgasnization: A Structure And Process Perspective, *Electronic Journal Of Organizational Virtualness*, Vol. 4, No. 1
25. Sieber, P., Griese, J., (1999), Virtual Organizations As Power Asymmetrical Networks, Organizational Virtualness And E-Commerce, 2nd *International VoNet Workshop*, Zurich
26. Silva, J.P., Putnik, G.D. & Cunha,M.M. (2003), Technologies for Virtual Enterprise Integration, published in *Business Excellence: Performance measures, Benchmarking and Best Practices in New Economy*, Univ of Minho Press, pp.706-712
27. Timmers, P., (1999), *Electronic Commerce: Strategies and Models for B2B Trading*, John Wiley, Chichester

3 MULTI-PERSPECTIVE CHALLENGES ON COLLABORATIVE NETWORKS BUSINESS ENVIRONMENTS

Claudia-Melania Chituc
Americo Lopes Azevedo
Faculty of Engineering of the University of Porto (FEUP); INESC Porto
{cmchituc; ala}@fe.up.pt

New forms of collaboration emerged as response to transformations of the business environment and the rapid information and communication technologies developments. In this context, collaborative networks rise as a powerful mechanism to achieve strategic objectives in a time response, quality and cost effective manner. The aim of this paper is to present the most relevant challenges concerning collaborative networks paradigm analysis, and to advance a multi-perspective approach on collaborative networks (technological, semantic, social and business perspective), emphasizing the importance of the business view that allows collaborative networks to be regarded as combinations of inter- and intra-enterprise business processes. Balance Scorecard is seen as a powerful tool which can guarantee the strategic and business goal alignment within the network.

1. INTRODUCTION

The rapid development of information and communication technologies (ICT) and the transformations of the business environment determined new forms of collaboration, such as virtual enterprises, networked enterprises, or professional virtual communities. In this context, collaborative networks (CN) emerge as a powerful mechanism to achieve competitiveness, world-excellence and agility in today's turbulent market conditions, comprising various heterogeneous entities with different competences, but symbiotic interests. This motivated numerous research projects and studies aiming at understanding and implementing this paradigm. Despite the myriad scientific results in the area of business networking and the so-called "collaborative work", the scientific community agrees that more work needs to be done (Camarinha-Matos, *et al.*, 2004). Most studies on CN focus on technological aspects, such as supporting technologies, reference models, frameworks, infrastructures, often neglecting other issues, such as semantic, social and business aspects within CN (or partner organizations).

The aim of this paper is to address the most relevant challenges concerning CN paradigm analysis. This paper underlines the necessity to consider a multi-perspective approach on CN (technological, semantic, social and business perspective), emphasizing the importance of the business view on CN, that can be regarded as an aggregation of inter- and intra-enterprise business processes.

The paper is organized in five sections. After this introduction, the second section presents various types of networks arrangements usually considered by several researchers, and motives for participating in CN. The third section proposes a multi-perspective approach on CN: technological, semantic, social and business perspective, with emphasis on the business view on CN. The fourth section addresses issues on business processes in CN and business alignment. The fifth and last section contains the conclusions of the paper.

2. COLLABORATIVE NETWORKS

CN represent a valuable and effective approach to achieve strategic objectives in a time response and cost effective manner, with a high level of quality of delivery and customers' satisfaction, and generating value to stakeholders.

Current business trends determine a move from vertically integrated companies towards flexible network organizations, where the ability to quickly and efficiently set-up, maintain, develop and dissolve partnerships with business partners – networkability – is a critical success factor (Osterle *et. al.*, 2000). In fact, enterprises of all sizes are collaborating in order to fulfill client's demands, meeting their needs concerning cost, time response and quality, integrating various distributed business processes, and making relevant information available to all entities.

For the aim of this paper, in a broad sense, CN refers to a collection of heterogeneous organizations with different competences, but symbiotic interests, that join, efficiently combine, and coordinate their collective resources (*i.e* knowledge, skills, capital, assets, etc.) for a period of time in order to achieve a common objective, and use ICT to coordinate, develop and support their activities. The term CN is used in this article to represent collaborative forms such as virtual enterprises, extended enterprises, networked enterprises, professional virtual communities, and other emerging collaborative forms, with similar proprieties.

Miers (Miers, *et. al.*, 1997) identified three main types of networks arrangements (Azevedo *et al.*, 2002):

1. *Dominant organization with a network of suppliers*. This model is often used within large organizations, where one dominant player sets the main rules and uses a network of small firms to meet its needs and those of its customers. In this type of relationship, processes are usually focused on the repetitive supply of a service or product. The terms of the relationship are in general well defined in advance.
2. *Co-operative network* involves networks of small businesses undertaking together larger projects or services, which in turn may be supplied to larger or more dominant players. Processes are project-oriented and require a trust relationship between all co-operating entities.
3. *Virtual teams*. This type of network illustrates the trend of most large businesses to have teams managed on a project by project basis (seeking for a more agile structure).

Although an attractive option to undertake business, since they offer a number of advantages, CN face several difficulties, most obvious one being of technological nature, and referring mainly to issues such as inter- and intra-enterprise integration or interoperability. Alexakis (Alexakis *et al.*, 2004) identified several inhibitors and challenges for the adaptation of virtual organization concept, such as: clear organization, adequate workforce, finance, communication, loss of competence, development of the partnership, low acceptance, and intellectual property.

Since the effort required to integrate heterogeneous entities is relatively high, several benefits must be attained to justify this effort. The literature on collaboration identifies some motives and benefits associated with inter-enterprise collaboration:

• to increase market share; to increase asset utilization; to enhance customer service – reduction in lead times, customer complains, etc.; to share and reduce the cost of product development; to reduce time in product development; to increase quality of product; to increase skill and knowledge; to enhance skill and knowledge; to have technological gain as participating firm; to achieve economies of scale in production (Lewis, 1990)

• to decrease risk of failure of product development (Parker, 2000)

• to reduce inventory – in the face of increasing technological complexity and rapid rate product development and obsolescence (Parker, 2000; Holton, 2001)

• to gain rapid access to markets (Parker, 2000; McCarthy *et al.*, 2002)

• to increase flexibility; to attain international presence for small and medium size enterprises; to cope with changing dynamics; to have an effective knowledge management (Alexakis *et al.*, 2004)

The authors identified also other motivations for inter-enterprise collaboration:

• to have access to resources (skills, knowledge, etc.) that are usually well beyond those of a single player

• to learn (gain knowledge) form other participants in the network

3. MAIN PERSPECTIVES ON COLLABORATIVE NETWORKS BUSINESS ENVIRONMENT

3.1 Introduction

CN comprise several heterogeneous and world-wide spread organizations, with different ICT solutions. Its power consists of this association of different enterprises and institutions with different aims and different competences, but symbiotic interests, in the form of a CN. CN require tools, models and methodologies to support entities and employees to create just-in-time activity and exploit business opportunities.

The research undertaken allows the authors to consider four main perspectives on CN, comprising several aspects of these rich and powerful business mechanisms:

1. *technological perspective*, referring to technologies for inter- and intra-enterprise integration, interoperability, security, authentication, infrastructures supporting business, reference models and architectures, etc.;
2. *semantic perspective*, referring to semantic integration between business partners (data semantics, behavior semantics);
3. *social perspective,* which has a special emphasis on social actors (individuals and groups capable of performing activities and of interacting in order to pursue a specific goal);
4. *business perspective* concerning, among others, business alignment within the network, and inter- and intra-organization business processes.

Some other aspects of CN can be also considered, such as cognitive or knowledge perspective.

The following sub-sections detail the four above-mentioned main perspectives on CN, with emphasis on the business perspective.

3.2 Technological Perspective

CN are usually analyzed from a technical perspective, with focus on aspects such as:

messages format and content; activities for sending and receiving messages; specific negotiation messages and acknowledgement messages; time-out functionalities and catch-up attempts; supporting infrastructures, reference models and architectures.

In the context of CN, technologies such as Peer-to-Peer (P2P), Web services, workflow, semantic Web, intelligent agents, grid are core solutions for enterprise integration and interoperability, streamlining transactions while supporting process coordination and consistency. Despite the relatively high number of infrastructures and ICT solutions claiming to support enterprise integration and the numerous scientific results in the business networking area, more work needs to be done since available solutions are usually cumbersome and lack in flexibility to respond to the most recent technological outcomes, focusing on very specific aspects, and do not guarantee a natural operational environment. They often separate and isolate particular departments, companies, supply chains, authorities, research institutions and each individual of their surroundings (Chituc, *et al.*, 2005)..

Although intense research is being carried out on CN or related topics, and numerous distributed information technology infrastructures and distributed information systems architectures are available, the scientific community agrees that questions related to the formalization, conceptual development and semantic integration (namely concerning the formal description of the domain, ontology, behavior, etc.) are fundamental research topics waiting for a consistent development (Camarinha-Matos, 2003). The urgent need for new reference models, frameworks, business ICT solutions is illustrated also by several research projects, such as VOSTER (http://voster.vtt.fi) or THINKcreative (www.uninova.pt/~thinkcreative).

3.3 Semantic Perspective

Semantic perspective has little attention. Bussler (Bussler, 2003) launched as the grand challenge the issue of semantic integration among various organizations. Semantic integration encompasses data semantics and behavior semantics. Data semantics and ontologies are used to establish a formal semantic description of business domain concepts that allow an automatic transformation between them, without a human integration modeler. Process semantics concerns the match between communicating interfaces, so that their executions results in a consistent state after their execution is finished. In this context, when this grand challenge is met, the next (grander) challenge will be: how to achieve *self-forming* virtual enterprises, that is virtual enterprises where the detection of service providers, as well as their contracting is automated (Bussler, 2003).

3.4. Social Perspective

Social network analysis is not a completely new issue. The general theoretical framework of a networked society (Castells, 1996) determined intensive research developing and using networked-centric theories and methodologies. Wellman's work (Wellman *et al.*, 1996) on cooperative work and tele-work is directly based on social network concepts. Gitell's research (Gitell, 2000) also highlights the role of social networks and the use of ICTs to support forms of relational coordination.

Despite the current research trends, according to (Soares *et al.*, 2003), little attention has been paid to inter-organizational cooperation and the particular roles of the actors (individuals and groups). Nevertheless, relationships between enterprises will continue to involve people in key managing activities, taking operational, tactical and strategic decisions supported by conveniently distributed information systems.

3.5 Business Perspective

Business perspective in CN is often neglected. Research on business aspect of CN is scarce, and the few research studies available tackle very specific issues, such as value transactions in collaborative environments (Bititci, *et. al.*, 2004) or accounting models of economic relationships in virtual enterprises (Belak, *et.al.*, 2002).

CN analysis from a business perspective comprises business relationships within the network partners, as well as several attributes, such as:

- *competences* - refers to the expertise (skills, knowledge, etc.) one organization offers in a certain area/ domain, its capacity to disseminate and better advertise its capabilities, and also to its ways to make other entities discover its skills and knowledge;
- *availability*, which is concerned with its attainability in terms of negotiation, business operation, etc.
- *cost* – that concerns the shared production (development) cost, and also the costs to join the CN
- *value,* which according to (Martinez, 2003) has two components: internal value (i.e. shareholder perspective, where value is synonym to wealth), and external value (i.e. customer perspective, where value refers to clients' satisfaction)
- *functions and roles allocation and fulfillment.* This refers to organizations' functions and roles allocated within the CN, their performance, and functions and roles fulfillment during CN life-time and after their dissolution (i.e. support and maintenance services, exploitation strategies, etc.).
- *IPR* (Intellectual Property Rights) concerns, among others, issues related to the ownership of the information assets in a CN
- *trust* that refers to the confidence among CN partners
- *security* (i.e. security of information shared or exchanged)
- *business agreements* that concerns a (formal or informal) contract among CN partners setting out the terms of the collaboration
- *quality of service / quality of delivery* refer mainly to Service Level Agreement (SLA) that represents a contract between a service provider and an end-user, which stipulates and commits the service provider to a required level of service.
- *past performance* is related to the reliability of the partners considering their past accomplishments
- *legal issues* concern aspects such as risk management, tax payment, etc.
- *coordination and management.* CN coordination assumes a critical role, since a CN comprises heterogeneous entities, with different goals and cultures, but symbiotic interests.
- *development of new partnerships* that could determine the creation of a new CN based on past fruitful collaborations
- *business alignment.* Business alignment concerns one enterprise's business activity performance, within the CN, that should be in line with the activities developed by the rest of the partners.

The business perspective is of utmost importance within the CN and it is yet not fully explored, but has implication on technological, social and semantic aspects related to CN. In the context of a business networking environment, a CN can be described as a network of business processes (as illustrated in Figure 1) that can be identified, documented, controlled and improved. For the aim of this paper, it was made a distinction between intra-business processes (considered private business processes – PvBP) and inter-business processes (considered public business processes – PuBP).

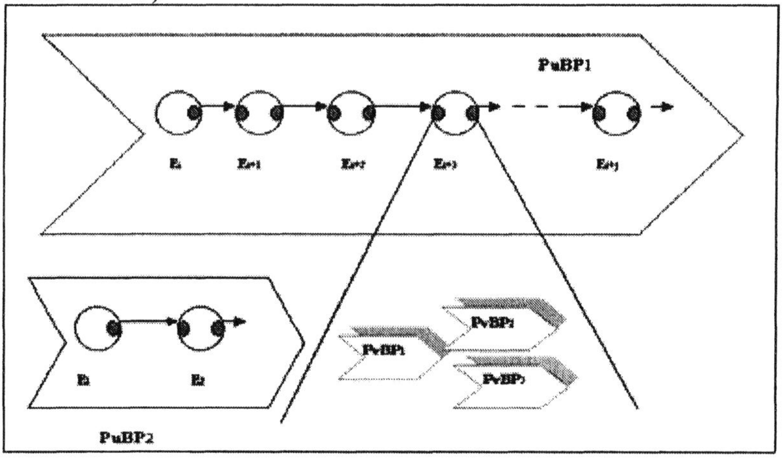

Figure 1. Collaborative Networks as Networks of Public and Private Business Processes

The main research questions inducing this paper are:
Question 1: Which business processes (inter- or intra- business processes) should one consider in order to operate the business model underlying the CN?
Question 2: How can one achieve an (technological and business) interface between several PuBP and a number of PvBP?
Question 3: How is it possible to align different PuBP with the strategic objectives of the CN, and to obtain a win-win situation for all parties involved (partners and end-users)? Which methodology and tools should be used or developed?
Question 4: How can one evaluate performance in a business environment supported by a CN?

4. BUSINESS PROCESS ORIENTATION AND BUSINESS ALIGNMENT

The process oriented organisation overcomes the problem found in traditional organizational structure where the information flows up the chain so that decisions can be made at the top. In fact, the goal of a process-oriented organization is to facilitate an "optimized" execution of processes.

However, such a process approach requires an effective management methodology and framework supported through a precision performance system to measure efficiency (resources consumed within the process) and effectiveness (quantify the ability of a process to deliver products or services according to their specifications).

The absence of meaningful goals and the use of wrong measures can drive organizations in the wrong direction. Thus, relevant perspectives and relevant objectives have to be selected and an adequate performance management system has to be designed and implemented. Nowadays, one of the trends is to consider a balanced approach to performance measure, namely taking into account past and future performance, financial and non-financial measures, soft and hard performance factors, internal and external indicators, etc. In this context, the Balanced Scorecard (BSC) concept plays an important and unquestionable role. The same applies to CN with probably a deeper interest due to the fact that in this environment interact different entities (autonomous, independent, heterogeneous, etc) which naturally limit the alignment level eventually necessary.

The BSC is an approach to performance measurement that combines traditional financial measures and instruments with non-financial measures to provide managers relevant information concerning the activities they are managing. First introduced in 1992 by Kaplan and Norton (Kaplan; Norton, 1992), the BSC concept has become widely known, and various forms of it have been widely adopted around the world. As Kaplan and Norton argue, no single measure can provide a clear performance target or focus attention on the critical areas of the business. The complexity of managing an organization today requires managers to view performance in several areas simultaneously. The selection of these performance measures should be linked to the organisation's strategic goals. One of the important characteristics of BSC design is the clustering of similar types of performance measures into groups (often called perspectives). In fact, BSC can be used, although requiring substantially different design and development processes, in two different applications:

1. *Management control.* BSC approach offers a holistic but focused view of performance measurement (extended to all business process);

2. *Strategic control.* BSC monitors the performance of all organisation as it implements activities associated with the implementation of strategic plan. The use of BSC in this context enables managers to establish their strategic objectives across a holistic view of the business, and to define relevant initiatives aligned with the goals defined at higher level.

In brief, BSC can be viewed as a multi-perspective strategic communication and performance measurement tool allowing translating strategy to key actions with the alignment of all relevant and critical activities. Concerning CN, the BSC approach can be a powerful framework to guarantee the right strategic and business goal alignment within the network and at the same time can work as a 'performance contract' between all partners involved.

5. CONCLUSIONS AND FURTHER WORK

Although there are numerous studies and research projects on collaborative networks (CN), most of them are focusing on technological aspects, undermining or even neglecting business, semantic or social aspects. No single perspective fully portrays or explains the complexity of a CN, this is why a multi-perspective approach should be adopted when analyzing a collaborative business networking environment.

Besides underlining the importance of the technical, semantic and social views on CN, this paper emphasizes the importance of the business perspective on a CN that can be regarded as a network of business processes. Thus, questions such as business process management, performance management and business process alignment are of most importance. In this context, the Balance Scorecard (BSC) becomes a powerful tool supporting a proper strategic and business goal alignment within a CN, while being a 'performance contract' among all partners.

Further work is being carried out in order to develop a holistic model on CN, trying to identify major critical success factors.

Acknowledgements. The author C.M. Chituc would like to thank FCT (Fundação para a Ciência e a Tecnologia) for the PhD scholarship.

6. REFERENCES

1. Azevedo, A.L.; Toscano, C.; Sousa, J.P., "An Order Planning System to Support Networked Supply Chanins". In Collaborative Business Ecosystems and Virtual Enterprises, Kluwer, 2002
2. Alexakis, S.; Kolmel, B.; Heep, T., "VO in Industry: State of the Art". In Collaborative Networked Organizations: A Research Agenda for Emerging Business Models", Kluwer, 2004
3. Belak,V.; Kolakovic, M.; Kovacevic, B., "Economic Relationships between the Members of Virtual Enterprises". In Collaborative Business Ecosystems and Virtual Enterprises, Kluwer, 2002
4. Bititci, U.S.; Martinez, V.; Albores, P.; Parung, J., "Creating and Managing Value in Collaborative Networks". In International Journal of Physical Distribution & Logistics Management, Emerald Group Publishing, Vol. 34 No. 3-4, 2004, p. 251-268
5. Bussler, C., "B2B Integration – Concepts and Architectures", Springer, 2003
6. Camarinha-Matos, L.M.; Afsarmanesh, H., "Collaborative Networked Organizations: A Research Agenda for Emerging Business Models", Kluwer, 2004
7. Camarinha-Matos, L., "New Collaborative Organizations and Their Research Needs". In Processes and Foundations for Virtual Organizations, Kluwer, 2003
8. Castells, M., "The Rise of the Networked Society", Vol. 1 of The Information Age: Economy, Society and Culture, Oxford: Blackwell, 1996
9. Chituc, C.M.; Azevedo, A.L., "Towards a Self-Forming Business Networking Environment", Proceedings ICEIS 2005 Conference (7th International Conference on Enterprise Information Systems), Miami (to be published in May 2005)
10. Gitell, J., "Organizing Work to Support Relational Coordination". In International Journal of Human Resource Management, 11(3), p. 517-34, Harvard University Press, 2000
11. Holton, J.A., "Building trust and collaboration in a virtual team". In Team Performance Management: An International Journal, Vol. 7 No. 3-4, 2001, p. 36-47
12. Kaplan, R.; Norton, D., "The Balanced Scorecard – Measures that Drive Performance", Harvard Business Review, January-February, p. 71-79, 1992
13. Lewis, D.J., "Partnership for Profit: Structuring and Managing Strategic Alliances", The Free Press, New York, NY, 1990
14. Martinez, V., "Understanding Value Creation: the Value Matrix and the Value Cube", PhD thesis, Strathclyde University, Glasgow, 2003
15. McCarthy, T.M., Golicic, S.L., "Implementing collaborative forecasting to improve supply chain performance". In International Journal of Physical Distribution and Logistic Management", Vol. 32 No. 6, 2002, p. 431-54
16. McLaren, T., Head, M.; Yuan, Y., "Supply chain collaboration alternatives: understanding the expected cost and benefits". In Internet Research: Electronic Networking Applications and Policy, Vol. 12 No. 4, 2000, p. 348-64
17. Miers, D., Hutton, G. "Technology Futures for the World Wide Web – Business Needs Something Better", http://www.cutter.com/concortium. Cutter Consortium
18. Osterle, H.; Fleisch, E.; Alt, R., "Business Networking: Shaping Enterprise Relationships on the Internet", Springer, 2000
19. Parker, A., "Interfirm collaboration and the new product development process", Industrial Management and Data Systems; Volume 100 No. 6; 2000
20. Soares, A.L.; Sousa, J.P.; Barbedo, F., "Modeling the Structure of Collaborative Networks: Some Contributions". In Processes and Foundations for Virtual Organizations, Kluwer, 2002, p. 23-30
21. Wellman, B.; Salaff, J.; Dimitrova, D.; Garton, L.; Haythornthwaite, C., "Computer Networks as Social Networks: Virtual Community, Computer Supported Cooperative Work and Telework", Annual Review of Sociology, No. 22, p. 213-38, 1996.

PART 2

BREEDING ENVIRONMENTS MANAGEMENT

4

A FRAMEWORK FOR MANAGEMENT OF VIRTUAL ORGANIZATION BREEDING ENVIRONMENTS

Hamideh Afsarmanesh [1], Luis M. Camarinha-Matos [2]

[1] *University of Amsterdam, THE NETHERLANDS, hamideh@science.uva.nl*

[2] *New University of Lisbon / Uninova, PORTUGAL, cam@uninova.pt*

Effective creation of dynamic virtual organizations requires a proper breeding environment to increase organizations' preparedness. After introducing some basic concepts related to collaborative networked organizations, the concept of breeding environment for virtual organizations is discussed and the key elements and requirements for its support management system are presented. The initial modeling needs and the required functionality are identified. Finally some important open challenges are addressed.

1. INTRODUCTION

Collaboration among autonomous and geographically disperse entities is a process that is clearly facilitated by the advances in computer networks and related technologies. A growing number of collaboration networks, including the "classical" virtual enterprises [11],[3], virtual organizations [10], and professional virtual communities [1],[6], as well as new organizational forms [2], are emerging. As a result of intense R&D in this area, new operating and governance rules as well as support environments are being developed.

Dynamic collaborative networks able to rapidly form and adapt to changing conditions provide good intuitive approaches to face the challenges of turbulent markets [10]. A key question is however how to guarantee the basic requirements to enable such collaboration. Among others, the formation of any collaborative coalition depends on its members sharing some common (or compatible) goals, possessing some level of mutual trust, having established common (interoperable) infrastructures, and having agreed on some common (business) practices and values. Achieving these conditions is a pre-requisite for **agility** and **integratability** in collaborative networks.

One discussion point is whether such organizations shall be temporary or long-term establishments. Temporary organizations seem to better fit the dynamics of the market and the typically short duration of business opportunities, while long-term organizations better cope with the trust building process and the investment on common infrastructures and practices. Traditional supply chains and some forms of extended enterprises in stable mass-production oriented businesses are examples of long-term organizations. Some interesting experiments combine both types of organizations: A long-term club of organizations that are prepared for cooperation and the short-term coalitions involving different subsets of these organizations that are dynamically assembled in order to respond to business opportunities. These new organizational forms are early manifestations of *breeding environments* for dynamic virtual organizations and emerge as an evolution of the industry clusters and industrial districts [9], [4], [12], [13].

This paper discusses this combined approach in detail, identifying its components and requirements, and proposing the necessary modeling and functional requirements for a supporting management system as well as extending it with further facilitating component and services. This research is being developed within the framework of the IST Integrated Project ECOLEAD which aims at creating necessary foundations and mechanisms for establishing an advanced collaborative and network-based industry society in Europe.

2. BASE CONCEPTS

Early works have assumed that partners for a new VO could be easily identified and selected from the wide open universe of available enterprises / organizations, and merged into a collaboration network. This assumption however overlooks a number of important obstacles in this process among which the following can be mentioned: How to know about the mere existence of potential partners in the open universe and deal with incompatible sources of information? How to acquire basic profile information about organizations, when there is no common template or standard format? How to quickly establish an inter-operable collaboration infrastructure, given the heterogeneity of organizations at multi-levels, and the diversity of their interaction systems? How to build trust among organizations, which is the base for any collaboration? How to develop and agree on the common principles of sharing and working together? How to quickly define the agreements on the roles and responsibilities of each partner, to reflect sharing of tasks, the rights on the produced results, etc.?

As a basic rule, in order to support rapid formation of collaborative networks, e.g. a business consortium, it is necessary that potential partners are ***ready and prepared to participate*** in such collaboration. This readiness includes common interoperable infrastructure, common operating rules, and common cooperation agreement, among others. Any collaboration also requires a base level of trust among the organizations. Therefore, the concept of **breeding environment** has emerged as the necessary context for the effective creation of dynamic virtual organizations. We define the **Virtual organization Breeding Environment (VBE)** [9] as:

an association of organizations and their related supporting institutions, adhering to a base long term cooperation agreement, and adoption of common operating principles and infrastructures, with the main goal of increasing both their chances and their preparedness towards collaboration in potential Virtual Organizations.

A main general aim of the VBE is focused on the transition from point-to-point connections among organizations to a network structure, in order to increase the chances of its member organization's involvement in opportunities for collaboration. Traditionally, breeding environments are established within one geographic region, in the tradition of industry districts, with the advantage of having common business culture and sense of community, as well as focusing on one specialty sector of the region. But, this restriction can today in most cases be overcome by VBEs.

VBEs primarily constitute two categories of regional and global. While regional VBEs mainly involve organizations (of different sizes) from one geographical region, a global VBE incorporates the involvement of geographically distributed organizations. In this paper, we address global VBEs. Furthermore, both regional and global VBEs can be either single-sector, i.e. specializing in a single focus area, or multi-sector, i.e. covering a number of focus areas.

Efficient creation of VOs is the main purpose for the existence of the VBEs. Therefore, the motivation for creation of VBEs primarily depends on identification / creation of opportunities for organization collaborations in certain sector(s). There are two kinds of opportunities pursued by a VBE, namely those that can be identified in the market/society, and those that can be created by the VBE for the purpose of innovation. The main actors in creation/identification of opportunity are either the VBE members who broker the VOs, or the VBE administrator who promotes the initiation of some VOs that seem to be beneficial for the market/society.

Establishment of VBEs provides the ten advantages listed and exemplified below, that are further described in the paper:

1. Agility in opportunity-based VO creation
   - Supporting reduction of needed efforts and complexity, flexibility for VO re-configurability, and cost effectiveness
2. Provision of base effective IC technology infrastructures for VBE members
   - The common grounds for interoperability / inheritability / collaboration
3. The VBE bag of assets, providing properties of interest for its members
   - General sharable information/knowledge (e.g. standardized product definitions and processes), software tools, lessons learned
4. Provision of mechanisms, guidelines, and assisting services to both motivate and facilitate configuration and establishment of VOs
   - Creating system of incentives, mechanisms to create positive reputation, and services for partners search, contract negotiation, etc.
5. Proactive management of competencies and resources available in VBE
   - Assuring coverage of the needed competency/resources within the VBE
6. Provision of related consulting/life maintenance support for VBE members through its support institutions
   - Supporting insurance, branding, training, etc.
7. Introduction of approaches/mechanisms to build trust among VBE members
   - By recording the performance history, and definition of criteria for organizations' trust worthiness
8. Provision of general guidelines for collaboration
   - Constituting rules of conducts, working and sharing principles, value systems, collaboration ethics and culture, IPR protection, etc.
9. Increasing the chances of VO involvement for VBE members, even from remote geographic regions
   - Through provision of members' profile in the VBE catalog, including their competencies, resources, products, services, etc.
10. Improving the potential / capacity of risk taking by the VO initiators
    - Due to the reduction of the VO setup efforts/time, availability of both a wide variety of competency/resources as well as indicators of the level of trust worthiness and past performance of the VBE members

A VBE is a regulated open, but *controlled-border* association of its members. It aims at improving the preparedness of its member organizations for joining potential future VOs, hence providing a cradle for dynamic and agile establishment of opportunity-driven collaborative networks. As represented in Fig. 1, it is far less costly and much more effective to quickly build a VO in a breeding environment context (branch 1b) than through a generalized partners' search (branch 2). In other words, VBEs substantially contribute to the increase of the level of preparedness of their members for participation in potential collaborative processes.

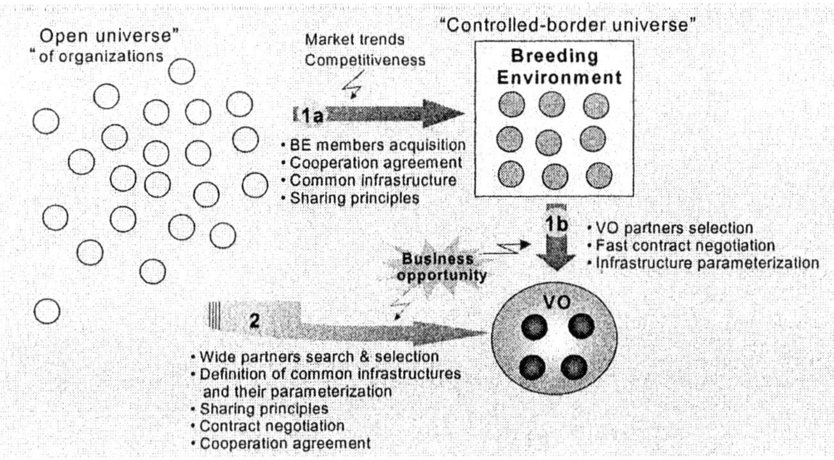

Figure 1 - Two approaches to the formation of virtual organizations

A VBE must have a controlled boarder, but does not need to be closed boarder; namely at any time new members can join the VBE association by complying with its general operating principles. Therefore, there may be different levels of membership defined and supported by the VBE administrator, each corresponding to different set of rights and responsibilities. In principle, different levels of VBE membership may constitute a range, with loose-membership on one end and tight-membership on the other end of the spectrum. For instance, a *loosely associated member* of the VBE may need to adhere to nothing more than a minimum level of organization "preparedness" that is necessary for getting involved in a VO, and to making some minimum information available to the VBE administration, e.g. about their activities related to the VO. At the same time, typically a *fully active member* of the VBE contributes to its promotion, growth, and the enrichment of its bag of assets, and can take an active role from brokerage and planning of VOs in a niche market, to being involved in the expansion of the VBE into new sectors, and initiating VOs towards innovation.

Similarly, for the formation of a VO that is initiated within the VBE, while preference will be given to the VBE members, it might be necessary to find some *external organizations*, for example when some skills or capacities are not available inside the VBE. Nevertheless, before becoming a partner in such a VO, an external organization shall be invited to join the VBE, at least at the loosest level (e.g. as a loosely associate member), in order to cover its minimum necessary VBE compliance. In some cases, it may be even desirable (either by organizations or by the VBE administration) that the names of the restricted members (e.g. the loosely associated members) of the VBE are not publicized as the VBE members. For instance if the association of an external organization with the VBE is *only* due to the fact that they are currently involved in one running VO initiated by the VBE, and this membership will not continue after the VO dissolves.

In addition to the enterprises, a VBE might include other kinds of organizations (such as consulting/research institutes, sector-associations, governmental support organizations, etc.) and even free-lancer individual workers that represent a one-person small organization. Furthermore, VBE can include and serve as the hosting environment for some support-institutions that will provide some specialized related services/expertise to the VBE members, such as the legal services, marketing expertise, etc. for the VOs configured within the VBEs, or the insurance services, training support, etc. (also called "life maintenance" support) for the free-lancers involved in the VBE.

Members of the VBE are the organizations that are registered at the VBE (traditionally bound to a sector). In summary, organizations in VBE represent:

- *Business entities* providing products and services to the market that get involved in the VOs to gain quantitative profit.
- *Non-profit institutions* that get involved in the VOs to gain qualitative profit.
- *VO Support institutions*, for example: legal and contractual service providers, companies supporting life maintenance to individuals (e.g. insurance and training companies), ministries, sector associations, chamber of commerce, environmental organizations, etc.

VBE members must comply with the general VBE rules and policies, e.g. adopting the common ICT infrastructure. At the same time, once joined the VBE, member organizations have access and shall benefit from the following available elements among others: Common information, services, and tools constituting its bag of assets; Common market and distribution channels; Common resource and labor pool; Common VBE cultural ties; Facilities to share the cost of new experiences; Facilities to share lessons learned.

A variety of **roles** can be assumed by a large number of actors in the VBE, where an actor represents either a VBE member organization or an individual representing a VBE member organization [9],[10]. Due to the autonomous nature of the VBE member organizations, at different times (or even simultaneously) the same organization may assume different roles, e.g. acting as a VO participant, a VO coordinator, etc. where each role requires assigning different rights/responsibilities within the VBE. Supporting these actors with their roles is a high priority in the VBE, and providing needed information and assisting tools for their support is among the VBE environment challenges. The following main roles are considered for the VBEs:

- ***VBE Member*** – this is the basic role played by those organizations that are registered at the VBE and are ready to participate in the VBE activities.
- ***VBE Administrator*** – performed by the organization responsible for the VBE operation and evolution, promotion of cooperation among the VBE members, filling the skill/competency gaps in the VBE by searching and recruiting/inviting new organizations into the VBE, daily management of the VBE general processes, e.g. assignment/reassignment of rights to different actors in the VBE based in their responsibilities, conflict resolution, preparation of a bag of VBE assets, and making common VBE policies, among others.

- ***Opportunity Broker*** or simply ***Broker*** – performed by a VBE actor (a VBE member organization or an individual representing a VBE member) that identifies and acquires new collaboration opportunities (of business nature or others), by marketing VBE competencies and assets and negotiating with potential customers. There is also the possibility of this brokerage function being played by an entity outside the VBE as a service to the VBE.
- ***VO Planner*** or business integrator – performed by a VBE actor that, in face of a new collaboration opportunity (designed by an opportunity broker), identifies the necessary competencies and capacities, selects an appropriate set of partners, and structures the new VO. In many cases the roles of opportunity Broker and VO planer are performed by the same actor.
- ***VO Coordinator*** – performed by a VBE actor that will coordinate a VO during its life cycle in order to fulfill the goals set for the collaboration opportunity that triggered the VO.

A number of other roles might be also useful to be considered in a VBE, including: the VBE Advisor (or an advisory board), the VBE Service Provider, the VBE Ontology Provider, the VBE Expertise Provider (through a support institution) involved in the VBE, and the last but not least is the role of VBE Guest played by an organization outside the VBE that is interested in finding general promotion information about the VBE, either interested to become a VBE member or interested in contacting the VBE in relation to a business opportunity, etc.

Because of the dynamic nature of both the VBE's environment and its member organizations, the defined roles for member organizations cannot be static. Every role taken by a VBE member organization represents: a set of responsibilities, a set of required rights/authorization, and further requires a set of assisting tools for the actor in that role. For instance, a VBE member, acting in the role of a VO broker, has accepted the responsibility to configure and negotiate a VO, for which it requires a set of access/visibility rights to the information regarding competency/past-performance of other member organizations available in the VBE, and requires an assisting tool to search for best fit organizations matching the required skills.

Considering the rights that need to be associated with every role of an actor in the VBE, it is necessary that the VBE members inform the VBE administrator about every new role they plan to assume (starting with becoming a VBE member organization) in order to request for proper rights to be associated to them.

The **life cycle** of the VBE represents all the stages that a VBE may go through, from its *creation* stage, to its *operation*, and possible *dissolution* (see Fig. 2 for VBE life cycle stages). In fact VBE, being a long-term alliance, and considering its valuable bag of assets gradually collected in the VBE, its dissolution is a very unusual situation. Instead, it is much more probable that the VBE goes through another stage, that we call the *metamorphosis* stage, where it can evolve by changing its form and purpose. The creation stage can be divided into two phases, namely (i) *initiation and recruiting*, dealing with the strategic planning and initial incubation of the VBE; (ii) *foundation*, dealing with the constitution and start up. The VBE creation needs to be properly supported considering the increasing variety of VOs, and the fact that usually every VBE serves a specific sector/domain and has specific aims. In the coming time, there will be a large number of different sector/domain-dependent VBEs needed to be established, in order to better support the creation of different forthcoming VOs. The VBE life cycle stages, as seen in

Figure 2, include: the VBE creation – composed of the VBE initiation/recruiting and the VBE foundation, the VBE operation/evolution, the VBE metamorphosis, and the VBE dissolution.

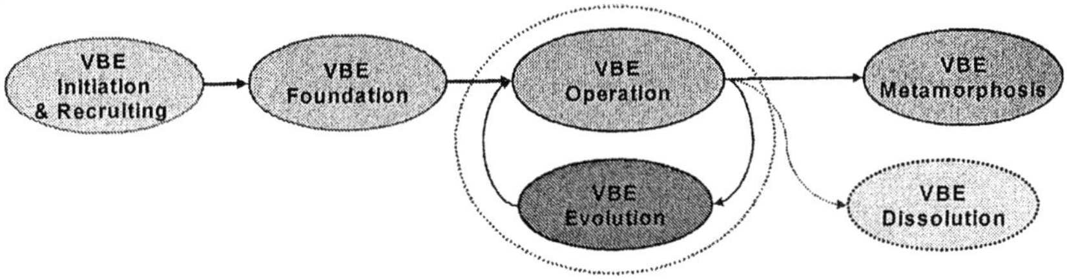

VBE Initiation & Recruiting – planning and incubation
VBE Foundation – constitution and start up
VBE Operation – the "normal" phase of the VBE existence
VBE Evolution – small changes in membership and daily operating principles
VBE Metamorphosis – major changes in objectives, principles, membership and/or mergers, leading to a new form of organization
VBE Dissolution – when the collaborative entity ceases to exist; Being a long-term entity, this stage of VBE is typically replaced by the metamorphosis stage, preserving the gained knowledge.

Figure 2 - VBE life cycle stages

Table 1 shows some effective examples of traditional breeding environments that provide substantial evidence for the need to establish VBE frameworks and the necessity of developing VBE support functionalities.

Table 1 – Examples and potentials of VBEs

Case	Members	Location	Domain
Virtuelle Fabrik	100	Switzerland, Germany	Mechanical industry
Kiesel	>15	Germany	Services, Environment
Virtec	>9	Brazil	Manufacturing
CEFAMOL	136	Portugal	Plastic moulds
Virtual Enterprise Networks Yorkshire	>25	UK	IT, Machinery, Bio-tech, e-Learning
Bipolo Ticino	>13	Switzerland	Life sciences
Virtual Biotech Company	>150	Germany	Biotechnology
PVC	45	Australia	Plastics
Regional Net for Ontario	-	Canada	Telecommunications
VIRFERBRAS	>12	Brazil	Moulds
Fenix Cluster	>250	Mexico	Electronics, metal & plastic
Biotechnology cluster	411	USA	Biotechnology
Biotechnology cluster	>160	Canada	Agro-food, biotechnology
Advanced Business Services	>6	USA	Credit, lending, investments
Helsinki ICT cluster	79	Finland	Telecommunications
CARPI	2068	Italy	Textile / clothing
Mining Cluster	-	Chile	Mining industry
Motorsport Valley	40	UK	Motor-sport
Verkko A	12	Finland	Process industry
Automotive cluster	54	Slovenia	Automotive industry
Plasttechnics cluster	>60	Slovenia	Plastics

3. MODELING NEEDS

In order to design and develop a management system for VBEs it is necessary to first identify and model the main elements of this collaboration environment. A wide variety of entities and concepts co-exist in a typical VBE environment, as graphically represented in Fig. 3. VBEs include heterogeneous organizations of different sizes and a number of support institutions. The VOs are from time to time created and will interact with the VBE. Furthermore, the VBE management system controls the base running environment enforced by a number of policies and regulations, as well as providing a set of general common tools, facilities and information that constitute the bag of assets for the VBE. Therefore, a large variety of information and knowledge must be properly modeled, organized, and applied to manage the VBE.

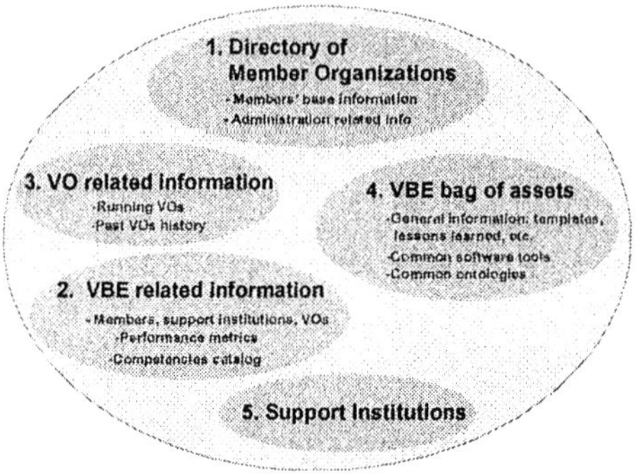

Figure 3 – Main categories of information in a VBE management system

For most of the elements in the categories identified in Fig. 2, generic sector-dependent/application-independent specifications can be provided, namely a common ontology can be defined for those categories and included in the VBE management system, to be used for all sectors and applications. However, some of the identified elements in Fig. 2 cannot have a common sector-dependent/application-independent definition. These elements include the competencies, resources, products and services of the VBE, for which their modeling and ontology need to be handled differently, as addressed below.

VBE Products and services specification is widely varied among different sectors. Furthermore, different products or services have different specifications and their respective properties describing each product or service differ widely, and thus their definition/conceptualization (ontology) will be completely different as well. In the best case, if there are standard meta-data / ontology defined for a specific sector for which the VBE is established, these standard models can be stored within the VBE as a part of its general assisting information, in its bag of assets. Otherwise, an alternative approach is needed to generate/define their ontology. For this purpose, some text mining tools can be developed to help discover ontology-related concepts and keywords. The approach planned for the ECOLEAD, **semi-automatic mechanisms** will be developed to mine and derive concepts from the online corpus related to VBE member organizations, in order to present to the human experts in the sector, assisting them with gradual / incremental building up of such meta-data and ontology for the VBE.

Similarly, competencies and resources offered by the VBE are also not easy to generalize. Consider for instance the differences in competency definitions (meta-data/ontology) that describe the skills / knowledge / potential of the organizations related to examples provided in Table 1. Furthermore, consider and notice the wide variety and heterogeneity among resources owned, such as facilities/machineries related to different domain/sectors. Clearly neither Competencies nor resources of the organizations in the VBE for Healthcare (e.g. hospitals, care centers, Doctors' practice office, insurance companies, ambulance services, etc.) can be defined by the same ontology (specification) that defines these aspects of the organizations in the VBE for production and assembly of bicycles (e.g. the raw material provider, mould maker, paint manufacturer, factory, marketing firm, packaging company, etc.).

Therefore, in the above case, only a minimum common meta-data can perhaps be defined and modeled, as the starting point for defining the competency and resources meta-data. This common meta-data includes a generic upper ontology plus some minimum profiling information common to all potential VBE member organizations. From that point on, similar to the product/services, some semi-automatic mechanisms need to be applied to VBE to continuously support the derivation/discovery of its domain/sector meta-data, and incrementally build and expand some common ontology for the competencies (and resources) of the organizations involved in that sector. For instance, semi-automatic mining of on-line texts, either directly through questionnaires and brochures provided by the current VBE members or through their web sites, can discover common elements of the competency related to the VBE sectors.

Nevertheless, it is important to notice that for proper modeling of the VBEs information, the development of a strong and detailed ontology for organizations' competency (related to the sector represented in the VBE), as well as the proactive management of this competency catalog are significant. This is due to the need to assist the opportunity brokers and to increase the effectiveness of the search/match-making process, necessary for creation of VOs within the VBE.

4. LIFE CYCLE SUPPORT FUNCTIONALITY

Defining a comprehensive and generic "reference model" for VBEs is a big challenge. Nevertheless, based on the initial empirical knowledge gathered from existing cases (see examples in Table 1), it is realistic to design the first steps for gradual definition of a **"reference framework for VBEs"**, addressing aspects such as the VBE behavior, topology, and structure.

In this direction, in addition to identification of constituting entities and concepts in VBEs that are briefly addressed earlier in the paper, so far a first list of *required functionality* for a **VBE management system** is identified in the ECOLEAD in relation to different stages of its life cycle. A subset of this list is addressed below and partially represented in Fig. 4.

Base functionality supporting the VBE creation – This phase includes two main steps: (1) *initiation / recruiting*, which requires the establishment and setup of a common base ICT infrastructure, and establish some base ontology / thesaurus of the domain, once the vision and strategic objectives of the VBE are defined; (2) *VBE foundation*, requiring support for parameterization of the used systems, setting up the necessary links, recruiting potential organizations to join the VBE (founding members), creation of the necessary databases (with initial meta-data / ontology), and populating these information structures.

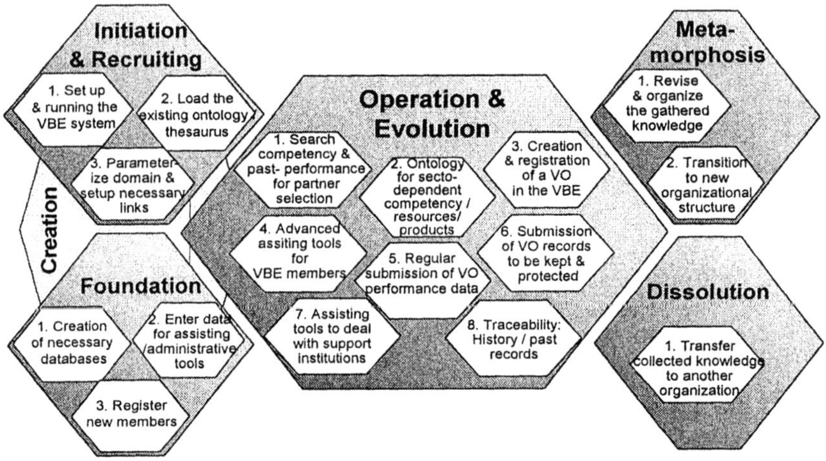

Figure 4 – Examples of VBE life cycle support functionalities

Base functionality supporting the VBE operation and evolution – This phase requires support for: management of competencies and assets, registration of new members (including incremental profiling, characterization of competencies, products, services, etc.), assisting VO creation, incremental generation / evolution of ontologies for the domain / sector, keeping records of past performance and collaboration processes, assessment and assistance tools, collaboration support (e.g. newsgroups, discussion forum, common information repositories, etc.), management and evolution of working and sharing principles and rules, acquisition and management of common knowledge and assets.

Base functionality supporting the VBE metamorphosis – This phase will require assistance for the design of the aimed new organizational structure, selection and reorganization of the information and knowledge collected during the VBE operation, and that might be transferred to the new organization, analysis and adjustment to the new context, etc.

Base functionality supporting the VBE dissolution - In the case of dissolution there is a need to plan the transfer of its collected knowledge, information, bag of assets, etc. to its members, or another entity based on defined agreements.

Clearly, considering the existing technological approaches, more than one system architecture can be designed for the VBEs, and many different ICT tools and mechanisms can be applied to develop this architecture [8].

5. SOME OTHER CHALLENGES

A number of important challenges can be identified in the design and development of a replicable VBE framework, where competency management, value systems, system of metrics, and trust management are among the main elements.

Competencies Management: Competencies represent the "capacity" for existing resources plus the available capabilities/skills to perform some task or activity. Competencies are thus the combination of **capabilities and capacities**. Proper management of the set of competencies is fundamental for a VBE management system. The VBE Competency Management System (CMS) shall include a catalog of competencies and a set of functionalities to manage it. In VBE, potential users of the CMS include the VBE Administrator, Broker, VO planner, VO Coordinator, and VBE Adviser. Table 2 summarizes some of the important issues needed to be considered in the CMS.

Table 2. Issues in Competencies Management

Competencies catalog:

- Ontology of competencies / skills – competencies need to be properly specified and organized in some taxonomic structure, supported by suitable navigational interface
- Related competencies/ skills must be identified as means for replace-ability or equivalence of skills
- Some hierarchy of competencies must be defined and supported for search, for instance the more generalized (e.g. welding) as well as some specializations (e.g. spot welding).
- Furthermore, the inter-relationships (e.g. the IS-A, the whole-part, etc.) among competencies / skills must be defined.
- Properties aggregation to characterize each competency.
- Basic catalog entities manipulation – flexible search (multi-criteria), add, remove, edit, etc.
- Internal Core and some non-core – For each member we can distinguish between the core and the non-core competencies.
- External valuation of VBE competency – Considering the global market level of the competency of the VBE as a whole.
- From an "operational" point of view, how to determine / collect competencies? Automatic? Manual? How to update them?
- Dynamic properties?
- It may be interesting to consider levels of competencies / skills. For a given competency C, does our VBE master it to the level of setting strategic developments, or is it only able to "follow" what is suggested by a customer, for instance.

Competencies Management functionalities:

- Competencies appraisal functionality - How "robust" or "sustainable" is the competencies base?
  - Skills' gap analysis. What if one member leaves? Specific indicators of skill robustness? Skill robustness inside an organization – skill possessed by one employee or part of the "culture" of the organization? How to rate the skills base?
- Marketing support functionality - How to "sell" it to the outside?
  - Identification of strengths and weaknesses? (Dynamic) Identification of new potentials?
- Acquisition of complementary skills? Which support functionality?
- Internal competencies & external but "easily" accessible competencies
- What is the "unit"? Enterprise? Department? Group?
- Relationship to processes and roles
- Endorsement / "accreditation" of competencies. Or rating their quality/past performance?
- Notion of joint competency (when one specific competency results from the contribution of 2 or more partners, and such competency cannot be provided by a single partner). Or is this represented by the notion of complex competency (see above)?
- Others to be determined.

Value Systems. It is commonly accepted that the behavior of an individual, society, or ecosystem is determined by the underlying value system. It is intuitively understood that the values considered in a business-oriented VBE are different from those in a non-profit context (e.g. disaster rescue and incidence management network). Taking the simplified view that the goal of a VBE is to maximize some "attribute" of its value system, within a business context the dominant value is the profit (in economic sense), while in other cases the objectives are altruistic and compensated by the amount of prestige or social recognition, etc.

A value system is in essence *the ordering and prioritization of a set of values that an actor or a society of actors holds*. However, the values that a group or an actor holds may fall into several different categories since the concept of value is multifaceted. In order to define a value system for a VBE, we need to first define the characteristics of values that could be represented in a value system. A number of characteristics can be considered for the values of a value system:

- *Subjective* – For an identical context, distinct members may apply different values.
- *Personal vs. social* – The personal values can be applied only to one member (e.g. assets, capacity, and price) while social values can be applied to a set of members at VBE or VO level (e.g. ethical code, cooperation agreements, contracts).
- *Normative* – The purpose of normative values is to define a set of rules ("rights/duties") that contribute to assure the stability and the cohesion of the group since they transmit norms in a persuasive way and present an unquestionable form (e. g. trust, ethical code, and law).
- *Exchange* - The purpose of exchange values is to "measure" the objects exchanged among partners in a certain context and moment.
- *Dynamic* - The values can change along the time. They can fade out, increase their worth or can appear for the first time.
- *Measurable* - The values can be measured using a quantitative or a quantitative scale.

Definition of a value system in a VBE context is based on the notion that each product/service requires a set of value creating activities to be performed by a number of actors, forming a "value creating system" through a VO. As a result, value system needs to be defined at the VBE level, to provide:

- A regulation mechanism – for instance, to assure social cohesion, to understand members' behavior and to build performance indicators.
- A transactions mechanism between partners – such as, to assure an equality utility between objects exchanged.

For managerial purposes it is important to identify which values (within list of values) shall be part of the value system for each specific VBE (or application domain). Another related research challenge is the elaboration of some significant performance indicators - for VBE members, VOs, and the VBE as a whole – to be computed through some combination of values / variables of the adopted value system. Also, a related issue is the elaboration of procedures for distribution of profits resulted from some activities in the VBE (and VOs) [7].

System of incentives: The definition of a system of incentives is important for attracting and maintaining partners and members. In general, for business-related contexts, the key incentives to participate in a VBE are **business benefits** and **knowledge**. Incentives for members are mainly associated with costs, and some examples could be: (i) Guaranteed participation in a given number of VOs during a given period of time (although difficult to materialize in practice), (ii) A set of basic tools provided in the VBE bag of assets, (iii) On-demand VBE Product and Services, (iv) Tutorials, Courses and Conferences to enhance productivity (and core competencies) in companies, (v) An initial evaluation of the member and a commitment for constructive suggestions/advice to better its status in a given period of time.

The development of a set of performance indicators, as mentioned above, can complement these incentives by providing a more objective measure of the benefits of being involved in a VBE. As an incentive for member organizations to become more active in the VBE, a set of rules can be defined to collect points (e.g. a broker collects X points when

Incentives for government involvement are directly related to the social and economic impact of the VBE. Examples of this type of incentives are the increase in employment rates, increase in gross product, better infrastructures, and SMEs' development. For universities, the key incentives for participation in a VBE are the openness of VBE projects looking for student practices and an early introduction to industry practices. A better link between industry and academia can also be offered in order to improve research results. For R&D organizations, the key incentive is the exploitation of their technological advances. This link between research and market is needed in order to sustain the research and development activities. Brokers are closely involved in materialization of this incentive.

Trust management. Trust is a critical antecedent for more efficient and effective communication, collaboration and knowledge creation. In fact innovation cannot be managed hierarchically because it depends on knowledge being offered voluntarily rather than on command. Therefore knowledge creation is social in nature; social exchange is a core process in knowledge creation.

Building trust is not an easy task, it requires mechanisms supported by the VBE, and usually takes time. Trust can be generated as an outcome of organization's past/present performance information recorded in the VBE. Therefore, trust is a component of the desired preparedness to participate in VOs. Trust plays an important role in order to create competitive advantage by reducing governance costs (management costs), costs for internalization (acquisitions), transaction costs between organizations, and impact positively in knowledge creation. Trust enables open communication, information sharing, and conflict management in a clear way, and also helps to speed up the contract process [5]. A set of well-established policies and criteria to follow in collaborative processes can help in creating / increasing trust among partners.

Several other challenges need to be also addressed including VBE marketing, ethical issues, management of VBE assets, contracts/collaboration agreements, etc.

6. CONCLUSIONS

For competing effectively in today's fast and rapidly changing business environment, organizations must organize people and processes to enhance responsiveness and flexibility and quickly react to a business opportunity. Advanced ICT and recently cutting edge web technologies have enabled new options in organizational structure and manifestations. Boundaries of location, time and individualization, and even organization have become less confining, allowing dramatic changes in the current work environments in form of VOs.

The Virtual organization breeding environment (VBE) is an emerging challenging area of research. Most elements comprising VBEs are not yet properly defined, and there are no reference models or reference architectures addressing the constituting elements and behavior of the VBEs. The multidisciplinarity of research on VBEs further adds to its complexity. Consequently, even discovery and identification of VBEs' requirements and proper definition of this problem area itself becomes challenging. Furthermore, to handle its wide variety of requirements, innovations in several areas are needed. Among others, endogenous to the VBEs, there are four key characteristics of VBEs that need careful attention. First, VBE entails the development of relationships with a broad range of potential partners, each having particular competency, resources, products, services, etc. that complements the others. Second, VBEs shall be regulated by a set of governing rules and principles for participation, and enforced by the VBE management system. Third, life cycle stages of VBEs determine its required functionality and services. And finally, there must be trust between VBE actors separated in space, for effective VO creation and operation. In this direction, ECOLEAD is contributing to the definition and establishment of a framework for VBEs that can be replicable to different application domains.

Acknowledgments. This work was supported in part by the ECOLEAD project funded by the European Commission. The authors thank the valuable contributions of their partners in the ECOLEAD consortium.

7. REFERENCES

[1] Afsarmanesh H., Guevara-Masis V., Hertzberger L.O., Virtual Community support in TeleCARE, in *Processes and Foundations for Virtual Organizations*, Kluwer, Oct 2003.

[2] Afsarmanesh H., Kaletas E.C., Hertzberger L.O., The Potential of Grid, Virtual Laboratories and Virtual Organizations for Bio-sciences, in *proceedings of 28th Conference on Current Trends in Theory and Practice of Informatics,* SOFSEM 2001, Piest'any, Slovak Republic, 2001.

[3] Afsarmanesh H., Camarinha-Matos L.M. Future Smart-Organisations: a Virtual Tourism Enterprise. in *proceedings of 1st International Conference on Web Information System Engineering - WISE'2000*, Hong Kong, China, 2000.

[4] Bremer, C.; Mundim, A.; Michilini, F.; Siqueira, J.; Ortega, L. - A Brazilian case of VE coordination, *in Infrastructures for Virtual Enterprises*, Kluwer, Oct 1999.

[5] Blomvist, K. – Partnering in the dynamic Environment: The role of trust in asymmetric technology partnership formation, PhD thesis, Lappeenrant University of Technology, 2002.

[6] Camarinha-Matos L.M., Afsarmanesh H., TeleCARE: Collaborative virtual elderly care support communities, in *The Journal on Information Technology in Healthcare*, Vol. 2, Issue 2, London, Apr 2004, pp 73-86, ISSN 1479-649X.

[7] Camarinha-Matos, L.M.; Abreu, A. - A contribution to understand collaborative benefits, in *Emerging solutions for future manufacturing systems*, Springer, 2004.

[8] Camarinha-Matos, L.M.; Afsarmanesh, H. (Ed.s) - Collaborative networked organizations – A research agenda for emerging business models, Kluwer, 2004.

[9] Camarinha-Matos, L.M.; Afsarmanesh, H. - Elements of a base VE infrastructure, *J. Computers in Industry*, Vol. 51, Issue 2, Jun 2003, pp. 139-163.

[10] Camarinha-Matos, L.M.; Afsarmanesh, H.; Ollus, M. (Ed.s) – Virtual Organizations: Systems and Practices, Springer, 2005.

[11] Garita C., Afsarmanesh H., and Hertzberger L.O., The PRODNET Federated Information Management Approach for Virtual Enterprise Support. in *Journal of Intelligent Manufacturing*, vol. 12, pp. 151-170, 2001.

[12] Mejia, R.; Molina, A. - Virtual enterprise broker: Processes, methods and tools, in *Collaborative business ecosystems and virtual enterprises*, Kluwer, May 2002.

[13] Plüss, A.; Huber, C. – Virtuellefabric.CH – A source network for VE in mechatronics, in *Virtual Organizations – Systems and Practices*, Springer, 2005.

5

CO-DESNET: AN APPROACH TO MODELING COLLABORATIVE DEMAND AND SUPPLY NETWORK

Agostino Villa and Irene Cassarino
Dipartimento di Sistemi di Produzione ed Economia dell'Azienda
Politecnico di Torino, c.so Duca degli Abruzzi, 24, 10129 - Torino (Italy)
Phone: +39-011-564.7233; fax: -564.7299; e-mail: agostino.villa@polito.it

Present evolution of multi-firm supply chains and industrial districts urges to have at disposal procedures and methods for the organization and management of a ***CO***llaborative ***DE***mand & ***S***upply ***NET***work (***CO-DESNET***. The crucial point in organizing and managing such networks is "to assure good collaboration among partners": interactions among the firms as well as the connecting information pattern have to be designed accordingly. The presentation of a new model of a CO-DESNET is the scope of the paper: based on this model, conditions verifying how collaborative operations of the firms included in the network will occur, are derived.

1. INTRODUCTION

In several European countries, groups of Small-Mid scale Enterprises (SMEs) aim to cooperate together, forced by the globalization of markets. The result of these agreements usually is a *Demand & Supply Network (DESNET)*, which is structured as an "extended virtual enterprise", i.e. a temporary network of several firms which decide to cooperate together in a common given value chain for a limited time horizon.

A special interest of the industrial bodies is reserved to networks of firms characterized by "co-operation agreements" signed for a finite time horizon, and stated such that each firm could partially interact with the other network partners (i.e. each firm could also have a proper market share, thus involving in the network only a part of their own core business). The resulting new *DESNET* can have a finite life and it does not completely reduce the autonomy of any component firm, because each one can still produce items for proper clients, and then operate in a proper market segment (Villa, 2001). More precisely, all the enterprises which agree to be included into a *DESNET* and then be active inside the same supply chain, must sign an agreement to co-operating together in defining common production plans for specific products.

The design, organization and management of a "temporary *DESNET*" requires to apply new models of the network operations, based on the concepts of the multi-agent organizations (Zheng & Possel-Dolken, 2002) and defined in formal terms according to the theory of large-scale dynamic systems optimisation (see Sethi & Zhang, 1994).

Depending on above mentioned requirements, a *DESNET* will be here formally stated as a *virtually connected chain of service stages*, each one containing either a firm or a set of parallel firms, each firm with its proper autonomous decision-maker, denoted "*agent*" (Huang and Nof, 2000, Farantin et al, 1998, Yung & Yang, 1999): each *agent* aims to cooperate with the others, but also wants to obtain the best profits for his own enterprise. Each service stage is connected to the upstream stages and to the downstream ones through a *virtual market place* (Wellman, 1993): it means that each firm will negotiate contracts for producing goods with downstream (buyer) firms as well as contracts for acquiring materials with upstream (supplier) firms. This *negotiation opportunity* is a qualifying character of a *DESNET*. Since each firm aims to gain its own best income, it utilizes the *DESNET* to which it belongs as a frame within which a "good negotiation" can be performed. Here "good negotiation" means that an agreement between each pair of "*consecutive agents*" (belonging to two consecutive stages of the chain) can be found such as to satisfy both agents, because both aim to being cooperative but, at the same time, want to make profits: then the desired agreement should assure a sufficient income to both of them.

The concepts above introduced allow detailing the real problem now facing supply chain designers and organizers (Villa, 2002): under which conditions does an individual enterprise find convenient to sign a temporary agreement for becoming a partner within a multi-agent *DESNET*?

Industrial experience suggests that this is a multi-faced problem depending on economic, technological and managerial considerations (Simchi-Levi & Kaminski, 2000). This paper will approach the problem according to the management point of view. And the goal is to develop a model of the multi-agent management problem in a *DESNET* such as to analyse how cooperation of partners could be enforced.

The paper contents are as follows. Section 2 introduces a model of the problem of managing interactions among the component firms of a *DESNET*. Section 3 will discuss the inter-firm negotiation problem, in order to derive conditions which can motivate cooperation among firms. The Section 4 will summarize final considerations about a collaborative management of local autonomous agents.

2. MODELING THE *DESNET* MANAGEMENT PROBLEM

The proposed model of a *DESNET* is based on the idea that such a networked industrial system consist of an "open commercial system" within which two component firms interact together by exchanging material and financial resources. For each material resource (i.e., parts of a common final family of products), a proper market place exists on which this resource is negotiated through a proper monetary value, between the supplier (i.e., the resource producer) and a customer (i.e. the purchaser who will utilize the resource in its own production sequence).

In a *DESNET*, considering the complete production cycle of a final product, each buyer will purchase at least a resource to apply his own manufacturing operations in order to transform it into a new item with more added value, to be sold in a downstream market place. So, the principal functions of any component firm are: purchasing, transforming (through either manufacturing or servicing), and selling of items. In a *Collaborative DESNET* (denoted in the following *CO-DESNET*[1], as the European project to which the paper is referred), this set of dynamic commercial interactions occurs into a co-ordinated protected industrial network. Partners indeed are connected together through collaboration agreements, which reflects into effectiveness of the commercial negotiations. These agreements should give each component firm a sufficient assurance of economic survival, by suitable management of usual "hard" business relations between large-scale and small-scale firms.

The model presented in the following aims at allowing an easy but correct evaluation of costs and advantages of the above sketched regulated industrial system. To this aim, a *CO-DESNET* composed by 4 enterprises, belonging to 2 different stages, is considered, together with a final customer. Two market places, one internal and one between producers and the final customer, define the interactions among the agents. At the material input stage, two firms (denoted by index $n=1,2$) produce parts to be sold to the two firms belonging to the following stage (denoted by index $n=3,4$). These last ones apply final operations to transform parts into products, to be sold to the final customer. The customer's exogenous demand is denoted by A_t.

Each agent n is modelled by a production optimisation problem: to maximize the firm profit (i.e. the difference between selling return and production costs) with respect to produced volume and price, under the constraints describing the inventory dynamics and the production capacity saturation.

The model for the first stage component firms $n=1,2$ is as follows:

$$\min_{X,P,Y} J_n = \sum_t (-P_{n,t} X_{n,t} + c_n I_{n,t,F} + r_n Y_{n,t}) \tag{1}$$

$$I_{n,t,F} = I_{n,t-1,F} + Y_{n,t} - X_{n,t} \tag{2}$$

$$Y_{n,t} \leq C_n \tag{3}$$

$$X_{n,t}, I_{n,t,F}, Y_{n,t}, P_{n,t} \geq 0 \tag{4}$$

where the following notations have been used, for the first stage component firms $n=1,2$, (all referred to time period t): $P_{n,t}$ is the price to sell items from supplier n to the second-stage buyers; $X_{n,t}$ is the volume sold from supplier n; $Y_{n,t}$, the volume produced by supplier n; $I_{n,t,F}$, the output storage of finished parts at supplier n; c_n, the storage unitary cost; r_n, the production unitary cost, and C_n, the production capacity of supplier n.

Referring to the second stage component firms, $n=3,4$ (denoted as "buyers"), the related models are as follows:

---

[1] *CO-DESNET* is the acronym of the Coordination Action (CA) project n° IST-2002-506673 / Joint Call IST-NMP-1, supported by the European Commission, Information Society Directorate-General, Communication Networks, Security and software, Applications, under the coordination of Politecnico di Torino, Prof. A. Villa, and with EC Official Dr. F. Frederix. This paper refers to research results developed for preparing the CA proposal at Politecnico di Torino.

$$\min_{Q,Z,W,D} J_n = \sum_t (Q_{n,t} Z_{n,t} + r_n W_{n,t} + c_{n,M} I_{n,t,M} + \\ + c_{n,P} I_{n,t,P} - S_t D_{n,t}) \tag{5}$$

$$I_{n,t,M} = I_{n,t-1,M} + Z_{n,t} - W_{n,t} \tag{6}$$

$$I_{n,t,P} = I_{n,t-1,P} + W_{n,t} - D_{n,t} \tag{7}$$

$$W_{n,t} \le C_n \tag{8}$$

$$Z_{n,t}, I_{n,t,P}, I_{n,t,M}, W_{n,t}, S_t \ge 0 \tag{9}$$

with the following notations: $Q_{n,t}$ is price to purchase items by buyer n from the first-stage suppliers at the internal market place; $Z_{n,t}$, the volume purchased by buyer n; $D_{n,t}$, the volume sold by buyer n to the downstream final client; A_t, the external demand from final client; $W_{n,t}$, the volume produced by buyer n; $I_{n,t,P}$, the output storage of final products produced by buyer n; $I_{n,t,M}$, the input storage of parts to be used by buyer n; S_t, the unitary price for selling final products during period t; $c_{n,P}$, the unitary cost of final products storage and $c_{n,M}$ is the unitary cost of input storage of parts.

Since the four enterprises belong to the same *CO-DESNET*, the network model is completed by introducing some conditions regulating interactions among the partners.

I. Conditions stating that production volumes must be balanced with internal and final demands:

I-a. All parts produced by firms in the upstream stage have to be purchased by firms of the second stage:

$$\sum_{n=1,2} X_{n,t} = \sum_{n=3,4} Z_{n,t} \tag{10}$$

I-b. The final client demand has to be fully satisfied:

$$\sum_{n=3,4} D_{n,t} - A_t = 0 \tag{11}$$

II. Conditions stating that prices of parts in the internal market place have to be balanced:

$P_{1,t} - P_{2,t} = 0$ (12); $P_{1,t} - Q_{4,t} = 0$ (13); $Q_{3,t} - Q_{4,t} = 0$ (14).

III. Condition stating that the production volumes of the firms belonging to a same stage have to be balanced according to the respective efficiency:

$$\frac{1}{C_1}(X_{1,t})^2 - \frac{1}{C_2}(X_{2,t})^2 = 0 \tag{15}$$

IV. Condition stating that the volumes of final products sold by the firms belonging to the final stage, to the end customer, have to be balanced according to the respective efficiency:

$$\frac{1}{C_3}(D_{3,t})^2 - \frac{1}{C_4}(D_{4,t})^2 = 0 \tag{16}$$

Note that these last two conditions state the effective collaborative rules for the enterprises belonging to a *CO-DESNET*. In practice, the agreement to be a network partner states that each firm agrees in producing, for the network needs, by using its own production capacity at a rate which must be balanced with the capacities of the other network partners: no enterprise will receive a demand for products "unbalanced" with respect to the others. In addition, conditions (12) to (14) will impose an equilibrium on the network internal prices.

The global management problem results from the whole set of conditions (1) to (16) above stated. It consists of a large-scale non-linear optimization problem: existence of an optimal solution can be proven according to standard optimisation theory results (Brandimarte & Villa, 1995).

By applying Lagrangian relaxation, the complete optimisation problem can be split into four optimization sub-problems, all interrelated together, each one linked to a component firm n, namely:

- for the firm $n=1$

$$\begin{aligned}\min_{X,P,Y} \Pi_1 = \sum_t (&-P_{1,t}X_{n,t} + c_1 I_{1,t,F} + r_1 Y_{1,t} + \\ &+ \alpha_t X_{1,t} + \gamma_t \frac{1}{C_1}[X_{1,t}]^2 + (\upsilon_t - \delta_t)P_{1,t})\end{aligned} \tag{17}$$

- for the firm $n=2$

$$\begin{aligned}\min_{X,P,Y} \Pi_2 = \sum_t (&-P_{2,t}X_{2,t} + c_2 I_{2,t,F} + r_2 Y_{2,t} + \\ &+ \alpha_t X_{2,t} - \gamma_t \frac{1}{C_2}[X_{2,t}]^2 - \upsilon_t P_{2,t})\end{aligned} \tag{18}$$

- for the firm $n=3$

$$\begin{aligned}\min_{Q,Z,W,D} \Pi_3 = \sum_t (&Q_{3,t}Z_{3,t} + r_3 W_{3,t} + c_{3,M} I_{3,t,M} + \\ &+ c_{3,P} I_{3,t,P} - S_t D_{3,t} - \alpha_t Z_{3,t} \\ &- \eta_t \frac{1}{C_3}[D_{3,t}]^2 + \beta_t Q_{3,t} + \omega_t D_{3,t})\end{aligned} \tag{19}$$

- for the firm $n=4$

$$\begin{aligned}\min_{Q,Z,W,D} \Pi_4 &= \sum_t (Q_{4,t} Z_{4,t} + r_4 W_{4,t} + c_{4,M} I_{4,t,M} + \\ &+ c_{4,P} I_{4,t,P} - S_t D_{4,t} - \alpha_t Z_{4,t} \\ &+ \eta_t \frac{1}{C_4} [\mathrm{D}_{4,t}]^2 + (\delta_t - \beta_t) Q_{4,t} + \\ &+ \omega_t D_{4,t})\end{aligned} \quad (20)$$

In above stated formulations, the newly introduced variables (in Greek letters) denote the Lagrangian variables, by which the constraints have been included into the augmented global functional to be minimized. *Maximization with respect to Lagrangian variables will allow to obtain the co-ordination conditions.*

3. COOPERATION CONDITIONS AMONG PARTNER FIRMS

Conditions which assure collaborative operations of the firms belonging to a *DESNET*, can be obtained by analysing the Lagrangian variables, introduced in the relaxed formulation, since Lagrangian variables denote co-ordination costs. Some particularly interesting examples of such conditions are outlined in the following.

(a) The variable α_t denotes the co-ordination cost concerning the volumes exchanged between the two suppliers and the two buyers, as stated by constraint (10). In case the offered volume is greater than the requested demand, such cost is greater than zero. Then, from (17) and (18), both first-stage producers are pushed to reduce their throughput. For the second-stage buyers, from (19)-(20), the effect is opposite.

(b) The variable γ_t refers to the co-ordination cost concerning volumes of production to be shared between the two first-stage suppliers, related to condition (15). The squared valued functions in (17) and (18) force a split of production volumes respectively depending on the rate between the production throughput $X_{n,t}$ and the firm capacity utilization, estimated by $\frac{1}{U_{n,t}} = \frac{X_{n,t}}{C_n}$, for *n=1,2*.

Then, cost γ_t forces to minimize unbalancing between concurrent producers. The Lagragian variable η_t operates in a similar way as γ_t, on the two firms belonging to the second stage, as in constraint (16).

(c) The variable υ_t represents an "horizontal co-ordination" cost concerning a potential difference between prices offered by the concurrent first-stage suppliers, as referred to constraint (12). In case such cost will increase, the first supplier (*n=1*) is compelled to pay an adjoint quantity of production for each unit sold by the second supplier (*n=2*), as shown in (17) and (18). A similar effect is due to the second-stage "horizontal co-ordination" cost β_t, as in (19)-(20), now associated to constraint (14). This effect is a demonstration of how a *CO-DESNET* should operate in order to regulate the financial transactions between concurrent producers: prices must be maintained as equal as possible otherwise a "dumping" attempt will be paid in terms of reduction of the planned throughput.

(d) Again referring to price management within the network, the variable δ_t is referred to the "vertical co-ordination" between the price proposed by upstream producers (*n=1,2*) and the price which downstream buyers (*n=3,4*) could agree to pay, i.e. associated to constraint (13). As soon as δ_t decreases, buyer 3 should pay an additional cost per part to supplier 1. The price-coordinating costs are strictly interrelated together. Any price variation between two firms of the same stage should immediately imply price unbalancing on the other stage and between the firms belonging to the other stage, as well. This effect is evidenced by the Lagrangian variables associated to the "triangular conditions" (12-(14).

(e) The variable ω_t is the co-ordination cost associated to the equilibrium requirement between volumes offered by downstream firms (*n=3,4*) and demands of the end customer in (11), the real exogenous input of the whole *DESNET*. The sensitivity of the network management to ω_t can be read as a cost paid by end products' producers to the end customer if the volumes offered are greater than the demand (i.e., a discount to push sales).

4. FINAL CONSIDERATIONS

The performance evaluation of the *DESNET* above presented has to be completed by better specifying profitability conditions. In practice, a potential manager of a network of this type should be able to prove that the required investment for the network organization should be so advantageous as to promote a real collaboration among partners (Bullinger et al., 2002; and Supply Chain Council, 2001).

It should be approached, indeed, the problem of validating the economic advantage of an investment devoted to promoting a *DESNET*, by investigating if there is clear interest to increase as much as possible its dimension, as it could be useful from the structural point of view of acquiring even larger production capacity and wider market share. An answer is that complexity-induced costs cannot overcome advantages offered by the "protected market", advantages consisting of the reduced global transaction costs. Once the most relevant transactions costs are recognized as those due to the procurement of information about the market, the monitoring of the trade partners performance, the addressing of problems that might arise in trade relationships and the risk of partners opportunistic behaviour (V.Grover, M.K. Malhotra, 2003), then enterprises can be convinced of the advantage to stipulate multi-agent contracts, by specifying the contribution of each partner and the respective rate of the global income. This is the first suggestion that the presented network model gives in terms of "equilibrium-assuring management".

A further problem concerns how to evaluate the investment for the development and innovation of a *DESNET*. Several classic criteria have been introduced to perform an analysis of the return of investment, generally based on the balancing between costs and return flows (Rossetto & Villa, 2003). Recently, a method based on the concept of "real options" (i.c. by noting that, when an investment is decided, the decision-maker still has the opportunity to choose at which time to invest as well as in which type of realization) became more and more interesting. Referring to a *DESNET*, this method seems to be even interesting, because it allows a supply chain organizer to analyse alternatives: if to enlarge the chain, or to improve the connections among agents, or to promote specific technologies at some partner. Obviously, a robust estimation of the return of investment, at any option time and for any potential option, is mandatory. The model proposed in the previous Sections can be used as a "planner" of the network operations over a future time horizon: thus, it can be applied as an "observer" of the network evolution in front of modification hypotheses, and an "estimator" of the network innovations' advantage.

Acknowledgements: This research has been partially supported by the Italian Ministry of Education, University and Research, within a national-interest research programme PRIN.

REFERENCES

Brandimarte, P., and Villa, A. (1995). *Advanced Models for Manufacturing Systems* Management, CRC Press, Boca Raton.

Bullinger, H-J., Kuhner, M., and Van Hoof, A. (2002). Analyzing supply chain performance using a balanced measurement method, *Int. Journal of Production Research*, **40**, 3533-3543.

Faratin P., Sierra C., Jennings, Nick R., (1998) Negotiation decision functions for autonomous agents, Robotics and Autonomous Systems, 24, 159-182

Grover, V., Malhotra, M.K. (2003), Transaction Cost Framework in operations and supply chain management research: theory and measurement, *Journal of Operation Management*, **21**, 457-473.

Huang, C-Y., and Nof, S. Y. (2000). Autonomy and viability – measures for agent-based manufacturing systems, *Int. Journal of Production Research*, **33**, 4129-4148.

Rossetto, S., and Villa, A. (2003). Evaluating capital investment for worldwide supply chain organization, in Proc. IFAC Int. Workshop on Intelligent Assembly and Disassembly, T. Borangiu (ed), Bucharest, pp. 215-220.

Sethi, S.P., and Zhang, Q. (1994). *Hierarchical Decision Making in Stochastic Manufacturing Systems*, Birkhauser, Boston.

Supply Chain Council (2001). *Supply Chain Operations Reference Model*, see the web site: http://www.supply-chain.org.

Simchi-Levi D., Kaminski P., Simchi-Levi E., (2000) Desining and managing the Supply Chain – Concepts Strategies and Cases Studies, McGraw-Hill.

Villa, A. (2001). "Introducing some supply chain management problems", *Int. J. Production Economics*, **73**, 1-4.

Villa, A. (2002). "Emerging trends in large-scale supply chain management", *Int. Journal of Production Research*, **40**, 3487-3498.

Wellman, M.P. (1993), Market Oriented Programming Environments and its Applications to Multicommodity Flow Problems, *Journal of Artificial Intelligence.*

Yung S.K., Yang, C.C., (1999) A new approach to solve supply chain management problems by integrating multy agent technology and constraint networks, *Proceedings of the 32nd Hawaii International Conference on System Science.*

Zheng, L., and Possel-Dolken, F. (2002), *Strategic Production Networks*, Springer-Verlag, Berlin.

6 COORDINATION OF COMPETENCIES DEVELOPMENT WITHIN NETWORKS OF SMEs

Xavier Boucher, Emilie Lebureau
Ecole des Mines de Saint-Étienne - Centre G2I
158 cours Fauriel,42023 Saint Etienne Cedex 2, France
{boucher, lebureau }@emse.fr

That paper tackles the issue of competence increase in networks of firms, taking advantage of collaborative relationships. By hypothesis we limit our approach to competence increase for individual firms within a network, and we don't cover the increase of collective competence of the network itself. We develop a framework of decision support system, which objective is to compare alternative plans of actions for the collaborative development of competencies. We use a multi-criteria decisional method, and we formalize the decision process based on five criteria including the evaluation of value creation, cost generation and equity between partners. We apply the approach to an industrial case study of SMEs, in the field of software development.

1. INTRODUCTION

At the beginning of the 90's (Prahalad & Hamel, 1990) defined core competences as the "collective learning in the organization, especially how to coordinate diverse production skills and integrate multiple streams of technologies". Such definition seems to be really pertinent in many cases of emergence of networks of firms, where several firms often try and cooperate in order to make operational a new "collective corpus of competences". Indeed a network of firms provides an intermediary way of coordination between the coordination of the integrated firm and the coordination by the market. It gives the advantage of a real flexibility in the composition of the network, due to potential changes in the partners. Taking advantage of the cooperation, it provides higher innovation capabilities as well as opportunities of savings on transactions costs, which can even be applied to competencies transfers (Tuma, 1998) .

(Doz & Hamel, 1998) point out that « companies often turn to alliances to win the learning race. These are often faster and more effective than alternative approaches to learning...Alliances are often the best way for companies to quickly acquire and deploy new skills ». The approaches of « Resource-based view » initiated by B.Wernerfelt (1984) and « Competence-based view » by R.Sanchez & al. (1996) are the more coherent for this exchange vision of inter-organizational exchanges and also for competencies development. The Winner /Winner relationship makes possible to increase individual performances for each partner, induced by the collaborative growth. In that perspective, firms should consider cooperation as a central element of their competencies development processes.

Thus, (Peillon, 2001) synthesizes the main characteristics of those networks aiming at competence development :

- The partnerships between firms are durable and motivated by a shared strategy on competence development, even if each partner keeps its own goals.
- The network consists in relations characterized by interdependencies and by shared investments, for which the notion of equity between partners is a major issue for a good coordination of collaborative actions.

Through recent research, several contributions have underlined the necessity of formal decisional methods applied to competence management (Manthou & al, 2004), (Fischer & al, 2004), (Szegheo & Petersen, 2000). In that perspective, we propose below a regulation mechanism for the competencies exchanges within networks of firms to search optimum gains on learning and costs for the partners as well as equity in the share of those gains within the network. Indeed, even if cooperation provides an interesting reduction of costs and risks linked to inter-organizational learning processes, we must not forget the necessity of balancing mechanisms in order to ensure equity between the partners on gains and losses. The notion of equity has been largely applied in the economic transactions, but we propose to formalize it for an application to the evaluation of inter-organizational learning processes.

However, by hypothesis, we limit the approach to the collaborative development of competencies for individual firms within a network. We don't deal with the concept of collective competence of the network itself, which would require models not available yet.

The paper is divided into 5 sections. Section 2 introduces the industrial case study. We deal with the issue of competence identification and evaluation in section 3. Then, section 4 introduces the notion of scenario for collaborative competence development, and formalizes the decisional process to compare alternative scenarios. Section 5 provides conclusions and perspectives.

2. CASE STUDY

The case study presented here stems from a collaboration with a network of firms named ARTIC. The origin of the network was the necessity of collaboration between very small to small firms in order to ensure on the long run their position on the competitive market. The association ARTIC gathers about twenty firms from similar sectors : the SMEs considered in that paper are all working in design and sell of software products. We will focus the formal study on the case of 3 of those companies For confidentiality, the concrete information we use is juggled.

In order to manage the creation of tighter cooperation within the network, ARTIC has launched a systematic identification of competencies' maps of the firms and an evaluation of their competencies levels. The identification and evaluation of competencies in use was based on an internal audit procedure clearly defined in (Grecopme, 2003). In order to make possible a systematic comparison between distinct firms' profiles of competencies, the audit was based on competencies reference grids linked to their specific activity field as we underlined in section 3.1.

3. COMPETENCE QUALIFICATION

That section aims at explaining the evaluation of firms' competencies used as a basis to analyze potential competence-based cooperation. The qualification of competencies we propose provides an evaluation of the needs of competence development for each firm of the network.

3.1 Competence model and competence sets

Our research focuses on a systemic view on competence, using the s-a-r-C model (Boucher & Burlat, 2003) to describe firms competencies without restricting the notion of competence to actors' skills. On the contrary, we consider that the competence of a firm depends on three main aspects : the methods deployed in the firm (modellized with the concept of professional situations), the skills of employees (modellized with the concept of actors) and the technological context (modellized with the concept of material resource). Thus, the s-a-r-C competence model formalizes that the competence emerges from the interaction between these 3 major components: "the professional situations, the actors, and the material resources".

Each firm of the network is to be described by a set of competencies. The identification of sets of competencies requires competencies dictionaries or competencies reference grids. In France, the national reference grid ROME (Répertoire Opérationnel des Métiers et de l'Emploi) offers the advantages to provide a national standard and to be based on aggregated descriptions of competencies. However it keeps very general. For the industrial case study we needed to develop competence grids more detailed and more specific to the activity field of the firms (Grecopme, 2003). Such reference grids make easier a systematic identification of competencies as well as the systematic decision aid we propose.

Further more, referring to a formalism developed in (Boucher & Burlat, 2003), the sets of competencies identified with the audit are formalized using the fuzzy subsets theory (Zadeh, 1965). Indeed, we are considering that a firm E can be described by an h-rank finite set of competencies $C(E) = \{C_1, C_2, \ldots C_h\}$. Let C_i be an element of C(E). We note $\tilde{X}$ the fuzzy subset defined by $\tilde{X} = \{C_1|\mu_X(C_1), C_2|\mu_X(C_2), \ldots, C_h|\mu_X(C_h)\}$ where $\mu_X(C_i)$ is the characteristic membership function of C_i in $\tilde{X}$, $\mu_X(C_i)$ takes its values in [0,1]. The characteristic function will be used to assess the levels of competencies of a given firm.

3.2 Qualification of competencies

Our goal is also to provide an evaluation of firms' competencies levels. Competencies can be characterized by different measures of "competencies levels". For a given application in an organization, the evaluation of the three components {s-a-r} provides a first qualification of competencies that we call the "theoretical level of competence". To calculate this theoretical level of competence we have defined in (Boucher & Burlat, 2003) indicators on situations, actors, and resources. We consider :

$S = \{S1, S2, \ldots Sp\}$ a finite p-rank subset of situations, characterized with an indicator named firm "expertise level" on the professional situation. That indicator can be assessed referring to several factors like the degree of rationalization on the professional situation and the frequency on such situation.

A = {A1, A2, ... Aq} a finite q-rank subset of actors, characterized with an indicator named "actor suitableness" to the situation, relating to the availability of the actors and to the cognitive abilities required.

Q = {Q1, Q2, ... Qr} a finite r-rank subset of resources, characterized by an indicator named "service level", relating to the availability of the technical resources and the technological capabilities required for the situation.

Those three indicators provide us with control parameters, later used for the competency development actions plan. We defined in (Boucher & Burlat, 2003) and in (Grecopme, 2003) various ways to aggregate those indicators in the final theoretical level of competence, referring to the fuzzy subsets theory we are using. Table 1 presents the notations used for the three indicators as well as for the Theoretical competence level $\mu_{\tilde{N}(E)}(C_i)$ resulting from the aggregation.

3.3 Targets on competence development

We consider that the competence development strategy for each firm directly depend on the top management of the firm. The managers are asked to make explicit that strategy, by providing a set of target competencies levels to be reached.

The target level of the competency C_i for the firm E within the network provides the value of the characteristic membership function $\mu_{\tilde{O}(E)}(C_i)$ (Table 1). For the entire network, we formalize various sets of targets, each set representing a competence development strategy for one of the partners.

Table 1 - Basic mathematical characteristics

Data	Explanation
$\mu_{\tilde{Q}(E)}(C_i)$	"Resource service" level in a competence C_i for a firm E.
$\mu_{\tilde{A}(E)}(C_i)$	"Actors suitableness" level in a competence C_i by a firm E.
$\mu_{\tilde{S}(E)}(C_i)$	"Expertise level" of the actors in a competence C_i by a firm E.
$\mu_{\tilde{N}(E)}(C_i)$	Theoretical level of competence : $\mu_{\tilde{N}(E)}(C_i)=Min(\mu_{\tilde{S}(E)}(C_i),\mu_{\tilde{A}(E)}(C_i),\mu_{\tilde{Q}(E)}(C_i))$
$\mu_{\tilde{O}(E)}(C_i)$	Target on competence level by a firm E of the network, on a competence C_i

3.4 Competence developments needs

Within the network, each enterprise E is characterized by a set of competencies C(E) ={C_1, C_2, ... C_n}, with i taking values from 1 to n. Using a comparison between the target levels and the theoretical levels of competence we can calculate a pertinence indicator ρ_1, defined in (Boucher and Burlat, 2003) which measures for each enterprise the overall gap between the competencies available and the targets.

$$\rho_1=1-\frac{1}{n}\sum_{i=1}^{n}\left|\mu_{\tilde{N}(E)}(C_i)-\mu_{\tilde{O}(E)}(C_i)\right|$$

This indicator corresponds to a notion of "pertinence", i.e. the appropriateness of the means implemented with respect to the targets. In the case of ARTIC, the firms have identified 10 basic competencies (both technical and managerial competencies) to be potentially developed in cooperation within the network. Table 2 indicates the gap between target and competence for the three firms considered (with $\mu_{\tilde{O}(E)}(C_i)$ the target level for each competence and $\mu_{\tilde{N}(E)}(C_i)$ the theoretical competence level).

Table 2 - Initial data for the case study "ARTIC"

		Enterprise 1			Enterprise 2			Enterprise 3		
Competencies	*Name: "To be able to...*	$\mu_{\tilde{O}(E)}(C_i)$	$\mu_{\tilde{N}(E)}(C_i)$	e_i	$\mu_{\tilde{O}(E)}(C_i)$	$\mu_{\tilde{N}(E)}(C_i)$	e1	$\mu_{\tilde{O}(E)}(C_i)$	$\mu_{\tilde{N}(E)}(C_i)$	e_i
C 1	Conceive business software	1	0,5	0,5	0,75	0	0,75	0,5	0,35	0,15
C2	Achieve programming	0,5	0,5	0	0,5	0,5	0	1	0,72	0,28
C3	Master software adaptability and evolution	1	0,63	0,37	0,5	0	0,5	0,75	0,4	0,35
C4	Control quality	0,75	0,5	0,25	0,75	0	0,75	0,5	0,38	0,12
C5	Bring under control quality-costs-lead times	1	0,5	0,5	0,75	0	0,75	0,5	0,5	0
C6	Keep in line with quality standards	0,25	0	0,25	0,5	0	0,5	0,5	0	0,5
C7	Stage campaigns for quality continuous improvement	0,5	0	0,5	0,5	0	0,5	0,5	0	0,5
C8	Achieve marketing	1	0	1	0,25	0	0,25	0,5	0,5	0
C9	Manage customer relationship	1	0	1	0,75	0,38	0,37	0,75	0	0,75
C10	Manage sales	1	0,25	0,75	1	0,64	0,36	0,75	0	0,75

Such data provide us with the identification of the competence development needs of each firm. Then we can define **actions of competence development** aiming at reducing that pertinence gap, and of course we will take advantage of the network to implement cooperative actions of competence exchanges. Section 4.3 underlines the procedure used to identify potential actions for a specific network.

We deal with elementary actions, each of them only applied to one of the three components of the competence "situation", "actors" or "resources". A given action of competence development w_j has an impact on the level $\mu_{\tilde{Q}(E)}(C_i)$ or $\mu_{\tilde{A}(E)}(C_i)$ or $\mu_{\tilde{S}(E)}(C_i)$. So the theoretical competence level shifts from a $\mu_{\tilde{N}(E)}(C_i)$ to a new value $\mu_{\tilde{N}'(E)}(C_i)$. The action of competence development creates an increment $\Delta(E_i,w_j)$ of the theoretical competence level for a enterprise E_i, with ($\mu_{\tilde{N}'(E)}(C_i) \geq \mu_{\tilde{N}(E)}(C_i)$) because the w_j are improvement actions.

4. COOPERATIVE SCENARII OF COMPETENCE INCREASE

4.1 Hypothesis on competence development

The decisional process we propose below refers to the following restrictions :

- We only deal with the development competencies of the firms considered individually ;
- Therefore, the actions of competence development are based on competence

similarities. They don't cover potential complementarities of competencies which could lead to a collective competence.

- The decisional process will support the equitable identification of collaborative actions of competence development. Those actions could also be completed in each firm by complementary investments if necessary.

The goal of the decisional process presented below is to select competencies development actions in order to improve the pertinence, i.e. in order to reduce the gap between the targets and the available levels of competence. In this perspective, we formalize various alternatives of cooperation on competencies, and we define a decision support procedure to guide the collaborative building of plan of actions. The alternative plans of action to be compared are called "scenarios". The selection of a scenario within a network will respect the two following principles:

(1) Maximization of the increase of competencies for each enterprise (with regards to their targeted goal for competence development) by a conceptual use of actions in cooperative mode.

(2) Equitable balancing between the increases of competencies of each partner.

Indeed we underlined before that even if the cooperation provides an interesting value-added to inter-organizational learning processes, we can not forget the necessity of equity between the partners to share the gains and losses.

4.2 Decisional criteria

To fit both principles, the classification of scenarios for collaborative development of competencies can be processed in a systematical way referring to several criteria including equity measures. In that perspective, we define in that section five decisional criteria to make possible the comparison of the alternative scenarios. Each scenario (i) includes a set of competence development actions (w_j), (ii) can have impact on several competencies, and (iii) can have impact on several partners. Thus, to proceed to scenarios comparison, we need global indicators concerning all the partners and all the actions in each scenario.

Furthermore, we decided to distinguish between equity on value creation and equity on costs because both constitutes two different regulation variables : a more aggregated vision would reduce the precision of the decision to be taken.

- **Value induced by a plan of actions**

First, for each action, we need to evaluate the local improvement on the competency components. As underlined in section 3.4, a given action will change the theoretical competence level from $\mu_{\tilde{N}(E)}(C_i)$ to the new value $\mu_{\tilde{N}'(E)}(C_i)$. Thus, for a set of actions W(R) selected by the network of SMEs, we have a global increment of the theoretical competence level written:

$$\Delta(E,W(R)) = \sum_{i=1}^{n}\left(\mu_{\tilde{N}'(E)}(C_i)-\mu_{\tilde{N}(E)}(C_i)\right)$$

This increment $\Delta(E,W(R))$ measures the increase of competence due to the scenario W(R) for a specific partner E. Considering k firms within a network, the indicator I_1 measures the overall competence increase induced by W(R) on all the partners:

$$I_1(\mathrm{W(R)}) = \sum_{j=1}^{k} \Delta(\mathrm{E}_j, \mathrm{W(R)}) \quad (1)$$

- **Equity on competence increase**

The equity on competence increase is an equity between the value transmitted by each partner to the network and the value he acquires on its side. In fact, we measure the homogeneity of the ratios between the transmitted value and the acquired value (one ratio for each partner). As an hypothesis, we consider that a "transfer of value" is an organizational learning action, where a firm E induces a competence increase for its partners in the network, without any competence increase for E. We call "acquisition of value" the opposite mechanism.

Equity would be that the global competence increase would be fairly shared between all the partners. For every action w_j and for every enterprise E_i, we use the variable $v(E_i, w_j)$ to indicate if the action w_j is a transfer of value (in that case $v(E_i, w_j)=1$) or an acquisition of value (in that case $v(E_i, w_j)=0$) for Ei. Considering m actions and k enterprises, the ratio R between the transmitted value and the acquired value for the firm E_i is given by:

$$R(E_i)=\left(\sum_{j=1}^{m}(\mathrm{v}(\mathrm{E}_i,w_j)\times\Delta(E_i,w_j))\right)\Big/\left(\sum_{j=1}^{m}((1-\mathrm{v}(\mathrm{E}_i,w_j))\times\Delta(E_i,w_j))\right)$$

For a partner when that ratio tends to 1, there is a good balance between the competence he provides to its partners and the competence he can get from them. But we need an overall indicator, to compare two scenarios taking into account all the partners. Within the network, the equity indicator I_2 gives an estimation of the dispersion on the ratios $R(E_i)$ by a classical variance measure:

$$I_2(\mathrm{W(R)}) = 1/(k-1)\sum_{i=1}^{k} (R(E_i)-M_R)^2 \text{ with } \mathrm{M_R} \text{ the mean of the ratios.} \quad (2)$$

- **Overall costs induced by a scenario**

This function is the sum of the costs stemming from the implementation of the actions of competencies development, supported by the k enterprises of the network.

$$I_3=\sum_{i=1}^{k} costs(E_i) \quad (3)$$

The different costs are determined thanks to a system of reference which specify the calculi parameters to provide for each action.

- **Equity on costs**

We deal here with the equity on the costs stemming from the competence development actions. This equity is a measure of costs dispersion between the partners, with regards to the average cost for all of them. This indicator of equity I4 is calculated from the standard deviation of each partner E_i costs to the average cost:

$$I_4 = 1/k \times \sqrt{\sum_{1=1}^{k} (\cos ts(E_i) - Mc)^2} \text{ with } Mc = I_3/k \tag{4}$$

- **Feasibility of the scenarios** Each action of competence development can be characterized by its feasibility. The feasibilities are determined thanks to a system of reference which specify the calculi parameters to provide for each action. Then we evaluate the global feasibility of a scenario, by the average feasibility considering every action included in the scenario.

$$I_5 = \sum_{j=1}^{k} \frac{feasibility(wj)}{k} \tag{5}$$

4.2 AHP method

The comparison of potential scenarios (i.e. sets of actions) uses the AHP (Analytic Hierarchical Process) developed by T.L Saaty. The decision-makers keep the possibility to provide different weights to the five previous indicators. This method presents the advantages to model the articulation between the individual objectives of each partner and the collective ones of the network, to give a clear visualization in the decision-makers preferences, and to easily generate various ranking of scenarios, according to the weights given to the five indicators.

4.3 Application

As we underlined before, the concrete application of the approach starts with an internal audit of the firms which provides us with the necessary data on sets of competencies, level of competencies et targets on competence development. The decisional process starts with a systematic analysis of the gap e_1 between the targets and the actual theoretical competence levels (table 2).

A second phase of the decisional process consists in the systematic identification of potential actions on the situations, actors, and resources' of each firm, to try and reduce those gaps. The process we use for a systematic identification of potential actions has been described in (Boucher & Lebureau, 2004). We use a generic typology of actions for the development of competencies and the concrete evaluations on situation, actors and resources for each competence to generate an exhaustive set of actions aiming at fulfilling the needs of the partners. Then, the actions set is also filtered using strategic, logical, or operational constraints concerning competence development to eliminate inconsistencies. Concerning the case study, that process result in a dozen of possible actions shown in table 3.

The resulting set of actions gathers all the possibilities of cooperative competence development. However depending on technical or economical constraints, all the actions can not always be implemented together. Therefore, the third stage of the decisional process is the generation of consistent scenarios, with regards to such constraints. Those scenarios are subsets the initial set of potential actions. In this example, we consider that a budget constraint induces the selection of only 3 cooperative actions among the 12 possible identified. Thus in this case, there are 220 possible scenarios consisting of 3 actions (C_3^{12}) that we have to compare in order to establish the most relevant in the cooperation objectives. The reader must remember that beyond selected cooperative actions, each company will supplement its action-plan with autonomous actions. Of course a change in this budget constraint would only modify the combinatory without modifying the proposed method.

Table 3 - Potential actions[1] of competencies development for ARTIC case study.

Actions	Actions definition
w_{1c}[A; C4; E_s 3; E_b1/ E_b2]	Inter-enterprise competencies transmission for individual actors
w_{2c}[A; C8; E_s 3; E_b1/ E_b2]	Inter-enterprise competencies transmission for individual actors
w_{3c}[S; C8; E_s 2; E_b1]	Best practices diffusion
w_{4c}[A; C1; E_s1; E_b2/ E_b3]	Inter-enterprise competencies transmission for individual actors
w_{5c}[A; C3; E_s3; E_b2]	Inter-enterprise competencies transmission for individual actors
w_{6c}[S; C4; E_s1; E_b2/ E_b3]	Best practices diffusion
w_{7c}[S; C9; E_s1; E_b2/ E_b3]	Best practices diffusion
w_{8c}[A; C9/C10; E_s2; E_b1/ E_b3]	Inter-enterprise competencies transmission for individual actors
w_{1m}[S; C1; E1UE2UE3]	Common Investment on methods
w_{2m}[S; C4; E1UE2UE3]	Common Investment on methods
w_{3m}[R; C4; E1UE2UE3]	Common Investment on one resource hold by the network
w_{4m}[A; C9/C10; E1UE2UE3]	Mutual formation of the individual actors

The last decisional phase consists in the selection of the most favourable scenario for competence development. For all the 220 scenarios, we calculate the five decisional criteria thanks to the formula (1) to (5), and we apply the analytic hierarchical process. If the decision-makers give the same weight to every criterion, we get the following results :

Table 4 - Some scores of the best scenarios after multi-criteria ranking.

Scenarios	SCORE	I_1 **(1)**	I_2 **(2)**	I_3 **(3)**	I_4 **(4)**	I_5 **(5)**
Scenario_59	75.79 %	[1.5/2[	[0.5/1[	[15000/20000[	[0.25/0.5[	[0.08/0.12[
Scenario_116	74.74 %	[1/1.5[	[0.25/0.5[	[15000/20000[	[0/0.125[	[0.08/0.12[
Scenario_90	74.74 %	[2/2.5[	[0.25/0.5[	[20000/25000[	[0.125/0.25[	[0.04/0.08[
Scenario_175	72.63 %	[1.5/2[	[0/0.125[	[20000/25000[	[0/0.125[	[0.04/0.08[
Scenario_58	72.63 %	[1.5/2[	[0/0.125[	[20000/25000[	[0.125/0.25[	[0.04/0.08[
Scenario_190	72.63 %	[1.5/2[	[0.125/0.25[	[20000/25000[	[0/0.125[	[0.04/0.08[

It is between these 6 scenarios that we find the better balance in the competence gains, costs, feasibilities and equity, since they get the three best notes. The final decision of the scenario to implement is to be taken by the network's managers. Their decision could be oriented by a qualitative analyze of the better noted scenarios : the scenario_90 is better for the global competence gain, but it is the worth for the global costs, the scenario_59 et scenario_116 are comparable in term of global costs and feasibilities, and if we choose to favor equity on the competences gains and costs, we would prefer the scenario_175.

The analysis of scenarios also shows the influence of interactions between competencies. For instance the actions w_{8c}[A; C9/C10; E_s2; E_b1/ E_b3] and w_{4m}[A; C9/C10; E1UE2UE3] appear often in the best scenarios. It can be explained by the fact that they have impact on two competencies (the same actor supports C9 and

[1] In table 3, the notation w1c[A; C4; Es 3; Eb1/ Eb2] indicates that the action w1c has an impact on the actor (A) for the competence C4, with the firms E1 et E2 as beneficiary-firm and E3 as root-firm.

C10 competencies and shares knowledge on both competencies). The decision aid method presented here shows that interactions between competencies are a key element of our approach. Interactions between learning actions on actors, resources or situations within a same competence are taken into account in the calculation of the theoretical level of competence; and interactions between actions on distinct competencies (common actors or resources of distinct competencies) are taken into account in the calculation of actions impacts.

5. CONCLUSION

That paper is based on a formalization of the notion of firms' competencies, and it points out a collaborative decision process aiming at enhancing the competence development of partners within a network. On a conceptual point of view, the main value added consists in the decisional criteria which provide both an objective measure of the organizational learning a network of firms and a measure of equity concerning the transfer of competencies. Of course the approach is based on several restrictive hypothesis concerning the model of competencies, the way to make explicit a strategy of competencies, and the decisional process. Such hypothesis induce several perspectives which could enlarge the application field. The most important would be to take into account not only the development of similar competencies between firms, but also complementary competencies. On an applicative point of view that paper demonstrates the possibility to develop quantitative decision tools applied to the notion of competence management.

REFERENCES

1. Boucher X, Burlat P. "Vers l'intégration des compétences dans le pilotage des performance de l'entreprise". Journal Européen des Systèmes Automatisés 2003: 37(3). 363-390.
2. Boucher X, Lebureau E. "Practical Aspects of Knowledge Management". 5th International Conference PAKM 2004, Vienna, Austria, December 2-3, 2004. ISBN: 3-540-24088-8.
3. Doz Y, Hamel G. Alliance advantage: the art of creating value trough partnering. Boston : Harvard Business School Press, 1998.
4. Fischer M, Jähn H, Teich T. "Optimizing the selection of partners in production networks". Robotics and Computer-Integrated Manufacturing 2004 : 20. 593-601.
5. GRECOPME II, Burlat P (coord.). Rapport final du projet de recherche GRECOPME II à la région Rhône-Alpes. Thématique prioritaire « Productique ». September 2003.
6. Manthou V, Vlachopoulou M, Folinas D. "Virtual e-Chain (VeC) model for supply chain collaboration". International Journal of Production Economics 2004: 87. 241 – 250.
7. Peillon S. Le pilotage des coopération interentreprises : le cas des groupement de PME . Thèse de l'Ecole Nationale Supérieure des Mines de Saint Etienne. October 2001.
8. Prahalad, CK., Hamel G. "The core competence of corporation". Harvard Business Review May-June 1990. 79-91.
9. Sanchez R, Heene A, Thomas H. Dynamics of Competence-based Competition. Elsevier,1996.
10. Szegheo O, Petersen SA. "Extended Enterprise Engineering – a model-based framework". Journal of concurrent engineering research and applications 2000: 8. 32-39.
11. Tuma, A. "Configuration and coordination of virtual production networks". International Journal of Production Economics 1998: 56-57. 641-648.
12. Wernerfelt B. "A Resource-Based View of the Firm". Strategic Management Journal 1984: 5. 171-180.
13. Zadeh L. A., " Fuzzy sets". Information and Control 1965: 8. 338-353.

PART 3

VO CREATION - FRAMEWORKS

7

TOWARDS A FRAMEWORK FOR CREATION OF DYNAMIC VIRTUAL ORGANIZATIONS

Luis M. Camarinha-Matos [1], Ivan Silveri [2], Hamideh Afsarmanesh [3], Ana Inês Oliveira [1]

[1] *New University of Lisbon, PORTUGAL, cam@uninova.pt, aio@uninova.pt*

[2] *TXT e-solutions SpA, ITALY, ivan.silveri@txt.it*

[3] *University of Amsterdam, THE NETHERLANDS, hamideh@science.uva.nl*

Effectiveness of the virtual organization (VO) creation process is the base for the possibility of having truly dynamic VOs in response to collaboration opportunities. A realistic approach to materialize agility in VO creation is the assumption of a VO Breeding Environment. In this context, a discussion of the process and suggested functionalities towards a VO creation framework are presented.

1. INTRODUCTION

The possibility of rapidly finding a set of partners that best fit a business opportunity and quickly configure them into a collaborative network to exploit that opportunity seems indeed a desirable scenario to face the challenges of market turbulence. The same idea is also very appealing in other non-business oriented contexts. An extreme case being the incident management and disaster rescuing processes, when it is necessary to very rapidly engage and coordinate activities of a large number of entities (e.g. fire brigades, police, hospitals, local government, non-governmental organizations). This very idea of groups of organizations being able to rapidly configure themselves into some form of mission/goal-oriented collaborative form embeds the notion of great agility.

Finding the right partners and establishing necessary conditions for starting the collaboration process might however be costly and a time consuming activity, and therefore an inhibitor of the aimed agility. Among others, obstacles include lack of information (e.g. non-availability of catalogs with normalized profiles of organizations) and lack of preparedness of organizations to join the collaborative process. Overcoming the mismatches resulted from the heterogeneity of potential partners (e.g. different as in infrastructures, corporate culture, methods of work, and business practices) requires considerable investment, building trust, a pre-requisite for any effective collaboration, is not straight forward and requires time.

Furthermore, partners' selection is not a simple "optimization" problem. More than a matching process based on potential and abilities (e.g. competencies, capacities, recommendations), many other factors, some of them of subjective nature (e.g. personal preferences and established trust based on previous experience), suggest that fully automated processes are not at all a realistic approach. It is rather preferable to conceive a computer-assisted framework to help the human planner in making decisions.

The ECOLEAD project is designing a VO creation framework which represents an approach to minimize the mentioned difficulties by conceiving the VO creation within a VO Breeding Environment context. After a brief analysis of related work, the following sections summarize the approach being followed in ECOLEAD as well as the preliminary results of this ongoing initiative.

2. PAST APPROACHES

Three approaches are so far addressed in the R&D as alternatives for VO creation.

2.1 Manual or assisted approach

Manual or assisted approaches in VO creations are derived from the traditional methods adopted in working group creation for big organizations or for extended enterprises, mostly based on "competency" matching.

The adoption of a competency-based approach in Human Resource Management was initially determined by the acknowledged inability of traditional psychological and cultural tests in predicting successful job performances. In the early seventies, McClelland and his research group demonstrated that traditional measures, primarily based on candidates' cultural background, were not meaningfully correlated to excellence on job and, moreover, the results were strongly biased by racial, social and sexual prejudices [10]. McClelland's approach was based on two fundamental rules: (1) To compare groups of excellent or best performers with group of average performers in order to determine which characteristics could be associated to successful job performances. (2) To elicit operational cognitive schemata and behaviors that can be related to the job performance on a causal and objective basis.

The competence-based approach has received a wide consensus in Human Resources Management practices because it allows overcoming the typical pitfalls of the traditional job-based approach where the basic mechanism to identify the right person for the right job was the following: (1) To describe precisely the set of tasks, activities and responsibilities characterizing a given job; (2) To find the individual that best fits the job description: this is done applying the matching selection.

The set of required skills of a potential partner is usually called "profile". A skill is the ability to perform a physical or mental task, i.e. what we can do. A competence is knowledge and / or skill, plus capacity to apply it and the ability to make others applying it. It is characterized by managerial capabilities and personal qualities. Competency is strictly connected to work situations (e.g. information diffusion in inter-functional team). It is how we behave when performing a task, how we go about it and the application of our knowledge and skills.

A profile is moreover influenced by other external factors, not directly related to the candidate's skills, but which are affecting its matching index: namely, the behavioral aspects. These are very relevant and cannot be classified and categorized in the form of competence, but they should be traced in historical records that must be considered when a candidate's ranking is made. Such aspects could be for instance:

- Past performance experiences: how was the candidate behavior, for instance if it was collaborating, active, proactive in providing contributions as well as in performing the task.

- Human Competencies: what affects the human being sphere, if the candidate is keen in team working, etc.

The candidate's matching/selection is typically done in two steps: (1) a matching algorithm is applied to the candidates' list based on the skills that can be well defined (the competencies), (2) these candidates are filtered applying the second type of competencies, which affect the human behavior.

Most of the considerations made in the context of human resources management apply as well to the selection of organizations as partners for a VO. Other aspects to consider include the interoperability readiness, size of organization, "robustness" of its skills base (i.e. critical mass), geographical location, costs, etc.

A typical difficulty is the access to reliable profile and performance information as well as the time spent with the preliminary filtering of potential candidates. An earlier example of attempt to move from a manual approach to a computer assisted one can be found in the PRODNET project [6]. Recently there has been a considerable effort put in the so-called electronic procurement [4]. The main objectives in this area include the definition of "normalized" procedures for public announcement of business offers, reception, and management of bids. Standardization is in fact the main obstacle in electronic procurement. The VO partners' search and selection activity shares several similarities with the classic electronic procurement. Both areas require the identification of potential suppliers / partners to be addressed, the adoption of normalized specification of requirements and bids, management of directories of potential partners, management of bids, and decision support functionalities.

2.2 Multi-agent based approaches

A growing number of works are being published on the application of multi-agent systems (MAS) and market-oriented negotiation mechanisms for the Virtual Enterprise (VE) formation [4].

Figure 1 – Enterprise represented as an agent

One early example can be found in [13]. This work assumes a virtual market place where enterprises, represented by agents that are geographically distributed and possibly not known in advance, can meet each other and cooperate in order to achieve a common business goal. A MAS architecture is proposed to model the electronic market to support the formation of the VO. In addition to the agents representing the enterprises, there is a market agent – coordinator or broker – that is created and inserted in the MAS community when a business opportunity is found. A multi-round contract-net protocol is followed and the most favorable bids are selected based on a multi-criteria mechanism and constraint-based negotiation. Examples of considered criteria are lower-cost, higher quality, higher availability, etc. Utility values are associated to each of these criteria and a linear combination of attribute values weighted by their utility values is used. Multiple negotiation rounds can take place. At the end of each round bidder agents receive indication whether their bids are wining or loosing and a rough qualitative justification, allowing them to change the parameters of their proposals.

A similar work is found in [9] where a more detailed analysis of the problem of goal decomposition, leading to a hierarchy of VE goals, is done. In addition to the enterprise agents and VE coordinator agent (broker), an information server agent is introduced to keep public information related to common organizational and operational rules, market environment, enterprises and products / services provided, etc. The need for a common ontology to support the communication among agents is explicitly introduced and a multi-attribute, constraint-based negotiation / selection process is implemented. The work described in [14] identifies the need for yellow pages agents that are responsible to accept messages for registering services (similar to the information agent server mentioned above). They also consider the concept of Local Area, a quasi-physical division of the network that can be controlled by a local area coordinator. This is a similar concept to the Local Spreading center first introduced by the HOLOS system [11, 12]. Finally [8] elaborates further on the application of market-oriented principles, with particular reference to the principles of general equilibrium in micro-economics.

More recent works have attempted to progress with new negotiation protocols, auction mechanisms, distributed matching processes, etc. In order to improve the effectiveness of the contracting process and to dynamically form VOs the need to develop forms of e-contracting has been identified. Several significant characteristics for the e-contracting process can be found in [1]. These proposals are however still limited by a number of factors which affect their practical implantation including: (i) Lack of common standards and ontologies, a situation difficult to overcome in a general "open universe" of enterprises; (ii) None of these proposals takes properly into account more subjective facets (soft computing issues) like trust, commitment, successful cooperation history, etc.; (iii) In general they pay little attention to the implantation aspects and the management of the yellow pages / market place; (iv) Security issues in the negotiation process are not addressed, which is a critical point as the agents are only partially cooperative (they might be self-interested, competitive, and even exhibit antagonistic behavior). On the other hand, the attempt to reach a fully automated decision-making process, although an interesting academic exercise, is quite unrealistic in this application domain. Furthermore, as agents are designed and developed independently, it is quite difficult to guarantee their coordination unless common rules ("social laws") are adopted. Agent-based approaches can lead to an interesting simulation tool.

2.3 Service federation based approach

Figure 2 illustrates the basic principles behind the service federation approach [5]. According to this model, companies (potential members of the virtual organization) are considered as "service providers", i.e. the potential collaborative behavior of each company is "materialized" by a set of services. The approach assumes the existence of one entity that keeps a catalog of services where service provider companies publish their service offers. This entity is sometimes called a "service market", a "service promoter node", or even "service portal". Regardless the different implementation approaches the general three major functions – publish, discover, invoke – are usually considered.

This approach reflects an indirect partners' selection – what is selected is the service (not the provider), i.e. the immediate task is the composition (or orchestration) of complex services, not the consortia. Partners are implicitly selected via the specific services that are chosen. One example of this approach applied to the tourism sector can be found in [2].

Although the "popularity" of the web services paradigm give this approach some relevance, there are still a number of limitations in the current service model including: Are services always available? How is the workload balanced? What is the level of awareness of the service provider? Can all skills be represented as services? Does it make sense to consider specific services for the partner search / negotiation phase? Furthermore, most example developments so far are for e-commerce, not for collaborative activities.

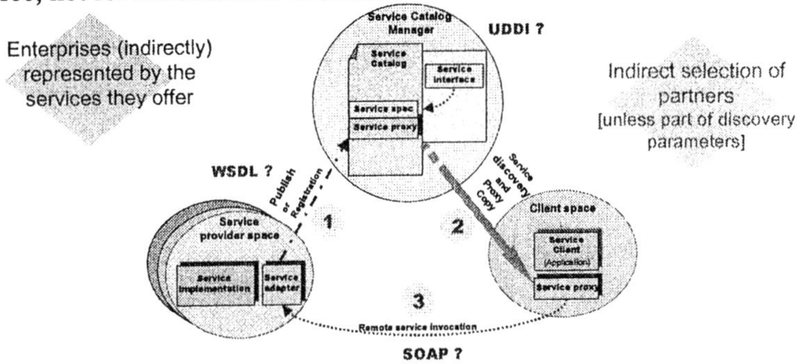

Figure 2 – Service federation approach

One important feature for the service catalog is the opportunity to provide the broker with an intelligent search / selection filtering lookup functionality based on the services attributes. Another main issue is the access rights, that is, who are allowed to access the information in the catalog. The service providers shall keep the autonomy and the right to specify whom and under which conditions has access rights to their registered services.

3. VO CREATION PROCESS

In ECOLEAD the VO creation process is considered to happen in the context of a VO Breeding Environment (VBE) [3, 5, 12]. This long term collaborative association is composed of organizations that are prepared to collaborate and thus rapidly respond to a collaboration opportunity.

As illustrated in Fig. 3, it shall be noted that VBE creation and VO creation are different processes, triggered by different motivations. A VBE is created as a long term "controlled border" association and its members are recruited from the "open universe" of organizations according to the criteria defined by the VBE creators or administrators. A VO is a temporary organization triggered by a specific business / collaboration opportunity. Its partners are primarily selected from the VBE members. In case there is a lack of skills or capacity inside the VBE, organizations can be recruited from outside. Considering that each company might have its list of "acquaintances" outside the VBE (i.e. other partners or former partners in activities outside the VBE), the search space can be seen as first composed of the VBE members, then with less probability by acquaintances of the VBE members (a kind of "extension" of the VBE borders), and finally by the "open universe" of organizations. For difficulties of preparedness, trust, etc, this last category will, of course, be the last resort.

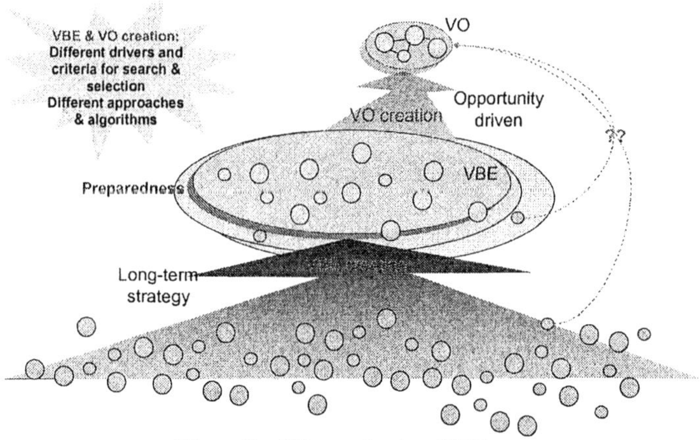

Figure 3 – VO creation in a VBE context

In this context the following main steps (Fig. 4a) are suggested for the VO creation process:

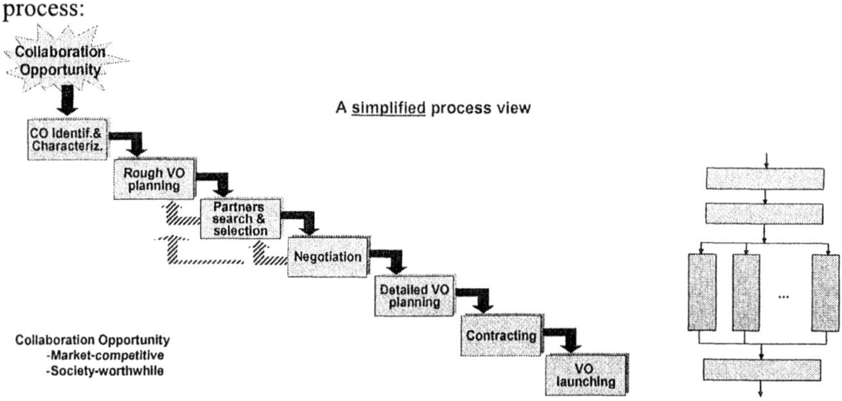

Figure 4– a) VO creation process b) Alternative solutions

♦ *Collaboration Opportunity Characterization*: this step involves the identification and characterization of a new Collaboration Opportunity (CO) that will trigger the formation of a new VO. A collaboration opportunity might be external, originated by a (potential) customer and detected by a VBE member acting as a broker. This is the case, in the business world, when the possibility to satisfy a customer, gaining money, rises from collaboration between members. Some opportunities might also be generated internally, as part of the development strategy of the VBE. This could happen in order to improve the VBE overall quality and competitiveness or the profitability of some members. As an example of this class of collaborations it is the case when a manufacturer company would like to reduce the failure rate of its production process. In order to do this it will approach a problem solving process involving other members of the VBE, which have equal or similar production process.

Four main collaboration modalities were identified, namely: (1) Collaborative business process (BP) model, (2) Project model, (3) Problem solving model, (4) Ad-hoc collaboration model.

A ***collaborative BP*** model can be defined as a set of heterogeneous activities normally distributed in cross-organizational sub-processes. These activities can be categorized as in the following: *Automatic Activities*, implemented by ICT services; *Interactive Activities*, implemented by Collaborative Work plus ICT services; *Co-operative Activities* implemented by Co-Work; *Manual Activities*, implemented by Humans; *Decisional Activities*, followed by "or" branches, alternatives (Fig. 5).

A ***collaborative project*** model can be defined as the support for multi-projects towards the definition of a work break down structure (WBS), composed by multi-projects, workpackages, tasks and activities and the support for the human resource management where Human Resources belongs to multi-organizations (Fig. 6). VOs, which will adopt this model, will need a set of supporting tools: *Technical/Financial Control*, control primitives for progress, technical (percentage of completion) and financial (budget); *Co-Work Integration*, integration with co-work services, collaboration measurement and rewarding; *Knowledge Management Integration*, integration with document and multi-media material exchange/sharing; *project management* facilities, nice presentations, re-planning and re-scheduling facilities for project managers.

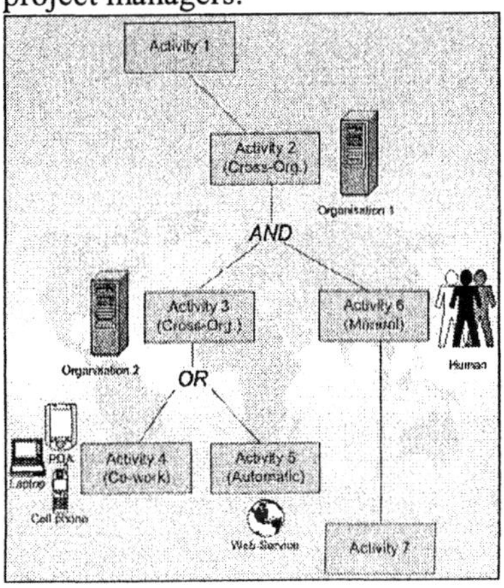

Figure 5 - Collaborative BP

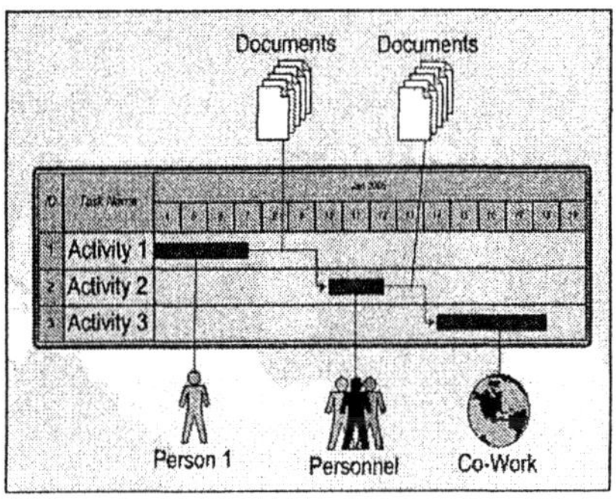

Figure 6 - Collaborative Project

In a ***collaborative problem solving*** a roadmap model must be established defining the as-is situation and the to-be scenario, performing the gap analysis and identifying the working groups (Fig. 7). In this case a VO will need: a Mediated Collaboration Model, where the mediator identifies contributors, collects and evaluates contributions; Collaboration Measurement & Reward, that is identification of value metrics, rewarding of experts contributing decisively towards the roadmap's goal achievement; Personal Time/Work Organizer, that is the possibility to integrate Project-Problem Solving Ad-Hoc collaboration sessions and/or off-line e-work; Specific Tools for Problem Solving, that is the integration with specific Problem Solving tools, like Diagnosis Tools, Case-based Reasoning, Expert Systems and Continuous Improvement.

The ***ad-hoc collaboration*** model can be very useful when big organizations, not used to tightly collaborate one with the other, are required to joint their efforts in order to rapidly give a quick response to an external request (e.g. like fire brigade and red cross in an emergency case) (Fig. 8); in this model only few persons are required to take decisions and in this way addressing their organizations towards the common goal. Supporting to this model is given by: *Integration and Composition of Co-Work*, several Co-Work services to be combined and integrated as atomic services; *Co-Work Logging*, primitives for multi-media Co-Work logs recording (text, speech, image, video); *Co-Work Analysis*, advanced services for Co-Work logs analysis (speech-to-text; MPEG analysis); *Ubiquitous Access*, as far as possible to integrate the Co-Work services with PTO/PWO (personal time organizer/ personal work organizer) in an AAA (Anybody-Anywhere-Anytime) scenario.

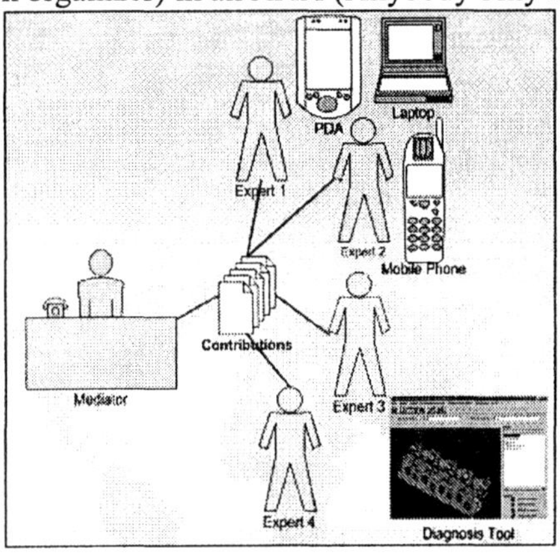

Figure 7 - Collaborative Problem Solving

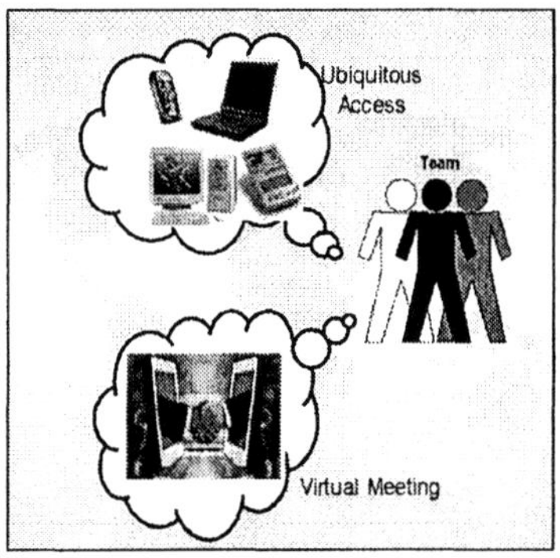

Figure 8 - Ad-hoc collaboration

Therefore the main issues to consider in this initial step are: Identification and categorization of the CO (external/explicit, internal/implicit), Collaboration modality, CO representation, CO feasibility analysis, Interaction with customer, Support (rapid) quotation / bidding, etc. The main actors involved in this step are the broker and the customer.

♦ *Rough VO planning*: determination of a rough structure of the potential VO, identifying the required competencies and capacities, as well as the organizational form of the VO and corresponding roles.

At this stage it is important to define the partnership form which is typically regulated by contracts and cooperation agreements. Fig. 9 illustrates some typical organizational forms for collaborative consortia [4].

Case 1: Explicit consortium. Collaboration is regulated by a joint contract with the customer and a consortium agreement. The Client cares about who is part of the consortium.

Case 2: Internal consortium. There is a contract between one representative of the consortium and the Client. The Client doesn't necessarily know about the way the consortium is organized. The consortium is also formalized using an agreement and an internal contract. Only one partner (the one that signs the contract) is committed to the Client. The other partners are committed to the one that signs the contract.

Case 3: Sub-contracting. There is a contract between one partner and a client and subcontracts between this partner and the other service / product providers. The Client doesn't necessarily know about the way the contracted partner is organized.

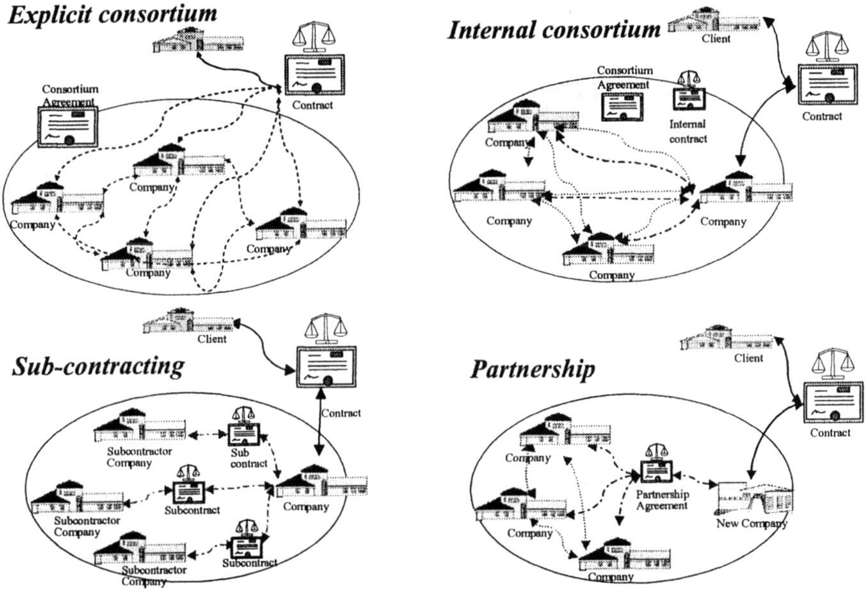

Figure 9 – Different types of collaborative consortia

Case 4: Partnership. The partnership creates an entity (new company) using a partnership agreement. The new company establishes a contract with the Client. Only the new company is committed to the Client. The partnership may continue after the end of the initial client contract.

Cases 1 and 2 are the most typical situations for dynamic VOs.

Other issues to be considered at this stage: Identification of needed competencies and capacities, Rough VO structure / topology / levels and associated roles, macro governance rules, Representation of rough VO model, Top-down (planning) vs. bottom-up (emerging), Simulation (to assess different configurations), etc. Main roles involved in this step: Broker role and VO planner role.

♦ *Partners search and selection*: perhaps one of the most addressed topics in past research, this step is devoted to the identification of potential partners, and their assessment and selection.

Issues to consider: Elements for search and selection (technical, economical, reliability indicators, preferences); matching algorithms; (multi-criteria) selection criteria; optimization; assessment (preparedness, etc), consideration of collaboration history / record; external search (if the internal offer is insufficient); etc.

Multiple strategies / algorithms can be considered to support this task (Fig. 4.b). For instance a frequent solution follows a top-down approach in which the VO planner designs the VO, deciding on which roles and selecting the partners that best fit his plan. An alternative would be a bottom-up (competition) approach in which the VO planner or the broker announces the collaboration opportunity to the VBE and waits till some consortia spontaneously form (by the initiative of some members) and then analyzes their global bids.

Nevertheless, it is not only in the creation phase that the selection is important, as in the operation phase it also might be needed some new partner to execute some sort of task that no other partner can perform; or even there might be the case where a partner needs to be replaced. The main roles involved are the VO planner role, the VBE member role, and in some cases the broker.

♦ *Negotiation*: is an iterative process to reach agreements and align needs with offers. It can be seen as complementary to the partners' selection process and might in fact require going back to the previous step(s) if a solution cannot be found with the current configuration of partners.

Important issues to consider at this stage include: Determination of the objects of negotiation; Negotiation protocols; Decision making process and corresponding parameters; Representation of agreements; etc. BP negotiation, i.e. BP refinement and assignment to partners may also be considered at this stage (if not in the detailed VO planning). The main roles intervening in this step are the VO planner role, and the VBE member role.

♦ *Detailed VO planning*: once partners have been selected and collaboration agreements are reached, this step addresses the refinement of the VO plan and its governance principles.

This step involves the business / collaboration process modeling (depending on the type of collaboration - BP, collaborative project, collaborative problem solving, ...); Final VO representation; Assignment of roles and responsibilities; Definition of sharing principles, access levels (assets/resources, IP, benefits,...), preliminary operating policies; etc. The main contributors to this step are the VO planner role, and the VBE member role.

♦ *Contracting*: involves the formulation and modeling of contracts and agreements as well as the contracting process itself, before the VO can effectively be launched.

A **contract** is an agreement between two or more competent parties in which an offer is made and accepted, and each party benefits. A contract defines the duties, rights and obligations of the parties, remedy clauses as well as other clauses that are important to characterize the goal of the contract. An **agreement** is an arrangement between parties regarding a method of action. The goal of this arrangement is to regulate the cooperation actions among partners, and it is always associated to a contract.

In addition to the definition of the types of contracts and their representation, this step needs to deal with: Contracting process (manual, e-contracting); Contract enforcement mechanisms and institutions; Legal issues; etc. This step needs to be performed in close interaction (in parallel) with the Negotiation and Detailed VO Planning steps. Main roles involved: VO planner role, VBE member role, and VO coordinator.

♦ *VO launching*: the last phase of the VO creation process, i.e. putting the VO into operation, is responsible for tasks such as configuration of the ICT infrastructure, instantiation and orchestration of the collaboration spaces, assignment and set up of resources / activation of services, notification of the involved members, and manifestation of the new VO in the VBE. Main roles to be involved in this step: VO coordinator, VBE member role, and possibly the VBE administrator.

4. VO CREATION FUNCTIONALITIES

Based on the process and requirements described above, a number of support functionalities and information models can be identified, as illustrated in Fig. 10.

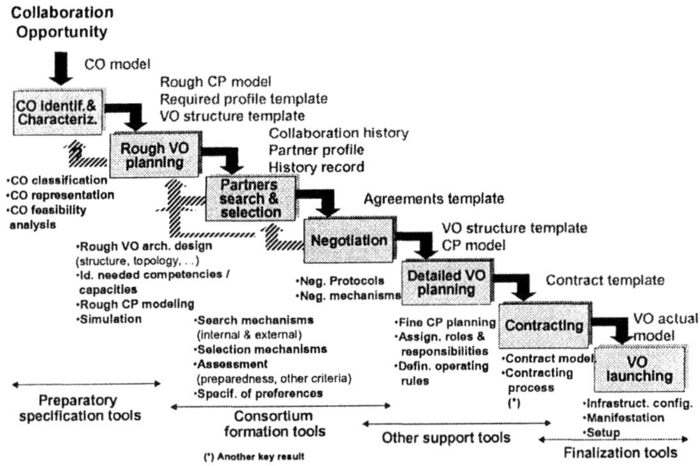

Figure 10 – Main functionalities and support models for VO creation

As preparatory specification tools and mechanisms (supporting the first two steps), the following examples have been identified: CO characterization and representation tool; CO feasibility analysis; Rough VO architecture design (structure, topology, main roles); Identification of needed competencies and capacities; Rough collaboration process modeling; and Simulation for preliminary assessment. Main information models for this phase include: Collaboration opportunity model, Rough collaboration process model, required partner(s) profile template, and VO structure template.

As consortium formation tools (next two steps), we can consider functionalities and mechanisms for: Partners search and selection (internal to VBE and external); Assessment of partners preparedness / fitness; Specification of preferences; Negotiation protocols and methods. Main information models for this phase include: A record of collaboration history, members profiles, agreements template, etc.

Some other support tools are important to help the detailed planning and contracting, such as for instance: Mechanisms to assign roles and responsibilities; Definition of operating rules for the VO; Contract modeling; and support the contracting process. Main information models for this phase include: VO structure template, Collaborative process (or business process) model, Contract template.

Finally as finalization tools we could refer: Configuration and setup of the infrastructure and resources; Manifestation of the VO; Notification of the partners; etc. Main information model for this phase is the detailed or actual VO model.

5. CONCLUSIONS

The time and amount of resources consumed during the VO creation process whenever a business/collaboration opportunity is acquired, give a good indication of the level of agility of a collaborative ecosystem. The effectiveness of this process mainly depends on the availability of adequate information about potential partners and their level of preparedness for VO involvement. The existence of a VO breeding environment facilitates these requirements and thus enables truly dynamic virtual organizations. The ECOLEAD approach to VO creation is developed under such assumption and proposes a detailed process covering all required steps from the identification of the collaboration opportunity till the actual launching of the VO that will exploit that opportunity. Ongoing research is aimed at developing a full VO creation framework and corresponding support tools.

Acknowledgments. This work was supported in part by the ECOLEAD project funded by the European Commission. The authors also thank the contributions from their partners.

6. REFERENCES

1. Angelov, S., & Grefen, P. - The 4W framework for B2B e-contracting. *Int. J. Networking and Virtual Organizations*, Vol. 2(No. 1), pp. 78-97. 2003.
2. Afsarmanesh, H.; Camarinha-Matos, L.M. - Future smart organizations: A virtual tourism enterprise, *Proceedings of WISE 2000 – 1st ACM/IEEE International Conference on Web Information Systems Engineering*, Vol. 1, pp 456-461, IEEE Computer Society Press, ISBN 0-7695-0577-5, Hong Kong, 19-20 June 2000.
3. Camarinha-Matos, L. M.; Afsarmanesh, H. – Elements of a base VE infrastructure, *J. Computers in Industry*, Vol. 51, Issue 2, Jun 2003, pp. 139-163.
4. Camarinha-Matos, L. M.; Afsarmanesh, H. – Virtual Enterprise Modeling and Support Infrastructures: Applying Multi-Agent System approaches, *in Multi-Agent Systems and Applications, Lecture Notes in Artificial Intelligence LNAI 2086,* Springer, ISBN 3-540-42312-5, July 2001.
5. Camarinha-Matos, L. M.; Afsarmanesh, H.; Ollus, M. – Virtual Organizations: Systems and Practices, Springer, Boston, 2005.
6. Camarinha-Matos, L. M.; Cardoso, T. – Selection of partners for a virtual enterprise, in *Infrastructures for Virtual Enterprises - Networking Industrial Enterprises*, Kluwer Academic Publishers, ISBN 0-7923-8639-6, Oct 1999.
7. Davidrajuh, R.; Deng, Z. Q. – Identifying potential supplier for formation of virtual manufacturing systems, *Proceedings of 16th IFIP World Computer Congress 2000*, Vol. ITBM, Beijing, China, 21-25 Aug 2000.
8. Kaihara, T. – Supply chain management based on market mechanism in virtual enterprise, in *Infrastructures for Virtual Enterprises*, Kluwer, Boston, 1999.
9. Li, Y.; Huang, B.Q.; Liu, W. H.; Wu, C.; Gou, H.M. – Multi-agent system for partner selection of virtual enterprises, *Proceedings of 16th IFIP World Computer Congress 2000*, Vol. ITBM, Beijing, China, 21-25 Aug 2000.
10. McClelland, D. C. - Testing for competence rather than intelligence. *American Psychologist*, 28, 1-14. 1973.
11. Rabelo, R.; Camarinha-Matos, L.M. - Negotiation in Multi-Agent based dynamic scheduling, *Int. Journal on Robotics and CIM*, Vol. 11, N. 4, Dec 1994.
12. Rabelo, R.; Camarinha-Matos, L.M.; Vallejos, R. - Agent-based brokerage for virtual enterprise creation in the moulds industry, *in E-business and Virtual Enterprises*, Kluwer Academic Publishers, ISBN 0-7923-7205-0, pp.281-290, 2000.
13. Rocha, A.; Oliveira, E. – An electronic market architecture for the formation of virtual enterprises, in *Infrastructures for Virtual Enterprises*, Kluwer, Boston, 1999.
14. Shen W. & Norrie, D.H. - An agent-based approach for distributed manufacturing and supply chain management, in Globalization of Manufacturing in the Digital Communications Era of the 21st Century:, Jacucci, G. (ed.), Kluwer, Boston, 1998.

8 AN INTEGRATIVE APPROACH FOR VO PLANNING AND LAUNCHING

Ricardo Camacho, David Guerra, Nathalie Galeano, Arturo Molina
DIA, Center for Innovation in Design and Technology, ITESM Campus Monterrey
A00788106@itesm.mx, david.guerra@itesm.mx, ngaleano@itesm.mx, armolina@itesm.mx
MEXICO

Virtual organizations (VO) have been rapidly growing within collaborative business environment. However, there is need to develop work related to VO planning and launching. This paper proposes a reference model to plan and launch VOs. The reference has a three dimensional structure. The first dimension is related with VO life cycle. Second dimension shows VO modelling views supported by UML. Third dimension presents VO knowledge management structure, VO knowledge assets are structured in procedural, organizational and operational domains, which enable knowledge creation and sharing within virtual organizations. A case study is presented in order to demonstrate reference model us in VO planning and launching.

1. INTRODUCTION

In an era where rapid changes have been guided by trends such as mass customization, agility, globalization and an increasing demand for extended products and services, the competitive focus of organizations is shifting to cooperation schemas in many different ways (Saabeel et al, 2002). VOs are a new organizational scheme that requires high levels of agility in order to achieve a competitive advantage when a business opportunity is identified. Due to VO characteristics it is important to establish a systematic approach for VO planning and launching.

The aim of this paper is twofold: to present a novel reference model as a mechanism for VO planning and launching using a systematic approach and to describe how this reference model is implemented in a study case.

2. BACKGROUND: VO PLANNING AND LAUNCHING

VO is a term being used to describe how different organizations come together to explore business opportunities, and collaborating on a temporary basis (Katzy and Obozinky, 1999). Several definitions have been explored for Virtual Organization, this work uses the following definition: "VO's are temporary alliances of organizations that come together to share skills or core competencies and resources in order to better respond to business opportunities and produce value-added services and products, and whose cooperation is supported by computer networks". (Camarinha-matos and Afsarmanesh, 2004)

One of the challenges in VO environment is to setup fast and efficient VOs. TØlle (2004) established that, the ability to create VE (VE is a particular case of VO) composed of the best competencies available, should be linked to a competitive setup, otherwise the virtual enterprise vanishes. This phenomenon is also presented in VO's. Thus, references, methods and tools that support and enhance the process of VO creation, especially in planning and launching stages are required.

Enterprise Reference Architectures helps in the process of VO planning and launching by providing an integrated approach for VO creation. The Generalized Enterprise Reference Architecture and Methodology (GERAM) framework is used in this work to support some elements of the Reference Model presented. GERAM is the major outcome of IFAC Task Force on Enterprise Integration (Bernus et al, 2003), which has become the basis of an international standard. "The purpose of GERAM is to serve as a reference for the whole community concerned with the area of enterprise integration providing definitions of the terminology, a consistent modelling environment, a detailed methodology, promoting good engineering practice for building reusable, tested, and standard models, and providing a unifying perspective for products, processes, management, enterprise development, and strategic management" (Vernadat, 1996).

Together with the need of having references and models that support the VO creation, VO knowledge management and information transfer among partners is an important issue to consider. The success of any VO will only come through optimizing the learning process of the VO (Jackson, 1999). In addition, it is important to mention that some authors have explored around the knowledge concept trying to obtain more understanding about this concept (Guerra, 2004).

Identification of types of knowledge helps for the analysis of knowledge management. According to Leonard and Sensiper (1998) knowledge types can be represented in a knowledge spectrum (See figure 1), "at one extreme it is almost completely tacit, that is, semiconscious and unconscious knowledge held in peoples' heads and bodies. At the other end of the spectrum, knowledge is almost completely explicit, or codified, structured, and accessible to people other than the individuals originating it. Most knowledge, of course, exists in between the extremes". Tacit knowledge consists of personal relationships, practical experience and shared values. Explicit knowledge is a formal and systematic type of knowledge consisting of basic facts and storable document sets (Guerra, 2004).

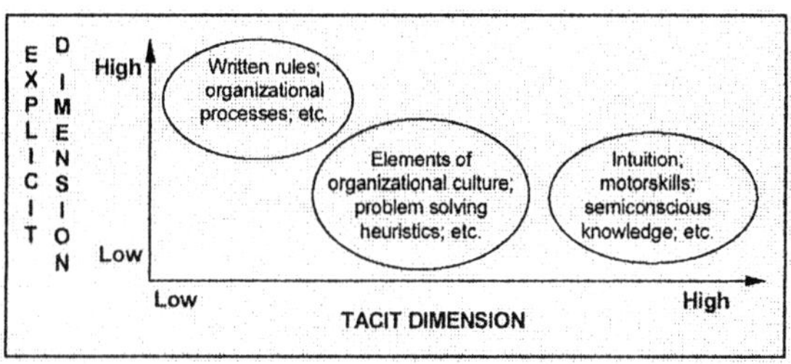

Figure 1.- Knowledge spectrum (Leonard and Sensiper, 1998)

3. REFERENCE MODEL FOR VO PLANNING AND LAUNCHING

The purpose of the reference model presented in this work is to provide guidelines for VO planning and launching activities. The reference model integrates the elements involved in VO creation in a three dimensional structure. First dimension represents the VO life cycle (Creation, Operation & Evolution and Dissolution). In this reference model only VO creation stage is included, this stage is divided into two sub-stages: Planning and Launching. Second dimension consists of four modelling views. These views provide the basis for the creation of a multidimensional model in order to represent the interactions of the VO elements involved in creation process. Third dimension establishes how the knowledge, generated during the process of VO planning and launching, is captured, shared and exploited. Three knowledge domains are included that act as filters to structure planning and launching knowledge.

3.1 First dimension: VO planning and launching within VO lifecycle

This dimension has a direct relationship with VO lifecycle (Creation, Operation/Evolution & Dissolution); within this dimension five main activities are included, the activities are: (1) Analysis of Business Opportunity, (2) Partners selection, (4) High WBS (Work breakdown structure) and (5) VO Setup. Methods, tools and models are customized according to the characteristics of the VO for each activity. It is important to select suitable methods and tools that support this dimension, some example of IT tools are: (1) Web-enabled project management tools, (2) Workflows, (3) simulation tools and Matchmaking engine.

3.2 Second dimension: VO modelling.

This dimension is composed by four modelling views based on GERAM, these views support the creation of a multidimensional model (VO model). The modelling views are: 1) Resource: This view represents all the resources (Human, Technological, etc.) employed by the processes developed by the Virtual Organization in order to achieve their objective. 2) Organization: Represents the responsibilities, authorities and relationships of all the entities involved in the Virtual Organization. 3) Functional: This view represents the behaviour of the entities involved in the processes developed in the life cycle. 4) Information: This view represents the information and knowledge structure among the entities involved in the Virtual Organization, and the relationships among these entities.

To enable the creation of a VO model an enterprise modelling language is needed. In this work Unified Modelling Language (UML) is the language that will support the creation of the models for each modelling view. Examples of IT tools that enable the creation of this model are: ARIS Toolset, UML and IDEF modelling tools, among others.

3.3 Third dimension: VO knowledge management.

Third dimension establishes the mechanism that supports knowledge management during VO planning and launching, to enable knowledge capturing and sharing among VO partners. Three knowledge domains are defined based on the work of Fischer and Rehm (2004). The purpose of the knowledge domains is to act as filters for the knowledge generated during VO planning and launching. Through the action of these domains it will be possible to display in a structured way the knowledge among VO partners, here is a brief description of the three domains:

Organizational Knowledge: This domain includes all knowledge related with VO structure, members profile, roles, competencies, authorities and available resources.
Procedural Knowledge: This domain includes knowledge which represents the way the VO's work; this can be procedures, member's responsibilities, business processes, etc.
Operational Knowledge: This includes knowledge related with the status of the activities been developed within VO, can be Gantt Charts, quality inspections reports, etc.

To enable knowledge capturing and sharing among members it is important to translate knowledge domains characteristics into specific IT tools; examples of these tools are Object-Oriented Databases and Ontology Managers.

3.4 Reference Model Relationships among dimensions

Important elements in the reference model are the relations that exist between the dimensions. Figure 2 depicts how planning stage activities (First dimension) are developed and how knowledge domains (Third dimension) capture the knowledge generated during these activities. For facilitate and enable knowledge exchange among VO members it is important to create a knowledge repository based on the knowledge domains mentioned in section 3.3, the knowledge repository should be able to allow distributed access to the VO members involved in planning activities. This knowledge repository will capture and share the knowledge generated during planning and launching activities. The relationship between these two dimensions is guided by planning activities because the knowledge to be captured in the domains is generated during the activities of the first dimension.

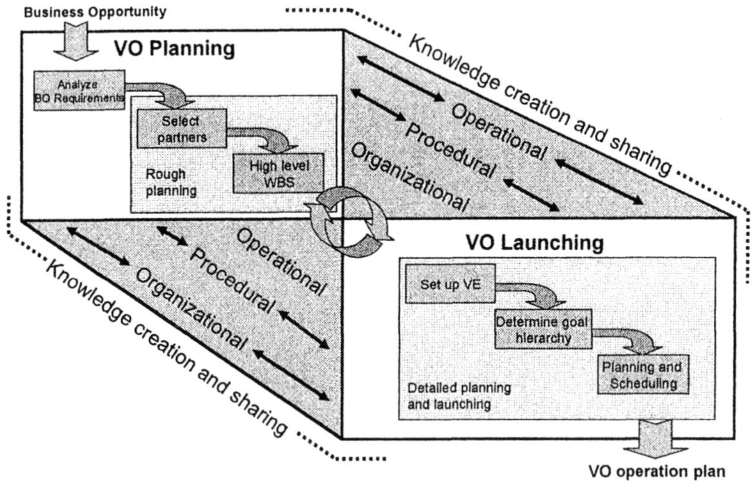

Figure 2. - Description of the relationships between reference model dimensions

The relationship between first dimension (Planning and launching activities) and second dimension (modelling views) are based on the models required for each activity. Each activity required in VO planning and launching should be accompanied by a set of models according to the four modelling view (information, organization, function and resource). The purpose of these models is to represent the interaction of VO members and define the resources required to develop planning and launching activities.

Third and Second dimensions have a relationship based on the UML diagrams used to build the VO model, this diagrams are related to the knowledge domains. Knowledge domains support VO modelling by providing diagrams developed during past VO models that can be used in order to enhance the creation of new models.

4. STUDY CASE: VO PLANING AND LAUNCHING IN IECOS COMPANY

IECOS (www.iecos.com) is a broker company located in Monterrey, México who has three main competencies: Supply Services, Engineering Services and Construction Services. The study case analyzed on this work is using IECOS Supply Services (IECOS-SS) division. IECOS-SS identified a Business Opportunity related with the fabrication of Aerospace Maintenance Tooling (*inspection equipment*). This product has different components. The components are mainly machined and plastic injection parts.

Following the description of the reference model for VO planning and launching is described in each dimension according to IECOS characteristics. First dimension was developed based on VEM-Virtual Enterprise Methodology (TØlle, 2004) as a basis for VO planning and launching. This methodology was adapted according to

IECOS particular characteristics (See table 1), including 4 main stages: (1) Analysis of Business Opportunity, (2) Partners selection, (3) High WBS and (4) VO setup. A detailed description of each activity is presented in table 1.

Table 1. - IECOS Study Case planning and launching methodology stages.

Methodology Stages	VO Specific Sub-Stages	Description
Analysis of Business Opportunity	Analysis of Cluster Members capabilities	Seven Virtual Industry Clusters were analyzed and two of them where identified as possible sources of suppliers
	Drawings analysis	All product related drawings were analyzed and comments about product characteristics were captured
	Identification of required processes	Based on product characteristics, the required manufacturing processes were defined
Partners selection	Evaluation and selection of members competencies	Two clusters were analyzed, within these cluster two members were selected according its capabilities
High WBS	Product Work Breakdown Structure	Using a project management tool, the product was break down into specific needs that VO members should accomplish.
VO Setup	VO Structure Definition	During this stage four activities were developed: Members role definition, quotation process, Definition of contractual issues and operating rules.
	VO Project Definition	This stage established the VO project plan, to develop this plan several activities were developed: Project strategy definition, implementation plan development, definition of project schedule and project plan development among VO members

A VO model was created in order to represent the interaction of VO elements. To create this model four UML diagrams were developed: 1) Use case diagrams to represent organizational view, the use case diagram was used because for this study case it was required to identify how the VO members are involved in VO planning and launching activities; 2) Activity diagrams for functional view, representing how planning and launching activities were developed and which members was responsible to develop an specific activity; 3) Class diagrams to represent resource views of all members involved in the VO; 4) Sequence diagrams for information view that represent information exchange among members. Through the integration of these UML diagrams was possible to build a multidimensional model (VO model) which represents how VO members are involved in planning and launching stages. The type of diagrams used depends of the modelling requirements defined for specific VOs. Figure 3 shows how UML diagrams were integrated in IECOS Aerospace Product VO model.

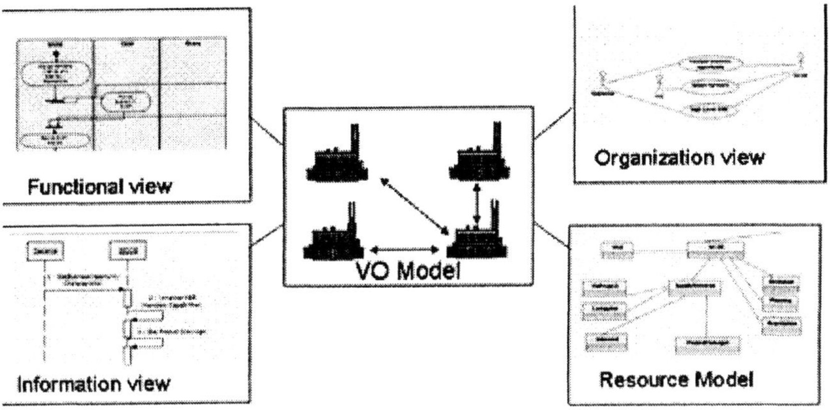

Figure 3. - UML diagrams within VO model

Regarding to the third dimension, to enable knowledge capturing and sharing among VO members, a knowledge repository was created using an object oriented database. The architecture of the database was based on the knowledge domains mentioned in section 3.3. General Knowledge Base software (www.baltsoft.com) was used to create the knowledge repository. The database was set up for capturing and sharing knowledge among VO members. IECOS was the administrator of the knowledge repository structure and access privileges of VO members. Through this database it is possible to structure the knowledge generated during VO creation process; VO members involved in VO planning and launching activities were interacting with the knowledge repository through uploading and downloading the knowledge generated during the development of VEM activities.

The outputs after VO model implementation were: 1) A detailed VO project plan deployed among VO members in order to develop specific activities related with the product; 2) A VO knowledge repository which can be used during operation and dissolution stages; 3) A VO model that clearly represents how all VO entities are involved in VO planning and launching.

4. CONCLUSIONS

This paper presents a reference model which has the capability to systematically plan and launch VOs. Through this reference it is possible to integrate all the information related with VO planning and launching.

Enterprise Modelling is achieved by creating a VO reference model. This model provides a global view of all the entities involved in planning and launching process.

Based on the case study developed it was shown that the reference model could be easily implemented if the methods and tools required for VO planning and launching are available. However, it is important to generate enough trust among VO members in order to enhance VO creation lead time and there is need to have defined the tools required for VO planning and launching prior to use the reference model in order to only use the required resources.

VO reference model provides a modular structure for VO methodologies and tools. These modules should develop and implemented for specifics VOs requirements.

Future research activities should be developed in order to validate VO reference model in several virtual enterprises in México and other countries.

VO reference model feasibility has been demonstrated by the results obtained in IECOS operation. By implementing VO reference model in IECOS it was possible to enhance the process planning and launching, the creation of a knowledge repository helps in future project planning and launching decisions.

The methodology proposed by TØlle (2004) provides a good general basis for this work, however is important to consider VO specific requirements to complement planning and launching stages.

In the study case presented in this paper, an object oriented database was used to create a knowledge repository; however, the use of ontology managers should be further analyzed.

6. ACKNOWLEDGEMENTS

The authors acknowledge ECOLEAD project (European Collaborative Networked Organizations Leadership Initiative), Baltsoft Corporation, and the "IBM SUR Program" for their funding and support in the development of this research.

5. REFERENCES

1. Bernus P. , Nemes L. and Schmidt G. Handbook of Enterprise Architectures, Springer, 2003, New York, USA, pp. 22-60
2. Camarinha-matos L.M. and Afsarmanesh H. Collaborative Networked Organizations: a research agenda for emerging business models, Springer, 2004, New York, USA, pp. 7-10
3. Fischer T. and Rehm S., A Cibernetic approach towards knowledge-based coordination of dynamically networked enterprises; Virtual Enterprises and Collaborative Networks: IFIP 5th Working Conference on Virtual Enterprises, Kluwer Academic Publishers, 2004, Toulouse, Fr.
4. Guerra D., A Manufacturing Model to Enable Knowledge Maintenance in decision support system, Phd Dissertation, Mechanical and Manufacturing Engineering, Loughborough, Loughborough University of Technology, 2004, p. 12
5. Jackson, Paul J; Virtual Working: Social and organizational dynamics, Routledge, , London, 21-22, 1999
6. Katzy R.B. and Obozinski V. Designing the Virtual Enterprise, ICE conference, 1999, Den Haag, Netherlands.
7. Leonard, D. and Sensiper, S. The Role of Tacit Knowledge in Group Innovation. California Management Review. Special Issue on Knowledge and the Firm, v. 40, n. 3, p. 112-132, Spring 1998.
8. Saabeel W., Verduijn T.M., Hagdorn L., Kumar K., A Model of Virtual Organisation: A Structure and Process Perspective, Electronic Journal of Organizational Virtualness, 2002, Volume 4
9. Tolle M.; Management and Engineering of Virtual Enterprises, Phd Dissertation: Department of manufacturing engineering and management, Technical University of Denmark, 2004, Denmark, 157-162
10. Vernadat F.B., Enterprise Modeling and Integration, Chapman & Hall, London, 1996

9 THE FORMATION OF COLLABORATIVE CHAINS FOR CONCEPTUAL DESIGN

Antonio P. Volpentesta, Maurizio Muzzupappa
Università della Calabria, volpentesta@deis.unical.it, muzzupappa@unical.it
ITALY

In this paper, we propose a collaborative and joint approach for the identification of partners and the formation of virtual enterprise for concept designing, without compromising design rights or proprietary knowledge. Besides, we introduce a framework for a Multi-Agent System model which is capable of supporting such an approach. The approach described in this paper enables the formalization of distributed processes which lead to the emergence of both conceptual design chains and functional architectures of an innovative product.

1. INTRODUCTION

Previously proposed Virtual Enterprise (VE) models in advanced manufacturing are generally oriented to the management of initial phases of a product lifecycle, but there is also an increasing interest in the exploration of the management processes of a VE that is specifically devoted to the generation a product concept in the initial design phase.

The current tendency for gradual moves towards collaborative commerce increasingly leads one to study VEs which can efficiently operate in an e-design market involving more complex exchanges, i.e. not reducible to buy/sell transactions. For these VEs, a more effective conceptual design phase incorporating the management of a wider range of competencies and knowledge becomes crucial to achieve new and innovative results.

Conceptual Design refers to the creative phase of the design process which, according to authoritative contributions to the established literature (Ulrich, 1995, Rodgers, 2001), is placed between the product planning phase and the embodiment design phase. In other words, it includes all logical processes starting from the task clarification phase, which lead the designer or the project team, to formulate hypotheses, and search for solutions, and thus define the product architecture during the ideation phase. The scenario we focus on is based on the assumption that an enterprise has identified, in a knowledge market place, specific opportunities which can be addressed in the formulation of a product concept. In this case, new decision problems arise in VE management processes, particularly in the selection of partners and the identification of the organizational-informational structure. They should deal with the management of distributed knowledge management in an entire network of Design Offices and which cannot be tackled separately and sequentially, as happens when the classical life cycle of a virtual enterprise is adopted. As matter of fact, this life cycle comprises the identification, formation, operation and termination phases and the decision processes are sequentially related (Strader, 1998). Its adoption seems to be appropriate when the VE goal is essentially to deliver more timely and qualitative services and products (Weigand, 2002). It is less effective in a knowledge market (Davenport, 1998), i.e. where the VE business goal is basically to sell knowledge-professional services or knowledge products (i.e. innovative product concepts) and possible interactions between VE members are knowledge based transactions.

In particular, in a concept design market, the classical sequential approach to the identification and formation phases in the VE life cycle cannot be applied for the following reasons:

- a full description of the required product concept cannot be provided in advance (as it assumed in the identification decision process);
- enterprise rarely give away valuable concept design knowledge without expecting something in return. The formation process should utilize only information that is strictly needed to define a VE architecture (members, their interactions and their roles in contributing toward the VE goal, namely, the generation of a new concept), but it could not rely on complete product part concepts description without compromising enterprise private knowledge.

To satisfy these new challenges we propose:

- a multi-agent system model for a concept design knowledge e-market;
- a collaborative and joint approach for the identification of partners and VE formation, without compromising design rights or proprietary knowledge.

This work has allowed the authors to develop in a companion paper a formal definition of logical structures and processes which arise in the formation of VEs in a Conceptual Design Knowledge e-market (Volpentesta, 2005).

2. CONCEPTUAL DESIGN KNOWLEDGE E-MARKET

We assume that a product is not yet available on the market, cannot be produced by assembling a different set of parts during production, and cannot be obtained by the addition of some application engineering to a basic design. In other words, to achieve a better response to such business opportunities, the enterprise needs to develop an innovative product concept by exploring the product functions and properties with regards to consumer preferences. This enterprise decides to rely on a Conceptual Design Knowledge market, where knowledge circulation enables the blending of the collaborative contributions of a set of enterprise partners, in order to form a VE which is, in principle, capable of bringing new product concepts to life. Extending the Yamamoto (2001) notion of knowledge market, we assume that a Conceptual Design Knowledge market consists of a set of Design Offices (DO) which supply Requests for Concept (RFCs), conditioned undertakings to respond to an RFC, and responses to RFCs. An RFC defines a set of requirements for a functional concept, by specifying characteristic parameters and their value range. These parameters generally refer to technical/functional requirements of a product element or part. However, they may also refer to requirements that a DO must satisfy when responding to the RFC, or to assessment criteria that may be used for ranking the concepts received from respondents to the RFC. Conditioned undertaking to respond to an RFC is an expression of interest to respond conditional on obtaining responses to other related RFCs. An answer to an RFC consists of a functional concept description including, if necessary, other additional useful details. Moreover, we hypothesize that the execution of VEs formation processes may be supported by a technological infrastructure with some self–organization abilities, and for this reason we use the term "e-market". An e-market can be seen as a virtual marketplace where geographically distributed business participants possibly unknown to each other advanced can meet and cooperate to the purpose of achieving a common business goal. In our case, business participants are DOs interlinked by a network infrastructure and the goal is the formation of a VE with the capacity to generate an innovative design solution.

3. THE APPROACH

In our approach, two main distributed processes should be sequentially executed in order to identify a set of VEs each of which is potentially able to generate the required product concept, with distinctive properties and functional features. A further characteristic is that the product's functional architecture generated by a VE is isomorphic to the logical structure of the VE itself (see figure 1).

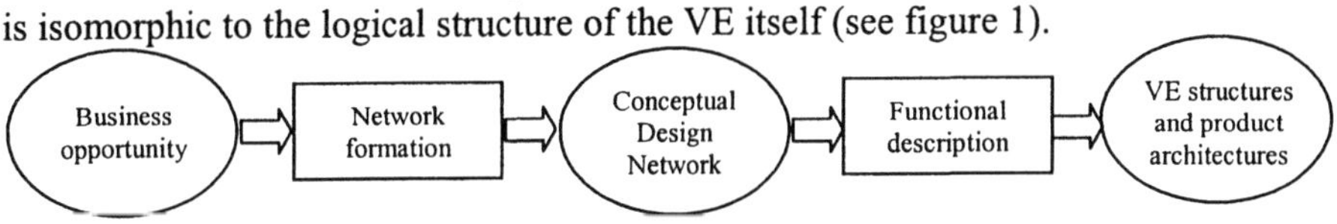

Figure 1. Objects and processes in our approach

The first process starts as soon as a DO, participating in the e-market, launches an initial RFC.

Conceptual Design Network formation. In this process each DO may carry out a task which leads to conditional undertaking to respond to an RFC: once the DO has viewed RFC, it carries out an exploratory consideration of functional features to decide should respond to the RFC. In such a case, it may issue related RFCs to the e-market and will respond to the initial RFC only if the related RFCs generate appropriate and sufficient responses to enable it to do so; contextually, it expresses its undertaking to respond to the RFC, provided that it can receive the required responses to its RFCs. Multiple executions of this task, carried out by different DOs, induce a recursive formation of a Design Request Network which is a set of relations between RFCs, expressions of interest and DOs. Finally, the process extracts the Conceptual Design Network from the Design Request Network. The Conceptual Design Network consists of all logical structures of a VE which, relying on a collaborative and minimal organization, are potentially capable of responding to the given RFC coming from the e-market. On the one hand, the logical structure of a VE defines a decomposition of the initial RFC in other less complex ones, on the other hand it identifies the DOs and the requirements of their knowledge exchanges and their collaboration in order to respond to the given RFC.

Product Concept Functional Descriptions. Such a process is a recursive composition of Functional Description Tasks carried out by DOs along the

Conceptual Design Network. A Functional Description Task consists of a more or less detailed description of a new product or a specific sub-system in accordance with requirements set out in RFC to which the DO is responding. It is important to underline that the execution of this task does not necessarily involve designing sharing. The task could be carried out by a DO on the basis of both the organizational information of the VE which the DO seeks to join and the condition of the information used in the entire Functional Description process occurring along the VE structure. Of course the task can start only if the DO has received all the required RFCs responses.

At the end of process, all possible architectures of VEs, capable of generating an innovative product concept, are obtained. Moreover, the DO issuing the initial RFC has access to all the responses. Only in a subsequent phase, VE members are required to exchange design and useful technical details to get a fully description of the product concept (Volpentesta, 2004). Such separation between the functional description phase and the one concerning full design definition, guarantees an adequate security level in the interaction between DOs, i.e. an interaction that allows sharing only of the information which is required for a functional description of a product concept, without compromising design rights and DO proprietary knowledge. Furthermore, technical information exchange is always restricted between two DOs, so that no DO can get a complete knowledge of all the functional features and so obtain a competitive advantage over other DOs. Of course, once a VE is established, a negotiation protocol has to be defined to initiate the operating phase in the VE life cycle.

4. THE MULTI AGENT SYSTEM MODEL

During the past decade, MAS modelling has emerged as promising discipline and many MAS have been proposed in distributed manufacturing (Hao, 2005). In conceptual design, the usage of a MAS, which fully automates the formation of collaborative chains, seems to be very challenging. Our proposal has more limited goals: the MAS should be intended only as a tool which reduces administrative time spent by a DO on managing RFCs, expressions of interest and RFCs responses and which allows the market broker to offer a set of a e-services for the formation of a VE. In what follows, we sketch a Multi-Agent System model in order to support the above mentioned processes that lead to the establishment of VEs oriented to the generation of an innovative product concept in the Conceptual Design Knowledge e-market. The general architecture of such a system includes several heterogeneous and semi-autonomous agents representing the several independent DOs, and also a special agent, called a Market Broker Agent, that assists the VE's formation processes. In our proposed system, only managerial information is exchanged between DO agents and the Market Broker agent, while technical information, i.e. RFC responses, may be exchanged only between two DO agents.

✓ **Market Broker Agent**

When a specific opportunity is identified, a DO activates a Market Broker Agent in the e-market system and sends an initial RFC to it. This agent plays the role of coordinator in the e-market where it is placed and its main goal is the VE's formation. Its structure includes three principal modules "*RFC Management*", "*Design Structure Formation*" and "*Functional Description Process Control*".

The *RFC Management* module contains a database of DOs participating in the e-market. Once a new RFC has been received from some member of the market the module forwards it to all DOs. Besides it archives expressions of interest from DOs submitting conditional undertakings to respond to certain RFCs. By analysing data collected in the RFC Management module, the *Design Structure Formation* module builds the Design Request Network, representing the relationship between RFCs, expressions of interest and DOs. More importantly, such a module is responsible for:

- extracting the Conceptual Design Network, which underlies an organizational model for the development of the collaborative/competitive conceptual design,
- identifying all VE logical structures, which are potentially able to collaboratively generate the required product concept,
- transmitting information to a DO agent about other DOs that are potentially eligible to participate in the formation of VE. In particular, it informs a DO of the partners that are required to exchange RFC responses with it.

The last module is devoted to gather data about Functional Description Tasks carried out by each DO in the Conceptual Design Network. In such a way, the Market Broker Agent is able to control the behaviour of the Functional Description Processes that are carried out somewhere along the VE structure. In particular, at any time, this module is able to determine the state or condition (on going, aborted or completed) of each Functional Description Process and to communicate it to all DOs involved in the related VE that is being formed.

✓ **Design Office Agent**

A DO agent structure comprises different functional modules: "*RFC Handler*", "*DO Knowledge*", "*VE Knowledge*" and "*Response Handler*".

The *RFC Handler* receives RFCs from the Broker. Once the DO has looked over an RFC, say r, it carries out a functional features exploration, on the basis of its experience and skill, and decides whether it will respond to it. In such case, the DO may formulate some other RFCs, say $r_1, \dots, r_k$, and forwards them the Broker. The RFC handler module sends to the Broker a message of expression of DO's interest to respond to r; such a message should be interpreted as conditional undertaking to respond to r: the DO could respond to r, provided it receives the responses $r_1, \dots, r_k$.

The *VE Knowledge* includes information, coming from the Broker about the formation process of each VE which the DO could belong to:

- Profiles of potential partners and their commitments;
- State of the Functional Description Process which is carried out by VE's potential partners

The *DO Knowledge* contains information about the agent itself (the selected RFCs which the DO has expressed an interest to respond to, the RFCs forwarded to the Broker, the RFCs responses coming from *Response Handler* module of the agent itself, the state of the functional description tasks which are carried out by the DO itself). The *Response Handler* receives from other DO Agents responses to the RFCs previously forwarded by the DO. Once the DO has carried out a Functional Description Task related to RFC such a module is capable of sending the RFC answer to DO Agents which have required it and, contextually, a message notification to the Broker (see figure 2).

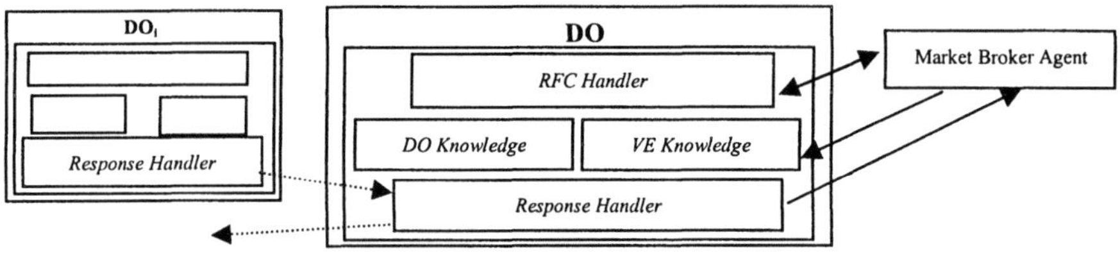

Figure 2. The DO Agent structure.

5. EXAMPLE SCENARIO

A certain enterprise has identified a specific opportunity which can be addressed by the design of an innovative vehicle to be used exclusively in shopping centres, airports or campuses. This enterprise (DO_0) activates the Market Broker Agent that forwards the initial RFCo (see table 1) to the market. Different Design Offices give conditional undertakings to respond to this RFC. The DO_1 proposes a concept consisting of a three wheel vehicle with a compressed-air engine of small dimensions, a seat for the passenger and a rack for bags. The DO_1 proposes to develop innovations in the product's style, in the stacking procedures and in the recharge system of the parked vehicles. To achieve those proposals, the DO_1 requires the collaboration of other DOs and decides to communicate a set of RFCs to the Market Broker Agent (see table1). The Market Broker Agent forwards these requests the market and will communicate to DO_1 any resultant expressions of interest in these RFCs. A second DO_2 plans to design a four-wheel vehicle with an intelligent driving system located under the pavement of the place of operation: this forces the vehicle to move only over an invisible "path". The vehicle is equipped with a laser which signals the presence of obstacles on the road in order to stop it. Since the DO_2 does not have the know-how in an appropriate electronic control system, it searches for collaboration on the market and forwards appropriate RFCs to the Market Broker Agent (see tab.1). DO_3 proposes to design an innovative trolley-like vehicle which can covert to an electrical three wheel vehicle. DO_3 is not able to design a transmission system and wishes to make use of skills available on the market to respond to the initial RFC.

Table 1 – RFC_0 and proposed concepts

RFC_0 by DO_0	I concept by DO_1	II concept by DO_2	III concept by DO_3
design of an innovative vehicle: • available for anyone with the place of operation, • very easy to drive, • easily stored and re-charged when not in use.			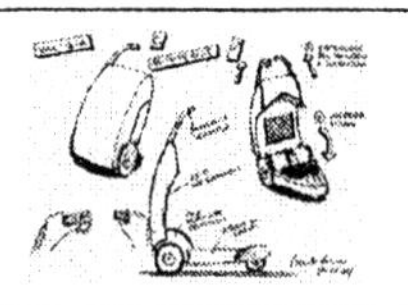
	RFC_1: request to design an electronic control system	RFC_4: request to design a laser system for automatic obstacle recognition	RFC_6: request to design a transmission system
	RFC_2: request to design a plastic mould	RFC_5: request to design a steel framework	
	RFC_3: request to design a compressed air engine		

The formation process of the Design Request Network starts with the launch of RFC_0. Figure 3 represents the state of the network after some DOs have given conditional undertakings to respond to RFC_0. The notation (RFCo :- RFC_4 RFC_5) indicates that, in order to respond to RFCo, answers to RFC_4 and RFC_5 are necessary. The other notations are interpreted in a similar manner.

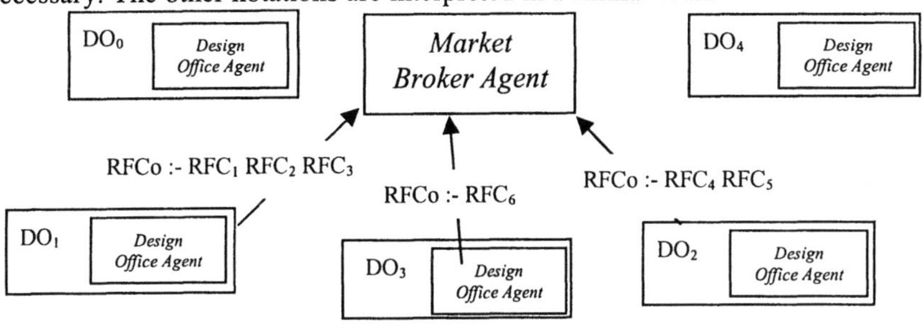

Figure 3. Expressions of interest.

At the end of this recursive process, a Design Request Network is formed. It is possible to use a hypergraph to represent this logical structure. In this hypergraph, a node is associated with RFC, while a hyperarc is associated with a DO that has expressed interest in responding to the RFC associated with its head. In the hypergraph, there is a special node associated with a RFC_{dummy} for which no answer is required. In figure 4, we have represented a particular Design Request Network in which no DO expresses an interest in the RFC_3 (request of a compressed air engine). It follows that the first DO will not be able to produce a solution to RFC_0, notwithstanding an expression of interest to do so.

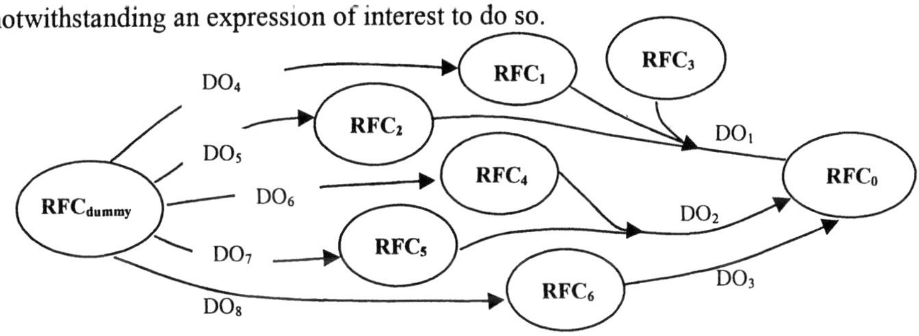

Figure 4. The Design Request Network

The definition of this hypergraph is essential to the extraction of all logical structures of Virtual Enterprises that are able to generate a new concept to respond to the initial RFC. At the end of the process, the Market Broker Agent has also collected all the information about substructures of VE which cannot be successfully completed. Figure 5 shows clearly how DO_2 -DO_6 -DO_7 and DO_3 –DO_8 can form two VEs capable of producing a concept responding to the initial RFC. This example has shown how structured aggregations of distributed design offices may emerge in a conceptual design market. Such aggregations are eligible candidates to form a VE. Starting from this point, the phase concerned with Product Concept Functional Descriptions should be executed. Only those aggregations which succeed after this phase would be able to activate managerial procedures aimed at forming a VE.

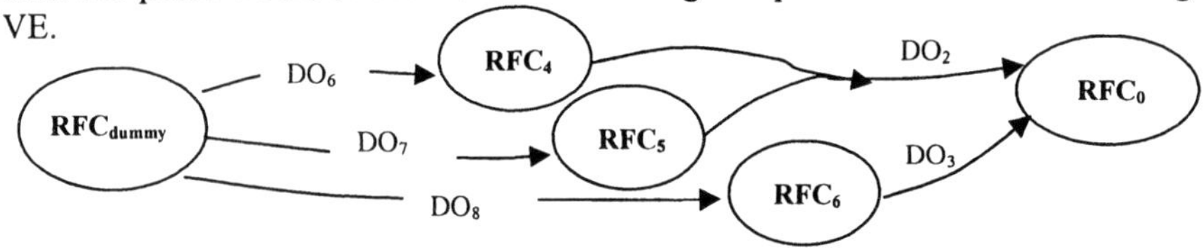

Figure 5. The Conceptual Design Network

6. CONCLUSIONS AND FUTURE WORK

We have presented a collaborative approach and a support MAS for the formation of a VE in a Conceptual Design Knowledge e-market. By adopting such an approach, the functionality of a new product and the structure of a VE which is capable of designing it, take shape in a circular way. In particular, we have focused on collaborative and distributed analysis of the first phases of the design activity which lead, on the one hand, to the identification of DOs and informational exchanges which take place between them, and, on the other hand, to the definition of possible functional architectures for the product. A fundamental feature of the proposed approach is the guarantee of an adequate level of mediation security among the DOs involved in the processes which we have considered to occur in the Conceptual Design Knowledge e-market. Finally, it is important to point out that the results of the present study may be used for further investigations in order to:

- give a complete formal definition of logical structures and processes which arise in the formation of VEs in a Conceptual Design Knowledge e-market;
- indicate a feasible implementation of the proposed MAS architecture, on the basis of emerging technologies, such as business objects and peer to peer; this problem is strongly felt by researchers and software producers who are involved in collaborative commerce along a Design Chain (*Dhbrown.com, Ptc.com,...*);
- define economic models and negotiation protocols for Design Chain management in a design phase, successive to the phase treated in this paper.

7. REFERENCES

1. Davenport T., Prusak, L., Working Knowledge, (Harvard Business School Press, 1998).
2. Hao Q., Shen W. Wang L., Towards a Cooperative Distributed Manufacturing Management Framework, Computers in Industry, **vol. 56**, pp.71-84, (2005).
3. Rodgers P.A., et al., The Management of Concept Design Knowledge in modern product development organizations, Int. Journal of Computer Integrated manufacturing, **vol. 14**, n.1, pp.108-115, (2001).
4. Strader T. J., Lin F., Shaw M.J., Information Infrastructure for Electronic Virtual Organization Management, Decision Support System, **vol. 23**, pp. 75-94, (1998).
5. Ulrich K., Eppinger S., Product Design and Development, (McGraw-Hill, New York, 1995).
6. Volpentesta A., Muzzupappa M., N. Frega, S. Rizzuti, Product Design Data Modelling for Review Process Management, J. of Engineering Design, **vol.15**, n.1, pp.53-67 (Taylor&Francis Ltd, 2004).
7. Volpentesta A., Muzzupappa M., Identifying Partners and Logical Structures for VEs Oriented to Conceptual Design, *submitted for publication*.
8. Weigand H., Van den Heuvel W.J., Cross-Organizational workflow integration using contracts, Decision Support System, **vol. 33**, pp. 247-265, (2002).
9. Yamamoto H., Ohta T., Development of a knowledge market based on reputation, and absorption of uncertainty in electronic commerce, Proc. of the 5th World Multi-Conference on Systemics, Cybernetics and Informatics, **vol.8**, pp. 394-399, (2001).

PART 4

VO CREATION – PARTNERS SELECTION

10

A SYSTEMATIC APPROACH FOR VE PARTNERS SELECTION USING THE SCOR MODEL AND THE AHP METHOD

Felipe Bittencourt, Ricardo J. Rabelo
Federal University of Santa Catarina, BRAZIL
felbit@das.ufsc.br, rabelo@das.ufsc.br

This paper presents an approach to help VE managers in the selection of the most suitable enterprises to compose a VE (Virtual Enterprise). Applying the Analytic Hierarchy Process (AHP) method having as basis metrics presented in the SCOR model, the VE manager can have a more robust view upon the partners' importance and bill of material's items criticality in a given business opportunity.

1. INTRODUCTION

The enterprises have faced markets in constant changing, global competition, and shorter and shorter technologic cycles. With the popularization of the Internet and the proliferation of the electronic markets, the ability to have competitive advantage and to survive in so dynamic markets, depends on its organization flexibility, information availability, effective coordination of decisions and actions, and permanent or sporadic relations with other enterprises willing to face new business opportunities (Pereira, 2000). Besides that, looking at reducing costs and other correlated objectives, like changing fixed cost to variable and reducing its assets, many enterprises are allocating some of its less critic activities to third part firms (ATKearney, 2003). The concept of Virtual Enterprises (VE) emerges from this scenario. Actually it is relatively new in the literature and very new yet in terms of industry acceptance.

A VE is a dynamic, temporary and logical aggregation of autonomous enterprises that cooperate with each other as a strategic answer to attend a given opportunity or to cope with a specific need, and whose operation is achieved by a coordinated sharing of skills, resources and information, totally enabled by computer networks (Rabelo et al., 2004a).

Many efforts have been spent by the scientific community in order to address each new dilemma that the Virtual Enterprise paradigm brings up. Since VEs are composed of autonomous entities and frequently created with short and medium term objectives, the process of creating VEs must be carried out with more and more agility while the global cost for that must be minimized (Davulcu et all., 1999). However, the VE creation is a complex problem. The traditional ways enterprises select their suppliers are no longer adequate at all in a VE scenario regarding the weaker trust among newer partners, the metrics used to evaluate them, and the need for a much quicker selection of them out of potential dozens of candidates.

In this sense, this paper proposes a systematic approach to assist the so called VE Manager in the selection of the most suitable partners for a given VE. For that, the SCOR model and the AHP (Analytical Hierarchical Process) method are applied in a combined way once the enterprises have bid for a given proposal.

This paper is organized as follows. Chapter 1 has highlighted the new trend for collaborative work and the need for more agile selection of partners. Chapter 2 stresses a bit the problem of VE partner's search and selection. Chapter 3 introduces the proposed systematic approach for partner's selection. Chapter 4 comments some results already achieved in terms of prototype implementation. Finally, Chapter 5 presents some conclusions.

2. PARTNERS' SEARCH AND SELECTION PROBLEM

Nowadays there is a clear trend towards business collaboration. Enterprises are building long term relationships in order to benefit from preferences or exclusivity when bidding to an item. It is assumed that enterprises should help to each other improving their own processes in order to beneficiate both sides, even if it demands a short term effort (Neverwire, 2002). Here trust arises in importance. In very concrete terms, collaboration in a trustful environment involves the sharing of principles. One perspective of these principles involves the sharing of metrics to measure the partners′ performance and the way they are measured and understood. On the other hand, in a more volatile relationship, usually done among partners who are collaborating for the first time and perhaps will no longer work together again, it is quite difficult to guarantee a minimum basis of trust.

Under this perspective of trust, some works divide enterprises into two main groups (Neverwire, 2002): large enterprises, and SMEs. The first group uses to work in a *Collaborative Commerce* environment. They build long term relationships with their suppliers and eventually with their suppliers' suppliers, providing low tax financing for raw-material purchase, production line improvement, employees training, etc. In this group there is time for establishing common principles and rules, including continuous improvement and learning processes. The second group, generally represented by SMEs, use to focus more on a *Market Oriented* approach, where transactions are only an exchange of goods for payment. Usually this is about the singular delegation of a task from a buyer to a seller. Enterprises stay autonomous and do business per individual transactions. There are no formal agreements binding the seller to the buyer. It might have some kind of cooperation between them, but this lasts only until that business opportunity is finished. This kind of relationship requires from enterprises to be more agile and flexible as a way to guarantee their survival in the increasingly competitive environment. In this group there is not much room for establishing wider principles of trust, which makes them to be connected via a fragile line of common conduct and sometimes working with a not recommendable level of risk.

More recently, and perhaps as a third / hybrid group, there is the Virtual Breeding Environments (VBE) (Camarinha et al., 2004). In general, VBEs can be seen as an evolution of the classic concept of cluster of enterprises. A VBE is a group of enterprises from any sectors that decides to make part of a long-term collaborative community where they can benefit from each other in common business opportunities, in the sharing of technologic knowledge, in training activities, and many other advantages. Nevertheless, for partners' selection purposes, the key aspect here is that they share the same code of conduct on how to make businesses together as well as on how they can be evaluated. Despite these common rules, enterprises keep autonomous for leveraging businesses with outsiders, both working with long term relations with a given large enterprise and to make businesses with other SMEs opportunistically.

When partners should be selected to create a Virtual Enterprise, this is made using the same decisions that purchase departments take daily when selecting bid suppliers for the involved products. The purchasing literature states that selection and management of the right supplier is crucial to obtain the desired level of quality, comprising delivery time, right price, the necessary level of technical support, and the desired level of service. According to (Dobler and Burt, 1996), buyers must take six important supplier-oriented actions in order to satisfy these requirements:

1. Develop and maintain a consistent supplier base;
2. Address the appropriate strategic and tactical issues;
3. Ensure that potential suppliers are carefully evaluated and that they have the potential to be effective suppliers;
4. Decide whether to use competitive bidding or negotiation as the basis for source selection;
5. Either select the appropriate help or be the team leader responsible for this task;
6. Manage the selected supplier to ensure it fulfills the order's requirements.

A considerably number of firms does this by the means of suppliers' performance measurement programs that are based on *metrics*. Metrics are used to evaluate past performance of processes in order to take control actions or only to do benchmarking (Goranson, 1999). There are hundreds of metrics that can be applied to select partners. One of the most comprehensive set of metrics is provided by SCOR (Supply-Chain Operations Reference model). What are the most suitable metrics to be applied to and upon a given set of suppliers for a given business? Do suppliers implement metrics in the same way? Are there semantics conflicts on how to interpret them? Are there some metrics more important than others for that given business? If so, how much important are they? Can I also make some qualitative analysis instead of a purely quantitative computation? These are examples of answers that a manager should have for a proper selection of VE partners when using metrics.

Actually, the suppliers' evaluation varies in nature, criticality, complexity, and monetary value of the purchase to be made. Seeing the literature, it seems there is a clear lack of supporting methodologies to help managers in those decisions. Besides that, it has been observed that several works make that analysis focusing on adequate metrics for each process/partner of the chain or VE instead of considering the VE as a whole.

Aiming at contributing to this problem, next chapter presents the proposed approach to assist VE managers in the partners' selection. It considers the VE as a whole as well as that in a VE scenario every business opportunity is *per se* different from one to another hence requiring a careful analysis about the metrics to be used.

3. THE PROPOSED SYSTEMATIC APPROACH

When a partner is clearly better then its competitors the selection becomes a very simple task. However, practice shows it is quite rare. The choosing of the best partner is becoming complex and complex as modern business requires the application of a number of metrics against partners simultaneously with metrics having different degrees of importance (weights) in each business.

The identification of the key metrics and their respective weights is typically accomplished by a committee of individuals involved in the purchasing. Regarding the difficulty to assign weights to metrics, this work applies the *Analytic Hierarchy Process* – AHP – method (Zahedi, 1986).

Three important assumptions are considered in this work. The first one is that all enterprises would belong to a given VBE, so VEs are to be created based on a VBE′s rules. The second one is that, as a VBE, the SCOR model was chosen as the source of metrics that cold be applied in the partners′ selection and evaluation. The third one is the existence of a global historical database (HDB) in the VBE, which would contain an historic of all the transactions among the VBE members, keeping the metrics' set updated and contributing to measure the performance of each of the enterprises.

In general, the proposed systematic approach is carried out in ten almost totally sequential steps, within which the AHP method is used. Actually, these steps fit the main phases of the VE creation life cycle: collaboration opportunity characterization, rough VE plan, partners' identification, negotiation, detailed VE planning and VE launching (Camarinha et al., 2005).

i) Business Opportunity Specification (BO):
This phase is characterized by the identification of an opportunity to do business with the enterprises inside the VBE related to a given product. The enterprise which has identified this BO, by default, will act as the VE manager and so will be responsible for searching and selecting the partners that match the product's global specifications.

ii) Bill of Materials (BOM): Having on hands he BO's specifications, the VO manager is provided with its BOM in order to compose a preliminary VE plan. It is through this BOM that the potential partners will be found, ranked and later selected. This VE plan must embody all the aspects to attend the BO, from the delivery and transport service (when necessary) to the last level of product decomposition.

iii) First Call for Tenders: By means of using BOM it is necessary to find suppliers interested and capable of supply each of its items. Calls for tender containing basic (but essential) information about the product's parts, dates, price limits and other preferences are spread out over the VBE (partners search phase) and potential / interested partners can make a bid for them. The sending of only basic information is interesting as it avoids enterprises to receive a bunch of unnecessary information (and sometimes huge ones in the case of CAD models) for their preliminary analysis. Besides that, some pre-processing in the VBE's members list can be made considering the members' profiles so that even this basic announcement can be sent to potential members only.

iv) Analytic Hierarchy Process (AHP): In parallel to step iii, the VE manager should evaluate the criticality of the BOM's items in the context of every / specific BO. For that, the *Analytic Hierarchy Process* (Zahedi, 1986) is applied. The VE manager is then assisted with the AHP method in order to 1) assign a weight for the product's parts and then for the partners, 2) to choose the most suitable metrics and weight them 3) to assign a weight for the metrics' scales.

Figure 1 illustrates part of the idea / process. The *FBTextile* is a product composed basically of four parts: *buttons*, *embroidery*, *fabric* and *labels*. The VO manager assigns (in a subjective way) the levels of importance (in the form of weights) to each product's part. Besides that, (s)he selects the most suitable metrics for each part. In the case of buttons, the metrics would be *price*, *quality* and *delivery date*. These metrics in turn should also have different levels of importance considering that specific BO. For instance, the VO manager assigns 55%, 20% and 25% for those metrics, respectively. Finally, each metrics has some specific ranges that will be used to classify the bidders. Having all these weights settled, the VE manager can realize, for instance, that, considering the weights of the buttons and of the delivery time, if s(he) could find some partner who can deliver buttons at the contracted date with at least 95% of certainty, then 1.2% of the whole "success" of the VE is "guaranteed".

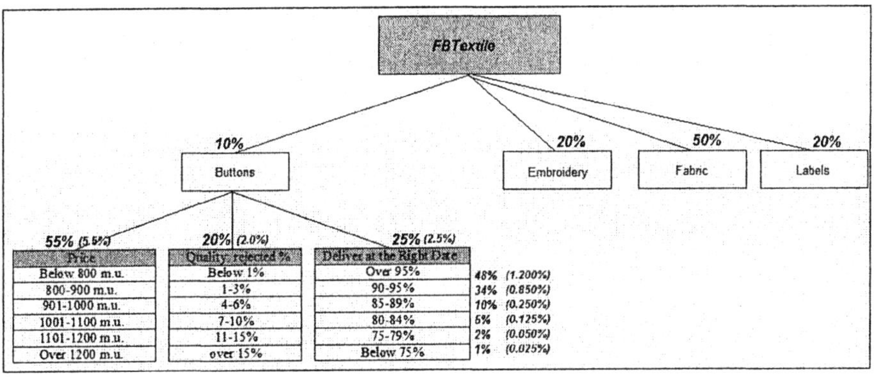

Figure 1 – The Analytic Hierarchy Process to weight a Virtual Enterprise

iv.1) Weighting the importance of each Supplier: Comparing the different possible VEs that can be formed with the bidders is not an easy task. Suppose we have a configuration where the supplier of Buttons, in Figure 1, is an outstanding enterprise, but the Fabric quality of another supplier is very poor. In another configuration, the Button and Fabric suppliers are both good, but not the best. Which the configuration is the most suitable to address the BO? The AHP method is used here to weight the importance of each kind of supplier, and the result is that the Buttons supplier is responsible for 10% of the BO success.

iv.2) Choosing the Best Metrics to evaluate each Supplier: A common problem faced by the enterprises when doing business is the lack of standardization among the metrics used to evaluate the processes. It is recommended that the decision makers from all the enterprises get together to create, discuss and analyze these metrics, trying to foreseen the future businesses that will be carried out among the VBE participants. The SCOR model presents a comprehensive and huge set of metrics (called "criteria" in Figure 2) and respective ratings that can be used in the partners' selection. Anyway, the VBE Board can decide to use some additional particular metrics regarding its specificities. Metrics should be selected and agreed by the VBE members, prior to any business, no to only as a mean to provide further evaluations, but also, and extremely important, as a mean to have decision criteria transparent and homogeneous so reinforcing trust building. Metrics must reflect the success factor, the competition basis, of the given sector, which is more and more customer-driven (Raynor, 2003).

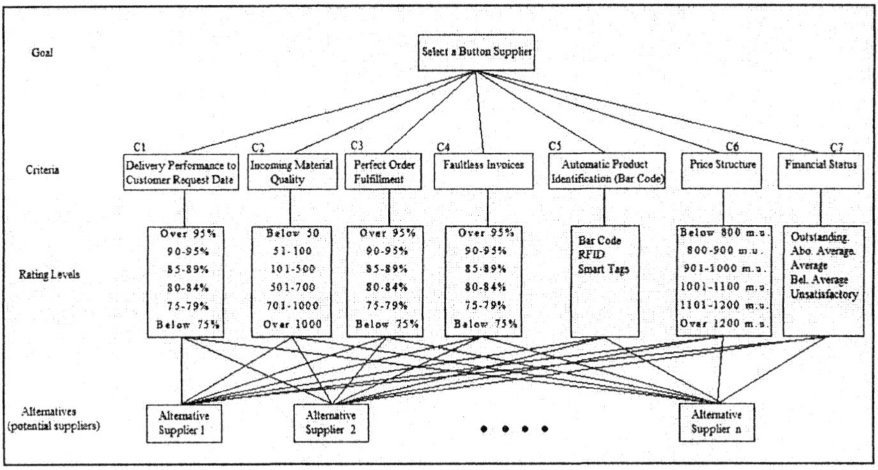

Figure 2 – SCOR metrics to measure suppliers for a BOM item

Once the metrics are selected, it is necessary to assign weights of importance to each of them. The graph in Figure 3 shows the resulted weights for the metrics presented in Figure 2. As stated by (Lee, Ha and Kim, 2001), where a set of hierarchical metrics are used with the AHP Method, it is not necessary to consider *all* the metrics presented in the Figure 3 to continue a deeper analysis. Applying the Pareto's principle, it is easy to verify that C6 (47%), C1 (21%) and C2 (15%) represent together 83% percent of the weights. Thus, they represent the "key metrics" when selecting the Button suppliers for this specific BO.

iv.3) Weighting the Metrics' Scale: The metrics' scales are used to place the supplier value for the metric in a pre-specified range. The scale, in the same way as its metric, must also be chosen previous to the VBE conception. One could suppose that the scales presented in Figure 1, are all part of a linear function, but it is usually not true. For instance, a Delivery with 95% of certainty must be strongly preferred than a 90% delivery. However, anything below 85% could have the same preference since it would not feet to the BO in consideration. Then, the AHP is once again employed to give weights for each of the scales' steps. In Figure 1, the Delivery at the Right Date criterion with more than 95% of certainty was weighted with 48% of importance.

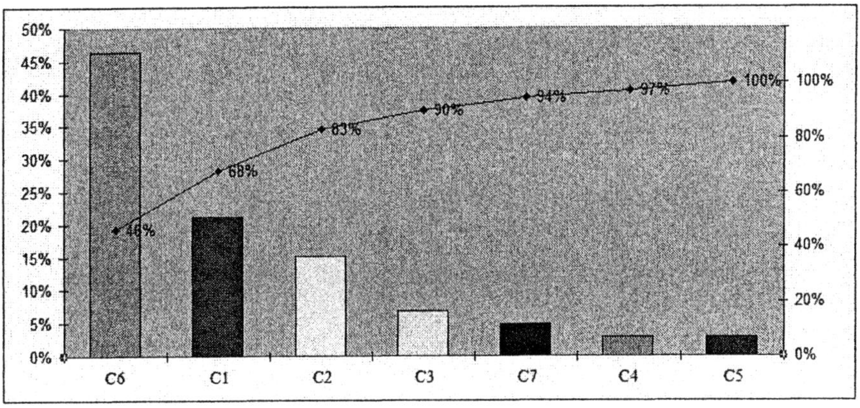

Figure 3 – Weight for the metrics selected to measure suppliers for a BOM item

It is important to highlight that these considerations represent the main basis for selecting partners as a non-isolated, single process, but rather, as a part in the whole. Yet, because product's parts are inter-related and are dependent to each other. It is also important to consider here the matter related to metrics that are "feasible" to be applied in long-term relationships and in short-term relationships. As mentioned in Chapter 2, a SCOR-based model is more robust and can be applied in BOs whose accomplishment will be done by the VBE's members. This means that the metrics used by its members should be implemented in their enterprises with a common criteria and interpretation and that this will be constantly audited by the VBE Board in order to guarantee that members are applying them properly in-house. This is fundamental for the trust building process inside the VBE as partners will only participate in businesses which they are sure that competitors will be evaluated/selected having the same interpretation about the metrics. Therefore, it is feasible to require for a given BO metrics like stocks turn-over, scrap average, lead-time, financial health and others. Besides this, benchmarking can be (as has been more and more) used to compare partners as well as a mean to make partners to compare with each other. On the other side, when enterprises need to work with non-VBE members, especially in very short-term relationships (only for that BO), metrics like those ones are not feasible, not useful at all and not trustful as enterprises don't have them implemented and, if they have it, they may have it using different interpretations and ways of measurement. Therefore, in these cases, the only choice is the application of "common sense" metrics, like general quality, final price and delivery date.

<u>v) Send Complete Announce:</u> After having the metrics chosen and weighted, the complete announce is sent to the enterprises which have bidden positively so that they can refine their bid now being aware about the global criteria that will be indeed used in the selection of partners. This awareness is very much important for trust building. After receiving the tenders, those enterprises make their final offer.

vi) Generate possible scheduling alternatives: As many enterprises can bid for the same product item, it is natural to have a number of possible VEs and hence different valid schedule alternatives.

vii) Instantiate the Metrics values: Applying a function on each possible VE for a given BO, the VE manager can instantiate the metrics matrix according to the partners current bit and their past performances. This is executed consulting the VBE's historical database. This function can be a simple average mean, or a weighted average mean, giving higher values to more recent performances.

viii) VE Schedules Ranking: With the instantiation of those metric values and their respective weights in every possible VE, it is possible to go through the BOM list giving values for each node, from the BOM bottom to the top. The value achieved at the top represents the overall score for that given VE configuration. Therefore, the highest score would express the most suitable set of enterprises and VE plan. Some authors, like (Goranson, 1999), defend that is not very secure to estimate the future performance of an enterprise by its past accomplishments, but rather for the capacity it has to perform well in the future. Figure 4 illustrates this idea. In this figure, is quite obvious that Enterprise A has much more probability to perform better than Enterprise B in the future. Applying this principle at the VE level, it means that a set of "snapshots" taken along the time with the ranking generated could be shown to the VE Manager so that he could have complementary information for his decision. In order to better present this multi-level perspective, the Figure 4 below, besides showing snapshots of individual enterprises along the time, could be used to show instantiations of VE alternatives/composition along the time as well. For example, enterprise A would represent VE alternative A and enterprise B the VE alternative B.

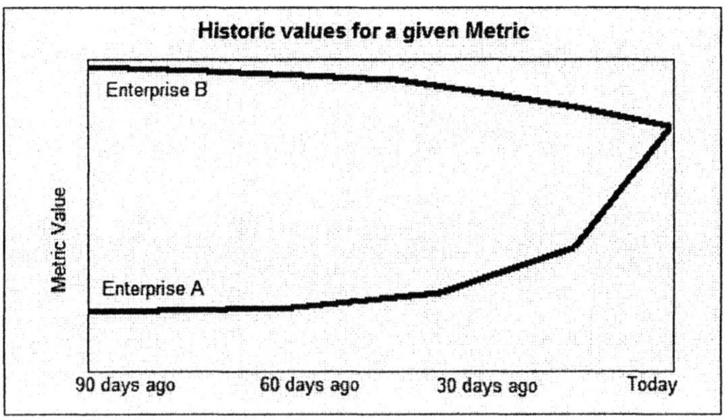

Figure 4 – Comparison between two enterprises past performances

ix) Negotiations: Sometimes, even after have ranked the possible VEs and the results announcement, there is some room for negotiation and eventual refinements in the VE plan.

x) Operation phase: Once the VE is settled and partners contracted, the operation phase can start. Ending this proposed systematic approach, the VE manager should monitor the partners' performance and update the VBE historical database for further use in next BOs.

4. PRELIMINARY PROTOTYPE

In order to exercise the framework, a multi-agent system prototype has been developed. This system was developed having the Schmidt's system as the basis (Rabelo et al., 2004b). Each enterprise of the VBE is modeled as an agent and the information gathering from the enterprises to compose a VE is provided by means of sending mobile agents to them. The system uses the AGLETS platform and uses KQML and XML to exchange information between the VBE members. The system has two main classes of agents: VBE Manager, and the Enterprise Agents.

The VBE Manager agent is responsible for keeping the historical database containing the information about all the businesses carried out in the VBE, and also for handling the request for information from the Enterprise Agents.

The Enterprise Agent is composed by the BOM Module, AHP module, Scheduling module and Rank module. Once a given enterprise acts as the VE Manager of a given BO, this agent is allowed to send mobile agents to the other enterprises to collect their biddings. The BOM module is used to create the list of materials which will be the input for the AHP and Scheduling modules. The mobile agent is responsible for delivering and requesting announces for bidding, and metric values from the VBE Manager. The AHP module assists decision makers to weight the most important criteria to select suppliers for that specific BOM. The Scheduling module generates all the possible VE based on the delivery constraints of the BOM items announced and on the answers from the interested enterprises. Finally the Rank module works together with the mobile agent to gather the metric values, computing the weighted criteria and generating a rank based on the results of each VE scheduled by the Scheduling model.

5. CONCLUSIONS AND OUTLOOKS

The right partner's selection is extremely important, and it should not be based only in cost and delivery, but also in other metrics which must be aligned with the enterprise strategic planning. This work has proposed a systematic approach for the partners' search and selection, based on the history of past trading metrics. Those metrics were selected from the widely accepted model, SCOR – Supply Chain Operational Reference, by the use of a multi criteria decision making called AHP – Analytic Hierarchy Process.

As it has been explained, the application of the AHP method in the VE context seemed quite appropriate for partners' selection. However, it requires a good experience from the VE manager when assigning weights to products' items and partners. Some other methodology could then be applied to assist him in this process.

The use of the bill of materials as the main supporting bases for the proposed systematic approach seems to fit very well "stable" / already existing products. Other types of "products", like services and one-of-a-kind, can make use of this approach but perhaps with several additional considerations and different time constraints to form a VE.

The effective coordination and integration between the VE functions are also far beyond the desired level. There are many gaps regarding the mastering of logistics' costs, and the monitoring and improvement of enterprises' internal processes. It is not possible, in that case, to skip essential evolution steps. This means that enterprises should envisage specific initiatives focused on the VE paradigm requirements.

Acknowledgments

This work has been developed in the scope of the Brazilian IFM project, funded by MCT/CNPq, and IST IP FP6 ECOLEAD project, funded by EC.

6. REFERENCES

A.T.Kearney, GEO Awards Special Survey – As Novas Fronteiras da Gestão da Cadeia de Suprimentos na América Latina, 2003.

Camarinha-Matos, L.M.; Afsarmanesh, H.; Ollus, M. (Eds) - Virtual Organizations, Springer, 2005.

Davulcu, H., Kifer, M., Pokorny, L. R., Dawson, S. - Modeling and Analysis of Interactions in Virtual Enterprises, Ninth International Workshop on Research Issues on Data Engineering: Information Technology for Virtual Enterprises, March 1999.

Dobler, D.W., Burt, D. N., "Purchasing and Supply Chain Management: Text and Cases", McGraw-Hill, Sixth Edition, 1996.

Goranson, H.T., The Agile Virtual Enterprise – Cases, Metric, Tools, 1999, Quorum Books.

Lee, E. K, S., Ha, S., Kim, K., "Supplier Selection and Management System Considering Relationships in Supply Chain Management", IEEE Transactions on Engineering Management, vol. 48, no 3, August 2001.LEE and KIN, 2001,

Neverwire, Inc., Collaborative Commerce: Compelling Benefits, Significant Obstacles, 2002.

Pereira, A. M. C., Formação de Empresas Virtuais com Agentes Inteligentes, tese Doutorado, Faculdade de Engenharia da Universidade do Porto, novembro 2000.

Rabelo, R. J.; Pereira-Klen, A.; Klen, E. R., Effective Management of Dynamic Supply Chains, in International Journal of Networking and Virtual Organizations, 2004a.

Rabelo, R. J.; Wangham, M. S.; Schmidt, R.; Fraga, J. S., Trust building in the creation of virtual enterprises in mobile agent based architectures, Proceedings PRO-VE'2003, Kluwer Academics Publishers, pp. 65-72, 2004b.

Raynor, M. E., Deloitte Research – Inside Outsourcing, Deloitte Consulting, 2003.

Supply-Chain Council: http://www.supply-chain.org

Zahedi F., "The analytic hierarchy process: a survey of the method and its applications", Interface 16, 96-108, 1986. http://www.interfaces.smeal.psu.edu/

11 THE ROLE OF ENTERPRISE MODELLING IN VIRTUAL ENTERPRISES

Sobah Abbas Petersen
Dept. of Computer and Information Science, Norwegian University of Science and Technology, Trondheim, NORWAY
Email: sap@idi.ntnu.no

The partners of a Virtual Enterprise are selected based on how well they meet the skills requirements to fill a specific role. Enterprise Modelling is a suitable means of supporting this, first by defining the Virtual Enterprise and the skills requirements of the partners and second, by using the information in the model to drive the partner selection process. The enterprise model provides information about the requirements of the partners as input to any system that supports the selection of partners. Once the partners are selected, the system can provide information about those partners back to the enterprise model. This is illustrated using a case study and by creating an enterprise model using a commercially available modelling environment.

1. INTRODUCTION

Enterprise models have played a central role in the design of enterprises and the management of the business processes of enterprises. With advances in distributed information technology and the ever-changing needs of the global business environment, enterprises have been challenged to adopt agile and flexible organisation models to be able to adapt to the dynamic business environment. Enterprise modelling has become a significant part of supporting enterprises' success in such an environment.

Virtual Enterprises (VEs) is a means of meeting the new challenges. While there are several descriptions of a VE, (e.g. [2], [6] and [16]), the project-based view of a VE, [1], is considered in this paper. A VE is defined as *a team of partners that collaborate to achieve a specific goal.*

Enterprise modelling has long been used to understand and represent traditional enterprises and their behaviours, [15] and [3]. While enterprise modelling plays a significant role in traditional enterprises, its role becomes even more important in VEs. Unlike traditional enterprises that are established and continue to exist over a long period of time, VEs are established to answer more contingent needs and can have a shorter span of life. Due to the dynamic and flexible nature of VEs, there is a greater need to build models to help understand them and their evolution. Enterprise models provide the support that is required in the design and analysis of VEs and the interactions within a VE and they are powerful tools for analysing and understanding the flexible nature of VEs.

VEs have a shorter lifespan and for them to succeed, they need to be formed as quickly as possible. The need for the rapid formation of VEs has been emphasized and support for this have been proposed by reference architectures and frameworks, an example of one is VERAM (VE Reference Architecture and Methodology). VERAM identifies modelling as one of its key components, which can be used to describe and capture a VE, [17].

An overview of approaches and techniques for modeling a VE is provided in [7]. One of the early examples of applying enterprise modeling to describe VEs is TOVE (Toronto Ontology for VEs), [4], where they defined a formal model to describe the goals, activities and other components of an enterprise. A goal and actor-oriented "intentional" organisation model is presented in [5]. The notion of Active Knowledge Modelling (externalisation of enterprise aspects) is used in [9] to model a VE.

In this paper, we illustrate how enterprise modelling can be used to support VEs in the various phases of their lifecycles, by presenting a case study. A commercially available enterprise modelling environment is used. The rest of this paper is organised as follows; the model of a VE and the modelling approach that is used is described in Section 2. Section 3 describes the case that will be used to illustrate how the model of the VE can be created as an enterprise model using a commercially available modelling environment. Section 4 presents the enterprise model and illustrates the advantages of having such a model.

2. MODELLING VIRTUAL ENTERPRISES

A VE can be described as an entity that has a goal or a set of goals that need to be achieved. An example of such a VE is a project team. The VE is formed to achieve the goals of the VE. Thus, the VE needs "partners" that need to perform some work to achieve the goals. A VE can be modelled as an entity that has a goal (and sub-goals) that need to be achieved by some activity (or activities). The activities are performed by a role which is filled by a "partner" that meets certain skills requirements. A partner, in this case can be a person or an organisation. Such a model of a VE is shown in Figure 1. The model can be described using first order logic, see [13] for details. It can also be considered as a VE ontology, such as TOVE, [4], and the Edinburgh Enterprise Ontology, [14].

This model describes a VE prior to its formation. The model helps identify the work that needs to be done by the VE and the types of partners that are required to perform the work. Consider a VE from a lifecycle perspective. A very simplified lifecycle of a VE can be assumed to have the main phases, design, formation and operation, see Figure 2. The model shown in Figure 1 can be created before the VE is formed and used to support the formation phase of the VE. One of the main activities during the formation phase is the selection of partners for a VE; i.e. to match partners to the requirements for the roles. Once the VE is formed, the information about the partners that fill the roles of the VE can be modelled, thus providing information to complete the model of the VE.

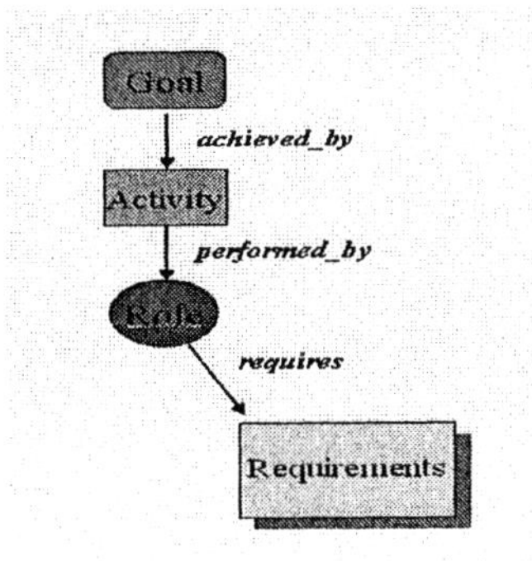

Figure 1: Enterprise Model of a Virtual Enterprise

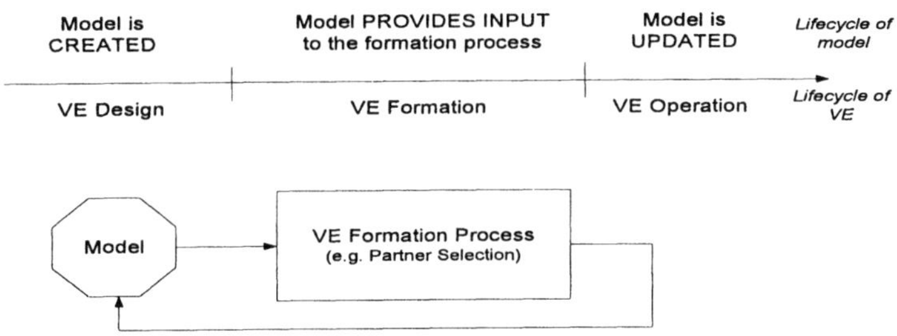

Figure 2: The Model and VE from a Lifecycle Perspective

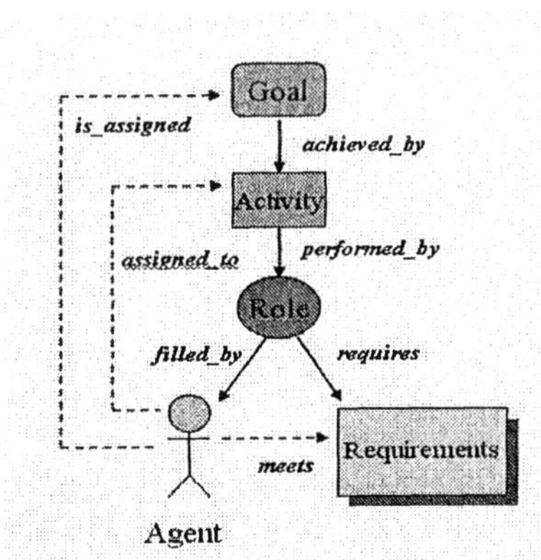

Figure 3: Model of a VE and its Partners

When information about the partners is available, additional relationships can be established in the model. For example, the model can now show the goal(s) that is/are assigned to any particular partner and the activity (or activities) that a partner is assigned to. See Figure 3.

3. CASE DESCRIPTION

Summer projects at Statoil[1] are an organised form of summer jobs for university students in their 3rd year of study. The idea is that better results are achieved by putting students together in interdisciplinary project teams. The teams work in groups of 2 to 6 students per project, for 8 weeks. The case that is modelled is "Summer project 2002 New Statoil, Use of Fibre Optics and Subsea Visualisation". The main goal was to generate ideas on how Statoil could use new technologies, such as fibre optics, to control remote production installations. 800 students applied; 75 were selected for 25 different projects. Here, each project could be considered as a VE.

Each VE is represented by its goals, the activities to achieve the goals, the roles that perform the activities and the skills that are required to fill the roles. For example, the goal of one of the projects was to explore new technologies, which could be achieved by studying different technologies and by selecting one. This activity can be performed by a group of technologists that have skills in cybernetics, telecoms technology, process control and physical electronics.

4. MODELLING THE CASE

The projects were well-defined. Thus, Statoil was able to identify the types of skills that they required, i.e. they could identify the requirements for the roles in the VE. Although the projects were well-defined, due to the nature of the work that was required of the students, the activities and roles were defined at a high-level.

4.1 Modelling Environment

The Metis modelling environment, by Troux Technologies AS, Norway, has been used. Metis provides a graphical modelling environment with powerful visualisation and analysis capabilities. It is based on Active Knowledge Modelling, [8]. The models are created using objects to represent the entities in the example and by creating relationships among these entities. For example, the activities of a VE can be represented as process objects and related to goal objects. Additional information on Metis is available from [10].

4.2 Model of the Virtual Enterprise

The high-level information provided by Statoil has been used in the model shown in Figure 4. The goals of the VE are represented as goal objects, activities as processes, roles as role objects and skills that are required to fill the roles are represented as requirement objects. The relationships among these entities are the lines (or arrows)

---

[1] Statoil ASA is an integrated oil and gas company. Statoil Research Centre in Trondheim Norway organises summer projects for university students to work as teams.

in the figure. For example, a goal is achieved by an activity, an activity is performed by a role and the role has skills requirements.

The model shown in Figure 4 represents the model of the VE during the design phase of the VE, prior to its formation. The goals, roles and the requirements for the roles are important during the formation of the VE, to select the appropriate partners for the VE and assign roles to them. This information can be extracted from the model and used during the formation of the VE. For example, the formation of the VE can be supported by a system that takes this information as input and provides a list of partners. A multi-agent system that provides such capabilities is described in [11] and [12].

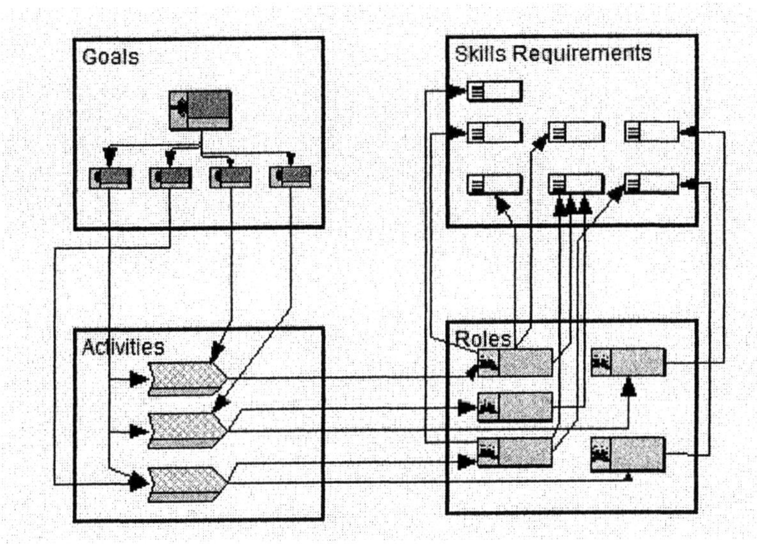

Figure 4: Model of VE Design

The list of partners and their skills can be incorporated into the model, once this is available. Figure 5 shows how the partners of the VE can be modelled and related to the roles that they fill and the skills requirements that they meet. Once the partners for the VE have been selected and modelled, additional relationships can be established between the partner objects and the rest of the model. For example, the goals that can be assigned to the partner and the activities that the partner is assigned to. This information can be obtained by tracing the relationships between the partners and roles, roles and activities and activities and goals.

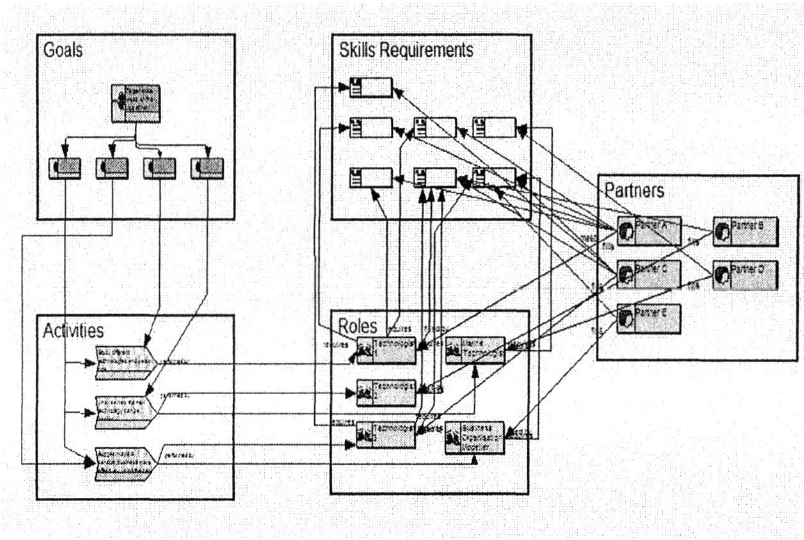

Figure 5: Model containing VE Partners

4.3 Using the Model

The model can be used for several purposes. As described in section 4.2, it can be used to find out which goals of the VE a partner must try to achieve by performing which activities. In addition to this, the model can also provide an overview of all the partners and their skills; see Figure 6. Similarly, the model can also be used to see the role(s) that is/are filled by a partner by meeting the requirements for the role(s); see Figure 7.

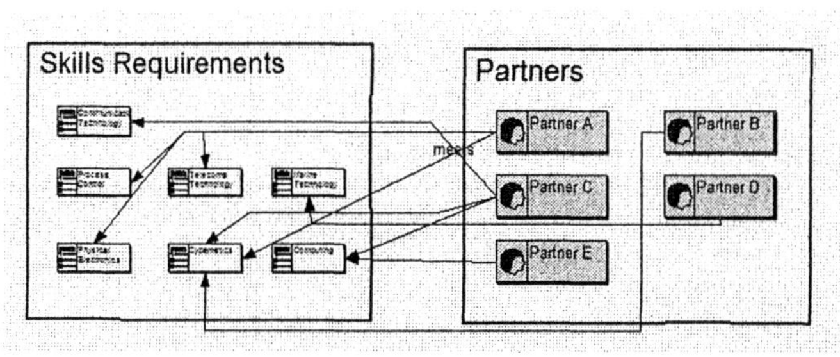

Figure 6: Overview of Partners and their Skills

The availability of an enterprise model makes it easier to ensure that all the roles in a VE are filled by partners; i.e. that the VE formation is completed. For example, if one role is unfilled by a partner or some skills requirements of a role are not met, it will be easy to detect this using the model.

Metis also provides capabilities to export information from the model, thus, making it possible to use information in the model in other systems within a company or use another system to perform some specialised functions using input from the model, e.g. supporting the partner selection process, [11] and [12].

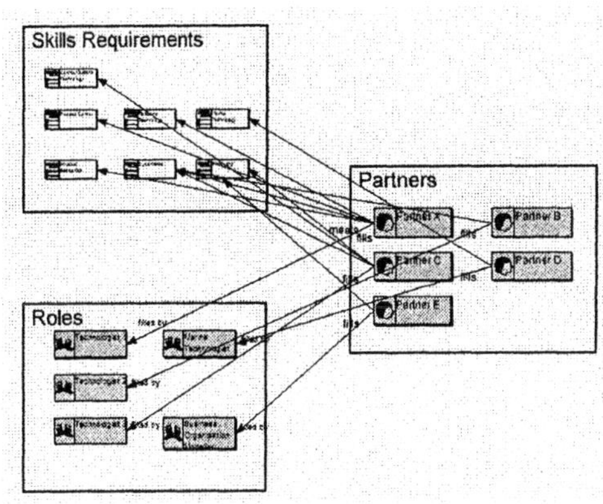

Figure 7: Roles filled by Partners

5. CONCLUSION

This paper describes how enterprise modelling can be used to support VEs. A VE can be described in terms of its goals, the activities that achieve the goals, the roles that perform the activities and the skills that are required to fill the roles.

The role that an enterprise model can play in the lifecycle of a VE, in particular to support its formation, is discussed. The model provides varied support during the lifecycle of a VE. A VE can be described as an enterprise model during its design phase, which helps identify the skills requirements that must be met by the partners of the VE. This information can be used in the selection of the partners and once the partners have been selected, information about the partners can be modelled, thus providing additional information about the VE and its partners. This supports in providing a more complete description of the VE.

The model can also be used to detect if the VE formation is complete, e.g. if all the roles of the VE have been filled by partners. It can also be used to identify the goals of the VE that a partner is assigned and which activities of the VE a partner should perform. Thus, the model also provide information that can be used to support the operation phase of the lifecycle of a VE.

The model presented in this paper focuses on the aspects of a VE that are relevant during the formation phase of the lifecycle of a VE. However, during the operation phase of the lifecycle, the activities can be considered from a process modelling perspective and enhanced to incorporate information for monitoring and control of the process.

6. ACKNOWLEDGMENTS

I would like to thank Dag Sjong, Statoil, Norway, for providing this case and Troux Technology AS, Norway, for letting me use the Metis modelling environment for describing the case.

7. REFERENCES

1. Bernus, P., Bertok, P. and Nemes, L., "Modelling Dynamic Management Features of Virtual Enterprises", in *Computer Applications in Production Engineering*, eds. Plonka and G. Olling, Chapman and Hall, London, 1997, pp.643-655.
2. Fischer, K.,Muller, J., Hemmig, I. and Scheer, A., "Intelligent Agents in Virtual Enterprises", in Proceedings of 1st International Conference and Exhibition on the Practical Applications of Intelligent Agents and Multi-Agent Technology, April, 1996, London, U.K., pp. 205-204.
3. Fox, M.S., Gruninger, M., "Enterprise Modelling", *AI Magazine*, AAAI Press, Fall 1998, p. 109-121.
4. Fox, M.S., Barbuceanu, M. and Gruninger, M., "An Organisation Ontology for Enterprise Modelling: Preliminary Concepts for Linking Structure and Behaviour", *Computers in Industry*, Vol. 29, 1996, pp. 123-134.
5. Fuxman, A., Giorgini, P., Kolp, M. and Mylopoulos, J., "Information Systems as Social Structures", 2nd International Conference on Formal Ontologies for Information Systems (FOIS-2001), October 2001, Ogunquit, USA.
6. Garita, C. and Afsarmanesh, H., "A Study of Information Management Approaches for Support Infrastructures", Cove *Newsletter*, (1), 2001.
7. Gastinger, A. and Szegheo, O., "Enterprise Modelling Approaches", *Enterprise Modeling: Improving the Global Industrial Competitiveness*, eds. A. Rolstadås and B. Andersen, Kluwer Academic Publishers, 2000, pp. 55-70.
8. Lillehagen, F. "The Foundation of the AKM Technology", Concurrent Engineering: Enhanced Interoperable Systems, eds. Jardim-Goncalves, Cha and Steiger-Garcão, Balkema, The Netherlands, 2003, pp. 700-715.
9. Lillehagen, F., Dehli, E. and Fjeld, L., "Utilising Active Knowledge Models in an Infrastructure for Virtual Enterprises", in eds. L. M. Camarinha-Matos, *Collaborative Business Ecosystems and Virtual Enterprises*, Kluwer Academic Publishers, pp. 353-360.
10. Metis: http://www.trouxmetis.no
11. Petersen, S. A., Rao, J., Matskin, M. "Virtual Enterprise Formation with Agents – an Approach to Implementation", IEEE/WIC International Conference on Intelligent Agent Technology, IAT2003, Halifax, Canada, October 2003, p. 527-530.
12. Petersen, S. A., Divitini, M., "Using Agents to Support the Selection of Virtual Enterprise Teams", Proceedings of 4th International Bi-Conference Workshop on Agent-Oriented Information Systems (AOIS-2002) (at AAMAS 2002), Bologne, Italy, July 2002.
13. Petersen, S. A., Gruninger, M., "An Agent-based Model to Support the Formation of Virtual Enterprises", International ICSC Symposium on Mobile Agents and Multi-agents in Virtual Organisations and e-Commerce (MAMA 2000), in Woolongong, Australia, 11-13 Dec. 2000.
14. Uschold, M., King, M., Moralee, S. and Zorgios, Y., "The Enterrpise Ontology", *Knowledge Engineering Review, Special Issue on Putting Ontologies to Use,* 13, 1998.
15. Vernadat, F. B., *Enterprise Modeling and Integration Principles and Applications*. Chapman and Hall Publishers, 1996.
16. Vesterager, J., Larsen, L. B. and Gobbi, C., "Architecture and Methodology for Creating Virtual Enterprises" - Results from Globeman 21, Presented at the IMS Globeman 21 Open Day, Time24, Tokyo, Japan, March 1999.
17. Zweger, A., Tølle, M. and Vesterager, J., "VERAM: Virtual Enterprise Reference Architecture and Methodology", *Global Engineering and Manufacturing in Enterprise Networks GLOBEMEN*, eds. I. Karvonen et. al., Julkaisija Utgivare Publisher, Finland, 2002, pp. 17-38.

12 TOWARDS ONTOLOGY-BASED CNO MATCHING APPLIED TO SQUADS

W. Mulder,
LogicaCMG Netherlands, University of Amsterdam, wico.mulder@logicacmg.com
P. H. H. Rongen,
IBM Netherlands, erik@nl.ibm.com
G. R. Meijer,
University of Amsterdam, LogicaCMG Netherlands, Geleyn@science.uva.nl

As the interest in Collaborative Networks grows, and the number of organizations participating in a Virtual Breeding Environment increases, tools will be needed to support the creation of Collaborative Network Organizations. An important driver for this support is that in modern commercial environments a rapid response to changes in the market is essential to remain competitive. We are working on a domain-ontology and a model that supports the composition of CNOs using semantic capability descriptions. We apply this model in the field of software development, where multiple expertise teams form dynamic task-forces, called Squads, in order to build and manage computer applications. In this paper, we focus on the development of the domain-ontology and the elements of the composition model. We are working on a prototype that supports the creation of Squads by means of capability matching.

1. INTRODUCTION

The trend in the ICT market in shifting revenues from the sales of products towards the provision of on-demand services continues. In order to remain competitive in an agile market, organizations need to be able to respond rapidly to changes. As a result, collaborative strategies and flexible forms of cooperation between organizations emerge.

The discipline of collaborative networks (CNs) is defined to focus on the structure, behavior, and evolving dynamics of networks of autonomous entities that collaborate to better achieve common or compatible goals [Camarinha]. Variants of CNs, such as Virtual Enterprises (VEs), Virtual Organizations (VOs) and Virtual Breeding Environments (VBEs) form part of our research.

Today, the concept of VOs is familiar, and related environments, such as VBEs, are getting significant momentum. A VBE represents an association (also known as cluster or pool) of organizations that have the potential and the intention to cooperate with each other through the establishment of a long-term cooperation agreement and interoperable infrastructure [Camarinha]. In case a business opportunity is identified by one member, a subset of these organizations can be selected to form a CNO.

If the number of organizations in a VBE is large, the selection and formation needs to be supported by a semi-automatic system. Such a system might relieve an initiator inside a VBE from unnecessary complexities of specifying the organizations to form the CNO that has to fulfill the job. The objective of such a system is to match a particular business case, for example a customer problem, with the capabilities of the VBE-members. We are developing a model and a prototype to support this kind of matching. It is here where we enter the field of domain ontologies, semantics, and reasoning.

Ontologies are a popular research topic in various communities such as knowledge engineering, natural language processing, cooperative information systems and knowledge management. They are used to share a common understanding of a domain that can be communicated across people and computers. They are also used in the field of team matching and competence management [Posea,Hefke].

In previous work [Mulder] we described the concepts of collaborative organizations that develop and maintain software. We defined the term *Squads* as mobile teams that operate in the field of software development and application management. Here, in this paper, were we discuss the ontology-based composition support, a Squad is described as a task-force consisting of one or more expertise teams.

While the size of expertise teams varies from a single person to teams that can be identified as sub-organizations within a large company, they can be grouped in Squads. Note that the model can be applied to expertise teams from different organizations, but can also be applied to expertise teams within one single organization. A mechanistic view on expertise teams models them in the form of a processing unit with an interface containing input and output parameters. A Squad can be seen as a chain or network of expertise teams each having an input and output interface.

Figure 1 shows a VBE containing a set of expertise teams. The teams are willing and have potential to participate in Squads. They have registered themselves as a member of the VBE. In case a customer provides one of them with a problem, the process of selection and matching takes place. This will be followed by the formation of a Squad whose mission is to provide a solution for this customer.

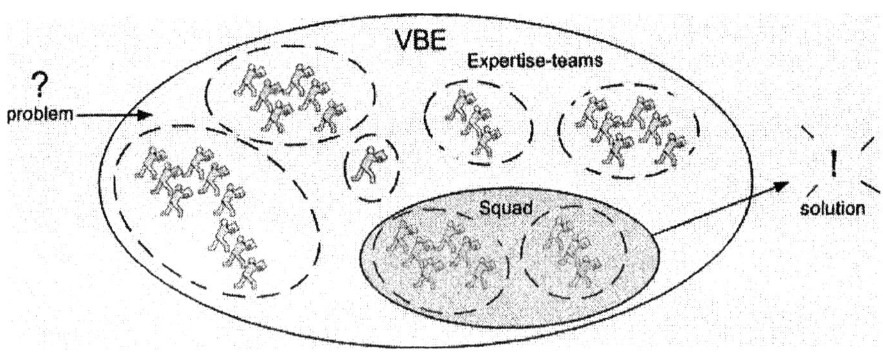

Figure 1 - A VBE containing expertise teams.

The field of automatic composition of small entities to provide end-to-end services [Rabelo] is not new. In [Kvaloy] the ontology based composition and selection of semantic web-services is described. Individual web-services are grouped together in an application flow to perform the requested task. In the area of semantic web-services, ontologies are being used intensively [owl-s]. The ideas of expertise team matching show remarkable similarities with this area. Also in the field of agent technology strategies exist to automate the process of negotiation [Chen, Dignum, Norman]. We adopt the results from these areas in the new area of collaborative networks. Driven by the need for tools that support CNO-management, we work on ontology-based support for the creation of Squads.

Figure 2, contains four phases as part of a Squad-life-cycle-model. The matching phase starts with the analysis of an incoming customer problem and is followed by the selection and optimization of expertise teams that have subscribed themselves as members of the VBE. In case a match between the expertise team capabilities in combination with the problem is found, the phase of physical Squad-formation might begin. This paper focuses on the support for selecting candidate squads, denoted as the matching phase.

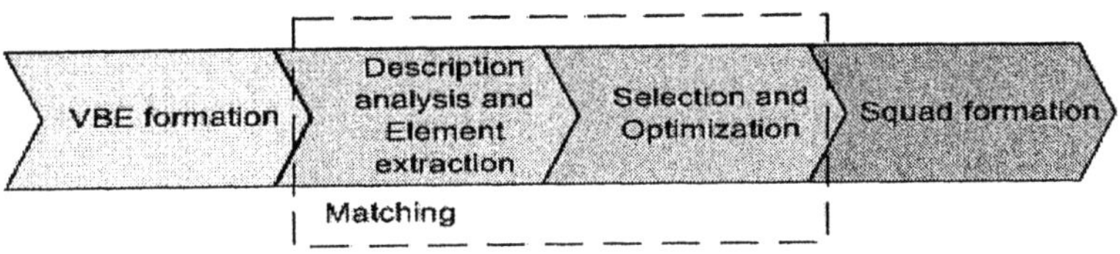

Figure 2 - The matching phase

The rest of the paper is organized as follows: section 2 describes the structure of the expertise team capability descriptions, which forms the basis for our domain ontology. In section 3 we describe the model for the automated matching process and mention our prototype of the matching tool. Section 4 contains results, section 5 contains discussion and future work, and section 6 ends with the conclusions.

2. A DOMAIN-ONTOLOGY FOR SQUADS

In general, collaborative parties have to use common terminology to express their role and contracts. This terminology, represented by a domain-ontology, is necessary for each type of interaction between organizations. In our approach the organizations are reflected by expertise teams, and the collaborative environment is a software development VBE. By describing the capabilities of individual expertise teams we are developing a domain-ontology that reflects the knowledge and expertise of the VBE. Motivated by ideas of web ontologies [owl-s], we distinguish three types of descriptions:

- The profile: the needs from others and the deliverables of the team.
- The model: description of how an expertise team performs its tasks.

- The grounding: describes the context of the team in which it operates

The *profile* describes capabilities, conditions and prerequisites. On one hand it tells what the expertise team can deliver, on the other hand it expresses needs from others in order to deliver its service.

The *model* describes how the expertise team works, and the steps involved while carrying out its service. The description can be used to perform a more in-depth-analysis, or to enhance capability descriptions.

The *grounding* describes in what situations the team is normally involved, and how they can be reached during their operation.

An example is a Java web-development team subscribing itself as a member of the VBE. The profile may describe that the team provides web interfaces for existing systems, based on use cases and technical designs. The model describes that they use RUP as a development methodology, the types of common frameworks they use and their development environment tools. The grounding describes that the team is usually involved in development projects for customers in financial markets and that they can be accessed by their organization's local management. Other examples are architect-teams, C++-teams, database-teams and teams of functional analysts.

In our model the capabilities of expertise teams are written in the language that is represented by our domain ontology. We use this ontology in an environment that supports the creation of Squads by matching customer requests with expertise team capabilities. The relations between the entities in the model allow us to analyze the capability descriptions and apply a form of description logic reasoning. We believe that the three kinds of descriptions not only lead to proper matching possibilities, but also reflect our domain-ontology in a good sense. The focus on capabilities and the development of the ontology will go hand in hand.

3. CAPABILITY MATCHING

We distinguish two important aspects of matching; capability analysis and configuration optimization.

The first aspect, capability analysis, covers the analysis of problem descriptions and expertise team capabilities. As shown in Figure 3, the domain-ontology is used to extract key-elements from a particular problem description. The same is done for the expertise team capability descriptions. The elements (denoted with K's) that occur as classes in the ontology are called *direct* elements. These elements are used to infer other domain elements by means of relationships and attributes described by the ontology. For this, an inference engine can be used. Comparing the elements found for the problem description with those derived from the expertise team capabilities, results in a similarity-score that represents the level of matching.

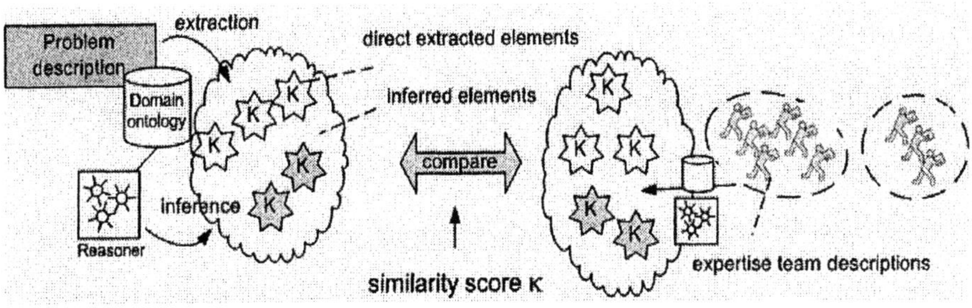

Figure 3 - Matching using (inferred) domain keywords

The second aspect of matching contains preferences and optimization rules in order to combine expertise teams into candidate squads. In our analysis we work towards a utility function that can be used to find the most suitable Squad.

The capabilities of a squad are reflected by the capabilities of its constituting expertise teams. Some capabilities depend on each other, for example the ability to program Java applications is necessary for the ability to create J2EE applications. Other capabilities are independent, which means that having one capability does not imply the presence of another. We represent the requested and available capabilities in a multi-dimensional space. The individual, independent capabilities of the expertise teams in the VBE span a multi-dimensional space schematically shown in Figure 4. Part (a) shows the volume within that space containing the required capabilities to build a solution. This volume, represented by the dashed line, will hereafter be called the requirements space. The goal is to combine expertise teams to fill the requirement space in the best possible way.

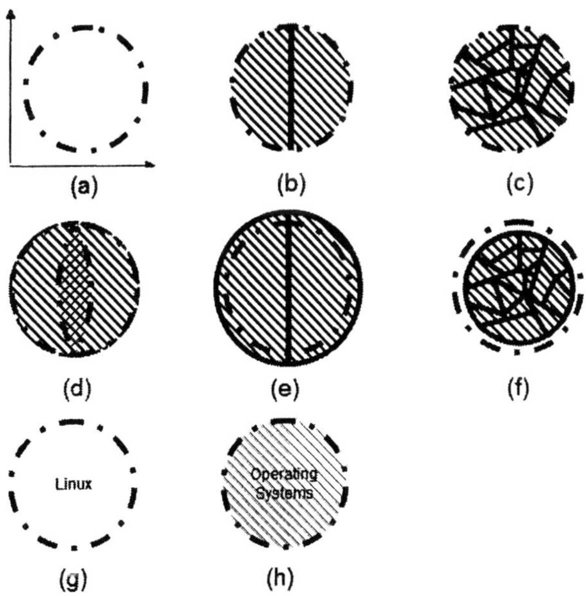

Figure 4 - Capability matching and squad formation.

Figure (b) shows the situation where two expertise teams are combined into a candidate squad. The combined capabilities, represented by the dashed area of these two expertise teams exactly match the requirements space. In (c), the requirements space is also exactly matched, but now the Squad consists of many small expertise teams. In (d), the requirements space is again exactly matched by a squad, but now the expertise teams of the candidate squad have an overlap in their expertise. In situation (e) the combined capabilities of the squad are partly outside of the requirements space, meaning the squad has capabilities that are not asked for, and are possibly irrelevant for the task at hand. Figure (f) shows the situation where the squad does not match the total requirements space. Figures (g) and (h) represent the situation where a requirement (e.g. Linux skills) is not matched, but expertise of a more general concept in the ontology is present (e.g. Operating systems).

The goal of our system is to define the best squad for a given task as specified by the requirements space. In many cases, there will be various alternatives to form Squads out of expertise teams that match the requirement space.
In our current work we focus on three kinds of considerations:

- Many expertise teams versus a few expertise teams
- Overlap of relevant capabilities of the expertise teams in the Squad
- Capability coverage of the requirement space

Figure 4 (b) and (c) show the requirements that are met by a few or many expertise teams. The disadvantage of having a Squad consisting of many expertise teams could be that more agreements between the teams have to be made. It is likely that it will take a lot of effort to come to these agreements, and also that during the tasks performed by the Squad, communication between these expertise teams will consume a considerable amount of time. On the other hand, having more expertise teams result in less supplier-dependent solutions.

A different consideration is about expertise teams having overlapping capabilities (d). Although this might be an overkill of required skills, Squads are more able to compete and communicate, improving the quality of the solution.

The third consideration describes the capabilities required versus those that can be provided. Figure (e) shows the case that the expertise teams have more capabilities than required. This might be more expensive, since the expertise teams have experiences in fields which are not required for the task at hand. However, if those capabilities are related to the ones in the requirements space, this can also be an advantage, because the Squad can deal with unexpected problems that are related to the problem it is being created for.

Opposite to this situation is the case in which not all capabilities are available in the VBE to fulfill the task (f). Here, none of the possible squads can fulfill the requested tasks, which brings us to the third kind of coverage-problems: only capabilities of a more general concept in the ontology are available (g) and (h).

The above discussion tells that there is no unique way of describing these features in terms of positive or negative influence on the utility of a Squad to achieve its goal. This means that in most cases preferences are needed to find the optimal Squad for a particular task. Also, personal preferences about the teams might be of influence.

In our model the optimization will be achieved by maximizing a particular utility function with parameters representing the features of a Squad as discussed above:

- Number of expertise teams in the Squad
- Overlap size of capabilities of the expertise teams forming the Squad
- Capability coverage of requirements and capabilities

4. RESULTS

We are implementing the model described above in a prototype environment called SqoMMe, which stands for Squad ontology-based Matching and Managing environment. While identifying candidate expertise teams and making suggestions about optimal Squad configurations, the environment interacts with the user.

We are in the process of developing our domain-ontology using the PROTÉGÉ [protege] environment. The first version consisted of two groups of classes. One group is process-related, containing expertise-team, capabilities, task and mission. The other group is technique-related, containing programming languages, software components and their relationships. In parallel with these ontology-explorations, we are working on implementations of matching mechanisms in Java, mainly to study the effects of various approaches. A third activity, which is also in early-stage, is to find a proper way for doing inference reasoning.

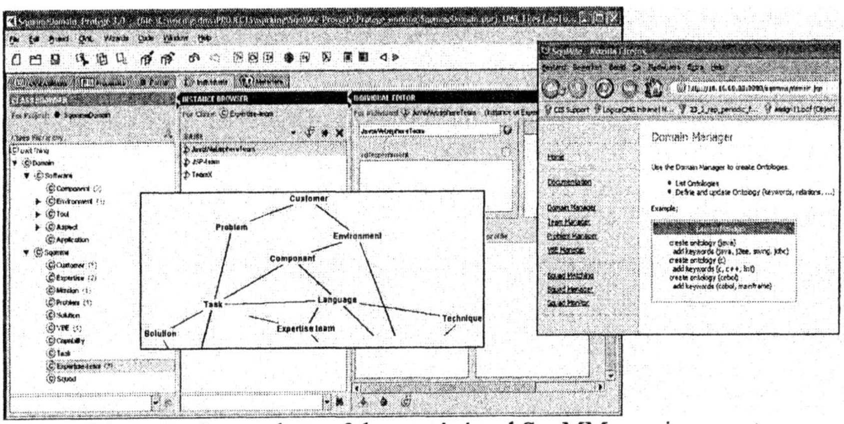

Figure 5 - Screenshots of the protégé and SqoMMe environment

5. DISCUSSION

At the moment the model does not involve availability issues and service level agreements (SLAs) of the individual expertise teams. In our current work we prioritize to focus on the matching of capabilities. For the same reason the aspect of costs is left out. We recognize that it might have a strong influence in the matching phase, although it might also have its main relevance in the formation phase. In future work, we want to include both aspects in our model, together with the lessons learned from testing the environment in our own company.

We also study whether the ontology used for matching can support the monitoring and management of Squads as well. Therefore we will investigate the use of the same domain-ontology to enable the automation of Squad performance measurement, which contributes to the support for monitoring and managing the Squads during their operation.

6. CONCLUSION

In this paper we presented a model to support the creation of Squads, dynamic task-forces that operate in the field of software development.
We discussed the way of describing the capabilities expertise teams, and the use of a domain-ontology for matching these capabilities with problem descriptions. We are applying the model in a prototype and study the use of a utility function to find the best suitable configurations of Squads. Our research on this subject is in early stage, but is expected to be of important value in the creation of CNOs.

7. ACKNOWLEDGEMENTS

This work is supported by the Ecolead project.[1]
We would like to thank Ron de Kruijff and Tim van Soest for their suggestions, and René Kuipers for all the fruitful discussions and technical efforts.

8. REFERENCES

1. Camarinha-Matos, L.M., Afsarmanesh H, The emerging discipline of collaborative networks, In Virtual Enterprises and Collaborative Networks, (L. M. Camarinha-Matos, Editor), Kluwer Academic Publishers, ISBN 1-4020-8138-3, IFIP Vol. 149, Aug 2004
2. Chen, Y et al, 1999, A negotiation-based multi-agent system for supply chain management, Proceedings of the Agents'99 Workshop: Agent-Based Decision-Support for Managing the Internet-Enabled Supply-Chain, Seattle, WA, 15-20.
3. Dignum, M.V., Dignum, F.P.M., & Meyer, J-J.Ch. 2004. An Agent-Mediated Approach to the Support of Knowledge Sharing in Organizations. UU-CS-2004 (Ext. r. no. 019). Utrecht: UU-CS-Technical Report
4. Hefke M, Stojanovic L., An ontology-based approach for competence bundling and composition of ad-hoc teams in an organization, in K. Tochtermann and H. Maurer, Proceedings of the 4th International Conference on Knowledge Management (I-KNOW'04), Journal of Universal Computer Science (J.UCS), Graz, Austria, June 2004.
5. Kvaloy, T.A., R.H.H. Rongen, Automatic Composition and Selection of Semantic Web Services, Proceedings EGC, Amsterdam, 2005
6. Norman, T.J. et al., Agent-based formation of virtual organizations, Knowledge-Based systems 17 (2004) 103-111
7. Mulder W., Meijer G.R., SQUADS: Software Development and Maintenance on the Grid by means of Mobile Virtual Organizations using Adaptive Information Services, Virtual Enterprise and Collaborative Networks, Proceedings PROVE04, WCC 2004, ISBN 1-4020-8138-3, p. 379-386
8. (Owl-s) http://www.daml.org/services/owl-s/1.0/
9. Posea, V., Harzallah M., Building an Ontology of Competencies, in Workshop on Ontology and Enterprise Modelling: Ingredients for Interoperability Proceedings,Vienna, Australia, Dec 2004
10. (Protégé) http://protege.stanford.edu
11. Rabelo R. J., Baldo F., Tramontin R. Jr., Pereira-Klen A., Klen E.R., Smart Configuration of dynamic, Virtual enterprises, Proceedings PROVE04, WCC 2004, ISBN 1-4020-8138-3, p. 193-203

[1] www.ecolead.org

PART 5

VO CREATION - OPTIMIZATION

13

A MULTI-CRITERIA MATHEMATICAL PROGRAMMING MODEL FOR AGILE VIRTUAL ORGANIZATION CREATION

Toni Jarimo and Urho Pulkkinen
VTT Technical Research Centre of Finland
toni.jarimo@vtt.fi, urho.pulkkinen@vtt.fi

This paper studies virtual organization (VO) creation through an application of mathematical programming. We present a mixed integer linear programming (MILP) model to support VO configuration in a virtual organization breeding environment (VBE). The model allows for multiple criteria, of which we give several examples: One objective is to minimize total fixed and variable costs. Another objective is to maximize expected cooperative efficiency using collaboration history as reference data. We model collaboration history with bilateral cooperation indices forming a weighted graph of VBE members. Furthermore, we incorporate capacity risk-measures in the model, allowing capacity risk minimization.

1. INTRODUCTION

Collaborative network organizations (CNO's) have become a necessity for companies who have decided to concentrate on core competencies, outsourcing other operations. This trend has attracted researchers to study the phenomena related to CNO's, and more specific virtual organizations and virtual enterprises (Camarinha-Matos and Afsarmanesh, 2005). In their earlier paper, Camarinha-Matos and Afsarmanesh (2003) introduced the concept of virtual organization breeding environment (VBE), being the platform for agile virtual organization (VO) creation. The idea of a VBE is that a set of organizations has commonly agreed cooperation structure, including for instance common ICT infrastructure, strategy, and processes for agile VO creation.

Our paper focuses on supporting decision-making concerning VO partner selection. When a VBE identifies a business opportunity, it faces the problem of finding a good VO configuration that is able to meet the needs of the customer. In this paper we approach this optimization problem through a mixed integer linear programming (MILP) model. This approach has been chosen for two reasons. First, a reasonable size MILP model is computationally solvable and second, it is flexible to modifications.

Earlier literature presents several optimization-based approaches to VO configuration. For instance, Wu et al. (1999), Ko et al. (2001), Ip et al. (2004), and

Wu and Su (2005) have applied integer programming in supporting VO selection. All of them use total costs as optimality criterion. Extending the solitary cost-criterion, e.g. Mikhailov (2002), Fischer et al. (2004), Lin and Chen (2004), and Sha and Che (2005) present models that account for multiple criteria, such as organizational competitiveness and social relationships. This paper contributes to the existing literature by, firstly modeling inter-organizational relationships as a selection criterion, and secondly assessing failure risk of VO operation.

Inter-organizational relations, such as collaboration history, distinguish the case of VBE based VO creation from traditional supplier selection. This is explained by the long-term agreements between the VBE members, which enable the collection of collaboration data. In contrast, in the non-controlled global supplier markets the collection of such data is practically impossible.

The rest of this paper is structured as follows. Section 2 presents a mixed integer linear programming model for VO creation. Sections 3 and 4 extend the basic model catering for inter-organizational relationships and risk measurement. Section 5 concludes and suggests directions for further research.

2. A MIXED INTEGER LINEAR PROGRAMMING MODEL

Our main concern is in VO partner selection. We consider this as a work-allocation problem, for which we present a mixed integer linear programming (MILP) model. Sections 2.1-2.3 present the basic model, which Sections 3 and 4 extend by taking collaboration history and risk measurement into account.

2.1 Variables

Let M = {1,...,m} denote the set of organizations, i.e. the members of a VBE. Assume the VBE identifies a business opportunity, which will be performed as a project to a customer (for more discussion on VO coordination, see e.g. Camarinha-Matos and Pantoja-Lima, 2001). We model the project with a set of tasks, denoted by N = {1,..., n}. Tasks 1,...,n constitute the whole project to be carried out. Each task $j \in N$ has a work load w_j, which describes the amount of work required (e.g. person months) in order to perform that task.

In VO creation, the information gathered from VBE members $i \in M$ and from databases includes the following parameters:

$c_{i,j}^k$ = capacity, or amount of work that member $i \in M$ can perform on task j (e.g. person months), with probability $p_{i,j}(k)$

$p_{i,j}$ = probability measure on set $C_{i,j}$, which includes $c_{i,j}^k$'s for given i and j

$v_{i,j}$ = variable costs of member $i \in M$ working on task j (e.g. €/person month)

f_i = fixed cost of member i becoming part of the VO, i.e. working on at least one task of the project

$f_{i,j}$ = fixed cost of member i starting to work on task j.

The actual decision variable is the work-allocation matrix $X_{m\times n}$, whose element $x_{i,j}$ denotes the amount of work that VBE member i performs on task j. In addition, we define the following dummy variables, whose values depend completely on x's.

First, let

$$y_i = \begin{cases} 0, & \text{if } x_{i,j} = 0 \forall j \in N \\ 1, & \text{if } x_{i,j} > 0 \text{ for at least one } j \in N. \end{cases}$$

That is, y_i is binary, denoting whether any work in the project is allocated to VBE member i. Furthermore, let

$$y_{i,j} = \begin{cases} 0, & \text{if } x_{i,j} = 0 \\ 1, & \text{if } x_{i,j} > 0. \end{cases}$$

In words, binary $y_{i,j}$ denotes whether any work on task j is allocated to i.

2.2 Objective Function

In the basic model we present one criterion, which is cost. Therefore the objective is to minimize total costs related to each organization's variable and fixed costs:

$$\min_{X,Y} \underbrace{\sum_{i=1}^{m} f_i y_i}_{(I)} + \underbrace{\sum_{j=1}^{n} \sum_{i=1}^{m} \left(v_{i,j} x_{i,j} + f_{i,j} y_{i,j} \right)}_{(II)} \tag{1}$$

where X is m×n matrix consisting of x's and Y is m×(n+1) matrix of y's. Interpretation of the sum terms is the following.

(I) Sum of fixed costs for adding a new member to VO

(II) Sum of fixed and variable costs of each member's work on tasks

It should be noted, however, that the model is flexible in the sense that some costs can be ignored if considered irrelevant. On the other hand, the model allows accounting for completely new criteria, of which some examples are given in Sections 3 and 4.

2.3 Constraints

The constraints of the optimization problem are divided into three categories, namely 1) constraints that assure the demands of the project are met, 2) constraints that care for the feasibility of decision variables, and 3) constraints related to additional features. Beginning with the project constraints, first the work load of each task has to be covered:

$$\sum_{i=1}^{m} x_{i,j} \geq w_j \quad \forall j \in N.$$

The work allocation may not exceed expected capacities:

$$x_{i,j} \leq \sum_{k=1}^{|C_{i,j}|} p_{i,j}(k) c_{i,j}^{k} \quad \forall i \in M, j \in N. \tag{2}$$

Work loads are non-negative (unless capacity can be transferred inside the VBE):

$$x_{i,j} \geq 0 \quad \forall i \in M, j \in N.$$

Second, we present the feasibility constraints. The correct values for binary y_i's are assured with the following constraints:

$$y_i \geq \frac{\sum_{j \in N} x_{i,j}}{\sum_{j \in N} w_j} - \varepsilon \text{ and } y_i \leq \frac{\sum_{j \in N} x_{i,j}}{\sum_{j \in N} w_j} - \varepsilon + 1 \quad \forall i \in M,$$

where ε is a lower bound for the amount of work allocated to i in order to have i considered as an *essential* VO member.

The following constraints assure binary $y_{i,j}$'s have correct values:

$$y_{i,j} \geq \frac{x_{i,j}}{E[C_{i,j}]}, \quad \forall i \in M, j \in N \text{ s.t. } E[C_{i,j}] > 0,$$

where $E[C_{i,j}]$ is i's expected capacity for task j, defined as in (2).

Lastly, the MILP model allows numerous additions and modifications, of which we give two examples. First, *common capacity* between several tasks is captured with a simple additional constraint, e.g. $x_{i,a}+x_{i,b} \leq c_{i,ab}$.

Second, *overwork pricing* is captured with a new variable $x_{i,j}^+$ denoting work that exceeds expected capacity $E[C_{i,j}]$. The capacity constraint transforms to $x_{i,j}-x_{i,j}^+ \leq E[C_{i,j}]$ and $x_{i,j}^+ \leq x_{i,j}$. Objective function takes an additional cost term $v_{i,j}^+ x_{i,j}^+$, where $v_{i,j}^+$ is the variable cost of overwork.

3. COOPERATIVE EFFICIENCY

Organizational collaboration is seldom completely frictionless when compared to work performed by a single organization. Since organizations have different physical and social relationships to each other, it is not justified to assume that two distinct groups of organizations would perform equally well, even with equivalent intra-organizational competencies. We denote this phenomenon by cooperative efficiency of organizations.

3.1 Cooperation Measures

We define the bilateral cooperation measure as follows.

Definition 1 *Let* M *be a set of organizations. For each* a, b, c, d ∈ M, a≠b, c≠d, *bilateral cooperation measure* $e_{a,b}$ *satisfies the following conditions*

(i) $e_{a,b} \in \mathrm{IR}$

(ii) $e_{a,b} = e_{b,a}$

(iii) $e_{a,b} > e_{c,d}$ *pair* (a,b) *has higher expected cooperative efficiency than pair* (c,d).

Suppose there is a documented collaboration history between the organizations of VBE M. This can be modeled for instance as a graph, where nodes are the organizations of M and edges between the nodes represent successful/unsuccessful collaboration history. More generally, the edges are weighted corresponding to the success/failure of past collaboration, measured by a bilateral cooperation measure. Recently, Lavrač et al. (2005) have modeled trust in a VBE through an application of multi-attribute decision analysis. For instance, their work provides a means for measuring efficiency of bilateral cooperation, whereas Pearson et al. (2002) present a model for the evolution of bilateral relationships.

In the following, we suggest that the cooperative efficiency of a network can be obtained from bilateral cooperative efficiencies. Let G = (M,E) be a graph whose nodes are the members of VBE M and edges are weighted with bilateral cooperation measures between members of M. Let $E = \{e_{a,b} \mid a, b \in M, a<b\}$ denote the set of edges, i.e. the bilateral cooperation measures of each pair $(a, b) \subset M$. Furthermore, let P^M denote the power set of M, and let $G_P(P^M \setminus M, E^P)$ denote a graph whose nodes are the elements of P^M excluding set M itself, and edges exist between every two nodes $\alpha, \beta \in (P^M \setminus M)$, such that $\alpha \cup \beta = \varnothing$. Figure 1 illustrates a $G_P(P^M \setminus M, E^P)$ with M = {a, b, c}.

Definition 2 *Network cooperation measure is a mapping* γ: $G_P(P^M \setminus M, E^P) \rightarrow IR$ *with the following property. Let* $A,B \subseteq M$, $A \neq B$, *then* $\gamma(A) > \gamma(B)$ *network organization A has higher expected cooperative efficiency than B.*

Hence, the network cooperation measure accounts not only for bilateral cooperative efficiencies between individual organizations, but also for bilateral cooperative efficiencies between possible coalitions inside a network. This is necessary, for instance if a, b, and c get along well twosome, but cannot work together as a triplet.

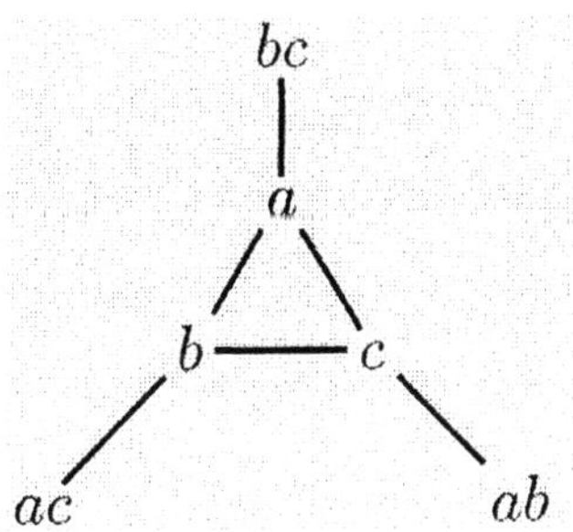

Figure 1 – Graph $G_P(P^M \setminus M, E^P)$ with M = {a, b, c}

3.2 Two Examples of Network Cooperation Measures

The following additive measure is defined for $e_{a,b} \in (-\infty,1]$:

$$\gamma^{ADD}(A,E) = \frac{1}{\left\lceil \frac{|A|(|A|-1)}{2} \right\rceil} \sum_{\substack{(a,b)\subset A \\ a<b}} \lambda_{a,b} e_{a,b},$$

where $\lambda_{a,b} > 0$ is a weight attached to cooperative efficiency of pair (a,b). The weights sum up to one. The weighted sum is normalized with the number of edges in complete graph with |A| nodes. Hence, a network with perfect relationships would attain a value of one. This measure enables the comparison of two different size networks.

For our MILP model we would like to have a linear measure. For that purpose, let us first define a binary variable $z_{a,b} \in \{0,1\}$, such that

$$z_{a,b} = \begin{cases} 0, & \text{if } y_a = 0 \text{ or } y_b = 0 \\ 1, & \text{if } y_a = 1 \text{ and } y_b = 1. \end{cases}$$

In words, $z_{a,b}$ denotes whether both a and b have work allocated. For z, we need the following constraints:

$$z_{a,b} \le \frac{y_a + y_b}{2}, \text{ and } z_{a,b} \ge y_a + y_b - 1 \;\; \forall\{a,b\} \subset M, \text{s.t. } e_{a,b} > 0.$$

Then, the following cooperation measure is linear:

$$\gamma^{LIN}(Z,E) = \sum_{\substack{a,b \in A \\ a<b}} e_{a,b}(f_a + f_b) z_{a,b},$$

where Z is m×m matrix of z's. The bilateral cooperative efficiencies are weighted with fixed participation costs.

However modeled, the purpose of collaboration data is to highlight such subsets of a VBE that, based on e.g. historical evidence, have a higher expected cooperative efficiency than those with unsuccessful or negligible past collaboration. This phenomenon can be included in our MILP model using cooperation measures.

4. CAPACITY RISK MEASURES

Apart from financial portfolio optimization problems, where risk is usually measured through fluctuations in profit, in our case it is meaningful to define risk through fluctuations in capacity. This is reasoned with two facts. Firstly, project income, i.e. payment from customer, is normally risk-free, excluding force majeure reasons, e.g. customer's bankrupt. Secondly, almost all project failures, e.g. quality defects, material shortages, and unexpected raise in demand, can be reduced to capacity shortfall.

We shall review two linear risk measures, which are therefore applicable to our MILP model. First, Eppen et al. (1989) suggest *expected downside risk* (EDR) be used for capacity-risk measurement. Applied to our model, expected downside risk of i's work on j is

$$\rho_{i,j}^{EDR} = \sum_{\forall c_{i,j}^k < x_{i,j}} p_{i,j}(k)\left(x_{i,j} - c_{i,j}^k\right)$$

In words, EDR is the expected value of downside difference between allocated work and capacity. Hence, the summation is taken over such events $c_{i,j}^k$ that imply a shortfall in capacity, if work $x_{i,j}$ is allocated.

Explicitly, EDR is incorporated in our model as follows. For each $c_{i,j}^k \in C_{i,j}$, let $c_{i,j}^{k+} \ge 0$ and $c_{i,j}^{k-} \ge 0$, respectively, denote the positive and negative difference of $c_{i,j}^k - x_{i,j}$. The correct values of $c_{i,j}^{k+}$ and $c_{i,j}^{k-}$ are assured with constraints:

$$x_{i,j} - c_{i,j}^{k-} + c_{i,j}^{k+} = c_{i,j}^k \, \forall i \in M, j \in N, c_{i,j}^k \in C_{i,j}.$$

Formula for EDR becomes

$$\rho_{i,j}^{EDR} = \sum_{\forall c_{i,j}^k \in C_{i,j}} p_{i,j}(k) c_{i,j}^{k-}.$$

The other risk measure we shall review is *lower semi-absolute deviation* (LSAD), which was presented by Gustafsson and Salo (2005) in the context of financial portfolio selection. For our model, LSAD of i's work on j is calculated as follows:

$$\rho_{i,j}^{LSAD} = E\left[C_{i,j}\right] - \sum_{\substack{k \\ c_{i,j}^k < E[C_{i,j}]}} c_{i,j}^k.$$

Hence, LSAD is the expected downside deviation from expected capacity.

Both EDR and LSAD are interpreted as expected shortfalls from a target value; in EDR the target value is allocated work, whereas in LSAD the target value is expected capacity. Both can be incorporated in our MILP model either as linear constraints, e.g. $EDR \leq r_1$, $LSAD \leq r_2$, or as additional costs in the objective function. However, both approaches require parameter estimations; in the former the accepted risk-levels (r's) are to be defined, and in the latter the cost of capacity risk is to be determined.

5. CONCLUSIONS AND FURTHER RESEARCH

In this paper we have presented a mathematical programming approach to virtual organization creation. The use of such models helps obtain better understanding of prevailing conditions and helps answering questions such as "What would be the structure of an optimal VO?", "Should the project be performed in a centralist rather than in a distributed manner?", "What are the risks related to distributed manufacturing?".

We have formulated a mixed integer linear programming model for the optimal VO creation problem. The objective of the model is to match the core competencies of different VBE members with the requirements of a project and thereby select the optimal VO to serve the customer. The most important contributions of our model are first the modeling of inter-organizational relationships and second, measuring risk of VO failure.

Topics for future research are manifold. First, our optimization model could be improved by several features. These include for instance dynamic decision-making and uncertainties, interdependent risks, hedging against capacity risk, etc. Second, the effect of incentives, e.g. profit sharing rules, on VO creation should be studied. Third, VBE member performance measurement models are needed in order to most efficiently use operative models. For instance, our model raises the need to measure factors related to cooperative efficiency.

ACKNOWLEDGEMENTS

The European Integrated Project ECOLEAD, and the funding of National Technology Agency of Finland (Tekes) and the National Workplace Development Programme (Tykes) through COBTEC project are acknowledged.

REFERENCES

1. Camarinha-Matos LM, Afsarmanesh H. Elements of a base VE infrastructure. Computers in Industry 2003; 51: 139–63.
2. Camarinha-Matos LM, Afsarmanesh H. Collaborative Networks: A New Scientific Discipline. Journal of Intelligent Manufacturing 2005; to appear.
3. Camarinha-Matos LM, Pantoja-Lima C. Cooperation coordination in virtual enterprises. Journal of Intelligent Manufacturing 2001; 12: 133–50.
4. Eppen GD, Martin RK, Schrage L. A Scenario Approach to Capacity Planning. Operations Research 1989; 37(4): 517–27.
5. Fischer M, Jähn H, Teich T. Optimizing the selection of partners in production networks. Robotics and Computer-Integrated Manufacturing 2004; 20: 593–601.
6. Gustafsson J, Salo A. Contingent Portfolio Programming for the Management of Risky Projects. Operations Research 2005; to appear.
7. Ip WH, Yung KL, Wang D. A branch and bound algorithm for subcontractor selection in agile manufacturing environment. International Journal of Production Economics 2004; 87: 195–205.
8. Ko CS, Kim T, Hwang H. External partner selection using tabu search heuristics in distributed manufacturing. International Journal of Production Research 2001; 39(17): 3959–74.
9. Lavrač N, Ljubič P, Jermol M, Papa G. A Decision Support Approach to Modeling Trust in Networked Organizations. In Proceedings of the 18th International Conference on Industrial & Engineering Applications of Artificial Intelligence & Expert Systems, Bari, June 22-24, 2005, Springer Verlag.
10. Lin C-WR, Chen H-YS. A fuzzy strategic alliance selection framework for supply chain partnering under limited evaluation resources. Computers in Industry 2004; 55: 159–79.
11. Mikhailov L. Fuzzy analytical approach to partnership selection in formation of virtual enterprises. Omega 2002; 30: 393–401.
12. Pearson DW, Albert P, Besombes B, Boudarel M-R, Marcon E, Mnemoi G. Modeling enterprise networks: A master equation approach. European Journal of Operational Research 2002; 138(3): 663–70.
13. Sha DY, Che ZH. Virtual integration with a multi-criteria partner selection model for the multi-echelon manufacturing system. The International Journal of Advanced Manufacturing Technology 2005; 25(7-8): 793-802.
14. Wu N, Mao N, Qian Y. An approach to partner selection in agile manufacturing. Journal of Intelligent Manufacturing 1999; 10(6): 519–29.
15. Wu N, Su P. Selection of partners in virtual enterprise paradigm. Robotics and Computer-Integrated Manufacturing 2005; 21: 119–31.

14 HIERARCHICAL MULTI-ATTRIBUTE DECISION SUPPORT APPROACH TO VIRTUAL ORGANIZATION CREATION

Toni Jarimo (1), Peter Ljubič (2), Iiro Salkari (1), Marko Bohanec (2), Nada Lavrač (2, 3), Martin Žnidaršič (2), Stefan Bollhalter (4), Jiri Hodik (5)

(1) VTT Technical Research Centre of Finland, toni.jarimo@vtt.fi, iiro.salkari@vtt.fi

(2) Jožef Stefan Institute, Ljubljana, Slovenia, peter.ljubic@ijs.si, marko.bohanec@ijs.si, nada.lavrac@ijs.si, martin.znidarsic@ijs.si

(3) Nova Gorica Polytechnic, Nova Gorica, Slovenia

(4) Virtuelle Fabrik AG, Arbon, Switzerland, stefan.bollhalter@virtuelle-fabrik.com

(5) Czech Technical University, Prague, Czech Republic, hodik@labe.felk.cvut.cz

The process of virtual organization (VO) creation can be seen as the selection of a set of organizations from a larger set, called a VO breeding environment (VBE). Often a VBE provides several possible VO configurations whose efficiency differs. The ultimate task is to evaluate all possible configurations in order to select the optimal VO configuration. The contribution of this paper is twofold. First, we formalize the VO creation process as a multi-attribute decision-making problem. Second, we suggest a hierarchy of attributes for computer-supported VO creation. Finally, we illustrate our approach using a subset of criteria, through a case of an existing VBE, the Virtuelle Fabrik AG.

1. INTRODUCTION

The process of creating Virtual Organizations (VO) has recently attracted the attention of researchers from various fields. One approach is that of Camarinha-Matos and Afsarmanesh (2003), who suggest that a pool of proactively cooperating organizations, called a Virtual Organization Breeding Environment (VBE), would be an efficient platform for creating VOs. Their idea is that a VBE provides a common structure for repeated VO creation, hence decreasing the costs related to ad hoc VO creation. Such a VBE structure includes, for instance, a common infrastructure, contracting templates and decision-support tools for agile VO creation.

This paper builds on the VBE context, focusing on supporting the selection of a good VO configuration from among the members of a VBE. Since the notion of VBE is relatively new, VO creation in a VBE is not yet well understood. Therefore, this paper proposes a general formalization of the problem, which can serve as a basis for future tool development.

The need for VO selection arises when the VBE, or its *broker* who is a marketer of the VBE (e.g. Katzy and Dissel, 2001), identifies a value creation opportunity[i] and is willing to create a VO for performing the job. Like many other decision-making situations, VO selection necessitates the definition of case-specific selection criteria, some of which are likely to be conflicting. Common examples of conflicting criteria are the usual project measures, i.e. cost, time and quality.

Multi-criteria decision-analysis (MCDA) is a well developed mathematical theory providing methods to cope with conflicting objectives (see e.g. Keeney and Raiffa, 1976). Therefore we suggest MCDA as one possible approach to support decisions related to VO creation. In this paper, we restrict ourselves to the case of a single decision-maker, whose ultimate task is to evaluate several alternatives, i.e. feasible VO configurations, with regard to multiple criteria. Naturally, the evaluation of alternatives leads to their ranking, which supports the selection of the most suitable one. Often, the decision criteria are structured in an attribute hierarchy, which divides the general criteria into subcriteria and sub-subcriteria etc.

The remainder of this paper is structured as follows. Section 2 formalizes VO creation as a multi-attribute decision-making problem. Section 3 suggests an attribute hierarchy for the problem and Section 4 illustrates the model through a real-life example. Section 5 concludes and suggests topics for future research.

2. A MULTI-CRITERIA MODEL FOR VO CREATION

2.1 Two Phases of VO Creation

We consider VO creation as a two-step process. Phase 1 defines the set of all possible VO configurations that are capable of performing the value creation opportunity addressed. Specifically we say that a VO is *capable* of performing a task if it has the necessary competencies and resources available to the extent the task requires. We denote the set of capable VO configurations as the *feasible set*. We assume that a broker has made a work breakdown structure of the value creation opportunity, including competency and resource needs. This naturally has consequences for the feasible set, hence emphasizing the role of the broker.

Phase 2 attaches a *value* to each VO configuration in the feasible set, thus defining a preference order of feasible VO configurations. The value of a VO configuration is an aggregation of its scores on given criteria. For instance, the *set of criteria* could be {skills, efficiency, network relations}, which can be further developed into a *attribute hierarchy*. We discuss the attribute hierarchy in more detail in Section 3.

2.2 Mathematical Modeling

Following the notation of Liesiö et al. (2005), let X denote the set of organizations, i.e. the VBE. All possible VO configurations from VBE X is the power set $P=2^X$. We denote the feasible set by P_f, ($P_f \subset P$), and its elements, i.e. the capable VO configurations, by $\{p^1,\ldots,p^m\}$.

We let n be the number of criteria against which the elements of P_f are evaluated. For each $p^j \in P_f$ there exists a score vector $\mathbf{v}^j=[v_1^j \ldots v_n^j]$, whose element v_i^j denotes the score of configuration p^j corresponding to the i-th criterion. The different criteria are weighted with weights $w_i>0$. Weights are normalized so that $w_1+\ldots+w_n=1$. The value of configuration p^j is given by the *additive value function* $V^j=\Sigma_{i=1\ldots n}\, w_i v_i^j$.

We divide the criteria into two categories: 1) Node Attributes and 2) Network Preparedness Attributes. The difference between these two groups is that Node Attributes are related to a single VBE member (node), whereas Network Preparedness Attributes reflect the overall (decrease in) efficiency of a VO configuration, due to difficulties that multilateral working induces. Hence a VO configuration consisting of a single VBE member has the highest possible score on all Network Preparedness Attributes. Section 3 provides an example of such a criteria hierarchy.

The requirement for existence of an additive value function is that the attributes are *mutually preferentially independent*. To clarify this concept, we first give an example of *preferential independence*: Say the quality level *p'* that a VO provides is deemed better than quality level *p''*, at cost level *z'*. If this holds for any cost level *z*, then quality is preferentially independent of costs. Furthermore, if every subset *Y* of these attributes is preferentially independent of any other subset *Z*, then the attributes are mutually preferentially independent. (Keeney and Raiffa, 1976)

In some cases, the feasible set P_f may be very large and the evaluation of all feasible configurations becomes practically impossible. Therefore we need approaches that efficiently distinguish good alternatives from P_f. One way to diminish the number of alternatives is to identify *dominated* VO configurations, i.e. configurations which are worse than another configuration on every criterion (Keeney and Raiffa, 1976). For instance, Liesiö et al. (2005) have developed "Robust Portfolio Modeling" for identifying all non-dominated options from among a large sct of alternatives.

3. ATTRIBUTE HIERARCHY

This section proposes an attribute hierarchy, which illustrates the division of the common problem into 1) Node Attributes and 2) Network Preparedness Attributes (Figure 1). In addition, it gives an insight into the two-phase process of firstly defining the feasible set and secondly attaching value to the configurations.

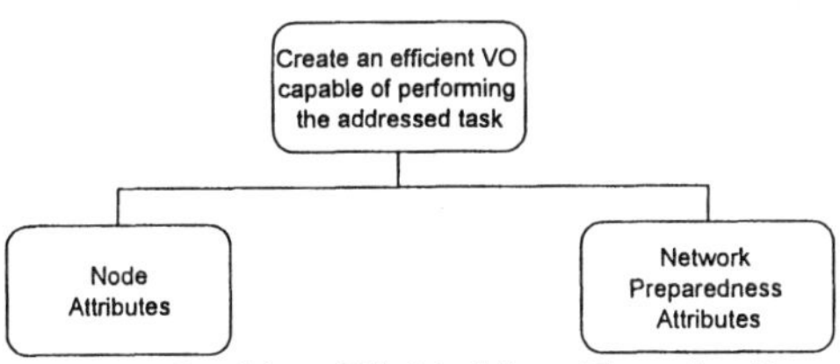

Figure 1 – Common Problem Divided into Two Attribute Categories

As discussed in Section 2, if a node has the required expertise for conducting some task defined in the work breakdown structure, the node is capable of the task. If the node has the required expertise, it is expected that the node has the necessary competencies, resources and availability for the task. We refer to these attributes as *feasibility attributes*. Reviewing the feasibility attributes reveals the feasible set, i.e.

phase 1 of the VO creation process. Figure 2 presents the Node Attribute hierarchy, in which the feasibility attributes are marked with an asterisk (*).

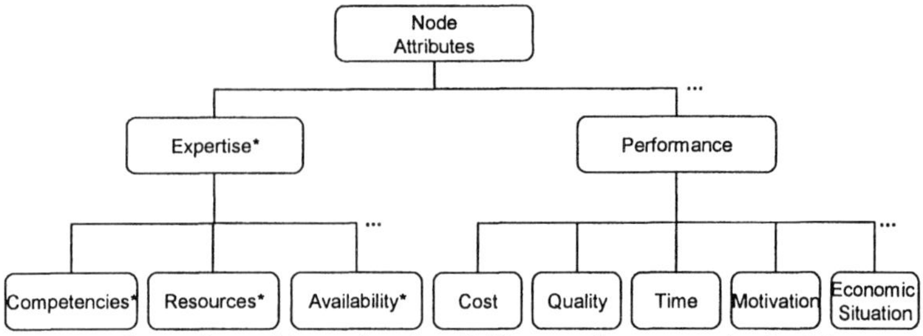

Figure 2 – Node attribute hierarchy, feasibility attributes marked with asterisk (*)

Phase 2 of the VO creation process attaches values to the different VO configurations of the feasible set. This takes place by assessing node performance individually and network preparedness as a whole. The performance of a single node is a node attribute and the related hierarchy is depicted in Figure 2. We propose that for instance cost, quality, time, motivation and economic situation effect the performance of a job the node is capable of.

The network preparedness attributes reflect the difficulties of multilateral working (Figure 3). They indicate the performance of a capable VO configuration. We propose that the network preparedness attributes can be divided into e.g. business characteristics, social characteristics and miscellaneous attributes. This division is not clear at every point nor is it exhaustive, but it illustrates our idea of network preparedness. Potential other attributes are identified by e.g. Lin and Chen (2004). Network preparedness attributes are issues that may make collaboration more difficult.

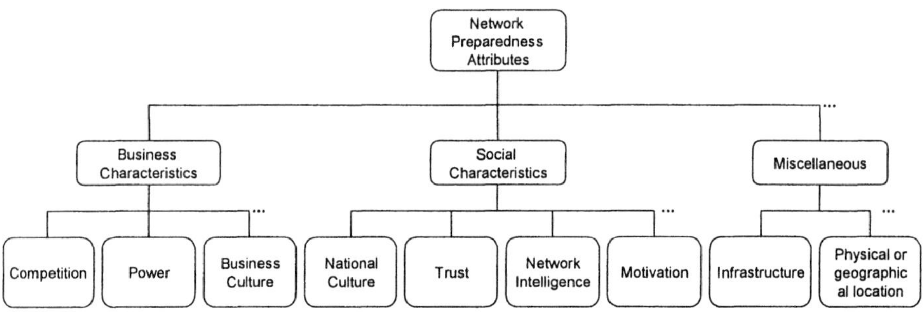

Figure 3 – Network preparedness attributes

Business characteristics consist of competition, power and business culture. If companies compete for the same customers, it may be hard for them to collaborate, or even competition (or antitrust) law may prevent some companies from collaborating. Depending on the objective of the VO that is being created, the power difference of the companies may play a role: it may be desired, equal or restrictive from collaboration viewpoint. Companies that have interoperable infrastructure are in better situation when collaborating than companies with dissimilar or non-interoperable infrastructure. By network intelligence we mean accumulated experiences from past collaboration. Similarly, the rest of the attributes reflect the challenge of multilateral collaboration.

There is no general order of preference for attribute values. For instance, in the case of power, in a subcontracting type of collaboration, the power difference may even be desired by the principal company, whereas in joint R&D efforts, the power difference may be considered as a drawback. Therefore, the decision-maker needs to elicit case-specific preference weights for attributes.

Weight elicitation methods for numerical MCDA models are numerous and well developed, such as WSM, ELECTRE, TOPSIS (Triantaphyllou, 2000), SMART and SMARTER (Edwards and Barron, 1994), and similar. A well-known method in this field is the Analytic Hierarchy Process (AHP) (Saaty, 1993), in which weights are elicited by pairwise comparison of attributes. AHP is interesting for its ability to estimate the consistency of assessment.

In addition, weight elicitation may require the use of qualitative variables as a complement to more typical quantitative ones. Qualitative variables are often denoted by words like "low", "appropriate" and "acceptable". The qualitative attributes are evaluated to suit decision-making problems that are less structured and formalized (Bohanec and Rajkovič, 1999). For qualitative (symbolic) multi-attribute models, a suitable method is implemented in the system called DEXi (Bohanec, 2003). The method approximates numerical weights from qualitatively assessed decision rules (Bohanec and Zupan, 2004). Regarding the decision support system, this implies that the system should be capable of analyzing both numerical and qualitative variables.

4. AN ILLUSTRATIVE EXAMPLE CASE

In this example case we tried to construct a rule-based hierarchical model using functional decomposition, which is focused on discovering novel concepts in the data. To build such a structure we used a hierarchy induction tool HINT (Zupan et al., 1999) from a data mining suite Orange (Demsar and Zupan, 2004). Its purpose is to decompose a complex function into a hierarchy of simpler ones. The result of such decomposition is a concept hierarchy with a number of tables that help to provide an extensional definition of concepts.

We provide an illustrative example using data of the Virtuelle Fabrik (VF) industry cluster in the area of mechanical engineering. The key question we would like to answer is the following: Can we not only predict, but also understand how a company's attributes influence its cooperation with other companies?

The data consists of two tables shown in Table 1. The first table describes a sample of 62 partners collaborating in VF and their attributes. The attributes are the following: *activity*, *punctuality*, *reliability*, *motivation*, *love of risks* and *economic situation*. All attributes can take values from 1 (very bad) to 6 (very good). The second table represents a cooperation matrix showing cooperation between companies. Values vary from 0 (no cooperation) to 3 (intense cooperation). Since input to the HINT functional decomposition should be in one table, we prepared the data in the following fashion. In the new table there is one row per each cooperative action of companies. Consequently, each company may appear in more than one row. Each row also holds information about the intensity of such cooperation, as shown in the lower table of Table 1. For simplicity we discretized companies' attribute values so that numbers 1 and 2 were changed to nominal value *low*, 3 and 4 to *mid*, and 5 and 6 to *high*. The rows with missing values were skipped (e.g. company 1 in table 1) and the attribute *reliability* with only one value (6) was removed. The resulting input table for HINT consists of 58 rows.

Table 1 – Information about companies (upper left-hand side table) and their cooperation (upper right-hand side table). For simplicity, zeros are omitted in the cooperation matrix. Below is the HINT input table, where shadowed rows represent the cooperation of company 4 (the shadowed row of the upper left-hand side table).

id	activity	punctuality	reliability	motivation	love of risks	econ. situation
1	2	5	6	4		5
2	4	5	6	5	3	5
3	2	5	6	5	4	5
4	5	6	6	6	6	6
5	5	5	6	6	5	6
6	2	5	6	4	4	6
7	5	5	6	6	6	4
8	4	5	6	6	3	4

cooperation matrix

	1	2	3	4	5	6	7	8
1				3			1	
2								1
3						1		
4	3					2	2	
5							1	
6			1	2				
7	1			2	1			
8		1						

id	activity	punctuality	motivation	love of risks	econ. situation	cooperation
...						
3	low	hi	hi	hi	mid	1
4	hi	hi	hi	hi	hi	3
4	hi	hi	hi	hi	hi	2
4	hi	hi	hi	hi	hi	2
5	hi	hi	hi	hi	hi	1
...						

A result of HINT is a rule-based model for a hierarchy of concepts, shown in Figure 4 (note that due to space restrictions, inference rules are not listed). In the hierarchical structure, three new concepts are introduced (shown as ellipses in Figure 4), the numbers in brackets denote the number of different values for each new concept. What is the benefit of such a structure? We can use it as a classifier to estimate a new company's cooperation. However, a much greater value of this model lies in its transparency and the capability of using various analysis methods that work on multi-attribute decision-models (e.g. what-if). Such an automatically obtained model can serve as the first approximation of a model and as a starting point for an improvement in collaboration with a domain expert. An expert should recognize and label concepts according to his background knowledge, delete senseless concepts and possibly improve the data gathering for another iteration of concept formation.

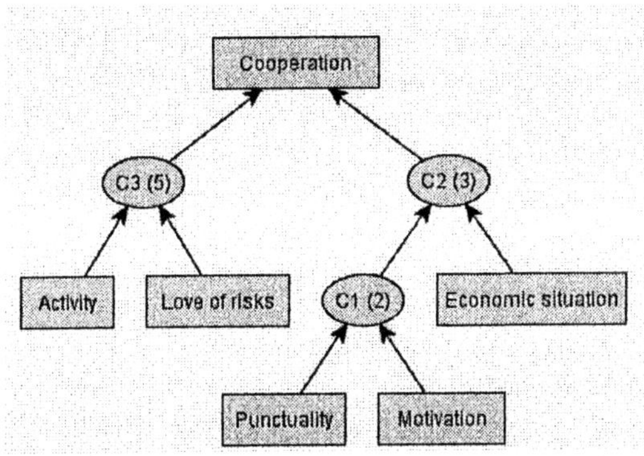

Figure 4 – Hierarchical structure obtained by HINT showing that *Activity* and *Love of risks* more directly influence *Cooperation* than *Punctuality* and *Motivation*

5. CONCLUSIONS AND FURTHER RESEARCH

In this paper we proposed a general multi-attribute decision-making model for VO creation. We first formalized VO selection as a multi-criteria portfolio-selection problem and secondly suggested an attribute hierarchy for selection criteria. The approach was illustrated through an example of an operating VBE, the Virtuelle Fabrik AG, Switzerland.

The multi-criteria decision-analysis methodology seems to work as a good approach for supporting VO selection. Its advantages are strongly developed theory, transparency of decision criteria, an ability to use models for various analyses and simulations, such as what-if analysis, and for improved communication and documentation between decision-makers themselves as well as between decision-makers and other interested parties. Usually, decision-making models are applicable as software tools, albeit computational challenges may arise if the set of alternatives becomes very large. In addition, the existence of multiple decision-makers makes the problem very difficult (e.g. Arrow, 1951).

This paper suggests several avenues for future research. First, performance measurement, especially for network-related attributes, is called for. Second, suitable methods for attribute-weight elicitation are needed. For instance, we have identified the need to cope with qualitative variables and combine both quantitative and qualitative criteria. Third, the practical value of multi-attribute decision-support methodology to VO creation should be evaluated through an extensive real-life case study, which could additionally lead to tool development.

ACKNOWLEDGEMENTS

This work was supported by the 6FP Integrated Project ECOLEAD, the Slovenian Ministry of Higher Education, Science and Technology, and the National Technology Agency of Finland (Tekes) and the National Workplace Development Programme (Tykes) through the COBTEC project.

---

[i] This term was suggested by Mario Martínez in an ECOLEAD project meeting in Rome, January 2005.

REFERENCES

1. Arrow K. Social Choice and Individual Values, PhD Thesis, Columbia University, 1951.
2. Bohanec M. "Decision Support". In Data Mining and Decision Support: Integration and Collaboration, Mladenić D, Lavrač N, Bohanec M, Moyle S, ed. Kluwer Academic Publishers, 2003.
3. Bohanec M, Rajkovič V. Multi-Attribute Decision Modeling: Industrial Applications of DEX. Informatica 23(2), 487-491, 1999.
4. Bohanec M, Zupan B. A Function-Decomposition Method for Development of Hierarchical Multi-Attribute Decision Models. Decision Support Systems 2004; 36: 215-33.
5. Camarinha-Matos LM, Afsarmanesh H. Elements of a base VE infrastructure. Computers in Industry 2003; 51(2): 139-63.
6. Lin C-W, Chen H-Y. A fuzzy strategic alliance selection framework for supply chain partnering under limited evaluation resources. Computers in Industry 2004; 55(2): 159-79.
7. Demsar J, Zupan B. Orange: From Experimental Machine Learning to Interactive Data Mining.White paper, Faculty of Computer and Information Science, University of Ljubljana, Slovenia, 2004. http://www.ailab.si/orange
8. Edwards W, Barron FH. SMARTS and SMARTER: Improved Simple Methods for Multiattribute Utility Measurement. Organizational Behavior and Human Decision Processes 1994; 60: 306–25.
9. Katzy BR, Dissel M. A Toolset for Building the Virtual Enterprise. Journal of Intelligent Manufacturing 2001; 12: 121-31.
10. Keeney RL, Raiffa H. Decisions with Multiple Objectives: Preferences and Value Tradeoffs, John Wiley & Sons, 1976.
11. Liesiö J, Mild P, Salo A. Preference Programming for Robust Portfolio Modeling and Project Selection, working paper, Systems Analysis Laboratory, Helsinki University of Technology, 2005. http://www.sal.hut.fi/Publications/pdf-files/mlie05.pdf
12. Saaty TL. Multicriteria Decision Making: The Analytic Hierarchy Process. RWS Publications, 1993.
13. Triantaphyllou E. Multi-Criteria Decision Making Methods: A Comparative Study. Kluwer Academic Publishers, 2000.
14. Zupan B, Bohanec M, Demšar J, Bratko I. Learning by discovering concept hierarchies. Artificial Intelligence 1999; 109: 211-42.

15

A MULTI-CRITERIA DECISION SUPPORT SYSTEM FOR THE FORMATION OF COLLABORATIVE NETWORKS OF ENTERPRISES

José António Crispim
Universidade do Minho, PORTUGAL
crispim@eeg.uminho.pt

Jorge Pinho Sousa
INESC Porto, Faculty of Engineering Univ. Porto, PORTUGAL
jsousa@inescporto.pt

In this paper we present a Decision Support System (DSS) to deal with the partner selection problem taking place in the formation or re-organization of a Virtual Enterprise (VE). This DSS is based on a multi-criteria model and handles several types of data (numerical, interval, linguistic and binary). This approach is used to facilitate the expression of the decision maker's preferences and assessments about the potential partners and can be performed individually or by group. The system also allows the assignment of a degree of confidence to each linguistic statement. The operation of the DSS is structured in two phases. In the first phase it determines the set of non-dominated alternatives (potential VEs) through the use of meta-heuristics. The second phase ranks the alternatives for a possible network of enterprises configuring the VE. This is achieved through a procedure based on linguistic analysis and distance measures.

1. INTRODUCTION

In the information age competition is expected to take place less among single companies, and increasingly among groups of enterprises working together to explore emerging business opportunities (Katzy and Dissel, 2001). This new reality is in fact giving smaller companies the possibility to compete with large multinationals. A Virtual Enterprise (VE) is a temporary alliance between globally distributed independent companies working together to improve their competitiveness by sharing resources, skills, risks and costs. Since each partner brings a strength or core competence to the consortium, the success of the VE strongly depends on the achieved level of co-operation. The creation of a VE is usually triggered by a market opportunity, giving rise to a "project". Projects are usually decomposable in relatively independent sub-projects or activities. The work needed to "fulfil" a project involves a set of collaborative activities that can be dependent, when relations of precedence between activities exist, or independent, if that is not the case. Therefore, before a VE is formed, the different input and output characteristics of each activity have to be clearly defined, particularly the required degree of synchronisation, the actors involved and the resources needed.

The success of a project is strongly dependent on the composition of the VE. Hence, the selection of the partners becomes a crucial part of its lifecycle. This phase is even more important when, due to the multiplicity of opportunities the dynamic environment can create, the VE has to be formed very quickly in order to meet deadlines or when an enterprise can participate in various VEs at the same time. The problem of partner selection also arises when the VE needs to be reorganized by adding/expelling some members or by re-assigning tasks or roles in order to better cope with new market circumstances. During the VE formation, different obstacles can arise such as lack of a culture of cooperation, lack of trust, existence of different behaviours, different perceptions of the environment and different (and even competing) priorities and motivations. To overcome these obstacles, Camarinha-Matos and Afsarmanesh (2003) suggest the creation of breeding environments (BE) consisting of long-term networked structures with common infrastructures, common ontologies, and mutual trust.

In this paper we present a Decision Support System (DSS) to deal with the partner selection problem under a multi-criteria perspective, where several types of information (numerical, interval, linguistic and binary) are allowed, in order to facilitate the expression of the decision maker's preferences or assessments about the potential partners, in an individual or group decision making scenario. This is in practice an important requirement as the multiplicity of factors considered when selecting partners for a business opportunity, such as cost, quality, trust and delivery time, cannot be expressed in the same measure or scale.

The DSS starts by considering that all companies (the potential partners) are present in a network (the breeding environment), interacting with each other. However, it is assumed that not all pairs of companies are linked. The main objectives of the DSS are to facilitate the rapid VE formation (or re-organization), and to improve the informal cooperation between the enterprises of the network through the simulation of alternative operating scenarios. The DSS also handles the existence of several VE formation processes inside the network, simultaneously or at different moments. Its operation is structured in two phases. In the first phase it determines the set of non-dominated alternatives (potential VEs) through the use of metaheuristics. The second phase ranks the alternatives for a possible network of enterprises, thus configuring the VE. This is achieved through a procedure based on fuzzy clustering, linguistic analysis and distance measures.

The remainder of the paper is organized as follows. In Section 2 the problem is described, in Section 3 the DSS is presented, in Section 4 an illustrative example is provided and finally, in Section 5 some preliminary conclusions are presented.

2. PROBLEM DESCRIPTION

The VE formation process can be described in the following way. Assume a network A representing all potential partners (companies) and their relationships. Companies and links are characterised by a set of m attributes, some assigned to the nodes and some assigned to the edges of the network. These attributes will be used to define the criteria for evaluating solutions (i.e. VE configurations). The first step in this modelling process is to carefully define what attributes are going to be considered on both subsets. The Decision Maker can weight the attributes according to his believes about their relative importance to the project under consideration.

The network includes a set of n companies connected with each other, capable of handling activities and of providing a finite amount of resources, available over specific intervals of time. Two types of connections between enterprises are allowed: a) a direct relation exists when a pair of companies has had a previous commercial relation; b) assume that enterprise *J* has a direct relation with *I*, and *I* has a direct relation with *K*, then an indirect relation exists between *J* and *K*.

Moreover assume project *P* involving *k* activities that demand a specific amount *Q* of resources and have to be performed within a determined interval of time *S*.

The partner selection problem consists of choosing the best group of companies to perform all *k* activities of project *P* taking into account a set of evaluation criteria based on the *m* attributes established for the network. The main constraints of the problem are time windows limitations and the minimum amount of resources required.

Partner selection can be viewed as a multiple attribute decision making (MADM) problem (Li and Liao, 2004), i.e. a process where the DM must choose from a set of limited alternatives that are typically defined explicitly in terms of attributes. In this problem, the alternatives correspond to groups of enterprises that have the resources and skills needed to carry out the project. Infeasibility is not considered, i.e. groups of enterprises that are not able to carry out the project are not accepted. The DM's preferences are often used to rank alternatives, with the best alternative being usually selected by comparisons through the various attributes that are often hard to quantify (Pohekar and Ramachandran, 2004). In this work the DM has the possibility to use different types of variables (numerical, linguistic, interval and binary) to express his preferences. Given the multi-criteria nature of the problem, there is generally no "optimal" alternative, and a good compromise solution must therefore be identified. Figure 1 gives an overall idea about the VE formation problem, namely the network, the companies, the relationships and the groups of enterprises that are potential VEs.

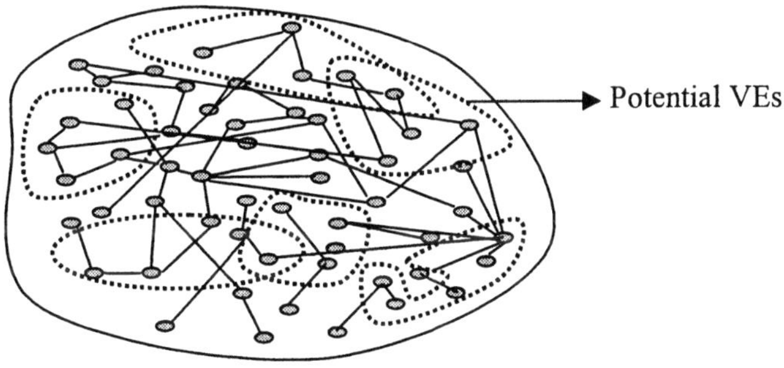

Figure 1: Multiple potential VEs within a network

3. THE DECISION SUPPORT SYSTEM

The DSS briefly described in this paper follows a simple architecture (figure 2) that comprises an interface with the DM, a data base, an output report area and three "functional" modules: the generation module, the ranking module and the simulation module. Its operation follows a 2-phase approach consisting of running the generation module first, and then the ranking module. The simulation module is an auxiliary module of the ranking module and is used to determine weight vectors for the attributes by Monte Carlo simulation.

This architecture aims at: i) supporting the DM in structuring the problem through the definition of the project (Goals that are to be achieved by performing Activities, requiring Skills and Competencies, developed by Enterprises described by their attributes and by the attributes of their relationships); ii) generating a ranking of potential VEs capable of performing the project (market opportunity); iii) providing support for *"what if"* analysis; and iv) analysing, in a given time horizon, how the network reacts when various projects take place, simultaneously or not. The DSS supports the existence of different types of data, individual and group DMs, and allows the DM to choose the number, kind and type of attributes to use in order to describe the network and the solution. Next, we will briefly describe each element of the DSS that was implemented in C++.

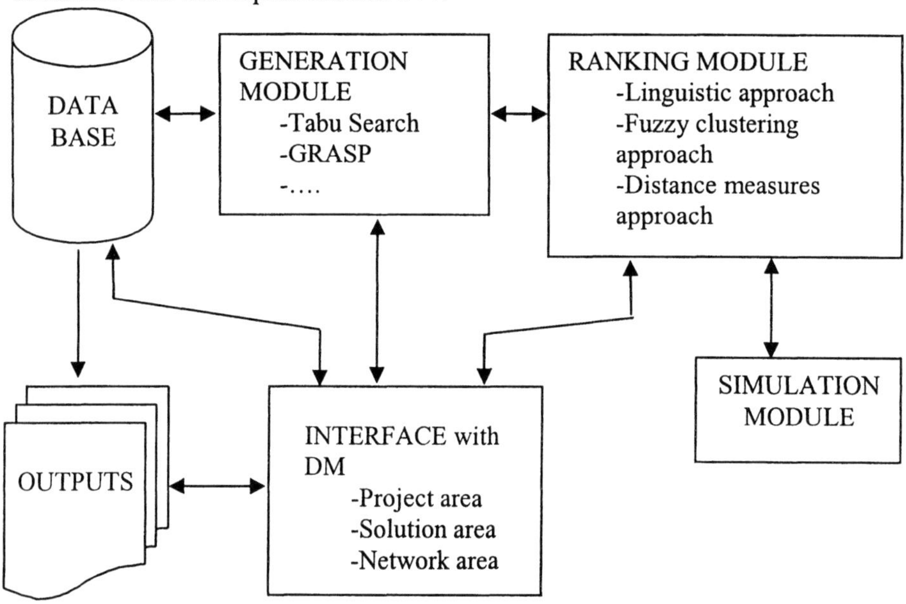

Figure 2: Architecture of the DSS

3.1 Interface

The DSS interface is formed by three distinct areas (Project area, Network area, and Solution area) and allows the introduction of data by text files or directly by the keyboard. The Project area is used to introduce information about the business opportunity being analysed, i.e. information about its activities (what activities, if there are precedences in their execution, execution interval times and quantities involved). The Network area is used to define the attributes that characterise the enterprises (nodes) and their relationships (arcs, edges). The Solution area is used to introduce information about the attributes used to compare and evaluate groups of enterprises (potential VEs). These attributes can be those considered in the Network area, all or only some of them, or they can be the result of an expression/combination of the Network area attributes. The Solution area can also be used to introduce constraints such as time windows and to introduce weights or to impose thresholds for trust, risk, etc.

3.2 Generation Module

This module is built around some metaheuristic algorithms, used to find a set of non-dominated alternatives to perform each project. Metaheuristics are approximate methods designed to solve hard combinatorial optimisation problems (Reeves, 1993). A metaheuristic is an iterative generation process that guides a subordinate heuristic while exploring the search space. It combines sophisticated rules to search different neighbourhood structures, memory structures and learning strategies in order to efficiently find near-optimal solutions (Osman and Kelly, 1996). The most well known metaheuristics are probably "simulated annealing" and "tabu search".

By repeatedly running these algorithms, it is possible, for the same project, to generate a large set of diverse solutions according to the type and number of attributes considered. However this set should also be small enough to be treatable and understandable by the DM. Moreover, it should cover the entire "solution curve", i.e. contain solutions that represent well the different possible compromises between the attributes. This can limit the number of alternatives to be kept by the system, leading to the deletion of the most similar ones.

In this work, we have implemented a Tabu Search (TS) metaheuristic (see e.g. Glover, 1989, 1990, 1993 and Glover and Laguna 1996, 1997). By a memory mechanism, TS is able to forbid certain movements during the search process, in order to diversify it. To do this, it stores the recently accepted solutions or attributes of these solutions in memory (tabu list) in order to prevent cycling. The main competitive advantage of Tabu Search with respect to alternative heuristics, also based on local search, is the intelligent use of the past history of the search to influence its future steps.

In our problem, a solution is represented by a set of companies in the network associated to the different activities, along with the values of the corresponding attributes.

The initial solution is generated through a simple process consisting of the following steps:

- Create a table of enterprises, activities and constraints (e.g. capacities). A given activity may be performed by a group of enterprises if, for example, separately they do not have enough resources. In this case, the group of enterprises is added to the network as a single unit and the attribute values that describe it result from the attribute values of the different enterprises.
- From that table randomly select one enterprise or a group of enterprises capable of handling the first activity of the project.
- Search, for the next activity, the enterprises with direct relations with the enterprise previously chosen and select the one which has the higher value for one or a group of attributes (for example, the higher value of trust). If no direct relations exist, search for an indirect relation and, if it does not exist, search for any other feasible enterprise.
- Repeat the previous step until all the activities of the project have been assigned to enterprises. If there is an activity not performed by any enterprise, ask the DM to introduce a new enterprise in the data base in order to overcome this problem.

The improvement of a solution is done by local search, where the neighbourhood structure consists of swapping an enterprise in the solution with an enterprise outside the solution. In this way, the search starts by exploring an enterprise that can do the first activity. If this replacement leads to a non-dominated alternative, this new set of enterprises is saved in the table of alternatives. The activities are explored by the order they have been defined in the project. Two tabu lists are used, the first forbids the utilization of the enterprises recently chosen, and the second forbids the choice of the last activity selected. This exploration of the neighbourhood structure is repeated until the search cannot achieve any alternative solution during 5000 consecutive iterations.

The strategy used in the neighbourhood search is similar to the first improvement and only accepts feasible solutions. An intensification strategy is adopted after a given number of consecutive dominated solutions is found and consists of re-starting the procedure with one of the non-dominated solutions saved in the table of alternatives randomly chosen. The algorithm only saves those non-dominated solutions that are significantly different. For that purpose, we consider an *"indifferent zone attribute value"* which consists of admitting that the attribute values are similar if their difference in percentage is smaller than a given value (±5%, for example). This percentage is provided by the DM, and can be different for each attribute.

3.3 Ranking Module

3.3.1 Linguistic Approach

There are decision situations in which the information cannot be assessed precisely in a quantitative form, due to its nature (e.g. trust) or because either information is unavailable or the cost of its computation is too high. In these situations an "approximate value" may be acceptable and so the use of a linguistic approach is appropriate (Herrera et al., 2004). "Linguistic variables" will represent qualitative aspects, with values that are not numbers but words or sentences in a natural language, thus making it easier to express preferences.

For our DSS we have adopted a 2-tuple fuzzy linguistic representation model (see Herrera and Martinez, 2000) as it allows the management of non-homogeneous information (numerical, linguistic interval, binary). This model is based on symbolic methods and takes as the base of its representation the concept of Symbolic Translation. It represents the linguistic information by means of a 2-tuple (s, α) where s is a linguistic term and α is a numerical value with $\alpha \in [-0,5; 0,5]$, representing the original result translated to the closest index label in the linguistic term set.

In the linguistic decision analysis of an MCDM problem, the solution scheme should involve the following three steps (Herrera and Herrera-Viedma, 2000): the choice of the linguistic term set with its semantic (meaning), the choice of the aggregation operator of linguistic information, and the choice of the best alternatives. *The linguistic term set*, usually called S, comprises a set of linguistic values that are generally ordered and uniformly distributed. For example, a set S of seven terms could be given as follows: S = {s_0 =none; s_1 =very low; s_2 =low; s_3 =medium; s_4 =high; s_5 =very high; s_6 =perfect}, in which $s_a < s_b$ if $a < b$. The semantics of the elements in the term set (the meaning of each term set) is given by fuzzy numbers defined on the [0, 1] interval and described by membership functions. Since the linguistic assessments given by the individuals are approximate, because it may be impossible or unnecessary to obtain more accurate values, Delgado et al. (1998) and Herrera et al. (2002) consider that trapezoidal or triangular membership functions are good enough to capture the vagueness of those linguistic assessments. In our DSS we have adopted triangular membership functions and accept different cardinalities for S, and different semantics in the term set, depending on the DM and/or the attribute in question. This becomes an advantage of the DSS because it allows the DM to be more or less detailed, when in presence of distinct attributes. For example, for "trust" use the term set S = {s_0 =none; s_1 =very low; s_2 =low; s_3 =medium; s_4 =high; s_5 =very high; s_6 =total} and for "prestige" S = {s_0 =none; s_1 =medium; s_2 =total}.

The 2-tuple approach implemented follows a scheme composed by three phases: unify the information into fuzzy sets over a basic linguistic term set (BLTS), aggregate them in a decision matrix, and rank the alternatives. Our implementation of this technique is slightly different from the original since we allow multiple attributes and eventually multiple DMs. In this way, to unify information, first, we have to aggregate (through a simple arithmetic mean) the attribute values of each enterprise. This aggregation can be complemented by attribute weights provided by the DM or by running the simulation module. After that, we transform the mixed information into fuzzy sets over a BLTS that corresponds to the term set with more linguistic values. Then, a transformation of the aggregate fuzzy sets into 2-tuples (s, α) is performed. Finally the ranking is achieved by calculating the dominance degree.

3.3.2 Distance Measures

Fuziness is inherent to most decision making processes when linguistic variables are used to describe qualitative data. Since linguistic labels, such as "very high", to describe the "trust" linguistic variable can be represented using positive triangular fuzzy numbers, a new approach to rank alternatives based on distance calculations can be used. This approach consists in comparing fuzzy numbers through the use of a fuzzy distance measure computed between each alternative and a crisp ideal solution (Tran and Duckstein, 2002) or a fuzzy positive ideal solution (Li and Yang, 2004; Ding and Liang, 2004). According to Tran and Duckstein (2002), the ranking order of all alternatives is obtained by comparing the distances of each alternative to two points, the crisp maximum and the crisp minimum, and the alternative first rank has the smallest distance to the maximum and the highest to the minimum. These two points of reference could be predetermined targets. Therefore in the *Distance measures area* we calculate the distances between each attribute value in the vector solution and its associated ideal maximum and minimum (values defined in the database for each attribute or introduced by the DM). For linguistic variables, we can use the distance between two triangular fuzzy numbers (the membership functions used in this DSS), presented by Li and Yang (2004), identical to the euclidean distance. In the case of interval values, we follow the distance formula presented by Tran and Duckstein (2002). In the case of numerical values, we use the distance between real numbers (Li and Yang, 2004). The main problem here is how to aggregate in a single value the non-homogeneous distance values we obtain, an issue that the previous studies do not take into consideration. To overcome this problem, after determining the distances, a normalization is performed and therefore all the distances are in the [0, 1] interval. Then an average is calculated and a final list, ranking the alternatives, is presented to the DM.

3.4 Simulation Module

This module is used when the DM wants to weight attributes in order to express their relative importances but is only capable of providing their rank order, or if the DM desires to perform some sensivity analysis on the weights. In this case, the module randomly computes weights for each attribute respecting the attributes rank order introduced and calculates the new alternative ranking. This process is repeated for a number of iterations (5000). A matrix containing the alternatives (rows) and the positions they assume (columns) is used to count every new alternative hierarchy. At the end a final alternative ranking is obtained according to the matrix information (for example, alternative *D* is the "best" because it occupies the first position 3500 times, the second 1400 times, ...). The simulation process, similar to that described by Butler et al. (1997), can be summarized as follows:

1. Repeat until stop criterion is satisfied
   - Generate n-number attributes random weights (w_i) on the interval [1, 99].
   - Normalize the weights, with $0 < w_i < 1, \forall i$, and $\sum_{i=1}^{n} w_i = 1$.
   - Order the weights and assign them to the attributes respecting the attributes hierarchy provided by the DM
   - Through the use of the additive model, compute the new alternative hierarchy.
   - Save this new hierarchy in a matrix of results.
2. Obtain the final rank order list of alternatives according to their counter.

4. ILLUSTRATIVE EXAMPLE

Assume we would like to form a VE to perform a project decomposed in 5 activities as shown in Table 1.

Table 1: Project data

Activities (code)	Precedent activities	Standard duration	Earliest start time	Latest finish time	Quantity of resources
8	-	24	111	171	121
4	-	9	101	160	181
5	-	35	28	295	146
6	4	48	160	298	280
3	4	47	160	228	62

Suppose a network composed by 100 companies described by a set of numerical variables (activities that each enterprise can execute, its capacity considered in terms of an available quantity, years of existence), an interval variable (time window during which the resources are available), and some linguistic variables (global performance, dimension, and management prestige). There are direct and indirect connections between the companies, comprising information such as distance, capacity of the link (in quantity), cost, price, trust and risk. For the linguistic variables we assume triangular membership functions with a cardinality of 5 with the correspondent term set {none, low, more or less, high, perfect}. The values of indirect connections are estimated as half of the direct connections. Attributes have an equal weight and there is a single DM. By applying the tabu search procedure, we have obtained the non-dominated alternatives set shown in table 2.

Table 2: Non-dominated alternatives data

	company number					price interval		cost	distance	trust	prestige	risk	global performance
	Act1	Act2	Act3	Act4	Act5								
VE1	74	9	13	22	47	9	48	4564	193	ML	P	ML	ML
VE2	35	9	13	22	47	35	49	4314	233	L	L	L	L
VE3	82	9	13	22	47	6	69	4180	224	L	H	H	P
VE4	92	9	13	22	47	66	87	4431	219	H	H	L	N
VE5	102	9	13	22	47	9	11	4977	191	ML	N	ML	L
VE6	102	8	13	22	47	41	97	3554	185	ML	H	N	N
VE7	102	21	13	22	47	9	92	3859	228	H	H	N	ML
VE8	92	21	87	22	47	7	38	2783	248	L	ML	ML	H
VE9	102	71	87	22	47	18	84	2506	243	L	H	ML	L
VE10	74	21	48	22	47	43	50	3156	179	H	H	ML	H
VE11	92	21	48	22	47	11	92	3255	195	L	H	P	ML
VE12	92	9	48	22	47	14	51	2405	294	N	L	P	ML
VE13	35	8	48	22	47	38	47	2464	226	ML	L	L	P
VE14	92	71	48	22	47	24	84	2336	233	ML	ML	ML	L

To illustrate the MADM techniques here we only use one variable of each type to rank the alternatives (price, cost and trust).

Linguistic 2-tuples approach

- First we have normalized the numerical and interval variables, then applied the membership function to transform them into fuzzy sets, composed by 5 fuzzy numbers according to the cardinality previously chosen. After the information has been unified, we have transformed the fuzzy sets in linguistic 2-tuples, and then, we have calculated the aggregate grade evaluation (through an arithmetic mean operator). The membership function considered is:

$$\mu_i = \begin{cases} 1 & \text{if } b_i = x \\ 0 \text{ if } & x \notin \text{to term label} \\ \dfrac{x - a_i}{b_i - a_i} & \text{if } a_i \le x \le b_i \\ \dfrac{c_i - x}{c_i - b_i} & \text{if } b_i \le x \le c_i \end{cases} \tag{1}$$

Table 3: Fuzzy sets, linguistic 2-tuples and the dominance degree

	price	cost	trust	price	cost	trust	aggregate grade evaluation
VE1	(0.64,1,0.07,0,0)	(0.37, 0.63,0,0,0)	(0,0,1,0,0)	(VL,-0.33)	(L,-0.37)	(ML,0)	**(VL,0.1)**
VE2	(0,0.59,0.98,0,0)	(0,1,0,0,0)	(0,1,0,0,0)	(ML,-0.37)	(L,0)	(L,0)	**(VL,0.21)**
VE3	(0.74,1,1,0.75,0)	(0,0.79,0.21,0,0)	(0,1,0,0,0)	(ML,-0.5)	(L,0.21)	(L,0)	**(VL,0.24)**
VE4	(0,0,0.37,1,0.48)	(0.17,0.83,0,0,0)	(0,0,0,1,0)	(VH,0.06)	(L,-0.17)	(H,0)	**(ML,0.29)**
VE5	(0.63,0.45,0,0,0)	(1,0,0,0,0)	(0,0,1,0,0)	(N,0.42)	(VL,0)	(ML,0)	**(VL,-0.19)**
VE6	(0,0.37,1,1,0.86)	(0,0,0.84,0.16,0)	(0,0,1,0,0)	(VH,-0.27)	(ML,0.16)	(ML,0)	**(ML,0.3)**
VE7	(0.64,1,1,1,0.69)	(0,0.31,0.69,0,0)	(0,0,0,1,0)	(ML,0.02)	(ML,-0.31)	(H,0)	**(ML,0.24)**
VE8	(0.74,1,0.51,0,0)	(0,0,0,0.68,0.32)	(0,1,0,0,0)	(VL,-0.1)	(VH,0.32)	(L,0)	**(ML,-0,26)**
VE9	(0.27,1,1,1,0.34)	(0,0,0,0.26,0.74)	(0,1,0,0,0)	(ML,0.04)	(P,-0.26)	(L,0)	**(ML,0,26)**
VE10	(0,0.29,1,0,0)	(0,0,0.24,0.76,0)	(0,0,0,1,0)	(ML,-0.23)	(VH,-0.24)	(H,0)	**(VH,-0.49)**
VE11	(0.56,1,1,1,0.70)	(0,0,0.39,0.61,0)	(0,1,0,0,0)	(ML,0.07)	(VH,-0.39)	(L,0)	**(ML,-0.11)**
VE12	(0.44,1,0.04,0,0)	(0,0,0,0.1,0.9)	(1,0,0,0,0)	(VL,-0.27)	(P,-0.1)	(N,0)	**(ML,-0.46)**
VE13	(0,0.47,0.89,0,0)	(0,0,0,0.19,0.81)	(0,0,1,0,0)	(ML,-0.34)	(P,-0.19)	(ML,0)	**(ML,0.49)**
VE14	(0.06,1,1,1,0.35)	(0,0,0,0,1)	(0,0,1,0,0)	(ML,0.17)	(P,0)	(ML,0)	**(VH,-0.28)**

The results obtained suggest that the group of companies chosen to carry out the project should be those in alternative VE14, because this is the one with higher linguistic label (VH - very high) and with the less negative value of the symbolic translation (-0,28).

Distance approach

Distance measures formulas:

- For interval numbers (Tran and Duckstein, 2002)

$$D(A,B)=\sqrt{\left[\left(\frac{a_1+a_2}{2}\right)-\left(\frac{b_1+b_2}{2}\right)\right]^2+\frac{1}{3}\left[\left(\frac{a_2-a_1}{2}\right)^2+\left(\frac{b_2-b_1}{2}\right)^2\right]} \quad (2)$$

- For triangular fuzzy numbers (Li and Yang, 2004)

  Let $A=(a_1, a_2, a_3)$ and $B=(b_1, b_2, b_3)$ be two triangular fuzzy numbers.

$$D(A,B)=\sqrt{\frac{1}{3}\left[(a_1-b_1)^2+(a_2-b_2)^2+(a_3-b_3)^2\right]} \quad (3)$$

- For real numbers

  Let A and B be two real numbers

$$D(A,B)=\sqrt{(a-b)^2} \quad (4)$$

Table 2: Normalized distances

	price		cost		trust		average	
alternatives	max	min	max	min	max	min	max	min
VE1	0,38	0,15	0,84	0,16	0,43	0,43	0,55	0,25
VE2	0,71	0,25	0,75	0,25	0,68	0,20	0,71	0,23
VE3	0,51	0,29	0,70	0,30	0,68	0,20	0,63	0,27
VE4	1,00	0,20	0,79	0,21	0,20	0,68	0,67	0,36
VE5	0,00	0,00	1,00	0,00	0,43	0,43	0,48	0,14
VE6	0,91	0,53	0,46	0,54	0,43	0,43	0,60	0,50
VE7	0,63	0,41	0,58	0,42	0,20	0,68	0,47	0,50
VE8	0,25	0,84	0,17	0,83	0,68	0,20	**0,37**	0,62
VE9	0,72	0,93	0,06	0,94	0,68	0,20	0,49	0,69
VE10	0,79	0,69	0,31	0,69	0,20	0,68	0,44	0,69
VE11	0,66	0,65	0,35	0,65	0,68	0,20	0,56	0,50
VE12	0,47	0,98	0,03	0,97	0,84	0,00	0,45	0,65
VE13	0,72	0,96	0,05	0,95	0,43	0,43	0,40	0,78
VE14	0,78	1,00	0,00	1,00	0,43	0,43	0,40	**0,81**

The DM is now in a position to choose one particular alternative among these fourteen (potential VEs), according to his preferences: smallest distance to the ideal maximum (1) or the highest to the ideal minimum (0). If the ideal maximum is the purpose, VE8 is chosen (0,37 - distance to maximum) but, if it is the ideal minimum, VE14 is chosen (0,81 - distance to minimum). In case that the DM wants to take into consideration both points, the ranking order of all alternatives can be obtained by calculating the amplitude between the two average distance measures, maximum and minimum, and so VE14 may be considered the best one (0,41 – higher amplitude distance). Generally the rank order found is subjective and depends of the DM judgements. The linguistic 2-tuples approach has as major advantage (when compared with the distance measures approach) the fact that it presents a precise rank order to the DM.

5. CONCLUSIONS

The selection of partners is a critical issue in the formation of a VE, i.e. the choice of entities to be involved in an emergent business opportunity, according to their attributes and interactions. This work is a first step in the development of an integrated DSS capable of handling this problem. Moreover such a DSS will hopefully become a simulation tool encouraging informal cooperation between the companies of the network. The system provides the necessary support to structure the VE formation (or re-organization) problem, allows the existence of different types of data (numerical, linguistic, binary, interval), individual and group decision makers, and performs several MADM techniques in order to generate a ranking list of potential VEs. It allows the analysis, for a given time horizon, of how the network reacts when various projects take place, simultaneously or not, and it enables different types of *"what if"* analysis. The system was designed in a modular way, allowing an easy incorporation of different metaheuristics for the generation of alternatives, or other MADM techniques for supporting the ranking and choice of those alternatives.

6. REFERENCES

1. Katzy BR, Dissel M. A toolset for building the virtual enterprise. Journal of Intelligent Manufacturing 2001; 12, 2: 121-131.
2. Camarinha-Matos LM Hamideh Afsarmanesh. Elements of a base VE infrastructure. Computers in Industry 2003; 51: 139–163.
3. Scheubreina R, Ziontsb S. A problem structuring front end for a multiple criteria decision support system. Computers & Operations Research, In press, Corrected Proof, Available online 16 july 2004.
4. Climaco J, ed. "Multicriteria analysis". New York: Springer-Verlag, 1997.
5. Zanakis SH, Solomon A, Wishart N, Dublish D. Multi-attribute decision making: a simulation comparison of select methods. European Journal of Operations Research 1998; 107, 3: 507-529.
6. Pohekar SD, Ramachandran M. Application of multi-criteria decision making to sustainable energy planning—A review. Renewable and Sustainable Energy Reviews 2004; 8: 365–381.
7. Li Y, Xiuwu, L. Decision support for risk analysis on dynamic alliance. Decision Support Systems, In press, Corrected Proof, Available online 18 December 2004.
8. Fan Z-P, Hu G-F, Xiao S-H. A method for multiple attribute decision-making with the fuzzy preference relation on alternatives. Computers & Industrial Engineering 2004; 46: 321–327.

9. Reeves CR, ed. "Modern Heuristic Techniques for Combinatorial Problems". John Wiley & Sons, Inc. NY, USA, 1993.
10. Osman IH, Kelly JP. "Meta-Heuristics: An Overview. In Meta-Heuristics: Theory and Applications, Osman IH, Kelly JP ed. Kluwer Academic Publishers. Boston, USA, 1996.
11. Glover F. Tabu Search, Part I. ORSA Journal on Computing 1989; 1: 190-206.
12. Glover F. Tabu Search, Part II. ORSA Journal on Computing 1990; 2: 4-32.
13. Glover F. A user's guide to tabu search. Annals of Operations Research 1993; 41: 3-28.
14. Laguna M, Glover F. What is Tabu Search. Colorado Business Review 1996; 61: 5-12.
15. Glover F, Laguna M. "Tabu search". Kluwer Academic Publishers. Boston, USA, 1997.
16. Herrera F, Martıınez L, Sanchez PJ. Decision Aiding Managing non-homogeneous information in group decision making. European Journal of Operational Research 2004; 166, 1: 115-132.
17. Herrera F, Herrera-Viedma E. Linguistic decision analysis: Steps for solving decision problems under linguistic information. Fuzzy Sets and Systems 2000; 115: 67–82.
18. Delgado M, Vila MA, Voxman W. On a canonical representation of fuzzy numbers. Fuzzy Sets and Systems 1998; 93: 125–135.
19. Herrera F, Lopez E, Rodriguez MA. A linguistic decision model for promotion mix management solved with genetic algorithms. Fuzzy Sets and Systems 2002; 131: 47 – 61.
20. Herrera F, Martınez L. A 2-tuple fuzzy linguistic representation model for computing with words. IEEE Transactions on Fuzzy Systems 2000; 8, 6:746–752.
21. Degani R, Bortolan G. The problem of linguistic approximation in clinical decision making. International Journal of Approximate Reasoning 1998; 2: 143–162.
22. Herrera F, Herrera-Viedma, E, Martínez L. A fusion approach for managing multi-granularity linguistic term sets in decision making. Fuzzy Sets and Systems 2000; 114: 43-58.
23. Xu Z. A method based on linguistic aggregation operators for group decision making with linguistic preference relations. Information Sciences 2004; 166, 1-4: 19-30.
24. Ding J-F, Liang G-S. Using fuzzy MCDM to select partners of strategic alliances for liner shipping. Information Sciences. In press, Corrected Proof, Available online 28 August 2004.
25. Butler J, Jia J, Dyer J. Simulation techniques for the sensitivity analysis of multi-criteria decision models. European Journal of Operations Research 1997; 103: 531-546.

PART 6

TRUST MANAGEMENT

16 TRUST BUILDING FOR SMES THROUGH AN E-ENGINEERING HUB

Z. Ren, T. M. Hassan and C.D. Cater
Dept. of Civil & Building Engineering, Loughborough University, UK, z.ren@lboro.ac.uk

Trust building is a vital issue and enabler for e-Business. It has been studied at various stages of e-Business from initial trust establishment, contract negotiation and formation, fulfilment to closure. Current studies mainly focus on building trust through the improvement of the social business environment and online security by adopting latest technologies. This paper introduces a new trust building approach developed in the eHUBs (e-Engineering enabled by Holonomic and Universal Broker Services) project. Unlike most of the current trust building studies, this approach fosters trust building between Small and Medium sized Enterprises (SMEs) and their clients through collaborative project planning (PP). The e-Hub provides a transparent, traceable and predictable collaborative PP and contract negotiation platform.

1. INTRODUCTION

Small and Medium sized Enterprises (SMEs) are considered the backbone of the European economy, as well as an important key source of jobs and a breeding ground for the knowledge-based economy. By focusing on their core competencies and knowledge, the flexible integration of resources and engineering collaboration of SMEs is expected to facilitate the strengthening of the competitive position of SMEs in their struggle for the future. Recent surveys (e-HUBs Technical Annex, 2001) also show large companies are willing to consider the outsourcing of non-core competency tasks to specialized SMEs. Rather than adopting the "extended enterprise" formula, SMEs are often involved in 'on-the-fly' partnerships. Efficient integration of engineering services on an ad-hoc basis into engineering projects is of strategic importance for SMEs. The knowledge intensive businesses that SMEs are often involved in are characterized by flexibility, decentralization and networking of organizations. These factors have led SMEs to look for platforms to initiate partnerships that are remote, time-critical and volatile.

The emergence of B2B e-Markets is expected to provide such platforms. By taking advantage of e-Markets' services, SMEs are able to conduct procurement and collaboration online, and therefore reach a wider market than ever before. However, despite the assurances of technological security mechanisms, there appears to be a perception that business through e-Markets may be both insecure and unreliable due to the uncertainties inherent in the e-Business environment, particularly for SMEs as they are more vulnerable to external threats than their larger counterparts. Risks exist not only due to the ad-hoc and volatile pattern of business, but also due to

SMEs' unfamiliarity with the technology and not commonly, a shortage of resources.

Although considerable research on trust in e-Business is ongoing, much of it concentrates on trust building in B2C environments; very few studies have been undertaken on trust in the context of e-collaboration for SMEs in dynamic business environments. Moreover, current trust building studies in e-Business focus either on technology aspects (e.g. improvement of online payment security, information access and authority) or social aspects (e.g. involvement of trust third party, self-regulations and legal systems). No study has been done on trust building through collaborative engineering activities (e.g. collaborative project preparation) or e-Engineering platforms (e.g. increasing the transparency of e-Engineering market), which has been identified as a key trust contributor in engineering procurements and collaborations (Elo, URL1; Andersson and Sörvik, URL2; Ong, URL3; EC, 1997).

This study developed a novel approach, the e-Engineering Hub, to facilitating trust building between Engineering Service Providers (ESPs) and their clients through collaborative project preparation and planning performed on the e-Hub workspace. The e-Hub provides a transparent, traceable and predicable collaborative workspace. By conducting collaborative project planning (PP) on the e-Hub, both partners can clearly understand what to do, how to do it, and when to do it. This provides a chance for project partners to understand each other more clearly. This is particularly important for SMEs to demonstrate their expertise and competence to their partners. Trust is fostered through the effective collaborative PP.

This paper first reviews the trust concept, key trust building issues, and trust building approaches in e-Business; then introduces the e-Hub concept and presents the functional architecture of the e-Engineering Hub. It then discusses the trust building process in a seismic engineering testbed with focus on the functional architecture. Finally, conclusions are drawn based on the result of the study.

2. TRUST AND TRSUT BUIDLING

Trust is seen as the coordinating mechanism which binds relationship together, provides the necessary flexibility, lowers transaction costs and reduces the complexity of relationships. Particularly, trust is a key determining factor for commercial relationships wherever risk, uncertainty, or interdependence exist (McKnight and Chervany, 2001). Given its importance, trust has become a major concern in the e-Business environment over the past decade.

2.1 Trust Definition

Due to the different research perspectives and constructs adopted to conceptualize trust, trust has been defined in literally dozens of ways. Inconsistent and incomplete conceptualization leads to problems in the development, operation and measurement of trust. In an e-Engineering Hub context, two kinds of trust definitions have been adopted as below. The first type is used to define users' trust to the e-Engineering Hub whilst the second type is used to define the trust among business partners.

- Blau (1964): "The belief that a party's word or promise is reliable and that a party will fulfil his obligations in an exchange relationship".
- Mayer *et al.* (1995): "The willingness of a party to be vulnerable to the actions of another party based on the expectation that the other will perform a particular action important to the trustor, irrespective of the ability to monitor or control the other party".

2.2 Trust Building Issues

After clarifying the trust definition, this section further explores the nature and characteristics of trust, key trust building issues and the trust development process.

1) Schumacher (URL4) summarised that most conceptualisations of trust identify several main factors:

- Firstly, trust exists in an environment of uncertainty and risk. If parties could undertake a transaction with complete certainty, then trust would not be required and the concept would be trivial;
- Secondly, trust implies the vulnerability of a partner. The extent of the potential loss due to untrustworthy behaviour is typically much greater than the anticipated gains from honest actions;
- Thirdly, trust describes some degree of predictability. It reflects a prediction of a party's behaviour, and implies that the expectancy that it will perform a specific action is high enough for another party to consider engaging in interaction;
- Fourthly, trust exists in an environment of interdependence and mutuality. The parties to an exchange have to believe that their own objectives cannot be realised without reliance upon the other; and
- Fifthly, trust is inherently a positive and good notion. When people refer to trust, they are making a statement about the likelihood of positive outcomes.

2) Blomqvist and Ståhle (URL5) summarised that competence, goodwill, behaviour and self-reference are four key components of trust in technology partnerships. Trust is increased by, and decreased by the lack of, evidence of these components in partners' actual behaviour and communication.

- Competence represents a party's technological capabilities, skills, expertise and know-how. It is a necessary antecedent for trust in the business context, especially in technology partnerships, where complementary technological knowledge and competencies are a key motivation for partnership formation.
- Goodwill implies a partner's moral responsibility and positive intentions towards the other. Expected goodwill is a necessary and active component for trust in any business partnership formation.
- When the relationship is developing, the actual behaviour (e.g. that the trustee fulfils the positive intentions) enhances trustworthiness. The capability and goodwill dimensions of trust become visible in the behavioural signals of trustworthiness.
- Self-reference means a system's capability of autonomy and dependency. Self-reference is demonstrated by the system's ability to define its own existence, the basic idea for being and doing, values, principles and goals, as well as abilities.

3) McKnight and Chervany (1996) provided a typology of interrelated types of trust constructs that helps to distinguish and capture the conceptual meanings of trust and the key trust construct factors. They identified three major trust types: dispositional,

institutional, and trusting beliefs: Dispositional trust, Institutional trust and Trust beliefs.

Trusting beliefs means that one believes that the other party has one or more characteristics beneficial to oneself. It reflects the idea that interactions between people, and cognitive-emotional reactions to such interactions, determine behaviour. There are four types of trusting beliefs: competence, benevolence (i.e. believes that the other party cares about one and is motivated to act in one's interest.), integrity (i.e. believes that the other party makes good-faith agreements, tells the truth, acts ethically, and fulfils promises.) and predictability.

These studies point out the key components and conditions for trust building from various aspects. It is always a hard topic to identify or demonstrate these factors so that trust, especially for SMEs, can be built in e-Business / e-Engineering.

2.3 Trust Building Approaches in e-Business

Compared with trust building in general business, trust in e-Business has at least three different perspectives: trading partner trust as between organisations in e-Business (e.g. psychological or behaviour trust, interpersonal/organisational trust and product trust); technology assurances (e.g. security-based mechanisms provided by e-Business platform); and external legal situations (e.g. legal systems and self-regulation). To attract more business opportunities, e-Market providers have taken both business approaches and technology approaches to overcome trust barriers. For example, some of the business approaches include:

- Providing unconditional guarantees of safety with an offer to cover any losses due to credit card fraud (e.g. Amazon);
- Providing detailed explanations of privacy policies on their Websites (e.g. Travelocity);
- Capitalizing on existing brand reputations in the case of established businesses (e.g. Microsoft Expedia, Barnes and Noble);
- Including suppliers only approved by Trusted Third Parties (TTP), trust seals, trust signals or intermediaries (e.g. Consumer Reports, Trust-e);
- Building community based self-regulation systems (e.g. e-Engineering Hub); and
- Providing online dispute solutions (e.g. Cybersettle, WebMediate).
- Many technologies are also adopted to foster trust building in e-Business by improving online security and privacy (e.g. confidentiality of sensitive information, integrity of critical information, prevention of unauthorized copying or use of critical information, traceability of digital objects, management of risks to critical information, and authentication of payment information), which include:
- **Identity :** Public key infrastructure (PKI) based certificate authorities are commonly used to underpin digital identities. Companies (e.g. Verisign, ValiCert) provide mechanisms and services to outsource validation and verification.
- **Digital Credentials :** Emerging privilege management infrastructures (PMIs) address the very basic need of certifying attributes associated to users and enterprises such as credit card numbers, certified credit limits, ranking information, etc.

- **Anonymity:** Anonymity services are becoming important on the Internet to protect customers' privacy and security. Companies (e.g. Zero-Knowledge Systems) offer an online anonymity service based on encryption mechanisms and IP masking techniques.
- **Guaranteed message delivery:** Technologies are adopted to assure secured message exchanges between business partners. For example, EDI and WebEDI messaging and business interaction infrastructures provide reliable and trusted infrastructures underpinning interactions.
- **Notarisation:** Notarisation services provide evidence of the existence of documents and messages at particular points in time. Surety enables users to notarise electronic files, guaranteeing the content and verifying it for a long period. Timestamp.com provides a service to digitally timestamp documents.
- **Storage:** The storage of critical digital documents is extremely important, especially for long periods of time, as it is the foundation of accountability. Infrastructure technologies (e.g. Storage Area Networks and Network Attached Storage) provide high availability, replication and survivability of stored documents.

Despite the considerable efforts in both business and technology aspects, lack of trust is still a major barrier for the development of e-Business, particularly for SMEs due to the shortage of resources and low creditability (e-Hub Technical Annex, 2001). Much research still needs to be performed to improve trust building in e-Business, particularly in the complex B2B domain. For example, researchers (e.g. Andersson and Sörvik, URL2; Ong, URL3; EC, 1997) point out the importance of building transparency and predictability e-Business platforms to trust building. Another more important area is the integration of trust building services with e-Business processes. These are particularly important for the complex e-Engineering environments. It is desired that e-Engineering platforms facilitate the trust building between ESPs and their Clients through the engineering services it provides.

Trust building is one of the major concerns for the development of the e-Hub project. Particular attention is paid to how the e-Hub could facilitate SMEs to build and strengthen the (initial) trust with their potential client(s). This project not only adopts the existing business and technology approaches (e.g. self-regulation, legal conditions, TTP, data access right, time stamps, PKI, etc.), but also emphasizes building trust through collaborative PP conducted on the e-Hub, which offers a transparent, predictable and traceable collaborative workspace.

3. THE E-ENGINEERING HUB

The aim of the e-HUBs project was to develop a universal collaborative engineering platform which offers a system-based approaches to e-engineering trust building, enterprise modelling and process sharing, SME services hosting and re-engineering of collaborative workflows. There are five business steps in the e-Hub facilitated collaboration process: 1) deciding what to partner; 2) finding the right partner; 3) agreeing with that partner what, how, when to do it; 4) executing the plan developed in stage 3; and 5) dissolving the partnership. The e-Hub is based on the observation that stage 3 is underdeveloped, under recognised and hence the biggest obstacle between potential partnering and actual partnering. The central concept of the e-Hub is mainly to address the problem raised at this stage.

3.1 The Role of the e-Hub

As illustrated in Figure 1, the e-Hub, through its value added services, provides some dedicated e-Engineering brokerage services for distant co-engineering. In general, there are three kinds of services:

- A Basic Collaboration Platform (BCP), which offers various basic collaborative services such as email, fax, diary, calendar, online chatting room, secured messaging exchange, secured data storage, authority and access right control, language translation, etc.
- A collaborative project preparation, planning and contract negotiation platform, which is the core of the e-Hub. Essentially, the e-Hub workspace is a generic negotiation platform allowing users to define, plan and negotiate various engineering and contractual issues during the project preparation stage.

A group of human specialists/organisations which form the e-Hub community. The community is responsible for verifying the qualifications of the companies that register to it and could provide endorsement to the registered members according to their performance and ratings.

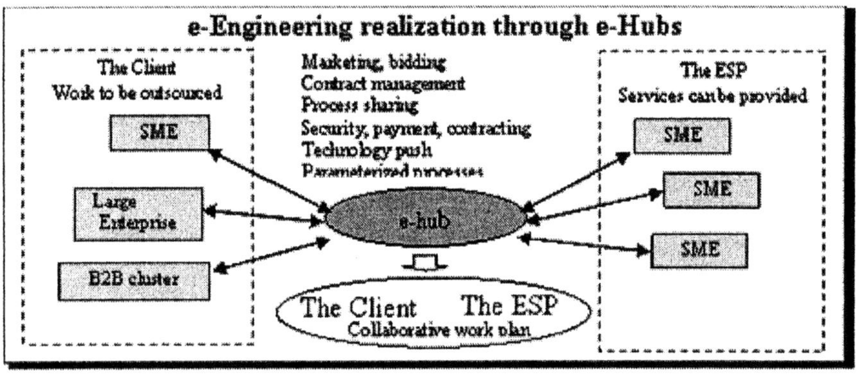

Figure 1. The Collaborative/Intermediating Role of the e-Hub

This study focuses on how the e-Hub's functional architecture could foster the trust building between ESPs and clients. Advanced information technologies and Web-hosted collaborative engineering form the baseline of the core of the e-Hub. On top of that, incremental layers of additional services are built. Each service system offers dedicated e-Engineering functions at increasing subsystem scales. The e-Hub is configured by offering transparent collaboration templates to each of these systems. Its services are defined and developed for process sharing and configuration based on the process templates for effective collaboration.

3.2 The e-Hub's Functional Architecture

Collaborative PP is viewed by the e-Hub as a managed process that transparently generates a set of comprehensive planning documents. They may contain both structured models and unstructured documents. The added value of the e-Hub is that the generation process is collaborative in nature and logically ordered, driven by structured content exchange. Both aspects are embodied in a formal Project Planning Model (PPM), which is a collection of models. Each of these models consists of a PP process model, representing with workflow (WF) models that incorporates the coordination logic of how the project partners negotiate and reach a resolution on one of the aspects that need to be agreed. Each of the WF models operates on one or more content templates, which controls who has read or written access to which field (Figure 2).

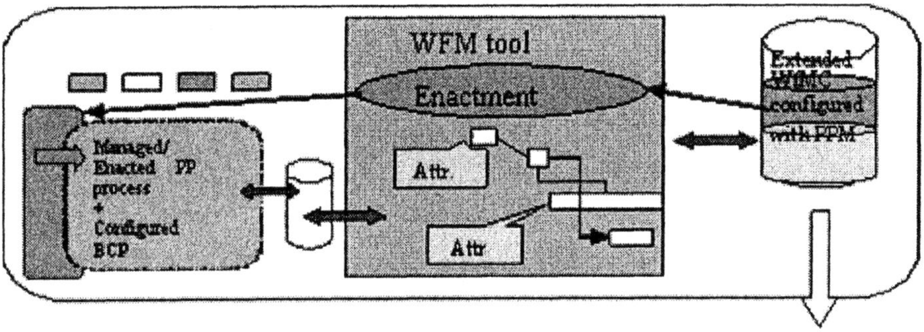

Figure 2. The conceptual model of the e-Hub's functional architecture

The key features could be summarised as follows (Figure 3):

- To facilitate project definition and planning, a meta workflow, developed based on the generic PP process, is embedded in the e-Hub workspace as a generic PP process template. This workflow will guide users going through every key project definition and planning stage such as briefing project charter, clarifying scope statement, and defining execution plan. Various essential PP issues are covered in the execution plan such as project schedule, quality plan, risk plan, communication protocol, and resource plan, with each guided by a sub-workflow.
- Meanwhile, a generic negotiation workflow is also embedded in the e-Hub platform. The enactment of this workflow guides users through the general negotiation process (e.g. propose, check, modify, re-check, re-modify, etc.).
- Besides the generic PP process workflow, various attribute templates for each of the PP issues have been developed and embedded in the e-Hub. These templates, built based on both theoretical studies (e.g. PMBOK & Process Protocol) and industrial scenarios (D5.1, 2003), specify all the key elements which every project plan should address. The negotiation between the Client and the ESP regarding each project plan is basically to address these attributes specified in the templates.
- To facilitate contract negotiation, the e-Hub contains various engineering service contract templates covering different engineering areas and situations. Users can negotiate and specify the details of the contract and legal issues through the e-Hub's Online Contracting System (OCS). The collaborative work plans generated through the e-Hub platform will be integrated into the OCS and form the core of the engineering service contract. Moreover, the e-Hub also provides a contracting workflow which

highlights the key contractual issues for each particular engineering service outsourcing situation so that users can finalise all the key issues before they sign the contract.

- On a technical level, the e-Hub provides some unique tools facilitating collaborative PP such as PP whiteboard and annotation functions. The annotation function allows users to mark all the changes made in proposals and the reasons of changes during the negotiation process. This information will be stored in the history folder for future checking. This also contributes to the effort of making e-Hub a transparent and traceable environment for joint work plan definition and negotiation.
-

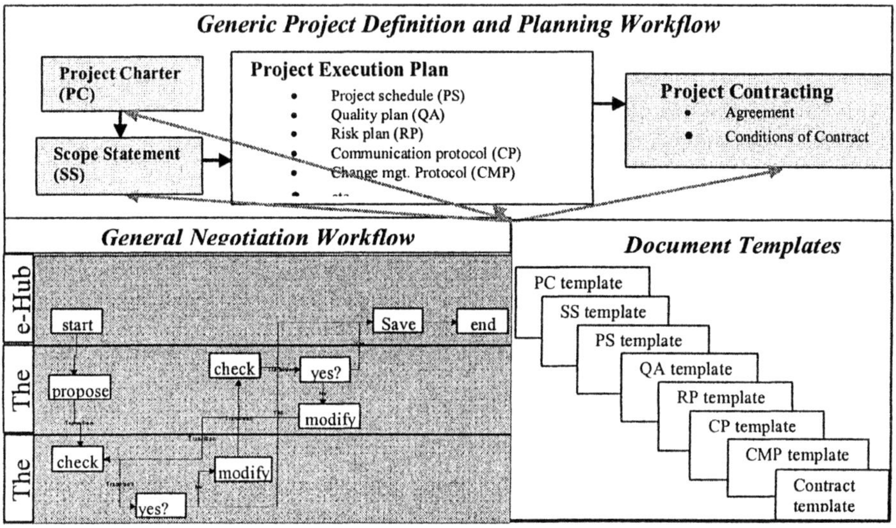

Figure 3. Generic project definition and planning workflow embedded in the e-Hub

4. DISCUSSION

The e-Hub's functional architecture provides a unique approach to fostering trust building between clients and ESPs. Some of the key advantages can be summarised as follows:

- First of all, the collaborative project definition and planning process conducted on the e-Hub workspace provides an opportunity for both parties to further strengthen the initial trust built through other approaches (e.g. company profiles and certificate from TTP). Although it might not be necessary for a B2C environment, the collaborative PP is particularly important for the engineering outsourcing environment, which, as the first step of collaboration, evidences both party's capabilities, goodwill and integrity. This cannot be achieved through any existing initial trust building approaches/services.
- Secondly, the collaborative PP is guided by a generic PP workflow and related attribute templates, which are specific to each particular engineering outsourcing situation. Such an approach is open, transparent, traceable and predictable to all the project planning participants. For those SMEs who are not familiar with the project

planning process, this approach will help them to develop the project plan, and further build the Client's trust to the ESP. Meanwhile, the negotiation parties are not passive during the PP process, they can suggest, modify and improve the project plan attributes during the negotiation process. This leaves them enough flexibility to conduct the PP. A collaborative project plan developed based on such an approach is helpful to build confidence for project execution.

- Thirdly, the particular technologies adopted in the e-Hub platform such as the annotation function and PP whiteboard improve the transparency, traceability, and predictability of the e-Hub workspace. For example, changes made by any party will be marked with ownership, reasons/suggestions for change and time highlighted with different colours. Furthermore, the generated project plan will be exported to other systems (e.g. e-room or other WFM systems), which will be used to monitor the overall project execution process.
- Finally, the contract negotiation conducted on the e-Hub platform also contributes to the trust building between clients and ESPs. Some of the major advantages include: 1) the contract signed based on the collaborative project plan is firm and solid; 2) the contract template and the contract negotiation process templates provide a transparent contract negotiation background. This avoids the problem caused by using any party's existing contract templates. A relatively fair contract is the basis for trust building.

The seismic engineering testbed demonstrates how the e-Hub could facilitate the trust building between the Client and the ESP through both general trust building services and the collaborative PP facilitated trust building approach. This testbed has been evaluated through both expert evaluation clinic and online demonstrations. The results (D6.3) show that the experts from both academia and industry are very positive about the trust building approach though some of the technical details need to be further improved. It is particularly pointed out that building services should not only be limited to current business and technology approaches, engineering service based trust building models should be developed to foster trust building in an e-Engineering environment.

5. CONCLUSION

This paper presented the engineering e-Hub's functional architecture and discussed its particular role in fostering trust building for SMEs in engineering outsourcing environments. Unlike general e-Markets, where trust services focus on building a social trust environment (e.g. legal systems and community self-regulation) and adopting latest technologies (e.g. security and privacy protection approaches), this study emphasizes the importance of collaborative project planning as an approach of trust building for SMEs involved engineering outsourcing service. The emphasis is the seamless integration of trust building services into the e-Business/ e-Engineering process.

The engineering e-Hub, through a particularly designed functional architecture, provides an open, transparent, traceable and predicable workspace for project participants to conduct collaborative project planning. Guided by the generic PP workflow and related attribute templates, project participants are able to conduct collaborative project planning systematically. This is particularly important for complex e-Business situations like engineering outsourcing with the involvement of SMEs. Partners could demonstrate their expertise, resources, willingness of cooperation and integrity during the collaborative PP process. This will strengthen the initial trust gained through other trust services. Furthermore, the e-Hub online contracting system not only helps users to focus on the key contract issues, but also provides a fair basis for contract negotiation. The contract signed based on the collaborative project plan paves the way for the smooth transaction of the project.

Although the concept of the e-Engineering Hub and the particular trust building approach developed in this project are still immature, it has demonstrated the great potential for the enhancement of trust building in B2B environment. The key concept has been adopted in the EU-funded SEEMseed project (Study, Evaluate, and Explore in the Domain of the Single Electronic European Market, IST-1-502515-STP).

Acknowledgements

The e-Hubs project is supported by the European Commission under the IST programme (Contract no: IST-2001-34031). The authors would like to acknowledge the financial support of the European Commission, and record their appreciation to the e-Hubs project partners for their contributions to the project.

6. REFERENCES

Andersson, T. and Sörvik, J. Enabling *Trust in the Digital World.* URL2: http://www.iked.org/pdf/GlobalTrustCenter.pdf, accessed 25/01/05.

Baessler, E., Mejía, R., Grop, A. V. , Crehan, P., and Ren, Z., 2004. D6.3: Evaluation Approach and Benchmark Results. *e-HUBs Project Deliverable. IST project: (IST-2001-34031).*

Blau, P. (1964). *Exchange in Power and Social Life.* John Wiley, New York.

Blomqvist, K. and Ståhle, P. *Trust in Technology Partnerships.* URL5: http://www.stahle.fi/material/Trust_in_technology_partnerships.pdf, accessed 25/01/05.

e-HUBs Project Technical Annex-1 (2001) e-Engineering enabled by Holonomic and Universal Broker Services, *Description of Work. IST project: (IST-2001-34031).*

Elo, M. (2003). *National Culture and Its Impact on Trust and Cooperation in International Business Networks: Some Empirical Evidence from a Greek-Finnish Business Network.* URL1: http://www.impgroup.org/uploads/papers/4328.pdf, accessed 25/01/05.

European Commission (1997). *Fifth Annual Report of the European Observatory for SMEs.* Brussels.

Mayer, R.C. Davis, J.H. & Schoorman, F.D. (1995). An Integrative Model of Organizational Trust, *Academy of Management Review*, 20(3), 709-734.

McKnight, D.H., and Chervany, N.L. (1996). The Meanings of Trust, *University of Minnesota MIS Research Center Working Paper Series, WP96-04*, Minneapolis.

McKnight, D.H., and Chervany, N.L. (2001). Conceptualizing Trust: A Typology and E-Commerce Customer Relationships Model, *In Proceedings of the 34th Annual Hawaii International Conference on Systems Science*, Maui, Hawaii, IEEE Computer Society Press.

Ong, C.E. B2C *E-Commerce Trust in Redress Mechanism* (Cross Border Issues), URL3: http://proceedings.informingscience.org/IS2003Proceedings/docs/018Eang.pdf, accessed 25/01/05.

Project Management Institute, (2000). A Guide to the Project Management Body of Knowledge (PMBOK). *Project Management Institute Inc.* Newtown Square, PA.

Ren Z., Anumba C.J., Hassan, T.M., (2003). D5.1: Basic Collaborative Engineering Web Services and Functional Architecture to Embed in the e-Hubs. *e-HUBs Project Deliverable. IST project: (IST-2001-34031).*

Ren, Z., Anumba, C.J., Hassan, T.M., (2004). D5.2: Set of Working e-Engineering Services dedicated for Seismic Engineering Demonstrator. *e-HUBs Project Deliverable. IST project: (IST-2001-34031).*

Schumacher, C. *The Influence of Trust on SMEs Co-Operation Structuring and Performance.* URL4: http://nzae.org.nz/files/%239-SCHUMACHER.PDF, accessed 25/01/05.

17 A DECISION SUPPORT APPROACH TO TRUST MODELING IN NETWORKED ORGANIZATIONS

Nada Lavrač (1, 2), Peter Ljubič (1), Mitja Jermol (1), Stefan Bollhalter (3)
(1) Jožef Stefan Institute, Ljubljana, Slovenia
(2) Nova Gorica Polytechnic, Nova Gorica, Slovenia
(3) Virtuelle Fabrik AG, Arbon, Switzerland

The main motivation for organizations to e-collaborate is to enable knowledge and resource sharing in order to effectively solve a business task. Virtual organizations (VOs) can be formed dynamically from a cluster of experts/organizations when a new business opportunity arises. The main strength of a VO lies in the range of competencies the partners are able to offer jointly through collaboration. One of the difficulties in VO creation is appropriate partner selection with mutual trust, as well as the support for trust estimation and monitoring. High trust is a necessary prerequisite for VO creation, knowledge sharing, resource sharing and taking joint risks. This paper presents a decision support approach to modeling trust in a network of collaborating organizations.

1 INTRODUCTION

The main motivation for organizations to e-collaborate is to harness dispersed expertise, enable knowledge sharing, learning and flexible resource management in order to effectively solve a new business task. This leads to more flexibility, at a cost of increased complexity of a virtual business environment. E-collaboration requires a different set of management processes since collaboration is a fundamentally voluntary process. Collaborative networked organizations are non-static (continually evolving) networks enabled by Information and Communications Technology (Camarinha-Matos, 2003; McKenzie and van Winkelen, 2001). Virtual organizations (VOs) are a form of collaborative networked organizations.

The main strength of a virtual organization lies in the range of competencies the partners are able to offer jointly through collaboration. To fully exploit this advantage, problems of efficiently storing, updating, sharing, promoting and transferring knowledge need to be solved. These problems are solved by appropriate knowledge management which – in addition to the technological solutions provided by knowledge technologies – needs to address also organizational, economic, legislative, psychological and cultural issues (McKenzie, 2001).

Virtual organizations (VOs) can be formed dynamically from a cluster of experts/organizations when a business opportunity arises. As a VO is formed to meet a specific demand, it dissolves once the demand is fulfilled. VO creation is a difficult process, requiring the strategic and management decision making processes to be substantially different from those in traditional organizations, where decisions are made at the top and implemented at the bottom. One of the difficulties in VO creation is appropriate partner selection with mutual trust, as well as the support for the management of trust. High trust is a necessary prerequisite for knowledge sharing, resource sharing and taking joint risks. It is also one of the most important aspects to be considered in the VO creation process.

Establishing trust is one of the most important mechanisms in collaborative projects, since the possibility of opportunistic behavior of partners cannot be eliminated by formal contracts. In moderately sized VOs of a few dozen partners, means for trust building include personal meetings, regular communication, sharing of information and knowledge, and stable rules of the game, whereas computational means can also be beneficial to support trust modeling. Computational means for trust modeling are, however, indispensable in large VOs in which personal meetings and communication are hindered by the size of the VO.

In order to propose a mechanism appropriate for modeling trust between collaborating partners, the conditions for trust building and management need to be analyzed first. Some of the factors that affect mutual trust and need to be acquired to enable mutual trust estimation include: partner's competencies, reputation and performance in previous collaborations.

This paper proposes a decision support approach to modeling trust in a network of collaborating organizations, aimed at improved trust management in VOs and decision support in the process of creating virtual organizations. In our paper, the term "trust modeling" is used to denote a simple model of trust relations between networked organizations. The model is represented by a graph, where notes denote reputation and arcs indicate collaboration between organizations. Visualization of the graph enables a useful insight of "trust relations" to a VO broker when creating VO for a specific business case.

A trust model of networked organizations is created through following steps:

1. Each organization is given a simple questionnaire in which it estimates experience in collaboration with other organizations.
2. For each questionnaire, a numerical estimate of reputation, collaboration and trust are computed by a multi-attribute decision support system DEXi, for each pair of organizations.
3. A graph of nodes (organizations) and arcs (collaborations) is formed. Size of the node represents the reputation of a partner, whereas the weight of the arc represents the collaboration between the connected partners.

The paper is organized as follows. Section 2 presents a questionnaire-based decision support approach to trust modeling, illustrated by a study of trust modeling in Virtuelle Fabrik, an industrial cluster in the area of mechanical engineering, followed by the lessons learned from this study. Section 3 presents related work, followed by conclusions and plans for further work.

2 A HIERARCHICAL MULTI-ATTRIBUTE DECISION SUPPORT

This section present an approach to trust modeling, based on hierarchical multi-attribute decision making, applied to modeling trust between partners of an industrial cluster in the area of mechanical engineering.

2.1 The proposed approach to trust modeling

For trust modeling, the decision making problem of trust estimation can be decomposed into decision sub-problems; e.g., a mutual trust estimate can be computed as a weighted sum of values of different decision criteria. This computation can be performed by a utility aggregation functions used in hierarchical multi-attribute decision support systems in which values of top-level decision criteria are computed by aggregating values of decision criteria at lower levels of a hierarchical tree, which can be used to decompose a decision making problem into sub-problems. A hierarchical decomposition of a decision problem into sub-problems is shown in Figure 1.

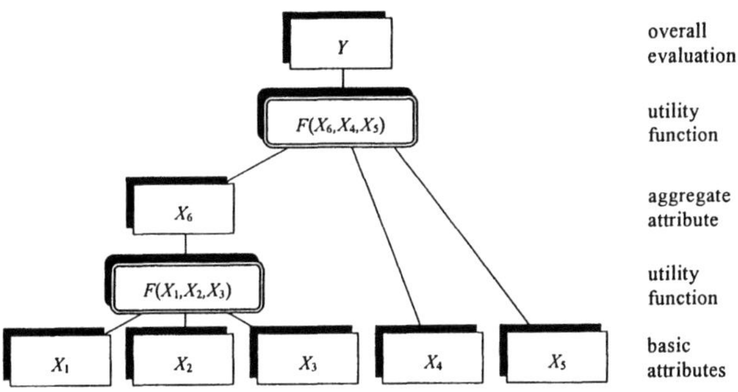

Figure 1 - Components of a multi-attribute decision support model.

Decision support system DEXi, used in our approach to trust modeling, enables the development of qualitative hierarchical decision support models. DEXi is based on the DEX (Bohanec and Rajkovič, 1990) which is used to evaluate incompletely or inaccurately defined decision alternatives, by employing distributions of qualitative values, and evaluating them by methods based on probabilistic or fuzzy propagation of uncertainty. While DEXi is a simpler variant of DEX, lacking some of the DEX functionality, it has better graphical and reporting capabilities, and has therefore been used for decision support in our study.

Knowledge about mutual trust can be acquired through a simple questionnaire that a partner of a networked organization can fill-in to describe the competencies of his own organization and the collaborating partner's performance in previous joint collaborations (for a set of organizations with which the partner has collaborated in past joint projects).

The proposed fields of a questionnaire are listed below:

- partner's own competencies (list of competencies)
- competencies of the collaborating partner (list of competencies), and
- collaborating partner's trust estimate based on: estimated collaborating partner's reputation (image, market share), number of successful joint past collaborations, estimate of the profit made in joint collaborations, estimate of the partner's timeliness in performing assigned tasks, estimate of the partner's quality of performance and products, and estimate of the partner's appropriateness of costs of performance and products.

A set of questionnaires, filled-in by a partner, results in a star-shaped network: a partner who has filled-in a questionnaire for N collaborating partners is represented by a node, and links to nodes representing collaborating partners. If the questionnaires are filled-in by M partners, this leads to a multi-star network of collaborations in which thick links represent partners with highest mutual trust. In accordance with the link analysis approach to the analysis of social networks (Kleinberg 1988), nodes with most incoming links of high value represent the most trusted partners in the network (the *authorities*), while the nodes with most outgoing links represent the best connected nodes (the *hubs*). Hubs and authorities exhibit what could be called a *mutually reinforcing* relationship, computed through iterative relaxation of the following equations:

$$\text{Hub}(p) = \sum_{q:p\rightarrow q} \text{Authority}(q)$$

$$\text{Authority}(p) = \sum_{q:q\rightarrow p} \text{Hub}(q)$$

2.2 The Virtuelle Fabrik trust model: Estimating business reputation and collaboration of VF partners

The DEXi modeling approach was applied to trust modeling in Virtuelle Fabrik (VF), an industrial cluster of companies in the area of mechanical engineering. In the actual questionnaire, only the questions about each VF partner's reputation and collaborations were taken into the account. The selected multi-attribute decision support model for trust estimation is shown in Figure 2.

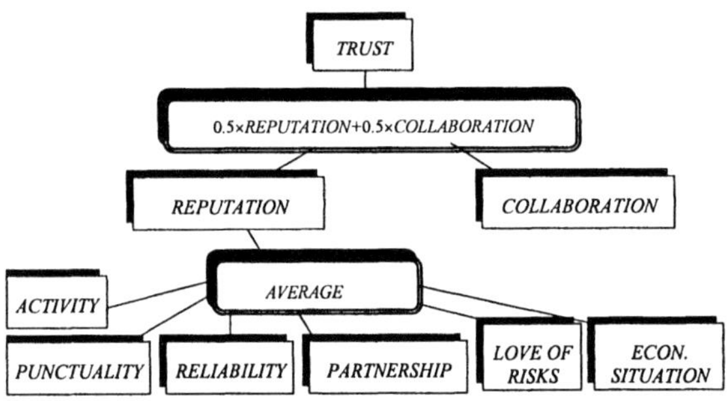

Figure 2 - The selected trust estimation model for Virtuelle Fabrik.

Reputation was modeled through the following VF partner's properties: activity, punctuality, reliability, partnership, love of risk and economical situation. Each of the properties had values from 1 to 6 (1 – very bad, 6 - very good), and the overall reputation was computed as the average of values of the basic input attributes. Collaboration between VF partners was evaluated by values 0 to 3 (0 – no collaboration, 3 – strong collaboration), as shown in Table 1. For trust estimate calculation, normalized values of properties are used.

Figure 3 shows the Virtuelle Fabrik trust network. In the visualization tool developed for this application, higher trust can be estimated, when the node representing an organization is wider and/or the connection between two collaborating partners is thicker. 'Non-trustful' partners (below the user-defined threshold) do not appear as nodes of the trust network. Specifically, in Figure 3, reputation estimates are depicted by the size of nodes representing individual companies, and the collaborations estimates by the width of arcs between two collaborating companies.

Table 1 – Information about companies (left-hand side table) and their cooperation (right-hand side table). Missing values in the property table are ignored in the model, while, missing values cooperation matrix denote zero values (no collaboration) , which are omitted for clarity only.

id	activity	punctuality	reliability	partnership	love of risks	econ. situat.
1	2	5	6	4		5
2	4	5	6	5	3	5
3	2	5	6	5	4	5
4	5	6	6	6	6	6
5	5	5	6	6	5	6
6	2	5	6	4	4	6
7	5	5	6	6	6	4
...						

cooperation matrix

id	1	2	3	4	5	6	7	8
1				3			1	
2								1
3						1		
4	3					2	2	
5							1	
6			1	2				
7	1			2	1			
...								

2.3 The lessons learned

In the Virtuelle Fabrik trust modeling application the following lessons were learned.

- The developed decision support approach and trust visualization tool are useful for VF trust estimation.
- The graph developed by the visualization mechanism shows an accurate picture of the status of Virtuelle Fabrik and its potential VO configurations.
- Some known partner relationships were confirmed.
- Data collection has to be done carefully, as it is a very sensitive issue. There is a certain offending potential of collecting trust modelling data and graphically depicting partner relationships.
- Despite a potential danger of offending non-active and non-connected partners, the approach can also have the opposite, motivating effect: non-active partners may explain the reasons for their situation and the desire for becoming more active members of the network.

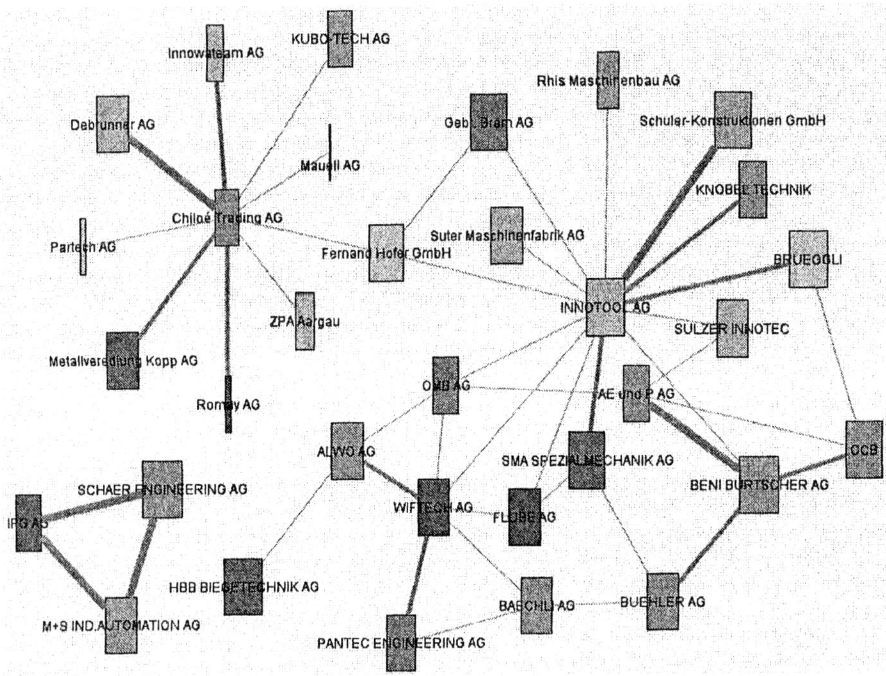

Figure 3 - Visualization of the Virtuelle Fabrik trust network, with node labels corresponding to company names. The figure shows he best connected subset of organizations of the Virtuelle Fabrik industry cluster.

3 RELATED WORK

Recent applications of knowledge technologies show their potential for improved trust modeling, knowledge and competence mapping, competence directory formation, partner selection and matching, partner and competency search. Managing trust for the Semantic Web has been of particular interest of researchers [Richardson *et al.,* 2003; Domingos and Richardson, 2001]. Some of these approaches can be used for trust modeling aimed at facilitating the partner selection process and the matching of competencies for a new business opportunity.

Of special significance to our current approach of evaluating trust (using a utility function) is the work of Richardson *et al.* [2003]. Drawing the analogy from the semantic web, different organizations in a network can be viewed as information sources (of varying qualities) and the competencies of each organization can be treated in a similar way to those of contents on the semantic web in the form of logical assertions or statements. For each organization, which is directly linked to its partner, trust between them can be computed using a utility function like the one proposed in Section 2. Every organization also has a certain belief in its own statements asserted (which are basically its competencies). The belief of an organization in its partner's competencies is then computed and is used as a basic criterion for selecting partners when a new business opportunity arises.

Social network analysis aimed at modeling network phenomena is an established research field [Wasserman and Faust, 1998; Barabási, 2002]. In addition, trust modeling research (see links to research on trust and reputation at http://moloko.itc.it/trustmetricswiki/moin.cgi/AnalyzedTrustMetrics) has also gained much attention. There has recently been a flood of networking tools made available to individuals and organizations. Selected approaches are described in some more detail below. Other approaches (e.g., accessible at www.zerodegrees.com, center.spoke.com) can also be checked.

LinkedIn (http://www.linkedin.com) is the premier provider of online networking tools, currently used to network over 1.7 million professionals all across the globe. By managing their existing professional networks on LinkedIn, professionals can discover new inside connections and reach business people through referrals from people they know and trust. LinkedIn facilitates hiring, business partnerships and access to industry experts through referrals based on strong and mutually confirmed connections.

Knowmentum (http://www.itsnotwhatyouknow.com) is a tool that supports business, career, and social networking. It is intended to be used by motivated individuals world-wide. CEOs, directors, executives, department managers and sales persons, as well as students, alumni and college associations use Knowmentum to establish communications between job seekers and available positions.

Ryze (http://www.ryze.com) helps people make connections and grow their own networks, with the intention to increase their businesses, build careers, find jobs and make sales. They can also join special networks related to their industry, interests or location. More than 200 organizations host networks on Ryze to help their members interact with each other and enable the growth of their organizations.

4 CONCLUSIONS AND FURTHER WORK

The proposed approaches to trust modeling can be used for several purposes, such as ranking of partners according to their research reputation, joint collaborations and the overall trust estimate, visualization of the entire trust network, and finding well-connected sub-graphs with high trust utility value, representing 'cliques' of partners with strong mutual trust.

Using the proposed approaches for ranking, visualization of the trust network and cliques of partners is relatively straightforward. Implementation of other functions – such as finding the best partners with respect to their competencies and mutual trust, request the computation of the utility function based on the match between the requested expertise with the partners' competencies, and the overall mutual trust of the selected partner sub-graph. This functionality will be developed in further work. One of the outcomes of this trust modelling study is the design of a future awareness raising platform for Virtuelle Fabrik. The main function of the future Automatic Collaboration Trigger (ACT) tool is the activation of VF partners, based on on-line information collection, securing permanent awareness of collaborative business opportunities. The development of the ACT platform is planned in future work.

Acknowledgments

The support of the Slovenian Ministry of Higher Education, Science and Technology programme Knowledge Technologies (2004-2008) and the European Integrated Project ECOLEAD (European Collaborative Networked Organizations Leadership Initiative, 2004-2007) are acknowledged.

5 REFERENCES

1. Barabási, A. L. Linked. The new science of networks. Cambridge: Perseus Publishing, 2002.
2. Bohanec, M. and Rajkovič, V. DEX: An expert system shell for decision support, Sistemica, Vol. 1, No. 1, 145–157, 1990.
3. Camarinha-Matos, L.M. and Afsarmanesh H. Elements of a base VE infrastructure. J. Computers in Industry, Vol. 51, No. 2, 139-163, 2003
4. Domingos, P. and Richardson, M. Mining the network value of customers. In Proceedings of the 7th International Conference on Knowledge Discovery and Data Mining, 57-66, 2001. San Francisco.
5. Grobelnik, M. and Mladenić, D. Analysis of a database of research projects using text mining and link analysis. In Mladenić D, Lavrač N, Bohanec M, and Moyle S. (editors) Data Mining and Decision Support: Integration and Collaboration, 157-167, Kluwer, 2003.
6. Kleinberg
7. McKenzie J. and van Winkelen C. Exploring E-collaboration Space. Henley Knowledge Management Forum, 2001..
8. Richardson, M., Agrawal, R. and Domingos, P. Trust management for the Semantic Web. In Proceedings of the 2nd International Semantic Web Conference, 351-368, 2003. Sanibel Island.
9. Wasserman, S. and Faust, K.: Social Network Analysis. Methods and applications. USA: Cambridge University Press, 1998.
10. Kleinberg, J. Authoritative sources in a hyperlinked environment. In Proc. 9th ACMSIAM Symposium on Discrete Algorithms, 1998.

18

TOWARD WEB SERVICES PROFILES FOR TRUST AND SECURITY IN VIRTUAL ORGANISATIONS

Alvaro E. Arenas, Ivan Djordjevic
CCLRC Rutherford Appleton Laboratory, UK {A.E.Arenas, I.Djordjevic}@rl.ac.uk
Theo Dimitrakos, Leonid Titkov
British Telecom, UK {theo.dimitrakos, leonid.titkov}@bt.com
Joris Claessens, Christian Geuer-Pollmann
European Microsoft Innovation Center, Germany {jorisc, chgeuer}@ microsoft.com
Emil C. Lupu, Nilufer Tuptuk
Imperial College, UK {e.c.lupu, nt102}@doc.ic.ac.uk
Stefan Wesner, Lutz Schubert
High Performance Computing Centre Stuttgart, Germany {wesner, schubert}@hlrs.de

The rise in practical Virtual Organisations (VOs) requires secure access to data and interactions between their partners. Ad hoc solutions to meet these requirements are possible, but Web services hold out the potential for generic security solutions whose cost can be spread across several short lived dynamic VOs. This paper identifies trust and security requirements throughout the VO lifecycle and analyse current Web Services specifications to show their suitability to meet these requirements. Although they demonstrate the potential for generic security support, there are uncertainties concerning different level of interoperability and stability of implementation for different specifications, which may slow down their exploitation for security-critical business applications. However, research in Web services developments are well timed to avoid losing first adopter advantage when they become stable.

1. INTRODUCTION

Virtual Organisations (VOs) have been the focus of business research for several years (Goldman et al, 1995; Saabeel et al, 2002; Roberts and Svirskas, 2005). In this paper, a VO is understood as a temporary or permanent coalition of geographically dispersed individuals, groups, organisational units or entire organisations that pool resources, capabilities and information to achieve common objectives (Dimitrakos et al, 2004). Enterprise Computing systems increasingly operate within VOs similar to the scientific collaborations that originally motivated Grid Computing (Foster et al, 2001). Depending on the context, dynamic ensembles of the resources, services, and people that comprise a scientific or business VO can be small or large, short- or long-lived, single- or multi-institutional, and homogeneous or heterogeneous.

Service Oriented Computing frameworks allow for the creation, maintenance, and application of the service ensembles that VOs maintain. Key business functions are treated as services: *globally identifiable and discoverable network-enabled entities providing a capability through the exchange of messages over standardized, extensible protocols that allow data-encapsulated cross-application invocations.*

The TrustCoM[1] IST project (Dimitrakos et al, 2004) is developing a framework for enabling secure collaborative business processing in on-demand created, self-managed, scaleable and highly dynamic VOs. The project is built on the convergence of emerging technologies such as Web services and Grid. As a part of this project we have done an analysis of the Web Services Security Specifications as an enabling technology to build secure and trustworthy dynamic VOs. This paper identifies trust and security requirements throughout the VO lifecycle and analyses current Web services specifications with respect to meeting these requirements.

2. AN AGGREGATED SERVICES SCENARIO

This section introduces the example of a VO created for the purpose of offering aggregated services. It is an abstraction of the real-world scenario on aggregated services in the telecommunication domain, which is currently being developed in TrustCoM.

A *consumer* requests a complex service **S** which has been advertised by provider **SA** (Service Aggregator). The latter has a pre-defined business process describing the decomposition of **S** into a number of sub-services that interact with each other (potentially sharing resources) in order to realise **S**. From this point of view, **S** can be also understood as the enactment plan of a collaborative business process **BP** which consists of a number of tasks, some of which are outsourced to other providers and require the consumption of resources, and others which will be rented.

Figure 1 depicts the case where **BP** consists of three tasks: the first one corresponds to the first instance of an action $\mathbf{s_a}$ followed by two concurrent actions which respectively correspond to the first instances of actions $\mathbf{s_b}$ and $\mathbf{s_c}$ followed by a second instance of action $\mathbf{s_a}$. The Service Aggregator **SA** then discovers the services that match the specification of $\mathbf{s_a}$, $\mathbf{s_b}$ and $\mathbf{s_c}$. This involves locating the appropriate service providers and inspecting their reputations and the SLA template characterising their service, security and access policies they publish about their services. The **SA** (or a broker acting on its behalf) forms a collection of candidate services and assesses whether their terms of service provision collectively allow **SA** to offer satisfactory terms for the provision of service **S** to the consumer at an acceptable risk. In **Figure 1**, we assume that **SP1**, **SP2**, **SP3** is such a set whereas **SPx**, **SP2**, **SP3** is not.

The scenario includes a number of actors. The external actor is a *Service Consumer*, who requests a service **S** from a service provider **SA**. *Service Providers*, (**SP1**, **SP2**, etc.), offer specific services. A particular kind of service provider, which plays a significant role in this scenario, is the one that is able to *aggregate services* provided by other providers. This actor, called *Aggregator*, has the capability to act as manager of the VO, discovering the appropriate services, negotiating with service providers, setting up the VO and managing the whole operation.

Once an agreement is reached between **SP1**, **SP2**, **SP3** and **SA, the SA** confirms its agreement with the *consumer*, and prepares for the enactment of the process.

[1] http://www.eu-trustcom.com/

Preparation includes planning the formation a VO community. This can be understood as a collection of reputable services containing at each time only those services, which are active in performing a business process task and assume a specific role that is defined for this purpose. The community is managed by the federation of service providers contributing to the aggregation, and which is coordinated by the Aggregator. Notably VO community membership evolves following the progress of the business process enactment: services that are needed for performing some task enter the VO community, those that have fulfilled their role leave and those which committed terminal violations are expelled and replaced, should the business process enactment continue.

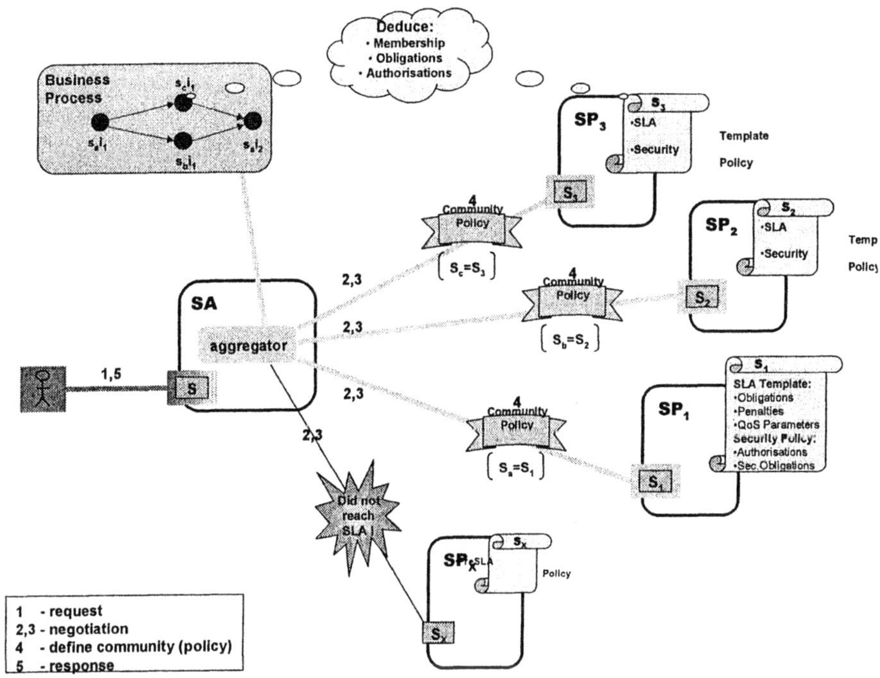

Figure 1 The Aggregated Services Scenario

Each member in the VO community is assigned to some roles which consist of a set of obligations, access permissions and prohibitions that are derived from the business process enactment plan, the service level agreements of the corresponding services and security policies of the collaborating service providers.

Furthermore, adaptation policies enable automatic updates to membership (e.g. expulsion due to violation of SLA or security obligations), to roles (e.g. an existing member also assuming a role that was previously assigned to a member that is now being expelled), to reputation (e.g. a member has just successfully completed service provision to other members of the community) or to policy (e.g. strengthening the performance thresholds so as to compensate for previous underperformance, or obligation to encrypt communication if intrusion is suspected, etc.).

Once the business process enactment is completed, all agreements are nullified and the VO community is dissolved.

Note that a VO community does not act in isolation, but rather is part of a wider system in which its members may have their credentials revoked or reputations altered as a result of actions undertaken outside the VO community. Such changes may have an impact on the VO community during its lifetime.

3. AN OVERVIEW OF WEB SERVICES

The TrustCoM project is exploiting Web services to develop frameworks to implement scenarios like the one described previously. Web services offer us an interoperable framework for stateless, message-based and loosely coupled interaction between software components. These components can be spread across different companies and organisations, can be implemented on different platforms, and can reside in different computing infrastructures.

Web services expose functionality on via XML messages, which are exchanged through the SOAP protocol. The interface of a Web service is described in detail in an XML document using the "Web Service Description Language" (WSDL). Further, a Web service is registered at a "Universal Description Discovery and Integration" registry (UDDI), and is as such discoverable.

A key element in the Web services technology is the so-called composability. Web services specifications are being created in such a way that they are mostly independent of each other, however they can be combined (composed) to achieve more powerful and complex solutions. Reliability, security, transaction capabilities and other features can be provided without adding unnecessary complexity to the specification. Moreover, the specifications are easily extended with new concepts, tools and services, by adding new layers and elements.

Section 4 summarises the main Web service specifications, when explaining the needed technology to realize the scenario of the previous section. For a more comprehensive description of the Web Services Security specifications we refer the reader to (Geuer-Pollmann and Claessens, 2005).

4. VO Lifecycle

TrustCoM is following the life-cycle model developed in the VO roadmap project (Camarinha-Matos and Afsarmanesh, 2003), including phases such as identification, formation, operation/evolution and dissolution.

The identification phase is dealing with setting up the VO; this includes selection of potential business partners by using search engines or looking up registries. VO formation deals with partnership formation, including the VO configuration by a VO Manager, who distributes information such as policies, Service Level Agreements (SLAs), etc, and the binding of the selected candidate partners into the actual VO. After the formation phase, the VO can be considered to be ready to enter the operation phase where the identified and properly configured VO members perform accordingly to their role. Membership and structure of VOs may evolve over time in response to changes of objectives or to adapt to new opportunities in the business environment. Finally, the dissolution phase is initiated when the objectives of the VO has been fulfilled.

In the rest of this section we analyse these phases for our scenario, identifying the main challenges from the trust and security perspective, and explaining how Web services specifications may help to meet those challenges.

4.1 VO Identification

The identification phase includes defining VO wide policies and VO agreement templates as well as selecting potential business partners who are both capable of providing the required services and of fulfilling the trustworthiness requirements of the VO by using search engines and or looking up registries.

In the case of our aggregated services scenario, the Aggregator first analyses the Business Process Template, identifies roles, and deduces the security requirements for the VO: obligations, permissions and prohibitions. Then, the Aggregator selects the collection of potential Service Providers for the business process tasks that it would like to outsource; this selection may include assessing the trustworthiness of the service providers. The selection of the potential providers is based on abstract service descriptions of the business process template. The Aggregator and the Service Providers will also need to negotiate further details of the agreement, including the security and access requirements. Finally, the Aggregator will need to correlate the security negotiation responses of the service providers to make sure they can collectively fulfil the requirements of the VO.

Web services technology may be useful in the realisation of this phase. In relation to the representation of the business process we can use "Business Processes Execution Language for Web Services" (BPEL4WS)[2] to specify the behaviour of both executable and abstract business processes; BPEL4WS provides a language for the specification of business processes and business interaction protocols, extending the Web services interaction model and enabling it to support business transactions. The selection of potential business partners involves looking at repositories. The usual Web service technology to be applied is WSDL/UDDI, WSDL describes messages and operations while UDDI offers a discovery mechanism. To include the provision of SLA, "Web Service Level Agreements" (WSLA)[3] has been developed, a XML language for specifying and monitoring SLA for Web Services, which is complementary to WSDL. Determining the required service providers and a proper negotiation requires secure communication. WS-Security[4], a specification defining mechanisms for integrity and confidentiality protection, and data origin authentication for SOAP messages can be used between the entities to secure the communication.

4.2 VO Formation

If the identification phase is successful, the selected set of Service Providers needs to be configured so that they can perform accordingly to their anticipated role in the VO. During the VO Formation phase the Aggregator disseminates configuration information such as VO security and adaptation policies. The VO security policies

[2] http://www.oasis-open.org/committees/tc_home.php?wg_abbrev=wsbpel

[3] http://www.research.ibm.com/wsla/about.html

[4] http://www.oasis-open.org/committees/tc_home.php?wg_abbrev=wss

include obligations –what the VO member needs to do, permissions –the access rights, and prohibitions –negative policies defining negative authorisations. These requirements are derived from the Business Process Plan and the security policies of the contributing Service Providers. Adaptation policies include rules encapsulating actions that need to be performed in case of security breaches, SLA violations and any other changes in the VO context, such as new members joining the VO. The adaptation policies are defined by analysing the collaboration agreement clauses, Business Process adaptation rules and other conditions that assist in detecting and responding to violations.

The Web Services Policy Framework (WS-Policy[5]) provides a general-purpose model to describe Web service related policies. The realisation of the VO requires the creation of federations, where two or more security domains agree to interact with each other, specifically letting users of the other security domain accessing services in the own security domain. For example, in our scenario Service Providers **SP1**, **SP2** and **SP3** may form a federation. The WS-Federation[6] specification deals with federations by providing mechanism to manage and broker trust relationships in a heterogeneous and federated environment. This includes making use of WS-Trust[7] to support for federated identities, attributes and pseudonyms. The dissemination of configuration information requires secure communication as provided by the WS-Security specification.

4.3 VO Operation

This phase can be considered as the main life-cycle phase of a VO. During this phase the identified partners contribute to the actual execution of the VO tasks by executing pre-defined business processes. Important features in this phase are the monitoring of the performance of the VO as well as the enforcement of policies.

Throughout the operation of the VO, service performance will be monitored. This will be used as evidence when constructing the reputation of the service providers. According to the predefined roles of the VO, the Aggregator or other VO members can perform monitoring. Any violation –e.g. an unauthorised access detected by the access control systems- and security threats –e.g. an event detected by an intrusion detection system- need to be notified to other members in order to take appropriate actions. Unusual behaviours may lead to both a trust re-assessment and a contract adaptation. VO members will also need to enforce security at their local site. For example, providing access to services and adapting to changes and the violations.

Monitoring can be supported by event management and notification mechanisms using the WS-Eventing[8] and WS-Notification[9] specifications. This allows the monitoring service partner to receive messages when events occur in other partners. A mechanism for registering interest is needed because the set of Web services

---

[5] http://msdn.microsoft.com/ws/2004/09/policy/

[6] http://msdn.microsoft.com/ws/2003/07/ws-federation/

[7] http://msdn.microsoft.com/ws/2005/02/ws-trust/

[8] http://msdn.microsoft.com/ws/2004/08/ws-eventing/

[9] http://www.oasis-open.org/committees/tc_home.php?wg_abbrev=wsn

interested in receiving such messages is often unknown in advance or will change over time.

In addition to WS-Policy and the possibility of authorization decisions through WS-Trust, to gain access control to service resources we use constructs provided by the eXtensible Access Control Markup Language (XACML[10]). The XACML policy language is used to express access control policies written in form of XML for expressing requirements to access particular resources.

VO Evolution is part of the VO Operation phase. When a VO member fails completely or behaves inappropriately, the VO manager may need to dynamically change the VO structure and replace such partners. This evolution may involve discovering new business partners, re-negotiating terms and providing configuration information, as done in the identification and formation phases. One of the main problems involved with evolution consists in re-configuring the existing VO structure so as to seamlessly integrate a new partner, possibly even unnoticed by other participants – this involves revoking security tokens, issuing new tokens, etc.VO Evolution is close related to adaptive security. In term of specifications, currently there exists little work in this area that can be directly leveraged.

4.4 VO Dissolution

The dissolution phase is carried when the objectives of the VO has been fulfilled. During dissolution, the VO structure is dissolved and final operations are performed to annul all contractual binding of the partners. From a trust and security perspective, this involves resolving federations, revoking security credentials, invalidating VO context information, and updating reputation of all participants. According to agreement on historical information, audit trail information and provenance information may be stored.

5. CONCLUSIONS

In this paper we have presented a case study of a Virtual Organisation for aggregated services. We have analysed trust and security requirements for this kind of VO through a VO life cycle and shown how Web services specification can be used to meet such requirements, summarised in Table 1.

Trust and security aspects of a VO framework span a large number of concerns such as reputation, certification, access control, authentication and secure connection. Web Service Secure Specifications aim at producing a composable solution to these issues. Every specification aims to solve very particular problem; security solutions are created by combining the approaches from different specifications.

6. ACKNOWLEDGMENTS

The results presented here are partially funded by the European Commission under contract IST-2003-01945 through the project TrustCoM. The authors would like to thanks members of other organisations working in TrustCoM AL1: SAP, Swedish

[10] http://www.oasis-open.org/committees/tc_home.php?wg_abbrev=xacml

Institute of Computer Science, ETH Zurich, Kings College London, University of Milano, University of Salford, and IBM.

Table 1. Analysis of challenges and Web service technologies for the Aggregated Services Scenario

VO Life Cycle	Trust and Security Challenges	Technology
VO-Identification	VO interactions	SOAP/WSDL/UDDI; WS-Security to support integrity and confidentiality protection
	Defining VO and its participants	BPEL to define business process; WSLA to select potential partners based on the ability to deliver QoS
VO-Formation	Aggregator disseminates configuration information	Dissemination of information requires secure communication provided by WS-Security
	Creating federated cross-organisational realms	Use architectural paradigms of WS-Federation, combined with WS-Trust.WS-Policy to support managing security tokens/ assertions
VO-Operation / VO-Evolution	VO interactions	WS-Security to support integrity and confidentiality protection
	Authorisation and Access Control	WS-Trust, WS-Policy, XACML
	Monitoring & event management	WS-Eventing, WS-Notification
VO-Dissolution	VO interactions	WS-Security to support integrity and confidentiality protection

7. REFERENCES

1. Camarinha-Matos LM, Afsarmanesh H. A Roadmap for Strategic Research on Virtual Organizations, PRO-VE'03, Lugano, Switzerland, 2003; pp.33-46.
2. Dimitrakos T, Golby D, Kearney P. Towards a Trust and Contract Management Framework for Dynamic Virtual Organisations. In *eAdoption and the Knowledge Economy: eChallenges 2004*. Vienna, Austria, 2004.
3. Foster I, Kesselmann K, Tuecke S. The Anatomy of the Grid: Enabling Scalable Virtual Organizations. International Journal of Supercomputer Applications, MIT Press, 2001.
4. Geuer-Pollmann C, Claessens J. Web Services and Web Service Security Standards. Information Security Technical Report, Elsevier, 2005, 10(1)15:24.
5. Goldman SL, Nagel RN, Preiss L. Agile Competitors and Virtual Organisations: Strategies for Enriching the Customer. Van Nostrand Reinhold, 1995.
6. Roberts R, Svirskas A. Implementation Options for Virtual Organisations: A Peer-to-Peer (P2P) Approach. In *Virtual Enterprise Integration: Technological and Organisational Perspectives*, Idea Group publishers, 2005.
7. Saabeel W, Verduijn TM, Hagdorn L, Kumar K. A Model for Virtual Organisation: A Structure and Process Perspective. In *Electronic Journal of Organizational Virtualness*, volume 4, 2002.

19

A SECURE MODEL TO ESTABLISH TRUST RELATIONSHIPS IN WEB SERVICES FOR VIRTUAL ORGANIZATIONS

E. R. Mello, M. S. Wangham, J. S. Fraga, R. J. Rabelo
Federal University of Santa Catarina – Department of Automation and Systems
PO Box 476-CEP 88040-900- Florianópolis(SC) Brazil
E-mail: {emerson, wangham, fraga, rabelo}@das.ufsc.br

This paper introduces a model making use of the security proposals based on Web Services architecture that aims to provide guarantees authentication and authorization transfer among different security domains. The model describes a flexible, scalable and secure way to establish trust relationships among Virtual Organization partners and to assign the access rights or roles to each partner in the VO. This model serves as a mediator for the interoperability among of security technologies that are found in a Collaborative Network.

1. INTRODUCTION

A large variety of Collaborative Networks (CNs) have emerged during the last years as a result of the challenges faced by both the business and scientific worlds, such as Virtual Enterprises (VE), Professional Virtual Community (PVC) and Virtual Laboratory (VL) (Camarinha et al., 2004). Within the CN scenario, cooperation in the form of Virtual Organizations (VO) represents a modern strategy which has been adopted by many enterprises, professionals and laboratories over the world to accomplish a given business opportunity, to take part in new markets and/or reach scientific excellence for innovative developments. Actually, a VO corresponds to a temporary set of independent organizations that share resources and skills to achieve its objective as none of them is able to attend to it alone The selection of the most suitable VO members has been often supported by partner's search and selection systems that are applied over a pre-defined group of organizations - a VO Breeding environment (as an evolution of the *cluster* concept).

However, despite this trend for collaborative works, most of organizations (companies and/or professionals) are still quite skeptic to share sensitive information when there is a need to collaborate with previously unknown partners. Actually, Collaborative network organizations demand the development of relationships with a broad range of potential partners each having a particular competency that complements the others. Therefore, the establishment of **trust relationships** among the partners is essential to the effectiveness of the VO Creation process.

The infrastructure to support the full life cycle of the VO in networked environments can be seen as a Services Oriented Architecture (SOA). A group of (web) services must attend different VO needs such as creation, operation and dissolution functionalities. It must also provide mechanisms to support coordination and collaboration functionalities, interoperable and secure information exchange, legacy systems integration, and so forth.

Collaborative Networks are usually characterized as an open, heterogeneous and large-scale system which makes a wide use of the Internet. In this way, there are some inherent advantages that make Web Services the ideal programming technology for building virtual organizations, which include: (1) it makes easy the integration and interoperability among different local systems; (2) it is based on well-accepted standards such as XML and HTTP; and (3) it provides services for discovering business partners to VOs. The Web Service's integrative feature allows existing VO applications, including legacy application, to be available and visible without any great cost being involved.

The management of distributed applications (such as VO applications) built according to the *Web Services model* is a great challenge. In a VO, since the companies' administrative boundaries get crossed, the involved applications will be under control of several security management, policies and mechanisms. Each security domain crossed by a distributed application can provide its own set of security credentials, based on its underlying security technology.

This paper presents an approach that aims at improving the trust on the infrastructure's services. It is seen as one of the necessary directions to reinforce the trust building process. The proposed model provides a flexible and secure way to establish trust relationships among VO partners as soon as it is formed as well as to assign the access rights / the roles to each partner in the VO. Its main goal is to deal with different security technologies and to allow the interaction among organizations that usually have their security services based on different technologies. This article describes an example in which three organizations are interacting, having domains based on different security technologies: X.509 PKI (ITU-T, 1993), Kerberos (Kohl, 1993), and SPKI certificates (Ellison et al., 1999), respectively. These technologies usually express identities and rights in a varied and non-interoperable way.

2. THE SECURITY MODEL

The following paragraphs illustrate a scenario where each organization in the CNO has a Web Services-based infrastructure to support the VO life cycle.

In Collaborative Networked (CNs), each organization can receive a business opportunity. Therefore, each one can become a Virtual Organization's Manager (VO Manager) and anyone can potentially be one of the VO partners. As soon as one organization is chosen to be a VO manager, it will search and select the partners. In the Web Service technology, the UDDI service (UDDI, 2002) can be used to locate these partners. UDDI has three registry types and each service (organization) can publish on it information about its functionality, capabilities and business area (e.g. molds, textile, automotive).

Once the partners have been selected, the trust relationships among them should be established. These relationships are essential to provide security guarantees such as authenticity, confidentiality and integrity of communication channels. In a CNO environment, each organization, including the VO manager, has its own security technologies and it is able to work only with them.

In order to enable a secure communication among the VO partners, a flexible solution would be to allow the VO Manager to establish trust relationships with its partners even if these partners use different technologies. Yet, the VO Manager could assign its roles in the VO by issuing a generic security token to each partner.

Figure 1 illustrates a CNO where the organizations are grouped according to security technologies. When a VO is going to be created as an answer to a certain business opportunity (BO), the involved organizations should support an interoperation among these technologies.

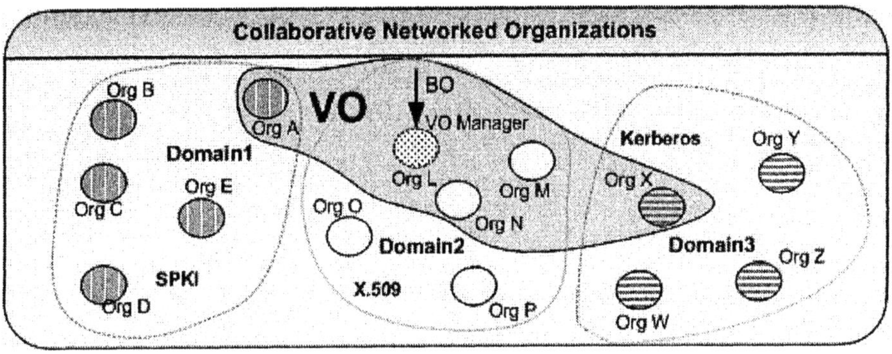

Figure 1 – A VO immersed in different security domains

In the proposed model, the infrastructure to support the VO is fully based on Web Services and its security specifications, such as WS-Trust (WS-Trust, 2004) and Security Assertions Markup Language (SAML) (OASIS, 2002). WS-Trust defines a Security Token Service (STS), which is responsible for issuing standard security tokens that should be understood by all CNO participants. In the present model, security tokens are represented by SAML assertions and used to establish the trust relationships among the VO partners. Access rights or roles to each partner in the VO are dynamically assigned by the VO Manager and expressed in SAML assertions. Therefore, it means that the security technologies present in the underlying layer is not important to the communications inside of a VO. In all communications in a VO the only security token used will be the SAML tokens issued by a VO Manager.

In the scenario depicted in Figure 1, the problem is that each partner has a different security technology. The VO Manager supports only X.509 and for all partners communicate with the VO Manager, should be necessary present tokens/certificates X.509. In addition to that, these tokens must be issued by an organization that the VO Manager trusts. The main difficulties are (1) locating the organizations that the VO Manager trusts, and (2) defining how the tokens/certificates will be issued. The next sections describe in detail the model that supports these tasks, by considering the components and services that will permit secure communication among organizations.

2.1 WS Domain in a CNO context

Security management in an environment composed of several types of organizations or professionals, each with different interests, it is hard work, mainly considering a large-scale environment. A classic way to facilitate the administration is to group individuals according to their skills and interests. An individual can belong to more than one group. In environments such as a CNO, the problem is how to organize these groups and the relationships among them.

Aiming at achieving scalability and hence being able to reach all the CN participants, groups must communicate with each other and trust relationships have to be established among themselves. These groups may be described in several ways, such as *federations*. In (Santin et al., 2003), (WS-Federation, 2003) and (Liberty, 2003), federations are proposed, whose objective is to group individuals who may have interests in common.

The trust model described in (Santin et al., 2003) is based on SPKI federations, and its objective is (1) to resolve chains of SPKI/SDSI authorization certificates (Ellison et al., 1999) and (2) the dynamic establishment of new chains of certificates. Federations must provide certificate repositories and support for certificate chain discovery. Scalability in this environment is achieved through associations among the federations (webs of federations). Such associations allow principals to carry out searches through these webs of federations, without having to join numerous federations. It is an equalitarian trust system which does not impose key hierarchy to gain in scale as those formed by X.509's PKI (Public Key Infrastructure).

The grouping of entities (services and clients) through federations, presented in the specifications (WS-Federation, 2003) and (Liberty, 2003), aims to reduce the complexity in the management of entities (names) of clients and service providers, however without requiring a central repository for storing these entities. Nevertheless, these proposals are negligent regarding the as dynamic establishment of trust relationships in heterogeneous and complex environments.

The proposed trust model is based on this concept of federation that, in this work, is called **WS Domain**. Each WS Domain is composed of a manager who groups its various affiliates according to their security attributes (credential, certificates, etc). The features of these managers depend upon the underlying security technology of the domain. For instance, if this manager is encapsulated in the SDSI/SPKI infrastructure, it becomes a simple repository of authorization certificates and names of this PKI. If this, on the other hand, corresponds to a Kerberos server, then the Ticket Granting Services of this server will be available through this manager. In other words, the manager of a WS Domain represents any PKI or security technology.

In any of these security technologies, the manager has control over the members and manages their joins and leaves, as members of the domains, as well as the queries performed by them. The WS Domain manager is a Web Service which makes possible the dynamic establishment of trust relationships. As parts of its functionalities, WS Domain manager provides the STS and XKMS (XML Key Management Service) (Ford, 2001) services.

The WS-Trust provides concepts, services and protocols which form the basis for the present trust model developed to cross management boundaries and security domains. The STS plays a fundamental role, mainly in the mediation of trust relationships involving two different security domains. The XKMS allows the localization and validation of keys, and works as an agent that makes the complexity of dealing with public key infrastructure transparent to the clients (organizations).

2.2 Trust relationships Intra-Domain and Inter Domains

After electing the most suitable VO composition, as showed in Figure 1, the VO Manager sends all participants a *challenge* aiming at mutual trust building between the VO manager and the VO members. In this model, the challenge is directly related with the security technology supported by VO managers. In the illustrated scenario, the *challenge* requires the participants present an X.509 certificate assigned by certification authorities which the VO manager trusts. In case a participant does not support the VO manager technology, the model provides means (1) to search the organizations that the VO manager trusts and (2) to negotiate the emission of security attributes required by the VO manager. Figure 2 illustrates the essential components and the steps involved in locating and negotiating security attributes.

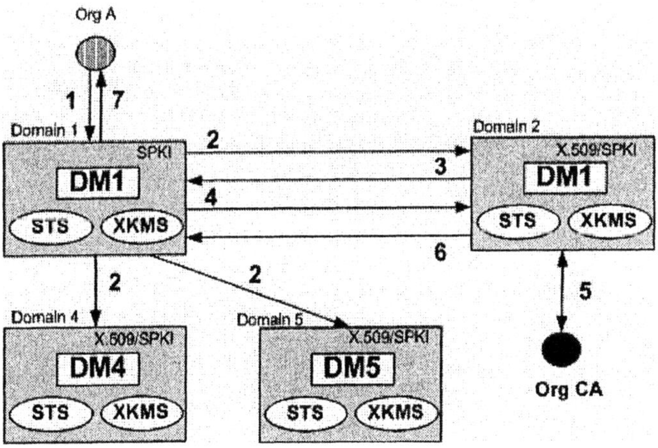

Figure 2 – Control flow for locating and negotiating security attributes

In the proposed model, the organizations have a passive role. Search and negotiation functionalities are available in its Domain Manager. Therefore, when *Org A* receives the challenge, this organization forwards it to its Domain Manager – *DM1* (**step 1**), which analyzes the challenge and verifies whether or not the requested security attribute (X.509 certificate) is supported by it. Then, *DM1* performs a search (a search heuristic as described in section 2.4) throughout the domains with which it has trust relationships, in order to find a trustworthy path which will lead it to the *Org CA* (**step 2**). *DM2* indicates, by replying to the query, that it has a trust relationship with *Org CA* (**step 3**). In **step 4**, *DM1* invokes *DM2*'s STS, by requesting an X.509 certificate (issued by *Org CA*) for *Org A*. After that, *DM2* forwards the *DM1*'s request to *Org CA* which replies a X.509 certificate (**step 5**). Hence, *DM2*'s STS issues a security token including the X.509 certificate (**step 6**). Finally, *DM1*, through its STS, provides *Org A* with all the necessary credentials so that *Org A* may respond to the challenge made by the VO Manager (**step 7**).

At this point, *Org A* did prove its identity, and then the VO Manager sends *Org A* a security token (SAML token) that will permit *Org A* to participate in VO. The steps illustrated in Figure 2, to the establishment of the trust in VO members, need to be executed to all VO members. When a VO member and a VO manager has the same security technology, this process is simplified because the interactions among Domain Managers are unnecessary.

After establishment the trust relationships with all participants, VO is fully formed. VO members' access control mechanisms are able to handle SAML tokens and implement a role-based access control (RBAC) (Sandhu and Samarati, 1994). Therefore, a VO Manager shall dynamically assign roles, expressed in SAML tokens, to each VO member and it sends all defined roles to all participants. Each VO member should map the VO Manager's roles into local roles.

2.4 Search Heuristic

In the case of the example illustrated in Figure 2, the manager of *DM1* wishes to locate, among the domains with which it has trust relationships, a trustworthy path that will lead it to *Org CA*. In the proposal in point, this search performed by the managers works similarly to the Gnutella protocol (Gnutella, 2001), which facilitates the navigation through the web of associates, in a way to achieve scale without requiring the manager to know all other likely partners in the web. The protocol which follows this model has two messages: *query*, which is used in the search for trustworthy path; and the *queryHit*, which informs that the path has been found. The algorithm shown in Figure 3 describes how the search for a path is performed, in this case the message "*query*".

Algorithm 1 $query(source, resource, P, ttl)$

Require: $T = \{$ Table with all nodes where there are trust relations$\}$
Require: $D = \{$ Local directory with information about security domain's members$\}$
if $(resource \subset D)$ **then**
  $queryHit(source, resource, P, p)$
else
  if $(ttl > 0)$ **then**
    $N \longleftarrow T$
    while $N \neq \varnothing$ **do**
      $x \longleftarrow getElement(N)$
      $P \longleftarrow source \cap P$
      $query(actualNode, resource, P, ttl - 1)$
      $N \longleftarrow N \setminus \{x\}$ {Removes the element x from the set N}
    end while
  end if
end if

Figure 3 – Query Protocol

The message *query* is comprised of four variables: (1) *source,* which indicates from where the request came; (2) *resource*, which describes which resource (target organization) needs to be searched; (3) *P,* which is a set containing the reverse sequence of all nodes through which the request passed; and (4) *ttl* which contains the lifetime for a search and thus limits its propagations. This prevents it from extending itself indefinitely.

A node (*p*), in this case a domain manager in the web, upon receiving a "*query*" message, verifies in its local repository (a set D of algorithm 1) if it has the "*resource*" searched and, if it does, sends a "*queryHit*" message to the node which originated the "*query*" message. Otherwise, a "*query*" message is sent to all the nodes (domains) with which it has trust relationships (set T, lines 6-11). For each new level that the "*query*" message descends, the value of "*ttl*" is decremented. With this heuristic it is possible to cover a great variety of nodes, without requiring a central repository to identify the existing trust relationships in a CNO.

3. RELATED WORK

Welch (2003) describes how to allow the dynamic creation of services as well as trust domains and has his application geared towards the Globus toolkit (a platform for grid computing architecture) (Foster and Kesselman, 1999). The security infrastructure specification for grid computing architecture assumes the integration with Web Services and benefits from the security standards, such as SAML and WS-Security. Some of the main security challenges present in grid computing architecture are shown as being the dynamics of the environment, since the service (resources) may be activated or deactivate dynamically during the life cycle of a resources-allocation session. This type of environment congregates several management and security domains, consequently different security technologies. In the proposal, security is provided as services, and is *The Credential Conversion Service* responsible for enabling different domains to communicate.

The security services described by Welch's work are similar to the services used in our proposal. However, Wlech describes neither how trust relationships are established, nor how to locate, if necessary, possible trust relationships. In the present study, such questions are addressed and the use of the proposed in grid computing architecture could be adopted without great changes.

In (Foley et al., 2004), a security infrastructure for heterogeneous middleware is presented. To coordinate the trust relationships among the different systems, the Keynote (Blaze et al., 1999) was adopted, however the infrastructure also provides support to SPKI/SDSI. The authorization policies of each middleware are coded in Keynote certificates and vice-versa. This allows heterogeneous security domains to be crossed, serving as the basis for a decentralized support of security policies. The work details the advantages of the systems which are based on the concept of trust management (Blaze et al., 1999) on systems which use the X.509.

Foley's objective is to cross the limits imposed by technologies through Keynote certificates. The present model seeks to overcome such limits through the use of standards for Web Services, in this case WS-Trust and SAML, which seem more adequate since it is a standard defined. The crossing of limits brought problems to the localization of rights needed by each domain, which enabled the description of how to overcome such problems through the concept of federations and the navigation heuristic.

4. CONCLUSION

The integration concept represents a defined set of industry-standard technologies that work together to facilitate interoperability among heterogeneous systems. Web services hold the potential of easily integrating legacy systems with distributed applications.

This article describes a way to integrate organizations which use different security technologies in the establishment of virtual organizations. The security proposals to Web Services along with XML security standards were adopted to form the basis of the proposed model. This model then provides (1) confidentiality, (2) integrity, (3) authenticity, and also (4) a means to locate security attributes, and thus enables the dynamic creation of trust relationships.

In the context of virtual organizations the privacy of each partner's properties may be desired. Organizations would like to take part in a business opportunity, but this implies the revelation of some important information, such as production capacity, abilities, and so forth. This information can be used in a malicious form. Once the deficiencies of this organization is known, a malicious organization can focus its business on providing a competitive solution, with the same kind of services, at lower cost.

In this work the privacy of organizations issue was not addressed. Specifications such as the Liberty Alliance (2003) and the proposal WS-Federation (2003) propose pseudonymous services which guarantee anonymity. Future studies may adopt and adapt the use of pseudonyms services.

Acknowledgments

This work has been developed within the scope of the Brazilian IFM (www.ifm.org.br) and European FP6-IP ECOLEAD (www.ecolead.org) projects.

5. REFERENCES

1. Blaze M, Feigenbaum J, et al. Decentralized Trust Management. AT&T Tech. Report 96-17, 1996.
2. Blaze M, Feigenbaum J, et al. The keynote trust-management system version 2. IETF RFC 2704, 1999.
3. Camarinha, L.M and Afsarmanesh. The emerging discipline of collaborative networks. In Virtual Enterprises and Collaborative Networks, Kluwer Academic Publishers, IFIP Vol. 149, Aug 2004.
4. Ellison C. M, et al. SPKI Certificate Theory. IETF RFC 2693, September 1999.
5. Foley S. N et al. A framework for heterogeneous middleware security. 18th International Parallel and Distributed Processing Symposium (IPDPS'04), 2004.
6. Ford W, Hallam-Baker P. XML Key Management Specification (XKMS), 2001. http://www.w3.org/TR/xkms
7. Foster I, Kesselman C. The grid: blueprint for a new computing infrastructure. A Toolkit-Based Grid Architecture. Morgan Kaufmann Publishers Inc., 1999; 259-278.
8. Gnutella. The Gnutella Protocol Specification v0.4, 2001.
9. ITU-T. ITU-T Recommendation X.509, 1993. http://www.mcg.org.br/mirrors/97x509final.doc.
10. Kohl J, Neuman C. The Kerberos Network Authentication Service (v5). IETF RFC 1510, Sept. 1993.
11. Liberty. Liberty Architecture Overview v1.1, 2003.
12. OASIS. Security Assertion Markup Language (SAML), 2002. http://www.oasisopen.org/comittees/tc_home.php?wg_abbrev=security.
13. Sandhu RS, Samarati P. Access Control: Principles and Practice. IEEE Communications Magazine.
14. Santin A, Fraga J, et al. Federation WEB: A scheme to compound authorization chains on large-scale distributed systems. 22nd Symposium on Reliable Distributed Systems, Florence, Italy, 2003.
15. UDDI. UDDI Version 3 Published Specification, 2002. http://uddi.org/pubs/uddi_v3.htm
16. Wlech C, Siebenlist, et al. Security for Grid Services. 12th IEEE Int. Symp. on High Performance Distributed Computing, 2003.
17. WS-Trust. Web Services Trust Language (initial draft), 2004. http://msdn.microsoft.com/library/en-us/dnglobspec/html/WS-Trust.asp
18. WS-Federation. Web Services Federation Language (initial draft), 2003, http://msdn.microsoft.com/ws/2003/07/ws-federation.

PART 7

VO MANAGEMENT

20

CHARACTERIZING VIRTUAL ORGANIZATIONS AND THEIR MANAGEMENT

Iris Karvonen, Iiro Salkari, Martin Ollus
VTT Industrial Systems
Iris.Karvonen@vtt.fi, Iiro.Salkari@vtt.fi, Martin.Ollus@vtt.fi
FINLAND

Virtual Organization (VO) Management aims to the achievement of the objectives of the VO. It can be seen as a set of mechanisms and activities directing and controlling VO operation. As different VOs have different objectives and environment, different approaches for VO management are needed. The paper discusses the concept of VO management and presents an outline for building VO management approaches based on VO characteristics or descriptive parameters. First analysis of practical cases against the characteristics has been performed. Further development is needed to specify the management methods and mechanisms for different approaches.

1. INTRODUCTION

The research in the area of Collaborative Networked Organizations (CNO) has been active during the last years. Especially information and communication technology solutions and infrastructure have been developed. VOSTER (VOSTER 2004) has analysed and structured some results and experiences of this research. In this paper, the term "virtual organization" is understood as it is defined by VOSTER (Kürümlüoglu et al., 2005): "Virtual organisation (VO) is a temporary consortium of partners from different organisations established to fulfil a value adding task, for example a product or service to a customer." Effective operation in VOs requires preparedness, which can be achieved by a long-term co-operation in the so called Breeding Environment (BE) (or Network).

This paper focuses on the VO management and discusses the configuration of the VO management for different circumstances. The concept of VO management is defined, and the supporting previous knowledge is briefly reviewed. As Virtual Organizations (VOs) respond to specific business opportunities, the VO management mechanism also needs to adopt to the cases. The paper aims to identify the main features affecting VO management and to define VO management approaches. This could support the end-users in the definition of cost-effective and dependable VO structures, management structures and mechanisms.

2. VO MANAGEMENT

2.1 Definition

The Virtual Organization Management (VOM) denotes the organization, allocation and co-ordination of resources and their activities as well as their inter-organisational dependencies to achieve the objectives of the VO within the required time, cost and quality frame.

The VOM applies knowledge, skills and/or tools in order to achieve the VO goals. Obviously, the management of Virtual Organizations to a large extent deals with humans and is performed by humans. In most cases the human aspect is considerable as the last decisions about management actions usually are done by the VO managers.

At a high level description, VOM can be seen as the management and control of the VO lifecycle. More detailed, VOM can be seen as a separate process interacting with the VO operational processes. VOM receives data and information of the status of the VO operation. Actions are based on the comparison of actual achieved behaviour compared to the wanted behaviour. They are supposed to be proactive in order to avoid also emerging deviations from the expected outcome.

Figure 1 expands the control loop view. In addition to the real-time VOM process (control loop), VOM includes mechanisms and rules, which influence the VO operation and can be seen as part of VOM. Most of these rules have to be developed in advance, typically in the VBE (Virtual Breeding Environment) behind.

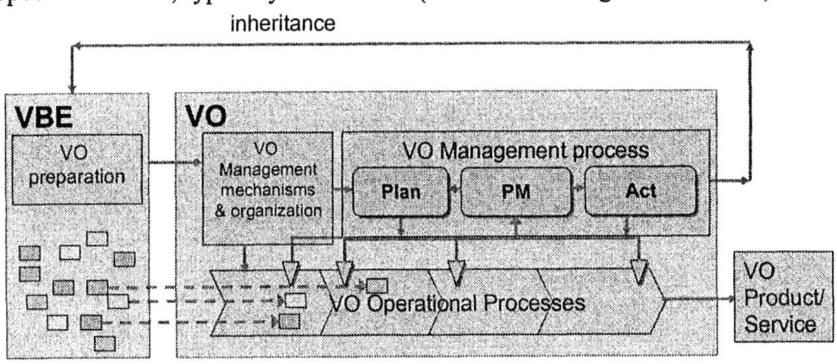

Figure 1. VOM

2.2 Views to Virtual Organisations Management

The VOM has to be based on the models of the processes to be managed. In order to get a comprehensive coverage, a structuring of the modelling views is needed. The structuring can be based on the views of model content defined in GERAM and also used as a basis in VERAM (GERAM, 1999):

1. Function View represents the functionalities (activities) and the behavior (flow of control) of the business processes of the VO. The function view includes functional models, process models and decisional models.

2. Information View collects the knowledge about objects of the VO needed for the management tasks.
3. Resource View represents the resources of the VO. Resources are assigned to activities according to their capabilities and are structured into resource models for VOM tasks
4. Organisation View represents the responsibilities and authorities on all entities identified in the other views.

In the implementation of a VOM these views need to be considered, but also other aspects like the division between human activities and activities performed by the system may have to be addressed.

2.3 Virtual Organisations and Project Management

Projects, as they are performed e.g. in the capital intensive production, have several similarities to Virtual Organisations. Project management can be considered as one basis for the development of management approaches for VOs. The Project Management Body of Knowledge (PMBOK) developed by Project Management Institute Standards Committee describes the generally accepted knowledge of projects.

The PMBOK (1996) defines that "a project is a temporary endeavour undertaken to create a unique product or service". The impermanence and a specific objective is common with the definition of a VO, but the inter-organizational precondition and preparation is missing. A dynamic VO is an outcome of a deeper preparatory cooperation between partners than a project, which is based on loosely defined principles, implemented to some extend ad-hoc, since no long-term preparatory cooperation exists. In the VO concept, proactive cooperation takes place in the VBE (Camarinha-Matos and Afsarmanesh, 2003).

According to PMBOK, project management consists of integration, scope, time, cost, quality, human resource, communications, risk, and procurement management. Further, PMBOK (p. 28) organises project management processes into five groups:

- Initiating processes, which recognise that a project or phase should begin
- Planning processes, which devise and maintain workable scheme to accomplish the business need that the project was undertaken to address
- Executing processes, which coordinate people and other resources to carry out the plan
- Controlling processes, which ensure that project objectives are met by monitoring and measuring progress and taking corrective action when necessary
- Closing processes, which formalize acceptance of the project or phase and bring it to orderly end

These processes are overlapping and dependent on each other, which mean that one process produces the input for another process.

During the lifecycle of a dynamic virtual organization, similar processes exist. Some of the identified processes may be conducted in the BE, some in a VO. It seems reasonable that initialising and planning processes belong to the BE. Initialising process would in the VO–concept be something more than just initialising for a project. This process might even be the core process of the BE. Initialising could include preparations for customer order, and the order itself would then trigger planning the process that is required to fulfil that specific customer need. Planning also includes set-up of the monitoring and management structures and it launches the executing and control processes. The closing of a VO is something more than just contract close-out and administrative closure. Further, part of the closing job continues surely in the BE and not all takes place during the VO.

Thus, even though the processes that are originally defined for projects can be found in VOs, rethinking is needed. The BE and VO concepts have different characteristics compared to traditional project networks (or CNOs). This implies that also the transition between these two concepts (from a BE into a VO) may need rethinking concerning the control processes.

2.4 Recent European Research Projects and VOM

As mentioned earlier, the approaches towards VOM in European projects were studied in the VOSTER project. In most of the analysed projects, the focus is on issues supporting the creation and management (frameworks, infrastructure, modelling, etc) of VOs rather than on management and management actions. However, in some of the reported projects (Camarinha-Matos et al., 2005), the management of VOs, and also the coordination and management issues, are addressed. For instance, the following relevant topics were addressed in these projects: inter-enterprise coordination, distributed engineering, scheduling in distributed (industrial) environment, cooperation planning in networked environment, monitoring in distributed environment and performance measurement, information and knowledge management, horizontal ICT infra and software tools.

Also organizational and social issues, including the creation and maintenance of trust, are considered in VO research. Trust can be seen as a success factor for co-operation, but trust as such does not make the operations less vulnerable. Justified trust is based on knowing the risk level. In VOs trust contributes to the efficiency of cooperation.

(Rezgui et al., 2005) consider organizations consisting of several interrelated elements, – strategy, staff, shared values, systems, skills, style and structure (The "seven S" model). Changes to any one element will have effects on the others. This can be seen as a socio-organizational equation, which must be balanced. The elements are expected to operate in harmony together for the organization to operate effectively. These issues must be taken into account also in VOM.

3. VO CONTINGENCY FACTORS & VO MANAGEMENT

3.1 Characterizing VOs

There are some approaches to describe different characteristics of networks and virtual organizations. The Globeman21 approach (Pedersen et al., 1999) identifies two kinds of descriptive parameters:

- situational factors: these are conditions coming from the environment (lead time requirements, types of needed competencies, ...); that is, factors which cannot be changed or selected.

- design parameters: these are selected parameters (rules for the management, for exposure of competencies, legal aspects...). Thus there is not only one possible VO solution.

In VERAM (Virtual Enterprise Reference Architecture and Methodology) the situational factors and design parameters are called contingency factors (Zwegers et al. 2003). They are factors to be analyzed when designing a network or a VO.

3.2 Feedback loop from VO to BE design parameters

A VO is usually based on a Breeding Environment (network), even if the level of preparation may vary. Thus the features of the BE behind are situational factors for the VO.

On the other hand, the experience gained in VOs gives information to the BE. The VO experience may affect the BE design parameters and be useful in the evolving process of the BE (Figure 2). Currently this feedback loop is usually missing or weak.

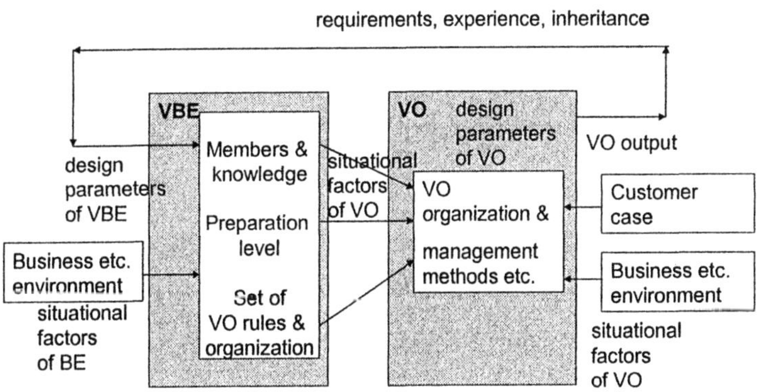

Figure 2. Feedback from VO output to BE design

3.3 Review of VO topology and coordination

3.3.1 Topology classification

The network or VO characterization applied mostly in the previous research is the topology classification. The topology is here understood as a structure describing all the different relationships between the partners (nodes of network), including information, material, monetary and control flows, responsibilities and power relationships. All the different flows do not always have the same routes and directions.

In CE-NET (Katzy & Löh 2003) and VOSTER (Katzy et al., 2005) projects, where experience and knowledge of VO research and development projects were summarized, the following topologies could be identified (Figure 3):

- supply-chain topology; interaction of partners follows mainly a chain, links are in a tiered structure with each partner relating to its upper and lower neighbours.

- star topology, or hub and spoke –topology, with one central partner (main contractor). Links are arranged predominantly star-like between a central partner and the other organisational entities.
- peer-to-peer topology; interaction between all nodes without hierarchy.

Typically each reviewed research project in VOSTER used one of these categories and most of the developed solutions made an assumption of a specific topology (Katzy et al., 2005).

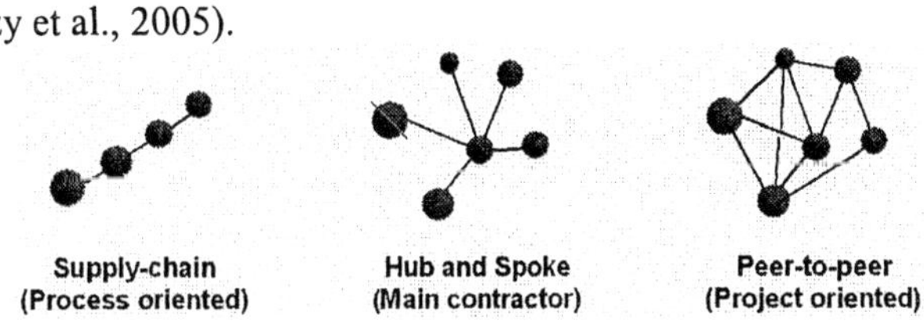

Figure 3. Topologies for Virtual Enterprises (Katzy et al., 2005).

The topologies can be applied both for BE (network) and VO. If the BE/VO processes are divided into operational processes and management processes, the following topologies are derived:

- BE/network operational topology and BE/network management topology
- VO operational topology and VO management topology.

The VO operational topology describes the physical and information flows needed for the production of the VO product (or service or value), and the VO management topology describes the information & control flows of guiding the VO to its objective. Monetary flows can be seen as part of both processes.

The topologies are not necessarily the same for different processes or for a BE and a VO created from it. For example, even if the management topology is a star, there may be peer-to-peer processes at the operational level. A network with peer-to-peer management may e.g. create a VO with star management topology.

From the VO management point of view the most significant topology is the VO management topology. Using the terminology above the topology is a design parameter of a VO, a feature that can be selected. On the other hand, there may be strong reasons (situational factors) why a certain topology is used and the selection is not totally free.

3.3.2 Examples of topologies in manufacturing industry

Henderson and Clark (1990) assume that the knowledge and information processing structure of organisations mirror the structure of the product that they manufacture. This assumption implies that the end product or purpose of the VO should be considered, when defining the structure and topology for the VO.

In recent research, the star VO topology has been identified in the field of one-of-a-kind manufacturing (GLOBEMEN, product-centric networks, Karvonen et al., 2002). When the products are extensive, complex systems, one of the partners typically has the responsibility of the product towards the customer. In the CE-NET study (Katzy & Löh 2003) star-type VOs are mentioned to appear e.g. in construction industry (also one-of-a-kind). A study from Northern Germany has identified this type "General Virtual Contractor" (Hausner et al., 2003) in the the construction industry and large equipment manufacturing, but also in automotive and telecommunication industry. The supply-chain topology is often used for mass type production. Even if many networks or VOs operate in peer-to-peer structure, there are not as visible practical examples of VOs with peer-to-peer management topology. However, future organizations may be able to operate also without any centralized management, for example supported by pre-defined rules or agent technologies. This may mean that the responsibility towards the customer also becomes distributed.

3.3.3 Structural holes and VOs aiming at innovation

Several researchers interpret positive network structures and relations as social capital. Coleman (1988 & 1990) and Burt (2004) take different viewpoints to social capital regarding networks. Coleman sees that cohesion in a network with numerous, and probably redundant ties between actors, yields social capital. The communication between the actors is effective, and trust and shared norms are strong. Burt considers, that an intermediary position between actors, which are away from each other, creates the best social value to the intermediary due to the rich information it receives and due to its control advantages.

In creating something new (R&D and innovation VOs), effective VO topology may be different from an effective VO that produces more standardised outcome. Ahuja (2000) e.g. discusses the implications to innovation output by studying organisation's direct ties, indirect ties and structural holes. Figure 4 (modified from Ahuja, 2000, p. 428) illustrates these concepts.

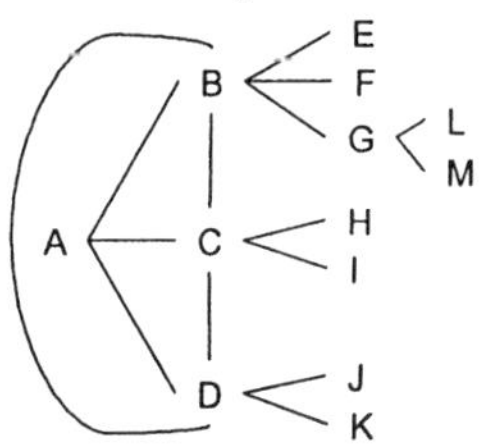

Figure 4. An example VO topology (Modified from Ahuja, 2000)

In Figure 4 organisations A, B, C and D all have direct ties between each other. They create a closed network with no structural holes from A's perspective. Organisation B has direct ties to E, F and G, which further have ties to L and M. These two latter ties are from B's perspective indirect. There are also structural holes (unconnected partners) between e.g. E, F and G.

The direct ties can provide knowledge sharing, complementary and scale, but having direct ties may add costs if maintaining the tie is costly. Indirect ties can, without significant costs, also provide benefits, like knowledge propagation. Structural holes then, as discussed earlier, and as Burt claims, enrich the information that an intermediary node in the network gains (e.g. organisation B may receive rich information from partners E, F and G).

Many researchers have studied the implications of these so called structural holes for the innovativeness (e.g. Ahuja, 2000; Burt, 2004). The results are not straightforward. The business context (e.g. matured – immature) seems to effect the preferable structure. The main finding is that the context in which the VO operates and the desired outcome of the VO should be considered when designing the VO structure, and that in some cases missing links may even be preferable. On the other hand, VOs with structural holes may be more vulnerable to opportunism and the extension of trust along the indirect ties is weaker.

According to the definitions, a VO is a temporary structure built from an existing BE (network). Additional consideration should be needed about the benefits or disadvantages of the crosswise combinations:

- creating a VO without structural holes from a BE with structural holes. In some cases this could support innovation, especially new ways of combining knowledge. A potential drawback is too low trust in the starting phase.
- creating a VO with structural holes from a BE without structural holes. Fewer links may, in some cases, be more effective, and the BE with the links creates a basis for trust.

3.3.4 VO coordination

The selection between star and supply chain VO management may depend on the VO operational topology, but the selection between peer-to-peer and the other topologies depends on the need for coordination. As the peer-to-peer management form has no central coordination, the VO coordination intensity can be considered as a key design factor for VO management.

Malone, & Crowston (1994) define coordination: "Coordination is managing dependencies between activities."

A VO has a specific task and goal and a distributed organization to achieve it. VO coordination then means management of the dependencies of partners' activities in order to achieve the goal of the VO. A conclusion could be, that if there are no dependencies, there is no need for coordination, and, if there are strong dependencies, intensive coordination is needed. Dependencies may come from different sources: the VO objective or product type (an integrated package, where parts should fit together), the process type (input-output relationships) and resource allocations and scheduling.

The importance of the coordination also depends on the risk or consequences of not achieving the VO objective, and the model of risk sharing. If there are no losses in case of failure of the VO, it is not cost-effective to invest in coordination. If there is high risk of not achieving the goal with self-acting methodology, coordination is more important. On the other hand, if each partner only needs to tolerate its own risk and their risks do not depend on the other partners, coordination is less important.

It can be concluded that although the VO coordination intensity is a VO design parameter, it is determined based on two factors:

- the level of dependencies (partly designed, but partly situational)
- the risk involved in the VO objective (mostly a situational factor).

Partly the dependencies can be affected by the VO design, but the BE behind and the VO objective or product itself cause important restrictions on the design. As the involved risk highly depends on the VO objective, it can be concluded that the type of the VO objective /product/ service often determine the VO design parameters, including the management models and methods.

3.4 From VO contingency factors to VO management approaches

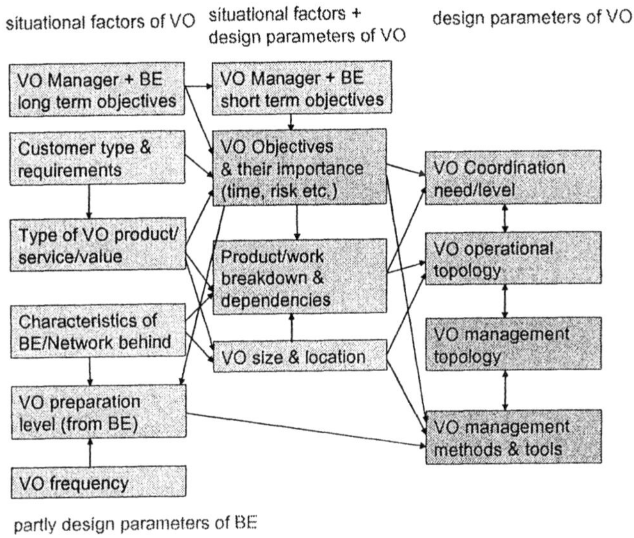

Figure 5. First map of VO contingency factors.

Figure 5 presents a map of VO contingency factors (situational factors and design parameters) relevant to VO management. The arrows between the entities present the influences between them. The elements on the left hand side mainly present parameters which are situational factors, the ones in the middle are partly situational factors (as the VO Objectives) and partly design parameters, and the ones on the right are VO design parameters. The aim is to identify the decisive entities and characteristics (situational factors) affecting recommendable VO methods.

The characteristics of Figure 5 were preliminarily analysed in 11 ECOLEAD VO scenarios/ cases with different types of products, sizes, locations, frequencies and operational topologies. For most of the cases the preparation level in the network/BE was considered low. Even if the products were different, all VO cases identified strong dependencies between the partners. Mostly this lead to high coordination intensity. The definition of used VO management methods and tools proved to be difficult in some cases; following a VO plan and reacting on exceptions were the most common methods. Measuring partners was described in some of the scenarios, but no well-defined VO management mechanisms / rules were defined.

Based on the analysis of scenarios some VO management approaches have been described for different combinations of VO objective & dependencies & risks in Table *1*. The different approaches partly overlap. To go further, proposals for VO management methods and mechanisms for different management approaches are needed.

Table 1. First VO management approaches

Approach	**Application area**	**Focus/ methods of management**
Project management – constrained approach	A specific task, a defined goal. Constrains with outcome, costs & schedule, high/ medium risks , considerable interdependencies of tasks/operations (capital projects), possibly strong technical dependencies (SW integration, capital projects)	Effective/ medium operational/ technical coordination Planning, allocation of resources, following a plan, monitoring & real time progress measurement, reactive & proactive, often focus on interfaces and dependencies. (Monitoring of results/ activities/ inputs) Fast, emerging VOs with standard detailed preplans/ stand-by state. Configurable / tailored plans and one-of-a-kind VOs.
Supply Chain Management approach	Supply chains, longer duration, no "final" plans,…	Forecasting, allocation of resources, planning, monitoring, reallocation …?
"Encouragement approach "	Abstract objective/ changing objective/ not constrained objective, first phases of innovation (invention), research, business development.	Clarification of objective, building of common visions. Management of scope & motivation, measuring motivation & performance? rules for knowledge ownership & utilization
"Self-organizing – internalized common objective"	Self-willing – all the partners have internalized the objectives -the objectives of partners support each other, no conflicts	No coordination – management of motivation & result, integration may be needed, rules for sharing of results, risks and knowledge are needed.
"Automatic control of VO"	Partners with no conflicting objectives/ predefined solutions, give decision power to the automated system.	Automated/ semi-automated follow-up of VO plan, (semi)automatic negotiation and decision making, no conflicts/ automatic resolution, agent systems?

4. CONCLUSION

4.1 Challenges for further work

To efficiently manage virtual organizations, a broad scope is necessary, which also can be seen in the definition of VO Management, presented in this paper. The main challenges in the management come from the temporary nature of a VO and the distribution of operations to several organizations. In addition, the VO is aimed to respond to fast changes in its environment, i.e. a dynamic management is needed, which also may include restructuring of the management approach or even the VO configuration.

The required dynamic management implies that needs of management actions are identified in real time. Consequently, an efficient performance measurement system should also be in place to give reliable, real-time indicators about the performance of the VO. The basic challenge for the work then becomes to develop real-time performance measurement based management approaches fulfilling the requirements and features described in this paper.

4.2 Acknowledgments

The paper is mainly based on work performed in the Integrated project ECOLEAD funded by the European Community under the Framework programme 6 (IP 506958).

5. REFERENCES

1. Ahuja, Gautam. Collaboration Networks, Structural Holes, and Innovation: A Longitudal Study. Administrative Science Quarterly, 45 (2000), pp. 425-455.
2. Burt, Ronald. Structural Holes and Good Ideas. American Journal of Sociology, 2004, pp 349-399.
3. Camarinha-Matos, L.M. and Afsarmanesh H., 2003. Elements of a base VE infrastructure. J. Computers in Industry, Vol. 51, No. 2, 139-163, 2003.
4. Camarinha-Matos, L., Afsarmanesh, H., Ollus, M. (eds.), 2005. Virtual organizations. Systems and Practices, Springer-Verlag. 2005.
5. Coleman, James S. Social capital in the creation of human capital. American Journal of Sociology, 1988, pp 95-120.
6. Coleman, James S., 1990. Foundations of Social Theory. Harvard University Press, Cambridge, MA. 1990
7. ECOLEAD D32.1 Challenges in Virtual Organisations Management. March 2005. www.ecolead.org.
8. GERAM, 1999. GERAM: Generalised Enterprise Reference Architecture and Methodology; Version 1.6.2; IFIP–IFAC Task Force, 1999
9. Hausner, U., Teichmann, K., Albers, S. & Hussla, I. Management of Virtual Enterprises: Results from Case Studies in Northern Germany. In Weber, F., Pawar, K. & Thoben, K.-D. (eds), Proceedings of the 9th International Conference on Concurrent Enterprising: "Enterprise Engineering in the Networked Economy", Espoo, Finland , University of Nottingham, 2003;. 337- 342.
10. Henderson Rebecca M., Clark Kim B. Architectural Innovation: The Reconfiguration of Existing product Technologies and the failure of Established Firms. Administrative Science Quarterly, Vol. 35, No. 1, Special Issue: Technology, Organisations, and Innovation. (Mar., 1990), pp 9-30.

11. Karvonen, I. & Jansson, K. & Ollus, M. & Hartel, I. & Burger, G. & Anastasiou, M. & Välikangas, P. & Mori, K. Inter-enterprise eCollaboration in Sales and Service of one-of-a-kind products. (In: Stanford-Smith, B. & Chiozza, E. & Edin, M. (Ed.), 2002). Challenges and Achievements in E-business and E-work, IOS Press / Ohmsha, Berlin, Germany, 2002; 1388-1395.
12. Katzy, B. & Löh, H. Virtual Enterprise Research State of the Art and Ways Forward. In Weber, F., Pawar, K. & Thoben, K.-D. (eds), Proceedings of the 9th International Conference on Concurrent Enterprising: "Enterprise Engineering in the Networked Economy", Espoo, Finland , University of Nottingham, 2003; 343-353.
13. Katzy, B., Zhang, C. & Löh, H. Reference models for Virtual organisations, in Camarinha-Matos, L., Afsarmanesh, H., Ollus, M. (eds.), Virtual organizations. Systems and Practices, Springer-Verlag. 2005; 45-58.
14. Kürümlüoglu M., Nøstdal R., Karvonen, I. Base concepts, in Camarinha-Matos, L., Afsarmanesh, H., Ollus, M. (eds.), Virtual organizations. Systems and Practices, Springer-Verlag (2005), pp.11-28.
15. Malone, T.W., Crowstron, K. The interdisciplinary Study of Coordination. ACM Computing Surveys, 1994 (March), 26 (1), 87-119.
16. Pedersen, J.D., Tolle, M. Vesterager, J. Final report on Models. Deliverable 1.3 of Esprit 26509 Globeman 21 project. 1999.
17. PMBOK, 1996. A Guide to the Project Management Body of Knowledge. Project Management Institute Standards Committee. 1996.
18. Rezgui, Y., Olphert W. and Damodaran L., 2005. Socio-organizational issues, in Camarinha-Matos, L., Afsarmanesh, H., Ollus, M. (eds.), Virtual organizations. Systems and Practices, Springer-Verlag (2005), pp. 187-198.
19. VOSTER: http://voster.vtt.fi/
20. Zwegers, A., Tolle, M, Vesterager J. VERAM: Virtual Enterprise Reference Architecture and Methodology., in Karvonen et al. Global Engineering and Manufacturing in Enterprise Networks (GLOBEMEN), VTT Symposium 224, 2003, p. 17-38.

21

UNDERSTANDING AND MANAGING SHARED PROJECTS IN SMEs NETWORKS

Carmen L.Villarreal L., Lionel Dupont, Didier Gourc, Hervé Pingaud
Centre de Génie Industriel, Ecole des Mines d'Albi-Carmaux, Albi, France
e-mail address: villarre@enstimac.fr

This research work presents a management framework applied to a network of SMEs which organizes its production like a shared project. Starting from a set of network definitions and considering the collective nature of their activities and the concentration on the own core competences, the study tries to specify what is expected from the management. Then, it proposes a framework to plan and manage the collaborative work using concepts coming from project and risk management theories and practices based on the results of an empirical study in a twelve SMEs network from the aeronautical sector located in Toulouse, France. A specific typology of risks that affect the operation of networks is proposed. Additionally, work planning recommendations are presented.

1. INTRODUCTION

Virtual enterprise concepts have gained considerable relevance in the last years. The virtual enterprise is founded in cooperation between independent enterprises that accept a temporary aggregation of all or part of their resources in order to achieve a specific goal, such as a business opportunity for example.

A distinctive feature of these organizations is the large spectrum of life duration. It could be a limited cooperation because a virtual enterprise is legitimated by particular common objectives and should be dissolved subsequently as soon as the objectives have been attained or are considered as not reachable. But it can also be composed of entities linked in long-term alliances such as in supply chains, when products exchanged by partners are of strategic nature with a high added value.

Enterprise networks are considered as a form of virtual enterprise. They could be classified depending on the size of the different members involved in the cooperation. Agreement could be done between a set of large companies, or between large companies and small- and medium-sized enterprises (SMEs), or only SMEs. This work deals with these last organizations, a set of relatively small companies, that decide to share some objectives. This field of investigation implies short or middle term life-cycles of the network, and the management should be quickly efficient and cannot mobilize too much energy and resources.

The study is limited to production SMEs networks which manage their collaborative work as a shared project. Each company preserves individual activities out of the collective project. The network production is executed by many firms, each one is responsible for a part of the whole set of operational activities. So, if classical project management theory and practice could certainly be applied to the shared project, by definition, sources of uncertainty are always more difficult to handle in such organizations, and risk management is emphasized by the need to react. Reactivity has to be rapidly included in the planning phase of project design. That is the reason why integration of risk to project management appears to this work as a key factor to conceive the management framework.

If many authors have discussed the strategic goals of SMEs networks, there are relatively few references dealing with tactical and operational management levels in such organizations. Unfortunately, if these management levels of networks have some similarities with the ones of a single enterprise, coordination of collective activities in a network at least leads to consider some adaptations and recommendations.

The goal of this work is to search the main features of a network management framework based on project management. The framework is realized from an empirical study in a twelve SMEs manufacturing network from the aeronautical sector, located in Toulouse, France. The study consisted in analyzing project documentation and developing interviews with project managers. The proposition is based on the results of this study.

This paper initially examines the main organizational characteristics of SMEs networks including advantages and restrictions that collective structure comes up to the SMEs. The paper then proposes a global structure and procedure for management including risk analysis and describes a risk typology developed. Finally, a set of recommendations for work planning is presented.

2. SMEs NETWORKS

2.1 Characteristics of SMEs networks

From an organizational point of view, SMEs networks are structures of independent firms related by vertical or horizontal agreements that jointly define a strategy to achieve some goals (Hammami *et al.*, 2004). Different types of networks can be identified according to the pursued objectives (Burlat, 2001): purchasing networks (economies of scale for purchases and supplies), production networks (joint production, product diversification, cost savings), new market oriented networks (sharing business services to increase the turnover), quality certification networks (sharing quality experts to obtain ISO certification), data exchange standardization networks (constructing and adopting common norms to exchange data), etc. These types of networks are not mutually exclusive. For example, a given network may have a strategy composed by both production and purchasing goals.

From an economical point of view, SMEs networks can be considered as particular organizations due to their hybrid form between market and hierarchy. In fact, network coordination is not carried out through a hierarchical organization (as in the firm) or through price regulation mechanisms (as on the market), but through cooperation and free interaction between independent firms (Hammami *et al.*, 2004). The robustness of the network is based on the win-to-win nature of the relationship with respect to individual performances and some autonomy to take decisions.

In the ideal case, partners are only able to develop new businesses and to acquire new competences together, by sharing technology, commercial structure, market locations, productions volumes, resources, skills or activities (Fischer, 2004). But to transform this strategic goal into real performances, some collaborative processes are necessary in order to affect resources properly, to communicate information correctly and to control the progress of realized work as well as to globally supervise the real investment of partners. It is vital to effectively keep the status of an hybrid organization by maintaining a consensus in the win-to-win game using collaborative processes.

2.2 Benefits and limitations

The pressure to face competitive challenges considerably increases, especially for SMEs, in order to secure their own survival. This also explains the reason for the high frequency of production networks in practice. The main benefits for SMEs in joining manufacturing networks are (Mallidi *et al.*, 1999):

- access to new markets by realizing products that are out of feasibility for the sole SME;
- increased productivity, by cumulating and optimizing the individual collective capacity;
- improved reactivity through joint response to perturbations that would be unbearable for the single enterprise;
- improved utilization of resources, by avoiding duplication of functions through the network.

Network emergence is favored by the intrinsic SMEs lean and flexible structure and, for most of them, by natural disposition toward cooperation, gained through stable subcontracting and partnership links (Mallidi *et al.*, 1999) (Burlat *et al.*, 2001). Nevertheless, the main obstacles to network emergence are the individualistic nature of SME management, the lack of contractual frameworks for these new forms of cooperation and the lack of suitable methods and tools for distributed production management.

Organizing this kind of development effort also poses significant challenges. Extensive reliance on virtual interaction makes it difficult to develop a basic operating structure and set of ground rules to get things up and running (Kovacs *et al.*, 2003).

Moreover, in the course of their work, participants will meet regularly and may iterate some of the decision-making processes in order to achieve consensus by conflict resolution, to anticipate expected disturbances by preventive actions, or to delete perturbation effects using an accepted corrective treatment. Such issues like supervision, re-organization, costs, or re-working, and timely resolution of these issues will be crucial because delay in any subsystem has the potential to delay and undermine work on any other (Adler *et al.*, 1999).

Research indicates that consensus and conflict resolution are especially difficult in time-limited virtual contexts (Maznevski *et al.*, 2000). For such reasons, networks need specific coordination tools to link together activities processed by different firms and to federate independent goals.

Moreover, there are a number of factors which militate against SMEs network project management:

- in comparison to large organizations, SMEs are generally less formal and 'scientific' in their organizational and managerial practices;

- many SMEs have less sophisticated capabilities and expertise than large companies;
- SMEs tend to have a shorter term focus, on medium term survival rather than on long term profit;
- SMEs commonly have fewer resources available, both financial and intellectual (and specially managerial), to invest in major initiatives and are dubious about the benefits of committing those resources to the painstaking planning, data gathering, reporting and analysis that larger organizations would consider essential to such undertakings;
- there is often a degree of reluctance among SMEs managers and owners to use complex computational systems and a tendency to await meaningful pressure from a major client as the necessary stimulus for implementation.

3. THE PROPOSED MANAGEMENT FRAMEWORK

3.1 Procedure modeling requirements

Many of the manufacturing SMEs networks observed organize their common production like a shared project: a complete set of activities and operations which must be carried out by the network in a definite time. In consideration of the above conditions, the operational management framework is defined as a procedure to organize the global process to coordinate activities into the production network in terms of cost, quality and delay time (short-term performance constraints) and to supervise directly the project development. The main problem consists in integrating those kinds of objectives in a unique coherent and collaborative procedure.

In the networks, partner firms are heterogeneous and structured according to a wide range of different organizations. As a consequence of their specific competences and resources, firms' offers are also largely heterogeneous. And normally, the competences' set of the network determines the offers and the type of projects and products (complexity and volume) that the network can develop. In a general way, two types of networks can be found in accordance with the competences of the firms involved (Burlat, 2001). Then, the networks can be composed of firms with similar competences and firms with complementary competences.

At first, the observations about networking lead to accept the following characteristics of work interactions in the networks.

If one considers a network involving firms with similar competences:

a) The same activity (or task) of the product development can be assigned to several enterprises and then realized with different performances. This kind of events occurs when the project objective is the augmentation of the production volume.
b) The total product development could be done in projects organized in a parallel way (with identical starting and ending dates).

If one considers a network involving firms with complementary competences:

a) Different activities are assigned to the firms, when the project objective is to develop a complex product that demands a set of different competences, that any firm involved in the network individually possesses.

b) The activities could be developed in a project organized in a sequential way (with links of precedence between tasks).

3.2 Project and risk management issues

The conventional methods of project control are based on what has already taken place, i.e. so-called historical information. They use trends to predict future events. Using trends, it is difficult to perceive unforeseeable changes or situations that are surprising or develop outside the scope of project plans.

All such conventional methods adhere to the principle of so-called deviation management. The situation becomes even worse if the project manager is willing to take action only after observing large deviations, such as delays of several weeks in a time management report.

However, the environment in which projects are developed has become increasingly characterized by turbulence relating market and economical pressures. This turbulence emphasizes more and more the possibility of appearance of unforeseeable events. This possibility is included in the concept of risk (Courtot, 1998). In this study, the risk is considered like the possibility of occurrence of events which could be threats or opportunities (Bakir *et al.*, 2002) (Jaafari, 2001).

The need of taking risks into account on project management was largely recognized (Miller *et al.*, 2001) (Ward *et al.*, 2003)] and it is considered like a pertinent operational answer. In the particular case of shared projects in SMEs networks, uncertainty increases because of common work organization, the multiplicity and heterogeneity of partners and the resource sharing (Peillon, 2001). Compared to traditional cooperation styles, there are more uncertain factors in a network (Li *et al.*, 2004).

While the network brings a lot of flexibility to partners, it also implies some unavoidable risks. For example, in the operation process of network, the core technologies of an enterprise will intentionally and unconsciously pass on to other member partners, which are likely to become competitors. In contract design process, it is inevitable that there are some ambiguous items, which are likely to result in the profit conflicts among partners and so on. In order to operate the network and achieve anticipated goal, it is necessary to know all kinds of risk factors that influence the operation of network and, furthermore, take appropriate measures to prevent and control them. Implementing the risk analysis process in network project organization could make sure the risk responsibility will be shared by the partners, help member enterprises to avoid bad cooperative relations and make network operate in lower cost and risk.

3.3 The global procedure proposed and the related structure

Because of the increasing cooperation between SMEs in so-called production networks, new concepts for the management of value chains need to be developed. Apart from the operational application of information technology realized so far, which only serves the optimization of the enterprise-internal processes (O'Sullivan, 2003), global management of networks needs to optimize the whole value chain in order to make sure that all the participants have the possibility to act successfully on the market.

According to discussed aspects and adapting different approaches such as the ones of Martinez (Martinez *et al.*, 2001) about virtual enterprise organization and

Mezgár (Mezgár *et al.*, 2000) about cooperative production, the model proposes a non-hierarchic structure in a collaborative environment to systematize the project development and control using risk analysis which could be applicable to the two configurations of networks mentioned above. A network management board usually assumes the general organization of the whole process, and particularly management, planning and quality, but to manage all these activities, procedures and interfaces have to be precisely defined, and a large investment in time and work is needed.

This could end up in a large system, which has many chances to be non-flexible, or with a chaotic one, where leadership and organization problems will appear. Then, at first a structure which must be linked to the procedure and that could make the general system more flexible is proposed (see Figure 1). This structure is composed of two project decision levels:

1. The Network Management Board (NMB), which will be in charge of strategic aspects of shared projects: the project decomposition in global process, evaluation of feasibility, negotiation, project refinement, establishment of the contract and the provisional planning. The actors of this Network Management Board must be representative of each firm and linked to network activities (normally, this structure exists already since the creation of the network). They must have the capacity to take strategic decisions ("go" or "no-go") and to financially engage their own enterprise.
2. The Project Management Board (PMB), which must supervise and control all the project phases (planning, procurement, delivery and site activity). It has to be composed of actors linked directly to shared project development in each enterprise.

And in relation to the operational management (including supervision and control) of the shared project, the approach is based on Project Management and Risk Management techniques.

Firstly, this approach will be based on initial planning carried out by the Network Management Board. A first risk identification action could be developed. Because at this time, aspects of the project may not be clearly defined, the identification may be applied as a purely qualitative approach if it is to test the viability of a new project, but if it is being used to assess budgets or bid prices, a quantitative approach may be required.

Secondly, a process of synchronization project/risk could be applied. This process is founded on the coexistence of the project planning process and risk management process. It explains the integration of methods and the information exchange between those two processes.

The Project Management Board can start the risk analysis process by identifying and evaluating possible events (risks). This identification-evaluation phase must allow to know:

- where the risk comes from, in terms of what effects might be experienced, and the mechanisms underlying these effects;
- what it could be done about it, in proactive and reactive response terms (risk mitigation).

In the third place, the PMB can organize information to begin the construction of a new planning taking risks into account. The objective of this step is to identify possible disturbances on initial planning caused by risks and to transform this planning by adding representation of alternative activities (the realization of these activities is conditioned by the appearance of anticipated events).

Afterwards, they can generate possible scenarios (taking risks into account) using a planning tool and simulating different manners of carrying out the project. In this way, the PMB team has project performance indicators integrating the identified risks and their possible effects.

The step of follow-up makes it possible to collect information while the project is in progress. If any of the anticipated events occurs, PMB could start a new risk analysis phase. So, the iterative nature of the work in the network meeting is naturally supported by an iterative feature of risk processes management. These new information elements lead the PMB to define and to insert new tasks and new decisions in project planning.

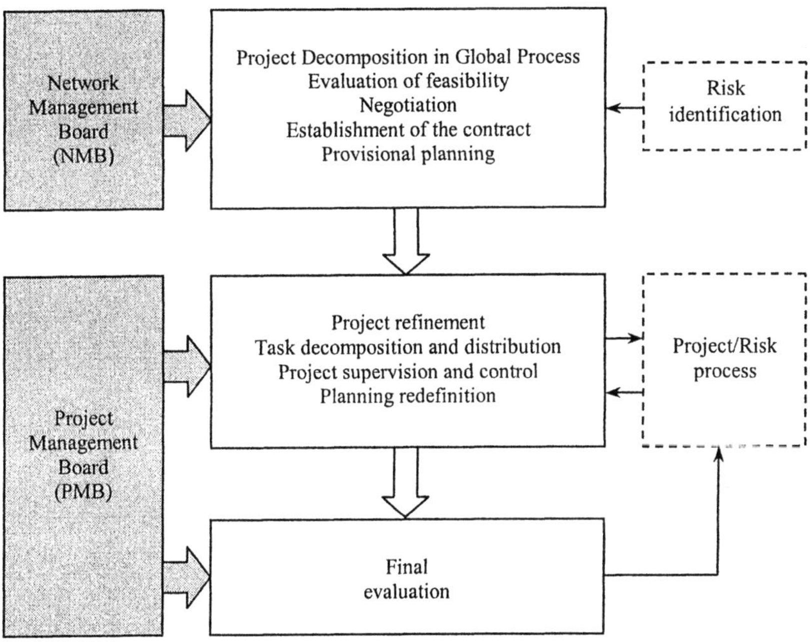

Figure 1: The proposed management procedure and related structure.

In total, this proposed work procedure allows the Project Management Board to deal with limitations related to inter-organizational nature of the common project because many scenarios are studied in order to solve effective problems and decisions are taken knowing the impact of each one on project performance.

At last, a final evaluation must be done to generate the necessary report and to obtain information about project development, modifications of initial planning and the occurrence of unforeseen events.

Thus, the total life cycle of a network, since the formation phase, is full of various risks. Then, it is recommended to implement some strategies of risk analysis in other aspects of network life such as policy definition, finance management, market analysis, competences organization, cooperation issues, operation and so on. The responsible of this monitoring would be the NMB.

3.4 Definition of risk typology

Further to the premises presented above of making risk monitoring of global aspects of the network and iterative risk analysis during project development, the initial set of risks is classified depending on the way a possible event is linked to network composition, organization and networking, external environment and the project internal processes.

As far as risk analysis is concerned, the study found that observations conforming to the idea of risk can be frequently made in project activity environments. The risk typology developed during this phase of research (presented in Table 1) indicates that the risks are observed to occur in all project phases, deliver information on all parts of the project, and show themselves in many ways with various sources: human ones, documents and situations.

This investigation also found that many project actors are already familiar with the existence of risk and they make use of these indicators in some unstructured and often unconscious way.

Table 1 - The description of risk typology

Risk domain	Risk factors
Structure	Selection of partners Partners relationship Size of partners Competences of partners
Organization	Strategic policies Marketing policies Financial procedures Established structure and role distribution *Know-how* capitalization Co-operative culture
External environment	Competitiveness Suppliers/Subcontractors Clients Public policies
Project internal processes	Collaborative planning Resources allocation and management Technical asymmetries Global project control

The main task of typology construction was to recognize all kinds of risk factors by analyzing a great deal of reliable information data. They not only include those obvious factors but also include those potential factors, which may be more difficult to identify. Otherwise, the domain concerns activities or entities associated with risk manifestation and identified as risk factors.

The first three domains correspond to risks associated to network characteristics and dynamics (that eventually could have influence in project) and the last domain presents the risks linked directly to project organization and development. This typology could be considered as a referential to risk identification. Periodic and continuous actions of risk analysis and the final evaluation of project could enrich and modify it.

3.5 Risk mitigation

One of the challenges of risk analysis and management is to find effective actions to deal with the possibility of events occurrence. If the risk is a menace that could have negative effects, preventive actions could be implemented. On the other hand, if risk involves an opportunity, managers could contemplate some actions to take hold of it.

For example, as it has been said, one of the principal features of networks is the heterogeneity of partner structure and offers due to their specific competences and ressources. The selection of a new partner could pose problems about competence compatibility of candidate in relation to global competence configuration of network. Then, one way to anticipate this kind of problems is to develop a detailed competence cartography of the network and also to meticulously evaluate the competences of possible partners to envisage their positioning in network configuration.

Another situation in network dynamics could be the absence of a defined framework for financial collective issues that could create cash flows problems. To anticipate, an accurate procedure could be developed and contractualised.

An example of project environment could be the difference between the technical performances of each partner when they develop a product that could have a negative impact in global performance. Such kind of situation could be treated with anticipation by establishing training around specific technical aspects or information exchange about practices and experiences lived in order to mitigate knowledge asymmetries.

3.6 Work planning recommendations

Each company is self-organized while the network's common structure is in charge of the global communication, the management of shared project and synchronization between activities. Projects undertaken by the SMEs networks are, by nature, decomposable in relatively independent sub-projects.

Then, at this phase, it is necessary to find the best combination of project decomposition and task allocation and to submit the answer to customer in the shortest process time. In a network structure this process can be achieved with the help of different methods and approaches (Martinez *et al.*, 2001).

First, the product could be decomposed according to its functions and analysis of each function cost is then carried out. Afterwards, the product technologies and design could be selected and with this information, the processes to develop the product and their cost could be deduced.

Sometimes, realizing successive processes decomposition to determine a set of tasks in which every task can be entirely assigned to a single organization by the network is needed.

The system cannot handle every elementary task. The PMB will have control on activities which are composed by these elementary tasks. These tasks are managed by the internal organization of each of the shared projects' actors, that means, the firms.

The product, the information procedure and protocols as well as the plan for process control must be distributed and utilized on the management systems of the partner firms. A task is locally managed by the responsible in the firm according to its own method and organization.

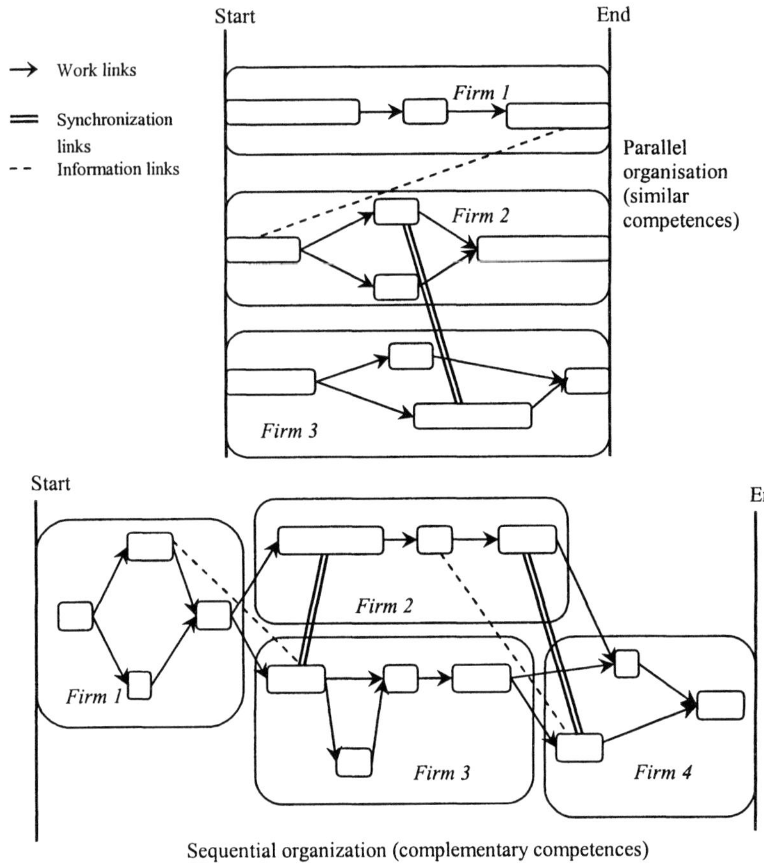

Figure 2. Task links

A distribution of task control among the network structure and the structure of partner firms should be achieved, as follows. The management of allocated tasks (task allocated as a whole to a firm) is assumed by the PMB. The following information must be defined for each allocated task:

- the synchronicity of tasks (a typical example of synchronization needs could be common purchases or tests of materials);
- the information needed and associated exchange procedures (the posterior assemblage of two pieces developed by different firms could be a reason to exchange information);
- the precedence links of tasks.

Both the case of a parallel organization of tasks (when similar competences are involved) and the case of sequential organization (when firms have complementary competences) can apply to these prescriptions (see Figure 2).

Nevertheless, the latter could become more difficult due to the complexity of decomposition and allocation of the task involved. To define this information, the firm in charge of a task must collaborate with the firms in charge of the previous or simultaneous ones. The collaborative work, which is difficult to manage at the network's global level, is made by the PMB.

4. CONCLUSIONS

SMEs networks is an emergent concept in manufacturing. The first objective of this paper was to present a management model that includes a global vision of the structure and an operational procedure centered in the organization of the common production.

The model presented proposes a possible answer to methods of project management in relation to shared projects in multi-organizational taking the network's short-term dynamics into account: real time constraints and risks.

The study hopefully adds elements that were previously known to project management, but not really treated. The realization of the risk analysis will contribute to anticipate events and to enrich a specific risk typology for shared projects in SMEs networks.

Anticipating problems and opportunities can make the decision-making process agile. In the particular case of SMEs networks, the organizational problems of shared projects linked to multiplicity (and heterogeneity) of the actors (partners) can be approached according to this *ex-ante* vision.

Moreover, one of the characteristics of virtual organizations such as the SMEs networks is time limitations that make a more dynamic, flexible and convenient decision-making process necessary.

These needs can be satisfied by the iterative and continuous character of the model proposed which can make a contribution to conventional methods of project management relating to shared projects.

In addition, project planning and task link definition in inter-firm projects could contribute to organizing project control.

Finally, this research work is the first part of a French regional SMEs development project (Midi-Pyrénées Région, France). This project is initiating cross research to support SMEs networks' creation and to assure their continuity.

5. REFERENCES

1. Adler P, Goldoftas B, Levine D. Flexibility versus efficiency? A case study of model changeovers in the Toyota production system. Organization Science 1999; 10(1): 43-69.
2. Bakir S, Gourc D, Pingaud H. Les méthodes de planification de projet en univers risque: apports et limites. Actes du 5ème Congrès International Franco-Québécois de Genie Industriel, Québec: Université de Laval, 2002.
3. Burlat, Patrick. GRECOPME II: Groupements d'Entreprises Coopérantes, Potentialités, Moyennes et Evolutions. Rapport de recherche. France: Ecole des Mines de Saint Etienne, 2001.
4. Burlat P, Boucher X. Pilotage distribué des groupements d'entreprises. Modélisation et perspectives. Journal Européen de Systèmes Automatisés 2001; numéro spécial.
5. Courtot, Hervé. La Gestion des Risques dans les Projets. Paris: Economica, 1998.
6. Fischer M, Jähn H, Tobias T. Optimizing the selection of partners in production networks. Robotics and Computer-Integrated Manufacturing 2004; 20: 593-601.
7. Hammami A, Burlat P, Campagne J.P. Evaluating orders allocation within networks of firms. International Journal of Production Economics 2003; 86(3): 233-249.
8. Jaafari, Ali. Management of risks uncertainties and opportunities on projects: time for a fundamental shift. International Journal of Project Management 2001; 19: 89-101.

9. Kovacs GL, Paganelli P. A planning and management infrastructure for large, complex, distributed projects –beyond ERP and SCM. Computers in Industry 2003; 51: 165-183.
10. Li Y, Liao X. Decision support for risk analysis on dynamic alliance. Decision Support Systems 2004; article in press.
11. Mallidi K, Paraskevopoulous AT, Paganelli P. Process modelling in small-medium enterprise networks. Computer in Industry 1999; 38: 148-158.
12. Martinez MT, Fouletier P, Park KH, Favrel J. Virtual enterprise – organisation, evolution and control. International Journal of Production Economics 2001; 74: 225-238.
13. Maznevski ML, Chudoba KM. Bridging space over time: global virtual team dynamics and effectiveness. Organization Science 2000; 11(5): 473-492.
14. Mezgár I, Kovacs GL, Paganelli P. Co-operative production planning for small- and medium-sized enterprises. International Journal of Production Economics 2000; 64: 37-48.
15. Miller R, Lessard D. Understanding and managing risks in large engineering projects. International Journal of Project Management 2001; 19: 437-443.
16. O'Sullivan, Alan. Dispersed collaboration in a multi-firm, multi-team product-development project. Journal of Engineering and Technology Management 2003; 20: 93-116.
17. Peillon Sophie. Le pilotage des coopérations interentreprises: le cas des groupements de PME. Thèse de Doctorat. France: Université Jean Monet, 2001.
18. Ward S, Chapman C. Transforming project risk management into project uncertainty management. International Journal of Project Management 2003; 21: 97-105.

22

A GENERIC FRAMEWORK BASED ON MACHINE LEARNING TECHNIQUES FOR VIRTUAL ORGANIZATION MANAGEMENT

Leandro Loss, Ricardo J. Rabelo, Alexandra A. Pereira-Klen
Federal University of Santa Catarina, Department of Automation and Systems
GSIGMA – Intelligent Manufacturing Systems Group
Florianópolis (SC), Brazil
{loss, klen}@gsigma.ufsc.br
rabelo@das.ufsc.br

The management of Virtual Organization (VO) brings some challenges. One of them is the appropriate and effective coordination and monitoring of distributed businesses processes. It is not easy or trivial to handle the enormous amount of information about and from VOs members. As a direct consequence, decisions are crucial and should be taken not only with agility, but also with intelligence. This paper introduces a framework to support an integrated decision-making environment through which managers will be able to take assisted and smarter decisions. The key element of this framework is the Intelligent Decision Support System, which applies Artificial Intelligence techniques (Data Mining and Machine Learning) to facilitate and to support the decision-making process.

1. INTRODUCTION

Enterprises are even more increasing their efforts in order to improve their (intra and inter) business processes, so that they can increase their own performance and at the same time become more competitive. In other words, this means that enterprises are exposed to a very competitive, demanding and global market. Some actions associated to this "movement towards competitiveness improvement" include: implementation of advanced information technology systems, reengineering task forces, e-commerce sites, integration of legacy systems, more powerful communication infrastructures, among others. On the one hand, all these actions provided to the companies a base for receiving and sending plenty of information. On the other hand, the more the companies use information the harder is the task to treat it in an efficient and smart way. According to Rabelo & Pereira-Klen (2002) managers have been plunged into so much information that, in opposite to the core objective, more difficulties have been brought for taking smart and agile decisions.

In this world scenario companies are being forced, due to the high level of competition, to take decisions not only with agility (an emergent requirement), but also with intelligence. Regarding the sort of problems that usually take place in the daily business management, it is observed that most of them are solved – when solved! – via ad-hoc actions. Actually, most of the available systems have been designed to be passive, don't offering any comprehensive supporting methodologies and/or systems guidance for decision-making. They use to be purely reactive, without considering neither the amount of knowledge the company already has about itself nor allowing the knowledge storing accordingly. Even the historical information about how decisions are taken and their related consequences is rarely stored. This means that systems are not yet enough prepared to help managers properly, regarding the issues that are indeed required in modern businesses, such as in alliances like Virtual Organizations (VOs)[1] (Rabelo, 2004b). However, despite that nowadays working collaboratively is fundamental to accomplish goals and to conquer new markets, the management of such alliances is of extreme importance but at the same time much more complex than "traditional" management.

This paper introduces a system architecture that aim to offer an integrated decision-making environment through which managers will be able to take smarter decisions based on the current data of VO members and on their past decisions/actions. Artificial Intelligence (AI) techniques properly combined serve as the basis to facilitate and to support decision-making process.

The paper is organized as follows: Section 2 presents a literature review related to the approached area. Section 3 briefly depicts the basic concepts of the AI concepts and techniques used. In section 4 the proposed system architecture is introduced and framed on an industrial scenario view. Finally section 5 provides preliminary conclusions and future steps.

2. LITERATURE REVIEW

According to Dobler & Burt (1996) the competition is (or should be) between value chains – not between members of a value chain. All efforts should be combined to motivate buyers and sellers to work in a collaborative mode where the forming and nurturing of buyer-seller partnerships and strategic alliances rise as a consequence. The key characteristics of such relationships are related to the interests' compatibility, mutual need, and willingness to be open sharing information as well as to the benefits resulting from the relationship and, perhaps of greatest importance, to trust[2] (Dobler & Burt, 1996).

Considering the partnerships and the management of strategic alliances, decision-making processes are crucial in order to achieve success. However, as stated by Dobler & Burt (1996), managers usually take decisions mostly based on "self-intuition", mental process, following a range of steps with no support tool. It makes this process, almost always, a blend of rational and emotional factors.

---

[1] A VO constitutes a number of cooperating independent organizations with certain common purposes that provides a set of services and functionalities to the outside world, as if together they represent one organization (Afsarmanesh, 2004).

[2] Trust is usually based on knowing the risk level in a business. Trust may speed up the inter-enterprise processes and decrease monitoring and coordination costs (ECOLEAD, 2005).

Several research projects have studied the Virtual Organization area. Usually the focus was on issues supporting creation rather than on management actions (ECOLEAD, 2005).

VO management refers to change how single enterprises view their way of doing business. Those enterprises must transform themselves from static and hierarchical to (semi-)dynamic and flexible network of organizations (Afsarmanesh, 2004). These networks must enable the involved organizations to develop the capability of setting up their needed processes in reasonable time in order to capture business opportunities, which no single company can do on its own (Afsarmanesh, 2004).

Relevant aspects concerning VO coordination were considered in previous works which aimed to describe the coordination issues. For example, Bremer (Bremer, 1999) argued that in order to achieve a successful partnership, a set of coordination aspects may be established, such as marketing strategy and game simulation. The research was performed using simulation which allowed the core competences description to each enterprise and visualized possible business opportunities when they rose up.

Actually, the complexity of managing VOs requires several managerial actions, some depends on the manager's skills, experience and capabilities, and others do not. It is believed that if those actions were analyzed and supported by an "adviser", like smart software tool, they will be much better.

The few approaches dealing with high level management miss smart procedures and/or functions to assist different kinds of VOs which are constantly changing over time. The duty to anticipate faults or unwished actions as well as the use of lessons learnt from experience or from available practices is still a challenge.

This paper presents a work being carried out in order to extend the SC^2 system (supply chain smart coordination) (Rabelo, 2004b). SC^2 is a support system built up to help the VO coordinator to achieve a better management, with an emphasis on the information flow. The SC^2 provides a set of approaches and techniques allowing managers to collect, analyze, and organize the information about multiple SCs and their individual chains in a VO context.

The developed functionalities allow VO members to access information – available at different levels according to some visibility criteria – about the whole VO. These functionalities aid to minimize the system global costs and to improve the transparency of the joint business, besides motivating trust building and cooperation among partners (Rabelo, 2004b).

SC^2 is a multi-agent system and it is composed by three classes of agents as shown in **Figure 1**: smart supervisor, chain supervisors, and supporting agents. The first one is the agent called Smart Agent, responsible for the global SC management. The second one has three instances: Production Agent, Sales Agent and Distribution Agent, responsible for dealing with the production, sales and distribution individual chains, respectively. The third one is represented by the XML Agent, which is responsible for dealing with the communication among the agents and with the "external environment".

Despite SC^2 helps the managers to overcome the problems of dealing with a vast amount of information, it offers very few pro-active actions. Whenever the manager desires some information (s)he must consult reports and functionalities. So far, the system does not provide/suggest plans in order to improve management skills or to solve existing problems. Our aim is to expand the Smart Agent functionalities offering an integrated decision-making environment within which AI techniques are applied to support some levels of intelligence.

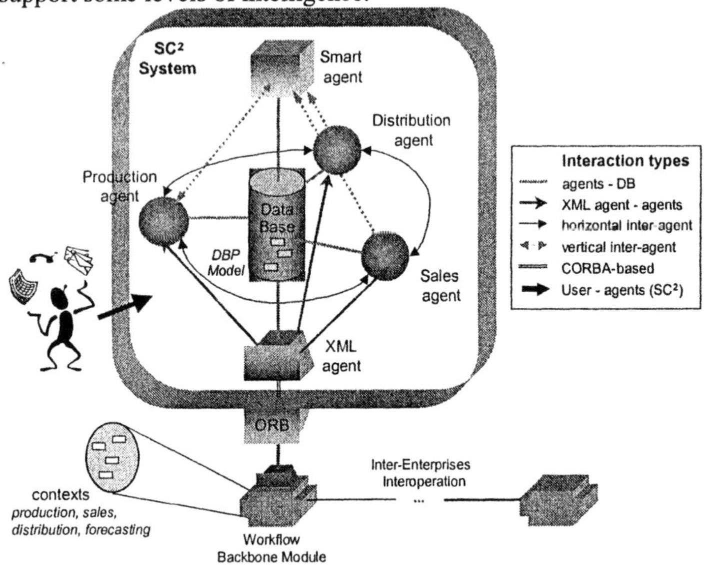

Figure 1 - The desktop SC^2 Architecture

3. IDENTIFYING RELATED TECHNOLOGIES

According to Lavrac (2002) the recognizing of partners' expertise, tools and skills as marketable knowledge assets are factors in which the success of knowledge intensive services are critically depend. Problems like efficiently storing, updating, as well as sharing should be solved by the VO in order to promote and to transfer knowledge among its members. Appropriate management will lead to a quick recognition of business opportunities and timely responses. In this section some relevant technologies are depicted in order to help to understand their use in the proposed architecture. These technologies are:

- Data Mining is concerned with finding patterns in data which are interesting and valid (Fayyad, 1996).
- Text Mining is about looking for regularities, patterns or trends in natural language text, usually texts for particular purposes (Intelligent-Web, 2005).
- Decision Support is related to developing systems aimed at helping decision-makers to solve problems and make decisions (Mallach, 2000).
- Benchmarking is a continuous and systematic process to evaluate products, services and processes against competitors or renowned organizations considered world leaders in their field (Zairi & Leonard, 1996).
- Machine Learning and the principle of learning that can be executed by computers and/or systems to improve their performance (Mitchell, 1997).
- Ontology formally represents domains of knowledge. Ontologies structures are formal explicit description of concepts in a domain of discourse, properties of

each concept describing various features and attributes of the concept, and restrictions on slots (Konar, 1999).

- Knowledge base may be used in order to store the knowledge obtained through the VO life-cycle in a systematic way. It is an approach to structure and to codify what is known about an area/issue (Rezende, 2003).

4. PROPOSED APPROACH

The existing tools have not used techniques, like Artificial Intelligence (AI), as an alternative approach to improve system's efficiency. AI techniques may help solve unpredictable and unexpected problems suggesting ad hoc solutions. It means that the system will work either anticipating future actions to improve efficiency and to avoid errors, or working as an integrated environment where decisions are taken in intelligent way.

This paper proposes a system architecture based on computational decision support system called *"Intelligent DSS"* which is divided in two layers (**Figure 2**). The first layer is responsible for the intelligent processes and is also called back-end. The processes running on the back-end, the ones that will help on decision-making process, are considered intelligent because they are able to generate new knowledge and to reason about them as well as to use knowledge to solve problems (Rezende, 2003). The second layer is responsible for the smart processes (it is not intelligent indeed). The smart level is the interface where the manager will interact with the system; it is also called here front-end.

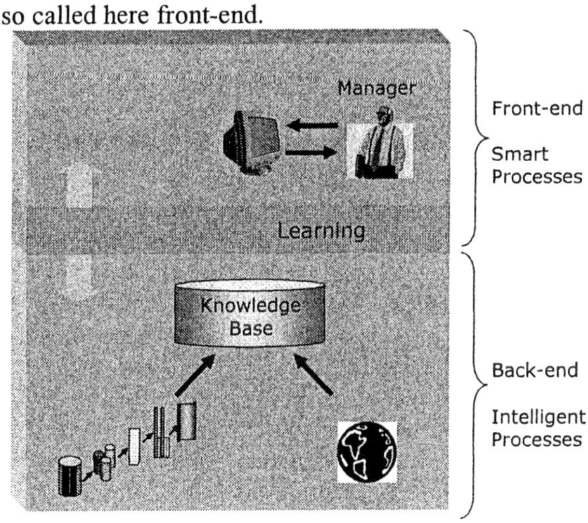

Figure 2 - Layers comprising the Intelligent DSS

The overall process is divided in two main steps, namely: off-line/intelligent processes, occurring in the back-end, and on-line/smart processes, occurring in the front-end. This division is necessary because before the manager starts to interact with the *Intelligent DSS* (on-line), the system must be fed with some knowledge, in a case-based learning way, (off-line) in order to attend the manager's requests.

The first step is executed off-line right after the VO had been created and had started its operation. The database is filled with current and historical data about each VO partner. The database is constantly updated as shown in Figure 3(a), despite this practice is not trivial, Rabelo *et al.*, (2004a) has already proved the feasibility of this process. Once data is stored, it is necessary to extract relevant information in order to help on future decision-making task. The process is carried out by applying data and text mining techniques as shown in Figure 3(b).

Figure 3(c) illustrates the inclusion of pieces of information coming from the experience got from benchmarking techniques (external world). It is important to emphasize that when feeding information in the knowledge base an ontology is required. The cross-functional team[3], on the other hand, is responsible to validate information and to include new information that seems to be relevant and/or to be useful for decision-making processes. In this approach the cross-functional team can also be called cross-organizational team because it includes people (experts) from each partner of the VO.

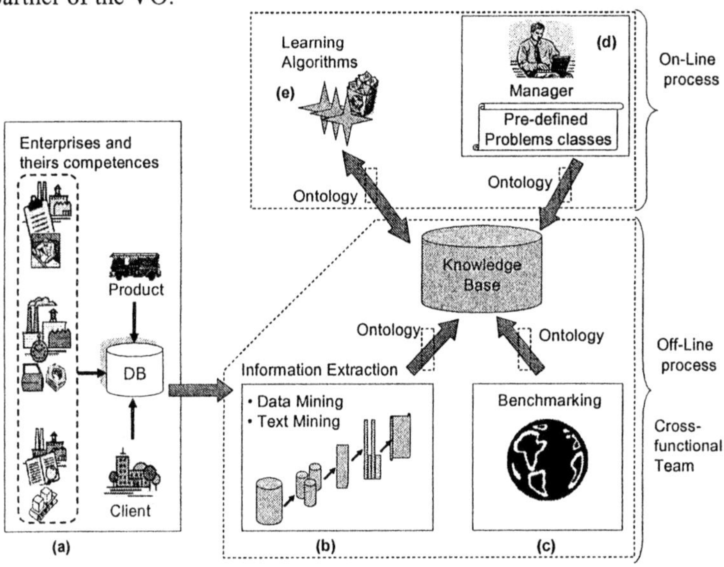

Figure 3 - Process to Obtain Information and Knowledge.

The second step, on-line, is started after all previous processes have been executed. At this time the manager interacts with the *Intelligent DSS* asking for advices in order to solve some problems (Figure 3 (d)).

Reinforcement learning algorithms are applied on this task (Figure 3(e)) and are responsible for the "intelligent processes" of the system suggesting actions to the manager. These algorithms monitor all actions taken on the system and they are executed whenever a new piece of information is included in the knowledge base. The algorithms are able to classify the information, detect errors and delays, and previously alert the manager(s). The analysis is done based on past decisions in order to suggest the best actions to be taken on the decision process, by the manager. The manager still remains with a very important role which is the responsibility to

[3] The cross-functional team of an enterprise is composed by people with knowledge and experience in many areas. (engineers and managers with knowledge and ability to "shape" new knowledge, IT people to support system's infrastructure, and so on).

validate the knowledge "created" by the system through the rank. The next section goes deeper in each phase where the steps are "instantiated" in a working scenario.

4.2 Example

In order to facilitate the comprehension, it is assumed that a VO is already created and is operating. The following illustrative situation is supposed: a large automobile enterprise wishes to contract a supplier to produce moulds and dies in order to build a new prototype in the Southern of Brazil. However, none mould and die industry placed in that area has enough resources to fulfill all requirements; rather, just part of them can be performed. The solution found by a group of five enterprises was to work collaboratively.

One enterprise (i.e. partner number 3) will take the role of a VO coordinator[4] and will concentrate all information from the other four partners to manage the VO. The manager entrusted to manage the VO is called Robert Landfill. It is important to emphasize that the proposed tool should be used only by the VO coordinator, so that, other members do not interact directly with the system interface, they only provide data to a common VO database (Figure 3(a)).

While the VO is under operation, the *Intelligent DSS* verifies that partner number 1 is delayed to deliver a mould (step 1, Figure 4). This delay is critical to the delivery time stipulated by the contractor. The problem is detected because the *Intelligent DSS* system has a specific module that continuously monitor each partner in the VO.

As soon as the *Intelligent DSS* detects the delay (comparing the actual data with the VO production planning), the system sends a standard alert message to Robert reporting the problem occurrence (step 2, Figure 4). At the same time the process to find possible solutions based on the knowledge stored on knowledge base is started.

The search for solutions is done comparing the detected problem in each class defined by the ontology against the knowledge base (step 3, Figure 4). Possible solutions are suggested to the manager through a report (step 4, Figure 4) i) to devote specialized employees to execute the task i.e. the system suggests to increase the working hours of a mechanical engineer to nineteen hours and of two material engineers to fourteen hours so that the production can be speed up (63% efficient), or ii) to reschedule the distributed process i.e. to anticipate the beginning of task "D" from partner 5 in three days and seven hours in order to compensate the delay on task "B" from partner 1 (71% efficient). The *Intelligent DSS* makes use of the knowledge obtained (and being acquired during the VO life-cycle) in order to help the decision making process.

These pieces of advices were obtained from the knowledge base according to the characteristics of the problem. So the *Intelligent DSS* concluded that this postpone may cause the bullwhip effect (Carlsson, 2002) resulting in nine days and two hours delay. Since those possible solutions were put in the knowledge base in the past in order to solve a similar situation, they were ranked by other managers with a "reward signal", which expressed how successful they were (63% and 71% respectively). Now they are available and are suggested to Robert by the system. In

[4] VO coordinator is the supervisor component related to VO activities.

the meantime the system is waiting for Robert's analysis and reply (steps 5 and 6, Figure 4).

Due to his experience, Robert knows that despite anticipating task "D" may be more successful (71% than 63%), partners rescheduling is a hard task, so he decides to accept the first option and calls the engineering sector delegating the task. Now Robert can come back to his normal job.

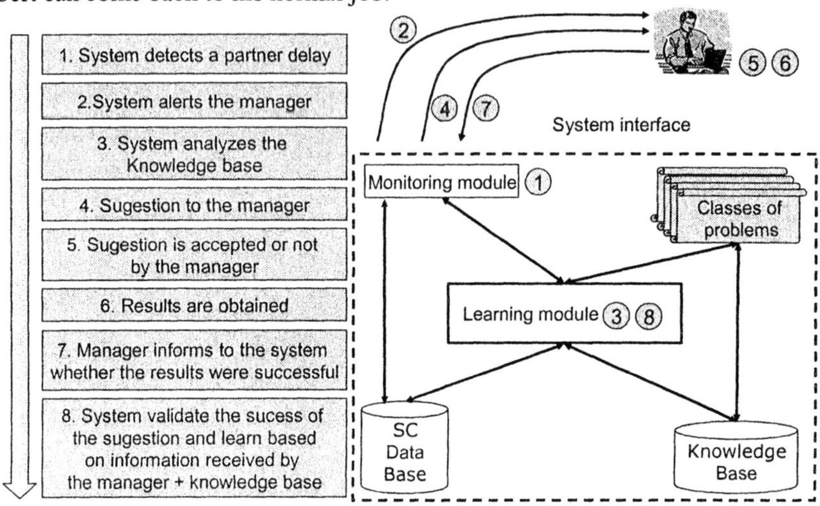

Figure 4 - Process of Decision-making and Learning

After task execution, Robert comes back to the *Intelligent DSS* and informs whether the results were successful or not (step 7, Figure 4). He accesses the system's options through the system interface and ranks how successful the options were. The rank ranges from -10 (*bad suggestion*) to 10 (*terrific suggestion*) where rank 0 means *"I did not use it"*. Here the learning algorithms are triggered, where Robert gives the rewards related to each suggestion. The first option receives the value 9,0, which means that it was a very good suggestion. The second option (rescheduling) receives value 0.0, which means that the suggestion was not used.

The *Intelligent DSS* analyzes the rewards given by Robert, stores them to use as a validation parameter when a similar occurrence emerge, and inserts them in the knowledge base (step 8, Figure 4). It is not intended to provide optimal solutions using the *Intelligent DSS*, actually there is no accurate knowledge for one specific situation.

This is the so called "on-line" phase. However, the global process described above was possible because Robert used and has fed the system at least once and the cross-functional team has been worked in a good way in the "foundation" of the system, maintaining the system knowledge base properly updated. This knowledge preparation is the one carried out in the so called off-line phase on the system.

During the off-line phase, the *Intelligent DSS*'s knowledge base must be fed with data in order to start effectively to work. The first action is to collect data from all partners to fill the VO database (Figure 3(a)).

After collecting data, the cross-functional team starts the process to extract relevant information from database. This is done applying data mining algorithms.

These algorithms will help in the information discovery process. Usually this kind of information is undercover in a large amount of tables and registers, so managers do not have in mind its existence and its relationships, and consequently do not use it.

Now the cross-functional team executes the DM algorithms several times trying to find any association among data. For example, one of these associations is verified when there is a relationship among the amount of sales, the number of employees, and delayed products in the period from ten years to now (for each partner). The final analysis shows the enterprises divided into two groups and each group has their own characteristics. The former group containing three enterprises had the same variation in the sales during the period according to the market and does not registered serious problems with delays. However, the two other enterprises comprising the second group had an interesting behavior: sales were under 5% when the number of hired employees increased above 10%.

By analyzing these data it is possible to conclude that the "phenomenon" occurs because hired employees do not had enough training to operate machines or they received insufficient trainings causing errors in the moulds during production and, consequently, delays in the delivery. At this point the cross-functional team has identified why delay has occurred.

Following the same line, text mining algorithms are also applied, but instead of searching for information in the VO database (like data mining), these algorithms look for information in internal documents and in web sites as an alternative source. Once again the cross-functional team specifies where the search must be done.

At this time, the cross-functional team realized that an important 50 pages document should also be comprised to complement the knowledge base. This document contains key indicators on how to improve efficiency on shop floor. Summaries are easier to use instead of the whole document when looking for possible solutions. i.e, results say that when a team which contains 10 employees working on the mould production is helped with 2 more senior engineers working 5 hours a day for 3 days, the final schedule are anticipated in 5 days and 7 hours.

Benchmarking rises up as an extra alternative to get information from outside and inside enterprises that are part of VO. This is done analyzing best practices. The cross-functional team evaluates actions taken during the bullwhip occurrence in well-known organizations, extracts how to proceed, and stores the information in the knowledge base. A best-practice says, for example, that enterprises should be transparent, strengthen strategic partnering arrangements with their distributors and customers, and should reduce order lead-times, besides to become a demand-driven enterprise through lean manufacturing.

All the processes executed by the cross-functional team are transparent to Robert. He does not to know how the *Intelligent DSS* works "downstairs". He just needs to know how to operate the system's interface.

It is important to emphasize that the more the *Intelligent DSS* is used, the richer are the knowledge to help the manager.

5. CONCLUSIONS AND NEXT STEPS

Collaborative Networks is an area that still requires much attention from the research community. This paper addressed the issue of managing virtual organizations as well as taking decision in a networked environment.

It was observed that most of the problems both in traditional organizations and in recent VOs are solved in an ad hoc way without neither specific methodologies nor supporting tools. Yet, the available tools are not enough designed to help managers in smart decision-making. It was verified that although efforts are being carried out towards the identification of needs and generation of research recommendations on how VOs can be managed, they are not based on intelligent tools. Thus, the main goal of this work was to propose an integrated decision-making environment based on an ample set of combined Artificial Intelligence techniques. The decision support interface provides means for smart decisions, whereas the base of the system acts intelligently in the supplying of useful knowledge to the manager. The prototype implementation as well as its validation are the next steps of this research.

5.1 Acknowledgments

This work was partially supported by CNPq – The Brazilian Council for Research and Scientific Development (www.cnpq.br), and it has been developed in the scope of the Brazilian IFM project (www.ifm.org.br) and the European IST FP-6 IP ECOLEAD project (www.ecolead.org).

6. REFERENCES

1. Afsarmanesh, H.; Marík, V.; Camarinha-Matos, L. M.; 2004. Challenges of Collaborative Networks in Europe. In:. Collaborative Networked Organizations. 1st Edition. KAP. 2004. p. 77-90.
2. Bremer, C. F..; Mundim, A. P.; Michilini, F. V. S. et al.; 1999. A Brazilian Case of Coordination. In: PRO-VE'99. Proceedings p. 377-386.
3. Carlsson, C.; 2002. Decision Support in Virtual Organizations: The Case for Multi-Agent Support. In: Group Decision and Negotiation. 11: 185-221, 2002. Kluwer Academic Publishers. Netherlands.
4. Dobler, D. W.; Burt, D. N.; 1996. Purchasing and Supply Chain Management. Text and Cases. 6th Edition. McGraw-Hill. 1996.
5. ECOLEAD, 2005: European Collaborative Networked Organizations Leadership Initiative Technical Report: D32.1 deliverable of ECOLEAD.
6. Fayyad, U.; Piatetski-Shapiro, G.; Smyth, P.; 1996. From Data Mining to Knowledge Discovery in Databases. AAAIMIT Press, p.37-54, 1996.
7. Intelligent-Web, 2005. Web site accessed in January, 29, 2005. URL: (http://intelligent-web.org/wsm/).
8. Konar, Amit; 1999. Artificial Intelligence and Soft Computing: Behavioral and Cognitive Modeling of the Human Brain. CRC Press LLC.
9. Lavrac, N.; Urbancic, T.; Orel, A.; 2002. Virtual Organization for Data Mining and Decision Support: A Model for Networking Academia and Business. In: PRO-VE'02. Proceedings p. 389-396.
10. Mallach, E. G.; 2000. Decision Support Systems and Data Warehouse Systems. McGraw-Hill, 2000.
11. Mitchell, T.; 1997. Machine Learning. McGraw-Hill.
12. Rabelo, R. Je.; Baldo, F.; Tramontin Jr, R. J.; et al.; 2004a. Smart Configuration of Dynamic Virtual Enterprises. In: 5th IFIP Working Conference on Virtual Enterprises (Aug.: 23-26) Toulouse, França.
13. Rabelo, R. J.; Pereira-Klen, A. A.; Klen, E. R.; 2004b. Effective Management of Dynamic and Multiple Supply Chains. In: International Journal of Networking and Virtual Organizations. Vol. 2. n. 3. p. 193-208.
14. Rabelo, R. J.; Pereira-Klen, A. A.; 2002. Business Intelligence Support for Supply Chain Management. In: BASYS02 Proceedings, Cancun 2002 p.437-444.
15. Rezende, S. O.; Pugliesi, J. B; Melanda, E. A.; et al.; 2003. Mineração de Dados. In: Rezende, S. O.; Sistemas Inteligentes – Fundamentos e Aplicações. 1st Edition. Barueri, SP: Manoele, 2003. p. 307-335.
16. Zairi, M.; Leonard, P.; 1996. Practical Benchmarking: The Complete Guide: London: Chapman & Hall, 1996.

PART 8

VO COORDINATION

23

HUMAN SUPERVISED VIRTUAL ORGANIZATION MANAGEMENT

Alexandra Augusta Pereira-Klen[1], Edmilson Rampazzo Klen[2]
GSIGMA – Intelligent Manufacturing Systems Group
UFSC – Federal University of Santa Catarina, Florianópolis-SC, Brazil
Automation and Systems Department[1]
Production and Systems Engineering Department[2]
klen@gsigma.ufsc.br[1], erklen@gsigma.ufsc.br[2]

This paper introduces the Virtual Organization Management (VOM) under the view that management is a liberal art. A dynamic and fluid VOM framework is proposed based on some management elements and having the Distributed Business Process (DBP) as its kernel. Then another dimension is added to the framework: the VO manager's behaviour. At the end some functionalities to support human-supervised VOM are presented.

1. INTRODUCTION

Management is an almost-50 years-old discipline. The Collaborative Networked Organization – where the Virtual Organization (VO) is inserted – is considered to be an emerging discipline. How to combine both in order to achieve an effective management of VOs? If this management is human-supervised and if different managers imply different management styles (even if they rely on the same management elements and on the same enablers), does this mean that there are different ways to manage a VO? And, if positive, can we personalize a VOM system? These issues are analysed in this work.

The paper is organized as follows: Chapter 2 introduces the VOM under the view that management is a liberal art and proposes a VOM framework. Chapter 3 describes the evolution of the business process from the enterprise-centric to the network-centric models and highlights its importance as the kernel element of the proposed framework. In chapter 4 some questions on how to manage complexity in dynamic environments are addressed and some – possible - answers are provided. Finally, chapter 5 presents some conclusions as well as further questions that need to be addressed in the near future.

2. MANAGEMENT: A LIBERAL ART

In the research area, where consensus building is far from being an easy task, there is a man who came very close to overcome this obstacle: Peter Drucker – also known as the "Father of Management" – is perhaps the deepest and most recognized thinker the world has known in the field of management. His ability to question assumptions and see connections among disparate forces and data has made him a visionary man (Drucker, 1999).

Management, according to Drucker, is a liberal art. It is not a science though it deals in technology. It is not only a humanity even though it deals with people.

"Management is thus what tradition used to call a liberal art – 'liberal' because it deals with the fundamentals of knowledge, self-knowledge, wisdom, and leadership; 'art' because it is also concerned with practice and application. Managers draw on all the knowledge and insights of the humanities and the social sciences – on psychology and philosophy, on economics and history, on ethics – as well as the physical sciences. But they have to focus this knowledge on effectiveness and results... For these reasons, management will increasingly be the discipline and the practice through which the "humanities" will acquire recognition, impact, and relevance." (Drucker, 1989 and 2001)

This work explores the view of Peter Drucker that management is a liberal art and therefore the authors define VO Management (VOM) as:

The intentional act bound up with the intuitive attitude of running Distributed Business Processes (DBPs) and dealing with people by means of applying knowledge, skills and/or tools in order to allow organization and coordination of resources, monitoring of activities as well as adequate reaction whenever needed so that VO goals can be achieved.

This definition suggests that Dynamic VOM should rely on technological, social-organizational and human enablers as well as on the existence of many different – but complementary – management elements. Figure 1 presents one alternative for this VOM Framework where DBP Management is the kernel and the other management elements (such as Risk Management, Trust Management, Knowledge Management, and so forth) contribute to reinforce the management basis as well as the knowledge sharing and the decision making process.

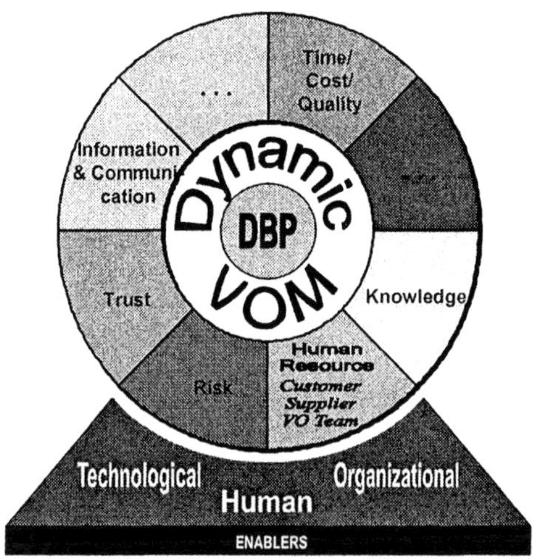

Figure 1: VOM Framework – a static vision of a dynamic framework

The next chapter is devoted to the main VOM element: the DBP. For the other management elements presented in figure 1 the reader is referred to: Malhotra, 2000; Capó et al, 2004; Karolak, 1998; Geber et al, 2004; PMBOK, 2000.

3. THE KERNEL ELEMENT

When enterprises started to see the activities they carried out for accomplishing their final business goal as small "pieces of business" and understood that these "pieces" behaved like processes, then the history of the enterprises began to be written from the *business processes* point of view. The information associated to the enterprises' activities as well as their relationships started to be modeled in such a way that the business processes could be represented according to different visions (organizational, technical, functional, etc). This representation (modeling) should enable enterprises to better understand their business processes in order to facilitate and improve the global business being run. The *business process* (BP) concept started to be exploited from many perspectives: BP implementation, BP monitoring, BP analysis, BP re-engineering, BP management, and so forth. Over decades this is still a very fertile field.

When the attention of industrial and academic worlds started to be deviated with more intensity (something about ten to fifteen years ago) from the enterprise-centric to the network-centric models, the *business process* area also followed this trend (with a small time-gap). The BPs were no longer confined to the enterprise borders. One more vision started to be considered: the meta-vision. This vision should allow the understanding of the Meta-BP carried out by a network of enterprises (or any other kind of organizations) which came together for a certain period of time (short or long) to attend to a business opportunity. Some of the definitions that appeared to describe the Meta-BP (or associated perspectives) include:

- Distributed Business Process (DBP) is a dynamic and temporary set of business processes (BP) which jointly gives rise to the end product of the virtual enterprise (Spinosa et al, 1998; Pereira-Klen at al, 1999).

  When a business process is executed by a virtual enterprise, parts of the decomposition of this BP (i.e., sub-processes) are assigned to different enterprises, becoming a Distributed Business Process (Camarinha-Matos, 2001).

- Distributed Business Process Management (DBPM) offers a new approach and allows organizations to link highly autonomous nodes, such as mobile users or partners, to a seamless process chain. This approach is ideal for manufacturing and supply chain related industries (BPE, 2004; Gensym Co., 2004).

- Collaborative Business Process Management (CBPM) addresses the weaknesses of current process logic models requires expanding the definition of process logic to include both explicit structured flows and the unstructured collaborative flows that characterize how people typically work. CBPM represents a new category of software that breaks down the barrier between the structured and unstructured world of collaboration and BPM. (O'Leonard, 2002).

- Collaborative Process Manager (CPM) supports decentralized, peer-to-peer process management for *inter-enterprise* collaboration at the business process level. A collaborative process is not handled by a centralized workflow engine, but by multiple CPMs, each represents a *player* in the business process. Each CPM is used to schedule, dispatch and control the tasks of the process that the player is responsible for, and the CPMs interoperate through an inter-CPM messaging protocol (Chen et al).

- Federated Business Processes (FBP) are understood as a concept to organise contract-based co-operations between independent organisations, which support the exchange of information, products and services. One of the key advantages of the concept of federation is the hiding of the internal structure of the individual processes and their internal knowledge from the participating organisations as much as possible. Only those objects that are to be exchanged will be disclosed to the collaborators. This means partners still have the freedom to change and improve their processes without violating the co-operation agreements. But to interoperate across organisational boundaries, process interfaces have to be provided that enable the desired exchange (Wagner, 2004).

- Global Process Model (GPM) shows how a process model is distributed. It abstracts details of local process models (Gruhn et al, 1998).

There are several other related definitions that could be included here. The above examples are just to give a flavor of the BP "movement" towards the Collaborative Networked Organization world. In this paper the term that will be adopted for referring to the Meta-BP is: "Distributed Business Process" (DPB) since its definition is in line with the work that has being carried out by the authors during the last years.

The evolution of the DBP is being much faster than one could imagine thanks to the experience gained through the BP history. Although there is still a lack of theoretical foundations as well as consolidations in terms of ICT support for CNOs many efforts surrounding the DBP concept have been done and are moving well forward. In this sense, DBP modeling, DBP implementation, DPB management and others are already a consistent part – in spite of still being "under construction" - of the CNO framework. Researchers will continue their search for standards or, at least, for well-accepted references in the DBP field. This means that the VOM kernel is in good hands. But VOM is not only about managing DBPs. It is also about reacting adequately whenever needed as well as taking decisions.

The next chapter will address these topics and introduce some thoughts on the liberal art of managing dynamic VOs.

4. SOME QUESTIONS AND – PROBABLY - SOME ANSWERS

It is not a trivial task to model something that is considered a "liberal art". How to come out with a VOM Framework? Actually, it is rather difficult to represent something that is dynamic by its nature. In this sense we have to do with two big issues: Management is dynamic; and so do the VOs... At every turn, in the middle of this dynamicity sits the VO Manager who, by the way, has its own way of being.

This means that different VO Managers imply different management styles (even if they rely on the same management elements and on the same enablers). So, if we take the VOM wheel represented in figure 1 and try to see it using the glasses of 3 different VO Managers we would probably get 3 different pictures (figure 2 - middle). It is like looking to the VOM Framework using a Kaleidoscope eye. Every time you turn it you will get different pictures. These pictures represent the VO Manager behaviour or the VO Manager profile (figure 2 – bottom).

All these parameters should be taken into consideration for an adequate VOM. But in order to accomplish this some questions[1] have to be addressed:

- How managers use skills and knowledge acquired in the liberal arts for the design and use of adaptive management systems also referred to as Management Coordination System (MCS)?
- How can the manager profiles and the management elements be combined and used?
- How do we connect all the involved parameters with "different ways on how to manage a VO"?
- Is there a way to define services (i.e. Web Services) and their allocation to specific VOM?
- Should (and if yes how) the services be coordinated or orchestrated in the categories?
- How to integrate the measurement systems that are necessary for communicating goals and objectives and for achieving alignment in adaptive organizations into the design of the MCS?

On the one hand it is clear that a broad range of skills is necessary to manage complexity in intense environments including technical, systems design, measurement, analytical and leadership skills (MGT 344, 2002). On the other hand the challenge remains: how to connect technology and performance measurement, including Internet technology, with knowledge of the humanities and social sciences acquired in the liberal arts?

This section intends to address the above raised questions and to provide some – probably – answers which include the following considerations:

- There is no single/fixed VOM Framework. The VOM framework is fluid/dynamic;
- The DBP management is the kernel of the dynamic VOM framework;
- Management elements – others than DBP management – reinforce the VOM basis. However, there is no complete or correct list of management elements. The management elements can be "elected" (risk, trust, knowledge, and so forth) and combined according to the managers/developers knowledge and/or priorities;
- The development of a MCS set of functions/services for dynamic VOM should focus on management elements in general and on DBP management in particular;

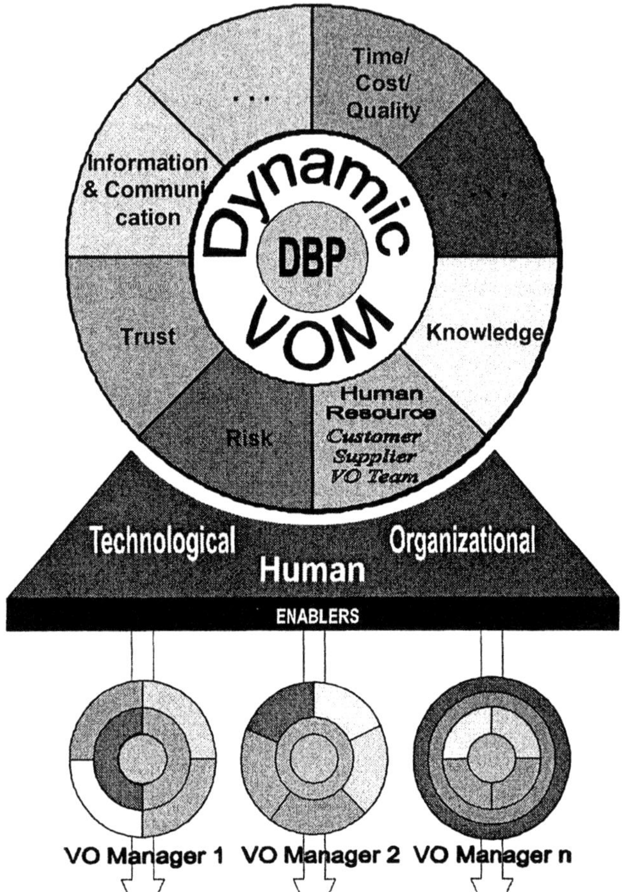

Management Elements / PROFILE	CONSERVATIVE	MODERATE	DARING	OTHERS
DBP	*	*	*	...
TIME /COST /QUALITY	1	1	2	...
KNOWLEDGE	3	2	1	...
HUMAN RESOURCE	3	2	1	...
RISK	1	2	3	...
TRUST	3	2	1	...
INFORMATION & COMMUNICATION	3	2	1	...

*IMPORTANCE: 1 – HIGH, 2 – MEDIUM, 3 – LOW, * KERNEL*

Figure 2: Dynamic VOM framework

- The behaviours of the VO Managers can be mapped with the management elements. In figure 2 the colours as well as the concentric and surface weighting denote the importance of the management elements (high, medium, low) in and for specific VO Managers' profiles (for instance, a "conservative" profile implies that the manager considers the risk management of high importance);
- Weighting the management elements for each manager profile is an exercise that requires knowledge of process as well as of human behaviours and which must be improved / fine tuned along the long-life management process;
- The services provided by the MCS for VOM are classified into Classes: I and II;
- VOM services class I includes all functionalities that support DBP management (to allow organization and coordination of resources as well as supervision and monitoring of activities);
- VOM services class II includes all functionalities that support decision-making and adequate reaction whenever needed including dynamism on negotiation process with adaptive behaviour. Therefore class II is based on the remaining management elements.

For some functionalities of class I, the reader is asked to refer to (Pereira-Klen et al 2002; Rabelo et al, 2002 and 2004). For VOM services class II, 3 possible functionalities[2] are described below:

Mining: "Torture the data till they confess..." The data/text/web bases have sometimes information "treasures". There is some valuable information that is hidden behind the enormous amount of data that are generated along the time. Data/Text/Web Mining allows the exploration and identification of relationships among variables that were originally independent. This potentiality combined with the Business Intelligence paradigm will allow to filter a great amount of data/text stored in the repositories, to establish relations among them as well as to organize and to transform them into useful information. This information, combined with some benchmarking techniques and with an ontology-based standardization, will form a knowledge base which in turn will support managers to take faster and at the same time smarter decisions.

Knowledge Map: The main idea behind this functionality is to take the most advantage possible of the VO cross-functional team. This means that the VO manager would not "just" manage the VO but would also manage knowledge. The VO members need to learn from their experience in a dynamic constellation as well as from the creativity and the intellectual capital from their organizations and from the individuals involved (the humanistic part of the management...). This knowledge which crosses boundaries may create a competitive advantage for the enterprises and may be a market asset for this new working environment. Different and complementary "kinds" of knowledge should be considered: knowledge of clients, of products, of processes, of relations and of businesses (Spinosa, Quandt, 2000). In this sense, all this knowledge extracted from the Knowledge Map should also be added to the knowledge base.

Negotiation (Fuzzy management): This functionality should support the fuzzy management (Filos, 2000) of the Dynamic VOs, acting in the negotiation process as well as helping the VO reconfiguration and in an eventual modification in the DBP contract. Therefore this functionality relies on the two previous ones.

There are many ways to proceed in a negotiation process until an agreement is reached. They are usually made by means of relaxation of some values specified in an "announcement", such as those related with the product tolerance, due date, prices, etc. This functionality should provide the manager with an environment to support an electronic and/or semi-automatic negotiation heavily relying on the knowledge base, on machine learning techniques as well as on DSS (Decision Support Systems) theories.

It is important to note that the knowledge base will encompass knowledge about the management elements (risk, trust, human resource, ICT, and so forth). This means that learning algorithms will be applied to the knowledge base and will be responsible for the 'intelligent processes' on the system suggesting actions to the VO manager (Loss et al, 2005). The possible solutions are given according to the characteristics of the problem and can be ranked by the managers (all managers that had faced similar problems) according to their own profiles. This means that the system will propose possible solutions and will link them with the managers' behaviours and their related efficiency coefficient.

The big deal is to create a reliable knowledge base and to feed it with VOM knowledge. Best practices, benchmarking, and adopted approaches in the VOM area are very few. The way to come out of this handicap seems to be to create a pilot knowledge base in which the experience of researchers will play the most important role. After that, like as for the weighting of the management elements, the knowledge base must be improved and fine tuned along its long-life process.

5. CONCLUSIONS AND NEXT STEPS

The work presented in this paper reflects in part the DBP maturation process, its close and direct relation to the VOM's sustained improvement as well as the awareness that has to be raised around this natural evolution stage. Functionalities to support DBP management – in this paper named as VOM services class I – were already identified, modeled, conceived and - in some cases – developed within the scope of some research projects (PRODNET II, 1999; Damascos, 2001; MyFashion, 2004). However functionalities to support the whole VOM framework and its dynamicity – VOM services class II - are missing.

The authors believe that a human-supervised VOM system can include the so-called class II functionalities which will grant to the system a personalized flavour. It is expected that this research path crosses in sometime not very far the path of the Ambient Intelligence vision (Pereira-Klen et al, 2005). But before that some further questions have to be addressed. Out of them two are of immediate priority: how can we bring in and integrate to this personalized VOM system the performance indicators? And, while waiting for the ambient intelligence space, how will we train VO Managers in the liberal art of managing VOs?

Acknowledgments

This work was supported in part by the IST FP-6 IP ECOLEAD project (www.ecolead.org) funded by the European Commission as well as by the IFM project (www.ifm.org.br) funded by the Brazilian Council for Research and Scientific Development - CNPq.

[1] Questions raised by the ECOLEAD WP3 team as well as by the course: "Adaptive Management Systems: Management as a Liberal Art"- MGT 344, held at the Drucker School of Management - Claremont Graduate University – Spring 2002

[2] These functionalities, identified in recent research projects according to end-users' requirements, are under development and should improve the Cockpit prototype developed by UFSC. The currently available functionalities of the prototype allow the managing of DBPs of Virtual Organizations by means of monitoring and supervision activities.

6. REFERENCES

1. BPE - Business Process Excellence. Web page: http://www.ids-scheer.com/usa/press/26175 - accessed in July, 19, 2004.
2. Camarinha-Matos, L. M.; Afsarmanesh, H.; Kaletas, E. C. ; Cardoso, T.; Service Federation in Virtual Organizations. In *Proceedings of The Eleventh International IFIP TC5 WG-5.2--WG-5.3 Conference (PROLAMAT 2001)*, 2001.
3. Camarinha-Matos, L. M.; Execution system for distributed business processes in a virtual enterprise. In: Future Generation Computer Systems 17 (2001) 1009–1021
4. Capó, J, Masiá E, Lario FC. "Inter-Organizational Knowledge Management. The Importance of Organizational and Environmental Context". Book: Virtual Enterprises and Collaborative Networks. ISBN 1-4020-8138-3, Kluver Academic Publishers, 2004.
5. Chen, Q.; Hsu, M.; Inter-Enterprise Collaborative Business Process Management. HP Labs, Hewlett Packard Co. qchen@hpl.hp.com
6. Damascos, 2001. http://www.inescporto.pt/~damascos/
7. Drucker, Peter. Management Challenges for the 21st Century, Harper Business, 1999.
8. Drucker, Peter. The Essential Drucker. HarperCollins, ISBN: 0066210879, 2001.
9. Drucker, Peter. The New Realities. Harper & Row, 1989, p. 231
10. Filos E.; Banahan E. "Will the Organisation disappear? The Challenges of the New Economy and Future Perspectives". Book: E-Business and Virtual Enterprises, Kluver Academic Publishers, 2000.
11. Geber A, Althaus K, Dietzsch M, Weidlich D, Steiner R. "Risk-Management of Product Development in Non-Hierarchical Regional Production Networks". Book: Virtual Enterprises and Collaborative Networks. ISBN 1-4020-8138-3, Kluver Academic Publishers, 2004.
12. Gensym Corporation and WebV2 Join Forces to Offer Rule-Intensive Solutions for Distributed Business Process Management. Web page: http://www.webv2.com/pr/040414_Gensym.html - accessed in July, 19, 2004.
13. Gruhn, V.; Wellen, U.; From Business Process Models to Distributed Software Architecture. In Proceedings of the third International Workshop on Software Architecture, pages 53--56, 1998.
14. Guide to Business and Information Modeling for the Development of Edifice Implementation Kits. http://www.edifice.org/REP/bigguide.pdf
15. Karolak, DW. "Global Software Development – Managing Virtual Teams and Environments". Los Alamitos, IEEE Computer Society, 1998
16. Loss, L.; Rabelo, R.; Pereira-Klen, A.A., 2005. For an Intelligent Decision Support System for Supply Chain Management. To appear in CIRP 2005 Conference. May, 2005 – Florianopolis, Brazil.
17. Malhotra, Yogesh. "Knowledge Management and New Organizations Forms: A Framework for Business Model Innovation". Book: Knowledge Management and Virtual Organizations. ISBN 1-878289-73-X, Idea Group Publishing, 2000.
18. MGT 344. Drucker School of Management - Claremont Graduate University – Spring 2002.

19. MyFashion, 2004. http://www.myfashion.org/ and/or http://www.fir.rwth-aachen.de/projektseiten/myfashion/
20. O'Leonard, J.; Business Process Logic: Half Empty or Half Full? December 02, 2002. http://www.bijonline.com/Article.asp?ArticleID=629&DepartmentID=7
21. Pereira-Klen, A. A.; Klen, E. R.; Loss, L. 2005. Challenging Scenario: Dynamic Supply Chains Supported by Ambient Intelligence System. To appear in CIRP 2005 Conference. May, 2005 – Florianopolis, Brazil.
22. Pereira-Klen, A. A.; Rabelo, R. J.; 2002. Business Intelligence Support for Supply Chain Management. In: Balanced Automations Systems in Manufacturing and Services (BASYS'02). Knowledge and Technology Integration in Production and Services. (Sep. 25-27,2002: Cancun, Mexico). *Proceedings*, p. 437-444.
23. Pereira-Klen, A. A.; Rabelo, R. J.; Spinosa, L. M.; Ferreira, A. C.; Distributed Business Process Management. In: working Conference on Infrastructures for Virtual Enterprises (PRO'VE 99). Infrastructures for Virtual Enterprises. Networking Industrial Enterprises (27-28.: Oct. 1999: Porto, Portugal). Proceedings. Porto, Portugal. p. 241-258.
24. PMBOK, 2000, - A Guide to the Project Management Body of Knowledge (PMBOK Guide). Project Management Institute. Four Campus Boulevard. Newton Square, USA.
25. Prodnet II, 1999. http://www.uninova.pt/~prodnet/
26. Rabelo, R. J.; Pereira-Klen, A. A.; Klen, E. R.; 2002. A Multi-Agent System for Smart Coordination of Dynamic Supply Chains. In: Infrastructures for Virtual Enterprises (PRO-VE'02). Collaborative Business Ecosystems and Virtual Enterprises. (May 1-3. 2002: Sesimbra, Portugal). *Proceedings*, p. 379-386.
27. Rabelo, R. J.; Pereira-Klen, A. A.; Klen, E. R.; 2004. Effective Management of Dynamic and Multiple Supply Chains. In: International Journal of Networking and Virtual Organizations. Vol. 2. n. 3. p. 193-208.
28. Spinosa, L. M.; Rabelo, R. J.; Pereira-Klen, A. A.; High-Level Coordination of Business Processes in a Virtual Enterprise. Prolamat'98 / The Tenth International IFIP TC5 WG-5.2 WG-5.3 Conference Trento, Itália
29. Spinosa LM. Quandt C. "An IT-based framework for Knowledge Management in Networked Organizations". Book: E-Business and Virtual Enterprises, Kluver Academic Publishers, 2000.
30. The ebXML Collaborative Business Processes. Web Page: http://www.schlegel.li/ebXML/linmagau_article/www/node6.html
31. Wagner, K. Schwarzenbacher. Föderative Unternehmensprozesse - Technologien, Standards und Perspektiven für vernetzte Systeme (Federated Business Processes - Technologies, Standards and Perspectives of Network Systems), (in German), Siemens, Publicis Corporate Publishing, Erlangen, 2004, ISBN 3-89578-231-9

24 IMPROVING CLIENT SERVICE RELIABILITY IN COLLABORATIVE SUPPLY CHAINS: A MAS SCHEDULER

Pedro Gómez, Raúl Rodriguez, Rubén Darío Franco and Angel Ortiz
Research Centre on Production Management and Engineering
Polytechnic University of Valencia
Camino de Vera S/N. Edificio 8G, Acceso D Planta 1°
Tel. (+34) 96.387.96.80/Fax: (+34) 96.387.76.89
{pgomez | raulr_|_dfranco | aortiz}@cigip.upv.es

The theory of network coordination provides a theoretical basis to explain how companies can overcome organizational boundaries and constraints to jointly manage business processes across supply chains. In particular, this paper focuses on Collaborative Scheduling, a collaboration process whereby Supply Chain trading partners activate on-line inter-firm coordination mechanisms to jointly plan key activities, from production and delivery of raw materials to production and delivery of final products to end customers.
By discussing a case study of ceramic tile the paper provides a theoretical framework that contributes to explaining the relations between inter-firm coordination mechanisms and the characteristics of interdependence among the actors involved in the implementation. To automate the coordination process a generalized agent-based framework that uses negotiation to dynamically schedule events is presented. Events can be created dynamically and event may potentially require collaboration or resources from one or more other actors/agents. The allocation of resources to the event will be negotiated iteratively until a compromise is found. The framework consists of a user preference model, an evaluation or utility function, and a negotiation protocol.

1. INTRODUCTION

This paper presents an introduction to the problematic of order management within extended collaborative selling chains (ECOSELL), and an identification of the objectives and requirements of this environment. Then, the main operations to be considered at the ECOSELL context are order planning, scheduling and monitoring, whose final goal is to meet the delivery date agreed with final customers.
Therefore, a proposal about the different roles of the actors and main processes detected within this ECOSELL environment is presented. Finally, a Multi-Agent System (MAS) architecture is introduced for dealing with the described problem.

2. SUPPLY CHAIN COLLABORATION

Nowadays, globalisation and enhanced national, European and worldwide competitiveness have promoted the creation and consolidation of the so-called EE, which transcend the single enterprise domain and build meta-enterprises [3].

Most existing EE have initially focused on reinforcing the links and flows between companies that are involved in the same value chain [6]. However, recently, the phenomenon has shifted toward the creation of EE that cross the barriers of a single value chain, and link different complementary value chains building collaborative selling chains. Many industrial companies have wanted to or have been selling and distributing jointly their aggregated products for a long time and now face the challenge of the complete integration of their value chains. [2].

This move from the meta-enterprise to the meta-value chain can be easily explained. In a world where the customer has become the new king, companies have to be fully customer-oriented, -customised and -governed in order to maintain their competitive advantage [4]. The starting point of any meta-value chain winning approach is consequently collaboration, where the concepts inherently implies agility and learn to learn capacity [7]

The selling chain focuses on the management of orders life cycle, from the initial order placement to the delivery and provision of physical goods, covering the part of the value chain that goes from manufacturers to end customers (including logistics platforms/operators, distribution, intermediaries, resellers and retailers). The order promising process comprises the set of activities that are triggered in order to give a response to the customer order requirements.

3. COLLABORATIVE PROCESSES IN THE ECOSELL FRAMEWORK

The business processes considered in this study include order planning, scheduling, and monitoring. The goal of these processes is the fulfilment of requested orders on agreed time (see Figure 1).

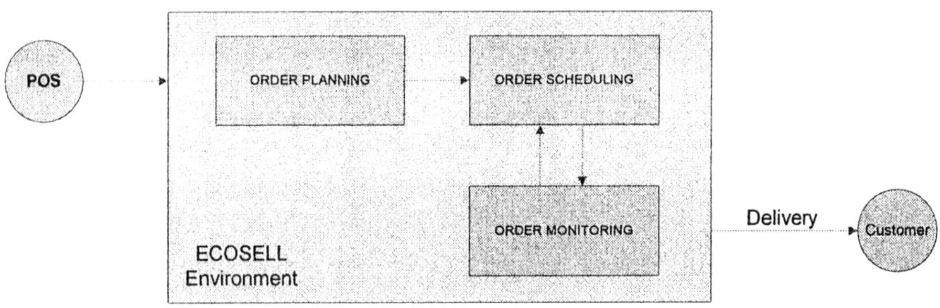

Figure 1 - ECOSELL environment

The Ecosell Environment must deal with a set of interrelated business processes, which are briefly described next:

1) Order planning: Customers look for packaged products in one Point of Sales (PoS). This process takes into account availability, capacity, constrains and stock already available in some store, in order to prepare the "installation program".
2) Order Scheduling: With such a calendar on hand, the system must check the requirements of the customer order at every distribution point (places with physical availability of products or available capacity for manufacturing it), always taking into account the specific conditions of the order (dates, capacity or costs).
3) Order Monitoring: The order's life cycle ends when the products that constitute the product pack are delivered to the customer. In the middle, several events may affect the original schedule (delays, temporary incapacity, quality problems). If one of these circumstances affects the "critical path" of the order, the system must initialize a re-scheduling process in order to allocate new dates on available capacities.

Then, the scenario of the problem can be depicted as follows (see Figure 2):

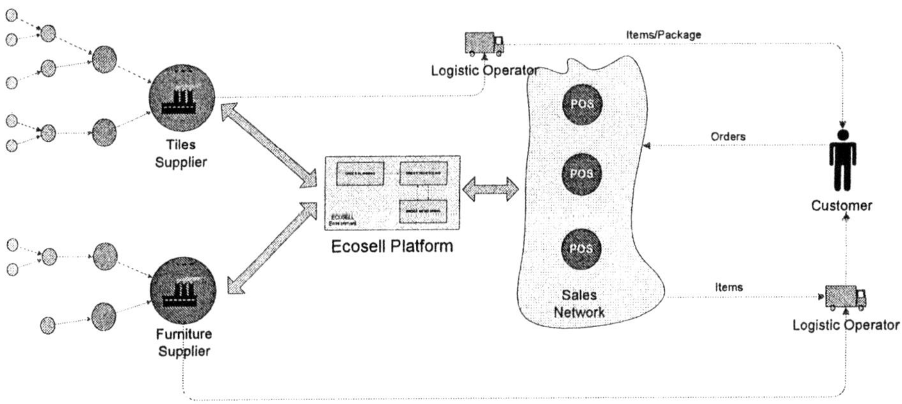

Figure 2 - Actors involved in the Ecosell Environment

This scenario presents a set of characteristics that highly increase the degree of complexity when proceeding to model it as:

- Companies must work cooperatively to properly coordinate decentralized scheduling activities for all SC involved because all of them may have heterogeneous scheduling systems
- The uncertainty about the actual "situation" in individual plants has to be regarded.
- Interdependencies between production processes that are performed in different plants have to be regarded.
- Existing (local) scheduling systems for individual plants that accomplish the local realisation of global requirements should be integrated.

4. MULTI AGENT SYSTEMS AS SUPPORT OF EXTENDED COLLABORATION

Conducting business transactions over the Internet is a well-known issue today (for projects and research trends see [10]), which has been addressed in vast research works. One of the most promising enabling technologies are those represented by the combination of human and system tasks in solving complex tasks [8].

All these features of the problem can be well addressed by an agent-supported ICT infrastructure. In fact, huge research work has been done in this sense, applying these concepts to several domains [1], [5]]. The main characteristics are:

- Decentralised and local task processing: Agents enable the automated distribution of formerly centralised programmes.
- Flexibility: On-demand software distribution / service provisioning – service.
- Automation of distributed task processing: Agents have got itineraries that determine what tasks they have to perform where without any user interaction.
- Reduction of network traffic and client processing power: Since massive data exchanges are locally handled at the nodes hosting, the data and client computers could concentrate on performing only limited local tasks,

Next section introduces an innovative approach by applying Multi-Agent System principles when product-packs are sold through a Sales Network and effective and efficient mechanisms of negotiation and co-ordination for assuring proper order fulfilment are demanded.

5. CASE STUDY

This case study focuses on the order management process of the bathroom product. The goal is to sell product-packs, which can be constituted by ceramic tiles, furniture, bathroom fittings and lamps.

5.1 Conceptual Description

The process starts when a final customer walks into a selling point and identifies a conjoint of products that might constitute a product-pack for his bathroom. Such items must be delivered and installed at the customer's house by accomplishing a calendar, which must respect the following constraints:

(1) The range of delivery dates facilitated by the customer.

(2) The dependencies between the operations of installation of every product. There is a graph of dependencies that determines both the sequence and the relationships among the items.

(3) To minimise the time frame between the starting operation and the final installation at the customer's house.

The order management system must find a proper solution for every particular case according to the above stated constraints. It must also solve unexpected events by carrying out re-scheduling operations that respect the promised delivery date or, if it is not possible, to come up with a close one in time.

It is established as objectives for each offer to maximise B (Equation 1) and to minimise nweeks, where B is the sum of Bi (Equation 2), the obtained final benefit from each product, and nweeks is the number of weeks between the best delivery date (proposed by the customer) and the delivery of the pack-product. Equation 3 illustrates the proposed objective function.

(Eq. 1) $B = \sum_i B_i$

(Eq. 2) $B_i = \left(SP - \sum C\right)$, where PS is the fixed selling price (official) and C the total cost (from suppliers and carriers).

(Eq. 3) $f = \dfrac{\sum_i B_i}{nweeks}$

Table I shows an example of how the different values from the objective function change according to the benefits gained by each item and the worst delivery date that comes from the item with the worst time of response. The first row shows the results of the first petition (petition without re-scheduling).

Scheduling conditions:
Minimum Benefits: 500 Euros
Number of weeks from now: 10 weeks

	Function Value	Ceramic Tile	Bathroom Fittings	Furniture	Lamps
Initial Offers	Benefit: 1200 D. date: 6w F=200	Benefit: 350€ D. Date: 6 w.	Benefit : 200€ D. Date: 3 w.	Benefit: 500€ D. Date: 6 w.	Benefit: 150€ D. Date: 2 w.
Negotiation process on 2 steps	Benefit: 650 D. date: 3w F=216,7		Benefit : 200€ D. Date: 3 w.	Benefit: 300€ D. Date: 3 w.	Benefit: 150€ D. Date: 2 w.
	Benefit: 850 D. date: 3w F=283,3	Benefit: 200€ D. Date: 3 w.	Benefit : 200€ D. Date: 3 w.	Benefit: 300€ D. Date: 3 w.	Benefit: 150€ D. Date: 2 w.
Negotiation process aborted	Benefit: 250 D. date: 2w F=125			Benefit: 100€ D. Date: 2 w.	Benefit: 150€ D. Date: 2 w.

Table I. An example of the evolution of the objective function, in a process of negotiation.

The rows 2 and 3 show the first negotiation process in a two-steps process. The step 1 selects the item (furniture), it has the worst delivery time but provides the highest time of response, asking then for an offer with re-scheduling. The representative item answers with a delivery date of 3 weeks, reducing the benefit to 300€. As it is observed that this offer supposes an increment over the objective function (still without checking the ceramic tile's contribution), it is not rejected, establishing the second step for the offer negotiation with the ceramic tile representative. In the last row, it is aimed to carry on with the improvement of the objective function, starting to negotiate with the item that more benefit provides after the last round. The negotiation process is cancelled since it cannot either overpass the last value of the objective function nor to reach the minimum objective of 500€. Therefore, the two last negotiated offers are accepted: furniture (-300€, 3 weeks), ceramic tile (-200€, 3 weeks).

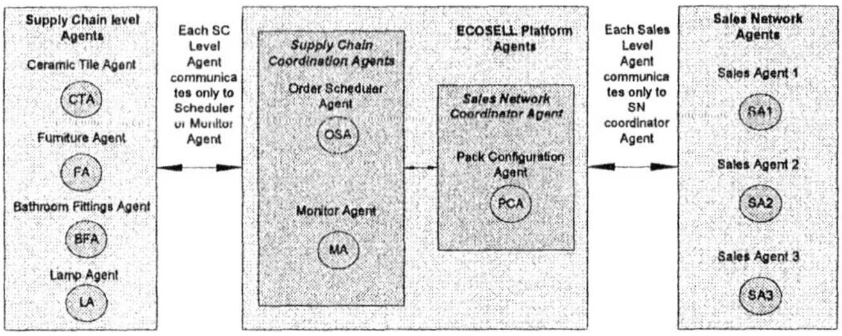

Figure 3 - Multiagent System Architecture

5.2 Mapping the organization and Roles to Multi-agents Architecture

In this case study, an ECOSELL environment is represented by a multi-agent system. In our case, each actor is represented by an agent. The agents created can be seen in figure 3.

Pack Configuration Agent

The Pack Configuration agent is the responsible for coordinating the order with the user interface agent (generator of an enquiry offer) and with the rest of agents. The Pack Configuration agent asks for the rest of selling points for asking about inventory levels from others warehouses; and also with the order scheduler agent for asking for the production of some item.

Order Scheduling Agent

The Order scheduler agent asks offer from the supply chain level agents for completing the offer already sent by the pack configuration agent. Then, it initiates a process of improving the received offers until to reach an adequate offer regarding the value of the objective function to be maximised.

Monitoring Agent

Finally, the Monitoring Agent is responsible of receiving from the supply chain level agent those events that could have relation with the different compromised orders.

5.3 Order Scheduler Agent-Supply Chain Level Agents Relationship

The Scheduler will ask from the supply chain agent offers enquiries for assessing them in its programme algorithm and then either to accept or to reject them. Two main difficulty levels within the SC level agents are distinguished when answering an order enquiry:

- When the supply chain agent does not carry out any sort of re-scheduling operations between its programs.
- When the supply chain agent allows assessing options that suppose re-scheduling. In this case, a change is forced, which can or cannot have consequences for other customer and which can suppose a higher cost in the offer.

5.4 Order Scheduler Agent – Supply Chain Level Agent: Negotiation Process
Finally the activity diagram showed in Fig. 4 represents the scheduler agent negotiating with all the SC level agents. The key actions stated in our algorithm are the steps enumerated in Figure 4.

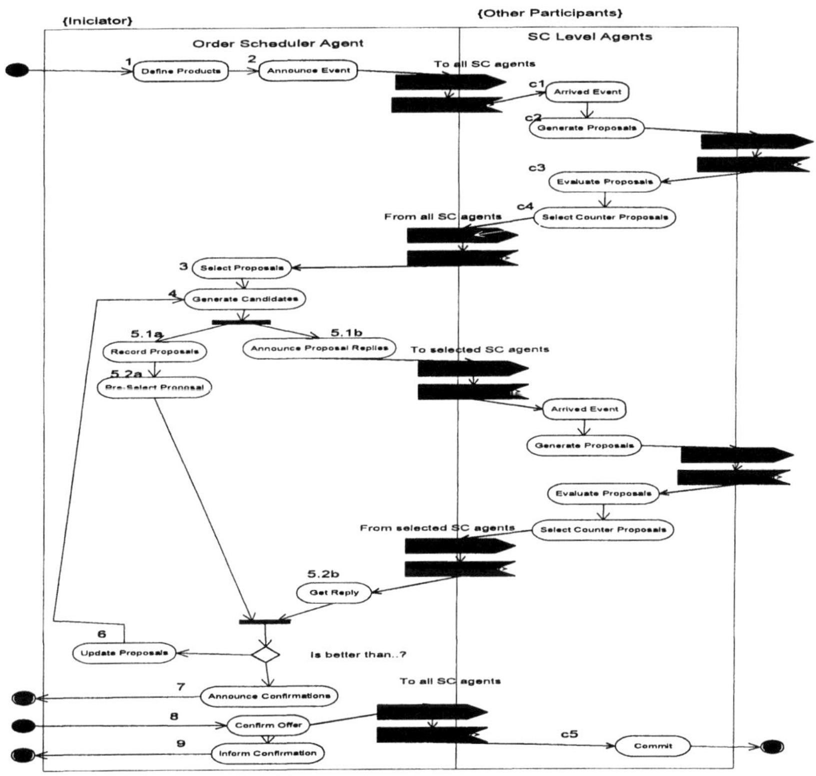

Figure 4. UML Activity Diagram of the Negotiation Algorithm.

6. CONCLUSIONS

Customers are acquiring more buying power as they access to more reliable and complete information about products. Nowadays, buying experiences requires mores skills form sales people. Points of sales are demanding more efficient tools to properly react to always evolving customer's needs.

This paper has presented an introduction to the problematic of order management within extended collaborative selling chains (ECOSELL), where an identification of the objectives and requirements necessary of this environment. Then, the main operations at the ECOSELL context (order planning, scheduling and monitoring) that need to be addresses were introduced. Therefore, a proposal about the different roles of the actors and main process detected within this ECOSELL environment was identified.

A Multi-Agent System (MAS) architecture was introduced for dealing with the described problems, focusing on the scheduler function and on the negotiation processes of such MAS with the different actors form the different supply chains in order to reach competitive offers.

Acknowledgements

This paper is based on researching developed within the EU-founded ECOSELL project (GRD1-2001-40692).

REFERENCES

1. Baker, A., Van Dyke Parunak, H. and Kutluhan Erol(1999)."Agents and The Internet: Infrastructure for Mass Customization". IEEE Internet Computing, Vol 3, N° 5

2. Burton, T.T. and Boeder, S.M (2003): The Lean Extended Enterprise: Moving Beyond the Four Walls to Value Stream Excellence. J. Ross Publishing, Inc. Florida.

3. Dyer, J. H. (2000), Collaborative Advantage: Winning Through Extended Enterprise Supplier Networks. Oxford University Press. New York.

4. Goranson, H.T. (1999)," The Agile Virtual Enterprise. Cases, Metrics, Tools", Quorum Books.

5. Kim, K., Paulson, B. Jr., and Petrie, Ch. Jr, (1999). "Agent-Based Electronic Markets for Project Supply Chain Coordination". Papers from the AAAI Workshop. Technical Report WS-00-04.

6. Macbeth, (1998), Partnering Strategy Implementation in the Supply Chain, Strategic Management of the Manufacturing Value Chain, Bittici U., Carrie A. (Edits.) Kluwer

7. Meier, J. (1995), The importance of relationship management in establishing successful interorganizational systems, Journal of Strategic Information Systems, Volume 4, Issue 2, pp. 135-148

8. Papazoglou, M. (2001). "Agent-oriented technology in support of e-business". Communications of the ACM. Vol 44, N° 4

9. Papazoglou, M.P., Laufmann, S. and Sellis, T.K. (1992) An organizational framework for cooperating intelligent information systems. International Journal of Cooperative Information Systems 1, 1.

10. Virtual Organizations Forum (2004). Research projects and issues. Reachable at www.virtual-organization.net.

25

SECURITY CONTROLS IN COLLABORATIVE BUSINESS PROCESSES

Jochen Haller, Yücel Karabulut, Philip Robinson
SAP Research, CEC Karlsruhe
Vincenz-Priessnitz-Str. 1
76131 Karlsruhe, Germany
[jochen.haller | yuecel.karabulut | philip.robinson]@sap.com

Virtual Organisations (VOs) are collaborative environments, encompassing different autonomous partners responding to a business opportunity with a focus on automation and flexibility. These are the sort of scenarios researched specifically in the EU IST project TrustCoM. Collaborative business processes are identified as the integrating component bringing together other required VO components and subsystems such as a policy infrastructure or contract management while still meeting the requirements regarding flexibility. eBusiness in such a complex, evolving environment as the one encountered in VOs can only prosper with an integrated security model, supporting various classes of VOs or catering for VOs forming in different business segments, for instance aggregated service provisioning or collaborative engineering. Such an integrated security model has to take the integrating component, collaborative business processes into account as well. This contribution deals particularly with the security model on the VO's enterprise layer. A business process model, offering means to controllably expose organisation internal processes is extended to interface with other security and contract management related VO subsystems (such as the policy infrastructure). The extended business process model supports process context aware security controls for and towards those subsystems within executable collaborative process instances.

1. INTRODUCTION

In today's economy, in many business areas, collaboration between organisations is becoming an essential requirement to meet business objectives. Collaboration between organisations typically involves extended negotiations between humans in order to come to terms with, for instance, a set of legal documents, formalising the collaboration in contractual form. Depending on the type of business objective, the collaboration has to be reflected to a varying extent on the Information and Communication Technology (ICT) layer as well. Some collaborations only require the exchange of simple communication, such as orders and invoices between collaborating partners' financial systems, while others require greater interaction like connecting supply chains across the administrative boundaries of organisations. In many business areas, speed and flexibility to adapt to dynamic situations is an important requirement to gain an edge on competitors. Involving supporting technologies from the ICT environment will help to meet these requirements.

In the above described ecosystem, the EU funded FP6 research project TrustCoM[1] investigates such collaborative environments which are termed as Virtual Organisations (VOs). A VO is defined as a temporary or permanent coalition of geographically dispersed individuals, groups, organisational units or entire organisations that pool resources, capabilities and information to achieve common business objectives. Since such a collaboration involves a great deal of exposure, in terms of an organisation exposing parts of its administrative domain, for instance confidential data or organisation-internal business processes, security requirements are of major concern. To make things even more complicated, otherwise independent organisations may even participate in more than one VO at a time where the VOs are in direct competition with each other. The presented work focuses on organisations participating in a VO, where their collaboration is covered by a contractual VO agreement. The inclusion and integration of Trusted Third Parties and external parties is not discussed within this paper. Neverthless, TrustCoM distinguishes different aspects of security and their management by the general term "TSC – Trust, Security and Contract – management".

- Trust - The collaboration has to be conducted in a reliable and dependable environment with partners having the same properties throughout the collaboration, e.g. based on reputation values.
- Security - The collaboration environment has to meet the security requirements of all participating partners and offer controls to monitor, adapt and enforce such requirements throughout the collaboration.
- Contracts - Contracts formalise the collaboration between partners and contract terms have to be enforced and monitored throughout the collaboration.

TrustCoM aims at developing a framework for enabling trusted, secure business collaborations in on-demand created, self-managed, scalable and highly dynamic Virtual Organisations.

Current VOs are supported in their collaborative efforts by at least partly available mechanisms on the service layer [10][11][12][13]. Currently missing is a strategy to coordinate these mechanisms. For example, consider the activation of a compensation mechanism, when a confidentiality requirement during enactment of a business transaction is violated using the optimal, minimal set of web service technology standards. How would this be specified using today's standards?

In this work, business processes on the top enterprise layer are foreseen as an integrating component, allowing for the optimal combination and configuration of service based TSC management mechanisms. Allowing for the business process to control TSC management on the service layer, we extended the chosen process model of Schulz et al. [7] by a so-called TSC task and a TSC context on the process level. In this paper we present the initial results of the extended collaborative business process model.

The rest of the paper is organized as follows. Section 2 presents the basic process model and introduces the Collaborative Business Process (CBP) model, including the description of the modelling methodology as far as necessary for the comprehension of the TSC task model. Section 3 exhibits the TSC management support in the CBP model and introduces the TSC task. Finally, section 4 analyses

---

[1] http://www.eu-trustcom.com

the related work, followed by section 5 concluding and providing an outlook on future work.

2. COLLABORATIVE BUSINESS PROCESSES

We introduce the Collaborative Business Process Model and the related modelling methodology in three phases, tailored for VOs. The following sections aim at executable Business Processes (BPs) which are executed at runtime in a business process execution engine.

2.1 Process Model

Business Process Management subsystem in TrustCoM plays a central role among other subsystems, such as the policy and monitoring subsystems, such that the modelling technique for business processes was chosen carefully to be aligned with the models created of other subsystems. Business processes are essentially comprised of tasks or activities executed in a coordinated order. The outcome or result of a task is able to influence the subsequent order of tasks in the process enactment. This ordering of tasks is represented as transitions between tasks. As depicted in Figure 1: Basic Process Model, business processes are modelled as UML activity diagrams [16].

The following components are the essential building blocks of processes:

Task: A task is the atomic business process component, describing an activity or altering the process' control flow, for instance splitting or joining the process flow. A process may contain different layers of detail. In the process model, a task can be an anchor or placeholder for a (sub-) process on a higher level of detail.

Transition or Arc: A transition is the second atomic business process component, connecting tasks with each other. Therefore, a transition always has a source and a destination. A transition is always unidirectional.

Figure 1: Basic Process Model illustrates the composition of the basic components in a simple business process. The diagram also contains a dedicated "begin" and "end" task. The process model can be visualised as a directed graph which is similar to the Business Process Modelling Notation (BPMN) [13] or various other established graphical BP modelling notations.

Figure 1: Basic Process Model

2.2 Collaborative Business Process Model

This basic model is extended to a process model catering for business process collaborations across administrative domains in a VO. The extension is based on work conducted in [7] on business process views in CBPs.

The following three classes of business processes are distinguished and modelled in three different phases of the derived modelling methodology:

Collaboration Definition Phase: The *Collaborative Business Process (CBP)* is the process describing the (message) choreography among different VO partners on the highest level of detail in the VO. The CBP describes the way to meet the business objective.

Distribution Phase: *External Business Processes (or View Processes)* are derived from the collaborative business process. They map to tasks in a CBP assigned to one particular partner in the collaboration.

Deployment Phase: Since highly optimised and tailored *internal (private) business processes* are assets of VO participants, these processes have to be protected. In the deployment phase views and internal processes are mapped to each other, including modelling rules to ensure consistency between both. Collaboration in a VO means that such assets like internal business processes have to be exposed in some way, but not necessarily in an uncontrolled fashion when they are required to contribute to the VO business objective. Views are in this respect the exposure technique for internal processes and are deployed in the administrative domains of assigned partners.

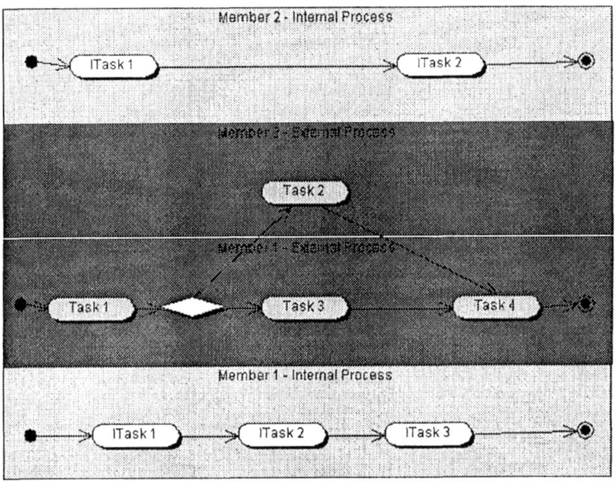

Figure 2: Basic concept of Deployment Modelling

Figure 2: Basic concept of Deployment Modelling shows a simple example of two collaborating partners with private business processes (outer swim-lanes) and associated views (external processes in inner swim-lanes). The CBP is not shown since such a choreography description is not required for enactment. In this example Member 1 chooses to expose all three internal tasks (iTask[1-3] in lowest swim-lane and corresponding Task[1-3] in swim-lane above) to the VO. The corresponding process view shows a mapping of all three tasks. Member 2 on the other hand wants to hide its two internal tasks (iTask[1,2] in top swim-lane). It only exposes the view task "Task 2", representing its two internal tasks, to outside administrative domains.

The described process model addresses security requirements in VO business process collaborations on a very basic level. Only exposure/privacy of entire private processes is addressed, which is not enough for realizing secure dynamic VOs. Secure business process enactment in a VO requires a more flexible security model that can dynamically react to events from other VO subsystems altering the process flow during runtime. Such events may originate from the monitoring subsystem, generating notification events, or policy subsystem allowing adapted policies. The TSC task in the following section introduces a conceptual model created at design time of the business process to meet TSC requirements even during business process runtime.

3. TSC REQUIREMENTS IN COLLABORATIVE BUSINESS PROCESSES

The following TSC requirements are identified in TrustCoM and the mechanisms addressing those requirements are provisioned by different VO subsystems. The implementations of those mechanisms and functionalities are hidden behind a web service interface and can be invoked by task activities from within the business process level. The actual invocation is conducted by a so-called TSC task, an introduced BP modelling extension described in the following section.

Contract Management
Contracts in the form of Service Level Agreements (SLAs) play a central role in the set up and administration of a VO. Most parameters for VO management processes are derived from SLAs even during business process runtime in an automatic fashion.

Policy Management
Besides the basic message security requirements, authentication, authorization, integrity, confidentiality and non-repudiation, policies are an integral part to declare and specify more complex security requirements. Policies facilitate the understanding and enforcement of declared TSC requirements across and within administrative domains.

Trust Management
The concept of trust in TrustCoM mainly deals with reputation. During runtime, trust levels of e.g. VO participants have to be verifiable. Therefore, the notion of trust is based on reliable behaviour of partners participating in the VO. In case of erratic or unexpected partner behaviour, differences are measured against the expected behaviour fixed in an agreed upon contract.

3.1 The TSC Task

The TSC Task is an initially generic, neutral task that is modelled at design time in the collaborative business process whenever a TSC specific functionality during later process runtime is required. The specific task functionality, called a TSC extension role, can be assigned in either one of above described BP modelling phases (see section 2.2), or even deduced at runtime.
A TSC Extension Role is a TSC specific functionality to be assumed by a TSC task in the scope of a collaborative business process. Specific TSC functionalities lie in the area of above identified TSC requirements. TSC Extension Roles can be classified into trust, security and contract management or monitoring related functionalities, shown by their service interfaces on the service layer in Figure 3: TSC Task. The latter is emphasised because the previous subsystems report notifications through a monitoring subsystem and affect TSC Extension Role assignments during process instance runtime.

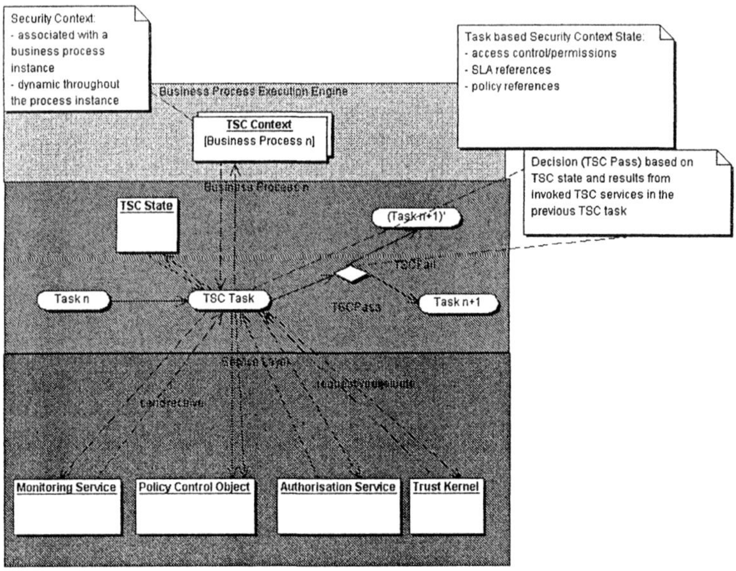

Figure 3: TSC Task

3.2 TSC Context

The TSC context captures the overall state of a business process instance and is used by the TSC task to fulfil its TSC extension role. The TSC context includes BP security control related metadata such as references to active policies or SLA's and provides interfaces to TSC Services like policy control object or SLA parser.

TSC extension roles are reflected in the TSC context content associated to a process instance. The TSC context content is the decision basis for TSC related control decisions during BP enactment, such as authorization, monitoring or policy adaptation decisions.

The TSC state captures, depending on the process configuration, the control decision relevant TSC context subset for a particular TSC task instance. Fields in the TSC context are conceptually modelled as task attributes. TSC tasks are intended to be used only locally, within one administrative domain and the lifetime of a particular TSC context instance is bound to the lifetime of a process instance. The TSC context by itself is designed not to contain confidential or security critical data, it is merely referencing such data, for instance active policies or access control lists which in turn are properly handled by their respective subsystems.

Figure 4: Business Process Component Classes summarises the described components and shows the overall UML information model of the presented work.

The upper half of the diagram shows standard building blocks of business processes, such as activities. Also, these building blocks are only shown on a higher level of abstraction. In more concrete business process models several elements would be refined and described in more detail.

The lower part illustrates the dependencies of the three phased modelling methodology and the TSC task (called also chameleon task) with related concepts in more details.

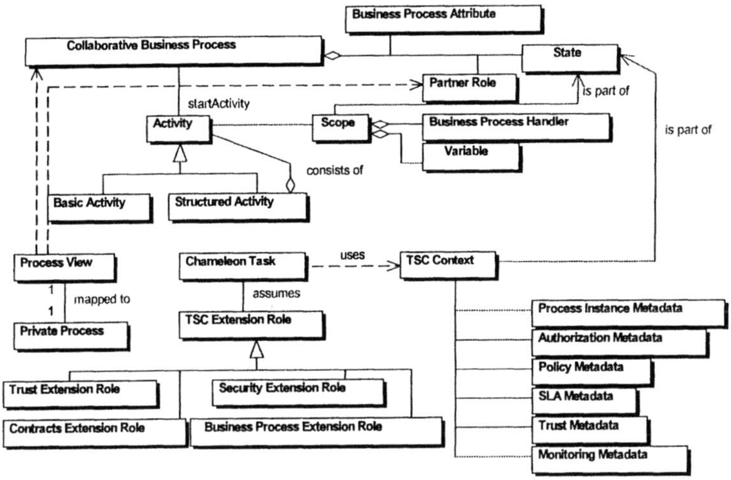

Figure 4: Business Process Component Classes

4. RELATED WORK

As mentioned above, the work introduced in this publication extends a collaborative business process model by Schulz et al. [7]. This work explicitly states security considerations as a high priority open issue. The authors of [8] and [9] independently worked on a view based process model and provide means to expose private processes, as a whole, in a controlled fashion to collaborating partners. This work still lacks an integrative component for process collaboration across administrative domains.

Executable processes in particular are addressed in [4] and [5], stating security requirements within business processes during enactment on the granularity of tasks, but focussing on authorisation. A generic model for more general security or even TSC requirements is not provided.

The work in [2] and [3] also remains with security as an authorization problem, but introduces already a SOA. The BPs are conceptually located on top of a (Web) Service Layer.

Different standards are available to model executable business processes. In [1] and [6] authors focus on BPs specified in the Business Process Execution Language (BPEL) [17] and addresses security requirements expressed as policies. BPEL specified processes, by language definition, require a SOA underneath and this work extends the scope of security requirements from authorisation decisions to policy requirements by means of service standards such as WS-(Security)Policy [12].

5. FUTURE WORK AND CONCLUSION

We introduced a conceptual model of the so-called TSC task addressing Trust, Security and Contract Management requirements in Collaborative Business Processes. The TSC Task leverages security related subsystems on a service layer by providing security controls within business processes. The TSC Task is embedded in an also described BP model and methodology.

The described work is not yet complete and has to be considered as a snapshot of ongoing work. The BP modelling is conducted within the TrustCoM project as a continuous effort throughout the entire project lifetime of three years. This snapshot was taken after the first year of work.

The next steps will include a refinement of the deployment model, including conflict resolution when TSC tasks are inserted in the three methodology phases and when TSC Extension roles are assigned. An initial TSC Context specification is already available, but has to be refined and evaluated against the TSC subsystems. An interesting development is pursued by including (a subset of) the TSC Context in the synchronisation messages of enacted process views across domain using standards such as WS-Coordination [13]. An implementation of the CBP model and methodology is under construction, comprised of a modelling tool and BP engine, which will be tested in the TrustCoM framework implementation with other implemented TSC subsystems. The framework evaluation will closely follow emerging technology standards, such as WS-CDL, the Web Service Choreography Description Language [15], and comparably mature ones, such as BPEL [17].

REFERENCES

1. Stefan Tai, Rania Khalaf, and Thomas Mikalsen. "Composition of Coordinated Web Services". IBM, 2004.
2. Leune, Kees. "EFSOC Framework Overview and Infrastructure Services". Infolab Technical Report, 2003.
3. Leune, Kees. "A Methodology for Developing Role-Based Access/Control to Web-Services". Infolab Technical Report, 2002.
4. John A. Miller, Mei Fan, Amit P. Sheth and Krys J. Kochut. "Security in Web-Based Workflow Management Systems". Technical Report #UGA-CS-LSDIS-TR-99-010, 1999.
5. R. K. Thomas, R. S. Sandhu. " Task-based Authorization Controls (TBAC): A Family of Models for Active and Enterprise-oriented Authorization Management". IFIP Workshop On Database Security, 1997.
6. Mendling Jan, Strembeck Mark, Stermsek Gerald, Neumann Gustaf. "An Approach to Extract RBAC Models from BPEL4WS Processes". WETICE, 2004.
7. Karsten Schulz, Maria E. Orlowska. „Towards A Cross-Organisational Workflow Model". Pro-VE, 2002.
8. Liu Duen-Ren, Shen Minxin. „Workflow Modeling for Virtual Processes: an Order-Preserving Process-View Approach". Information Systems 28(6), 2003.
9. Dickson K.W. Chiu, Shing-Chi Cheung, Kamalakar Karlapalem, Qing Li and Sven Till. " Workflow View Driven Cross-Organizational Interoperability in a Web-Service Environment". (ACM) Inf. Tech. and Management, 2004.
10. OASIS. URL: http://www.oasis-open.org/committees/tc_home.php?wg_abbrev=wss, 2005.
11. IBM/Microsoft/... URL: http://www-106.ibm.com/developerworks/library/specification/ws-trust/, 2005.
12. IBM/Microsoft/... URL: http://www-128.ibm.com/developerworks/library/specification/ws-polfram/, 2005.
13. IBM/Microsoft/... URL: http://www-128.ibm.com/developerworks/library/specification/ws-tx/#coor, 2005.
14. BPMI.org. URL: http://www.bpmn.org/, 2005.
15. W3C. URL: http://www.w3.org/TR/2004/WD-ws-cdl-10-20040427/, 2005.
16. OMG. URL: http://www.uml.org/, 2005.
17. OASIS. URL: http://www.oasis-open.org/committees/tc_home.php?wg_abbrev=wsbpel, 2005.

PART 9

NETWORK BENEFIT ANALYSIS

26

AN APPROACH FOR THE ASCERTAINMENT OF PROFIT SHARES FOR NETWORK PARTICIPANTS

Hendrik Jähn, Marco Fischer, Matthias Zimmermann
Chemnitz University of Technology, hendrik.jaehn@wirtschaft.tu-chemnitz.de
GERMANY

This paper introduces an approach for the automated calculation of profit shares for participants in non-hierarchical production networks under consideration of incentive and sanction mechanisms. Thereby the sanctions can be ascertained within an integrated approach for the evaluation of the performance of the individual value-adding units. Incentive mechanisms focus the interference of the behavior of the value-adding-units in order to act network-compliant. The discussed issues concern the two final phases of a typical life cycle of a virtual enterprise: the phase of the evaluation and the phase of the break-up of the network. Thereby the maximization of utility of the entire virtual enterprise serves as the main objective.

1. INTRODUCTION

The current economic situation is characterized by the requirement for a flexible and customer-oriented production of goods. As one reaction in order to bear that challenge, many enterprises intensify their engagement in virtual enterprises. At Chemnitz University of Technology, an innovative concept for the cooperation especially of very small organization units is elaborated within the scope of the Collaborative Research Centre 457 (Müller, 2003). That concept is called „Non-hierarchical Regional Production Networks". The cooperating organization units thereby are called Competence Cells (CCs). For operating and coordinating that kind of collaborative networks the management concept "Extended Value Chain Management" (EVCM) was developed (Teich, 2003). It guarantees the adherence to the non-hierarchical structure. That means that all CCs are legally and economically independent and dispose of equal rights and opportunities. Therefore the selection of the partners as well as the planning and execution of the value-adding process take place as far as possible in an automated way coordinated by EVCM. Because of the assumption of an asymmetrical distribution of information within the network it is expected that every network participant will act in favour of its own maximization of utility (Macho-Stadler, 2001). However for the success of the entire network the maximization of the network utility must be aimed at. Therefore suitable incentive and sanction mechanisms for the CCs are necessary to manage the problems caused by these behavior patterns.

In this contribution an approach for the automated calculation of profit shares in non-hierarchical regional Production Networks under consideration of incentive and sanction mechanisms is introduced. The consideration of incentives and sanctions within the calculation of profit shares for network participants describes an innovative approach. It has to be highlighted that the distribution of profit is a very important issue for the success of the entire network. However this problem is little discussed from the theoretical perspective. For that case only little literature exists (Rehkugler, 1972). The approach assumes that the CCs have well defined insulated tasks which is appropriate especially in the job-shop production in machine building.

2. DISTRIBUTION OF PROFIT

Although the topic of the distribution of profit only gains importance after finishing a value-adding process, the expectations of the CCs concerning profit already have to be taken into consideration during their selection phase. In the following, a model which focuses on the determination as well as the distribution of profits is introduced.

The basis of the model for a fair distribution of profit among partners in virtual enterprises is the phase of the preparation and submission of offers for every value-adding step. Therefore, a customer inquiry must have been made to the network for an exactly defined product. It has to be distinguished whether the customer expresses his idea of the price or not. In case, the customer states a desired purchase price, that price needs to be compared to the price that can be realized by the production network. That parameter can be calculated from the sum of the evaluated value-adding parts of all the CCs participating in the network plus a network profit, which is calculated as the sum of the profit expectations of the single CC. In case, the realizable price is higher than the price desired by the customer, it has to be expected that the customer does not accept the offer. In that case negotiations are necessary (Jähn, 2004). If the realizable price as oppose is lower than the desired price, the good is offered at the desired price for realizing a correspondingly higher network profit or to set up reserves.

In reverse, it is possible to ascertain a profit from the difference of the desired price and the realizable delivery price without profit. That profit amount can subsequently be distributed to the single CCs involved in the value-adding process by the means of a specific distribution key. After that, the CCs compare their individual idea of the profit and the planned profit share. If the majority accepts that amount, an offer can be submitted to the potential customer containing the desired price. The customer will probably accept that offer. In that case, the profit is calculated from the difference of the desired price and the realizable delivery price. The value-adding process can be started.

That procedure is more complicated in case several CCs are not satisfied with their profit share. This is similar to the case when the customer has no concrete idea concerning the desired price. In that case a new price must be ascertained. Here, the individual profit ideas of the single CCs serve as calculation basis. The profit ideas should be ascertained as a percentage of the value-adding share of a CC. An offer price for the inquired product can be calculated from the sum of the individual value-adding shares and the individual percentages of the profit shares. That price is reported to the potential customer. This customer has to decide if he accepts the offer or not. In case he accepts the offer, the profit is fixed and the production of the inquired good can be started. As oppose, if the customer cannot accept the offer because of the price, it has to be analyzed what can be modified. Thus, the customer might be convinced to pay a higher price. If this is not possible, the CCs need to reduce their profit ideas. Thereby, the question has to be answered whether a reduction is possible in order to realize the desired price of the customer. For the case that this is not possible and the customer is not willing to pay a higher price, the negotiation procedure is cancelled and no contract is concluded. That means the customer does not place the order. This should be an exception. In that case negotiations concerning the product can be started in order to realize an attractive offer, even the product differs from the original inquiry. Thereby it has to be paid attention that the requirements to the final product of the customer are fulfilled. In the next section the procedure concerning the distribution of profit is introduced.

Basically the total offer price is calculated from the sum of all the prices of the value-adding process of all CCs plus the expected profit shares per CC. After carrying through the value-adding process and delivering the final product to the customer, he is expected to pay the agreed purchase price. The agreed prices per value-adding process then are directly paid out to the participating CCs by EVCM. The remaining amount is the distributable profit *G*. It has to be mentioned that the distributable profit needs not to be equal to the expectations dependent on the procedure of the ascertainment of the offer price.

When ascertaining the individual profit share of a CC, a differentiation of a fixed and a variable profit share in networks seems to be efficient for every CC for the basic model of the profit distribution in non-hierarchical regional production networks. For the ascertainment of that distribution parameter α, it presents itself to compare the proportion of overheads and complete costs weighted with the realized value-adding p_i of a CC to the complete value-adding of the production network. Equation 1 shows these interdependencies. *G* represents the total amount of profit to be distributed.

$$g_i = \alpha \cdot \frac{G}{n} + (1-\alpha) \cdot \frac{G \cdot p_i}{P_{netto}} \tag{1}$$

If a finite number of CCs n in the production network is assumed, which were involved in a certain value-adding process, a fixed profit share results which is equal for all participating CCs $i=1,\dots,n$. As oppose, the variable part of a CC is calculated dependent on the individual share of value-adding p_i. Thus, this part is orientated on the corresponding offer price. Because a low offer price increases the probability of the participation in the network, it is avoided that single CCs might secure a too high share of the profit for themselves. The sum of the fixed and the variable profit share is the payable profit share g_i of a CC. Both parts of the profit are weighted by α.

That share g_i has to be compared to the expected share from the offer submission. If the payable profit share g_i is higher than the expected profit share $g_{i,e}$ of a CC *i*, only the expected amount is paid out and the remaining amount is kept as a reserve for the EVCM. However, if the payable profit share is lower than the expected profit share of a CC, an additional payment needs to be disposed that is financed by the reserves. Nevertheless, this must remain an exceptional case.

3. INCENTIVES

Incentive mechanisms are mainly (but not exclusively) financial benefits that are paid by an employer to a contractor. Thereby, the employer tries to influence the behavior of the contractor to convince him to act in his interest. The reason why the contractor does not automatically act in his sense could be that each actor aims at maximizing his own utility. In case the client and the contractor do not pursue the same or at least similar aims, incentives have to be given in order to synchronize their utility. The choice of the adequate amount of the financial incentive thereby is very important. If one succeeds to financially quantify the utility difference, the incentive amount should be at least as high as that utility difference. However, it is more efficient that the incentive amount is a little higher than the utility difference for giving the contractor an incentive to decide in favour of the aims of the client.

Reasons for that have to be identified before incentives can be quantified. Thus, however, if a CC abandons the participation in a value-adding process, it can be the best alternative for it, but not necessarily for the entire network. This would for example be the case if a competence or CC is missing in a value-adding chain for being able to submit an offer. In that case, the missing CC has to be given suitable incentives for the participation in the network. Because a too low price is no reason for not participating in the network, other reasons must be found. Those could for example be lacking production capacities, lacking personnel, a lack of interest in participating in the network or not meeting the profit expectations. Two reasons are exemplarily explained in the next section. In these cases, the additional costs for a rescheduling of the involved CC or a simple monetary incentive for extending the profit need to be compensated. This is the content of the following model.

When taking the case into consideration, that one or more CCs are not able or willing to participate in the network, they have to be convinced by the help of certain incentive mechanisms to participate in the value added chain. Because of the assumption that every enterprise works for maximizing its profit, a (monetary) incentive is the logical consequence. This however presupposes that the CCs that are willing to participate in the network from the beginning on have to pay for that. However, the complete network profit needs to be ascertained for finding out about the exact amount of possible incentive payments which every CC has to make. The costs for the incentive payments have to be financed from that amount. As can be seen from the profit distribution model, an acclamation procedure is necessary for the ascertainment of the profit G. For the CC lacking in the value-adding network, it presents itself to introduce so-called *CCsim* (simulated CC) for being able to submit an offer for the potential customer and to ascertain the profit. Thereby, however, the number of the *CCsim* must not be bigger than the total number of CCs cooperating in the network minus 1.

For the calculation, it is now assumed that the simulated CCs fulfill all the requirements (with regard to capacities, personnel, soft-facts etc.) and in the acclamations agree to the majority of the CCs concerning G. Thus, it is possible to ascertain the theoretically achievable network profit G_t. For realizing that profit, however, it is necessary to find suitable CCs also for the vacant value-adding processes. The following two cases can be distinguished in the selection of those CCs: In the first case the CC, which was replaced by a *CCsim*, exists in the pool of resources and disposes of all the necessary resources, but however does not want to participate in the network under the given conditions. In the second case the CC, which was replaced by a *CCsim*, does not exist in the network and / or does not dispose of all the necessary resources. There is the possibility that the CC-related share of value-adding p_i is published by the potential CC which is absolutely necessary for the further calculation. However, if there is no exact number for p_i, either experiences or estimations must serve for the first step of the calculation.

As mentioned above, the already engaged CCs have to pay for the incentives which are granted. However, it has to be assumed that those CCs also have ideas concerning their individual profit share. If they know that no network can be formed without the missing CC, they will nevertheless be willing to make the compensation payments. The reason results from the fact that no profit would be realizable at all without a network and thus a lower utility level would be achieved. Another acclamation procedure is carried through for the determination of the individual shares of the compensation payments (incentives). Within the scope of that process, the CC state to which amount (percentage of the complete result) they are ready to dispense with their profit. Equation (2) illustrates that coherence.

$$i_i = \frac{p_i}{\sum_{i=1}^{n} p_i} \cdot p_i \cdot i_{RPi} \tag{2}$$

Thereby i_i refers to the individual profit share and i_{RPi} the share a CC is willing to emit of its planned profit share in percent.

Subsequently, the amount of the available compensation payments I can be ascertained. That corresponds to the average compensation share a CC is willing to use for incentive payments. This is illustrated by Equation (3).

$$I = \sum_{i=1}^{n} i_i \tag{3}$$

Now, the single incentive payments can be distributed individually to the not yet participating CC, corresponding to their missing resources. The expenses for making available the resources have to be quantified for that. It thereby has to be considered that the CC won for the network also have to be involved in the compensation payment. After the available incentive budget I has been ascertained, it is now possible to replace the *CCsim* by real CCs, thereby the aforementioned cases are distinguished again. For the distribution of the compensation payments to the new CC, one starts with those from the second case. Those usually represent payments which are to make available the lacking resources and thus are only a little negotiable. The remaining amount of the available incentive budget I is proportionately distributed to the CC which belong to the first case. If the required costs are higher than the available compensation payments I, the already participating CC are again asked to state the profit share they are ready to dispense with. The condition for that is that this is higher than in the first acclamation. Subsequently, the compensation payments are distributed again aiming at finding missing network partners. This procedure can now be repeated as often as necessary until the required CCs have been found. However, the process is broken up if the sum of the compensation payments gets bigger than the achievable profit or if one or more of the existing CCs leave the network because of too low expected profits. This would again result in additional costs.

Incentive payments are based on the assumption that all the CCs aim at an individual maximization of utility. Thus, it must always be desirable to participate in a value-adding process if a profit is made. However, if a customer order cannot be realized because of lacking CCs, a profit of 0 would be achieved which is not desirable. Therefore, compensation payments as incentives are justified.

After introducing the model for distributing profit and the consideration of incentives a quantitatively orientated model for the calculation of sanctions for CCs, that have not performed a service as it was planned, is introduced in the next section. That model is based on a basic performance evaluation of each CC involved in the value-adding process.

4. SANCTIONS

If the evaluation of the performances of the network participants is aimed, the most important influence parameters need to be identified in a first and singular or at the most periodical work step. They include the price, the date of delivery and the specification of the quality. The quantity however is assumed as a fixed parameter and thus it is not included in the analysis. On the other hand, relevant parameters result from the social connection of such networked structures. Those for example include the quality of the cooperation and the confidential climate among the network participants. Thus, it is valid that there are *m* parameters K_j, $j=1,...,m$ $(m=5)$ to be investigated.

In order to manage the different relevancy of the single parameters, a weighting l_j has to be determined for every parameter in the second phase. The determination of the weights is based on the controlling target system. This is also a singular or periodical task. Rankings or empirical investigations might be resources for that. In order to achieve a possibility of comparison of the parameters in order to standardize the evaluation, in the regular case it is valid: $\Sigma l_j = L = 1$. Thus, it is guaranteed that the parameters can be compared with regard to their significance.

In order to be able to carry through a target-actual value-comparison of the parameters, the maximally achievable evaluation variable *tv* (target value) must be ascertained for every parameter *j* in phase three. This evaluation variable then must be compared to the actually achieved evaluation variable *av* (actual value) of every parameter *j* and of every CC *i* after each value-adding process in a dynamic network. That maximally achievable evaluation variable results from the product of the maximally achievable number of credits $r_{j,max}$ (usually 10) and the weight l_j, cf. equation (4).

$$tv_j = l_j \cdot r_{j,\max} \tag{4}$$

For managing that task, the degree of fulfillment, that justifies a maximal number of credits, must be fixed for every parameter involved. That task has a different difficulty for the single parameters. While keeping the price agreed upon and sticking to the determined quality justify an obviously maximal credit evaluation, the evaluation of the soft-facts is far more difficult. Therefore, an approach would be the evaluation with the maximal number of credits in case of an

„optimal“ confidential culture and an „optimal“ quality of the cooperation. Nevertheless, this issue remains subjective to a large extent. Most practicable for the evaluation of soft-facts in short terms is the individual rating of the parameters by the enterprises. However in this case data can be gerrymandered. The summed up target value (*TV*) can be ascertained by adding all tv_j for all considered parameters K_j. This value of comparison value is valid for several value-adding processes.

The following working steps need to be carried through for every process of value-adding and therefore they provide highly dynamic data for evaluating the performance of the enterprises during value-adding.

At first the five in the previous paragraph identified parameters are evaluated by the means of suitable points and evaluation measures with regard to their degrees of fulfillment for every CC. That credit evaluation is called r_{ij} and normally amounts to a value between 0 (extremely bad performance) and 10 (excellent / perfect performance). A connection between the degree of fulfillment and the credit evaluation needs to be fixed for every parameter. For considering the performance of the single CCs during the value-adding process the actual value is calculated. By multiplying the achieved credits r_{ij} and the corresponding weighting l_j, a weighted credit, the so-called actual value av_{ij}, results for every parameter and every CC, therefore cf. equation (5).

$$av_{ij} = l_j \cdot r_{ij} \quad (5)$$

Subsequently, the aggregated actual value of a CC i (AV_i) can be ascertained by summing up the av_{ij} for all the parameters K_j. Then, that value serves as a basis for the further analysis. AV_i describes in one variable the performance of an enterprise without giving any information about the quality of the performance.

Therefore finally the measure NC_i (network conformity) has to be ascertained in phase five by the comparison of the actual value AV_i and the target value TV for the evaluation of the behavior of a CC in the virtual enterprise. The network conformity represents a kind of level of fulfillment of the completed performances, because in the calculation, the aggregated actual value is compared to the aggregated target value. Thus, this variable can also be interpreted as the percentage of the fulfillment of performances. The calculation rule for that is illustrated in equation (6).

$$NC_i = \frac{AV_i}{TV} \quad (6)$$

The variable *NC* represents the degree of the network conformity of a CC and concludes in only one value the quality of fulfillment of the several performance parameters of the enterprises participating in a special dynamic network. That parameter is re-ascertained for every value-adding process for every participating CC according to the pattern described above. The comparability with other CCs as well as the consideration for the distribution of profit thus is guaranteed.

Finally, the NC_i of a CC must be allocated to the application in the profit distribution model within the scope of sanction mechanisms. In case of a poor performance of a CC, a proportionate shortage of the profit s_i seems to be an efficient measure. The sanction amount can be calculated according to equation (7).

$$s_i - (1 - NC_i) \cdot g_i \quad (7)$$

The remaining share of the profit has to be paid to the enterprises involved in the value-adding process in the network after the customer has paid the amount of an invoice. In case a CC has performed very well and has kept its delivery promises fixed in the contract it will receive the full profit share. An outstanding performance of the entire network is aimed at by allying this approach within the network controlling.

5. AGGREGATION

After the quantification of incentive and sanction payments, the final profit share z_i for every CC i can be calculated. That amount is finally to be paid to the CCs. Thus, after finishing a value-adding process, a CC is on the one hand given the individual share of the value-adding p_i and on the other hand the corresponding profit g_i. In addition, the incentives i_i are paid out and possible sanctions s_i are subtracted. It is stressed here that i_i as well as s_i might consist of several components. By realizing just one money flow including all components a clear calculation procedure realized by EVCM can be guaranteed. It has to be stressed that the calculation of profit shares is a very complex issue and the acceptance of the calculation scheme of all affected CCs is precondition for its implementation.

6. CONCLUSION

This paper introduced an approach for the profit distribution in non-hierarchical regional production networks taking into consideration sanction and incentive mechanisms. The described methodology is a starting point for dealing with a key issue in collaboration among independent partners. However further development will certainly be needed. This includes the procedure of evaluation and rating and the necessary instance for fulfilling that task. Furthermore a disturbance management has to be included in case a partner does not accept the ratings or sanctions. It has also to be clarified that monetary incentives are not the only ones.

However, the introduced approach can be arbitrarily expanded and adapted to certain structures within specific virtual enterprises. Future work will focus on the refinement of that approach as well as on its information-technical implementation in the EVCM. The realization of the approach makes possible a contribution to an automated and efficient network controlling and hereby supports the success of virtual enterprises in a rapidly changing world-wide economic environment.

7. REFERENCES

1. Jähn H, Zschorn L, Zimmermann M. An automated Negotiation Model for non-hierarchical Production Networks. In Proceedings of the 8th International Conference on Manufacturing Management, Vol.1, Salem S, ed, Gold Coast, Queensland, Australia, December 08-10, pp. 125-132, 2004.
2. Macho-Stadler I, Pérez-Castrillo, JD. An Introduction to the Economics of Information: Incentives and Contracts, Second Edition, Oxford: Oxford University Press, 2001.
3. Müller E, Wirth S. Innovative Production Nets based on a Competence Cell-based Approach. In Current Trends in Production Management, Zülch G et al., eds, 268-274, Aachen: Shaker, 2003.
4. Rehkugler, H. Die Verteilung einzelwirtschaftlicher Wertschöpfung. Dissertationsschrift, Ludwig-Maximilians-Universität zu München, 1972.
5. Teich T. Extended Value Chain Management (EVCM): Ein Konzept zur Koordination von Wertschöpfungsnetzen, Chemnitz: Verlag der GUC, 2003.

27 NETWORK ANALYSIS OF TERRORISM DEFENSE ORGANIZATIONS - A NETWORK APPROACH FOR DEVELOPING PERFORMANCE INDICATORS

Irma Borst, Joan Baaijens, Geleyn R. Meijer
LogicaCMG,
irma.borst@logicacmg.com;joan.baaijens@logicacmg.com;geleyn.meijer@logicacmg.com
THE NETHERLANDS

This document presents a newly developed approach for defining performance indicators for policy chains. Policy chains are collaborative networks in the government sector that develop, implement and administrate and/or control public bodies. The developed approach is based on two existing methods that we use frequently in our consultancy practice: a method for defining performance indicators for traditional (not virtual) public organizations and an approach for network analysis. By combining the methods an approach tailored to network organizations is constructed. The approach is being validated by applying it to a policy chain in the terrorism defense domain.

1. INTRODUCTION

Collaborative Network Organisations (CNOs) correspond to a very active and steadily growing area. These networks are also observed in the government sector and are called policy chains. Policy chains are multiple (governmental) organizations that work together in order to develop, implement, administrate and/or control public policies. Examples of policy chains are immigration administration chain, public safety chain and social security chain.

Policy chains seem to be characterized by a large number of actors that have to cooperate in order to fulfill the joint objective. Information exchange and coordination between the network actors is essential in order to achieve this.

Considering the large number of actors, we experienced that many policy chains struggle with non-transparency of the relationships between organizations in the network. With non-transparency we mean that actors in the network do not have a full overview of all actors involved, (inter)dependencies between actors, direct and indirect relations, formal and informal positions of actors (relative power) and performance of individual actors or of the network as a whole.

In order to overcome these non-transparencies we developed a network analysis tool (Baaijens, 2004) which visualizes different types of relations within a policy chain. The resulting network diagrams provide an insight in the practical dynamics of the day-to-day life in organizations and public policy settings. Specifically it enables communication on relation data with third parties and it improved understanding of the impact of embeddedness of individual actors in a network.

Besides the internal problems that involved actors experience as discussed above, we notice that there are external forces, such as accounting for government spending, which drive policy chains towards transparency, performance measurement and performance improvement. Based on existing theories for performance indicator (PI) definition, we developed a practical methodology (roadmap) tailored to public organizations (Wondergem, 2004). This roadmap for defining PIs is not tailored to *network* organizations. By combining the network analysis tool with this roadmap we developed a methodology which is suitable for policy chains. In order to validate the newly developed method, we will use it during a case study in the domain of terrorism defense organizations.

The case study in which we will apply the method to a policy chain in the terrorism defense domain will deliver relevant input to the ECOLEAD project (Ecolead).

2. TERRORISM DEFENSE ORGANISATIONS

Terrorism defense chains consist of two types of organizations:

Intervention teams
Intervention teams responsible for the fight of terrorism will be event-driven. This means that they are not permanently active, but will show a 'sleeping existence' until action is required. In this stage, members of the chain have to prepare themselves so that their action will be effective (and efficient). During this phase the policy chain can be considered as a Virtual Breeding Environment (VBE). A terrorism intervention team in action can be considered as a (short term) Virtual Organization (VO).

Intelligence organization
The terrorism intelligence organization responsible for data gathering and information analysis on (potential) terrorists and terrorist events can be considered (after its creation phase) as a longer term organization. The intelligence staff does not belong to one organization but are part of various Dutch Ministries and public bodies and can therefore be classified as a VO.

The behavior of both teams will be completely different. For example communication patterns, information needs, type and dependency on communication facilities will be incomparable. At the same time, the organizations are very much dependent on each other for being effective in their activities.

At the moment, the effectiveness of terrorism defense organizations is a very hot issue. We distinguish four kinds of motives for having PI implemented in terrorism defense organizations (AIVD report, 2004), (Fijnaut, 2004):

1. *Improve focus on results and transparency*
   The Dutch society requires a visible improvement of the results of terrorism defense organizations. In order to achieve improvement of results, responsible managers should have insight in processes that have an effect on results. If they steer on these processes they are able to improve the results. Besides internal

transparency there is also a need for external transparency, i.e. towards the citizens.

2. *Efficiency of processes*
   Besides the focus on results, the quality of processes should remain subject of attention and management. In times of scarcity (e.g. no unlimited government spending) it is crucial that resources and time are used in an efficient way. Otherwise terrorism defense organization will lose face and citizens will have a reduced perception of safety.
3. *Improve cooperation*
   In a recent report on the National Intelligence and Security Organization (AIVD), it is concluded that cooperation between AIVD and other bodies requires substantial improvement, both on information exchange and analysis and on operational consequences of these activities. Through process management it will become transparent what different actors are providing in the policy chain. After agreement on desired output, it will be easier for a staff member to contribute successfully. Process management will also support achievement of synergies because a chain approach replaces (sub) optimization of individual actors.
4. *Quality of processes*
   It is also concluded that management of AIVD is fragmented and unclear. This can be improved by introducing process management. Description of core processes enables communication, delegation and improvement of processes. This will lead to a 'self-learning' organization because changes of processes will have an effect on organization structure and on systems.

3. ROADMAP FOR DEFINING PI

There are many different methods for defining indicators. All methods assume a direct link between the organization's vision & strategy and indicators. This is visualized in figure 1.

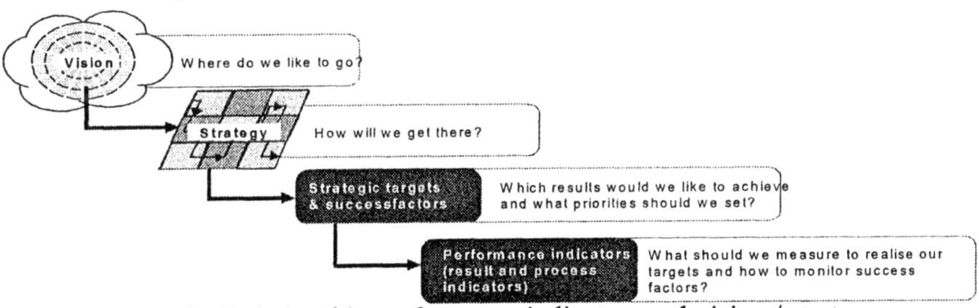

Figure 1 - Relationship performance indicators and vision / strategy

Examples of methods for defining PI are Balanced Scorecard method, strategy trees, process and system models, and methods that are based on customer value (Wondergem, 2004). Wondergem developed a roadmap for defining PI which reflects different basic methods (Wondergem, 2004) and validated this roadmap method within a public body, namely a Dutch police region.

Before describing this method, we would like to point out that PI can be classified in two groups (Wondergem, 2003):

- *Indicators related to processes*
  Process indicators measure the quality of the process, i.e. is the information gathering process executed by the right person of the intelligence team?
- *Indicators related to results*
  Result indicators refer only to characteristics of the results, i.e. the number of terrorism actions avoided.

In practice there seems to be a natural link between performance indicators and results while process indicators are sometimes forgotten. At the same time, process indicators might be harder to define and measure. Therefore explicitly attention is paid to process indicators in the roadmap.

The roadmap provides a detailed approach for the translation of strategic targets and success factors into PI. The roadmap consists of the following activities:

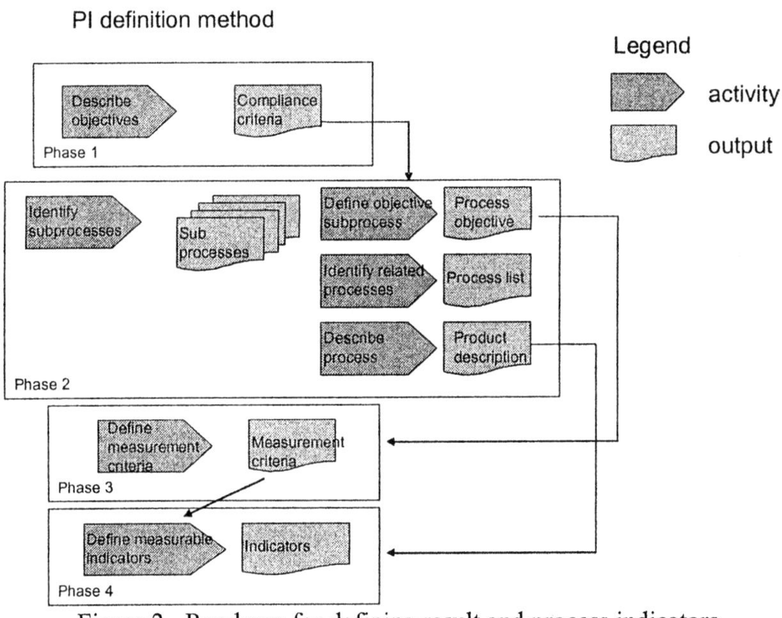

Figure 2 - Roadmap for defining result and process indicators

In phase 1 strategy objectives are described. This results in compliance criteria for processes. Both result oriented and process oriented objectives are included. The framework will be used in phase 2 when determining the objectives for sub-processes. In phase 2 the core process is divided in several sub-processes. For each sub-process, the objectives, underlying processes and the sub-process itself are described. The objectives of the sub-processes and the list of underlying processes are input for the definition of measurement criteria (activities in phase 3). Finally the list of products and the measurement criteria are used in the definition of indicators; per product one or more indicators will be defined.

Following the roadmap as described above will not be a guarantee for a successful PI definition process. At the same time the following conditions have to be fulfilled:

- PI should be developed through negotiation and consensus among key internal and external stakeholders at all steps in the process;
- PI should be simple to convey and broadly understood;
- PI should be based on data that are valid and consistent and that can be verified by third parties when necessary. PI should also be based on established data sources, where possible, in order to maximize credibility and minimize additional workload;
- PI should be established with wide recognition that are certain unavoidable ranges of error in any measurement activity; imposing a false sense of "precision" is counter productive;
- The system of PI should accommodate special circumstances (e.g. unique institutional missions) where possible;
- PI should be kept to the smallest number possible in order to minimize conflicting interactions among the indicators and to maximize the importance of each indicator;
- PI chosen should reflect industry norms and standards, where possible, in order to allow for benchmarking and peer comparison;
- PI system developed should incorporate both quantitative and qualitative measures in order to present the most complete picture of performance possible.

We would like to emphasis the importance of the first statement: PI should be developed through negotiation and consensus of key stakeholders. We believe that defining performance indicators is not exact science, there is room for interpretation. Therefore it is key to search for a shared and transparent definition of indicators. This requires involvement of stakeholders in the definition process: if many different indicators are possible then the selection has to be based on shared vision of stakeholders. Involvement of stakeholders will increase the acceptance of the indicators.

4. NETWORK GAMES

In order to apply the PI definition method to network organizations a network perspective on organizations and their environment will be required. This perspective is based on the idea that (organizational) actors are embedded within a network of interconnected relationships that provide opportunities and constraints on behavior (Brass, 2004). Actors can be individual persons, organized units or organizations connected by work flow ties. A network perspective therefore implies a multi-level perspective. In our approach this multi-level perspective is an effective framework for connecting individual actions with actions of organized or collaborative entities.

4.1 Multi-level aspect

In defining PI for policy chains, there are at least two levels of analysis. We consider:

Level of the individual actor
The orientation of an individual actor in a network is build upon the perception of that actor of the environment in combination with the historical path of experiences and interactions with other actors in a particular organizational field. The perception of the network at the level of one actor is a different perspective than the level of the network as a tangible set of organizations working together. An actor in a network has a structural different kind of interests than the interests of the entire network as a collaborative network.

Level of the network
The network as a set of actors interconnected by a set of ties has to be distinguished from the actor level. Analysis on the network level is about the size, the density, the composition and the hierarchy of the network.

Information on network level can be reconstructed on basis of the information on individual level. Actors in the network differ in terms of their position towards each other.

4.2 Network game

Crucial in the network game method (Baaijens, 2004) is the assumption that information on network level can be constructed on basis of information on individual level. Other essential elements of the method are interactive workshops, visualization of the network structure and the determination of a network score card. A network score card is a standard description of the network in terms of size, composition and hierarchy. We experienced that both the visualization of the network and the score card are powerful tools which increases transparency within the network organization. We distinguish three different formats for the network game:

The first format is a network game on the basis of '*ego nets*'. This means that the most prominent actors in a network organization are selected and individually interviewed. A complete set of interviews is processed in a database and analyzed. Next ego-nets step are reconstructed into network structure. The results are presented in a workshop where interviewed actors discuss the network reconstruction. We evaluate the networks with the network score card.

The second format is what we call a '*one actor game*'. We select the principal actor from a collaborative network for an interactive workshop. Input of this single actor results in the reconstruction of the network structure and the determination of the network score card.

The third and most advanced format of the network game is the '*multi-actor game*'. We select key actors from a virtual collaborative network. These actors provide their (joint) input on network structure and score card during an interactive workshop.

5. LINKING ROADMAP WITH NETWORK GAME

By combining the roadmap for defining PI and the network game approach we have a powerful method and road map for constructing and validating performance indicators on the level of collaborative networks. Our newly developed approach is visualized in figure 4.

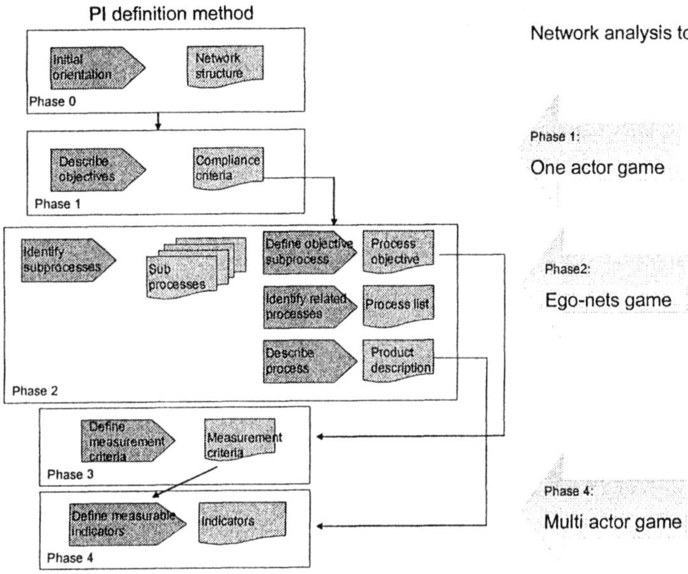

Figure 1 - Roadmap for defining PI tailored to policy chains

Phase 0: Orientation towards actors and network structure

Phase 0 is new compared to the initial roadmap. We added this step in order to anticipate on the non-transparency that is an observed problem within policy chains. Clarification of the characteristics of the network organization will be required before starting the process of defining PI.

Execution of this phase is mainly through desk research and some selective experts interviews. Output of this phase is a list of relevant actors, a list of domains for which PI can be defined and the choice of a principal actor in the field to work with in phase 1.

Phase 1: Description of objectives – One actor game.

The outcome of phase 0 is the selection of a principal actor, in casu an organization in the field of terrorism defense. With this actor we play the 'one actor network game' as indicated earlier. The output is a graph of the network as a perception of the principal actor. This includes a validated list of actors and their interrelations that structure the collaborative network under study.

Together with the principal actor we also determine the objectives and the compliance criteria. This is based on our assumption that the principal actor will be the best party to oversee the activities of the whole network and therefore able to fulfill this activity.

Phase 2: Description of processes – Ego nets

The actors in the network resulting from phase 1 will be interviewed in an individual mode. The questionnaire for these interviews will be focused on process objectives, descriptions and underlying processes. The outcome of this phase is a reconstruction of the structure of the collaborative network on the basis of the ego-nets. In reference of this reconstruction we also have the outline of process objectives, lists of processes and the process descriptions.

Phase 3: Definition of measurement criteria
Based on the results of the previous phase we will prepare measurement criteria independently from the actors.

Phase 4: Definition of indicators – Multi actor game
In this final phase we validate the reconstruction results and proposed measurement criteria with multiple actors. Next we will define the performance indicators in line with the network structure of the collaborative network organization in the terrorism defense field. As indicated before it is crucial that stakeholders are involved in setting the final PI. The multi-actor game in which stakeholder should reach consensus on the final results is the best option for this phase.

5. CONCLUSION

We presented two methods that we are currently using in our consultancy practice. In order to have a method for setting PI applicable to the domain of network organizations, we combined these two methods. We are now in the process of validating the newly developed methodology by using it in a case study in the domain of terrorism defense organizations. Unfortunately we can not yet present results. As a result of the case study we expect to deliver a set of metrics for terrorism defense organizations, practical guidelines for the use of the method (e.g. checklists of relevant issues per phase, process descriptions) and a software tool that processes interview and workshop results in a network score card and a visualization of the network structure. In addition we expect that defined PI for terrorism defense organizations will be examples of metrics applicable to other CNOs.

6. REFERENCES

1. Baaijens J.M.J., Lapré L.J. "Network analysis of policy chains in The Netherlands". Paper for the 20th EGOS Colloquium, Ljubljana, Slovenia, July 2004.
2. Brass D.J., Galaskiewicz J., Greve H., Tsai W. "Taking Stock of Networks and Organizations: A Multilevel Perspective". Academy of Management Journal, december 2004
3. Commissie bestuurlijke evaluatie Algemene Inlichtingen- en Veiligheidsdienst. "De AIVD in verandering", november 2004.
4. Ecolead (European Collaborative networked Organizations LEADerschip initiative), www.ecolead.org
5. Fijnaut Prof. dr. C. "De samenwerking tussen de lidstaten van de Europese Unie bij de bestrijding van het internationale islamitische terrorisme". Afscheidsrede Katholieke Universiteit, november 2003
6. www.ibhe.state.il.us/PerformanceIndicators/pdf/item%204%20Performance%20Indicators-Dec%202001/pdf.
7. Wondergem B.C.M. "What you measure is what you get – methoden voor het formuleren van prestatie indicatoren". Proceedings van de conferentie Informatiewetenschap, Technische Universiteit Eindhoven, november 2003.
8. Wondergem B.C.M., Vincent N. "Analysing transformation in performance management". Transformation of knowledge, information and data: theory and application, 2004.
9. Wondergem B.C.M., "Doelgericht presteren met processen: indicatoren voor proces en resultaat". Publicatie LogicaCMG/Politie Noord- en Oost Gelderland, januari 2004.

28

PERFORMANCE INDICATORS BASED ON COLLABORATION BENEFITS

Luis M. Camarinha-Matos, António Abreu
New University of Lisbon
Quinta da Torre – 2829 Monte Caparica, PORTUGAL
cam@uninova.pt, ajfa@fct.unl.pt

The identification and characterization of collaboration benefits is an important element for the wide adoption of the collaborative networks paradigm. This paper introduces an approach for the analysis of benefits in collaborative processes for networks of enterprises. The potential application of some indicators derived from this analysis is also discussed in the VO breeding environment context.

1. INTRODUCTION

The participation in a collaborative network of enterprises is commonly assumed to bring valuable benefits to the involved entities. These benefits include an increase of the "survival capability" in a context of market turbulence, but also the possibility to better achieve common goals. On the basis of these expectations are, among others, the following factors: sharing of risks and resources, joining of complementary skills and capacities, acquisition of a (virtual) higher dimension, access to new / wider markets and new knowledge, etc.

But it is also easily recognizable that collaboration introduces high overheads due to the higher coordination costs, diversity of working methods and corporate culture, which induces higher transaction costs, loser control structures, etc.

Is the balance between the potential benefits and the increased overheads substantially positive? Literature in the field, as well as a growing number of practical case studies, seems to indicate that the answer is yes. It is however difficult to prove. It is difficult to find some objective indicators in order to show to a SME that there are potential benefits in joining a collaborative network.

In order to address this problem, the issue of performance measurement and benefit analysis in collaborative networks started to attract attention. Being able to measure the performance of a collaborative network as a whole, as well as the performance of each of its singular members, could represent an important boosting element for the wide acceptance of the paradigm. However performance indicators tailored to collaborative networks or even an adequate conceptual basis for benefit analysis are not available yet [7].

Performance measurement depends on the premises of the measurement system used. Collaborative networks challenge the premises of the methods developed in the past, therefore the applicability of existing measurement systems in this area is questionable. This paper contributes to establish a basis for the analysis of benefits in collaborative networks, suggests some indicators, and discusses their measurability.

As a basis for this work inspiration is sought in the areas of social actor networks [12], transactions cost theory [13], and game theory [1,9]. Of particular relevance are the developments in graph theory tailored to social networks analysis, which have introduced a number of concepts such as prominence of actors in a network, members' centrality, prestige, etc, and approaches to measure / compute them [3]. Although these approaches are, in many publications, quite abstract, lacking some economic and practical focus, they be used as a source of inspiration to analyze collaborative networks of enterprises.

Other recent works have attempted to develop benchmarks for collaborative networks [8,11], although the limited data available is a major obstacle. In [10] (is discussed) an approach to develop a predictive performance indicators for VO.

The approach followed in this paper assumes the existence of a *VO breeding environment* (VBE) as a pre-condition for the effective establishment of dynamic virtual organizations (VO) [5], [6]. A VBE represents an association or pool of organizations and their related supporting institutions that have both the potential and the will to cooperate with each other through the establishment of a "base" long-term cooperation agreement. When a business opportunity is identified by one member (acting as a broker), a subset of these organizations can be selected and thus forming a VO. Various VOs can coexist at the same time in the context of a VBE. A breeding environment, being a long-term networked structure, presents the adequate base environment for the establishment of cooperation agreements, common infrastructures, common ontologies, and mutual trust, which are the necessary facilitating elements when building a new VO. In other words, a VBE represents a group of organizational entities that have developed a *preparedness* for cooperation, in case a specific opportunity arises. Industry *clusters* or industry districts are examples of such breeding environments.

The existence of this long-term environment can also provide the basis to record performance data about past collaboration occurrences, a source for computation of performance indicators. In this context, the definition of a cooperation benefits model and application of a set of indicators can be a useful instrument to the VBE manager, to a VO broker, and also to VBE members.

2. BENEFITS CONCEPT

The actual meaning of a benefit depends on the underlying value system that is used in each context. In order to illustrate this concept let us consider the following two examples:

Example 1 – Logistics area

Four transportation companies (E1, E2, E3, E4), as illustrated in Fig.1, have received, each one, an order from their respective customers (i.e. C1, C2, C3, C4). Each order requests 8 containers, while each transportation company has the capacity of delivering 1 container per day. The maximum delivery date for each order is, respectively, 8, 2, 12, and 4 days from now.

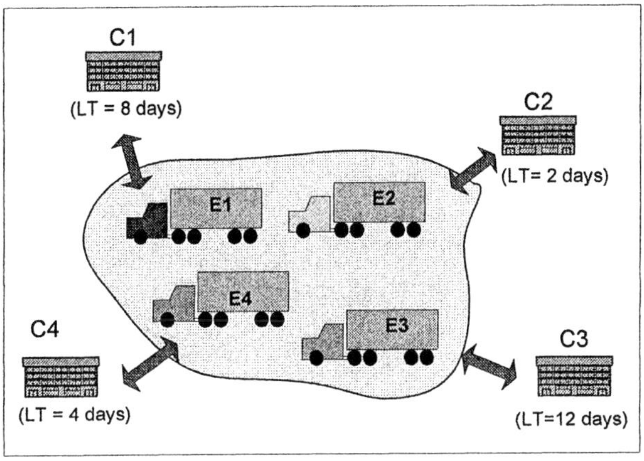

Figure 1 – Cooperation in transportation

In this case, without any cooperation agreement, only E1 and E3 have the capacity to satisfy their orders in time.

However, if the 4 enterprises decide to collaborate all orders can be delivered in time, as shown in Fig. 2.

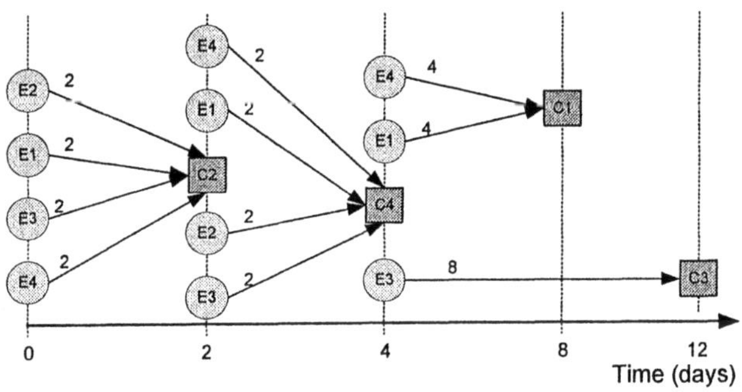

Figure 2 – Transportation collaboration over the time

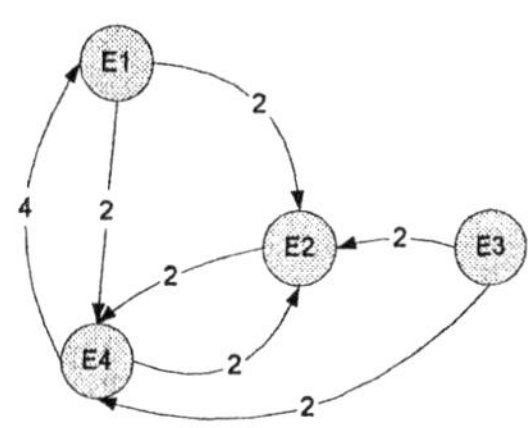

Figure 3 - Benefits exchanged among partners

In this case, enterprise E2 is the first one to receive help from the others as it has the smallest lead time and the next one is E4. After helping E2 and E4, E1 can no longer satisfy its order in time and also needs help. E3 can still fulfil its order even after helping the others. In this example, the value system consists only of one variable that is the quantity of containers, and the cooperation benefit is represented by the number of containers that one partner transports on behalf of another. Fig. 3 shows the exchange of benefits among partners for this case. A direct link represents benefits received by one enterprise form another enterprise.

Example 2 – Joint purchases

Three small enterprises in a given sector realize that one big competitor buys components from the same supplier at a much cheaper price as the supplier offers quantity discounts as shown in Fig. 4. Therefore, the three enterprises decide to establish a cooperation agreement in order to make joint purchases and thus getting higher quantity discounts. Fig. 5 shows the costs in case of individual and joint purchases. Fig. 6 shows, for each cooperative scenario, the total amount of money that can be saved, i.e. cooperation benefit value V, when embarking in a collaborative process. In this example, the collaboration benefit is represented by the amount of money that is saved when partners purchase in group.

Number of parts	Unit Price (€)
1500	35
2000	30
2500	29
3000	28
3500	27
4000	26
4500	25
5000	24
5500	23
6000	22
6500	21
7000	20

Figure 4 - Price of parts

Scenario	Number of parts	Unit Price (€)	Total price € – C
E1	1500	35	52500
E2	2000	30	60000
E3	3500	27	94500
E1+E2	3500	27	94500
E1+E3	5000	24	120000
E2+E3	5500	23	126500
E1+E2+E3	7000	20	140000

Figure 5 - Total price for each scenario

Scenario	Cooperation Benefit Value (€)
E1	$V(E_1)=0$
E2	$V(E_2)=0$
E3	$V(E_3)=0$
E1+E2	$V(E_1 \cup E_2)=C(E_1)+C(E_2)-C(E_1 \cup E_2)=18000$
E1+E3	$V(E_1 \cup E_3)=C(E_1)+C(E_3)-C(E_1 \cup E_3)=27000$
E2+E3	$V(E_2 \cup E_3)=C(E_2)+C(E_3)-C(E_2 \cup E_3)=28000$
E1+E2+E3	$V(E_1 \cup E_2 \cup E_3)=C(E_1)+C(E_2)+C(E_3)-C(E_1 \cup E_2 \cup E_3)=67000$

Figure 6 - Amount of saved money

Please note that the purpose of these examples was only to illustrate the concept of benefit and therefore a number of simplified assumptions were made.

In general the concept of benefit for the context of networks of enterprises most likely represents a measure of the economic benefits (in the sense of net profit), while in the context of a NGO it could represent a more abstract notion of acquired social prestige or peer recognition. Nevertheless, in most cases this concept could be expressed as a combination of multiple variables, as illustrated in Fig. 7.

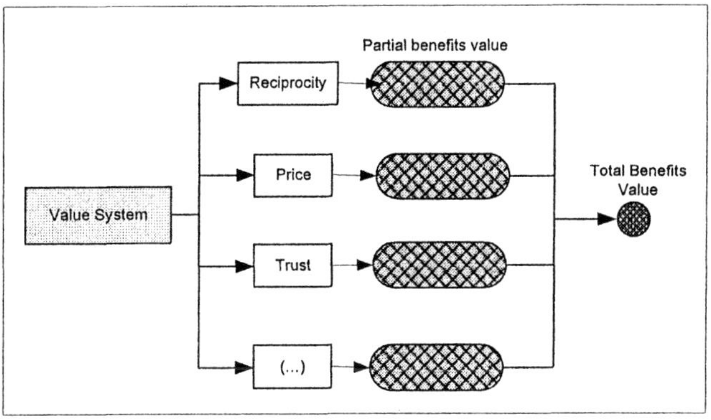

Figure 7 – Example of benefit as a combined abstract value

To illustrate this case, let us consider the following example:

Example 3 – Benefits as a combined abstract value
An enterprise needs to find a partner in order to accomplish a goal. For that purpose, it announces inside a VBE what its needs are. In order to select a partner, the enterprise builds a specific value system, decides on the relative importance of each variable and defines two reference levels – neutral and good (Fig. 8) and values worse than the neutral level are classified as "bad". Consider now that the enterprise receives bids from three other enterprises E2, E3, and E4, as shown in Fig. 9.

Value System v_j	Weight k_j	Reference level	
		Good	Neutral
Lead time	0,2	9 days	10 days
Unit Price	0,4	90 €	100 €
Guarantee	0,2	4 years	1 year
References	0,2	5 members	none

Figure 8 – Value system and reference level

Value System	E2	E3	E4
Lead time	10 days	8 days	8 days
Unit Price	100 €	120 €	80 €
Guarantee	5 years	4 years	3 years
References	7 members	6 members	6 members

Figure 9 –Received offers

In order to measure the benefits of each offer, consider that the enterprise applies the following criteria:

$$V(E_k)=\sum_{j=1}^{n} k_j \times v_j(E_k) \text{ with } \sum_{j=1}^{n} k_j = 1 \text{ e } k_j > 0 \text{ e } \begin{cases} v_j(good_j)=100 \\ v_j(neutral_j)=0 \\ v_j(bad_j)=-100 \end{cases}$$

Where:

$V(E_k)$ - Total benefits value from the bid of enterprise E_k

$v_j(E_k)$ - Partial benefits value from variable j of the value systems for the bid of enterprise E_k

k_j - Relative importance of variable j

As a result, the potential benefit of each offer is given in the table of Fig. 10.

Value System	Weight (k_j)	$v_j(E_2)$	$v_j(E_3)$	$v_j(E_4)$
Lead time	0,2	0	20	20
Unit Price	0,4	0	-40	40
Guarantee	0,2	20	0	-20
References	0,2	20	20	20
Cooperation Benefits Value $V(E_k)$		**40**	**0**	**60**

Figure 10 – Benefit of each offer

Unlike the previous two examples, in this case the concept of benefit is represented as an abstract combined value. Since, the enterprise that contributes with higher benefit value is E4 on this occasion E4 will probably be selected.

3. BENEFITS MODEL

3.1 Basic notions

Let's consider Task Performance Benefits (TB) as the combined benefits that result from the performance of a task in the context of a collaborative process. A collaborative process is understood as a set of tasks performed by the collaborative network members towards the achievement of a common goal (e.g. the business goal that motivates the creation of a Virtual Enterprise).

In this context it is also important to distinguish two set of tasks –dependent and independent. There is a task dependence when the realization of a task by one actor, and therefore the respective benefits, depends on other actors that are not involved in the execution but have an influence on that execution. An example of task dependence occurs when an actor with a good reputation in the market is present as member of a collaborative network and this fact helps others to acquire a contract (task) that otherwise would be lost. This task dependence (or influence from some actors) can be modeled as an enabling factor with a value between 0 (inhibitor) and 1 (enabler) (see, [5] for more details). For all other cases, the tasks are considered independent. For reasons of simplicity we also consider a level of granularity of tasks such that each task is performed by a single member of the network (single actor).

Based on this assumption we define the following set of intuitive concepts:

Self-benefit - benefits for actor a_i as a result of performing the task t_l.

Received benefits - benefits received by actor a_i when actor a_j performs the task t_l (perspective of a_i).

Contributed benefit – benefits from actor a_j to actor a_i as a result of performing the task t_l (perspective of a_j).

In the context of a collaborative network the total *self-benefits, received benefits or contributed benefits* for a actor a_i in a given collaborative process is given by the sum of the benefits obtained from all tasks performed inside of the collaborative network, as shown in table 1.

Table 1 – Classes of benefits

Name	Formula	Explanation of variables
Self-benefits **(SB)**	$(SB_{ii})=\sum_{l=1}^{L}TB_{ii}(t_{il})+\sum_{m=1}^{M}DTB_{ii}(t_{im})$	TB_{ii} - Task Performance Benefit for actor a_i. t_{il} – Description of a task t_l performed by actor a_i. DTB_{ii} - Dependable task Benefits for actor a_i. L – Total N° of independent tasks performed by a_i. M – Total of dependent tasks performed by a_i
Received Benefits **(RB)**	$(RB_{ij})=\sum_{l=1}^{L}TB_{ji}(t_{jl})+\sum_{m=1}^{M}DTB_{ji}(t_{jm})$	TB_{ji} - Task Performance Benefit from a_j to a_i DTB_{ij} - Dependable task Benefits from actor a_j to actor a_i. t_{jl} – Description of a task t_l performed by actor a_j L – Number of tasks performed by actor a_j M – Total N° of dependent tasks performed by a_j
Contributed Benefits **(CB)**	$(CB_{ij})=\sum_{l=1}^{L}TB_{ij}(t_{il})+\sum_{m=1}^{M}DTB_{ij}(t_{im})$	TB_{ij} - Task Performance Benefit from actor a_i to an actor a_j. DTB_{ij} - Dependable task Benefits from actor a_i to actor a_j. t_{jl} – Description of a task t_l performed by actor a_i L – Number of tasks performed by actor a_i M – Total N° of dependent tasks performed by a_i.

3.2 Indicators of collaboration

Table 2 shows a number of basic indicators that can contribute to establish a list of performance indicators tailored to collaborative networks.

Table 2 – Indicators of collaboration

Indicator	Short Description	Expression
Social Contribution Benefits **(SCB$_i$)**	The sum of benefits contributed by an actor a_i to all its partners as a result of its performance in the collaborative process.	$SCB_i=\sum_{j=1}^{N}CB_{ij} \quad i\neq j$ N – Number of actors involved in the collaborative process
External Benefits **(EB$_i$)**	The sum of benefits received by an actor a_i as a result of the activity of the other actors involved in the collaborative process.	$EB_i=\sum_{j=1}^{N}RB_{ij} \quad i\neq j$ N – Number of actors involved in the collaborative process
Total Individual Benefits **(TIB$_i$)**	The sum of external benefits plus self-benefits of an actor a_i	$TIR_i=SB_i+EB_i$
Individual Generated Benefits **(IGB$_i$)**	The sum of social contributed benefits plus self-benefits of an actor a_i	$IGB_i=SB_i+SCB_i$

Total Received Benefits **(TRB)**	The sum of external benefits achieved by a set of actors	$TRB = \sum_{j=1}^{N} EB_i$ N – Number of actors involved in the collaborative process
Total Contributed Benefits **(TCB)**	The sum of social contributed benefits generated by a set of actors	$TCB = \sum_{j=1}^{N} SCB_i$ N – Number of actors involved in the collaborative process
Total Network Benefits **(TNB)**	The sum of benefits achieved by a set of actors in a specific collaboration process or over a period of time.	$TNB = \sum_{i=1}^{K} (SB_i + SCB_i)$ K – Number of actors involved
Progress Ratio **(PR)**	This ratio is a macro indicator that represents the variation of the global benefits over a period of time. If: $PR_{[t_1,t_2]} \begin{cases} =1 \text{ there is no change} \\ >1 \text{ TNB increase} \\ <1 \text{ TNB decrease} \end{cases}$	$PR_{[t_1,t_2]} = \frac{TNB_2}{TNB_1} \quad t_2 > t_1$
Social Capital **(SC)**	Social capital can be defined as the sum of resources, that accrue to an individual or a group by virtue of possessing a durable network of more or less institutionalized relationships of mutual acquaintance and recognition [2]. In the context of a collaborative network, SC can be seen as the density of the network benefits relation.	$SC = \frac{2R}{K \times (K-1)}$ R – Number of collaborative relations in the network K – Number of actors involved
Cooperative Development Ratio **(CDR)**	The aim of this ratio is to measure the progress of collaborative benefits for a set of actors over a period of time. If: $CDR_{[t_1,t_2]} \begin{cases} =1 \text{ there is no change} \\ >1 \text{ cooperation benefits increase} \\ <1 \text{ cooperation beneits decrease} \end{cases}$	$CDR_{[t_1,t_2]} = \frac{\left(\sum_{i=1}^{N} SCB_i\right)_2}{\left(\sum_{i=1}^{N} SCB_i\right)_1} \quad t_2 > t_1$
Individual contribution index **(ICI_i)**	Normalized contribution of an actor a_i to the collaborative network	$ICI_i = \frac{SCB_i}{\sum_{j=1}^{N} SCB_i}$ N – Number of actors involved in the collaborative process
Apparent individual contribution index **(ACI_i)**	An indicator based on the number of contribution links (i.e. the *out degree* of the actor in the graph representing the collaboration benefits).This index gives an apparent and simple to compute measure of the involvement of an actor as a contributor to the collaboration process. An actor with an ACI close to zero is not perceived as a good contributor to the network (although the real value of its contribution is better expressed by ICI).	$ACI_i = \frac{N^\circ \text{ out links leaving } a_i}{N-1}$ N – Number of actors involved in the collaborative process
Individual external benefits index **(IBI_i)**	Normalized external benefits received by an actor. This index expresses the *popularity* or *prestige* of the actor [12] in the sense that actors that are prestigious tend to receive many external benefits links.	$IBI_i = \frac{EB_i}{\sum_{j=1}^{N} EB_i}$ N – Number of actors involved in the collaborative process

Apparent individual benefits index **(ABI_i)**	An indicator based on the number of received contribution links (i.e. the *in degree* of the actor in the graph representing the collaboration benefits). Similarly to IBI, this index also expresses the *popularity* or *prestige* of the actor.	$ABI_i = \frac{N^{\circ}\ links\ arriving\ at\ a_i}{N-1}$ N – Number of actors involved in the collaborative process
Reciprocity index **(RI)**	The balance between benefits credit (the sum of benefits contributed by an actor a_i to all its partners (or one specific partner)) and benefits debit (the sum of benefits received by an actor a_i as a result of the performance of all actors (or one specific partner) involved in the collaborative process). If: $RI \begin{cases} <0 & selfish\ behavior \\ =0 & null\ balance \\ >0 & altruistic\ behavior \end{cases}$	$RI = \sum_{j=1}^{N} CB_{ij} - \sum_{j=1}^{N} RB_{ji}$ N – Number of actors involved in the collaborative process

4. POTENTIAL APPLICATION IN VBE CONTEXT

Let us suppose we keep a record of the past collaborative processes where the benefits values are stored. Using simple calculations as illustrated in table 2, and some simple statistics, it is possible to extract several macro and micro indicators regarding the performance of the VBE and its members as a collaborative structure. These indicators can be determined for a particular collaboration process (a particular VO occurrence) or over a period of time (average values for the VBE) and can be used in decision-making processes, such as planning a new VO. For instance:

At the VBE management level: Global indicators (e.g. total network benefits – TNB, progress ratio - PR, social capital – SC, development cooperative ratio – DCR) or member specific indicators (e.g. reciprocity index – RI, Social Contribution index – SCB, Apparent individual benefit index – ABI, Apparent individual contribution index – ACI).

At the broker's level: Indicators that may help in partner selection for a specific VO (e.g. individual contribution index – ICI). For partners selection it is also important to analyze the history of dyads, an actor a_i might be more effective when collaborating with a specific actor a_j than with any other in the VBE, (reciprocity index – RI). For the analysis of the VO (e.g. total network benefits – TNB, total contributed benefits – TCB or total received benefits – TRB of the VO, etc.). For instance, if the benefits in a particular VO are mainly self-benefits it means the level of (explicit) collaboration is low (the work could be done in isolation).

At the member's level: Indicators that may help a member find answers for questions such as: Shall I get involved in this consortium? (e.g. Individual Generated Benefits – IGB); Was my participation in this collaborative process beneficial to me? (e. g. external benefits – EB, total individual benefits – TIB); What is my level of "popularity" or "prestige"? (e.g. individual external benefits index – IBI) What is the balance of my interactions with a specific member (dyad relationship)? Have I got reciprocity, in the past, from the potential members to be involved in the same VO? (e.g. reciprocity index - RI).

The main difficulty is naturally the determination of the benefits corresponding to each collaborative task/process. To collect and record those values without being intrusive in the network members "life" requires further research and development.

5. CONCLUSIONS

The characterization and understanding of collaboration benefits is a key pre-condition for a wide adoption of the collaborative networks paradigm in its various manifestation forms. This understanding is also a base for the establishment of proper performance indicators to be used in decision making processes at various levels: VO breeding environment management, VO brokering, and VO breeding environment membership. Some preliminary steps in this direction, inspired in the Social Networks analysis but also taking some insights from other areas such as transaction costs and game theories, were presented. Initial results illustrate the applicability of the suggested approach. The development of full practical framework for performance measurement and benefits analysis in collaborative networks still requires further work.

Acknowledgments – This work as supported in part by the ECOLEAD integrated project funded by the European Commission.

6. REFERENCES

1. Axelroad, R. (1984). The Evolution of Cooperation, Basic Books.
2. Bourdieu, P.; L. Wacquant, (1992). An invitation to reflexive sociology, Chicago: University of Chicago Press.
3. Borgatti, S.P., Everett, M.G. and Freeman, L.C. 2002. Ucinet for Windows: Software for Social Network Analysis. Harvard, MA: Analytic Technologies.
4. Camarinha-Matos, L. M.; Abreu, António (2004). A contribution to understand collaborative benefits - Emerging solutions for future manufacturing systems, Springer, ISBN 0-387-22828-4.
5. Camarinha-Matos, L. M.; Afsarmanesh, H. (2003). Elements of a VE base infrastructure, J. Computers in Industry, Vol. 51, Issue 2, Jun 2003, pp. 139-163.
6. Camarinha-Matos, L. M.; Afsarmanesh, H. (Ed.s) (2004). Collaborative Networked Organizations – A research agenda for emerging business models, Kluwer Academic Publishers, ISBN 1-4020-7823-4.
7. Evans, S.; Roth, N.; Sturm, F. (2004). Performance measurement and added value of networks, in Collaborative Networked Organizations – A research agenda for emerging business models, Kluwer Academic Publishers, ISBN 1-4020-7823-4.
8. Kolakovic, Marko (2003).VAVE – A model for measuring the business performance of virtual enterprise – Business Excellence I, performance measures, benchmarking and best practices in new economy, University of Minho, ISBN 972-8692-08-0.
9. Myerson, R. B. (1997). Game Theory Analysis of Conflict, Harvard University Press.
10. Seifert, Marcus; Eschenbaecher, Jens (2004). Predictive performance measurement in virtual organisations - Emerging solutions for future manufacturing systems, Springer, ISBN 0-387-22828-4.
11. Vallejos, Rolando Vargas; Gomes, Jefferson de Oliveira (2004). Applying a benchmarking methodology to empower a virtual organisation - Emerging solutions for future manufacturing systems, Springer, ISBN 0-387-22828-4.
12. Wasserman, S. and K. Faust. (1994). *Social Network Analysis - Methods and Applications*. Cambridge University press.
13. Williamson, O. E. (1985). The Economic Institutions of Capitalism: Firms, Markets, Relational Contracting, New York: Free Press.

PART 10

PERFORMANCE MEASUREMENT

29

A PERFORMANCE MEASUREMENT SYSTEM FOR VIRTUAL AND EXTENDED ENTERPRISES

Juan José Alfaro Saiz, Raúl Rodríguez Rodríguez, Angel Ortiz Bas
Department of Business Organisation, Financial Economy and Accounting, Polytechnic University of Valencia, SPAIN;
jalfaro@omp.upv.es, raurodro@upvnet.upv.es, aortiz@omp.upv.es

Nowadays, enterprises seek to improve their operations and results by collaborating within networks of enterprises. Then, it is necessary to have available a method for monitoring and controlling how both Virtual Enterprises (VE) and Extended Enterprises (EE) are performing. For doing so, an efficient and effective performance measurement system (PMS) should be applied. An extensive literature review was conducted to find out existing feasible PMSs that really covered this field properly. As a result, it was found out that there was not a framework that fully accomplished these tasks, being then developed the one called Performance Measurement System for Extended and Virtual Enterprises (PMS-EVE). The PMS-EVE framework is built on the concepts of trust and equity to be present within the relationships among the different components of the VE/EE.

1. INTRODUCTION

In the last years, market globalisation has been favoured for the advances experimented by Information and Communication Technologies (ICT), mainly with the apparition and huge spreading of the Internet. This fact has increased competitiveness among organisations, demanding a quick adaptation to face market requirements. Consequently, organisations seek to establish collaborations with others ones, aiming to strength their weaknesses by facing common objectives. Such organisations that cooperate and collaborate among them through their human capital and supported by ICT are known as Collaborative Networked Organisations (CNO) (Dyer, 2000).

Such collaboration maximise the combined capacities allowing each enterprise to reach its strategic objectives by providing integrated solutions to its customers' needs.

According to (Riis, 1997) these CNOs can be mainly classified into Extended Enterprises (EE) and Virtual Enterprises (VE). Additionally, (Moller et al. , 1997) identifies the EE with a Supply Chain and the VE with a Virtual Organisation.

EE span company boundaries and include complex relationships between a company, its partners, customers, suppliers and market (Browne, Sackett and Wortmann, 1994), (Caskey, 1995). As "Figure 1" shows, EE can be defined as an entity where the dominant company extents its vision and relies fully on others members for key aspects of the value chain such as distribution, logistics and direct sales to final customers. Companies in an extended enterprise must co-ordinate their internal systems (intra-organisational activities) with other systems within the supply chain, being flexible enough to adapt to changes.

On the other hand, (Preiss, 1996) defines a Virtual Organisation as a collection of business units where people and work processes from these business units interact intensively for carrying out work that mutually benefits all the parts. More specifically, numerous authors have defined VE, An obtained definition in "The Economist" (February, 1993) affirms that a VE is a temporal network of organisations that get joined to exploit a specific market opportunity supported by the technological capabilities of the companies that compose the network; (Riis, 1997) states that a VE is characterised by complementary contributions coming from different companies where one of these plays the broker role and without leader, relying their survival on the attitude of all the companies. "Figure 1" illustrates the mentioned concepts.

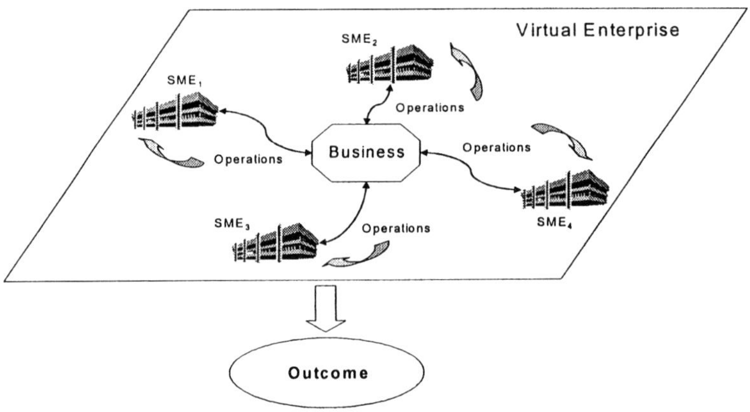

Figure 1: Virtual Enterprise

Due to the extensive degree of proliferation of these VE/EEs, it is very important to have a robust and reliable Performance Management System (PMS) that enables to control and monitor efficiently and effectively their performance. This is the main objective of the paper.

2. BRIEF LITERATURE REVIEW

Hence, it is possible to identify EE with Supply Chain level and VE with several enterprises (or business units) from different Supply Chains. The authors have conducted a breadth researching throughout the academic literature identifying the most significant existing frameworks for measuring performance at these two domains.

Thus, when measuring supply chain performance, several authors have identified that the usual practice was to extrapolate traditional individual performance measures, such as cost, flexibility or customer response (Beamon, 1999) to the supply chain context, concluding that this practice does not provide a proper PMS for the supply chain. Consequently, they developed several methods that tried to cover this lack. In this sense, Gunasekaran and Tirtiroglu (2001) presented a framework for measuring supply chain performance at the strategic, tactic and operative levels. On the other hand, Chan et al (2003) developed a supply chain model that counted with both tangible and intangible performance measures within multiple dimensions and cross-organisational. This model was improved by Chan and Qi (2003) with the introduction of the called Performance of Activity (POA), which was used to identify both performance measures and metrics, enabling the construction of processes models from the organisations' missions within the supply chain. On the other hand, (Brewer and Speh, 2000) developed a method that modified the traditional Balance Scorecard (BSC) developed by (Kaplan and Norton, 1992) for accomplishing the considerations stated as important ones by supply chain performance measurement experts (Handfield and Nichols, 1999) and (Lee and Billington, 1992). Finally, Burton and Boeder (2003) developed a good approach called Extended Enterprise Assessment Process based on the seven best practices and principle categories, each one having six more specific criteria (42 total criteria), but still not enough to define fully and properly the relationships among the components of the EE.

Only few frameworks deal with measuring performance within a network of enterprises. At this stage, the most relevant work is the one developed by Bullinger, Kühner and Hoof (2002), which presents a hybrid balanced measurement system, integrating both SCOR model (Supply Chain Operations Reference) and adapted balanced scorecards. The metrics of SCOR model focus on controlling both material and product flows by measuring logistic performance. The main motivation of network scorecards is to control logistic networks' business objectives by the measurement of management performance as stated by Gehlen (2002). Together, the metrics constitute a holistic instrument for the measurement of logistic process performance

Within this ambit, Leseure, Shaw and Chapman (2001) introduced the concept of Meta-performance to describe the performance at the network level. Such a concept is a two-dimensional construction, which encloses the concepts of performance and equity within a network. Under this vision, these authors defined a framework for meta-organisational performance measurement in vertical networks. They pointed out that equity should be present at all the levels of networked organisations, measuring both the contribution of each individual member to the VE/EE and the ability of each member to schedule its operations accurately.

The model developed by Zhao (2002) points in the same direction, determining whether the collaborative activities do transmit an appropriate value to all the involved partners of the network or not.

As a conclusion, it could be stated that there is a clear lack of robust and solid frameworks for both the VE and the EE, which establish solid relationships through equity and trust practices among the different actors of the VE/EE, by enabling also to keep a clear traceability among the parts.

3. PMS-EVE FRAMEWORK

From the above literature review is possible to think that one of the main problems that organisations find when facing the challenge of becoming either a VE or an EE is the lack of both methods and techniques for assessing the necessary efforts in terms of money, human capital, organisation, etc. Therefore, the PMS-EVE model presented in this work provides a definition of methods and techniques that enable evaluation of the organisation's current state as well as the migration model that will drive towards the VE/EE model, assessing at the same time the adequacy of such migration model for managing and achieving the change of state.

"Figure 2" shows the basics of the model, which clearly differentiates between the global or networked level and the local one. In the case of a VE the global level would be the conjoint of several individual enterprises (or business units) from different supply chains and the local one would be composed of every of these individual companies, whereas that in the case of an EE the global level would be the supply chain as a whole and the local one would be constituted by the different actors of the supply chain participating on the EE.

There are two axes, the vertical axis and the horizontal one. On one hand, the former defines the components of the PMS: Goals, objectives, strategies, plans, policies, critical success factors and derived KPIs at both levels global and local. On the other hand, the latter provides four different perspectives to be taken into account when defining the PMS components: Organisation, resources, information and function.

Hence, an objective is the current enunciate of a result that the entity aims to reach in the future, it responds to the question of 'What do we want to measure?'. Then, a strategy is the way of carrying out the entity's activities and processes and of managing the entity's resources to reach the objectives. It responds to the question of 'How do we want to measure the stated objectives?'. On the other hand, the critical success factors CSFs) are those factors that guarantee, through its monitoring and accomplishment, the entity's success. The CSFs are formed by a reduced conjoint of both measurable Objectives and Strategies. Once the Objectives, Strategies and CSFs have been defined, they derive into KPIs that are the final and most operative part of the PMS.

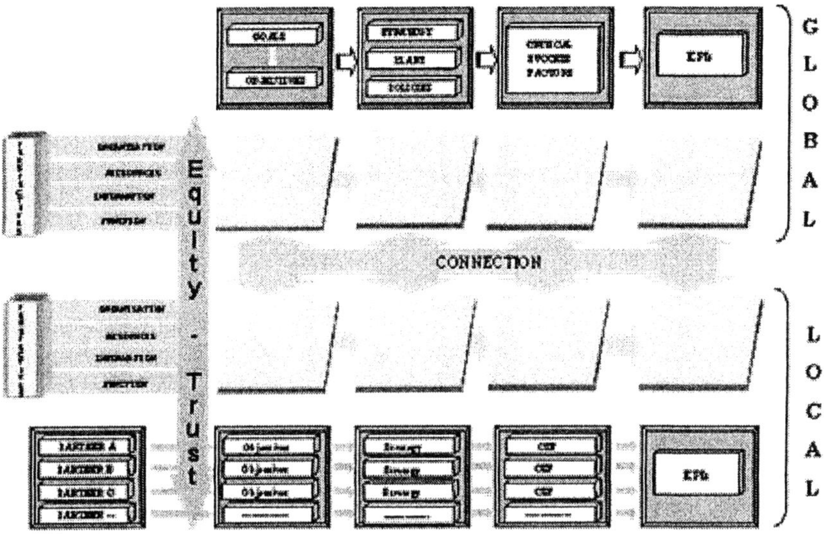

Figure 2: PMS-EVE Integrated proposal

Within a business level, the KPIs evaluate very important states of organisations aiming to join to a VE/EE since they control and assess the current or AS-IS state, the future ideal or TO-BE state, the migration path required for going from the AS-Is to the TO-BE state and the quality of the generated results. When carrying out the previous PMS components definition, it is necessary to bear in mind those factors or perspectives considered as of key importance for both the VE/EE and the individual enterprises/business entities forming the network. As "Figure 3" illustrates, we have considered four our model the next four perspectives to be taken into account: Function, Information, Resources and Organisation. These four perspectives are further explained next:

- Function: It is important to set up how the definition of the Objectives, Strategies, CSFs and KPIs will influence to the VE/EE regarding its functionality, and more concretely regarding processes, activities and inter-relationships.
- Information: It is necessary to find out what implications the Objectives, Strategies, CSFs and KPIs, from an informational point of view, will have for developing both processes and activities of the VE/EE, and more concretely regarding information needs and structure of the information systems.
- Resources: It is important to identify what needs, regarding resources, will be necessary for accomplishing the Objectives, Strategies, CSFs and KPIs and therefore being able to carry out both processes and activities of the

VE/EE, and more concretely regarding economic, human and material (tools) resources.
- Organisation: It is necessary to find out how the definition of Objectives, Strategies, CSFs and KPIs will affect to the VE/EE from an organisational point of view, and more concretely regarding organisational chart, responsibilities and decision-making.

These four perspectives correspond to the modelling skeleton of the Architecture of Open Systems, CIMOSA (Amice, 1989). In this way, our model aims to cover all the aspects that are susceptible of being measured and analysed under these four perspectives. Any element of a VE/EE can be allocated within these four views and therefore it will be a result of the definition of the different performance measurement elements used within the proposal.

As it can be seen in "Figure 3", at the Organisation perspective level, there are defined two objectives, and then three strategies, and then two critical success factors.

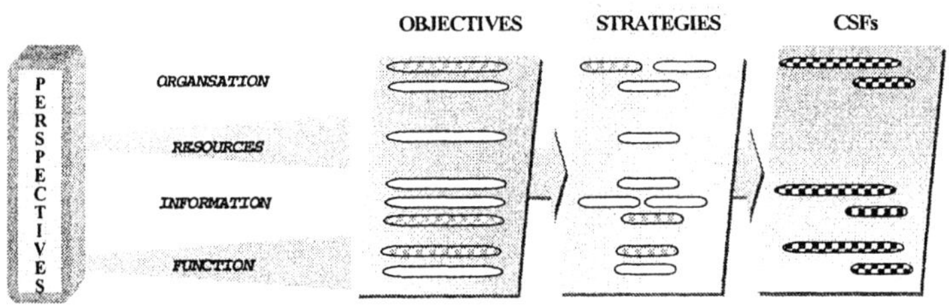

Figure 3: Relationships between Objectives, Strategies and Critical Success Factors and the four relevant perspectives

As stated in the literature review, one of the main objectives for establishing a solid and robust PMS within a VE/EE is to promote and achieve a state of coherence and equity among the partners constituting such VE/EE. In order to achieve such a coherence degree between the different levels, local and global, as well as among the different partners forming the network, the most important thing is to have a PMS that clearly shows the relationships among all the PMS components. Then, it would be possible to unequivocally control and monitor all such PMS components. For doing so, the system must provide a method that clearly shows the traceability from the defined KPIs until the upstream Objectives that these KPIs come from. As shown in "Figure 4", the PMS-EVE model allows such traceability among performance components. Then, it enables and foments coherence between the two main levels, global and local, as the Objectives, Strategies, CSFs and KPIs defined at the Global level are clearly identified with the Objectives, Strategies, CSFs and KPIs defined at the Local one. This approach also enables the easy control and follow-up of equity among the different enterprises forming the network.
Additionally, the PMS-EVE model is a very useful tool for making decisions within VE/EEs since it delivers to decision-makers the whole picture of both the global and the local level, being therefore pretty easy to find relationships and to assess the changes that will take place within the dynamic VE/EE overtime.

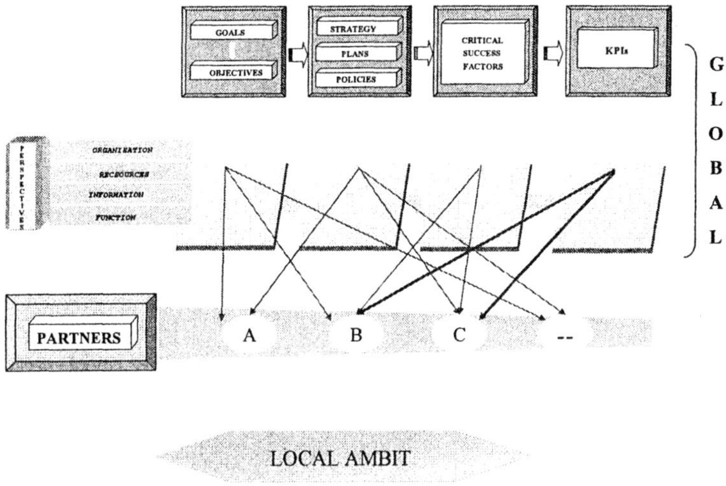

Figure 4: Traceability between the Global and the Local level.

4. CONCLUSIONS

This paper has briefly described the frameworks currently available to measure performance at both the EE and the VE. We then identified the gap that such frameworks present and justified the development of our model. Then, we presented the PMS-EVE model, describing its main parts and functionalities and how its application can deliver advantages to organisations that either have joined or are thinking of joining an EE/VE.

5. REFERENCES

AMICE (1989), Consortium 'Open System Architecture for CIM, Research Reports ESPRIT/Project 688 AMICE' Springer-Verlag 1989.

Beamon, Benita M. (1999): "Measuring supply chain performance", International Journal of Operations and Production Management, Vol. 19, N° 3, pp. 275-292.

Brewer, P.C. and Speh, T.W. (2000), "Using the Balanced Scorecard to measure supply chain performance", Journal of Business Logistics, Vol. 21, No. 1, pp. 75-94.

Browne, J.; Sackett, P.; Wortmann, H: (1994), Industry requirements and associated research issues in the extended enterprise, *Proceedings of the European Workshop on Integrated Manufacturing Systems Engineering*, IMSE'94, Grenoble, December 12-14, pp. 9-16.

Bullinger, H.J.; Kühner, M.; Hoof, A.V. (2002): "Analysing supply chain performance using a balanced measurement method", International Journal of Production Research; Vol. 40, N° 15, pp. 3533-3543.

Burton, T.T. and Boeder, S.M (2003): *The Lean Extended Enterprise: Moving Beyond the Four Walls to Value Stream Excellence.* J. Ross Publishing, Inc. Florida.

Caskey, K.R. (1995): Co-operative distributed simulation and optimization in extended enterprises, Proceedings of the IFIP WG5.7 *Working Conference on Managing Concurrent Manufacturing to Improve Industrial Performance*, Seattle, pp. 23-32.

Chan, T.S.; Qi, H.J. (2003): "Feasibility of performance measurement system for supply chain: a process-based approach and measures", Integrated Manufacturing Systems; Vol. 14, N° 3, pp. 179-190.

Chan, T.S.; Qi, H.J.; Chan, Henry C.W.; Ip, Ralph W.L. (2003). "A conceptual model of performance environment"; International Journal of Operations & Production Management; Vol. 21, N° ½, pp. 71-87.

Dyer, J. H. (2000): *Collaborative Advantage: Winning Through Extended Enterprise Supplier Networks.* Oxford University Press. New York.

Gehlen de Leao, A. (2002), "A business logistics approach to design performance evaluation systems", Papers from the Third International Conference on Performance Measurement and Management (PMA 2002), July.

Gunasekaran, A.; Patel, C.; Tirtiroglu, E. (2001): "Performance measures and metrics in a supply chain" measurement for supply chains, *Management Decision*; Vol. 41, N° 7, pp. 635-642.

Handfield, R.B., and Nichols, E.L. (1999), Introduction to supply chain management, Prentice may Upper Saddle River, NJ.

Jagou, P. *Concurrent engineering, French version*, Hermès, Paris (1993).

Kaplan, R.S.; Noron, D. P. (1992): "The balanced scorecard. Measures that drive performance", Harvard Bisiness review. Jan/Feb, pp. 71-79.

Lee, H.I. and Billington, C. (1992): "Managing supply chain inventory: Pitfalls and opportunities", Sloan Management Review, Vol. 33, Spring, No. 3, pp. 65-73.

Leseure M.; Shaw N.; Chapman G. (2001): "Performance measurement in organisational networks: an exploratory case study"; International Journal of Business Performance Management; Vol. 3, N° 1, pp. 30-46.

Moller, C.; Riis, J. O.; Hansen, M. (1997): Department of Production, Aalborg University, "A framework for studing industrial networks".

Preiss, K.; Steven, L.; Roger, N.N. (1996): "Cooperate to Compete Building Agile Business Relationships", Van Nostrand Reinhold,.

Riis, J.O. (1997): IFIP WG 5.7 Ascona Working Conference, Switzerland.

Zhao, F. (2002), "Measuring inter-organizational partnerships: The challenge of cultural discrepancy"; Papers from the Third International Conference on Performance Measurement and Management (PMA 2002), July.

30 VIRTUAL SCORECARD AS A DECISION-MAKING TOOL IN CREATING VIRTUAL ORGANISATION

W. M. Grudzewski
Correspondent Member of Polish Science Academy
w.grudzewski@orgmasz.pl
A. Sankowska
Warsaw University of Technology, Faculty of Production Engineering
e-mail: amsankowska@wp.pl
M. Wantuchowicz
Warsaw University of Technology, Faculty of Production Engineering
e-mail: monika.wantuchowicz@wp.pl
POLAND

Peter Drucker "If you cannot measure it, you cannot manage it". We want to elaborate the partners for co-operation in Virtual Organisation (VO). Our specific goal is to elaborate the Virtual Scorecard – a measure of organization abilities to form VO, which will give the answer for the following question – How well is the organization prepared to form VO?

1. INTRODUCTION

Today enterprises look for solutions that might secure them from more and more unpredictable changes in business environment and provide stable and successful existence. They search for various methods of decreasing risk and cost and benefiting from fast closing market opportunity. The virtual form of organisation could be one of the solutions that bring better understanding and new approaches to dealing with "ad hoc" cooperation (e.g. proper principles, formal models). The article distinguishes the special needs for measurement tool - Virtual Scorecard (VSc) - that focuses on three domains considered to be essential in effective Virtual Organisation (VO) and provides a large normative data set against which the potential partners for co-operation can be selected. Data derived from Polish IT sector enabled us to conceptualize VSc[1].

2. THE CONCEPTION OF VIRTUAL SCORECARD

2.1 Working definition

The composition of VO depends on requirements of a specific market opportunity and how other orgasniations may satisfy these requirements (Wywrocki, 1999,

[1]For more information and examples of the general partners selection tool interested readers are referred to e.g. "collaboration maturity audit" ("Cambridge Manufacturing Review", 2002).

Lipnack and Stamps, 1997). VO is temporary, ad hoc network of independent enterprises linked up by ICT and working together to exploit market opportunity.

2.2 Process of potential partners selection in VO model

In the cycle of forming VO we use a model (Saabeel et al., 2002) that consists of three layers (see Figure1), including: the universe of modules, the Dynamic Network (DN) and VO. According to this concept organizations forming the VO are a part of a larger network within which a selection is made[2].

Firstly, potential members are selected from the universe of modules - that is the set of all organizations that represent different objectives, strategies, competencies and resources and thereby different capabilities to act in the network. The ability to select potential partners from the universe of modules is essential for DN[3]. It allows to reduce complexity, interdependence and uncertainty. So far uncertainty of strangers is so huge, that decision-makers prefer to stay with already known partners form former collaboration (stable DN). Owning to that great number of new potential successful partnerships establishment will never occur[4].Therefore, providing a tool for selecting strangers to set of DN could enhance already existing connections in DN.

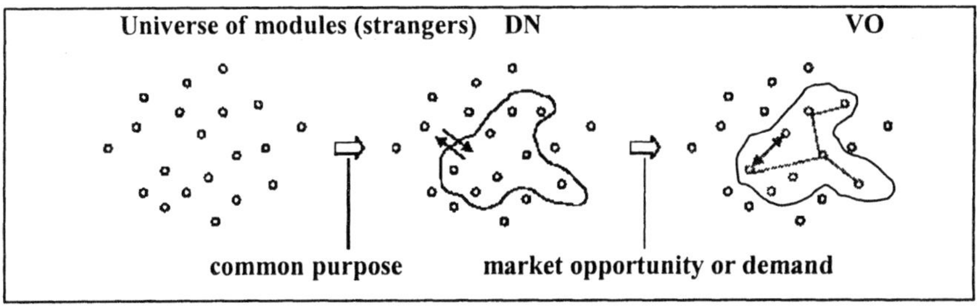

Figure 1 – Three layers in the process of partners' selection for VO (compare with Saabeel et al., 2002)

The pre-selection mechanism has to ensure that the DN members can work in VO by evaluating their capabilities to cooperate in form of VO. The crucial issue is the clearness of the assignment criteria. We obviously need to deliver to decision-makers final scores of strangers' crucial holistic collaborative competencies in order to make comparisons between strangers and more effective decisions.

2.3 Virtual –Scorecard in process of potential VO's partners selection

We define a Virtual Scorecard[5] as a measuring instrument of organizations'

---

[2] Many authors argue that there is a number of strategic effects of collaboration and co-operation (Dyer, 1996; Hamel et al., 1989). This model presumes that organizations are motivated to form VO at particular moment, when the market opportunity or demand occurs.

[3] The Dynamic Network is defined as an open-ended collection of pre-qualified organizations that are able to form VO in order to benefit from specific market opportunity.

[4] Notice that the map of Internet traffic looks similar to the maps of maritime and land transport.

[5] *Virtual* because it concerns the potential cooperation in reality in VO when there are suitable conditions and a lucrative market opportunity. *Scorecard* because it measures condition of the enterprise to collaboration.

capabilities used when organization want to participate in potential VO. It will allow the decision maker to find an open-ended collection of pre-qualified partners that have met defined criteria (Grudzewski and Hejduk, 2000). That means they are adopted to co-operate in future VO and agree to form a pool of potential partners in VO.

Our first step was defining the most important criteria verifying whether an organization is ready to work in the networks of organizations. To make the decision process more efficient we selected a subset from a wider set of criteria. Then, we found the most fit criteria which should be taken into consideration in the decision-making process. The selection of criteria from the "universe of criteria" was based on the results of survey conducted in IT companies that have got experience in temporary co-operation. There was an assumption that common proposal would be established.

VSc as a decision-making tool in the process of VO management allows to:

a. Make the process of partners' selecting more formalized and more efficient;

b. Create the DN database with potential partners for VO that have met specific criteria;

c. Make the process of selecting, pre-qualifying partners to VO clearer (the process of transition to the second layer – see Figure 1);

d. Make response to market opportunities more rapid (the choice from pre-qualified members is easier and faster than from the whole universe of modules);

e. Reduce the complexity and the uncertainty in the pre-selection process of business partners - standardized previously - which are from the universe of modules (risk management).

3. THE SURVEY

3.1 Objectives of the survey

There were two main phases in our survey:

a. Selecting the most important factors from the initial list, called testing factors, based on conducted survey. The thesis in this survey was as follows: selected factors, which would gain the highest ranks, were crucial for the success of VO. In this phase there was compiled a suitable questionnaire. It was completed in Polish IT companies by workers on managerial and non-managerial positions. These workers assessed the rank (the importance) of 48 factors which were considered while deciding in favour of initial list of partners for cooperation. A result of that phase was the final set of testing factors;

b. Creating VSc that is the tool veryfing if a certain enterprise is a suitable potential cooperant. The assessment and verification is based on fulfilling the conditions from the list of crucial factors. VSc can be also seen as a set of guidelines for developing these organizations which aspire to take part in relations based on the networks.

3.2 Methodology in the empirical study

The utilization of experts' opinions in a real world context has value (Bunn, Wright,

1991)[6]. This paper reports on a survey of 11 judges (experts) that are from IT-services companies in Poland (Warsaw) and are experienced in temporary "ad hoc" cooperation. This group represents a cross-section of staff working in VO in IT sector. All responses are made on an anonymous basis. The judges were asked to rank the importance of 48 initial factors which allow to evaluate the organizations' ability to become a potential partner in VO if there is a common purpose.

To face with the importance of factors we use a sum of ranks that each *j* factor receives according to the following formula from all experts:

$$R_j = \sum_{i=1}^{p} R_i$$

This way we identify which particular factors are the most important ones (those with the highest sum of ranks). In our study the maximum sum of ranks is 44. We pick up those factors that receive at least 80% of maximum sum that is 35.

The experts' answers analysis is based on the analysis of concordance of each opinion. The team is authoritative if the experts are at least moderately consistent in their opinions. We have got $p = 11$ of experts and $n = 48$ of factors which are ranked according to the scale with *k* degrees $(k=5)$. The starting point for the experts opinions analysis is the overall table with the survey results where R_{ij} means rank with *m* number $(m= 0, 1, \ldots, k)$ assigned to *j* factor by *i* expert $(i = 1, \ldots, p)$.

The analysis of the survey outcomes allows to:

a. Assess the concordance of experts' replies for each factor separately and for all factors in total;

b. Define the common opinion in the group of experts.

Regarding the analysis of the survey outcomes above the coefficient of dispersion was used. This coefficient measures the degree of agreement among judges within *j* factor. Formula shows the computation of this coefficient for *j* factor, represented as h_j :

$$h_j = \frac{k}{k-1}(1 - \sum_{m=0}^{k} f_{jm}^2)$$

where:

k – the number of ranks for each factor ($k = const = 5$);

f_{jm} - frequency of occurrence of *m* rank in *j* factor.

We used the Kendall Coefficient of Concordance *W* (Siegel, Castellan, 1988), to determine the overall agreement among *p* judges who were assessing the importance of a given set of *n* factors which were taken into consideration in the process of selecting members of DN. Kendall's *W* is obtained from the following formulas:

$$W = \frac{12S}{p^2(n^3 - n)} \qquad S = \sum_{j=1}^{n}(\sum_{i=1}^{p} R_{ij} - \overline{R})^2$$

---

[6] There is a large literature analyzing whether the predictions and assessments obtained from judges are more accurate than these from other statistical methods provided that the researchers obtain independent opinions from betweeen 5 and 20 experts (Armstrong ed., 2002).

$$\overline{R} = \frac{\sum_{j=1}^{n} \sum_{i=1}^{p} Rij}{n}$$

where:

p - the number of judges (respondents in the survey);

n – the number of factors ($n = 1, \ldots 48$)

$\overline{R}$ - average value of the ranks for all factors

R_{ij} - the rank of j factor ($j = 1, \ldots, 48$) of the analyzed feature measured with ordinal scale assessed by i judge ($I = 1, \ldots, p$).

To assess the significance of W ($0 \leq W \leq 1$) we use χ^2 statistics (chi-squared test) according to the following formula:

$$\chi^2 = p(p-1)W$$

with $(n - 1)$ degrees of freedom.

This allows us to test the statistical significance of W. The null hypothesis (H_o) was that the judges who produced rankings were independent from each other. In other words, H_o was that the $p = 11$ judges were not concordant with each other.

3.3 Results of the empirical study

After summing up the ranks for each factor from initial list of 48 factors we found 14 factors that achieved at least sum of 35. The coefficient of dispersion for 13 factors was from 0,58 to 0,79. One achieved more than 0,80 so we made a decision to remove it from our list of 14 the most important factors. Results for those 13 significant factors (testing factors) are presented in Table 1.

Table 1 – Testing factors

No.	Factor :	Sum of ranks	Coefficient of dispersion
1.	*Trusting relationships*	40	0,58
2.	*Openness to cooperation*	39	0,64
3.	*Fast feedback of information*	39	0,62
4.	*Honest and clear communication*	39	0,64
5.	*Communication via Internet*	38	0,70
6.	*Meeting the deadlines*	38	0,70
7.	*Format of transferred data*	37	0,79
8.	*Low failure rate of communications systems*	37	0,72
9.	*Advanced employees' skills to work in teams*	37	0,70
10.	*Competitive time of delivering products and services*	37	0,56
11.	*High throughput and transfer rate of communications channels*	36	0,70
12.	*Innovative technologies*	36	0,79
13.	*IT Systems Security*	35	0,79

As we see above the highest ranked factors are trust and openness to cooperation. Those two factors and fast feedback of information, honest and clear communication as well as working in teams are concerning the soft abilities. They embrace competences connected with high corporate culture and ethics. The other factors like: Internet, formats of data, low failure rate of communications systems, throughput and transfer rate of communications channels as well as security of IT unambiguously are embedded in technical facets of VO. Consequently, the rest of factors, that is meeting the deadlines, time of delivering services and products as well as innovative technologies, are rather connected with core competencies in the specific area of activity. The findings of our empirical study in IT sector clustered around three core domains important for VO.

As far as concordance of experts' opinion for these 13 factors is concerned we have:

$$W = 0{,}7$$

$$1\text{-}\alpha = 0{,}05 \qquad n' - 1 = 12$$

$$\chi^2 = 75 \qquad \chi^2_{(1-\alpha;n-1)} = 21$$

$$\chi^2 > \chi^2_{(1-\alpha;n-1)}, \quad \text{so we reject } H_o$$

Concluding - judges do agree on the factors and the results are not random in statistical sense. The team of judges is competent and helps to create VSc.

4. VIRTUAL SCORECARD FORMULATION

We had divided 13 important factors (testing factors) into three main domains: technical, cross-culture and core competence.

Virtual Scorecard is illustrated in Table 2.

In VSc should be determined weights for each factor in order to get the final assessment. This evaluation can help in deciding if an organization is capable of working in VO and to create the DN database.

We want to emphasize that it is initial outlook of VSc. Further survey should be carried on in order to find the correlation among all factors. Following the rule of diagnostic (testing) factors the ones that are strongly correlated should be removed and only their representative will appear in the final VSc. Moreover, VSc could be developed by finding quantitative/qualitative metrics (Parth, Gumz, 2003) for its factors. Due to the complexity of single factors , it can be necessary to define them through more than one performance measure, it order to characterize them sufficiently. These are the goals for the next research.

Thus, we are looking for score board that the multiplication of few very important not correlated weighted factors that each of them has got quantitative or/and qualitative measures. The less factor we have, the less time and money we spend on getting information about their values in potential partners.

Table 2 – Virtual Scorecard – *How well are the partners prepared to form VO?*

Domain	FACTORS	Measure	Weight	Weighted average
Technical competence	*Communication via Internet*			
	IT Systems Security			
	Format of transferred data			
	High throughput and transfer rate of communications channels			
	Low failure rate of communication systems			
Cross-culture competence	*Trusting relationships*			
	Openness to cooperation			
	Fast feedback of information			
	Honest and clear communication			
	Advanced employees' skills to wok in teams			
Core competence	*Meeting the deadlines*			
	Competitive time of delivering products and services			
	Innovative technologies			
TOTAL				

5. CONCLUSIONS AND SUGGESTIONS FOR FUTURE RESEARCH

The VSc is a clear, concise user-friendly and provides a useful information to select the potential partners for co-operation in VO. Our another research should improve and build up already existing VSc. We want to eliminate those factors that are correlated with each other. It would protect from repeating similar information.

Survey that led us to the formulation of VSc allows us to make some conclusions. After survey we acknowledged the great importance of trust and openness to collaboration for effective cooperation in VO. Furthermore, results provide a context for improvements in organization within its ability to participate in VO. Overall the general trust of the VSc has been well received by over ten experts from IT sector in Poland and they have acknowledged the importance of co-operants' selecting.

The problem is to find appropriate metrics for the selected factor as well as to find mechanism for their development. We can presume that in the area of the most important factors further studies must be undertaken to increase consciousness of these factors. Future research can consist of obtaining measures and methods of enhancing each factor with stress especially put on confidence factor.

6. REFERENCES

1. Bunn D, Wright G. Interaction of judgmental and statistical forecasting methods: issues and analysis. "Management Science", 37, 1991.
2. Dyer J. Specialized supplier networks as a source of competitive advantage: evidence from the auto industry. "Strategic Management Journal", vol. 17, no. 4, 1996.
3. Collaborate to innovate. "Cambridge Manufacturing Review", Summer, 2002, http://www.ifm.eng.cam.ac.uk/service/cmr.
4. Grudzewski WM, Hejduk I. Przedsiębiorstwo wirtualne (The Virtual Enterprise). Difin, Warsaw, 2002.
5. Hamel G, Doz YL, Prahalad CK. Collaborate with your competitors – and win. "Harvard Business Review", January-February, 1989.
6. Lipnack J, Stamps J. Virtual Teams: Reaching across Space, Time and Organisations with Technology. John Wiley and Sons, united Kingdom, 1997.
7. Makridakis S, Wheelwright SC. Forecasting – methods and applications. John Wiley and Sons, New York, 1998.
8. Parth FR, Gumz J. How Project Metrics Can Keep You from Flying Blind. www.ProjectAuditors.com, Project Management Institute, 2003.
9. Principles of forecasting, JS. Armstrong (ed.). Kluwer Academic Publishers, Massachusetts, 2002.
10. Przedsiębiorstwo przyszłości (The Enterprise of the future), WM. Grudzewski, I. Hejduk (ed.). Difin, Warsaw, 2000.
11. Saabeel W, Verduijn TM, Hagdorn L, Kumar K. A model of virtual organisation: a structrure and process perspective. "Electronic Journal of Organizational Virtualness", vol. 4, no. 1, 2002.
12. Siegel S, Castellan JN. Nonparametric Statistic for the Behavioral Sciences. Second Edition, McGraw – Hilll Book Company, New York, 1988.
13. Wywrocki A. Communication supported by Internet Technology between business parters in Virtual Organisations. Linköping University, 1999.

31

TOWARDS PERFORMANCE MEASUREMENT IN VIRTUAL ORGANIZATIONS
Potentials, Needs, and Research Challenges

Falk Graser
Bremen Institute of Industrial Engineering and Applied Work Science
grs@biba.uni-bremen.de, GERMANY

Kim Jansson
VTT – Industrial Systems
kim.jansson@vtt.fi, FINLAND

Jens Eschenbächer
Bremen Institute of Industrial Engineering and Applied Work Science
esc@biba.uni-bremen.de, GERMANY

Ingo Westphal
Bremen Institute of Industrial Engineering and Applied Work Science
win@biba.uni-bremen.de, GERMANY

Ugo Negretto
Enicma GmbH, Munich
ugo_negretto@enicma.com, GERMANY

Traditional Performance Measurement methodologies are designed to assess efficiency of intra-organizational processes. Those models are applicable for single companies or static networks running a streamlined set of performance indicators. Under the given changes in production paradigms, single enterprises and more static, long-lasting networks, e.g. Supply-Chains in the automotive industry, lose significance to dynamic, order-specifically configured Virtual Organizations that highly depend upon the efficiency of their collaborative processes. Measuring the performance of those processes is not feasible with traditional PM methodologies or at least an extension of those. Ongoing efforts in creating a PM framework for Virtual Organizations are facing several research challenges. This paper describes and analyzes challenges towards a Performance Measurement methodology for Virtual Organizations.

1. INTRODUCTION

Throughout the recent years, the degree of standardization in manufacturing is decreasing continuously, making the way for customized production of product-service conglomerates, so-called Extended Products [Thoben und Eschenbaecher. 2003]. The process of creating these Extended Products and bringing them to the market is too complex to be done by one single enterprise. Instead, this requires networks of companies temporarily joining their core-competencies for collaborative value-creation. These networks, so-called Virtual Organizations (VO), are dynamic (i.e. re-configurable within one order), order specifically configured, existing for the duration of one order only, and adherent to a specific life-cycle [Camarinha-Matos and Afsamarnesh 1999]. VO Management is strictly compelled by these characteristics: Due to their strict focus on one single business opportunity, time for corrective measures is limited – there is neither time to test and optimize collaboration of partners, nor to improve processes by trial-and-error procedures. This has significant implications on measuring and analyzing the VO performance.

2. PERFORMANCE MEASUREMENT

2.1 General Principles and Mechanisms

Performance Measurement is a toolkit providing methodologies, directives and indicators for measuring and evaluating the performance of business processes. This is done by indicators that are derived from an underlying process model. Applying a detailed set of indicators allows quick identification and assessment of weak-points within the value-chain and, by that, provides a basis for leveraging processes efficiency. With that, performance indicators prove to have traffic-light properties allowing conclusions on "go-" or "no-go"-items in value creation with the objective of being able to anticipate potential "no-go"-items as early as possible.

Generally, the challenge in Performance Measurement is the necessity to transfer highly complex real-world processes to a simplifying processes model, to derive performance information from the model, and to transfer these results back to the real world [Eschenbaecher and Seifert 2004]. Figure 1 highlights this loop of transfers.

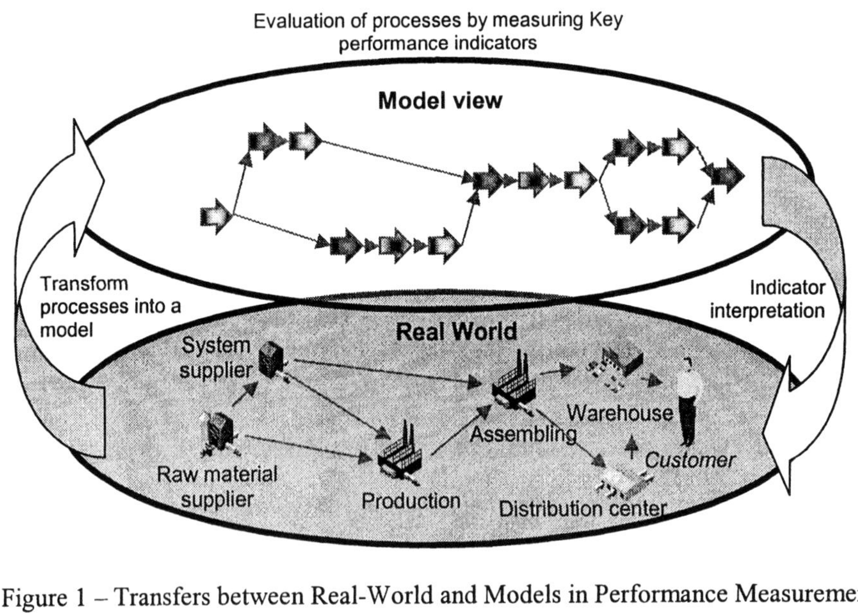

Figure 1 – Transfers between Real-World and Models in Performance Measurement

Theoretically, difficulties in Performance Measurement increase with the complexity of processes to be assessed. This implies that Performance Measurement within single enterprises in principle is easier as it is within a network of enterprises. On practical grounds, Performance Measurement is often tied-up by lacks of transparency in processes, misty process instructions, and inefficient communication between different business units even within one and the same enterprise. Between enterprises things are more complicated: Different cultural convictions, different standards, process models, performance indicators, gaps in technologies and incompatibilities in information systems create a clearly heterogeneous landscape among the partners that need to be harmonized to draw a transparent picture uniform to all partners of the entire distributed processes chain.

2.2 Existing Approaches in Performance Measurement

Performance Measurement can be applied for different purposes. In literature one can find examples for measuring performance for strategies, humans, tools, processes. In this paper the focus is on measuring performance of processes.

The origin of Performance Measurement (PM) could be found in financial accounting that gives information about one of the most essential performance indicators: the profit of an enterprise. The assessment of the financial performance was refined by indicators like Return on Investment (ROI), Economic Value Added (EVA, a trademark of Stern Stewart & Co.).

The major drawback of these approaches focusing only on financial performance is their retrospective character. In addition essential factors for a sustainable success are not covered as they are non-financial aspects.

To fill this gap several approaches are developed in then 1980s and 90s, which include essential PM components or rather build upon PM. The first approaches replenish existing PM with aspects of process performance. Examples are Benchmarking, Six Sigma, EFQM, and SCOR.

Benchmarking got popular in the 1980s. The basic idea is to compare performance indicators between different entities to obtain reference points for the optimization of processes. Typical indicators are for example productivity, efficiency, lead times or quality aspects.

The **Six Sigma** approach measures the process capability and stability by determining the rate of defects per million opportunities (DPMO) which is transferred into a Sigma-value. As a universal indicator the Sigma-value enables the comparison of processes in different functions of enterprises independent from the line of business.

A very comprehensive approach is **EFQM**. The European Foundation for Quality Management (EFQM) developed this reference model for quality excellence as a framework for a quality award. In addition to the process perspective it comprises eight further categories of indicators from leadership and people, to customers and financial results.

The Supply Chain Operations Reference Model (**SCOR** Model) was developed by the Supply Chain Council. This supply chain process model uses hierarchical decomposition into six layers, out of which the first three are generic (or implementation independent). An essential feature of SCOR is the connection of standardized performance indicators to the defined process elements on each level.

Most of these approaches are oriented to single processes or functions, focusing on few certain perspective and are not consequently linked to the enterprise's strategy. Therefore Kaplan and Norton introduced the concept of **Balanced**

Scorecard (BSC) [Kaplan; Norton 1992]. This approach provides a methodology that facilitates translation from strategy into appropriate actions [Kaplan; Norton 1996] by defining performance indicators that represent the fulfillment of objectives derived from the strategy. As BSC covers the perspectives of Financial Results, Customers, Internal Processes and Innovation it is very comprehensive approach that oriented towards the enterprise's long-term success.

The increasing importance of so called intangible assets for companies' values led to specific approaches for Intangible Assets Management. They pay special attention to indicators like know-how of specialists, strong brands or regular customers. Well-known examples are the Skandia Navigator, the Intangible Assets Monitor of Sveiby and the Intellectual Capital Monitor of Stewart [Klingebiel 2001].

The approaches described above are widely used and cover a very wide scope of aspects. However, none of them is aligned explicitly to collaborative business between independent partners. This gap was already identified and discussed by several research works [e.g. Gunasekaran 2001, Leseure 2001, Hieber 2002, Zhao 2002, MacBeth 2005]. Leseure for example developed an approach for meta-performance on network level, which comprises the two dimensions of aggregated performance and equity. Many of these research works considering collaboration in supply chains. Nevertheless a consistent PM approach for Virtual Organizations is still missing.

3. PERFORMANCE MEASUREMENT IN VIRTUAL ORGANIZATIONS

3.1 VO management general aspects

Virtual enterprises are the logical consequence of the shift from standardization to customization in production. In a world of customization characterized by a low vertical range of manufacturing enterprises are forced to collaborate with each other on an order-specific basis: For fulfilling a customer's demand those enterprises engage in a network that are considered to create the highest benefit to the customer [Miles, Snow, and Miles 2000].

Spoken in terms of process management, a VO is a temporary synchronization of processes and resources between different enterprises to achieve operational or strategic benefit from a specific business opportunity. For entities outside the network, a Virtual Organization appears not to be a network of various organizations, but one single entity.

VOs can be created either from an "open universe" of enterprises, or out of local clusters, so-called Virtual Breeding Environments (VBE). Being a strategic network itself, the VBE is an important concept for shortening lead-times in VO creation and supporting enterprises to quickly build-up infrastructures enabling them to collaborate efficiently [Camarinha-Matos; Afsarmanesh 2003]. Establishing a VO by going the road via a VBE appears advantageous predominantly for the following two reasons:

1. It is a process of down-sizing a completely "open" and almost infinite universe of potential VO candidate enterprises,
2. The VBE is a way of adjusting its enterprises to a common denominator of standards, infrastructures, management methods and tools, cultural

convictions, and mutual trust.

Figure 2 (left part) highlights the possible roads towards a Virtual Organization: either with (1a, 1b) or without (2) a VBE [Camarinha-Matos, Afsarmanesh 2003]. Once the VO is established, it is operated to a standard basic life-cycle. This cycle comprises the stages operation, evolution, and dissolution [Camarinha-Matos, Afsarmanesh 1999]. Eventually, all enterprises end-up where they came from: either in open universe or back in the VBE.

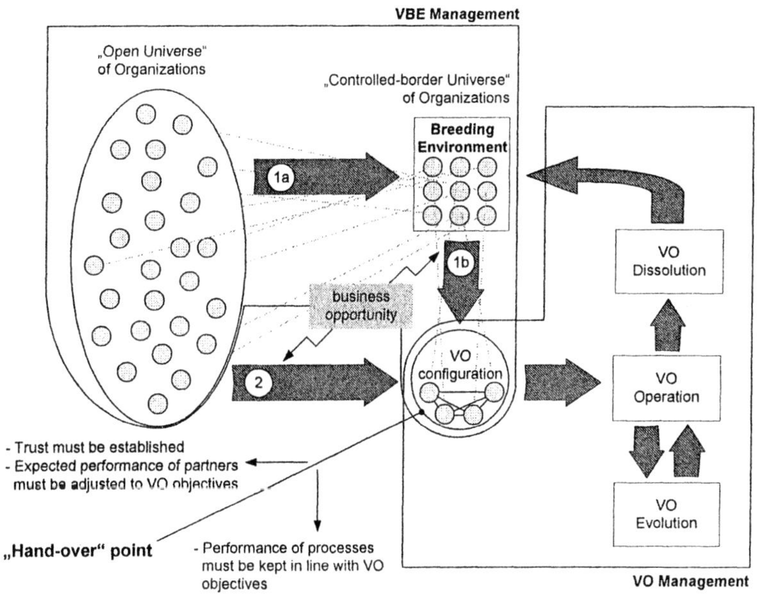

Figure 2: An integrated VBO/ VO lifecycle schema1

3.2 Needs for Performance Measurement in Virtual Organizations

Assessing Trust in Collaboration

In any kind of business network linking enterprises, individuals, or both, mutual trust is conditio sine qua non for fruitful collaboration [Blomqvist, Seppänen, 2003]. Trust is a prerequisite for both engaging in collaboration in general and especially for allowing other entities to view and assess enterprises' performance data. These two stages allow for distinguishing the following kinds of trust:

1. Trust in good behavior in daily business: Comprises for instance trust in timely delivery, responsiveness, reliability in payments
2. Trust in security of essential data/ information/ knowledge shared among the network partners.

[1] This figure is an extended composite of illustrations as stated within [Camarinha-Matos; Afsarmanesh 2003] and [Camarinha-Matos and Afsarmanesh 1999]

While the former is prerequisite for any kind of collaboration, the latter is the key momentum encouraging entities to share their performance data with the network partners: If the entity can trust that none of its partners will turn its information against itself, its propensity to participate in a VOPM increases. Vice versa, mistrust inhibits any kind of VOPM. Thus, efficiency of a VOPM system stands and falls with the trustworthiness of the partners applying it. For establishing VO's it is a critical question on how the entities can estimate their trust in the other partners, and how to enhance trust among them. Although detailed methodologies for trust building are available [Blomqvist; Staehle 2000], models for measuring trust are yet missing.

Predicting a VO's performance

Configuring a Virtual Organization and putting it into operations is more or less like playing jeopardy, because up to now it is uncertain how different partners will perform when interacting within a network that, in all of its parameters and environmental circumstances never existed before and will never exist again. This challenge is presently addressed by upcoming approaches of anticipative performance measurement which promises to be a beneficial asset in the process of partner selection: If you can assess how a partner's performance can contribute to the performance of the entire network, this is a crucial criterion for deciding on which candidate partner to involve in the VO. An approach for estimating the performance of a network before it actually exists must be based on experiences and data from the past that are somehow projected into the future. Emerging solutions to that problem are based on the idea of simulating the behavior of a certain VO based on historical data [Seifert and Eschenbaecher 2004]. In that model, trust and the concept of selecting the VO partners out of a VBE are indispensable for ensuring enterprises' willingness to share their performance data with other entities.

Measuring a VO's operational performance

Performance Measurement within a VO's operational phase must deliver information on its actual performance (retrospective to real-time perspective), and to anticipate and inhibit failures before they can occur (prospective perspective). Both aspects are crucial since partners do not have sufficient time to rehearse and improve collaboration in a pre-competitive environment. In fact, VO's are born of competition and must work efficiently from the scratch. The two perspectives in Performance Measurement condense as follows:

1. In the operation phase VO Performance Measurement is needed as a basis for detecting lacks in efficiency and potential threats endangering achievement of the partner's common business objectives. Here the problem is *that optimizing VO processes in operation is a highly time-critical issue due to restraints in time and resources.*
2. Proactive VO Performance Measurement is need for early detention of potential problems in partner's performance. Delays and problems in the performance of a partner my seriously endanger the operation of the whole VO. At this stage the problem is *to define relationships between tasks in work breakdown structure and how to forecast the impact of delays in on task on its subsequent and parallel tasks.*

PM Needs in VO Dissolution

A VO by definition is a temporary construct. After dissolution a VO's partners usually return to their VBE status, keeping ready to join forces with other VBE partners in other VO's. Looking back at the "old" VO it might be good for new VO partners to know the success of the old one and how every partner contributed to the VO's success. Information on that is highly sensitive and it is an open question to which VBE partners they should be made available. to comprises:

1. Retrospective assessment of the individual partner's performance
2. Retrospective assessment of the individual partner's behavior (for instance in terms of integration in the consortium, commitment, active vs. passive role in communication, etc)
3. Re-assessment of the partner's trustworthiness

This information is necessary input to the VBE managers and management systems for selection of partners for new VO's.

Another important topic even after dissolution of the VO is the quality of after-sales-services (for instance maintenance, warranty handling, reverse logistics). Assessing and evaluating the efficiency of after-sales-services is another important element of a Virtual Organizations Performance Measurement system.

4. OPEN RESEARCH CHALLENGES

Performance Measurement in virtual organizations can be considered as completely new research area. MacBeth (2005) discusses that performance measurement in supply chains is a non-solved problem which need to be addressed. Indeed performance measurement on VO is even more dynamic and a much bigger challenge. Consequently the next chapters provide an overview about the main general challenges which have been identified so far.

4.1 Cultural Challenges and Requirements

The following cultural challeges and requirements need to be addressed in developing a Performance Measurement approach for Virtual Organizations:

1. It is not enough to define the ability to co-operate in an isolated environment. The presence of other partners and concurrents other activites needs to be taken into account and reflected in the VOPM approach. *Consequently, a schema for measuring co-operational performance is needed.*
2. Performance Data are sensitive and normally confidential: Unauthorized delivery of performance data to third parties may cause fatal damage to the entire enterprise. Exchange of sensitive performance data is beyond the scope of normal ("operational") trust requiring a deeper confidence in the partners than just believing in his/ hers timeliness. Partners delivering these data must trust in the confidential usage of these data through the receiver/s. *Consequently specific trust-building models must be developed and enriched by organizational models ensuring trustful and secure performance data handling,*

4.2 Technical Challenges and Requirements

In the field of technical challenges towards VOPM, different issues are of importance. First, VOPM among different partners requires to a certain degree harmonized process models and a uniform set of metrics and indicators applied among the partners. Critical technical challenges towards a VOPM systems are:

1. *Harmonization of Process Models* among the network partners for creating a standardized set of performance metrics uniformly applied among the partners
2. *Real-time requirements* for PM in dynamic environments to allow for quick and reliable response to emerging problems in VO operational processes.
3. Procedures for *Ensuring Data Availability* for securing the process of gathering data from within the enterprise and sharing it with the network partners/ broker for further evaluation/ analysis
4. Data Integration → "Bridging" gaps between intra-enterprise Process Management/ ERP systems

4.3 Organizational Implications

From the organizational point VOPM is a very difficult task due to the distributed nature of the collaborating partners. Considerations and requirements on organizational structures mostly arise from the cultural and organizational challenges to be met for developing and implementing a VOPM methodology.

First, clear and uniform collaborative patterns and processes need to be implemented allowing for laying a clear and mutually accepted basis for VOPM. For instance, the business objectives and processes must be stated clearly and in an operable way for deriving suitable indicators for performance measurement.

Second, as seen before, the question of doing collaborative Performance Measurement touches questions of trust between the entities involved in the network. Generally, two ways of handling the problem are considerable:

1. *Centralized Performance Measurement:* Within the VO, one entity takes the part of a VO broker. This broker is responsible for setting-up the network out of the VBE, turning it into an operable network, and to keep this network in operation. Thus, Performance Measurement would be the task of this broker, and it would be the only entity that needs to know all partners' performance details. In this scenario it is sufficient that all entities trust their confidential data to the broker only.
2. *Decentralized Performance Measurement:* This is the most democratic way of managing the network. No obvious predominant power is visible, and every entity is able to access and to evaluate the network performance and the performance of all of its partners. In terms of trust this scenario is much more difficult to handle for everyone must be able to unconditionally trust everyone else within the network.

4.4 Summary

Authors such as MacBeth (2005) have identified a set of research issues for PM in supply chains which give first ideas about issues to be resolved:

- Who owns / can influence the network?
- Mutuality of consideration but are all partners of a VO equal?
- Dynamics of change in context of preferred solution?
- Can enterprise control in a classic sense ever work?
- Focus measurement of the output or input enablers?
- It is about rule sets agreed by all but who constitutes the all set might

change with time?

- What are the performance indicators and processes to replace a member of a network that are not longer appropriate or performing well enough?

Based on these research issues we have discussed the most prominent challenges. Figure 3 shows a summary of the discussion before. The identified challenges are a result of a common discussion about the most demanding challenges regarding PM in VO. Time restrictions, trust and the availability of data have been judged as most critical for the success of any VO.

The idea of complexity illustrates that uncertainties, dynamics, variation of goals and number of involved participants have a crucial impact of the performance of a VO.

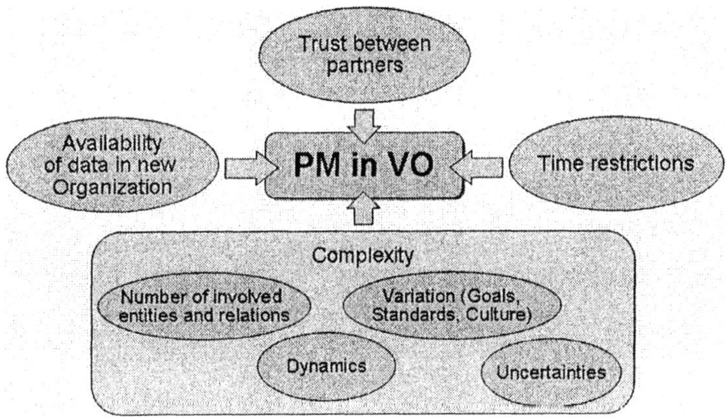

Figure 3 – PM in VO - challenges

PM in VO will be of major importance if a further dissemination of the VO concept should have any possibility to succeed. Only if managers of single organizations have instruments in hand allowing them to simulate and understand the high performance of a VO the further evolution of VO will be highly accelerated.

5. CONCLUSIONS

Performance Measurement in VO is a new scientific issue which needs to be solved. The discussion has shown that not even supply chains can be supported by proper instruments and tools. This is due to the fact that most of the available approaches for Performance measurement do focus on single organizations. Additionally the dynamism of a VO makes it very difficult to develop solid approaches. The challenges show that research is needed to solve organizational, technological and human aspects such as trust before a PM approach can really have a major impact on VO.

6. Acknowledgements

The paper is mainly based on work performed in the project ECOLEAD (FP6-IP 506958; www.ecolead.org) funded by the European Community within the IST-

Programme of the 6th Framework Research Programme. The authors would like to grant acknowledgements to the ECOLEAD consortium, especially to the participants of WP3 ("VO Management").

7. REFERENCES

[Blomqvist; Seppänen 2003]: Blomqvist, K; Seppänen, R.: Bringing Together the Emerging Theories on Trust and Dynamic Capabilities – Collaboration and Trust as Focal Concepts, 2003, 24 s., The 19th Annual IMP Conference, 4th-6th of September 2003, Lugano, Switzerland.

[Blomqvist; Staehle 2000]: Blomqyist, K; Staehle, P.: Building Organizational Trust - A paper submitted for the 16th Annual IMP Conference; 7th-9th September 2000 in Bath, UK

[Camarinha-Matos and Afsarmanesh 1999]: Camarinha-Matos, M.; Afsarmanesh, H., 1999. The virtual enterprise concept In: L.M. Camarinha-Matos and H. Afsarmanesh, Editors, Infrastructures for Virtual Enterprises—Networking Industrial Enterprises, Kluwer Academic Publishers, pp. 3–14

[Camarinha-Matos; Afsarmanesh 2003]: Camarinha-Matos, L. M.; Afsarmanesh, H.: Elements of a base VE Infrastructure; published in J. Computers in Industry, Vol.51, Issue 2, June 2003; pp.139 - 163

[Eschenbächer and Seifert 2005]: Eschenbaecher, J.; Seifert, M. (2005) Predictive Performance Measurement in Virtual Organisations. In: Emerging solutions for Future Manufacturing Systems, Edited by Luis M. Camarinha-Matos. Springer: New York 2005, S. 299-307.

[Gunasekaran 2001]: Gunasekaran, A.; Patel, C.; Tirtiroglu, E.: Performance measures and metrics in a supply chain environment., International Journal of Operations & Production Management, 2001

[Hieber 2002]: Hieber, Ralf: Collaborative performance measurement in logistics networks : the model, approach and assigned KPIs. In: Logistik-Management, Nürnberg, Vol. 4, No. 2, 2002.

[Kaplan; Norton 1992]: Kaplan, Robert S.; Norton, David P. The Balanced Scorecard--Measures that Drive Performance, Harvard Business Review, January-February, 1992

[Kaplan; Norton 1996]: Kaplan, Robert S.; Norton David P.: Balanced Scorecard, Boston 1996

Klingebiel, Norbert (Ed.): Performance Measurement & Balanced Scorecard. Vahlen, München, 2001

[Leseure 2001]: Leseure, M.; Shaw, N.; Chapman, G.: Performance measurement in organisational networks: an exploratory case study. In: International journal of business performance management. - Milton Keynes, Genève, Vol. 3, No. 1, 2001

[Macbeth 2005]: Macbeth, D.-K. (2005) Performance Measurement in Supply Chains. Presentation of the IMS-NOW SIg Meeting in Glasgow on Feb 24, 2005.

[Miles; Snow; Miles, 2000]: Miles, R. E.; Snow, C. C.; Miles, G.: The Future.org – Published in LRP-Long Range Planning – The Journal of Strategic Management; 33/3, June 2000

[Thoben; Eschenbächer 2003]: Thoben, K.-D., Eschenbaecher, J. (2003) Die Erweiterung des Produktbegriffs - Konzept und Praxisbeispiele. In: Industrie Management (19) 16, 4, S. 48-51, 2003.

[Zhao 2002]: Zhao, Fang: Performance Measures for Inter-organisational Partnerships. Presented at the 7th International Conference on ISO9000 & TQM (7-ICIT), 2002.

PART 11

PERFORMANCE MANAGEMENT

32

GLOBAL PERFORMANCE MANAGEMENT FOR SMALL AND MEDIUM-SIZED ENTERPRISES (GPM-SME)

Marc Alba[1], Luis Díez[1], Esther Olmos[1], Raúl Rodríguez[2]

[1]*DMR Consulting, P° de la Castellana, 141, Pl.13 Madrid*

[2]*CIGIP, Department of Enterprise Organization, Politechnical University of Valencia*

marc.alba@dmr-consulting.com, luis.diez@dmr-consulting.com

esther.olmos@dmr-consulting.com, raurodro@upvnet.upv.es

This paper refers to the project GPM-SME – FP6-005857[i], included within the 6th Framework Programme of the European Commission, in its CRAFT Programme. The goal of this document is to present the main concepts of Global Performance Management and how the GPM-SME consortium pursues to develop a framework to improve the competitive capability of companies and their network visibility, specially developed for Small and Medium sized Enterprises. This main aim will be achieved in two ways: allowing companies to include Innovation potential in their performance management, and defining new ways to share information among companies in Collaborative Networks(CN) and measuring the capabilities of Virtual Organizations (VO) as a whole.

1 INTRODUCTION

The new business ecosystem realities are the result of three major cyclones: globalisation, increasing competition moving more and more from enterprises to value chains, and even increasing customer dictatorship which is introducing an enriched definition of business excellence enhancing the traditional quality/cost/time variables with new views such as innovation and agility, eco-responsibility (environmental impact, green products and services), ethics and social responsibility (including gender issues).

This new environment is increasing pressure on companies which are involved in the so-called business visibility vicious cycle (see Figure 1) where large companies get bigger and bigger, and small companies smaller and smaller and thereby less and less visible. This vicious cycle often ends with the small company being dismissed from the marketplace.

To break this cycle, companies need to find a way to get visible even being small. The approach is necessary threefold: Companies must first of all improve their business excellence; then, they need to find a way to radiate this enhanced to the market (customers, consumers, competitors); finally, there is a need for the market itself to enhance its end-to-end transparency.

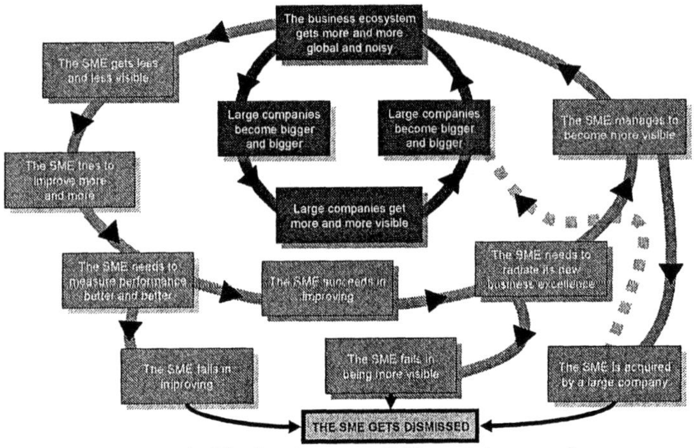

Figure 1: The business visibility vicious cycle

2 THE CONSORTIUM

In this environmental context a consortium of companies has launched the GPM-SME project, included within the 6th Framework Programme of the European Commission, in its CRAFT Programme.

This initiative is coordinated by DMR Consulting and involves several companies from different European countries and with different roles: R&D centres, industrial companies, software developers, consulting firms and standardization organizations (see Figure 2). The project is focused on two prime sectors for the European SME marketspace, Automotive and Consumer Goods.

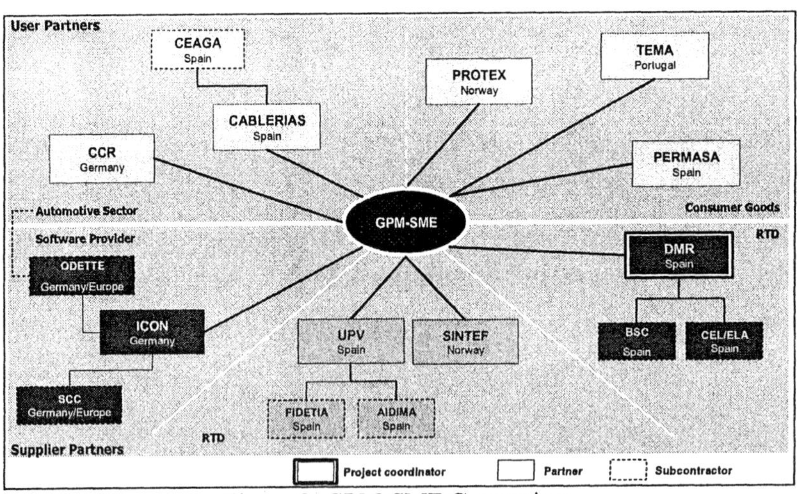

Figure 2: GPM-SME Consortium

These two sectors have been selected purposefully, being automotive the global best practice in terms of upstream value chain optimisation and performance tracking, and consumer goods the one for downstream value chain. By combining the conclusions and lessons learned in both sectors, the Consortium expects to deliver results with a broad range of applicability in new CNs and VOs.

3 THE GOAL

Most Companies nowadays know the importance of measuring accurately their main KPIs (Key Performance Indicators). However, a review of the classic performance management methods is a clear must in the new business context (Alfaro, 2002). The goal of the project is to **develop a new paradigm named Global Performance Management** (GPM) that combines two new performance management approaches: Extended Performance Management for CNs and VOs, and Enriched Performance Management. They are described in the next sections.

3.1 Extended Performance Management (ExPM)

Business players have evolved recently **from single enterprises to Collaborative Networks and Virtual Organizations**. More and more, companies need to get visibility about their clients, consumers, partners, competitors, and collaborate with them to create joint competitive advantage. This new business context requires companies to build new collaborative management and operational models.

To achieve this purpose, enterprises need to be able to measure, broadcast and monitor better performance, both internally and externally (with their partners in the CN and in the networks to which they belong), and VOs need to manage their performance in a global way (like a single enterprise) and benchmark with other VOs. The **goal of ExPM** is to **develop collaborative performance management instruments** (Hausman, 2003) relevant and reliable at the **internal** (single enterprise), **external** (one-to-one) and **network** (many-to-many) levels (see Figure 3).

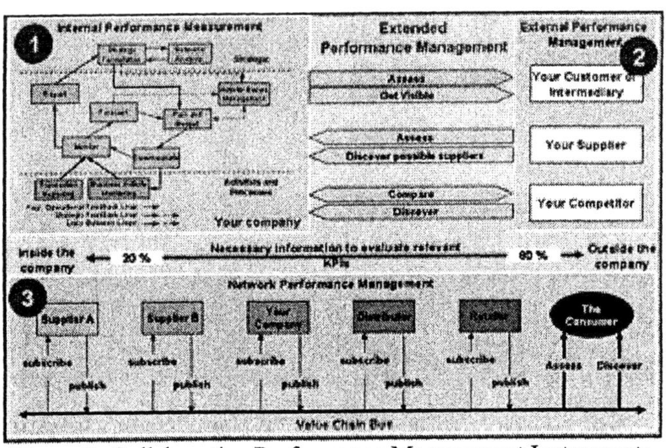

Figure 3: Collaborative Performance Management Instruments

The **main benefits** that ExPM provides for a company are the increase in its visibility with clients, benchmark with competitors, and assess its current suppliers or discover new ones. Moreover, the global network performance management can be applied to compare holistically different VOs which compete in the same market.

3.2 Enriched Performance Management (EnPM)

Companies have traditionally measured their performance in terms of Finance, Customers, Internal Business Processes and Learning and Growth (Kaplan, 1996), but the new business scenario reveals the need to create new **performance management views**, that can take into account new business paradigms such us **Innovation** and Agility (Beamon, 2003), **Environmental Care** and Green Operations (WBCSD, 2004), **Ethics** and Corporate Social Responsibility (GRI, 2002), subjects that can be considered as new business assets (Neely, 2001).

Within the scope of the project, we have decided to focus for the EnPM on the **Innovation and Agility performance management view**. Interests are put here on three types of innovation: product, process and business model innovation, as drivers and enablers of the Agility concept, which stands for the capability to quickly and continuously respond to internal and external changes.

The **main benefits** that EnPM provides for a company are to improve their business and reduce their costs/prices by the application of innovation with a global point of view. Moreover, it provides easy-to-use and affordable tools to react to the fast changing customer demand.

4 THE PRODUCTS

In order to achieve the goal of transforming the GPM paradigm into a common practice for SMEs (the so-called GPM-SME), in a first phase the Consortium has thereby centred its efforts in the analysis of the problem and in the definition of the solution, based on users' requirements collection and analysis.

In a second phase, focusing on two relevant sectors (Automotive and Consumer Goods), the Consortium has defined a set of products for GPM in SMEs in order to provide ready-to-use and easy-to-use instruments, including:

- A **methodology** to help SMEs in defining, developing, deploying and operating the GPM solution. It will enable the SME to manage efficiently and effectively continuous improvement and evolution. The GPM-SME Methodology thus becomes a complete and powerful tool to manage the whole lifecycle of the GPM solution in the SME.
- An SME-oriented **architecture** providing reference models, flexible and valuable analysis tools (best practices, checklists, guidelines, etc.), which complement the methodology to build a real model for the GPM solution.
- A **toolset** that offers to SME the GPM solution that bridges the engineering and conceptual environment, with the real-world operational and executable environment, following the path defined by the methodology and directly fed by the architecture. The GPM-SME

Toolset has been designed and developed as an affordable tool, free of cost, based on open source and standards-based IT tools.

- ❖ Pave the way for broad dissemination and exploitation of the results on a cross-sectorial basis. Among other actions and outcomes for this specific objective, the Consortium has defined the **GPM-SME Tutorial**. This product will bridge the current gap between existing market or R&D initiatives and SMEs awareness.

A requirement imposed by the European Commission in the CRAFT Programme of the 6th Framework Programme, is that all intellectual property rights of the research belong exclusively to the SMEs involved in the project.

4.1 GPM-SME Framework

In order to provide end users with necessary instruments to translate their strategy into operational objectives, the Consortium has defined the **GPM-SME framework**. This framework provides companies with a structured set of theoretical guidelines, methodologies and tools that support end users in their performance measuring and management (see Figure 4).

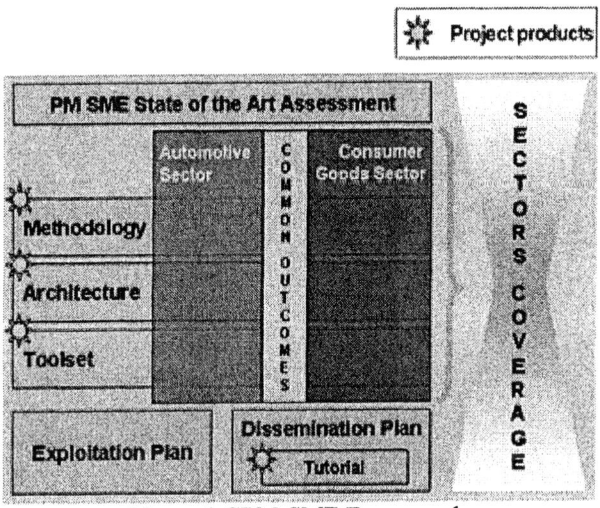

Figure 4:GPM-SME Framework

- ❖ The core of the framework is the **Global Performance Management System**, it is the IT tool that allows managers to implement their Extended and Enriched strategy and manage it in an automatic way.
- ❖ The partners have defined different base lines and a set of pre-packed experiences to support SMEs during the phase of **understanding** and **designing** their Global Performance Management System (for Extended and Enriched point of view). These instruments help companies during all the design process, from the definition of the strategy and competitive priorities to the implementation of indicators into the Norton and Kaplan perspectives (Kaplan, 1996). Companies

reduce their management effort because they measure only the indicators that achieve strategic goals.

- A set of questionnaires or checklists that help the companies with the **maintenance** of the GPM system. Two types of questionnaire are provided for the updating of internal and global performance management.
- Finally, the Consortium **supports** companies with a comprehensive and interactive guide for their **self-training** on the GPM concepts and toolset.

4.2 GPM Toolset

The GPM Toolset has been conceived as a modular and independent group of applications to provide companies with an affordable and easy-to-use IT solution. This Toolset covers the identified improvement areas to measure and manage the performance management of a company, regarding Extended and Enriched concepts, and it is represented by a cross module, the GPM Dashboard, over which repose the rest of applications (see Figure 5).

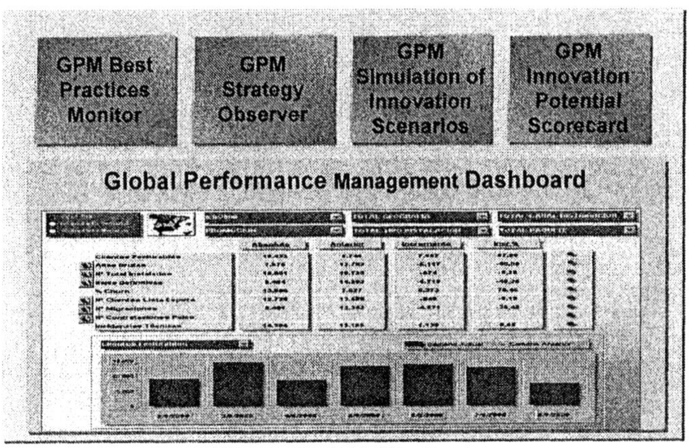

Figure 5: GPM Toolset

These products are independent and each one of them can be implemented alone or with others. According with one of the main requirements specified by the users partners, all these tools are easy-to-use and present information in an easily way. All these functionalities are developed using free licensed software, thus all SME can afford its own GPM Toolset.

The **Global Performance Management Dashboard** represents the core of the framework, id est the IT tool that allows managers to implement their Extended and Enriched strategy and manage it in an automatic way.

It consists of a multidimensional database, which is a repository with all the KPIs information, and a Front-end application (a Cockpit) that displays these KPIs.

This dashboard includes indicators, measures and goals, allows control by traffic-lights, the drill down navigation, displays the historical value of a selected

KPI, and establishes electronic communication of data eliminating the "paper management".

The **GPM Best Practices Monitor** is a graphical tool to detect where the best practices are in the company or in the CN, and allows the managers to know the reasons and good practices applied, and replicate them in other areas of the company.

The system automatically finds best practices using predefined rules and threshold values; it is based on comparable values of KPIs in the company or among different companies.

The **GPM Strategy Observer** is an automatic and graphical tool which identifies great values deviations integrated in the dashboard and provides a push alert system to the manager. This can be an automatic system to revisit the strategy of the company, because changes in the environment, the market, etc. can reveal the necessity of changing the company goals, based on new opportunities and risks.

New KPIs warning levels are designed and implemented in the tool with new five colours traffic-lights. The manager can quickly detect opportunities, great positive deviation, and risks, great negative deviation, and use it to make changes in the company strategy.

The alerts system manages KPIs roles, opening a communication channel between manager and responsible when an alert is released, manager knows the initiatives taken to eliminate the alert cause.

The **GPM Simulation of Innovation Scenario** is an environment to preview the temporal trends of the most important innovation indicators, based on business rules and mathematic algorithms.

What-if analysis allows previewing the behaviour and evolution of indicators as a function of variations on other related numeric variables.

This tool allows managers to prevent deviations of some indicators or measure the impact of innovation initiatives in the strategic KPIs.

The **GPM Innovation Potential Scorecard** is a framework to assess the innovation potential within the company, with qualitative values, obtained from surveys, and quantitative measures. Qualitative values are pondered to obtain numeric values that can be summarized. It consists of a graphical tool to represent the results of innovation potential assessment in different parts of the organization.

This tool reveals improvements or worsening trends of the company's innovation performance and hence its future growth and profitability potential, analysing the different results for areas or departments.

5 CONCLUSIONS

This paper presents the main concepts and the framework developed within the GPM-SME project, especially designed to help SMEs to improve their competitive capability by the effective measuring of their innovation and their network visibility in collaborative environments.

The **main benefits** that this set of methodologies, architectures and toolset provides for a company are:

- **Enrich the measurement and management of performance** helping industrial companies in integrating new management concepts required by end consumers and new legislations.
- **Extend the measurement and management of performance** helping industrial companies in including more and more all internal and external agents involved in the value chain/network of each firm, and increasing its visibility.
- **Provide ready-to-use and easy-to-use instruments** for industrial companies to improve on a daily basis the measurement and monitoring of their operations. This includes particularly the availability of open source and standards-based IT tools.
- **Enhance** the **level of homogenisation and consistency** of performance management across industrial companies through (even *de facto*) standard conceptual frameworks, reference models, indicators and methods.

At the present time, the GPM-SME Consortium is testing and validating the automotive and consumer goods pilots. These case studies will directly feed the best practices and lessons learned reports of the project.

6 REFERENCES

1. Alfaro JJ; Ortiz A; Poler R; Franco R. Performance Measurement for e-Business Enterprises. International Journal of Business Performance Management 2002; Vol. 4, N° 2, 3, 4.
2. Beamon BM. Supply chain design and analysis: Models and methods. International Journal of Production Economics 2003; Vol. 55, N° 3, pp. 281-294.
3. Global Reporting Initiative (GRI). Sustainability Reporting Guidelines. 2002
4. Hausman WH. Supply chain performance metrics; The practice of supply chain management: Where theory and application converge. Kluwer Academic Publishers, 2003.
5. Kaplan RS; Norton DP. The Balanced Scorecard. Harvard Business School Press, 1996.
6. Neely A; Adams C. Perspectives on Performance. The Performance Prism. Web Site of Neely A. www.som.cranfield.ac.uk/som/cbp/adn.htm, 2001.
7. World Business Council for Sustainable Development (WBCSD). WBCSD Annual Review 2004 - A decade of action and learning. Web site of the WMCSD: www.wbcsd.ch, 2004.

[i] GPM-SME web site can be accessed at: www.gpm-sme.org

33

COMBINING STRATEGIC, OPERATIONAL AND FINANCIAL PERFORMANCE IN THE VIRTUAL ORGANISATION

David Walters
Professor of Management
Sydney Graduate School of Management
AUSTRALIA
d.walters@uws.edu.au

The virtual business model is now commonplace across a range of industries and international boundaries. The attraction of the 'virtual' concept is well documented and numerous examples of its efficacy exist in the literature. Applications of the concept vary from the complete application of the virtual model to partial solutions to meet a need for specialist process and capability requirements. This paper identifies some of the issues that will have an impact on planning performance systems. Clearly the notion of 'asset leverage' and' zero working capital' are corporate ideals but before these can be anywhere near realities some problems must first be resolved. This paper addresses

1. INTRODUCTION

The growth of virtual business models has outpaced the ability to plan and to measure their performance. This paper reviews the growth of "new economy" business models and then explores the contributions of the planning, control and performance literature within the context of these new structures.

The paper will consider the implications for the virtual business organisation of integrating and coordinating the operating and cash cycles of component firms from not only an operational perspective but from the strategic directions and purposes of each constituent. While there is an inherent logic in the emerging virtual structure there appears not to be an accompanying "planning, performance and control" model with which to evaluate the efficacy of the alternatives. In recent months the major consultancy companies have been publishing articles that have paralleled the strategic issues for virtual business structures and performance management. What is now required is an attempt at combining both. This paper will identify recent contributions to both topics and demonstrate how they can be merged into a viable model.

2. STRATEGY, ORGANISATION AND THE 'PLANNING ENVIRONMENT'

Roberts (2004) suggests that achieving high performance in a business results from establishing and maintaining a fit among three elements; the firm's strategy, its organisational design and its environment. Roberts cites the seminal work of Chandler (1962) in which Chandler presented an argument that "structure follows strategy" and that organisation is the mechanism through which strategy is realised.

Over forty years have passed and while Chandler's proposition still holds there are a number of changes that have occurred to 'planning environment' with which the 21st century organisation now has to consider. The combined impact of knowledge, technology, process and relationship management are beginning to create a new environment, one in which an organisation is confronted with first identifying the strategic critical industry success drivers and then designing a business model that will offer a position that offers exclusive competitiveness – one of sustainable competitive advantage. There is evidence to suggest that these four generic frameworks appear to be becoming important features in planning in "new economy" business models. Disparate but linked threads are evident in the literature

These macro critical success frameworks should be used to help obtain a profile of industry characteristics against which it is then possible to measure 'organisational' performance and consider the influence of the drivers. Having identified the "critical success drivers" the next task is to identify where they are located – who owns them and how they can be accessed. A major skill in the management of a virtual enterprise is to establish the most effective position for a partner within the virtual community. Clearly no partner will agree to become involved unless the outcome will be to their benefit – that is they must be convinced that they will become "better off".

2.1 From Vertical to Virtual Structures

Problems with making shareholder value management effective coincided with the increasing appeal of virtual, or holistic, structures. The importance of achieving customer satisfaction *in order to achieve* shareholder satisfaction became very obvious and 'enlightened' management realised that the two should be seen as convergent rather than parallel and certainly not divergent. The virtual organisation offers an opportunity to identify the relationships that exist between customer satisfaction processes, capabilities and assets. With these linkages identified it is then easier to match the organisation's resources to a set of objectives that *optimise* customer and shareholder expectations. However two steps remain – that of identifying partners whose expertise and asset bases can make the "organisation" effective, more effective than that of competitors, and convincing the 'partners' to become involved in what has become known as the virtual business model

Roberts *op cit* suggests that essential to organisational interdependencies are two key tasks coordination and motivation and these becomes the role of the "vertical architect" or "virtual organiser". This role is larger than Roberts suggests. It combines *vision* and the ability to be able to *integrate* the relevant skills and resources (processes, capabilities and assets) to meet opportunities and the associated customer (and the broader base of stakeholders) expectations with a business model in which some exclusivity will offer a measure of competitive advantage. Two options emerge, product innovation or process innovation. Typically the virtual organisation is process innovation led. Strategically effective organisation structures are put in place that creates operationally efficient value delivery systems. Roberts identifies a number of such as Dell, Nike, Benetton, and the personal computer industry. Having found an acceptable structure successful integration is the dependent upon coordination and motivation

3. PERFORMANCE MEASUREMENT IN VIRTUAL ORGANISATIONS IS QUALITATIVE AND QUANTITATIVE AND DIFFICULT

3.1 Performance Planning and Management

Clearly it is more difficult to implement strategies in which a number of participants benefit but the growth of such structures is evidence of the fact that they can and are successful. Normann's (2001) argument concerning the *management* rather than the *ownership* of assets is fundamental to the virtual business. The attraction to all partners is the release from the burden of owning fixed assets and therefore being required to make decisions that are often volume oriented (a production orientation) rather than market based (customer centric). There is a strong incentive to reduce the burden of fixed costs and improve corporate performance through partnerships and alliances. The Australian Wine Industry this has proved to be a popular model, albeit one with problems.

The basic objective of any virtual organisation structure then is to provide value for both its customers and stakeholder partners. Given that both have clear views on what this comprises the structure should reflect the decision options available that can optimise this outcome. **Figure 1** models this process. The model identifies revenues as being a response to the relevance of the organisations' value proposition. This response will be based upon the added value content and 'worth' to the target customer(s). But as figure 1 suggests there are both *operational* and *strategic decision options* and these involve marketing strategy responses that in turn are influenced by the added value expectations of customers and partners. Clearly time perspectives are important and the model reflects these. The model also reflects the overall need to establish strong *competitive advantage* and this is measured by considering the impact of the potential (and feasible) operational and strategic decision options.

3.2 Managing for Strategic Cash Flow Effectiveness

It is suggested that the primary measure of corporate success should be free cash flow rather than notions of "profit" that are by definition artificial constructs. In this sense cash flow is defined more from a managerial perspective and differs from the accounting definition that has taxation and financial reporting requirements. Within the context and structure of a virtual organization the components of free cash flow should follow the decision-making processes. Figure two identifies four decision points; revenue generation, the operational decisions that are concerned with inventory levels, and receivables and payables. Changes to operations strategies result in changes to cash requirements for working capital and fixed assets, thereby changing the asset base and the cash flow from assets. Strategic decisions concerning the investment in tangible assets (processes, capabilities and assets) and intangible assets (such as R&D, brands, management and employee development) will impact on long-term cash flows. Free cash flow is influenced by funding structure decisions while value capture reflects the ability of the value organization to participate successfully and for each participant to meet its financial and marketing objectives.

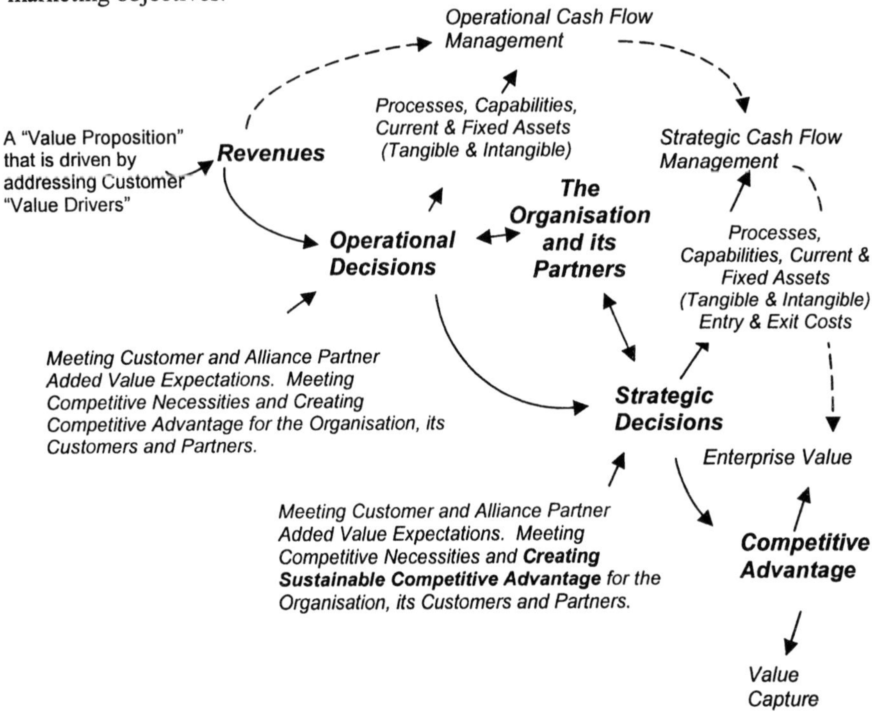

Figure 1: Successful Business Models Create Added Value for *all* Participants

Figure 2 reflects the structure and components of a virtual organisation cash flow model the model offers management an opportunity to evaluate alternative structures. For example *operating cash flow* profiles can be changed by modifying operations activities, a greater use of components and modules and focusing on assembly rather than component manufacturing can result in lower levels of inventories and decreased cash cycles. The introduction of JIT systems also change inventory and payables profiles. Supplier rationalisation can result in improved operating profit and credit terms. Decisions to outsource all or some of the manufacturing process will have similar effects.

In the long-term changes in strategic direction are likely to have implications for cash flow management. For example a decision to pursue an opportunity in an adjacent market segment can have significant implications for both working capital and fixed assets. A specialist cheese manufacturer found this at considerable cost. The mature cheddar segment appeared to have attractions. Competition was relatively low, and the market for specialist cheeses was being expanded by large multiple retailers. The costs of entry were an increase in both storage costs and inventory – the mature cheese market involved a maturing process period of nine months – a period of time in which the added value could not be realised and one in which the product required storage space. Large volume customers who used their size to protract accounts payment exacerbated the cash flow problems. Adjusting *cash flow from assets* and *strategic cash flow* profiles can have significant impact on *free cash flow*. As figure two suggests free cash flow is influenced by, not only the amount or size of the funding requirements, but also by the type of funds. Debt funding incurs interest charges *(an increase in operating cash flow)* while equity funding attracts fund raising costs *and* may dilute managerial control of the business. Clearly the virtual organisation concept is attractive as it offers a means by which financial performance can be planed and managed.

Revenues Less Discounts less Wages and Salaries less Materials, components and services Less Capital servicing and maintenance costs less Overhead expenses
= Operating Cash flow

↓

Operating Cash flow +/- Short-term Working Capital Requirements +/- Capital structure (restructuring) costs
= ***Cash flow from Assets***

↓

Cash flow from Assets +/- Fixed Assets (Tangible & Intangible) +/- Long-term Working Capital Requirements+/- "Entry and Exit" Costs
=***Strategic Cash flow***

↓

Strategic Cash flow +/- Changes in Equity & Debt funding = ***Free cash flow***

Figure 2: The determinants of free cash flow: *the primary business objective*

3.3 Managing Working Capital and Fixed Assets

Within the virtual organisation the deployment of both working capital and fixed assets is important. There are the cash flow implications that have been identified in the preceding paragraphs but there also issues concerning customer service. A significant aspect of customer value perceptions concerns service delivery and this has two characteristics. One is the traditional role of inventory in the supply chain but the other has implications for "value in use" and the customer's view of life cycle costs. Often the purchase decision is influenced by service packages (including installation, maintenance, staff training, etc) that can reduce the total costs of purchasing and operations.

Figure 3 explores these short and long-term decisions. Given a clearly defined demand chain profile results in specific value drivers that can be explored, not only in their ability to deliver added value to customers, but also for cost-efficient delivery alternatives. It follows that alternative formats for working capital, fixed assets and the implications for funding can be evaluated. However before a final decision can be made the impact on the operational gearing of the virtual business must be considered. If the resulting structure is one with a high fixed cost element there is inherent risk to the "organization" together with a lack of flexibility. Not could this result in excess capacity but it is likely to influence investors' funding decisions. This in turn can have implications for borrowing rates and the 'returns spread' of the organisation. Typically this is influenced by the relationship between debt and equity funding, however if investors (i.e. the banks) were to be concerned at the organisation's ability to respond to market fluctuations then the level of operational gearing could also influence their decision. Clearly one of the major benefits of the virtual organization is the ability to choose a structure that optimises return and risk.

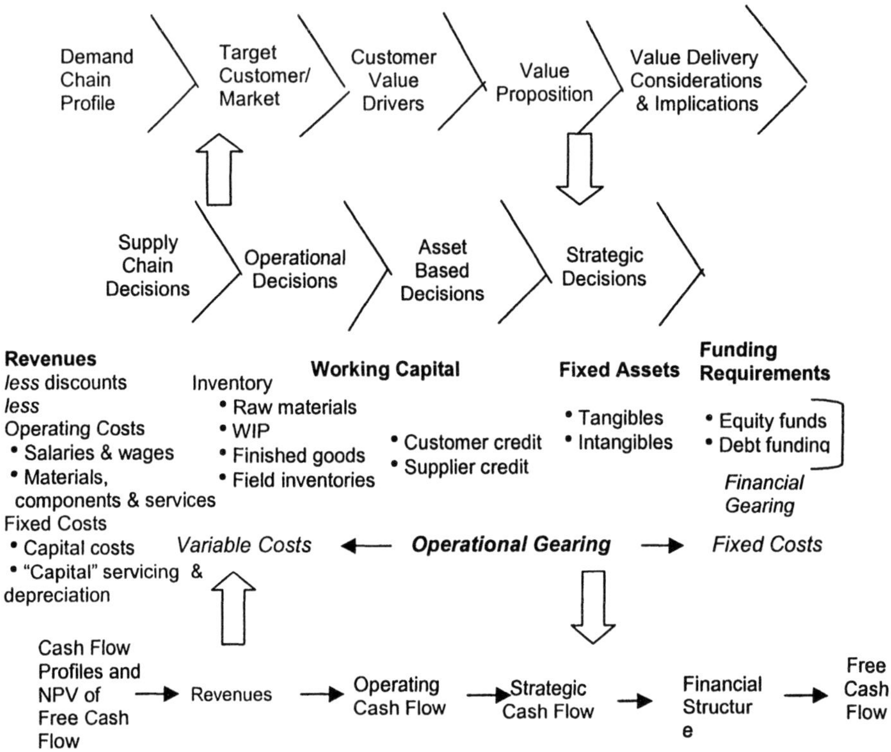

Figure 3: Managing Working Capital and Fixed Assets in the Virtual Business

4. AN EXAMPLE

Developments in the Australian wine industry are typical of a model based upon a virtual model with little or no fixed investment and the minimisation of working capital. The objective is to achieve a low investment to sales ratio. This takes into account assumptions concerning inventory levels that service target markets, realistic receivables and payables and a targeted pricing policy that generates target gross margins. The compelling philosophical attractiveness of the model can be demonstrated by the following two simple examples that compare a virtual wine business with a typical traditional wine business (which grows, makes and stores around 70% of its sales volumes).

In a low capital intensity (virtual winery) model the investment/sales ratio is typically lower than that of traditional models by a significant amount – 30 percent compared with as much as 120 percent. Assuming similar costs and product quality the *required* EBIT/Funds Employed ratio becomes a much lower figure. For example with a Capital Intensity Ratio of say 40/50 percent compared to the traditional level of between 100 to 200 percent the required EBIT/Funds Employed figure can be as low as 10 percent, considerably less than the 30 percent required for viability by the traditional model. It follows that target revenues are also lower, often by some 30 percent – in retail terms this may be as much as 25 percent less per bottle for the same quality wine! As a result the EBIT/Funds Employed ratio can show an impressive 75 percent for the 'virtual' model versus approximately five percent for the traditional winery model.

Cash flow improvements are equally significant. It can be calculated that, based on the assumptions of same revenues, EBIT/Funds Employed and debt, the cash generated can be shown to improve by a factor of between three and four times.

Clearly, the low capital intensity model begs the question as to whether a secure long term supply of input product and supplementary services are available from third parties. In the context of the Australian wine industry historically, a significant proportion of the wine industry's production volume has been traded between industry members as bulk "commodity product" and specialist bulk businesses have been established whose sole purpose is to supply bulk inputs (to other businesses). Huge volumes enabled these businesses to supply input product at very attractive prices on flexible payment terms. Rosemount is an example. Until the early 1990's Rosemount was a traditional wine business. It effectively adopted the low capital intensity model in the mid 1990's in order to fund its growth. This was achieved during a period of relative under supply and rising grape prices. The strategy is particularly attractive if it is perceived that over supply and falling prices have at least 3-4 years yet to run.

Under such circumstances a *virtual winery* would adjust the proportion of requirements supplied between "spot" purchases (under short-term contracts), and longer-term contracts. Supplementary services are typically available from third party sources for operational tasks such as facilities where it can "fine tune" and store "product" prior to final processing and contract storage of finished goods.

5. CONCLUDING REMARKS

This paper has set out some of the performance planning and control topics requiring resolution if the virtual business model concept is to become more widely accepted. It recognizes that the concept is not simply a co-operative response to market demands, but has its own tensions and conflicts. This need to be both identified and included in a firms strategic positioning and the construction of its business model.

REFERENCES

Blumentritt R and R Johnston (1999) "Towards a strategy for knowledge management," *Technology Analysis and Strategic Management,* September, Abingdon

Chandler A (1962) *Strategy and Structure,* Cambridge, MIT Press, MA

Hagel, J and M Singer (1999) "Unbundling the corporation", *Harvard Business Review,* 77(2).

Hacki R and J Lighton (2005) "The future of the networked company", *McKinsey Quarterly,* 11 February

Irani Z and P Love (2001) "The Propogation of Technology Management Taxonomies for Evaluating Investments in Information Systems" *Journal of Management Information Systems,* Winter 2000-2001

Jarillo J C (1993) *Strategic Networks-Creating the Borderless Organisation,* Butterworth-Heinemann, Oxford

'Normann R, (2001) *Reframing Business,* Wiley, Chichester

Roberts D J (2004) *The Modern Firm – Organisational Design for Performance and Growth,* OUP, Oxford

Zineldin M (1997) *Strategic Relationship Management A Multi-Dimensional Perspective: Towards a New Co-opetive Framework on Managing, Marketing and Organizing,* Almqvist & Wiksell International AB, Stockholm

34 PERCEPTIONS OF VALUE THAT SUSTAIN COLLABORATIVE NETWORKS

Ronald C. Beckett
The Reinvention Network & University of Wollongong, rcb@reinvent.net.au
AUSTRALIA

The author is involved in a multi-year program (called RELINK) to establish a number of large-scale collaboration) projects Potential economic benefits and who may receive them are mapped against three manifestations of a collaboration: a Breeding Environment, a Virtual enterprise, and an Agile Shop Floor. Some Potential participants have concerns that whilst the network may provide them with a vehicle to take on large tasks, but it may also create a new competitor, whilst others are concerned about losing their perceived source of competitive advantage if they start sharing knowledge. Some clients have concerns about large-scale collaborations reducing competyition. So despite a general acceptance of the need to collaborate, the balance between the value obtained and the market positioning of the individual participants needs to be understood.

1. INTRODUCTION

This paper is written from the perspective of a firm that has been invited to participate in a collaboration. The first question, however expressed, is WIIFM – "What's In It For Me". The response is – "an opportunity to more competitively position your business". The questions that follow in regard to specific kinds of benefits, how things will be organized, and how a particular firm may participate lead into the complexities of collaboration. There are different kinds of collaboration with different kinds of participants having differing levels of power and influence. The author is involved in an Australian multi-year program (called RELINK) to establish a number of large-scale (20 – 100 SME manufacturing firms) projects that demonstrate the benefits of collaboration in a real commercial environment. Three demonstration projects are to be centred on actual commercial activity for clients, so that serious buy-in by both clients and participants is necessary. This raises immediate questions by both parties of the value to be delivered by the collaboration.

2. PREVIOUS STUDIES

Previous studies by the author [1,2] have identified features valued by the participants that derive from economic, knowledge-sharing and social transactions. Transactions are the lifeblood of collaborations – no transactions, then no effective collaborations. Some housekeeping transactions are required, but whilst these are accepted as necessary, they are not perceived to add value. What sustains the collaboration is recurring value adding transactions. Table 1 shows a range of direct economic benefits observed

Table 1 Some Direct Economic Benefits observed in Sustainable Collaborations

Type of Economic Benefit	Specific Instance
Revenue enhancement	• Improved market access via a national brand (eg www.austmine.com.au) • Inter-firm trading to meet unique technical or schedule requirements
Cost reduction	• Joint projects focused on internal activities • Services that access best-of-breed through the network • Improved purchasing outcomes from buying as a group
Asset utilization	• Physical assets - participants acquire complementary assets rather than duplicate capabilities • Intellectual assets – participants may share some specialist staff • Operating infrastructure – buying some services (eg design) instead of duplicating them • Support infrastructure – shared or common software systems
Lead time reduction	• Concurrent engineering practices giving faster turnaround gives better cash flows • Supply chain alliances reduce lead time and inventory of incoming materials
Reliability enhancement	• Quality – collaborative improvement initiatives reduces scrap and rework • Schedule consistency supported by redundancy in resources • Client communications – single channel customer support improves consistency, reduces costs
Risk reduction	• Financial – higher utilization of new investments • Reduced dependency on a few key customers • Shared new market entry costs • Access to complementary competencies and larger experience base reduces technical risk • Inter-region cooperation may support distant customers better • Sustain individual firm reputation via improved schedule performance and broader range of capabilities available

3. MAPPING VALUE CREATION OPPORTUNITIES

Value adding transactions may take place at different stages of the evolution of a sustainable collaboration. Zwegers et al [3] see evolutionary stages as establishing networks from which virtual enterprises are formed to establish projects, which in turn provide goods and services. Previous studies by the author however suggest that a collaboration may not get past the network stage. No client projects emerge, but the network stays in operation because the participants are gaining sufficient benefit from inter-firm trading for example. In other cases, some participants only want to be involved for one project, or may be prepared to offer access to some resources, but do not want to participate in network activities. Camarinha-Matos and Afsarmanesh [4] have described a number of manifestations of collaborative networks (see Figure 1), and in the RELINK program three of these: a Breeding Environment, a Virtual enterprise, and an Agile Shop Floor have been used to map benefits observed in past cases studies in each of these manifestations.

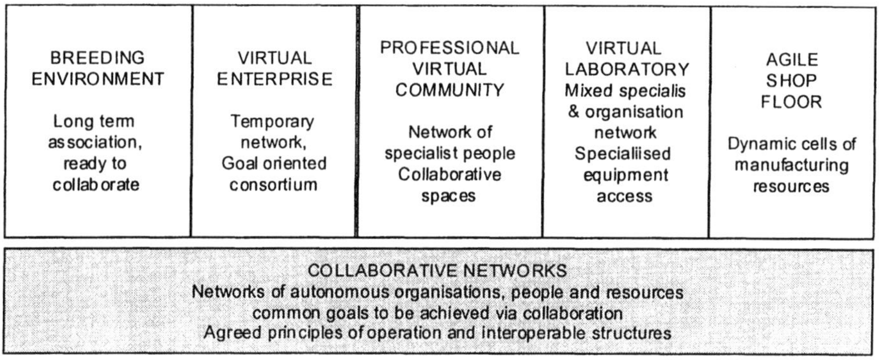

From Camarinha-Matos and Afsarmanesh(2004)

Figure 1 Some observed manifestations of collaborative networks

The other point to be made from these observations is that there is likely to be a heterogeneous mix of actors who may have quite different reasons for participating. These are characterized as:

- **Focal firms** that have demonstrated project management skills and can muster useful financial resources
- **Technology providers** that supply tools and methodologies to the participating firms
- **Regional networks** that may choose to operate outside their region as a single group
- **Communities of Practice** that operate across firms to identify collective capabilities and facilitate interaction between firms
- **Supporting firms** that add capacity by providing access to some of their resources on a flexible basis

Our objective is to summarize some likely combinations of these circumstances with potential direct economic benefits to encourage participation in network and virtual enterprise operations. Table 2 gives a summary example of the likely actors and benefits associated with three manifestations of a collaboration.

Table 2 Some Potential Economic Benefits from Multi-partner Collaboration

MANIFESTATION	TYPICAL ACTORS	ECONOMIC OPPORTUNITY
BREEDING ENVIRONMENT	- Focal firms - Technology Providers - Regional Networks - Firms offering supplementary capacity - Communities of practice supporting network establishment and operations	- Create Brands - Expand market access - Share tangible and intangible resources to improve ROI - Stimulate inter-firm trading - Reduce operating costs - Improve cash flows
VIRTUAL ENTERPRISE	- Client organisation - Focal firms - Supplemental firms - Communities of practice supporting focal firms	- Undertake client projects to grow sales - Undertake participant cost reduction or capability building internal projects
AGILE SHOP FLOOR	- Supporting firms - Communities of Practice marshalling candidate firms to access capacity	- Mobilize under-utilized capacity - Participate in cost reduction opportunities

4. SOME COMMERCIAL UPSIDES AND DOWNSIDES OF COLLABORATION

Many of the potential participants are competitors, and some of the larger firms have concerns that whilst the network may provide them with a vehicle to take on large tasks, it may also create a new competitor if some of the small firms get together. The small firms are concerned about losing their perceived source of competitive advantage if they start sharing knowledge with others. Some clients, whilst welcoming the benefits of being able to deal with fewer suppliers, have concerns about large-scale collaborations reducing competition in their supply base.

Biggiero and Sammarra [5] maintain that there are issues of identity and identification. at work too in inter-organisational networks, and this will influence the nature of transactions. They argue that the extent to which the network is seen as a discrete identifiable entity and the extent to which the participants identify with that entity influences the behavior of the participants. This helps to establish boundaries, determines who is in and who is out, and aids in sense-making, all of which improves the efficiency of operation and decision-making. Further Biggiero and Sammarra [5] argue that these factors will influence operational matters differently, depending on the extent of similarity or complementarity in the participants. In networks based on similarity, similar tasks can share common resources to increase efficiency through scale and technical specialisation. We see that housekeeping transactions will mainly relate to task coordination in this case.

In networks based on complementarity, the participant's tasks are different, but interdependencies help gain reduced coordination costs and increased returns. We see that housekeeping transactions here will mainly relate to interface coordination.

So despite a general acceptance of the need to collaborate, the tradeoff between the value obtained and the market positioning of the individual participants needs to be well understood. Bengtsson and Kock [6] have suggested that simultaneous cooperation and competition between business network participants can be successfully managed if the two aspects are separated and balanced depending on the degree of proximity to the customer and on the competitor's access to specific resources. They suggest that individuals within a firm may only act in one mode (cooperation or competition) at a time. This leads them to suggest that either the two roles are assigned to different individuals within a company, or that one role be controlled and regulated by an intermediate actor such as an industry association (community of practice). In small firms we see that the separation of roles may not be practical, and have observed that they may need to rely on an intermediate actor.

Client perspectives on working with supplier networks seem to be industry sector-specific. The author recently participated in a joint industry – academia workshop including people from the ICT and the Construction Industries. The ICT participants (from Oracle, Cisco and Intel) had titles like Vice-President, Strategic Alliances, reflecting a top-level focus on collaboration, but the impression given was that this consisted of a large number of one-to-one arrangements. Construction Industry participants described a growing enthusiasm for multi-functional team partnering with clients to jointly deal with issues in large, potentially risky infrastructure projects. Agreed target pricing and target schedules were the norm, and these were usually bettered. Frear and Metcalf [7] have reported on the evolution of supplier customer alliances in the Aerospace Industry, and Boeing have recently rolled out a number of extensive partnership arrangements in the new 787 aircraft development project. An Australian consortium of 3 larger toolmakers, supported by up to sixty others has been formed to bid for work with the tier one aerostructures suppliers on that project. At other conferences however, participants have reported a more adversarial approach to "partnering" in the Automotive Sector. It is speculated that such industry norms may also influence collaboration attitudes right down the supply chain.

5. DISCUSSION

In broad terms we see that participants derive value by participating in networking events and by undertaking internal projects or client projects. Whilst the focus is initially on building economic capital, knowledge capital and social capital enhancement also occurs, and this is also valued by some participants. In regard to aspiring participant questions about how things are organised and how they can participate, we have used an activity theory [8,9] framework to characterise some aspects of collaborations aiming to build economic, or knowledge or social capital. The author has found this framework to be a convenient way of comparing activities undertaken in different case study networks [10], and table 3 reflects observations from six recent case studies. It is noted that some commonly used tools are networking events, demonstration projects, celebrations of success, the creation of collective "brands", and ICT tools – a blend of socio-technical components.

Table 3 Activity Theory frameworks associated with building Economic, Knowledge and Social capital

	BUILDING ECONOMIC CAPITAL	**BUILDING KNOWLEDGE CAPITAL**	**BUILDING SOCIAL CAPITAL**
OBJECT (The motivation for and outcome sought from the collaboration)	- Better customer access to grow business - Pursuit of new cost reduction opportunities - Conserve capital	- Market intelligence - Technology intelligence - Find new combinations	- Making Connections - Building regional infrastructure and skill base
SUBJECT (The actors organising the activity)	-Typically a lead group of firms	- Typically a Community of Practice	- Typically an independent facilitator
TOOLS (Socio-net or Techno-net Devices used)	- Brands - Events - ICT for data sharing	- Events - Demonstration projects	- Events - Celebration of achievements
RULES (Behavioral, contractual or competency based rules for participation)	- Activities must make economic sense - Client interface - Trust - Incentives	- Knowledge sharing norms - IP Protection - Government incentives	- Ethical behavior - Participate as a team member - Incentives
COMMUNITY (The broader group of stakeholders supporting the activity)	- Global market drivers - Both private and public stakeholders	- Technology providers - Government support agencies	- Regional Governments - Regional Associations
DIVISION OF LABOUR (How some typical responsibilities are assigned)	- Focal firm leadership - Technology & Capacity support actors	- Community of Practice Leadership - Government facilitation - individual participant responsible for uptake	- Event (place & space) organization leadership - Content from event contributors - Individual participant responsible for uptake

We see that these tools also help address identity and identification matters raised by Biggiero and Sammarra [5]. "Incentives" have been noted under the rules category in table 3. These may relate to imperatives for survival or to government intervention strategies, but they often provide an initial stimulus for participation. Earlier in the paper some potential commercial downsides were noted – degradation of competitive position and restriction in client choice. Issues of trust and knowledge sharing were noted in the "rules" row of Table 3. The establishment of appropriate rules / norms can take some time, and this may be inconsistent with the rapid establishment of a collaboration. An approach taken by the author [11] in dealing with these matters is to jointly agree risks to be managed in establishing a collaboration. Discussion of this approach at events, via demonstration projects, at celebrations of success and by sharing information via a website help raise such important issues in an impartial way.

To achieve some knowledge sharing and social capital enhancement outcomes, it is highly likely that some people from the participating organisations will have to meet face-to-face. Consequently, despite the potential power of ICT tools, we see that properly designed (in terms of space, place and content) events that bring people together in an appropriate environment as a primary stimulation process

6. CONCLUDING REMARKS

Collaboration needs to make business sense, and a significant list of potential benefits has been presented in this paper. However realizing these potential benefits may be complex. Some firms enter into collaborations to implement company strategies, and are clear from the outset about what they hope to achieve. Others see collaboration as potentially beneficial but also potentially risky, and want a clear statement of benefits in relation to each specific manifestation of a collaboration. Following the formation of a "breeding network", some benefits may accrue from inter-firm trading, or from group purchasing without ever implementing a multi-partner client project. Winning significant sized client projects can however provide the greatest potential economic benefits, but the nature of client interaction may be dependent on industry sector norms. The initial focus is on direct economic benefits, but other indirect benefits may emerge – obtaining leverage from knowledge or social capital that might become assessable without ever jointly winning a new client project

Some issues arise in finding an appropriate balance between aspects of similarity and aspects of complementarity between firms. Similar firms tend to be competitors, and unless ways in which they complement each other can be found, having them work together can be difficult. At the same time, finding points of common interest between firms that have different kinds of capabilities is necessary to obtain focus. Both tasks and relationships have to be managed to deliver value

Finally, it is noted that most collaborations aim to service a market need, but the market view of collaborations seem to vary from sector to sector, as whilst the word "collaboration" is commonly used, what it really means may vary from client to client. In the RELINK project [12] referred to earlier in this paper, three different kinds of demonstration projects are planned. One is intended to promote small firms under a national brand, another seeks to combine complementary assets to access a greater depth of skills, and the third one seeks to demonstrate the agile shop floor concept via a virtual enterprise. The characterizations presented in this paper are being used to stimulate the interest of potential participants and to provide a framework for understanding potential roles and outcomes.

7. REFERENCES

1. Beckett, R.C; Hyland, P and Sloan, T (2003) "Mapping Collaborative Transactions in Networks that Yield Business Benefits" *Proc 19th Annual IMP Conference,* University of Lugano, Switzerland, 4-6 September (ISBN 82-7042-576-1)
2. Beckett, R.C. (2004), "Exploring Sustainable Virtual Enterprises". In "Virtual Enterprises and Collaborative Networks"(Ed L.M. Camarinha-Matos) Kwuhler Academic Publishers, the Netherlands, ISBN 1-4020-8138-3. pp 491-498
3. Zwegers A., Tolle M., Vesterager J., (2003). "Virtual Enterprise Reference Architecture and Methodology", *Global Engineering and Manufacturing in Enterprise Networks*, VTT Symposium 224, 9-10 December, Helsinki, pp.17-
4. Camarinha-Matos, L.M, and Afsarmanesh, H (2004) "The Emerging Discipline of Collaborative Networks" in "Virtual Enterprises and Collaborative Networks"(Ed L.M. Camarinha-Matos) Kwuhler Academic Publishers, the Netherlands. ISBN 1-4020-8138-3, pp 3-16
5. Biggiero, L. and Sammarra, A., (2001) 'Similarity and complementarity in inter-organisational networks' *APROS (Asia-Pacific Researcher in Organisation Studies)*, Hong Kong Baptist University, 3-5 December
6. Bengstsson, M and Kock, S (2000) "Coopetition in business networks – to cooperate and compete simultaneously. Industrial Marketing Management, Vol 29, Iss 5, p 411
7. Freer, C.R and Metcalf, L.E (1995) "Strategic alliances and technology networks: a study of a cast-products supplier in the aircraft industry" Industrial Marketing Management, Vol 24, Iss 5, p379
8. Vygotsky, L.S. (1978) "Mind and Society" Harvard University Press.
9. Engestrom, Y. (1987) "Learning by expanding: an activity-theoretical approach to developmental research" Helsinki: Orienta-Konsultant
10. Beckett, R.C (2004) "Exploring Virtual Enterprises using Activity Theory". Australian Journal of Information Systems, Vol 12, No 1, pp103 – 110
11. Beckett, R.C. (2005) "Collaboration now a strategic necessity: Handbook of Business Strategy, Emerald Publishing Group pp 327 – 332
12. RELINK (2004) http://relink.agileserve.com

PART 12

MODELING AND META-MODELING

35

A META-METHODOLOGY PROTOTYPE FOR COLLABORATIVE NETWORKED ORGANISATIONS

Ovidiu Noran
Griffith University, Australia
O.Noran@griffith.edu.au

The benefits of using various forms of Collaborative Networked Organisations (CNOs, or Collaborative Networks - CNs) to create agile virtual organisations, shop floors and laboratories, or to bring together professionals worldwide in virtual communities are commonly acknowledged in the academic and industrial communities. However, the advancement of the CN domain to a discipline *status essentially depends on the structuring of presently scattered and overlapping CN knowledge into a consistent framework, conveying a commonly agreed upon paradigm. The methodological aspect of this structuring effort can be greatly assisted by a* meta-methodology *integrating existing and emerging knowledge relating to the creation and operation of various concrete CN manifestations. This paper describes a milestone in the quest for a meta-methodology guiding the life cycle of CNs and their materialisations by explaining the final refinement and conclusions to a cyclic and reflective action research approach, which has resulted in the establishment of an implementable meta-methodology prototype for CN(O)s.*

1 INTRODUCTION

The current move towards market globalisation supported by pervasive computing and Internet-based information and communication technologies (ICT) has led to a significant proliferation of the practical manifestations of collaborative networked organisations (CNO)[1], such as virtual organisations (VO) and shop floors, professional virtual communities (PVC), value constellations, collaborative virtual laboratories, etc. It is nowadays clear that inevitably, organisations worldwide need to come together in order to complement their individual competencies when bidding for, or executing large projects. However, this action alone is not enough to ensure success. At a minimum, a CNO manifestation such as a VO has to form promptly, be agile and be based on sound underlying principles such as trust, common practices and infrastructure, interoperability, etc. Such requirements have deep organisational, cultural and technological implications. Collaborative business ecosystems (Camarinha-Matos, 2002), breeding / nesting environments or company

[1] also referred to as collaborative networks (CN) (Camarinha-Matos and Afsarmanesh, 2004)

networks (Globemen, 2000-2002) enable a prompt formation of CNOs; however, at present they are not properly supported by effective and integrated modelling techniques, including social and human aspects (Camarinha-Matos and Afsarmanesh, 2003). In this sense, a *meta-methodology*[2] helps integrate knowledge relating to CNO creation and operation methodologies and can suggest a customised set of steps to create and operate a CNO materialisation for a particular project type.

This paper describes a milestone in the search for a meta-methodology able to guide the life cycle of CNs and their various possible forms. The design of the research approach adopted is presented in (Noran, 2004d). The testing and validation of the successive prototypes have been performed in cyclic field tests described in detail in (Bernus et al., 2002) and (Noran, 2004c). This paper completes these research cycles by explaining the evolution, final refinement and conclusions resulting in an implementable meta-methodology prototype for CN(O)s.

2 META-METHODOLOGY PRIMER

2.1 Research Question, Strategy and Design

The main question of this research was whether a methodology describing how to construct customised modelling methods for CNOs (and their forms) may be built, and what factors may influence such an endeavour. This topic has provided an opportunity to employ Action Research (AR) (Galliers, 1992; Wood-Harper, 1985)) which allows for practical problem solving, and for generating and testing theory (Eden and Chisholm, 1993; McKay and Marshall, 2001).

The research was based on two cycles containing simulation, lab / field testing and reflections leading to theory extension (Checkland, 1991). The researcher saw himself as a facilitator and systems expert in an anti-positivist stance, guided by an interpretivist paradigm, seeing humans as voluntaristic and organisations as dynamic entities. The theoretical model adopted was ISO 15704 Annex A - GERAM[3] (ISO/TC184, 2000). The research strategy (design decisions, research stance justifications and methods adopted) is described in (Noran, 2001), while the initial conceptual development of the meta-methodology is presented in (Noran, 2004d).

2.2 Initial Meta-methodology Concept

The initial core concept of the meta-methodology comprised three main steps:

- identify entities relevant to the specific enterprise engineering task;
- construct a business model showing these entities *and their relations* in the context of their life cycles;
- 'read' the life cycle diagrams of the entities to be designed (e.g. CNO, VO) phase by phase, noting the relations of each phase with phases of other entities and constructing a list of activities expressing these relations.

These steps can also be found in the final meta-methodology concept (**Figure 1**). Note that the main meta-methodology deliverable is a functional model of types of tasks, built following the business model relations affecting the life cycle phases of the entity being designed and according to the AF elements selected from the Structured Repository (SR). The AF element selection and the further detailing of the functional model (down to a level executable by a human, a machine or a combination thereof, e.g. as an *agent*) are performed according to the *domain*

---

[2] a method (containing e.g. steps, rules and element repositories) on how to design a method.
[3] Generalised Enterprise Reference Architecture and Methodology

knowledge of the user, injected during meta-methodology application[4].

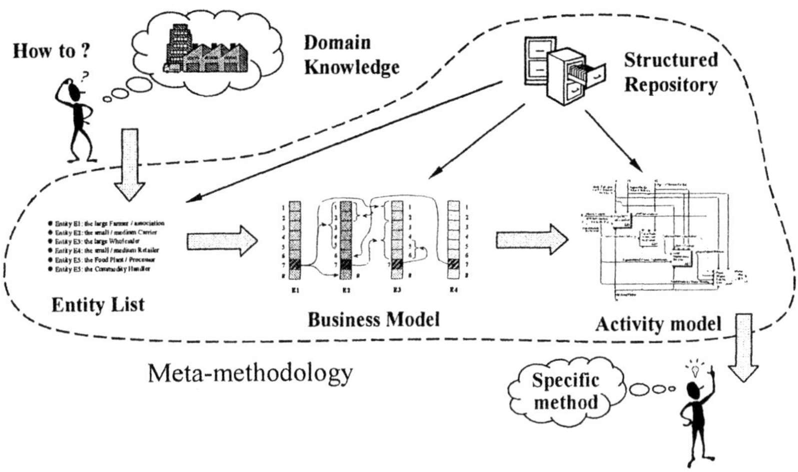

Figure 1. Meta-methodology concept

2.3 The Main Research Cycles

Simulation

The Enterprise Architecture (including CNO) area of research comprises substantial field testing turn-around times. Thus, such tests must be carefully prepared. The concepts to be tested must be mature, so as to obtain meaningful and potentially convergent results. Maturing can be efficiently obtained by simulation[5]; therefore, the preliminary meta-methodology prototype has been used to simulate the creation and operation of a virtual transport enterprise called FP-VITE, using an existing reference model (Chalmeta, 2000) and common architecture framework (AF) elements. This simulation has confirmed the feasibility and *usefulness* of the meta-methodology (Noran, 2004b), has refined its content and has uncovered the need for a Structured Repository (SR) holding the necessary AF elements.

A First Field Testing / Case Study

In this instance, the application of the meta-methodology has yielded a design (and partly operation) method for a Breeding Environment (BE) and the Service Virtual Enterprises (SVEs) created by it (Hartel et al., 2002). The lead partner(s) wished to retain control of the identification and the concept of the SVEs created, with the rest of the SVEs' life cycle phases covered by the BE. The audience (management and technical personnel) was partly familiar with the IDEF[6] family of languages and with a reference model developed by the Globemen[7] consortium.

The application of the meta-methodology has resulted in a multi-level IDEF0[8]

---

[4] e.g. via user's answers to questions on the scope of change, language / tool proficiency, etc
[5] note that the model thus obtained can only be checked for *internal* validity (Trochim, 2000)
[6] Integration DEFinition family of languages (Menzel and Mayer, 1998).
[7] Global Engineering and Manufacturing in Enterprise Networks (Globemen, 2000-2002)
[8] Integration Definition for Function Modelling (NIST, 1993)

model of the design methodology for the BE and the SVEs created by it, based on the Globemen reference model (due to the audience proficiency). The meta-methodology has also recommended to model the decisional aspect of the partners, BE and potential SVE(s) using GRAI[9] Grids and applicable reference models (Olegario and Bernus, 2003). More details (which are beyond the purpose of this paper) are available in (Bernus et al., 2002).

The Second Field Testing / Case Study

The second field testing has involved the application of the refined meta-methodology to the creation of a VO in the tertiary education sector (Noran, 2004a). Several schools of a Faculty within a University have formed a VO to capitalise on their shared knowledge, present a unique and stronger image to prospective students, industry and government, and thus improve their competitive level. The current (AS-IS) state of the schools was not fully understood by stakeholders. The future (TO-BE) state was to be obtained by evolving the AS-IS state, rather than by radical change. The audience of the meta-methodology deliverables was neutral in respect to a particular modelling formalism or reference model.

The main deliverable of this field testing was a customised VO creation method functionally expressed in IDEF0, supplemented by models of additional aspects (such as decisional and organisational, using GRAI Grid[10]) and by low detail models and guidelines for project management, human resources and organisational culture aspects. More details on this field testing are available in (Noran, 2004c).

3 THE META-METHODOLOGY EVOLUTION

3.1 Evolution of the Meta-methodology Steps

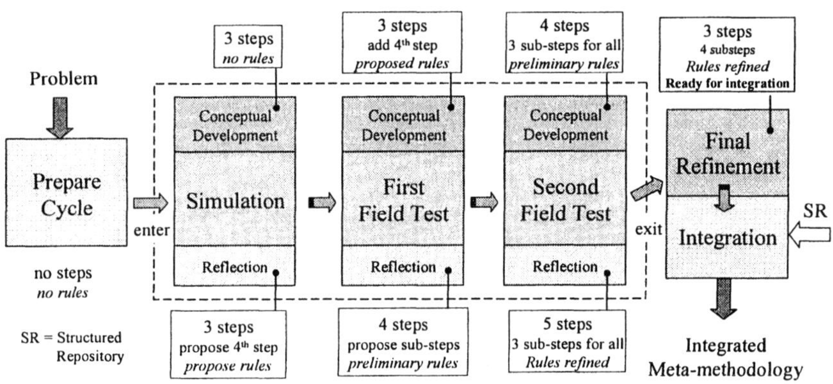

Figure 2. Evolution of the meta-methodology steps (Noran, 2004b)

As can be seen in **Figure 2**, in the initial conceptual stage of the first iteration (simulation), the meta-methodology contained three mandatory steps. Subsequent reflection has proposed an additional step (modelling of other aspects besides functional) and has uncovered the need for applicability rules, levels of modelling detail and representing management in life cycle diagrams.

---

[9] Graphs with Results and Activities Interrelated (Doumeingts et al., 1998)

[10] the use of IDEF0 and GRAI was warranted in view of the audience's formalism neutrality and ease of comparison with the first field testing and with the simulation

Conceptual work in the second iteration has added this step, has attempted to attach rules to the steps and has uncovered the need to *refine* the entity list obtained in step one, concurrently with step two. Subsequent reflection has proposed *sub-steps* to identify other aspects to be modelled using views contained in the modelling frameworks (MFs) of the AFs in the SR (e.g. Function, Information, Organisation, etc present in the MFs of GERA[11], Zachman[12], etc) and suitable formalisms / tools.

Conceptual work in the last cycle has proposed to shift modelling of additional aspects (e.g. decisional structure) into separate meta-methodology steps. However, subsequent reflection has found that these new 'steps' are in fact mere applications of other existing meta-methodology steps and thus, the modelling of additional aspects should become a *sub-step of all* main meta-methodology steps.

3.2 The Structured Repository Attached to the Meta-Methodology

Figure 3 illustrates the evolution of the SR. Its initial form was that of a repository containing elements grouped by categories, with attached 'IF / THEN' applicability rules that needed sequential testing by the meta-methodology user. Subsequent reflection has identified potential scalability problems and the need for additional AF elements (e.g. reference models), generic modelling languages / tools (non AF-specific) and additional attributes to rank AF elements by various criteria.

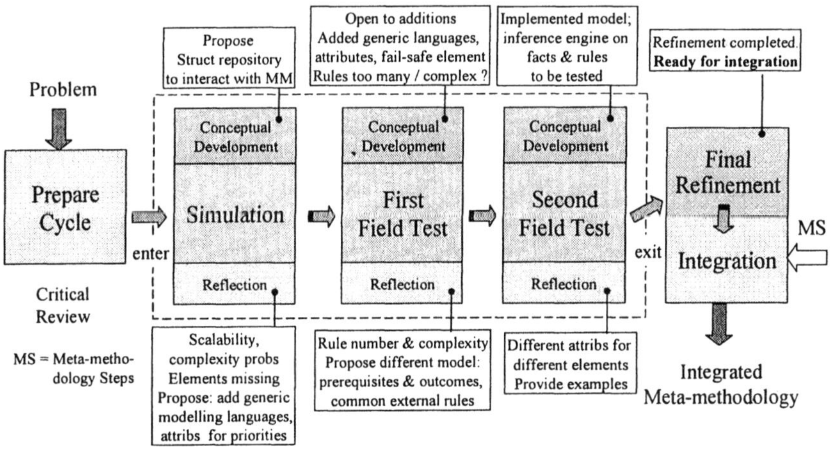

Figure 3. Structured repository evolution (Noran, 2004b)

Thus, subsequent conceptual work has added the proposed SR elements and high-level modelling elements (English text, rich pictures) for additional representations. However, the reflection ending this cycle has found flaws in the SR structure and has recommended that selection rules be common to the entire SR.

Therefore, the second field test has redesigned the AF elements in the SR to contain *prerequisites* and *modelling outcomes* (**Figure 4,** left), thus enabling their selection by external rules matching outcomes with user requests, and prerequisites with outcomes of other elements; the resulting SR structure was simple and scalable.

[11] the Generalised Enterprise Reference Architecture, a component of ISO15704 Annex A
[12] the Zachman Architecture Framework (Zachman, 2000)

4 FINAL REFINEMENT: THE PROTOTYPE

4.1 Meta-methodology Steps

In the final reflection and refinement phase, the number of steps and sub-steps and their content has been defined as follows:

Step1: *Identify a list of entities relevant to the EA project.* If one or more projects are set up to build the target entity (entities), consider including them;

Step2: *Create a business model showing the relations between the life cycles of the identified entities, while re-assessing the need for the presence of each entity in the diagram, and the extent of the life cycle set to be represented for each entity;*

Step 3: *Reading the life cycle diagram of the target entity, phase by phase, create a set of activities that describe the relations of the target entity with other entities.* For several target entities, determine the order in which they are created (from the relations in the diagram) and create the activity model in that order;

The meta-methodology sub-steps (applicable to all the main steps) are as follows:

Sub-step1: *Choose whether to represent only the present (AS-IS), the future (TO-BE), or both states (separately or combined).* The logic for this sub-step can be embedded in the SR, which can make recommendations if supplied with the step number and with answers to additional questions;

Sub-step2: *Choose aspect to model, depending on the meta-methodology step.* This sub-step can also be performed by the SR, which can resolve dependencies as well (e.g. the need to model aspect A, in order to be able to model the required aspect B);

Sub-step3: Choose modelling formalism (and tool) depending on the aspect selected and on modelling best-practice criteria. These criteria can be embedded in the SR.

4.2 Structured Repository

The refined form of the SR prototype has the structure shown in **Figure 4**.

Rules for Sub-Step 1: Modelling of AS and TO-BE states

These rules decide whether to model the present and / or the future (see **(1)**) and *how* to do it (separately or in a combined form, as shown in **(2)**):

(1) IF ((TO-BE_obtainable_from_AS-IS) OR (AS-IS_not_understood))
THEN (model_AS-IS)

Thus, *if the future state can be evolved from the AS-IS, or if the present state of the participants is not fully understood, then model the AS-IS state.* The IF / THEN structure can be simulated using modules similar to the formalism and tool elements, where the outcomes are the IF part, the module content is the THEN part, and prerequisites are any dependencies. E.g. - when should several TO-BE be modelled?

(2)
```
module several_TO-BE {          // the THEN part
      type rule_simulator       // this is a rule simulator module
            prerequisites (separate_AS-IS_TO-BE) // dependencies
            outcomes (undecided_TO-BE) } //  IF part
```

Rules for Sub-Step 2: Aspects to Model

The aspects (or views) of the MFs present in the SR may be modelled as outcomes in relation to the various life cycle phases, which are then matched against outcomes required by different meta-methodology steps. Thus, the MFs may contain functional, decisional, information, resources, organisation, behaviour, performance, culture, economic, infrastructure, etc aspects. However, some aspects are merely specialisations, or variants of others and therefore, their representation may contain prerequisites calling for the 'parent' aspect to be modelled as well. The selection of additional aspects necessary in each meta-methodology step is the result of the interaction of the user with the meta-methodology steps and SR (refer **Figure 4**).

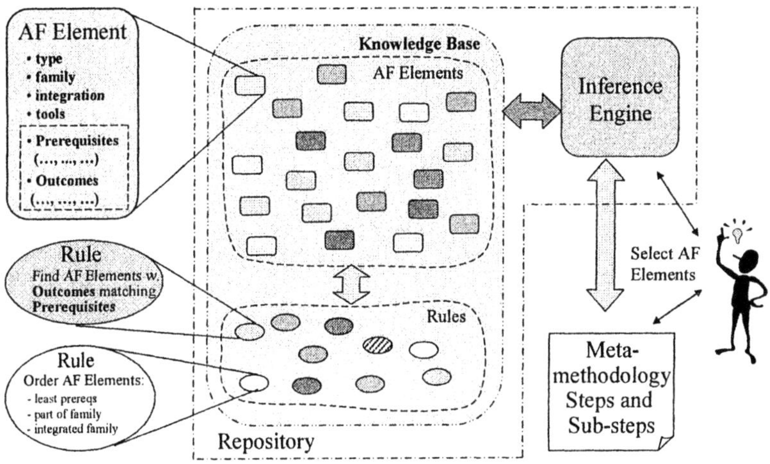

Figure 4. Structured Repository organisation and interaction with the user

Rules for Sub-Step 3: Choice of Formalisms

The criteria for formalism and tool choice can include: formalism previously used in the same modelling project, formalism being part of a family, integrated family of the formalism, tool support, availability and cost, staff literacy in that tool, etc.

5 CONCLUSIONS AND FURTHER WORK

The meta-methodology prototype has an open character. The SR knowledge base can be upgraded with new members, and the element representation in the SR and its rules may be changed to reflect various approaches to enterprise modelling. Interestingly, the open character of the meta-methodology makes it applicable to other EA tasks, or with suitable modifications, *to any task.*

Further testing and refinement is needed to completely define the SR, including the rules of selection for non-trivial aspects for the meta-methodology steps. The meta-methodology environment needs to be formalised (e.g. based on a metamodel) in order to achieve a complete integration, facilitating the envisaged implementation of the meta-methodology as a decision support system (Noran, 2004b).

The levels of refinement and usability of the meta-methodology prototype described in this paper essentially depend on further testing in case studies and regular updates with state-of-the-art knowledge in the EA domain.

6 REFERENCES

1. Bernus, P., et al. "Using the Globemen Reference Model for Virtual Enterprise Design in After Sales Service". In I. Karvoinen, et al. (Eds.), Global Engineering and Manufacturing in Enterprise Networks (Globemen). VTT Symposium 224 (pp. 71-90). Helsinki / Finland, 2002
2. Camarinha-Matos, L. M. (Ed.). Collaborative Business Ecosystems and Virtual Enterprises (Proceedings of PROVE02: 3rd IFIP Working Conference on Infrastructures for Virtual Enterprises). Sesimbra / Portugal: Kluwer Academic Publishers.2002
3. Camarinha-Matos, L. M., Afsarmanesh, H. "A Roadmap for Strategic Research on Virtual Organisations". In L. M. Camarinha-Matos, H. Afsarmanesh (Eds.), Processes and Foundations for Virtual Organisations (Proceedings of PROVE 03: 4th IFIP Working Conference on Infrastructures for Virtual Enterprises) (pp. 33-46). Lugano / Switzerland: Kluwer Academic Publishers, 2003
4. Camarinha-Matos, L. M., Afsarmanesh, H. "The Emerging Discipline of Collaborative Networks". In L. M. Camarinha-Matos, H. Afsarmanesh (Eds.), Virtual Enterprises and Collaborative Networks (Proceedings of IFIP 18th World Congress - TC5/WG5.5 (PROVE 04): 5th IFIP Working Conference on Virtual Enterprises) (pp. 33-46). Toulouse / France: Kluwer Academic Publishers, 2004
5. Chalmeta, R. Virtual Transport Enterprise Integration. Journal of Integrated Design and Process Science, 4(4), 2000
6. Checkland, P. "From Framework through Experience to Learning: the Essential Nature of Action Research". In H.-E. Nissen, et al. (Eds.), Information Systems Research: Contemporary Approaches & Emergent Traditions. Amsterdam: Elsevier, 1991
7. Doumeingts, G., et al. "GRAI Grid Decisional Modelling". In P. Bernus, et al. (Eds.), Handbook on Architectures of Information Systems (pp. 313-339). Heidelberg: Springer Verlag, 1998
8. Eden, M., Chisholm, R. F. Emerging Varieties of Action Research: Introduction to the Special Issue. Human Relations, 46, 121-142, 1993
9. Galliers, R. D. "Choosing Information Systems Research Approaches". In R. Galliers (Ed.), Information Systems Research - Issues, Methods (pp. 144-162): Alfred Waller Ltd, 1992
10. Globemen. Global Engineering and Manufacturing in Enterprise NetworksIMS project no. 99004 / IST-1999-60002. Available: http://globemen.vtt.fi/, 2000-2002
11. Hartel, I., et al. "Virtual Organisation of the After-sales Service in the One-of-a-kind Industry". In L. Camarinha-Matos (Ed.), Collaborative Business Ecosystems and VEs (Proceedings of PROVE02: 3rd IFIP Working Conference on Infrastructures for Virtual Enterprises) (pp. 405-420). Portugal, 2002
12. ISO/TC184. "Annex A: GERAM", ISO/DIS 15704: Industrial automation systems - Requirements for enterprise-reference architectures and methodologies, 2000
13. McKay, J., Marshall, P. The Dual Imperatives of Action Research. IT & People, 14(1), 46-59, 2001
14. Menzel, C., Mayer, R. J. "The IDEF Family of Languages". In P. Bernus, et al. (Eds.), Handbook on Architectures of Information Systems (pp. 209-241). Heidelberg: Springer Verlag, 1998
15. NIST. Integration Definition for Function Modelling (IDEF0) (Federal Information Processing Standards 183): Computer Systems Laboratory, National Institute of Standards and Technology.1993
16. Noran, O. Research Design for the PhD Thesis: Enterprise Reference Architectures and Modelling Frameworks, (Technical Report / Slides). School of CIT, Griffith University. Available: www.cit.gu.edu.au/~noran, 2001
17. Noran, O. Application of the meta-methodology for Collaborative Networked Organisations to a School Merger, (Technical Report / Slides). School of CIT, Griffith University. 2004a
18. Noran, O. A Meta-methodology for Collaborative Networked Organisations, (Doctoral Thesis). School of CIT, Griffith University. Available: http://www.cit.gu.edu.au/~noran, 2004b
19. Noran, O. A Meta-methodology for Collaborative Networked Organisations: A Case Study and Reflections. Paper presented at the International Conference on Enterprise Integration and Modelling Technology (ICEIMT 04), Toronto / Canada,2004c
20. Noran, O. "Towards a Meta-methodology for Collaborative Networked Organisations". In L. Camarinha-Matos (Ed.), Virtual Enterprises and Collaborative networks (Proceedings of the 5th IFIP Working Conference on Virtual Enterprises - PROVE 04) (pp. 71-78). Toulouse / France: Kluwer Academic Publishers, 2004d
21. Olegario, C., Bernus, P. "Modelling the Management System". In P. Bernus, et al. (Eds.), Handbook on Enterprise Architecture (pp. 435-500). Heidelberg: Springer Verlag, 2003
22. Trochim, W. M. The Research Methods Knowledge Base, (2nd Edition. Internet WWW page). Available: http://trochim.human.cornell.edu/kb/index.htm, 2000
23. Wood-Harper, A. T. "Research methods in IS: Using Action Research". In E. Mumford, et al. (Eds.), Research Methods in Information Systems - Proceedings of the IFIP WG 8.2 Colloquium (pp. 169-191). Amsterdam: North-Holland, 1985
24. Zachman, J. A. Enterprise Architecture - A Framework, (Web Page). ZIFA- Zachman International. Available: www.zifa.com, 2000

36

METHODOLOGY FOR BUSINESS MODEL DEFINITION OF COLLABORATIVE NETWORKED ORGANIZATIONS

Guillermo Jiménez[1], Nathalie Galeano[2], Teresa Nájera[2], José Manuel Aguirre[3], Ciprian Rodríguez[2], Arturo Molina[3]

[1]*CII-ITESM,* [2]*CIDYT-ITESM,* [3]*DIA-ITESM*

Ave. Eugenio Garza Sada 2501 Sur, Monterrey, N.L., Mexico

guillermo.jimenez@itesm.mx, ngaleano@itesm.mx, mtng@itesm.mx

jmaguirre@invitados.itesm.mx, A00790685@itesm.mx, armolina@itesm.mx

It is important for stakeholders to understand business potential and feasibility before investing in designing and implementing Information Technology services that support the enterprise operation. Ontologies for Business Models capture the essential elements and their relationships that contribute to provide value to all parties to validate the underlying rationale of the business opportunity. This paper presents a template and methodology to capture the elements and their relationships in a Business Model for Collaborative Networked Organizations. The template is a skeleton based on an ontological approach, and the methodology describes how the skeleton could be used to explain and illustrate the business models. Results and experiences of a real study case using this methodology are described.

1. INTRODUCTION

In the present world business have discovered that their competitiveness strongly depends on the relationships they establish and maintain with their customers and suppliers, and clearly identifying the value added to the products they sell. Collaboration is thus a necessary strategy that all business should pursue and manage. Information and communication technologies (ICT) provide the means to have organizations networked in collaborative environments to support their business interactions (ECOLEAD 2004). Consequently, a new breed of business organizations has emerged, arranged from once disperse elements, and now associated through ICT

The participants and their roles in a networked organization need a business model to describe how value is created and shared among participants. Different approaches could be used to describe the participants and their roles, such as textual, graphical, or combinations of both (Osterwalder 2004, Godjin 2002). A framework useful as reference to describe business models of networked organizations could be defined by an ontology. An ontology for business model provides a generic formal description of actors, their roles and their interactions to provide objects of value.

Ontologies by themselves are not enough to define business models. The representation needs a methodology to describe how actors and their roles are found, how value is assigned to objects, how relationships among actors are defined, how financial aspects should be considered, and how access to objects is provided by actors. This paper discusses the importance of ontologies for business models, proposes a methodology for business model definition supported by ontologies, and presents results and experiences using the methodology in a real study case of an enterprise who sells ICT based services for small and medium enterprises.

2. BACKGROUND: ONTOLOGIES FOR BUSINESS MODELS AND COLLABORATIVE NETWORKED ORGANIZATIONS

An ontology includes a set of concepts and their relationships that could be used to model a real world or business aspect using stated principles. Concepts are the things that are recognized in the domain of discourse, relationships define how concepts could be combined, and some guiding principles help to identify valid concepts and relationships. Several ontologies have been suggested in the business modelling domain (Godjin 2002, Osterwalder 2004, and OBELIX 2005). Rather than defining a new ontology for business model definition, we base our analysis on the ontology proposed by Osterwalder (2004). As we want to define a general methodology for business model definition, we consider that the ontology proposed by Osterwalder is the most general. In Osterwalder's ontology, generic concepts are: customers, products, value proposition, and financial aspects. These concepts are detailed in the elements that define each high-level concept.

Collaborative networked organizations are described as a planned arrangement of independent organizations around a core objective, associated via ICT technologies to perform harmoniously as one single establishment. Substantial research on CNO and Virtual Enterprise concepts have been done in the recent years (Camarinha-Matos et al. 2004, Molina et al 2005).

CNOs are formed from (and within) clusters of enterprises in similar industries, their existence might be temporary and devised to take advantage of a particular market opportunity. CNOs should be justified in such terms that the economic benefit for each participant enterprise should be superior to the benefit obtained working on its own.

CNOs demand a different approach of the business rationale (model) which considers entities separated by distance, with independent and distinctive management environments, and diverse needs, but working in cooperation to achieve one goal.

3. METHODOLOGY FOR BUSINESS MODEL DEFINITION

The methodology is a five steps process, where we propose the basics to construct a business model (figure 1).

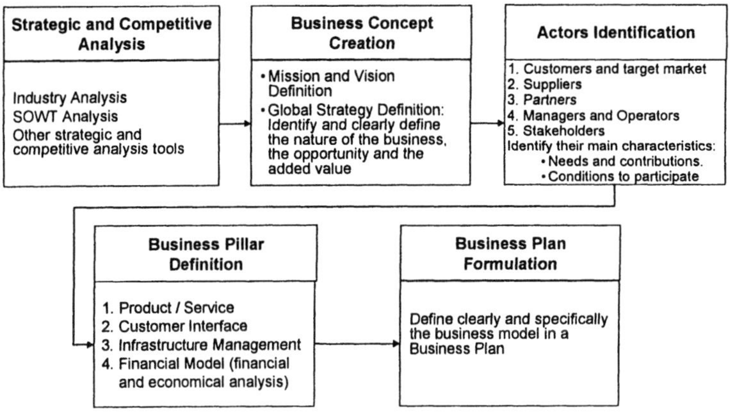

Figure 1 – Methodology for business model definition

3.1 Strategic and Competitive Analysis

Competitive analysis helps to identify and understand the current competitive condition of the collaborative network. This analysis should help to visualize the industry attractiveness, profit and collaboration potential of the CNO. The methodology suggest to use Porter (1985) five competitive forces to determine the state of CNO competition: threat of new entrants, bargaining power of costumers, threat of substitute products or services, bargaining power of suppliers and the number and position of competitors. These forces, some times called external drivers (Molina 2003), should be analyzed considering that new CNOs could arise as potential customer, suppliers or competitors. The overall attractiveness is considered by summarizing the five forces and identifying opportunities for the CNO in the market sector. Comparing the results found with the CNO potential and weaknesses determined through a SWOT analysis will provide a diagnostic picture that serves as foundation to support the CNO concept creation step.

3.2 Business (CNO) Concept Creation

In this task the market needs are identified thus validating the existence of a business/collaboration opportunity for the CNO. The definition of the mission, vision and strategy of the CNO is performed. Also, the CNO nature, the existing opportunities, and the value added of products/services are identified. Any CNO model will work with a real and sound collaboration opportunity (profit or non profit), and a real and sound market need that requires being satisfied. Four fundamental steps support the validation process of CNO concept creation: 1) the description of the need to be satisfied, 2) the identification of the main benefits provided, 3) the identification of the competitive advantage offered, and 4) a descriptive overlook of the product or service that the customer will be paying for. Once these steps are performed, conclusions should be drawn and the opportunity should be easily perceived. The results of these steps should be expressed in terms of market need, value chain impact and competitive advantages.

3.3 CNO Actors Identification

The quantification of the value offered through the product or service depends completely on the subjective perception of the customer; so, it is critical to understand the nature of this perception. Likewise, the customer often is not an individual, but a process of organizational decision making, and every player in the decision chain should be identified. Partners, suppliers, shareholders, managers and operators of the CNO should also be identified in terms of: main characteristics (profile), needs, conditions to participate on the business/collaboration, and the competencies that each actor is going to contribute to the CNO business model.

3.4 Business Pillar Definition

This phase consists in defining the four business model pillars and elements in accordance with a given CNO business model vision and objectives (Figure 2).

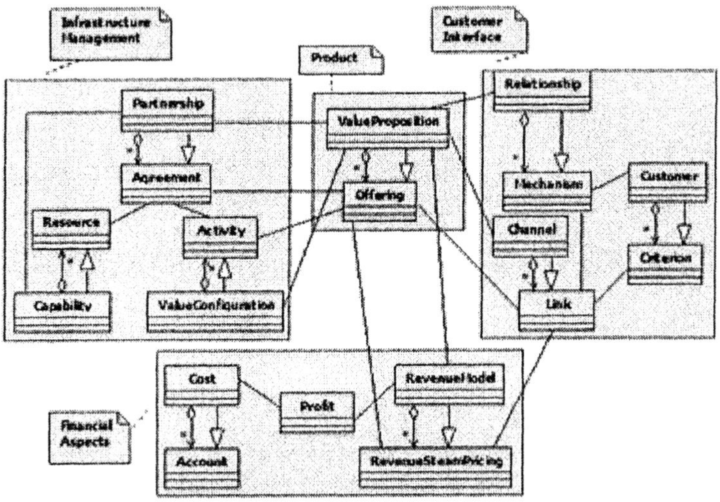

Figure 2 – Business Pillars and Elements (adapted form Osterwalder, 2004)

<u>Product Pillar</u>: this pillar includes one building block, which focuses on the "value" proposition of the product or service. The value proposition should be unveiled by the same primary questions used to define the nature and the opportunity of the CNO business (Customer Interface Pillar). The activities in this pillar includes: description of the needs to be satisfied, identification of the main benefits provided and description of the offering and the advantages of the CNO.

<u>Customer Interface Pillar</u>: this pillar defines all the characteristics and circumstances related to the customers of the CNO. The activities in this stage include: 1) identify target customers, its profiles and market characteristics, 2) definition of the means to get in touch with the customers (Distribution channels), and 3) identify the links between the CNO and customers (Relationships).

<u>Infrastructure Management Pillar</u>: refers to the organization and management aspects of the CNO venture. The principal activities include: 1) definition of the

activities and resources arrangement necessary to create value for the customer (Value Configuration), 2) definition of how the product/service will be deployed in terms of business capabilities (design, installation, operation, maintenance, management processes) and 3) determine the required partnerships.

Financial Aspects Pillar: refers to the definition of the revenue model, cost structure and CNO business model sustainability (financial performance and growth potential). Three activities are performed: 1) identification of the investment required; 2) identification, allocation and evaluation of cost elements, the capital budgeting needs, the procedure to assure the cost-effectiveness; 3) definition of: pricing policy, tariff structure, expenses policy, and analysis of the revenue stream; 4) conceptualization of the accounting / financial system, and determination of the financial and growth indicators.

3.5 Business Plan Formulation

The final phase is to formulate the CNO business plan. This document describes the CNO business concept and explains the opportunity in which is based the whole model, it also summarizes the objectives of the CNO, depicts why the CNO will succeed, identifies the CNO resources (money, people and technologies) that will be needed and the collaboration schemes that should be devised, as well as how those resources will be obtained, and defines the processes involved to succeed. Key sections to include in a business plan are: executive summary, CNO summary, products and services, market analysis, strategy and implementation, management summary and financial plan (Molina, 2003).

The business plan acts as the catalyst for the business development formal process; the business model explains how the model will be implemented, and describes the markets and project management information, including the cash flow. The business plan also validates and predicts the feasibility of the business model; intrinsically the business plan offers feedback to the business model, and input to revisit and change the model according to outcomes detected when planning the execution phase. Interaction between business plan and business model is virtuous circle.

4. CASE ANALYSIS: A CNO EXAMPLE UNDER THE BUSINESS MODEL FRAMEWORK ASSESMENT

The following case analysis is included as an example of how the business model approach has been applied to a CNO. The CNO described in the following section is a real virtual enterprise devised to foster small and medium enterprises (SMEs) competitiveness throughout sharing competitive managerial and operational resources The sustainability of this CNO, named PYME-CREATIVA (PYME as the Spanish acronym for SME), unconditionally depends on a feasible business model. Intuitive design of a CNO is replaced with our methodology. In the process, several potential flaws were detected and redesigned.

4.1 PYME-CREATIVA Project

The PYME-CREATIVA goal is the development of information technologies necessary for the creation of a HUB, which, through the integration of e-services, promotes the creation of virtual organizations based on value added networks of SMEs (small and medium enterprises). PYME-CREATIVA business concept is based on the Virtual Industry Broker business model and in its operation, focused on the creation of Virtual Organizations based on SMEs. This project is developing five integrated e-services: e-Marketing, e-Brokerage, e-Engineering, e-Supply and e-Productivity.

The operational characteristic of the HUB of integrated e-services was found during the strategic and competitive analysis of the project (focused on Mexican SMEs needs). In this analysis several analytical and strategic tool were utilized: five forces industry analysis, strategic benchmarking, strategic wheel, etc. This analysis identified that current individual e-services offered in the marked does not solve, in a systematically and integrated way, the problems and limitations of Mexican SMEs and the cost of access was out of reach for them. The four business model pillars of PYME-CREATIVA are described in the next paragraphs (Figure 3).

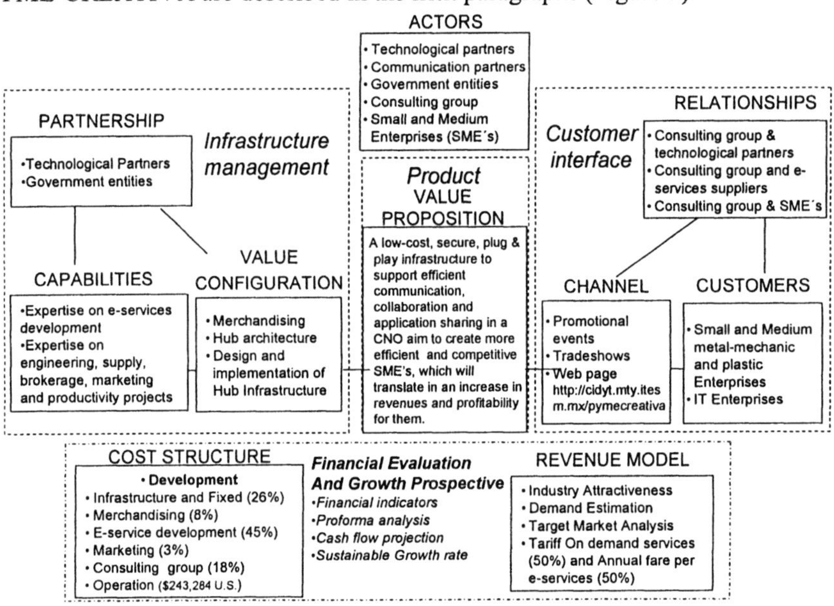

Figure 3 – PYME-CREATIVA Business Pillars and Elements

Value Proposition Pillar refers the characteristic of the five e-services that will be provided through a technological platform (HUB), which facilitates the creation of new business opportunities for SME manufacturing industries by sharing technology capacities and being able to access new global markets.

Customer Interface Pillar serves for the target customer definition, in our case, metal-mechanic and plastic automotive SME and, application services providers (ASP) that wish to utilize the HUB. Communication channels consist in means to make the project public; for this, promotional events, trade shows and also website advertising are used. The relationship defines the process for establishing strategic alliances with businesses aimed to reach and create value to customers.

The *Infrastructure Management Pillar* consists in identifying and managing the IT infrastructure needed to provide a reliable and valuable service. Partnership element analyses strategic alliance with business that develop generic software applications to provide interoperability between the HUB and the applications. Capabilities element correspond to expertises in the group to develop a product that creates value to an entity. In the value configuration element all data and process are managed by a central HUB, the advantage provided for SMEs is that they do not need to invest in expensive IT equipment to obtain services of this magnitude.

The elements of the *financial pillars*, cost structure and revenue model serve to identify, classify and allocate the cost elements of the Project and the cash generation respectively. Finally a financial evaluation of the business performance and the growth opportunities of the SME's will be done during the execution of the business.

Not all the necessary elements for the business plan development are yet defined for this particular case. Obviously, the business model shall be clear and consistent, and although the business opportunity and potential market demand have been tentatively established, the technological feasibility is still being explored, and a number of assessment tests will be performed in different market schemes. However, the results obtained to the moment are a demonstration business opportunity is being conducted in the correct direction.

Some of the contributions by the methodology proposed to PYME-CREATIVA are the following: Identifying pillars of PYME-CREATIVA business model helped to define the characteristic of the hub and the value proposition tended to add value to the customer. Determining the cost structure presented a clear panorama on the amount of cash flow that need to be generated for the business feasibility. Main contribution of customer interface's Pillar was the visualization and establishment of the target market and the ability to determine SME specific technological needs. Once, the value configuration and capabilities were determined, the need to establish technological, governmental and communication partners through strategic alliance arose in order to have a robust and efficient business, aim to offer a complete solution for the SMEs. In short, the Methodology proposed serve as a valuable tool in the strategic panning and the definition of PYME-CREATIVA's business model.

4.2 Related work

The need to base the operation of a networked organization in a clearly defined business model was evident from so called DotCom debacle (Glass 2001). There exist several examples of organizations whose success is the result of a competitive strategy reflected in their business models, e.g., Dell (Kraemer 2000), Southwestern Airlines (Kim 2002), and Walmart (Stalk 1992). The common denominator in these examples is that their strategy is the creation of a unique valuable position, involving a different set of activities (Porter 2000). The set of activities could be identified from a reference framework defined by an ontology for business model (Osterwalder 2004). The next step to assist companies in defining competitive and sustainable operation is a methodology based on an ontology for business model definition.

5. CONCLUSIONS

This paper proposes a methodology to describe business models for networked e-business. The methodology is unique in that it provides the steps that could be applied to describe business models in a systematic way. The elements of a business model and their relationships are described and used to show their use to elaborate a particular business model. The methodology is a guide for enterprises to define mission and vision, the strategy to implement them, and business models based on an ontology, which results in a detailed business plan. Neither of the steps is more important but instead all of them are necessary to define business models of networked organizations.

6. ACKNOWLEDGMENTS

The research presented in this document is a contribution for the ECOLEAD Project (European Collaborative Networked Organizations Leadership Initiative), funded by the European Community under the Information Society Technology Programme. We appreciate the collaboration of institutions involved in the WP6.2 of ECOLEAD project. Special thanks to the PYME-CREATIVA Project of ITESM University, for its support during the study case development.

7. REFERENCES

1. Camarinha-Matos, L.M; Afsarmanesh, H., Ed.s. (2004). *Collaborative Networked Organizations: A research agenda for emerging business models*. Boston-Dordrecht-London: Kluwer Academic Pub., 2004.
2. ECOLEAD DOW. (2004) *ECOLEAD: European Collaborative networked Organizations LEADership initiative*, FP IP 506958; Annex 1, DoW Description of Work, 2004.
3. Glass , Robert L. (2001). What can we learn from the dot-com debacle? *ACM SIGMIS Database*, Volume 32, Issue 2.
4. Gordijn, Jaap. (2002). Value-based Requirements Engineering: Exploring Innovative e-Commerce Ideas, *Doctoral Dissertation*, Vrije University, Amsterdam.
5. Kim, W.C. and Mauborgne R. (June 2002)Charting Your Company's Future. *Harvard Business Review*.
6. Kraemer, K. L., Dedrick J., and Yamashiro, S. (2000) Refining and Extending the Business Model With Information Technology: Dell Computer Corporation. *The Information Society*, 16:5–21, Taylor & Francis.
7. Molina, A Mejía, R, Galeano, N., Najera, T., Velandia, M. (2005). The HUB as an enabling IT strategy to achieve Smart Organizations, to be published in the Book*: Integration of ICT in Smart Organizations*.
8. Molina, A. (2003). Chapter 9: Developing the Enterprise Concept – The Business Plan, in *Handbook on Enterprise Architecture* P.Bernus, L.Nemes and G.Schmidt (Eds), Berlin: Springer; pp. 333 – 369.
9. OBELIX (2005) - Ontology-Based ELectronic Integration of CompleX Products and Value Chains, http://obelix.e3value.com/, visited on February.
10. Osterwalder, A. (2004).The Business Model Ontology: A Proposition in a Design Science Approach. *Doctoral Dissertation*. Universitè de Lausanne. Switzerland.
11. Porter, M.E. (1985). *Competitive Advantage; Creating and Sustaining Superior Performance*. NY: The Free Press, a division of Simon & Schuster.
12. Porter, M.E. (2000). What is Strategy. HBR, *On Point*, Harvard Business School Publishing Co., 2000.
13. Stalk, G., Evans, P., and Shulman L.E. (March-April 1992). Competing Capabilities: The New Rules of Corporate Strategy, *Harvard Business Review*.

37 A FOLDING SYNTAX FOR SEMANTIC MODELING

H. T. Goranson
Sirius-Beta, tedg@sirius-beta.com
USA

Enterprise integration is traditionally a matter of engineering to a framework. The virtual enterprise drives the engineering focus more to the semantics side of the equation. In our lab, we are dealing with a few experimental types of semantics for the virtual enterprise. Previous papers have indicated three of these: tactile semantic distance, introspective modeling and folded metaphors from film.

The need for advanced semantics plus the need for collaborative creation and management have forced us to re-examine model presentation for the virtual enterprise. In the past, if formal these have been based on graphical notations or sentential logic, often both. It is common to have annotative text associated with the formal structure.

This paper presents some ideas adapted from other communities and presents some ideas for an alternative presentation. The primary metaphor is nesting, and the motive is to conform in a natural way to XML formats. An outline presentation scheme is sketched and emerging collaborative editing methods adopted.

1. THE PROBLEMS

Our group works with modeling issues related to virtual enterprises. Our definition of what comprises a virtual enterprise is a fluid, opportunistic, presumably temporary aggregation of small businesses and individuals who are collectively addressing or seeking manufacturing opportunities. Our virtual enterprises often task partners to do things they don't ordinarily do in unfamiliar business sectors. Our enterprises are highly dynamic, and constantly evolving, meaning that optimization simulations are continuously run in parallel with operations. No central authority dictates, adjudicates or stores practices. Any process in any partner can trigger change in another process in another partner without central direction. The integration is intimate and proactive. No prestandardization occurs, nor any harmonization of business practices; indeed many of the partners never worked with (or even knew) the others.

This differs in both difficulty and promise from the notions of most other research groups. As a result we are identifying problems that may not be apparent in less ambitious virtual enterprises, like preharmonized bidding consortia.

1.1 Operational Dynamism

Enterprise modeling originated with a need to make processes explicit so that they could be comprehended and engineered. A later need, coincident with the appearance of enterprise integration, added the function of enterprise management. But still, in that current context, nearly all of the actual operational actions are taken outside of the modeling framework.

Virtual enterprises are different: there is no pre-existing operational infrastructure that can rumble on, parallel to the additional functions of modeling. That means that whatever models the virtual enterprise uses, they must do triple duty:

— they are a means for describing and revealing processes to partners or an assembly agent, and in this role often are referenced by contract documents and related metrics.

— they are a means, together with externally referenced procedures, for actually running the virtual enterprise, filling the role of operational infrastructure. In this role, the "models" become executable code.

— they are a means for re-engineering and optimizing the enterprise, perhaps by improving partners individually but also by making changes that could only be revealed via a system—level view. This might be seen as an extension of the first duty: after all, the original impetus for modeling was for process improvement. But functionally it is resourced as an extension of the second duty: enterprise management is a matter of both operating and improving the enterprise.

Those of us who do this in a practical context know that just managing the two roles is difficult enough, but to do that in the context of the third role is exceedingly challenging and unique to the virtual enterprise case. The key to this is the ability to explicitly capture the semantics of introspection. We'll return to that later.

1.2 Speculative, Federated Structure

Modelers like to change the world to be well-behaved. When they can, they'll force harmony in as many dimensions as possible: they'll use one modeling method, one presentation syntax, one ontology, one notion of business culture and ethics and they will perform all this harmonization (and settle all the models) well before actual work begins.

None of these things are true in the high payoff cases we encounter. Diversity is the rule (has been proven in fact to be a competitive advantage). As a result, many methods, ontologies and local cosmologies must be tolerated, even leveraged.

Usually work starts before many processes are well modeled or understood, so a way of discovering models by doing work is required. Agility is the name of the game, by which we mean extreme appropriate adaptability (rather than mere speed). Simulations of alternative strategies and configurations need to be hosted in parallel with real operation, using the same models.

This specific problem, also unique to the virtual enterprise case, is being addressed by the notion of "semantic distance," which we reported in an earlier Pro-VE. The basic notion is to have a semantics and related tools to represent certain aspects and assumptions about unknowns in models ranging from the misunderstood to the missing (data or process).

But how to represent this semantics?

1.3 Distributed, Low Level Comprehension

Virtual enterprises of the type we encounter are characterized by lean operation: the staffing and emphasis is on the expertise or core competency in question. Legal, enterprise engineering and managerial functions are slighted, certainly relative to the staid large organizations with which they compete.

It is also the case that decisionmaking and situational awareness is pressed to the lowest level possible, simultaneously "flattening" organizational charts.

These two reasons mean that whatever the sophistication and depth of the models, no matter how complex the introspection and distance (both being esoteric concepts that most professional modelers wouldn't comprehend), the results must be understandable by an ordinary partner. That translates into being understandable by an average human with a high school education but essentially no training in modeling, abstract mathematics or computer science.

In essence, they need a syntax as simple as a spreadsheet.

In the thirty-five years I have been doing modeling, the community has addressed every problem by ever-increasing sophistication in the theory and tools used. Real enterprise models are rarely used outside of large enterprises for the simple fact that only a large operation can afford to double-staff a process: one person who understands the process and another who understands the models and metrics associated with it.

Every year the community pays lip service to this need and every year it goes unaddressed (excepting tools that lack a formal basis). The virtual enterprise case forces the issue.

In the previous Pro-VE, we described a rather promising approach to this problem, the leveraging of sophisticated introspective abstractions from the movie world. This paper describes another approach, one more amenable to existing desktop computer tools. We will not discuss the combination of the two here for simplicity's sake.

Incidentally, at the same time that we have the comprehension problem, we have the need for models and their associated instances to be reportable in a number of formats for humans and machines. Practically, this means we need XML structure. What we propose here takes advantage of this structure visually.

2. THE OUTLINE VIEW

The modeling syntaxes we use today — graphic and sentential — originated in a print environment. There are good reasons for this. We need training and documentation material which is usually printed, and the sketching, exchange and archiving of models is often paper-based in ordinary or large enterprises. The virtual enterprise shifts the case from paper-based to desktop computer-based as the models and assembly of models is developed collaboratively, and the "use" of them is in a shared, networked environment.

Outlining, as it turns out, is possibly the first and probably the most mature paradigm for a display technique that is not tied to paper. Actually, there is a paper-based origin, but the conventions we mean here (collapsing, disclosure triangles, indented children, cloning, hypertext, transclusion and folding) exist only on a screen. Outlining is a way of allowing a focus on a single element, like a process, but also expanding the whole collection so that the entire system can be viewed, each element in a larger context.

The outlining paradigm goes back to coding tools at the MIT AI lab in the 1970's, but outlining came to the desktop on the Macintosh when it appeared in 1984. Since then, all the advances in this area have been on the Mac and the most robust user and developer communities are Mac-based.

Outlining has been added to the 100-year old Gantt chart format in a manner that has been adopted in essentially every project management software package.

Our expectation is that the outlining paradigm can be adapted as the basis for a basic virtual enterprise modeling tool that:

— can be widely supported on the cheapest hardware by a large number of software vendors

— will be accessible to someone in text mode who has essentially no special training in modeling

— but at the same time have the ability to be strictly formally based and have conventional graphic syntaxes

— be integratable into existing small business project management packages.

3. OUR ENGAGEMENT IN THE COMMUNITY

We started this project eighteen months ago. Our strategy was to engage a critical mass of the user and developer community, and having done that develop a set of principles and standards that can be leveraged by the developers. Our goal is to be as universally influential as fast as possible.

Our primary vehicle for this a monthly on-line column our project writes. It is part of an on-line "magazine" that focuses on Macintosh software. The periodical is free and can be read either on-line in html format or downloaded in screen or print-optimized PDF formats. Previous issues are well-indexed and persist on-line.

Our column on outlining (Goranson, 2005) gets a couple hundred thousand readers each month and about fifty readers a day thereafter. Though all the examples are Mac-based, it has quickly become the center of activity and theorizing about that specific interface convention for users of all desktop platforms. The columns have provided a definitive history of the paradigm and set an agenda for development and use. That agenda has been profoundly influential in the developer community by creating a market pull of educated users. Significant capability suggested by the column has appeared in more than a dozen widely varying outliner-based products in recent months.

Outlining is all about structure, so is almost universally employed in XML editors. We intend to open the collaborative modeling paradigm to our identified ontological needs for advanced virtual enterprise modeling. As it happens, outlining has historically been at the center of web-centric XML standards: XML-RPC, RSS, SOAP and OPML all came from the outlining world first, then found wider applications (especially SOAP and RSS) in the larger internet world.

OPML is an outline-specific XML format for the exchange of outline content (Winer, 2001).

We have initiated an effort to develop the replacement for OPML; because of the critical mass of developers involved we expect to be able to deliver the results in a very short time, together with compliant applications. We expect to have robust commercial and free products available to virtual enterprise users from this community in a short a time as a year.

4. THE SEMANTIC ISSUES

Some key elements to the new standard are typed links, semantic distance and attribute ontologies.

We keep the common notion that the primary hierarchy is used to describe the work breakdown according to existing conventions in the work breakdown and workflow communities. These breakdowns have legal legacies, associated contract law and accepted performance metrics. Secondary hierarchies are associated with human organizations and other resources, risks, costs and liabilities as also commonly used in the industry. We extend these as required for the virtual enterprise case, especially to cover transitional states where control over processes is distributed among several partners with different liabilities and rewards.

We also keep and extend the prevailing ontological infrastructures in the various enterprise functions. As is consistent in enterprise integration, we tag these to process ontologies. In the case of outlines, these appear as attributes, which express as XML types.

What is new is the notion of typed links. We type links among outline elements two ways. The first is a relationship link, for example a process or resource dependency for a process is linked to that process (and back) with the appropriate type link. These display as hyperlinks of different colors.

The second notion of type relates to the ontology employed in the outline element. We find all enterprises employ multiple ontologies, and we want to capture the "semantic distance" (Goranson, 2004) between the semantics of elements. In a typical enterprise, this might be the mismatch between how production and financial managers evaluate the quality of a given process. In a virtual enterprise, we find the ontological mismatches are amplified by different ontologies applied by similar actors over similar elements.

An international workshop was held in 2003 to identify the types of distance in a virtual enterprise, and these are the notions captured in the linkage types as alternatively a scalar or a geometric fit. The unsophisticated user usually chooses to see the semantic distance as a literal distance among elements in a map view of the outline elements.

5. CONCLUSION

The virtual enterprise has amplified needs for collaborative enterprise modeling. Such enterprises also have different, difficult needs. One of these needs is for many simple desktop modeling, project management and information collection tools. The basic structure of the outlining paradigm, existing tools, our role in the community and the possibility of a virtual enterprise-centric OPML 2 (or whatever it is called) may be the best way to address these needs.

6. REFERENCES

1. Goranson, HT, About This Particular Outliner series <http://www.atpm.com/Back/atpo.shtml>, 2003-2005.
2. Goranson, HT, "Semantic Distance," Proceedings of ICEIMT 04, to appear. 2004.
3. Winer, Dave, OPML Specification <http://www.opml.org/>, 2001.

38

TOWARDS A META-MODEL FOR COLLABORATIVE CONSTRUCTION PROJECT MANAGEMENT

Martin Keller, Karsten Menzel, Raimar J. Scherer
Institute of Construction Informatics, Technical University of Dresden, GERMANY
{martin.keller; karsten.menzel; raimar.j.scherer}@cib.bau.tu-dresden.de

Projects in the building industry are extremely dynamic and affected by several constraints. Therefore, common principles should be established throughout the construction industry that allows flexibly specifying and combining construction project information for the inter-organisational collaboration. New members should be supported to join and leave the project consortium by providing them with all relevant project information. Consequently, there is a need for an overall model representing the different design, construction and management activities as well as the building objects, organisational and IT infrastructure of the project. The paper presents an approach towards a common meta-model for collaborative construction process management. Relevant construction project constraints will be identified and classified in order to develop a Construction Network Meta-Model. Furthermore, a Framework for the instantiation of Construction Networks will be introduced.

1. INTRODUCTION

Projects in the AEC/FM[1] area are characterized by a variety of technical and structural boundary conditions. Furthermore, heterogeneous organisational structures and various IT-Systems influence the realisation of a construction project. Particularly, the organisational structure is of great dynamic, since a project life-cycle passes several phases, for example 'planning phase', 'construction phase', or 'operational phase'. Each phase is conducted by its own organisational structure involving international companies as well as SME´s. The need to rapidly establish new organisational structures and effectively manage this virtual organisation places high demands on the methods and models that are used for the specification of the project structure.

Large construction projects comprise thousands of individual building objects and activities, which are usually stored and managed in different information systems. Thus, to efficiently support construction project management and process coordination the project constraints should be described in a common and formal model with regard to domain specific requirements. By means of this model new

[1] Architecture, Engineering, Construction / Facility Management

project partners and their IT-systems should easily be integrated and adjusted to the project life-cycle and the relevant constraints.

The aim of the paper is to present an approach for the development of a meta-model for the management of collaborative construction processes. This *Construction Network Meta-Model* will support the construction project coordination and can be applied for the semantic interoperability between the project information and the specification of business processes. Therefore, domain specific project requirements and data models have been analysed and applied as references for the initialisation of a specific construction project. This comprises geometrical information and semantic descriptions of the construction objects as well as functional and organisational aspects.

The paper will start with the introduction of a framework that guide the instantiation of a *Construction Network Meta-Model*. By means of this framework a *Construction Network Instance* will be specified to describe the constraints and dependencies of a particular project.

2. A FRAMEWORK FOR CONSTRUCTION NETWORK INSTANTIATION

The specification of the relevant information for the coordination of a virtual organisation for a certain construction project is a demanding and complex task. Therefore, a framework that provides guidelines for this activity has been developed. Through this framework the definition of a *Construction Network Instance* will be supported by a methodology consisting of four major steps as indicated in Figure 1.

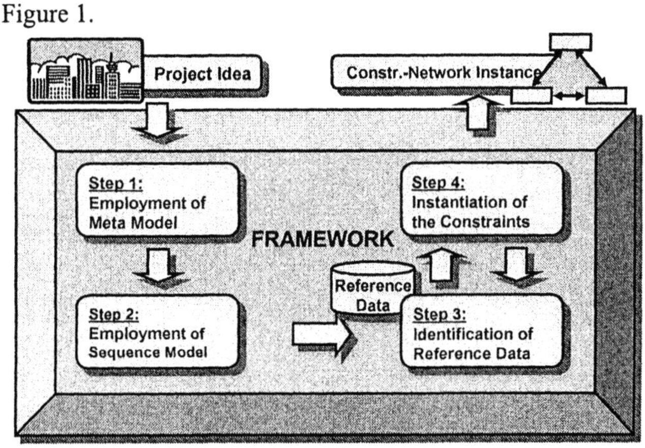

Figure 1 – Framework for initialisation of *Construction Network Instances*

Based on the project idea, a domain-specific meta model can be employed in step 1. This model identifies the elements, attributes and relations required for the description of the construction network. In step 2, a sequence model applicable for the employed meta model will be selected. The sequence model defines rules and constraints for the initialisation of the elements, attributes and their dependencies. In step 3, potential reference data for the meta model will be identified. For example the framework is providing different types of construction shapes, building functions or lifecycle phases. In step 4, the reference data will be applied and/or modified to specify the boundary conditions of the particular project.

3. CONSTRUCTION NETWORK CONSTRAINS

Construction projects are defined as complex one of a kind projects. Thus, to derive a common meta model for collaborative construction project management for the proposed framework, its complexity has to be reduced by subdividing it into integral / coherent sub-projects or project views. Therefore, the entire project has to be decomposed into its controlling elements and structured in a reasonable manner. Based on various sources, interviews and project analyses, three dimensions that control the project performances have been identified, namely *Project Organisation*, *Project Structure* and *Project Information*. Each of these dimensions can be subdivided again into two and three categories, respectively. The dimensions and the belonging categories are depicted in Figure 2.

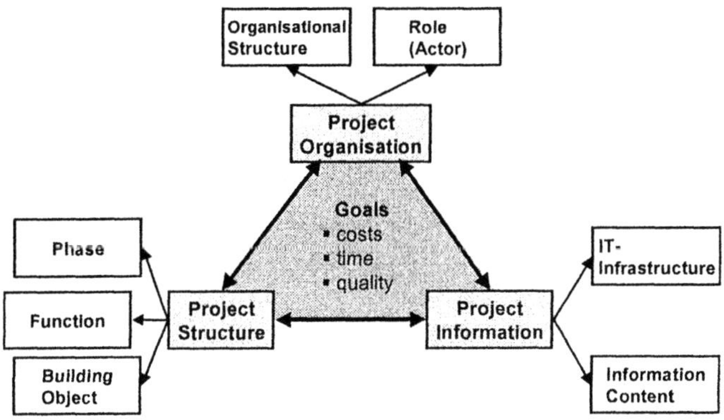

Figure 2 – Dependencies of the Construction Network constraints

Subsequent to the identification of the dimensions and categories, which influence the project development and construction management, typical models and data for these categories have to be identified and classified. Thus, several common building data standards and technical regulations were evaluated for its applicability to describe construction projects' constraints.

The following chapter gives an overview of the content and the requirements for the dimensions specifying a construction network. For each of these dimensions a partial model has been developed.

3.1 Content and Models of the Construction Network

Project Organisation

The project organisation determines the interrelationship between the participants and their roles/responsibilities in a project. It is usually set up by the project manager or the building owner in the beginning of the project, while considering legal and organisational aspects as well as best practise experiences.

The requirements for the project organisation within construction projects are considerable, since several independent phases are passed through. Each phase has its own organisational structure with different partners and roles. Thus, the project organisation has to be adapted for each phase. The predefinition of the organisational arrangement within the project phases mainly depends on the building owner. In practice distinct organisational structures are realised, such as:

- Conventional / classical organisation
- Bidding consortium and joint venture
- General planner
- General contractor

Five key roles /actors in a construction project have been identified:

- Building owner
- Project manager
- Planner / Architect
- Construction companies / supplier
- Facility Manager

Each role has dedicated rights and duties in the different phases of the project and might be subdivided into several sub roles like 'interior architect' or 'landscape architect'.

Project Structure

The structure of a construction project is classified by three categories: 1) phases, 2) functions and 3) building objects. In practise combinations of these three categories are common, since a single structure leads to misunderstandings and will not cover the complexity of a construction project.

Different national as well as international regulations and recommendations specify the phases of the building life-cycle. For example, in Germany the HOAI [2] standardizes the tasks and responsibilities of architects and engineers in construction projects. The HOAI is life-cycle oriented and catalogues the activities that have to be performed by architects and engineers in cooperation with other participants of the project. The required input and output documents, like technical drawings, are specified in the HOAI for each phase.

The focus of the function orientated project structure is on the performance of activities. This means that the overall project will be divided into its different activity-types. Each activity is performed by an actor of the project organisation and is linked to a building object. Within construction projects functions can be divided into primary functions and supporting functions. A sound example to structure a project by primary functions like 'masonry work' is provided by the German STLB[3].

Building objects are components of one build artefact. By means of the building objects the entire building can be decomposed into its elements. This structuring can have two different foci:

---

[2] HOAI – 'Official Scale of Fees for Services by Architects and Engineers'. The HOAI structures the construction design and realisation process into nine phases.

[3] STLB: The "Standardleistungsbuch" (Standard Construction Service Manual) is a general, standardised, and hierarchical catalogue of text modules specifying of construction activities.

- spatial focus (e.g. house -> floor -> room)
- element focus (e.g. wall, door or heating)

In consequence, to identify a certain construction item, it has to be localised in both foci; for example the 'window' in 'house IV, 2nd floor, room 201'.

Building Product Models (e.g. the IFC-2x model from the IAI[4]) provide a specification for the object oriented structuring of buildings. In addition, regulations like DIN 276[5] '*building costs*' and DIN 277[6] '*areas and volumes of buildings*' provide content for the building objects.

Project Information
The execution of larger building projects is nowadays hardly feasible without appropriate IT support. The information technology provides the means to carry out information exchange and data processing within and between the participating partners. In particular two scopes of information exchange among enterprises are of great importance for the inter-organizational management of building projects: 1) the IT-infrastructure systems and 2) the information content and structure.

The IT-infrastructure can be separated into IT systems for local information management such as building design software or calculation software and into IT systems for global information management such as document management server or 'building portals', accessible by several users. While the local systems are slightly influencing the construction processes the specification of the global systems are very important for the inter-organisational cooperation. Thus, addresses and interfaces of these systems have to be communicated to all partners.

For a sustainable exchange of project information it has to be structured in a coherent manner. Information standards serve for structured information exchange between application systems and should be specified by the partners in the beginning of the project. Katranuschkov et al. have identified several construction specific information standards for different construction activities [1].

4. CONSTRUCTION NETWORK META-MODEL

For a comprehensive specification of the constraints of construction projects the partial models for the identified categories of the construction network have to be integrated into an overall model, the *Construction Network Meta-Model.* By means of this model the required information for the collaborative project management is instantiated for a particular project and thus semantic interoperability between the dimensions is realized.

The general structure of the developed meta-model is depicted in Figure 3. In this model interrelationship between the categories of chapter 3 has been established according to the requirements that have been identified in the analysis of construction projects. The categories are represented by UML package diagrams to indicate that a more complex class diagram stands behind each package.

[4] 'International Alliance for Interoperability' within the construction and facilities management industries
[5] DIN 267 is used for the determination and classification of costs in building construction. It provides a structured list of building elements.
[6] DIN 277 provides a structured list for the occupancy of building spaces.

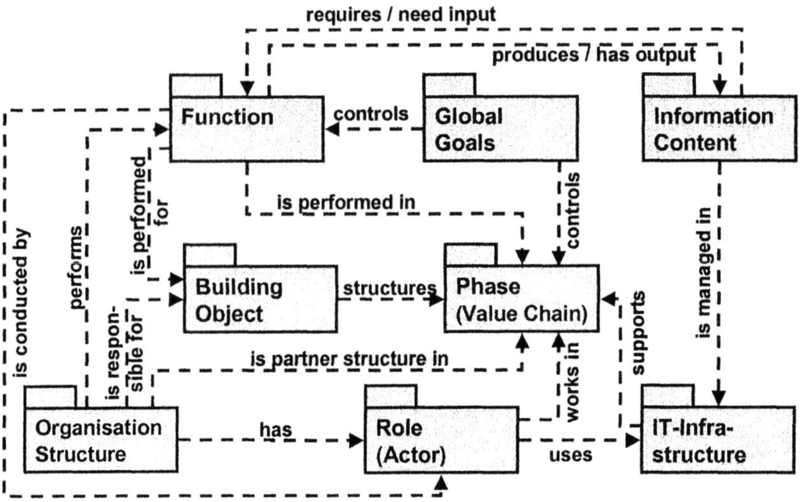

Figure 3 – UML package diagram of the *Construction Network Meta-Model*

The developed *Construction Network Meta-Model* will be capable to represent the following requirements for the inter-organisational collaboration of construction projects:

- The definition of the building life-cycle (phases) is the basis for the development of a construction project. Thus, the starting point for the construction network will be realised by the definition of the anticipated project phases on a high level (value chain).
- Building objects provide the spatial and element structure of a construction. However, each phase can have its individual focus on the object structure.
- Functions are the activities that have to be performed within each phase. A sequence of functions creates certain building objects. One function can contribute to the creation of multiple objects.
- Global goals will be defined to control the performance of the functions within the different phases. Thus, a comparison of the nominal with the actual goals is feasible.
- A specific role is responsible for the conduction of several functions within a certain phase of the project.
- The category organisational structure specifies the type of the co-operation and the project partners. The partners of the organisational structure are linked with one or more phases. Furthermore, one or more partners of the organisational structure can implement different functions, are responsible for several building objects and have one or more roles.
- Information content describes the required input and produced output information for each function.
- IT-infrastructure specifies the global services and systems that support the different phases of a project. Each role can have access to the IT-infrastructure with dedicated rights. The information content will be managed by the IT-infrastructure.

4.1 Sequence Model for the instantiation of a Construction Network

According to the proposed framework in chapter 2 the instantiation of a *Construction Network Instance* for a specific project can be enhanced by the employment of a sequence model. Such a model supports the project partners to specify the content and its relations for the different categories of the meta model in a structured manner. For construction projects the sequence model should support iterations (loops), concurrency (AND-junctions) and decisions (OR-junction). Figure 4 displays a section of a feasible sequence model for the developed meta model on high level. This model is based on the UML-sequence diagram notation.

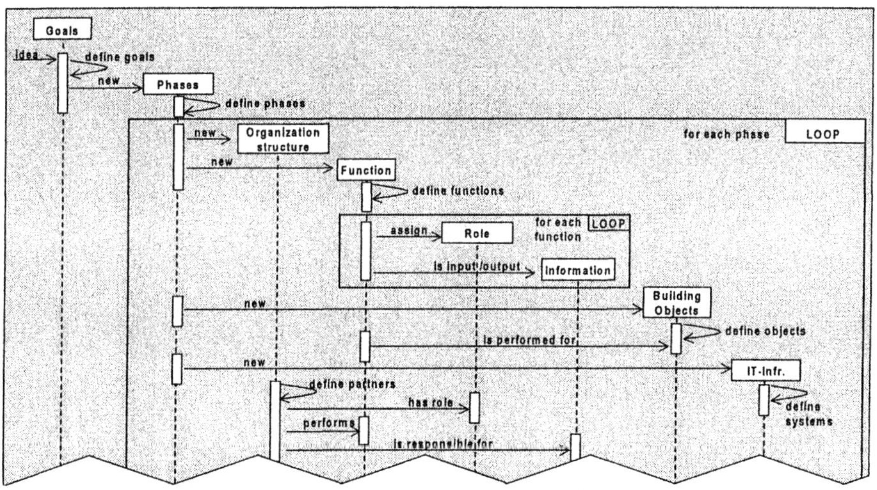

Figure 4 – Sequence model for *Construction Network* instantiation (example)

By means of the sequence model example in Figure 4 the instantiation of a *Construction Network* might be executed as follows (on a high level): After the definition of the project idea the global project goals will be specified. Next, the project will be divided into its mayor phases. For each phase the organisation structure and the functions including its belonging roles and the input/output information are defined. Following the definition of the building objects for a phase they can be linked to a specific function. Then, the different systems of the IT-infrastructure are identified.

4.2 Applicability of the Construction Network Meta Model

Once a *Construction Network Instance* has been instantiated, it can be applied to support the VO management of a construction project in several ways, e.g. by using predefined processes. Therefore, the *Construction Network Instance* provides the required context parameters for the selection and instantiation of the appropriate process module. Process modules are generally defined for the execution of a construction activity and can be adapted for constraints of a certain project. Flexible process-interfaces provide a seamless integration of instantiated processes modules into the existing workflow. An approach for the definition and use of process patterns for construction activities is described in Keller et al. 2004 [2].

5. VERIFICATION AND CONCLUSION

The management of projects in the building industry is influenced by several constraints. For example, the organisational structure of the projects is very heterogeneous. Partners and roles alter within the different phases of the building lifecycle. The need to rapidly establish new project structures and effectively manage these virtual organisations places high demands on the methods and models that are used for instantiation the project. Consequently, there is a need for an overall *Construction Network Meta Model* representing the different design, construction and management activities as well as the building objects, organisational and IT structure of the project.

The paper has demonstrated, that basically three dimensions, namely *Project Organisation*, *Project Structure* and *Project Information*, influence the performance of construction projects. Each dimension can be divided into categories that describe construction specific information like roles, functions, or data standards. Based on these results a *Construction Network Meta Model* has been developed. This meta model provides a schema for the definition of construction project constraints and can be integrated into a framework supporting the instantiation of a construction network. Several sources of reference data and models for the categories have been identified and can be used for the instantiation of a specific project in combination with a sequence model.

For the verification of the developed *Construction Network Meta Model* several projects with varying constraints about partner structure, functions, building components and IT-infrastructure have been analysed and evaluated. In particular the 'fault management process' has been investigated and decomposed into its categories and processes patterns.

5.1 Acknowledgment

This work has been conducted within the scope of the project 'Architecture for Collaborative Systems' (ArKoS) funded by the German Ministry for Education & Research. Within the project an holistic architecture for the management of inter-enterprise cooperation in construction projects is developed by the project consortium [5].

6. REFERENCES

1. Katranuschkov P. Gehre A. Scherer R.J. Wix J. Liebich T. „User Requirements Capture in Distributed Project Environments:A Process-centred Approach". In Xth International Conference on Computing in Civil and Building Engineering, Weimar, 2004.
2. Keller M, Katranuschkov P, Menzel K. "Modelling collaborative processes for Virtual Organisations in the building industry" In proceedings of ECPPM, Balkema, 2004.
3. Keller M; Menzel K, Scherer R.J. "Use of Workflow-Patterns for Process Modelling in the Building Industry". In proceedings of PRO-VE, Lugano Switzerland, 2003
4. UML – Unified Modelling Language "UML 2.0 – Superstructure Specification" www.uml.org, 2004
5. Zang S, Adam O, Hofer A. Hammer C. Jerrentrup M. Leinenbach S. "Architecture for collaborative business process management – enabling dynamic collaboration" In proceedings of ECPPM, Balkema, 2004

PART 13

PROCESS MODELING

39

SPECIFICATION MODEL FOR THE DEVELOPMENT AND OPERATION OF A VIRTUAL COMPANY IN THE AEROSPACE INDUSTRY

Barbara Odenthal
Chair and Institute of Industrial Engineering and Ergonomics (IAW)
at University of Technology Aachen (RWTH Aachen University)
e-mail: B.Odenthal@iaw.rwth-aachen.de

Meikel Peters
Chair and Institute of Industrial Engineering and Ergonomics (IAW)
at University of Technology Aachen (RWTH Aachen University)
e-mail: M.Peters@iaw.rwth-aachen.de

The reorganization of the supply chain in the aerospace industry has led to a new situation for small and medium-sized enterprises (SME). The suppliers are forced to deliver completed systems instead of components and assemblies. In order to react to the changed requirements, one possible solution is the project-oriented and temporary cooperation of SME by building a Virtual Organization in order to stay competitive and marketable. The research project AerViCo - Aerospace Virtual Company - is aimed at developing standard business processes, structures and tools to support a Virtual Organization in the aerospace industry.

1. INTRODUCTION

During the past years the development of the corporate strategy of manufacturers in the aerospace industry has led to a new situation for small and medium-sized enterprises (SME). In order to lower their costs, European consolidated companies in the aerospace industry (Airbus, EADS, astrium, Lagardere, ...) have re-organized their supplier network. The large number of direct suppliers caused enormous expenses regarding the coordination, the quality control and the auditing of the suppliers. By reducing the number of direct suppliers from several hundred to less than 10 strategic suppliers, the large enterprises expect not only better planning and control of their costs, an increase in output and a better quality of their products but also a decrease in their administrative work. In the long run, internationally operating enterprises are planning to reduce the number of strategic suppliers in all participating countries. Thus, one of the main requirements of aircraft manufacturers towards their strategic suppliers is an increasing international orientation. Furthermore, these strategic suppliers which have to be audited and certified are commissioned to deliver completed systems instead of components and assemblies.

In addition to the order processing, the first level suppliers are now also responsible for the monitoring and the compliance of second and third level suppliers with the quality standards. Consequently the above mentioned requirements are handed on to the second and the third level suppliers which are mainly SME. In order to respond to the new situation, one possible solution is the creation of a virtual network of SME which join forces in the case of an order processing flexibly adjusting to the requirements at hand (Peters/Bernhard, 2004). The cooperation within virtual companies on the other hand presents SME with new challenges concerning the work organization, the division of labor and the support by tools and methods in flexible networks.

To support SME with the development and operation of such virtual networks and to make the concept of virtual companies accessible to SME of the aerospace industry a research project - AerViCo - Aerospace Virtual Company – was initiated. The objective of the project is to develop a cooperation network of SME which is the basis for forming project consortiums to process a certain order. To do so, standard business processes, structures and tools to support a Virtual Company in the aerospace industry will be developed.

As one of the first achievements of the project, a specification model for Virtual Companies which meets the special requirements of SME in the aerospace industry was developed. Initially the model was set up literature based and provided a structure for a series of interviews with experts from the considered industry. The interview results were used to verify and further detail the model concerning the practical requirements of the aerospace industry.

2. SPECIFICATION MODEL FOR VIRTUAL COMPANIES

As a basis for the development and operation of Virtual Companies a specification model was developed based on a literature research (Albers et al., 2003) (Gerpott et al., 2000) (Kocian, 1999) (Ries, 2001) (Ringle, 2004) (Schuh et al., 2003) (Katzy, 1998) (Reid et al., 1996) (Camarinha-Matos, 2003) (Tølle, 2003). The model allows the description of all the relevant design areas of a Virtual Company in the aerospace industry which are namely (see figure 1):

- the core processes for building the cooperation platform and for the realization of concrete projects
- the supporting processes for administration and marketing of the network as well as project controlling and quality management
- in addition to the process level the IT-support plays an essential role in order processing in a distributed context
- finally the employee level must be considered carefully when designing Virtual Networks since especially in knowledge intensive networks the effective cooperation between employees is a success factor.

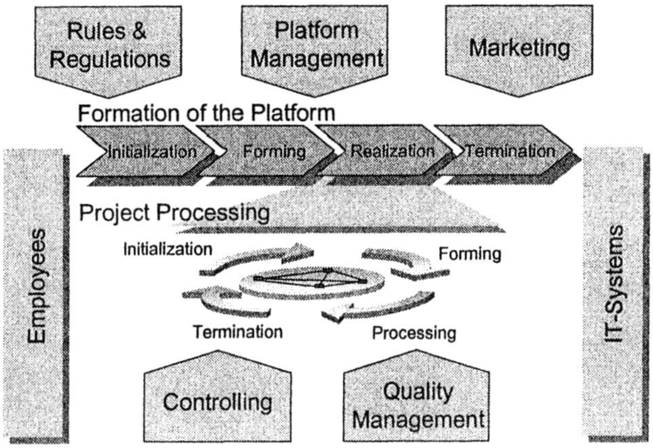

Figure 1: Specification Model for Virtual Companies in the Aerospace Industry

2.1 Core Processes and Supporting Tasks

The specification model for Virtual Companies was developed based on the phases of cooperation (Killich/Luczak, 2003). Regarding these phases of cooperation in Virtual Companies two levels can be distinguished: the platform level and the project level. On platform level the initialization, forming, realization and termination of the cooperation platform - the loose cooperation between potential project partners - are described. The phase of initialization starts with identifying potentials for a cooperation platform and defining goals of cooperation. The main tasks of the forming phase are the selection and assessment of potential network partners and the following negotiation with these. In the realization phase the cooperation platform carries out its original purpose, namely, the flexible configuration of project networks in order to achieve customer oriented order processing while concentrating on the network partners' core competencies. Finally, the termination of such a cooperation platform is possible. In this case the reasons for termination must be identified, collective resources must be divided and perhaps lessons learnt for future cooperations are generated.

The project level - the processing of concrete orders through flexible project networks - can also be described using four rather similar phases. A project starts with the identification of a market chance or an order by a customer in the initialization phase. According to the requirements of the market chance or the order, the project is defined, structured and planned in the phase of formation. A project network is configured considering the competencies required for the order processing and the existing core competencies of the members of the cooperation platform. The following phase of order processing mainly consists of the direct processes of the network partners and the project management for distributed projects. Finally the project network will be terminated, in most cases because the project goals were fulfilled. In consequence of the project, there might be further project related tasks, e.g. after sales services, that are carried out by one or several project partners.

The processes and tasks described so far are the direct processes on platform as well as on project level. In addition to these, supporting processes are necessary to ensure an effective and efficient cooperation based on the cooperation platform.

A number of problems often inhibit efficient collaboration in interorganizational networks. As a matter of fact, different goals and ethic values among the network partners as well as dynamic changes of processes are very complex to handle (Killich/Luczak, 2003). The higher the flexibility of the network, the more important the aspect of trust becomes, as it can no longer be built on extensive experience with the partners. Yet another major challenge is the overcoming of barriers due to different organizational cultures of network partners (Eppler/Sukowski, 2001).

The cooperation platform plays a main role in reducing these barriers. It provides a stable and long term pool of potential partners, supports the development of trust among partners and provides a certain degree of standardization to ensure efficient cooperative processes. To fulfil these requirements the cooperation platform must provide rules and regulations for the general cooperation between partners on platform level as well as on project level. The supporting processes also include the various tasks of platform management, e.g. finding new network partners, excluding partners from the network, measures of trust building and conflict management and also the development and operation of an adequate IT-infrastructure. Since one of the general characteristics of a Virtual Company is the collective market appearance of the network companies, the marketing of the cooperation platform is also an essential task on this level. These supportive and administrative tasks are usually carried out by the broker of the network.

Further, supporting processes that are important on platform level as well as on project level can be distinguished: controlling of all the activities of the platform is necessary to ensure the compliance with the goals of the platform and if necessary implement corrective measures. The different processes of quality management are particularly important since the aerospace industry strongly focuses on high quality standards.

2.2 IT-Support for Virtual Companies

Because of the collaboration in a distributed environment, an adequate IT-support of the processes of a Virtual Company is essential (Katzy et al., 2004) (DeSanctis/Monge, 1999) (Cohen/Mankin, 1999). The specification of the IT-support of a Virtual Company can be structured according to the life cycle as described above and the functions that are supported (see figure 2), namely information, communication, collaboration and coordination (Mertens, 1998). The initialization phase mainly requires support regarding informational functions, e.g. for identifying potentials for cooperation. These tasks can be supported for example by web-based databases or by electronic yellow pages. During the phase of formation communication systems – e.g. email, chat, ICQ, telephone and video conference, blackboard, news – gain importance in addition to information systems. In the following phase of realization the focus lies on the support of the operative project work by systems for collaboration and coordination. Examples for these are groupware document and Knowledge Management systems, newsgroups, Workflow Management Systems, Project Management Systems and Supply Chain

Management systems. The phase of termination finally requires support by systems providing mainly informational functions.
The main challenge, however, lies within finding adequate IT-support for the cooperative work that can be efficiently integrated into the existing operative systems of the network partners.

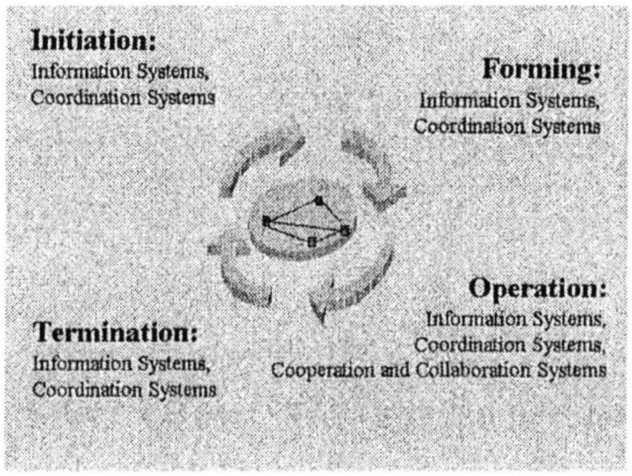

Figure 2: Description of the phases and of the corresponding IT systems (Mertens, 1998)

2.3 Employee-Related Aspects of Virtual Companies

As already mentioned interorganizational cooperation is always based on the actions of human beings. In a virtual context certain requirements towards employees are intensified and therefore should be considered carefully. In particular in knowledge-intensive cooperations the success depends on the efficient interaction of employees to a large extent. Because of this, the processes, structures and related tasks as well as supportive tools and instruments must be designed considering the effects on employee performance behavior.

In order to ensure compliance of employee behavior with the Virtual Companies' goals three aspects are of importance (Killich/Peters, 2003): commitment ("Are employees willing to act in a certain way?"), capability ("Are employees able to act in that way?") and conditions ("Do organizational and cultural conditions enable this kind of behavior?").

Regarding the area of commitment, structures, processes, areas of responsibility, decision authority should be reflected under motivational aspects.

The area of capability takes into account whether employees have adequate competencies to carry out the required tasks. This question is of particular interest since in a networked context social competencies, language and communication skills are needed in addition to excellent professional competencies.

With the third area, conditions, the view is extended to the surroundings of the employees. In this context for example aspects of organizational culture and trust between members of a virtual environment play an important role.

3. REQUIREMENTS OF THE AEROSPACE INDUSTRY TOWARDS A VIRTUAL COMPANY

The specification model provided a theoretical framework which had to be adapted to the particular requirements of a Virtual Company in the aerospace industry. Therefore, a series of interviews with involved companies from different levels of the supply chain (producer, 1st-tier supplier, 2nd-tier supplier and 3rd-tier supplier) was conducted.

In order to be able to cover the demands of SME towards the design of a cooperation platform, several potential network partners were questioned about their previous cooperations and the reasons for these. Furthermore, a particular focus lay on the prearrangements of the cooperation in respect to the selection and the rating of the potential partners and the contractual agreements. Finally, the order processing was analyzed regarding the role of the IT systems, the role of the employees and the contractual agreements during the cooperation.

The main reasons for cooperation given in the survey were the expansion of the product range and of the core competencies. Most of the companies announced that reciprocal specialization as well as know-how and knowledge transfer is highly important. All interviewees stated the long-term orientation of their past cooperations. Nearly all cooperations took place without a specific legal form but mainly on the basis of customer-supplier relationships.

Regarding the organization of the network respectively the cooperation platform, it appeared that the companies join forces in the case of a concrete project depending on the requirements at hand, so that the platform is often not managed explicitly. According to the questioned companies the important processes on platform level are the definition of corporate aims and merits, the fixing of rules and regulations, the strategy for the corporate marketing which must strictly market the product range of the cooperation platform and the integration of existing as well as the development of a new consistent IT structure.

In the case of an order processing, the following aspects are important for successful operating: finding the most promising combination of the partner companies, the clear structuring of the project and the definition of work packages, quality management and controlling supported by specialized IT systems and methods.

Because of the high quality standards of the considered industry, aspects of quality management must be integrated explicitly into the structures and processes of an Aerospace Virtual Company. The most important standards are the following:

- DIN EN ISO 9001: Quality Management Systems
- DIN EN 9100: Quality Management Systems in the Aerospace Industry
- ISO/TR 17400: Space systems – Space launch complexes, integration sites and other facilities – General testing guidelines
- JAR 21: Certification Procedures for Aircraft and related Products and Parts

As a result of the customer requirements and because of the conceptual formulation, most of the used IT tools are predetermined. In this regard, a secure well-structured electronic data interchange is one of the most important aspects concerning the configuration of a Virtual Company.

Because of the common customer request of being informed about each network partner involved in the order processing, the aim of the collective marketing cannot always be reached. Regarding the different roles in an Aerospace Virtual Company there is usually a prime-contractor who closes the deal **with the customer**. In order to fix the decisions and the work packages contractually, the prime-contractor is responsible for the arrangements with the cooperating companies.

In the context of working within a trans-national Virtual Company, the analysis of the interview results lead to the conclusion that the increasing importance of the role of the employees must be taken into consideration. The interviewees stated the increasing requirements regarding professional competencies as well as language skills, the flexibility concerning different fields of work and social competencies among other things due to the increasing international cooperation in the aerospace industry.

4. DISCUSSION AND OUTLOOK

To provide a basis for the specification of a Virtual Company in the aerospace industry a model describing all the relevant design areas was presented.

The model was detailed regarding the special requirements of the aerospace industry through a series of interviews with small and medium enterprises that have experiences with cooperative work in the respective industry. In order to also collect the requirements of potential customers of an Aerospace Virtual Company further interviews were carried out with aircraft manufacturers and their direct suppliers.

The next step in the project will be the development of concepts, IT-Tools, methodological support and framework agreements for the development and operation of a Virtual Company in aerospace industry according to the specification model. Accompanying the conceptual work the acquisition of a concrete evaluation project will be worked on by the project consortium. This project will be used to configure a Virtual Company according to the developed concepts and to apply and evaluate the supporting tools and methods.

As a result a complete and validated guideline for the development and operation of an Aerospace Virtual Company for small and medium enterprises will be provided.

5. ACKNOWLEDGMENTS

The Project „AerViCo – Aerospace Virtual Company“ is funded by the German Federal Ministry of Education and Research (grant number: 01HU0160 – 01HU0169). The other partners are: AIDA Development GmbH, Schwaebisch Hall, ALROUND e.V., Bonn, ANSYS Germany GmbH, Otterfing, Fraunhofer – Institut für Materialfluss und Logistik (IML), Dortmund, HEGGEMANN Aerospace AG, Büren, HTS GmbH, Coswig, IMA Materialforschung und Anwendungstechnik GmbH, Dresden, MST Aerospace GmbH, Köln, ProTec-Recycling, Werne.

6. REFERENCES

1. Albers, S., Bisping, D., Teichmann, K., Wolf, J.: Management Virtueller Unternehmen. Wiesbaden: Albers, S., Wolf, J. (eds.), Deutscher Universitäts-Verlag GmbH, 2003.
2. Camarinha-Matos, L., Afsarmanesh, M.H., Raselo, R.J.: Infrastructure developments for agile virtual enterprises, in: Int. Journal of Computer Integrated Manufacturing, 16, 2003, No. 4 – 5.
3. Cohen, S.G., Mankin, D.: Collaboration in the Virtual Organization, in: Cooper, C. L.; Rousseau, D. M. (eds.): Trends in Organizational Behavior, Vol. 6, Chichester, 1999, 105 – 120.
4. DeSanctis, G., Monge, P.: Introduction to the special issue: Communication processes for virtual organizations, in: Organization Science, 10, No. 6, 1999, 693 – 703.
5. Eppler, M.J., Sukowski, O. (eds.): Fallstudien zum Wissensmanagement: Lösungen aus der Praxis. St. Gallen: NetAcademy Press, 2001.
6. Gerpott, T. J., Böhm, S.: Strategisches Management in virtuellen Unternehmen, in: Albach, H. (ed.): Virtuelle Unternehmen, ZfB-Ergänzungsheft 2/2000, Wiesbaden, 13 – 35.
7. Katzy, B. R., Sung, G., Serrano, C.: Managing virtual projects – A benchmark study of collaboration tools, 2004. Internet source: http://www.ve-forum.org/, date: 17.12.2004.
8. Katzy, B. R.: Design and Implementation of Virtual Organizations, Proceedings of the 31st Hawaii International Conference on System Sciences, Maui, 1998.
9. Killich, S., Luczak, H.: Unternehmenskooperation für kleine und mittelständische Unternehmen. Berlin: Springer, 2003.
10. Killich, S., Peters, M.: The Interest of employees in Knowledge Sharing: A Theoretical Framework for the Integration of Motivation, Qualification and Organization for Knowledge Management in Networks. In: Luczak, H. ; Zink, K.J. (eds.): *Human Factors in Organizational Design and Management - VII. Proceedings of the Seventh International Symposium on Human Factors in Organizational Design and Management held in Aachen, October 1-2,* IEA Press, Santa Monica, CA, USA 2003, 373-378.
11. Kocian, C.: Virtuelle Kooperationen im Mittelstand, Wiesbaden, 1999.
12. Mertens, P.: Virtuelle Unternehmen und Informationsverarbeitung, Berlin: Springer, 1998.
13. Peters, M., Bernhard, J.: Virtuelle Zulieferkooperationen in der Luftfahrtindustrie – Entwicklung eines Konzeptes zum Aufbau und Betrieb Virtueller Unternehmen unter Berücksichtigung organisatorischer, technischer und personeller Faktoren. In: *Unternehmen der Zukunft*, Aachen, 5, 2004, 4; 3-4.
14. Reid, R. L., Rogers, K. J., Johnson, M., Liles, D.: Engineering the Virtual Enterprise. Fifth Industrial Engineering Research Conference. Minneapolis, Minnesota, 1996, 485 – 490.
15. Reinhardt, G., Mehler, B.: Organisatorische und informationstechnische Aspekte beim Aufbau virtueller Fabriken. In: Kaluza, B./Blecker, T. (eds.): Produktions- und Logistikmanagement in Virtuellen Unternehmen und Unternehmensnetzwerken, Heidelberg, 2000, S. 391-420.
16. Ries, A.: Controlling in virtuellen Netzwerken, Wiesbaden, 2001.
17. Ringle, C. M.: Die Virtuelle Unternehmung. Ausprägungsformen und Abgrenzung, in: Der Betriebswirt, 45, No. 2, 2004, 21 – 29.
18. Schuh, G., Kurr, M., Friedli, T.: Das Konzept „Virtuelle Fabrik" - Aufbau, Betrieb und Auflösung. In: Bullinger, H.-J.; Warnecke, J.; Westkämper, E. (eds.): Neue Organisationsformen im Unternehmen - Ein Handbuch für das moderne Management, 2nd ed., Berlin, 2003, 627 – 643.
19. Schuh, G., Millarg, K., Göransson, A.: Virtuelle Fabrik, Munich, 1998.
20. Tølle, M.: Reference models supporting enterprise networks and virtual enterprises, in: Int. J. Networking and Virtual Organisations, 2, 2003, No. 1, 2 – 15.

40

MODELING STRUCTURED NON-MONOLITHIC COLLABORATION PROCESSES

Willy Picard
Deparment of Information Technology
The Poznań University of Economics
ul. Mansfelda 4
60-854 Poznań, POLAND
<picard@kti.ae.poznan.pl>

Existing systems supporting collaboration processes typically implement a single, fixed collaboration protocol, and collaboration process takes place inside a single group. In this paper, we present a model which provides support for multiple collaboration protocols for non-monolithic collaboration processes, i.e. collaboration processes in which collaboration is spread among many groups. In the presented model, collaboration protocols include communicative, "acting", and social aspects of collaboration processes, and the introduction of group actions provides support for group dynamics. Conditions that collaboration protocols have to fulfill to be valid are also presented.

1. INTRODUCTION

From prehistoric tribes to trade unions, group structure has always been at the heart of human activities. Grouping their competences, humans are able to achieve great projects, from pyramids to railroad infrastructure construction. The keyword for group activities is *collaboration*. Collaboration is the process of sharing competences to achieve a common goal.

To a recent past, the collaboration process was limited by the requirement of a single location. People involved in a collaboration process needed to meet to exchange information. In reality, people are generally spread on large geographical area. Meetings are difficult to organize, because of schedule incompatibilities, and costly in terms of time and money.

Telecommunication networks provide a partial solution to the former problem. Telecommunication networks let collaborators be spread over various locations. The use of telephone allows collaborators to exchange information via voice communication. Documents can be exchanged via fax in a graphical format. Local area networks (LAN) are the basis of electronic information exchange inside enterprises, while wide area networks (WAN) - in between enterprises.

With the rise of telecommunication networks, collaboration models that rationalize the collaboration process have been developed. Most of them are document oriented, i.e. the fundamental object of the collaboration process is one or more documents. In enterprises' intranets, collaboration tools are currently widely used for sharing files, for group scheduling or for document collaborative writing.

Traditionally, research in electronic support for collaboration has concentrated on collaboration processes confined inside a single group. Little attention has been accorded to the case of *non-monolithic* collaboration processes, i.e. processes in which the collaborative activities are spread dynamically among potentially many groups. The term "non-monolithic" is taken from the negotiation vocabulary (see [10], pp. 4-5, 389-406), where a non-monolithic negotiation process is a negotiation process in which some parties do not behave as a unitary decision entity, i.e. a party consisting of many persons with various perceptions and goals.

In the field of computer support for collaborative work (CSCW), some works have addressed the issue of the group data organization in a dynamic way [3], the issue of non-monolithic collaborative document edition [8]. These works are usually poorly formalized and focused on very limited applications. In the field of electronic negotiations, some works addressed the issue of negotiation protocols [1][2][4][5][7][13]. According to [6], a negotiation protocol is "a formal model, often represented by a set of rules, which govern software processing, decision-making and communication tasks, and imposes restrictions on activities through the specification of permissible inputs and actions". One may consider a negotiation protocol as a collaboration protocol. Works in the field electronic negotiations are usually limited to monolithic negotiations, or address a single user's point of view and do not provide support for group collaboration. To our best knowledge, the issue of support for both structured and non-monolithic collaboration processes has never been addressed.

As stated in [14], "there can be no separate document and communication management for effectively supporting electronic negotiations". In the case of non-monolithic negotiations, a third aspect has to be taken into account: group dynamics. By extrapolating the case of cooperation from the case of e-negotiations, we argue that three elements have to be taken into account for an efficient support for non-monolithic cooperation: action management, communication management, and group dynamics. These three elements are required for computer support systems for non-monolithic cooperation processes as:

- the "acting" element is required to model the actions that the collaborators trigger during the cooperation process,
- the communication management element is required to model the meta-data about the cooperation processes,
- the group dynamics element is required to model social structures in which the cooperation takes place, i.e. cooperation groups.

The three elements presented above are not conclusive. Other components of a collaborative system, e.g computer support for proposition offer evaluation in the case of e-negotiations, may be included in the proposed model. However, it should be noticed that the three elements presented above are inherently related with the non-monolithic aspect of the cooperation processes, while other components are usually related with a collaborator's perceptions/goals concerning the cooperation process.

In this paper, we present a model which provides support for multiple collaboration protocols for non-monolithic collaboration processes. In Section 2, a model for collaboration protocols integrating communicative, "acting", and social aspects is presented, then group actions required to provide support for group dynamics are introduced. In Section 3, the proposed model is formalized. In Section 4, the question of protocol validity is addressed. Section 5 concludes the paper.

2. STRUCTURING NON-MONOLITHIC COLLABORATION PROCESSES

In non-monolithic collaborative processes, collaboration always occurs inside a group. Even when a single collaborator works alone, it may be considered as a group consisting of only herself/himself. Therefore, it may be stated that *a group is a non-empty set of collaborators*. An other aspect of this kind of collaboration is that collaborators are collaborating via message exchange. As we would like to structure non-monolithic collaboration processes, we have to address two issues: first, a mechanism to structure collaboration inside a given group has to be proposed, which means that message exchange has to be structured, second, group dynamics have to be addressed.

2.1 Collaboration Protocols

Three elements may be distinguished in collaborative processes: a meta-data aspect, an "acting" aspect, and a social aspect.

Meta-data is a major component of collaboration as collaborators need to exchange information to achieve their common goal [15][11]. The acting aspect of collaboration concerns the fact that collaborators not only exchange information to reach their common goal, but also act to achieve it. Finally, the social aspect of collaborative processes, captured via the concept of role, concerns relationships among collaborators, the perceptions they have of others collaborators.

The concept of *social behavioral element* captures all three aspects – meta-data, acting, and social – of collaborative processes.

Social Behavioral Element A social behavioral element is a triplet (User_Role, Meta-data_Type, Action).

- The User_Role addresses the social aspect.
- The Meta-data_Type addresses the meta-data aspect. The introduction of meta-data types allows to limit ambiguousness of communication [12].
- The Action addresses the acting aspect.

In the proposed model, collaboration processes result from exchange of social behavioral elements among collaborators. Collaborators are exchanging social behavioral elements, sending typed meta-data and acting, in a given role. Exchange of social behavioral elements causes the evolution of the group in which collaborators are working: each sent social behavioral element causes a transition of the group from a past state to a new state.

Transition A transition is a triplet (SocialBehavioralElement, SourceState, DestinationState).

It is now possible to define collaboration protocols, which may be used to structure collaboration processes.

Collaboration protocol A collaboration protocol consists of a set of transitions, a start state, and a set of terminating states.

One may notice that a protocol is a variant of finite state machines. A finite state machine (FSM) is usually defined as "a model of computation consisting of a set of states, a start state, an input alphabet, and a transition function that maps input symbols and current states to a next state". The set of states of the FSM can be easily deduced from the set of transitions of the protocol. The start state occurs in both the FSM and the protocol. The input alphabet of the FSM is the set of social behavioral elements which appear in all transitions of the protocols. Finally, the transition function of the FSM is defined by the set of transitions of the protocol. The only difference between FSMs and collaboration protocols is the existence of terminating states for protocols.

A collaboration protocol is a template definition for a set of collaboration processes. Using an analogy with object-oriented programming, one may say that a collaboration protocol is to a protocol instance what a class is to an object. In a given group, a given protocol instance regulates collaboration among group members/collaborators.

Protocol instance A protocol instance is a tuple (Protocol, CurrentState, UserToRoleMapping). The UserToRoleMapping is a function which associates a UserRole with a given user.

2.2 Group Dynamics

In non-monolithic collaborative processes, groups evolve: a collaborator may join or leave an existing group, a group may split in two or more groups, two or more groups may merge into a single group. Group dynamics may be modeled by a set of group actions. The following group actions have been identified:

- create action: creates a new group;
- join action: adds an author to the set of collaborators of an existing group;
- merge action: creates a new group consisting of the union of the set of collaborators of at least two groups;
- end action: deletes an existing group;
- leave action: removes a collaborator from the set of collaborators of an existing group;
- split action: creates at least two groups from an existing group and the union of the sets of collaborators of the created groups equals the set of collaborators of the existing group.

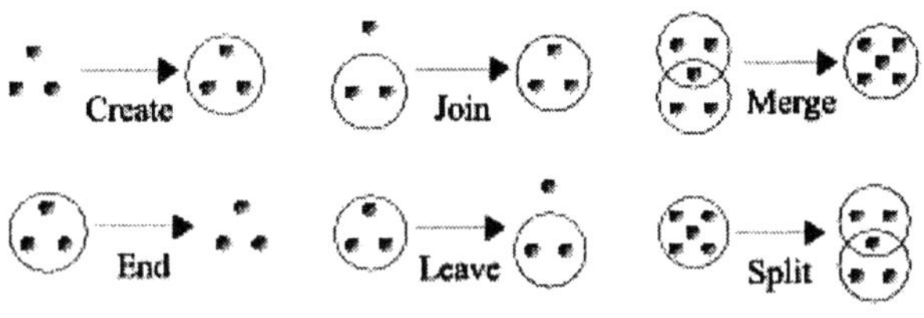

Figure 1. Group actions

Group actions are illustrated on Figure 1. Dots represent collaborators while circles represent groups. One may notice that, as shown on Figure 1 for the split and merge actions, a given collaborator may participate at a given time in many groups.

3. FORMAL MODEL

Let's first define the concepts of behavioral element and roles, which are the fundamental bricks of group protocols in the proposed model. The concept of *behavioral element* is required to model relationships between actions and meta-data types.

Behavioral element A behavioral element is defined as a couple (Action, Meta_data_type)

The relationship between actions and meta-data types is a *n-to-n* relationship. First, a 1-to-n relationship between action and meta-data types may exists: in an electronic negotiations case, one action – the leave action, triggered by a negotiator which wants to leave an existing group – may be associated with various meta-data types, such as a rejectOffer , when a negotiator wants to send a message concerning offer rejection, or a logout when a negotiator wants to log out the system. Reciprocally, a *1-to-n* relationship between meta-data type and actions may exists: a meta-data type – the rejectOffer meta-data type, triggered by a negotiator which does not accept a previously proposed offer – may be associated with various actions, such as a leave action to leave an existing group or an end action to delete an existing group. The concept of behavioral element enables *n-to-n* relationships between actions and meta-data types.

Role A Role r consists of a set of behavioral elements, denoted r_{be}, and a role name, e.g. buyer, seller, or moderator.

The relationship between behavioral elements and roles is a n-to-n relationship, as presented in Figure 2. First, in the presented example, one role – the moderator role – may be associated with various behavioral elements, such as "send message", "accept message", or "reject message". Second, on the same example, the behavioral element "send message" is associated with many roles, such as moderator or normal negotiator.

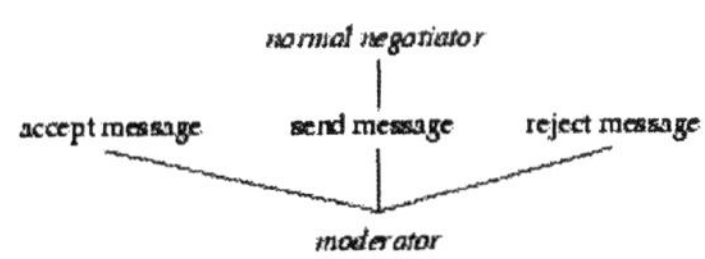

Figure 2. Example of n-to-n relationship between behavioral elements and roles

Social Behavioral Element For a given role r, the set of pairs *(role_name; be)*, with $be \in r_{be}$ is denoted r_{sbe}. A pair *(role_name; be)* is called a *social behavioral element*.

Using the example presented in Figure 2, the social behavioral element (moderator, accept message) is defined, while the social behavioral element (normal user, accept message) is not defined. For the role moderator, r_{sbe} is a set containing the following social behavioral elements: (moderator, accept message), (moderator, send message), (moderator, reject message).

Group Protocol A group protocol *p* consists of:

- a set of states *S*,
- one starting state $s_0 \in S$,
- a set of ending states $S_{ending} \subset S$, with $s_0 \notin S_{ending}$,
- a set of roles *R*,
- a transition function *t* from $(S - S_{ending}) \times S \times \cup_{r \in R} r_{sbe}$ to *{true, false}*.

4. VALIDITY OF COLLABORATION PROTOCOLS

The former definition specifies the basic requirements for collaboration protocols. It links the notions of states, roles, and behavioral elements. However, the former definition does not ensure that such protocols are valid, neither structurally, nor semantically.

Structural validity A protocol is *structurally valid* iff:

1) there is a path from the starting state to all states,
2) there is a path from every state to an ending state.
3) from a given state, there is only one transition associate with a given social behavioral element.

The two first conditions ensure that no state are neither non-accessible (and therefore should be suppressed from the protocol), nor leading to a lock in the negotiation process, i.e. forbids the negotiation process to be finished.

The third condition ensures that no ambiguity exists in a group protocol. An ambiguity may occur when two or more transitions associated with one social behavioral element *sbe* may lead to two or more states from a single state *s*. In this case, it is not possible to decide to which state the social behavioral element *sbe* leads to. Formally, the last condition for structural validity may be formulated as follows:

$$\forall s \in (S - S_{ending}), \exists (s_i, s_j) \in S^2, sbe \in \cup_{r \in R} r_{sbe}, \quad t(s, s_i, sbe) = t(s, s_j, sbe) = true \Rightarrow s_i = s_j$$

Semantic validity A protocol is *semantically valid* iff:

1) all transitions to ending states are associated with social behavioral elements containing an ending action,
2) social behavioral elements containing an ending action are associated only with transitions leading to ending states,

An action *a* is an *ending action* iff the life of the group *g* ends when action *a* is called in group *g*. The life of a group *g* ends when no more message can be sent to group g. The set of ending actions of a given protocol is denoted *EndingActions*. One may notice that the group action end is obviously an ending action.

The first condition ensures that a transition leading to an ending state really ends the life of the group. The second condition ensures that the group protocol cannot be "interrupted" by a transition associated with an ending action.

Formally, the first condition for semantic validity may be formulated as follows:

$$\forall (s_i, s_j, sbe_k) \in (S - S_{ending}) \times S_{ending} \times \cup_{r \in R} r_{sbe}, \quad t(s_i, s_j, sbe_k) = true \Rightarrow a_k \in EndingActions$$

where a_k is the action associated with the social behavioral element sbe_k.
The second condition for semantical validity may be formulated as follows:

$$\forall (s_i, s_j, sbe_k) \in (S - S_{ending}) \times (S - S_{ending}) \times \cup_{r \in R} r_{sbe}, \quad t(s_i, s_j, sbe_k) = true \Rightarrow a_k \notin EndingActions$$

The concepts of structural validity and semantical validity are illustrated on Figure 3. The case a) is an example of a valid group protocol, while the cases b) and c) are respectively examples of structurally and semantically invalid group protocols. In the case b), the group protocol is structurally invalid for two reasons: first, there is no path from the starting state to the state s_2. Second, there is no path from the state s_1 to the ending state s_4. In the case c), the group protocol is semantically invalid for two reasons: first, the transition t_1, which is not associated with an ending action, leads from the state s_1 to the ending state s_4. Second, the transition t_2, which is associated with an ending action, leads from the state s_2 to the state s_3, which is not ending state.

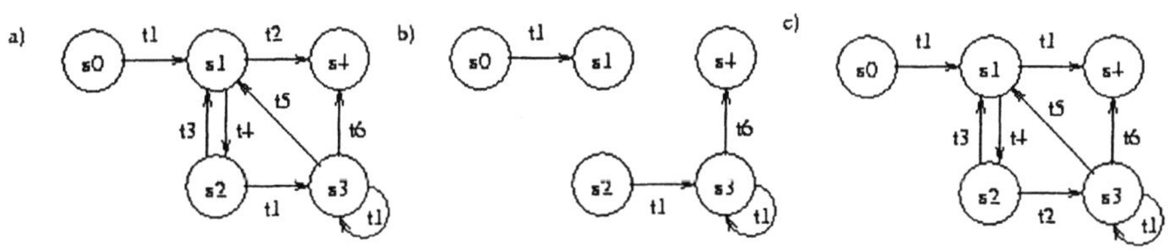

Figure 3. Examples of a) valid, b) structurally invalid , c) semantically invalid group protocols, where s_0, s_1, ..., s_4 are states, s_4 being the only ending state, and t_1, t_2, ... , t_5 are transitions, t_2 and t_6 being the only transitions associated with an ending action

5. CONCLUSIONS

The introduction of collaboration protocols and group actions allows to provide computer support to non-monolithic collaboration processes. To our best knowledge, it is the first model for electronic support for non-monolithic collaborative processes addressing the issues of group dynamics, meta-data management and protocol validity.

It would be possible to build complex support systems for complex collaborative processes using the model presented in this paper. The design of systems for non-monolithic collaboration processes may be resumed in the following steps: first, the roles involved in the collaboration process have to be identified. Next, the required actions have to be implemented. Then, meta-data types should be defined. Therefore, social behavioral elements may be defined. Finally, collaboration protocol(s) may be specified and their validity may be checked.

The presented model could be used in a broad spectrum of potential applications. The presented model may for instance be applied to non-monolithic negotiations, such as international negotiations or business-to-business contract establishment. Another field of applications is the legislative process in which various political parties, potentially presenting various opinions, are (or should) collaborate in order to establish laws in form of new or modified legal acts. The presented model could also be used to design support systems for collaborative documentation edition processes that often takes place between business actors.

Among future works, it would be interesting to investigate the possibilities to embed a protocol instance into another protocol instance. This would allow to modularize protocols, to design protocols using smaller protocols, to develop protocol libraries. Another field which could be the object of future works is the concept of role. The addition of relationships between various roles, such as inheritance or composition, would be an interesting work to be done. A prototype has already been implemented [9] and it would be interesting to evaluate the usability of the proposed solution in real-world cases.

6. REFERENCES

[1] M. Benyoucef and R. K. Keller, "An Evaluation of Formalisms for Negotiations in E-Commerce", Proceedings of the Workshop on Distributed Computing on the Web, Quebec City, Canada, pp. 45-54, 2000.

[2] W. Cellary, W. Picard, and W. Wieczerzycki, "Web-based Business-to-Business Negotiation Support", Int. Conference on Electronic Commerce TrEC-98, Hamburg, Germany, pp. 80-89, 1998.

[3] M. Ettorre, L. Pontieri, M. Ruffolo, P. Rullo, and D. Sacca, "A Prototypal Environment for Collaborative Work within a Research Organization", 3rd Workshop on Web Based Collaboration, associated to the DEXA Conference, Prague, Czech Republic, pp. 274-279, 2003.

[4] P. Hung and J.-Y. Mao, "Modeling of e-Negotiation Activities with Petri Nets", 35th International Conference on System Sciences, HICSS'02, Hawaii, USA, 2002. (http://csdl.computer.org/comp/proceedings/hicss/2002/1435/01/14350026.pdf)

[5] G. E. Kersten and G. Lo, "Aspire: Integration of Negotiation Support System and Software Agents for E-Business Negotiation", *International Journal of Internet and Enterprise Management (IJIEM)*, 1(3), pp. 293-315, 2003.

[6] G. E. Kersten, S. E. Strecker, and K. P. Law, "Protocols for Electronic Negotiation Systems: Theoretical Foundations and Design Issues", 5th International Conference on E-Commerce and Web Technologies, EC-Web 2004, Zaragoza, Spain, pp. 106-115, 2004.

[7] J. Kim and A. Segev, "A Framework for Dynamic eBusiness Negotiation Processes", IEEE Conference of E-Commerce: CITM, 2003. (http://groups.haas.berkeley.edu/citm/citm-home.htm)

[8] W. Picard, "Towards Support Systems for Non-Monolithic Collaborative Document Edition: the Document-Group-Message Model", 15th International Conference on Database and Expert Systems Applications DEXA 2004, Zaragoza, Spain, pp. 266-270, 2004.

[9] W. Picard and T. Huriaux, "DynG: Enabling Structured Non-Monolithic Electronic Collaboration", The 9th International Conference on CSCW in Design, Coventry, UK, 2005, to be published.

[10] H. Raiffa, J. Richardson, and D. Matcalfe, *Negotiation Analysis, The Science and Art of Collaborative Decision Making*, The Belknap Press of Harvard University Press, 2002.

[11] M. Schoop, A. Jertila, T. List, "Negoisst: A Negotiation Support System for Electronic Business-to-Business Negotiations in E-Commerce", *Data and Knowledge Engineering*, 47(3), pp 371-401.

[12] M. Schoop, "An Introduction to the Language-Action Perspective", *SIGGROUP Bulletin*, vol. 22, No.2, August 2001, pp 3-8.

[13] M. Schoop and C. Quix, "DOC.COM: a framework for effective negotiation support in electronic marketplaces", *Computer Networks*, vol. 37, No. 2, pp. 153-170, 2001.

[14] M. Schoop and C. Quix, "DOC.COM, Combining document and communication management for negotiation support in business-to-business electronic commerce", Proceedings of the 34th Hawaiian International Conference On System Sciences (HICSS-34), Maui, Hawaii, Jan. 2001, IEEE Press.

[15] H. Weigand, M. Schoop, A. De Moor, F. Dignum, "B2B Negotiation Support: The Need for a Communication Perspective", *Group Decision and Negotiation* 12, pp. 3-29, 2003.

41

QUANTITATIVE MODELS OF COLLABORATIVE NETWORKS

Dmitry Ivanov[1], Joachim Kaeschel[2], Boris Sokolov[3], Alexander Arkhipov[1], Lars Zschorn[2]

[1] *Saint Petersburg State Polytechnic University, RUSSIA*
dmitri.ivanov@mail.ru

[2]*Chemnitz University of Technology, GERMANY*
j.kaeschel@wirtschaft.tu-chemnitz.de

[3]*Russian academy of science,*
Saint Petersburg Institute of Informatics and Automation (SPIIRAS), RUSSIA
sokol@iias.spb.su

The paper deals with issues on mathematical modeling of collaborative networks (CN) caused by complexity and uncertainty of CN due to interactions of active elements (enterprises), high dynamics as well as external and internal disturbances. This paper introduces an integrated approach for CN complex modeling, and illustrates it on the example of production network design and control. The goal of this research is to develop generic model constructions for design and control of CN, and contribute to advancing of theoretical foundations of CN.

1. INTRODUCTION

The greater evolution of *production* concepts, based on advanced organizational principles and modern information technologies (IT), takes place. Collaborative networks (CN) can be classified under these conceptions. In recent years, the concepts and IT tools for CN have been strongly developed (Chandra and Kamrani, 2004, Kuhn, 2002, Virtual Enterprises, 2004). However, the research on quantitative modelling of CN is still very limited. In this paper we consider a concept of production networks, which are based on customer-oriented, temporary networking of core competences enterprises (Teich, 2003, Wirth, 2001). In such temporary networks, the special feature of *supply chain management (SCM)* lies in flexible configurable supply chains, conditioned by an enlargement of alternatives to search suitable partners for the cooperation. This paper introduces in a systematic way an *integrated approach for modeling and optimization of CN* based on combination of control theory, systems theory and operation research with multi agent theory, and illustrates it on the example of production network design and control.

2. RELATED WORKS

Development of quantitative models for CN is complicated by high degree of complexity and uncertainty in CN caused by interactions of *active elements* (enterprises), structure dynamics as well as processes oscillations as due to external and internal disturbances. Some of the issues on fundamental models for SCM can be found in (Tayur, 1999). The book seems to be the first attempt to provide a systematic summary of OR quantitative models of SCM, especially for inventory management and supply contracts.

The most researches on *vendor evaluation and selection* consider the vendor selecting separate for each product part (not from the point of view of the network as a whole). The researches predetermine a focal enterprise (centre), which selects the vendors, and the elaborated analytical approaches are suitable only when a number of product parts and vendors are limited. Few research deals with the methods and algorithms for value chain scheduling.

One of the highlights of past researches has been the application of *multi-agent approach* to SCM and VE (Fox et al., 2000, Shen et al., 2001, Swaminathan et al., 1998, Rabelo et al., 2002). A number of researchers have attempted to apply agent technology to manufacturing enterprise integration, supply chain management, manufacturing planning, scheduling and control, materials handling, etc. However, these researches was mostly concentrated on the software engineering and computer science rather than on the methodological problems of utilization of MAS to CN.

Few studies have integrated *risk management* into models of networking (Sorensen, 2005, Hallikas et al., 2004, Zschorn et al., 2004). The researches try to classify types of risk and uncertainty, and to develop some suggestions how to plan and control the networks taking into account risk factors.

Some recent research papers (Camarinha-Matos and Afsarmanesh, 2004) emphasise, that the proper methods of CN quantitative modeling have to combine elements drawn from various theories such as Systems Science, Control Theory, Operation Research, Distributed Artificial Intelligence etc. The combination of elements of various methods has been developed applied to complex technical systems for the last 30 years (Mesarovic and Takahara, 1975, Casti, 1979, Sokolov and Yusupov, 2004). In recent years, these ideas have been also used for development of generic models for information management in integrated enterprise systems (Chandra and Kamrani, 2004, Teich, 2003). Another approach to development of fundamental basis for SCM is being developed in the theory of system dynamics (Sterman, 2000). These researches are grounded in modern systems and control theories, which give extensive approaches to design and control of complex systems. However, their disadvantage regarding complex business systems is that the system elements are being controlled from a centre and cannot change their states and interactions of their own free will (the system elements are passive. In complex business systems the elements are active (their can compete and have contradictive aims, interests etc.) The classic methods do not allow developing of practicable complex quantitative models of open decentralized systems with active goal-oriented elements. That is why it is sensible to draw the elements from the multi agent theory, and construct the new techniques of CN modelling.

3. MODELING OF COLLABORATIVE NETWORKS

CN are described by various models. Besides, the CN operation is accompanied by perturbation impacts (*disturbances*), which influence the plan execution and the network environment. Moreover, additional uncertainty and requirements on models arise from the *activity of network elements* and their free-will interactions. The above-mentioned factors do not let produce an adequate description of design and control processes on a basis of single-class models. Consequently, the design and control of CN are to be considered interconnected, and the *adaptation* of models to the current execution environment is to be ensured. The other important feature of CN modeling is that the property of enterprise activity has to be taken into account.

The production CN management is composed of network design (network configuration and supply chain scheduling) and control (performance management, monitoring, regulations/change management) (Ivanov et al., 2004, Zschorn et al., 2005). The network design aims at forming supply chains through a partner selection from a pool of available suppliers based on the bid parameters of the enterprises (e.g. lead time, costs etc.) and customer requirements (delivery time, desired quantity, product technological structure etc.). The control phase targets at monitoring of supply chain execution and supply chain regulation (reconfiguration) in case of any deviations from the plan state.

The main parts of the proposed integrated modelling approach are:

- *multi-agent conceptual modeling framework* for the representation of active elements (enterprises) in graph-theoretical modeling,
- *multiple-model complexes* based for combination of various models (e.g. dynamical and static models, analytical and simulation models),
- *adaptive planning and control* for interconnecting of planning and control models.

The complexity and uncertainty of CN arise from the interactions of active elements (enterprises). The past researches on utilization of MAS to CN problems have been mostly dealing with agent based software architectures, where agents are autonomous, goal-oriented software processes. We propose to consider the agents *as not only software entities for negotiation support, but also as conceptual modeling entities*. We consider the agents as a part of the generic model constructions. It means that the agents are used not only on the stage of software simulation, but also at the levels of *the conceptual modeling, formalization and mathematical modelling*.

Due to complexity and uncertainty of CN modeling adequacy cannot be ensured within a single model, thus *multiple-model complexes* should be used. Each class of models can be applied to the objects for analysis of their particular aspects at a given level of detail. The interconnection between different models is ensured by means of functors (*F*) (see Figure 1).

The multiple-model complexes allow problem examining and solution in different classes of models, and result representation in the wishful class of models (concept of *"virtual" modelling*). It becomes possible under the terms of collective application of structural mathematical and categorical functoral conceptions. Paper (Sokolov and Yusupov, 2004) demonstrates the capabilities of the categorical-functoral approach to qualimetry of models.

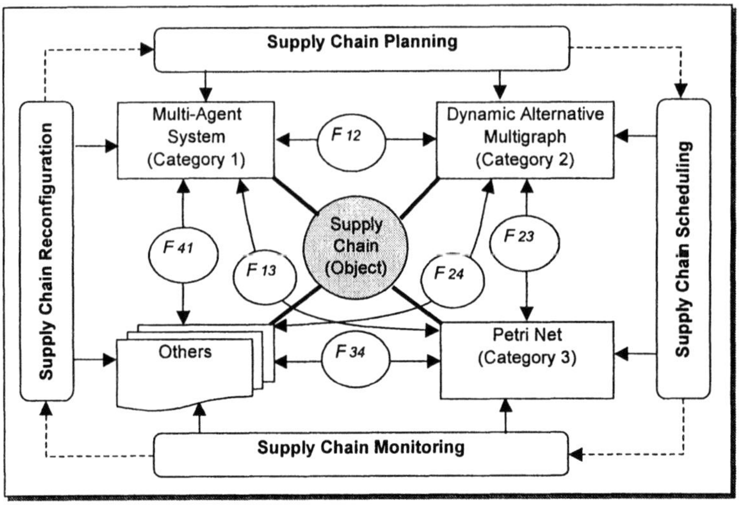

Figure 1. Example of a multiple-model complex

The adaptive planning and control is based on the system planning approach, which lets interpret planning not as discrete operations, but as continuous adaptive process. The concept of adaptive planning and control *incorporates* the phases of planning, monitoring and regulation, and makes it possible to adapt the models of planning and control in accordance with the actual execution environment by means of change of partner selection principles, change of selection algorithms, change of model parameters and criteria, etc.

The *general structure of quantitative models of collaborative networks* is shown in Figure 2.

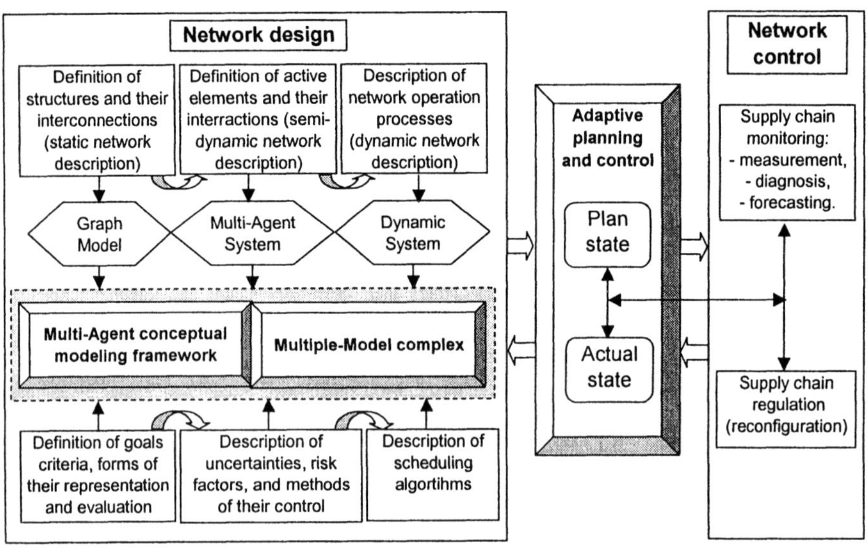

Figure 2. The general structure of quantitative models of collaborative networks

The modelling starts with the static graph-theoretical network description. The elements of the organizational graph (enterprises) are described as active agents in terms of multi-agent theory. So the model of enterprise interactions can be constructed. The next step consists of dynamic network description, which is composed of structure dynamics description and dynamic network operation description. Then the environment description is needed. By the definition of goal criteria it is essential, first, to define methods how to balance the global network criteria (from customers' orders) and local goals of the agents, and secondly, to elaborate forms of multi-criteria selection procedure. The next step of the environment description consists of uncertainty analyzing and integration of risk factors in the models. Then the scheduling algorithms can be elaborated.

The models of network control are comprised of supply chain monitoring and supply chain regulation (reconfiguration) models. Supply chain execution is a highly dynamic process complicated by structure dynamics, changes of network properties and parameters while decision-making, goal-oriented behaviour of enterprises. That is why it is necessary to formulate the models of monitoring and regulations of supply chains complex with the network design models in order to ensure the adequacy of models to the *current execution environment.*

Now let us illustrate the above-described principles. We consider dynamic supply chain building through partner selection from a pool of available suppliers in a CN. The network design is composed of: (i) selecting offers for each operation (formation of a set of alternative supply chains) and (ii) evaluating of alternative supply chains and selecting the best one. Let the number of initial data be denoted in the following way. CN is a set $B = \{B_\mu, \mu \in M\}$ of participant enterprises, which can fulfil a number of operations (jobs) $O = \{O_j, j \in L\}$. A pair (B_μ, O_j) is called *competence,* so that if the μ-enterprise can do the j-operation, so it posses competence $k_{\mu j}$. Each offer of the competence is characterized by available capacity $x_{\mu j}(t)$, costs $c_{\mu j}$, risk $q_{\mu j}$. So the offer network can be modeled graph-theoretically as a *directed graph (digraph).* The competences and their offers represent the nodes, and the edges between the nodes represent the corresponding allowed predecessor-successor-relations between the competences in the offer network.

Then we introduce the specific description of the *active objects in terms of multi agent theory.* For formal representations of agents three main functions are usually used (Kaihara, 2004): production function, profit function and bidding function. The agents try to fill up their capacities of each competence $x_{\mu j}(t) - \tau_j^\nu(\lambda_{\nu j}^\mu) \to \min, \lambda_{\nu j}^\mu \in \Delta, \lambda_{\nu j}^\mu \in \{0;1\}$, so as to maximize the discrepancy between price and costs $p_j^\nu - c_{\mu j}(\lambda_{\nu j}^\mu) \to \max$, where Δ - set of alternatives of resource allocation. For the set of orders, the profit function can be formulated as

$$J_1^\mu = \sum_{j=1}^{L} x_{\mu j}(t) - \sum_{j=1}^{I}\sum_{\nu=1}^{N} \tau_j^\nu(\lambda_{\nu j}^\mu) \to \min \qquad J_2^\mu = \sum_{j=1}^{I}\sum_{\nu=1}^{N} p_j^\nu - \sum_{j=1}^{I}\sum_{\nu=1}^{N} c_{\mu j}^\nu(\lambda_{\nu j}^\mu) \to \max$$

In order to take into account so called soft-factors (e.g., reputation, trust etc.), we consider also a reputation function of agents $r_{\mu j} = r_{\mu j}(W_{\mu j}, V_j)$, where $W_{\mu j}$ – knowledge about the agent B_μ to competence $k_{\mu j}$, V_j – importance of the job O_j. The bidding function of an agent B_μ, to competence $k_{\mu j}$ at the instant of time t can be formulated as $BF_{\mu j} = f(x_{\mu j}(t), c_{\mu j}, q_{\mu j}, r_{\mu j})$.

Now the *dynamic network operation models* have to be constructed. We propose to use a functorial transition from the category of digraphs that specifies the static network models, in the category of dynamic models, which describes the processes of supply chain execution. In this case, a constructive covariant functor establishes a correspondence between the nodes of the graph in the static scheduling model and dynamic models, as well as between the arcs and the mappings of dynamic models, called the adjacency morphism (Sokolov and Yusupov, 2004).

The supply chain is characterized by a set of structures which are formed while supply chain synthesis (organizational, informational, topological, technological structures etc.). Let us introduce in terms of the control theory a *dynamic alternative multi-graph* (DAMG) to relate these structures (Ivanov et al., 2004). The usage of DAMG allows representation of the graph-theoretical model in terms of dynamic linear system. It also allows forming of multi-structural macro states, and makes it possible to obtain a complex view on the network operation in dynamics.

Then we elaborate a complex of *dynamic network operation models* to describe the functioning of the supply chains (they will be discussed in one of our future papers). The dynamic network operation models let to describe the functioning of the supply chains (changing of order's states, changing of enterprise states with each operation to reflect the consumption of resources, as well as external operations to supply these resources from outside, etc.).

After the network description the goal criteria definition is needed. A set of orders to be planned is described as $A=\{A_\nu,\ \nu\in N\}$. Each order has a technology, which contains sequence of operations O_j $(j=1,2,\ldots,j_\nu)$. Realization of customer's orders is to finish in accordance with such parameters as desired delivery time, price limit, and accepted risk level (*reliability level* of a supply chain). The measure *supply chain reliability* is introduced in order to form and constrict set of Pareto optimal supply chains. It is also important to take into account some additional organizational constraints. For the optimal supply chain selecting is to define a principle of multi-criteria decision making, e.g based on the AHP-method. In our approach, the goal criteria (desired delivery date, costs, etc.) are represented as a multi-criteria selection structure. The optimal supply chain is selected with a scheduling algorithm, for example, an ACO-algorithm.

After the scheduling is finished, the *sensitivity analysis* takes place in order to analyze supply chain perceptivity and stability. Sensitivity theory lets analyze complex the uncertainty factors and integrate them in the models. The evaluation of *supply chain stability* is meant for the final decision making about the network design, and is the last step in the network design process. Special tools such as Workflow-systems support the sensitivity analysis. So the plan network state is generated.

However, the system and the environment can change during the operation, therefore it is necessary to correct plans periodically. In our approach, *monitoring of supply chain* is based on the monitoring of macro-structural states of the supply chains (Ivanov et al., 2004) as well on the *supply chain stability monitoring*. The particular feature of the SC monitoring in the terms of *macro states* is that at the each monitoring stage the parameters controlled are extracted from the parameter vector of the DAMG. The extracting rules depend on the management goals at the stage monitored. It makes it possible to consider all the parameters of supply chain execution described as the DAMG, and on the other hand to extract the necessary parameters to be controlled in a current execution situation. The other particular feature of the SC monitoring is analyzing of supply chain stability. Analysis of SC execution with the use of stability indicator lets determine the moment when reconfiguring of SC is needed.

Supply chain reconfiguration (real-time re-planning) is comprised of deviations analyzing, elaboration of compensating control actions and construction of a new plan and producing of appropriate correcting actions for transition from the actual supply chain state to the planned one. The model of supply chain reconfiguration is interconnected to the network design model. At the first phase of reconfiguration forming (generation) of allowable multi-structural macro-states is being performed. In other words a structure-functional synthesis of a new supply chain should be fulfilled in accordance with an actual or forecasted situation. At the second phase a single multi-structural macro-state is being selected, and adaptive plans of supply chain transition to the selected macro-state are constructed.

The above-named concepts and models are realized as software, e.g. EVCM (Extended Value Chain Management) (Teich, 2003, Zschorn et al., 2005), which provide IT-support for automatic network design, simulation tool SNDC (Supply Network Dynamic Control) intended for network design and supply chain scheduling, and computer-aided monitoring system (CMS). The EVCM-tool represents a web-based environment for the network design based on interaction between enterprises, and enterprises and customers. Software SNDC facilitates real-time planning and control of the processes and states of supply chains in CN. The obtained numerical results are satisfactory. The further direction of our researches is to provide the software SNDC with the agent oriented technologies.

4. CONCLUSIONS

The elaborated methodology provides the comprehensive quantitative modeling of CN. It allows taking into account activity of system elements (goal-oriented behaviour of enterprises) by their describing as agents. So the decentralized scheduling by means of agent negotiations is enhanced by the usage of control theory allows generating the ideal control programs for evaluating of the plans found by agents. The utilization of MAS to conceptual modelling framework also allows interconnecting the decentralized scheduling algorithms and learning algorithms. The usage of of multi-structural macro states makes it possible to obtain a complex view on the network operation in dynamics. The other advantage of the proposed approach is that the design process as well as the monitoring and reconfiguration of supply chains in CN are considered complex based on the unified methodological principles and systematic integrating factors of uncertainty in CN design and control models. It allows interconnecting of planning and control models as well as adaptation of supply chains and their models to the current execution environment. The presented approach allows development of vast model constructions for planning and execution in CN contributes to advancing of *theoretical foundations* of CN as well as to providing new advanced techniques for *practical management* in the areas of strategic planning, forecasting, and operative system management.

5. ACKNOLEDMENTS

The research described in this paper is partially supported by grants from Russian Fund of Fundamental Investigations (grant #05-07-90088), Institute of System Analysis (project 2.5), EOARD (Project № 1992p "Optimal Structure Reconfiguration"), and the Alexander von Humboldt Foundation. The authors thank also Collaborative Research Centre 457 at the Chemnitz University of Technology, which is financed from the Deutsche Forschungsgemeinschaft (German Research Foundation). The authors thank the contribution from their partners in such projects.

6. REFERENCES

1. Camarinha-Matos LM, Afsarmanesh H. The emerging discipline of collaborative networks. In: Virtual Enterprises and Collaborative Networks, edited by L.Camarihna-Matos, Kluwer Academic Publishers, 2004: 3-16.
2. Casti JL. Connectivity, Complexity and Catastrophe in Large-Scale Systems. Wiley-Intersc., 1979.
3. Chandra C., Kamrani A. Mass Customization: A Supply Chain Approach, Springer, 2004.
4. Fox MS., Barbuceanu M., Teigen R. Agent-Oriented Supply Chain Management System. International Journal of Flexible Manufacturing Systems, 12 (2000): 165-188.
5. Hallikas J., Karvonen I., Pulkkinen U., Virolainen V.-M., and Tuominen M. Risk management processes in supplier networks, International Journal of Production Economics, 2004, Vol. 90(1): 47-58.
6. Ivanov DA, Käschel J. Vernetzte Planung und kontinuierliche Lieferkettenoptimierung. PPS-Management, 2003, 4: 29-32.
7. Ivanov D., Arkhipov A., Sokolov B.: Intelligent Supply Chain Planning in Virtual Enterprises. In: Virtual Enterprises and Collaborative Networks, edited by L.Camarihna-Matos, Kluwer Academic Publishers, 2004: 215-223.
8. Kaihara T. Enterprise negotiation algorithm with walrasian virtual market, In: Virtual Enterprises and Collaborative Networks, edited by L.Camarihna-Matos, 2004: 227-224.
9. Kuhn A., Hellingrath B. Supply Chain Management: Optimierte Zusammenarbeit in der Wertschoepfungskette. Springer, 2002.
10. Mesarovic MD, Takahara Y. General Systems Theory: Mathematical Foundations. Academic Press, New York, Can Francisco, London, 1975.
11. Quantitative Models for Supply Chain Management, edited by S. Tayur, R. Ganeshan, and M. Magazine, Kluwer Academic Publishers, 1999.
12. Rabelo RJ, Klen AAP, Klen ER: A Multi-Agent System for Smart Coordination of Dynamic Supply Chains. PRO-VE 2002: 379-387.
13. Shen, Weiming et. al. Multi-Agent Systems for Concurrent Intelligent Design and Manufacturing. Taylor & Francis Group, 2001.
14. Sokolov BV, Yusupov RM. Conceptual Foundations of Quality Estimation and Analysis for Models and Multiple-Model Systems. Int. Journal of Computer and System Sciences, 6(2004): 5-16.
15. Sorensen L.B. How risk and uncertainty is used in supply chain management: a literature study, International Journal of Integrated Supply Chain Management, 2005, Vol. 1, No.4: 387-409.
16. Sterman JD. Business dynamics: systems thinking and modeling. McGraw-Hill, 2000.
17. Swaminathan JM, Smith SF, Sadeh NM. Modeling Supply Chain Dynamics: A Multiagent Approach. Decision Science, 1998, 29(3): 607-632.
18. Teich, Tobias. Extended Value Chain Management (EVCM). GUC-Verlag, 2003.
19. Virtual Enterprises and Collaborative Networks, edited by L.Camarihna-Matos, Kluwer Academic Publishers, 2004.
20. Wirth S., Baumann A. Wertschoepfung durch vernetzte Kompetenz. Huss Verlag, Munich, 2001.
21. Zschorn L., Jähn H., Zimmermann M., Teich T. and Gebhardt R., 2004, Monitoring in non-hierarchical Production Networks. Proceedings of the 8th World Multi-Conference on Systemics, Cybernetics and Informatics (SCI 2004), Orlando, Florida (USA), Vol. VIII, pp. 393-398.
22. Zschorn, L. Ivanov. DA. Jaehn, H. Fischer, M. An integrated modeling approach of supply chain planning and control in production networks. Proceedings of the 3rd international workshop on SCM and information systems, Thessaloniki, Greece, 2005 (accepted for publishing).

42 COLLABORATIVE HEALTHCARE PROCESS MODELLING: A CASE STUDY

José M. Framinan[1], Carlos Luís Parra[2], Margarita Montes[2], Paz Pérez[2]
[1]*Industrial Management, School of Engineering – University of Seville <jose@esi.us.es>*
[2]University Hospitals "Virgen del Rocío"- Seville
redtelemedicina.sspa@juntadeandalucia.es, SPAIN

Hospitals and health systems are trying to harmonise their information systems. However, most efforts have focused on data exchange, while little work has been carried out on the harmonisation of healthcare processes. Nonetheless, the latter may offer a number of advantages, such as the development of reference models containing best practices, and the fact that data exchange and systems integration can be more easily achieved on the basis of common (or similar) processes. In this communication, we present our experiences on collaborative modeling the current situation of healthcare process carried out within a national-wide network of Spanish hospitals. A methodology for collaboratively developing healthcare reference models is proposed, and the main findings in their application are presented.

1. INTRODUCTION

Many organizations consider electronic collaboration of distributed teams as a means to achieve higher productivity and improve the quality of their work products (Padgett, 2003). In this context, collaborative Business Process Redesign (BPR) appears to be a promising strategy for organisations to improve their products and services. BPR starts with a thorough understanding of the business processes of an organization (see e.g. Giaglis, 2001 for details). With this aim, the partners may share their expertise and develop a reference model that can be employed as benchmark for their Business Process and as a template for business process management. Healthcare environments have been involved in these changes too. Although hospital processes are complex and not very well known or categorised, the way to build a systemic view of hospital activities starts with the modeling of processes (Staccini et al, 2000). But individual process modelling is becoming insufficient. The need of enabling continuity of care among different hospitals and other healthcare providers has led hospitals and health systems to try harmonising their information systems. Establishing reference models for healthcare processes would make easier to manage and analyse current processes but it requires that a consensus among different workteams located in different hospitals or organizations must be reached. Our prime gain is to find an organizational ontology to inter-related healthcare processes and the characteristics they share. In addition to improve the way the services are actually delivered, for the healthcare sector there is another incentive for developing common reference models. Clearly, a process-based harmonisation may ease data exchange and systems integration, as data and functional requirements would be similar under a common process reference model.
In this communication, we present our experiences on collaboratively developing reference models for healthcare processes. These experiences have been collected

during the development of the FIS-G03/117 research project funded by the Spanish Ministry of Health. As part of the project, several healthcare organisations in Spain must develop common reference models for a number of processes, such as the care of certain chronic diseases. This collaboration among hospitals may be seen as a special type of Virtual Organization (VO), or even Virtual Enterprise (VE). Usually, in the VO/VE paradigm, a number of partners with *different* core competences collaborate to manufacture a product or deliver a service to what may be regarded as a *common* customer. In our case, the partners have common core competences (i.e. they all offer the same or similar services) while delivering their services to different customers (i.e. those citizens whose health is covered by the different hospitals).

1.1. OBJECTIVES AND REQUIREMENTS

The primary objective of our approach is to gain a global view of processes and to increase its comprehension, having people with different backgrounds and different approaches defining common processes with different viewpoints in different workplaces (Grützner et al, 2003). Specific objectives are to analyse patterns of healthcare activities, to build a systemic view of patient-centred processes, and to improve our knowledge and understanding of hospital organisation in order to achieve the effectiveness and efficiency of healthcare (Staccini et al, 2000).

Various requirements have been defined to successfully develop the virtual project:

1. The main requirement is to assist and advise the designers during their collective work. This is a key issue because the virtual process design we want to support is complex and structured, and most of process activities are creative and can be only modelled at a detailed level (Potts, 1989).
2. History-based assistance: all decisions, their rationale, and consequences are recorded as a basis for improving later decisions.
3. Flexibility and evolution: There are many decisions concerning how to structure the flow of tasks within a given context. Such structure must be incrementally constructed and dynamically evolvable. This is not only a technical issue but also an organizational question, particularly in a collective setting, for prescribing by whom, how, and why evolutions are undertaken (Longchamp and Denis, 1999).

Collaborative modelling focuses on the architecting and design of processes and systems using a formal modelling methodology. Three guidelines help to evaluate, compare and define collaborative system modelling solutions (Dori et al, 2004):

- *Concurrency*: The environment should allow team members to work on a shared system at the same time. The model should be available to all members in real-time, enabling them to get the most up-to-date view of the system.
- *Communication*: The environment should enable multi-way communication among the team members regardless of their physical whereabouts.
- *Security*: The environment should allow secure development, protecting the model under construction from unauthorized external entities and unauthorized changes by modellers.

2. COLLABORATIVE PROCESS MODELING

In Business Process Modeling, one should distinguish among methodology, technique, and tool (Kettinger et al, 1997). Modeling methodologies are supported by one or more techniques, and techniques can be supported by modelling tools (Giaglis, 2001). Despite the large number of vendors offering tools (see Kettinger et al., 1997), few –if any– of them offer some support for collaborative modelling (Walsh and Dickey, 2004). As it has been shown that employing a collaborative tool allows for wider user participation (Dean et al., 1997), we set this feature as a key one when selecting a tool for our project. Among the analysed tools, it turned out that only the IDS Scheer set of tools (ARIS Toolset™, and ARIS Web Designer™) supported, nonetheless only partially, the minimum requirements set for collaborative modelling. In ARIS, the modelling process itself can be achieved via Internet by employing a Java-based client (ARIS Web Designer™) that is able to interact with the ARIS Web Server and model a process through the Internet. Additionally, it can successfully integrate discrete-event simulation along with the static views of the models. The use of simulation for healthcare process modelling is often cited as a key issue, as then the models can capture the dynamic behaviour of the process (Ball et al, 2004). Finally, the software is probably the most extended tool in its class (see e.g. the survey by Gartner Group, 2001).

3. A CASE STUDY FOR COLLABORATIVE HEALTHCARE PROCESS MODELING

The healthcare quality paradigm requires not only the measurement of the outcomes of processes, but also the assessment of the means used to perform activities throughout each identified process. The needs for subsequent improvements in healthcare delivery, as for the reduction of variations in practices, stress the necessity for a continuous traceability of all care activities, and the detection, measurement and prevention of adverse events occurring during or after healthcare delivery (Staccini et al, 2000). The development of common reference models for healthcare processes is a challenging issue that differs from efforts in collaboratively modelling in other fields. Even if the main sketch of the process is similar to all hospitals, the large degree of freedom for organising resources in the hospitals has produced substantially different processes, particularly from the organizational and resource points of view. Other distinctive features are, among others: a high number of cooperating organizational units, limited resources, and a high ratio of manual activities (Amberg et al, 1996). Taking into account these specific features, healthcare process models can be assigned at various abstraction levels. In this project, we have considered three different levels:

- **Meta-model level**: a meta-model is an explicit model of the constructs and rules needed to build specific models within a domain of interest (Pidcock, 2003). It can be viewed as a set of building blocks and rules used to build models.
- **Process Definition Model level**. This level consists of a functional definition of healthcare processes built in each hospital or healthcare organization. Thereby, different points of view of the same process can be shared.
- **Reference Model level**. A reference model deals with a well-defined global representation of processes under consideration. Therefore, only one model, valid in any organization, will be used to describe a specific process.

3.1. STEPS FOR MODELLING

3.1.1. ORGANIZATION OF WORKING GROUPS

Collaborative work among geographically-distributed teams has been widely studied in literature, which recognizes that while dispersed teams can bring benefits such as increased flexibility they also represent challenges such as difficulties with coordination (Ghosh et al, 2005). Successful teams can be described in terms of the behaviours performed by members, i.e. task-oriented behaviours, and maintenance-oriented behaviours (Townsend, 1999). In our project, virtual teams are organised in a structural way. Hence, we have been distinguished three types of working groups:

1. **Design Working Groups (DWG).** DWG are work teams devoted to building Process Definition Models. Thereby, each DWG has to model a process. Consequently, there is one DWG per partner (hospital) and process. For each DWG, there is a person in charge of the model (Harmon, 2003) that must accomplish tasks related to model publishing and decisions balloting. The process of model building that these WG should accomplish is described later on.
2. **Coordination Working Group (CWG)**. Each CWG has to build and refine a reference model of a healthcare process. The CWG is composed by the Design Managers, who have been building the Process Definition Model of that process. The person responsible for the reference model is known as Coordination Manager, and the CWG members must consult him/her whenever weak points or potential improvements are discovered. Additionally, the CWG should develop a glossary of terms for the process, which contains all definitions of functions, event names and process information exchanged. We have selected SNOMED Clinical Terms® (Snomed, 2005) as common terminology, which is a validated clinical healthcare terminology and infrastructure that makes healthcare knowledge more usable and accessible. It provides a common language enabling a consistent way of capturing, sharing and aggregating health data across specialties and sites of care.
3. **Integration Working Group**. This group must revise and control different tasks being performed and build the first version of each reference model. The Integration Working Group supports maintenance-oriented behaviour, i.e. encouraging other group members; mediating differences among members; seeking to reach compromise with other members; encouraging contributions from reticent group members or limiting discussion on other subjects; evaluating the quality of group processes; or simply listening actively to discussion (Townsend, 1999)

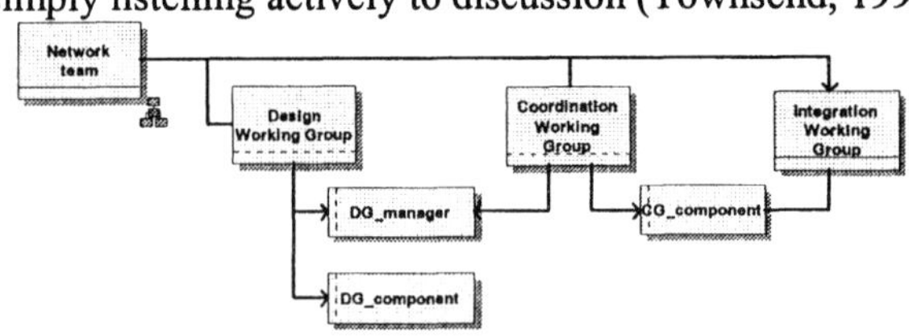

Figure 1 – Organizational Chart of virtual teams

We consider this WG to be a key issue for the involvement of all partners into the development of the reference models as it will help in developing a more representative model, which in turn will increase the chances of a successful implementation at a local level. The proposed structure for the virtual teams is shown in Figure 1 by means of an organisational chart.

3.1.2. META-MODEL BUILDING

The meta-model (see Figure 2) is used to describe entities that should represent the system elements: this is a key issue because each simulation tool has its own finite types of entities available to the modeller to be used in order to represent the real process components. It must include concepts for describing the aforementioned perspectives. The meta-model must rely on some consistent approach of design, and some homogeneity must be maintained without loosing creativity. A continuous feedback is required to keep the meta-model updated.

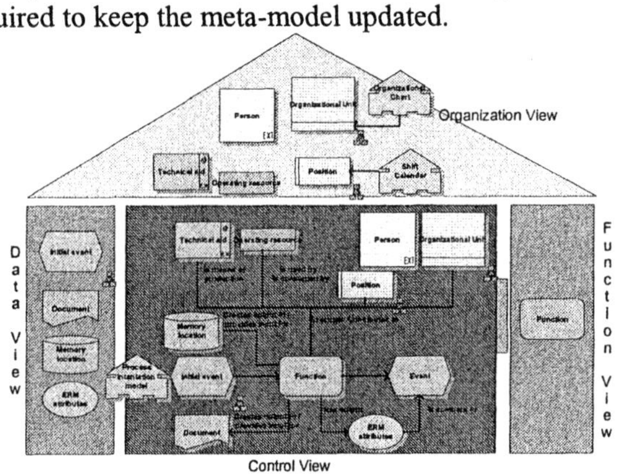

Figure 2 – Metamodel

3.1.3. MODELLERS' TRAINING

Training different modeller teams in the way they model their processes is a key issue in our collaborative modelling approach. Collaborative modelling requires enforcement of regulations that team members must follow in order to maintain the integrity of the process model under development (Townsend, 1999). Therefore, models cannot be built in an arbitrary way, but a commitment between freedom in modeling and the necessity of a guide followed by the project members to address the process modelling is required. For this reason, guidelines to build healthcare process modelling were developed within the context of the project, and two courses were held to explain them to all members.

3.1.4. MODELS BUILDING

According to the aforementioned guidelines, the following steps were accomplished:

1. Process selection: Each partner put forward the processes to be modeled, classified according to their importance, impact of their redesign on users, interest for continuous improvement efforts, etc. Then, after a consensus is reached, the processes to be modeled are assigned to different DWG, and the CWGs are created.
2. Modeling process objects description: In this step, stakeholders or organizational units whose value increases along the process, such as patients, relatives, professionals from another services or organizations, etc. are defined to facilitate reference model construction.
3. Setting the level of detail: The levels of detail required are established to each healthcare process. This level of detail depends mainly on the objectives of the

study. It has to be noted that most of the differences between the same process performed in different hospitals does not lay on the sequence of the activities that are performed, but on how these activities are actually performed.

3.1.5. REFERENCE MODELS BUILDING

As mentioned before, the IWG builds the first version of the process reference models according to the different process definition models of the DWGs. These reference models are published both in the Network Web page, and in the Network Web Server, so it can be edited using ARIS Web Designer. Once these reference models are published, CWG members contribute to its improvement. After analysing the models, the CWG may agree on proposing changes to the model. Once the CWG considers the reference model to be representative of the real world, its validation is required. To do so, we suggest simulating the process. Every DWG involved in the project should simulate the established reference model in order to ensure that it fits into different healthcare organisations. Then, validation is approved and the definitive reference model version is published. If validation cannot be performed, a new iteration is needed. The procedure is shown in Figure 4.

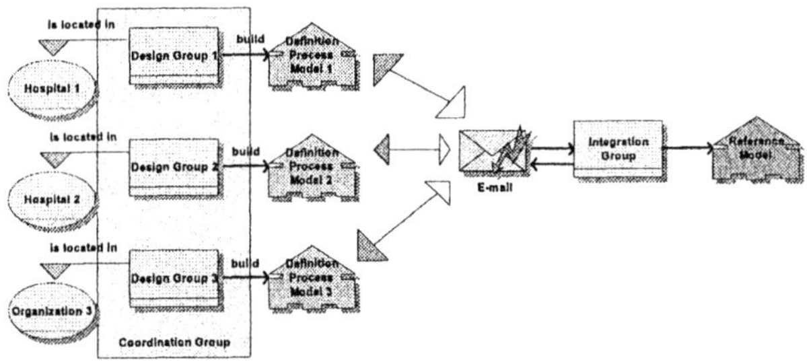

Figure 3 – Process Definition Process building scheme

3.2. CHANGE MANAGEMENT

An important requirement is the support of standard development processes, such as the spiral model. In such iterative development processes, each step in the process is based on refinement and modification of the output of the last step (Potok, 2002). According to this, the selected tool supports collaborative working by allowing models updates. Figure 4 shows a process model (described as an extended Event-Driven Process Chain) on how these tasks have been accomplished. In this figure it can be seen how proposals are collected, then subsequently discussed, and, if approved, finally implemented.

3.2.1. ACCESS CONTROL

Access control is the process of limiting access to the resources of a system only to authorized users, programs, or processes, and therefore preventing activities that might lead to a breach of the system's security. Access control assumes that authentication of users has been verified. Authentication services are used to correctly determine the identity of a user (Cera et al, 2004). Collaborative modelling requires protecting the model from inspection and changes by unauthorized entities. In a collaborative environment, it is required that only authorized team members who are responsible for a specific development stage will be able to refine artefacts created at that stage (Dori et al, 2004). Access control policies commonly found can be classified as Discretionary Access Control (DAC) (Sandhu et al, 1996), Mandatory Access Control (MAC), and Role-based Access Control (RBAC) (Osborn et al, 2000). Based on DAC and RBAC policies, three profiles for controlling accesses have been defined in our project (see Table 2).

Table 2. Profiles assigned to groups

Group	Access mode	Object	Task
DWG	Level 3	Their own Definition Process Model	Manage their own models
	Level 1	Reference models	Suggest improvement by mail
CWG	Level 2	Reference models	Suggest improvement
	Level 1	Definition Process Model from another CWG	Suggest improvement by mail
IWG	Level 3	Reference models	Manage reference models
	Level 1	Definition Process Model	Refine semantic mistakes by mail

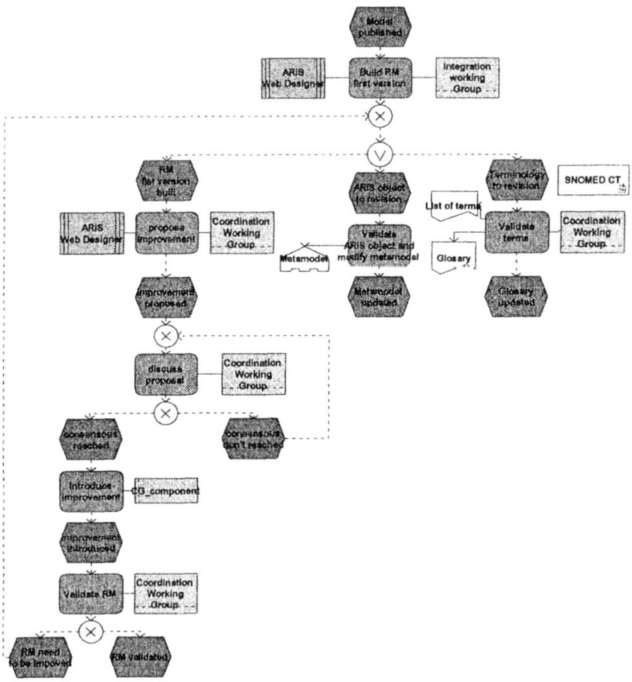

Figure 4 – Reference model

4. FINAL REMARKS

In this communication, we present an approach for collaboratively modelling healthcare processes. The approach stresses the need of participation of all partners so the model is representative, and a proper 'best practice' is really constructed. A number of mechanisms for carrying out the different steps in the approach, and the change management have been presented. Some ongoing work within this project includes developing common measures for assessing the impact that the implementation of the reference models may have on the hospital, and mechanisms for tracing the improvement after the implementation.

In this case study, the implementation of a virtual team has led to improve work developing, to decrease costs (for example, reducing travel time), to short life cycles (transforming from series processes to parallel processes), to encourage innovation (allowing the most diverse participation in the project and stimulating creativity) and to focus learning (capturing knowledge through natural course of working, developing or improving accesses to experts).

5. REFERENCES

1. Amberg, Michael and Gräber, Stefan. Specifying Hospital Information Systems Using Business Process Modeling. Brender, J., Christensen, J. P., Scherrer, J. R., and McNair, P. 1037-1041. 1996. Amsterdam, IOS Press. Medical Informatics Europe 96.
2. Ball, Peter, Albores, Pavel, and Macbryde, Jill. Requirements for modelling e-Business processes. Production Planning & Control 15[8], 776-785. 2004.
3. Cera, Christopher D., Kim, Taeseong, Han, JungHyun, and Regli, William C. Role-based viewing envelopes for information protection in collaborative modeling. Computer-Aided Design 36[9], 873-886. 2004.
4. Dori, Dov, Beimel, Dizza, and Toch, Eran. OPCATeam - Collaborative Business Process Modeling with OPM. 66-81. 15-7-2004. BPM 2004, Springer-Verlag.
5. Ghosh, Tanu, Yates, JoAnne, and Orlikowski, Wanda. Using communication norms for coordination: Evidence from a distributed team. Electronic Citation. http://seeit.mit.edu
6. Giaglis, GM. A taxonomy of business process modeling and information systems modeling techniques. International Journal of Flexible Manufacturing Systems 13[2], 209-228. 2001. Elsevier Science B.V.
7. Grützner, Ines, Münch, Jürgen, Fernandez, Alejandro, and Garzaldeen, Badie. Guided Support for Collaborative Modeling, Enactment and Simulation of Software Development Processes. 3-5-2003. Prosim 2003, Workshop. 2003.
8. Harmon, Paul. Business Process Change: A Manager's Guide to Improving, Redesigning and Automating Processes. Morgan Kauffman
9. Kettinger, William J., Teng, James T. C., and Guha, S. Business Process Change: a study of methodologies, techniques, and tools. MIS Quarterly 21[1], 55-80. 1997.
10. Osborn, S. L., Sandhu, R. S., and Munawer, Q. Configuring role-based access control to enforce mandatory and discretionary access control policies. Information System Security 3[2], 85-106. 2000.
11. Padgett, Gerson David. Informe resumen de tecnología de informaciôn para negocios Tecnología: Groupware. Electronic Citation. http://www.monografias.com
12. Pidcock, Woody. What are the differences between a vocabulary, a taxonomy, a thesaurus, an ontology, and a meta-model? Electronic Citation. http://www.metamodel.com
13. Potok, T. E. Extensions to the spiral model to support joint development of complex software systems. 2002. Proc. of the 30th Annual Southeast Regional Conference, ACM Press 2002.
14. Potts, C. A Generic Model for Representing Design Methods. Proceedings of 11th ICSE.
15. Sandhu, R. S., Coyne, E. J., Feinstein, H. L., and Youman, C. E. Role-based access control models. IEEE Comput 29[2], 38-47. 1996.
16. Snomed. SNOMED. Electronic Citation. SNOMED® International 24-5-0005. http://www.snomed.org/.
17. Staccini, Pascal, Joubert, Michel, Quaranta, Jean-François, Fieschi, Dominique, and Fieschi, Marius. Integration of Health Care Process Analysis in the Design of a Clinical Information System: Applying to the Blood Transfusion Process. Proc. AMIA Symposium 2000.
18. Townsend, Christine. Teams in Agricultural Education: An Assessment of Team Process Instruction. Proc. 26 Annual National Agricultural Education Research Conference. 1999.

PART 14

PROFESSIONAL VIRTUAL COMMUNITIES

43

THE ORGANIZATION AND BUSINESS MODEL OF A SOFTWARE VIRTUAL COMMUNITY IN CHINA

Jie Yan and Dimitris Assimakopoulos
Grenoble Ecole de Management, FRANCE
jie.yan@grenoble-em.com, dimitris.assimakopoulos@grenoble-em.com

With the increasing pervasiveness of communication among networked computers, scholars and practitioners alike recognize the value added of Internet based technical forums for enabling work in distributed communities (Hildreth and Kimble, 2000) and networks of practice (Brown and Duguid, 2001). China in particular is an interesting environment to explore the significance and role of specialised technical forums for software development beyond the firm boundary. Internet service providers' set up privately owned technical forums and software engineers join voluntarily such virtual communities for sharing information and knowledge. The organization and business model of such forums however has attracted very little research interest so far. Using a case study approach we present in this paper, the organization and business model of China Software Developer Net, one of the most successful Internet engineering communities in China with more than eight hundred thousands members in 2004. We also discuss how the system design and business model of CSDN service provider has helped to build up a sustainable distributed community and network of practice and creating a dynamic culture for extending information and knowledge sharing much beyond organisational boundaries.

1. INTRODUCTION

With the increasing pervasiveness of communication among networked computers, scholars and practitioners alike recognize the impact of Internet based communities to human society and economy. Virtual communities (Rheingold, 1993, 2000) and networks of practice (Brown and Duguid, 2001) provide interactive meeting places where people can pursue common interests and add value to work related practices. Virtual communities also show potential business advantages with their unique capacity of connecting people with common socio-demographic and professional characteristics across large geographical distances.

Using a case study approach we present below, the organization and business model of China Software Developer Net (CSDN), one of the most successful Internet based software engineering communities in China with more than eight hundred thousands members in mid-2004. We discuss in depth how the system design and management model of CSDN have helped to build up a vibrant virtual community adding value to the work of software developers in terms of knowledge sharing and daily technical problem solving. In particular, we highlight the business model of CSDN, showing how the community service operator makes use of the virtual community organisation to build up a diversified business portfolio, integrating the virtual community into their value chain and generating sustainable revenues from multiple sources.

2. VIRTUAL COMMUNITIES

Since the early 1990s, the Internet has been used as an enabling technology for long-distance communication and interaction, connecting people and generating a plethora of virtual communities. According to Rheingold (1993, p16) virtual communities are the 'social aggregations that emerge from the Net when enough people carry on those public discussions long enough, with sufficient human feeling, to form webs of personal relationship in the cyberspace'. Schubert and Ginsburg (2000) describe virtual communities as the union between individuals or organizations who share common values and interests using electronic media to communicate within a shared semantic space on a regular basis. The emergence of virtual communities rises from people's need to gather and participate in informal public spaces in everyday life and their primordial wish to look for a sense of 'community' (Rheingold, 2000). Jones (1995) has the same view, that Internet based discussion groups spring from the need to rebuild a sense of community. Community is not lost but transformed via the Internet (Wellman, 1979; Wellman and Gulia, 1997). Virtual communities have therefore taken various forms including computer mediated communication groups, such as mailing lists, Usenets (newsgroups), bulletin boards, chat rooms, and multiple user domains (Kollock and Smith, 1999).

Moreover, many virtual communities focus on work related professional practices, for example, scholars in academia (Koku and Wellman, 2002), lawyers (Hara, 2000), computer professionals (Wasko and Faraj, 2000), and open source software developers (Lakhani, and von Hippel, 2000; O'Mahony and Ferraro, 2004). These virtual communities provide opportunities, channels, and venues for professionals to share everyday work related resources, not just information, but also innovative ideas, solutions to specific problems, professional knowledge, and the latest thinking in their field of interest. Many participants treat such virtual communities as a place for learning and professional problem solving (Yan and Assimakopoulos, 2003; Teigland, 2003). Participants benefit from these communities by creating, accessing and exchanging new knowledge, expertise and innovative ideas not available in their local community of practice and working environment (Brown and Duguid, 2001).

From a business perspective, Hagel and Armstrong (1997) have emphasized the relationship-building aspects of virtual communities. The Internet community platforms work as a relational infrastructure providing a public meeting place to bring together people with similar interests, unrestrained by time and space. Many click and mortar retailers enhance their e-commerce web sites with chat rooms, bulletin boards, and other community building features as means of encouraging customers to spend more time, return more frequently, and make more purchases online and offline. It has been also reported that many retail web sites have seen their sales increase after they added such community features (Brown, Tilton and Woodside, 2002). From a commercial point of view, virtual communities of commerce (Bressler and Grantham, 2000) and virtual communities of transaction (Schubert and Ginsburg, 2000) highlight how groups of potential customers who share some common characteristics, may have similar purchasing interests and preferences and therefore regularly congregate in such communities of commerce. Business organizations often target virtual communities as potential customer groups for direct sales, or integrate these communities into their value chain as the source of information and ideas for product/service development and innovation (Franz and Wolkinger, 2003).

3. ORGANIZATIONAL MODELS OF VIRTUAL COMMUNITIES

Two types of interactive relationships are identified as important to the success of virtual communities: a) participant to participant, and b) provider to participant (Hagel and Armstrong, 1997; McWilliam, 2000). These two kinds of relationships generate two complementary types of organizational models for virtual communities: self-organizing communities, and, communities based on the organizational efforts of their service providers.

Some commentators emphasize the importance of self-organising virtual communities as they are fuelled both by volunteerism and self-interest of their participants. People join voluntarily such community, set up a virtual identity, and get involved in collective discussions, for exchanging information and sharing knowledge of common interest (Rheingold, 2000). Participants collectively create public goods (Kollock, 1998a; Wasko and Teigland, 2002), motivated by both altruistic and self-interested rationales (Wasko and Faraj, 2000). Altruistic volunteerism, the willingness to do a good thing for the others and also the personal interest surrounding a particular topic, often drive participants to actively participate and get involved in the collective activities of such self-organised virtual communities (Butler et al, 2002). Participants get out of such community both tangible and intangible returns, such as completing work tasks efficiently, and also gaining a sense of belonging, self-respect and reputation from the recognition of their peers. For example, Wasko and Faraj (2000) highlight reciprocity, as the key driver for motivating volunteerism in self-organising virtual communities.

Beyond the self-interested and/or altruistic nature of self-organized communities, successful virtual communities also take off as a result of the organizational efforts of their service providers, in particular with respect to the design and maintenance of a community platform (Kollock, 1998b). Kling (1996) summarizes four critical factors in building successful virtual communities, from a service provider's perspective: timely implementation of technology platform, promotion and empowerment of user interactions, reach a critical mass of users, and tailor the service to user needs. As Wellman (2001) points out, computer networks are social networks, and therefore the sustainability of a virtual community, regardless of whether it is a self-organised or service provider led, relies more on the quality of the social relationships within the virtual place, rather than its technological features (Kollock, 1998b). Besides the basic functions of far distance synchronous/asynchronous communication, the design and organization of virtual community infrastructure should take full consideration of the needs of users, supporting the social processes of human interaction and behavioural rules of real world communities, including components that enable such social relationships as friendship, reputation, trust, etc. (Kollock, 1998b, 1999; Resnick et al, 2002).

Key social components of virtual community infrastructure include electronic reputation components, group formation components, conflict resolution components and more generally any component that directly contributes to a social dynamic (Angehrn, Nabeth and Bubirana, 2001). Many of these social components have been applied in successful virtual communities, such as the transaction records of eBay, in which buyers can track the transaction history of the sellers and feedback of the previous buyers from these sellers. This has similar function as the reputation and credit system in real world communities. Many virtual communities also provide feedback channels for facilitating the communication between participants and service provider (Lollock, 1998b). In order to avoid information overload, segmentation of communication channels are built in the community platform, offering the participants the choice to select and 'tune in' into sub-groups of the broader virtual community (Jones and Rafaeli, 2000). To help members build up persistent relationships in the community, persistent IDs are also supported to further the sense of belonging (Blanchard and Markus, 2002) and build up trust and reputation (Resnick et al, 2002).

4. BUSINESS MODELS OF VIRTUAL COMMUNITIES

Any organization, real or/and virtual, ought to have the capability to generate sustainable profits for surviving competition and growing its business. A business model describes how an enterprise produces, delivers and sells its products or services. Above all, a business model shows how an enterprise generates sustainable revenues from its customer base by delivering value to its customers (Magretta, 2002). Virtual communities orchestrated by service providers, have followed the same business model of many other Internet related services. They were initially offered as a free service, but with the increasing popularity of 'doing business electronically' (European Commission, 1997), research has started demonstrating that virtual communities potentially represent a set of new business models for building successful enterprises (Hagel and Armstrong, 1997; Bressler and Grantham, 2000; Schubert and Ginsburg, 2000).

4.1 Virtual Community as a Stand-alone Business

For many service providers, virtual community is a stand-alone business. Three sources of revenue: advertisement, membership fee, and, direct selling, can be identified with such a business model.

Advertisement: an online community is often viewed as a target customer group with some similar socio-demographic characteristics and purchasing interests. It is therefore targeted by marketing using banner and pop up advertising, sponsorship and paying linkages as the main sources of revenues for many virtual as well as click and mortar companies (Laudon and Laudon, 2004). Although the expenditure of online advertising still represents a minority stake for the large majority of businesses, it has been continually growing since 1999 generating a sustainable source of income for virtual communities (WAN, 2002).

Membership fees: participants in an online community are increasingly seen as members who can potentially pay to enroll in the community for making use of its contents or taking advantage of special offers given to the community members. Differentiation of contents, functionality, and potential switching costs are identified as the key elements for a successful membership fee based community strategy. Social emotions associated with a community, such as sense of belonging, friendship, trust or reputation, are thought to increase the switching cost of leaving one virtual community for another, thus assisting in member retention (Blanchard and Markus, 2002; Resnick et al, 2002).

Direct selling: today virtual communities often choose a strategy of free membership, but charge for some specific services or contents. For example, some online newspaper communities such as the Economist and the Financial Times sell some exclusive, high quality articles, or analysis reports, to their online reader community, while they offer them free of charge to subscribers of the print edition. Similarly, in some academic and professional online communities, resources are only freely available to the members who pay membership fees, but chargeable to the non-member participants. In some retailing websites that have community features, community members are more likely to purchase online than non-member users. For example, Brown, Tilton and Woodside (2002) found in a recent study that community members accounted for one third of all users, but generated two third of all online sales.

However, very few virtual communities have been proven to be commercially successful so far (Franz and Wolkinger, 2003). In most cases, revenues from advertising and/or membership fees are not sufficient to cover operational costs, and direct selling has only recently been introduced in such virtual communities. For example, Bughin and Zeisser (2001) report that the marketing revenues of online communities are rather insufficient to sustain such communities. Hence virtual community, as a stand-alone business, seems an unsustainable business model. As a result of its limited capability of generating direct revenues it has become necessary to recognize from the outset that the real value of virtual community is not the direct revenues it can potentially generate, but the value added as an integrated element of a diversified e-commerce portfolio.

4.2 Virtual Community as Customer Integration

The revenues a virtual community can generate may not be shown clearly in balance sheets, but they do contribute in several intricate ways benefiting the community service providers as a whole. For e-commerce operators, virtual community is a fruitful strategy for increasing their traffic and repeat customers' visits on a website. Brown, Tilton and Woodside (2002) found that in media websites community members raise four times the amount of page views per person compared to the non-members. A survey conducted by Mckinsey shows that contrasting to the pure B2C websites that transfer 1% of the visitors into repeat customers, virtual communities have an average member retention rate as high as 18%, and these community members visiting the website frequently are more likely to purchase online and become repeat customers (Bughin and Hagel, 2000). In practice, many e-commerce websites that build up their own online communities have seen an increase of sales both in their online and offline business (Brown, Tilton and Woodside, 2002).

Compared to the traditional marketing media, including TV broadcasting, newspapers and magazines, Internet communication increases both richness of content and reach. A large amount of information can be provided to customers quickly and inexpensively, with additional capabilities of mass customisation (Evans and Wurster, 2000). Internet communication also provides two ways information flows, salient feature of virtual communities with such interactive infrastructure including chat rooms, bulletin boards, etc. Feedback of community members is often valuable for customer relationship management and help business organizations further tune in their services and products to meet the demand of niche markets. Information sharing about a specific product among community members is often more grounded on a particular customer base than the marketing efforts of business operators. For example, the member recommendation system within the Amazon online community plays a key role in the success of its e-commerce platform.

Virtual communities provide business organizations a direct channel to target specific customer groups and sell directly their products and services. For example, the virtual community babycenter.com, that enables communication among parents who need information with raising up their babies and toddlers, is an online place for both seeking advise and also direct online selling of products of the companies producing baby care products and services. Johnson & Johnson is marketing acne products using online communities of teenage girls (Kenny and Marshall, 2000). Virtual communities are also used to conduct marketing research, based on pop up tests, online questionnaire surveys, and so on (Hewson et al, 2002). Active members who benefit from a community are often willing to answer questions focusing on shared interests of the community. The cost of such online surveys is often much cheaper than offline marketing research. Additionally, the demographic information of members such as sex, age, address, etc., that is generally recorded upon online registration, it provides a sound basis for statistical analysis. By tracking the purchasing history of community members, statistical analysis can also be carried out to summarize customer behaviour in target niche markets.

The knowledge of community members can also help to tailor and redesign existing services or products. In some cases, the enthusiastic members of virtual communities are even directly involved in the innovation process. For example, Duotone, a well-known snowboard manufacturer, initiated a design competition in the online community of the Austrian youth radio station FM4 (Franz and Wolkinger, 2003). MIT virtual customer initiative (http://mitsloan.mit.edu/vc/), a multidisciplinary research project developing new theory and methods for improving new product development process, proposes the direct participation of customers into the product development processes through virtual communities, regards a virtual customer community as an important source of new innovative ideas (Dahan and Hauser, 2002). Knowledge-rich contents produced by community members have also the potential to be directly packaged and sold to other interested parties. For example, in the case of the software engineering community that we study below, the community service provider publishes outstanding technical solutions for all the community members in their own specialized technical magazines and CDs.

5. CASE STUDY: CHINA SOFTWARE DEVELOPER NET (CSDN)

5.1. Some basic figures about CSDN

CSDN (www.csdn.net) is one of the biggest Chinese language Internet software technology forums. It was established by Unisun MDM Digital Technology Company Ltd in 1999, with the aim 'to provide a venue for China software developers to communicate, learn and improve'. Up to June 2004, some 800,000 IT professionals, software developers, and system administrators from 19,000 IT organisations from all over mainland China, as well as Taiwan, Hong Kong, Singapore, and Malaysia, have been registered as members in the CSDN forum. The membership of CSDN quadrupled between March 2002 and June 2004. CSDN has 30 discussion sub-forums, specialising in different software technical areas. During working hours, there are always 5,000 - 8,000 software developers online in the forum. The large number of online members ensures a critical mass of technical backgrounds of participants in the ongoing online discussions.

5.2. Knowledge sharing in CSDN

With so many software professionals gathered daily in the forum, CSDN is more like a large knowledge factory in which many thousands IT professionals talk freely about their shared topics of interest. Every day thousands of software technical problems are posted and discussed in CSDN. Most of the online enquiries during working hours get replies within a few hours, if not minutes. The usual reply points out what is probably wrong and gives possible solutions. The senders are often professionals who have experience and knowledge of similar problems. It is easy for them to diagnose and solve problems. Most of the replies are less than 5 lines in length, but a few words often seem enough to help solve specific problems. Some posts with original software code may be longer, up to a few pages in length. In some other even longer posts, the contents are obviously copied from electronic technical documents. The senders advise referring to the documentation for finding information about solving the problem. The vast majority of messages are written in mixed Chinese and English language, i.e. the software program codes are in English, and the diagnosis of the problem and suggestions in Chinese.

In some cases, when the problem is rather complex, the questioning and replying often evolves into interactive discussion among many interested community members. The solutions are often collaborative group results. It is common after several suggestions are provided by different respondents for the engineer who initially asked the question to test these alternatives and report back to the forum results of proposed solutions, often including original code, compiler feedback, error logs, input and output, and so on. Although most of the discussions are completed within 10 exchanges, some enquiries get back 30 or more replies. Sometimes this interactive discussion lasts a few hours, even one or two days.

Most of the technical problems posted in CSDN are solved, and when a problem is solved, the service provider places the solution to a 'settled-post' board. Some frequently asked questions are moved to the FAQ board, and some with excellent technical solutions are moved to an 'elite post' board. Participants who do not like to ask a direct question to the forum can search in these boards and get some indirect technical support.

5.3. Organizational model of CSDN

The CSDN platform is based on a bulletin board system. The service provider has put forward a set of rules and accounts to fuel online discussions and keep well organised the forum and its sub-forums. The three most prominent organisational features are: expert point account, reputation point account, and membership grade system.

The Expert Account based on a point system gives a clear indication how expert a member is; and how much of a contribution s/he has made to the ongoing public discussions. Upon registration, each member is given an expert account with 200 points, which increases by 10 points every day. Posting a message adds 5 points to the account. When making an enquiry, the member must promise a number of expert points to the potential repliers, say 30, 50, or more, depending on how difficult the question is and how urgently the reply is needed. The promise has to be sufficiently attractive that other members will answer the question. In order to have enough points to ask questions, CSDN members must keep answering questions; otherwise, they lose the right to ask questions when individual expert points run out. Members with high expert points are well respected in the forum as they are considered highly qualified experts, have solved many technical problems, and have continuously helped other people in the forum. CSDN publishes online the names of its top 100 experts every week. In the No. 1 position is a member nicknamed *zjcxc*, with 630,881 expert points up to February 1st, 2005.

The Reputation Account based also on a point system assesses how well a member complies with the forum regulations. Every member gets 100 reputation points at registration. Bad behaviour causes deduction of reputation points, for example: breaking the promise to transfer expert points after a problem is solved, using impolite phrases, posting meaningless messages, and the like. In other cases, reputation points increase. When a member has few reputation points, no one cares to answer his/her questions, and the right to post messages is lost when reputation points run out.

The Membership Grade system is similar to a military ranking system but on the basis of expert points. It reflects the technical capabilities of individual members, and also what contributions members have made to the public discussion. The grade is often perceived as an honour and is classified in three categories: novices, middle- and advanced-level members, and multiple star categories. The novices, include the first, second and third levels, with members at these grades having less than 1,000 expert points; middle-level members include the fourth and fifth levels, plus level one and two star members who have more than 1,000 and less than 10,000 expert points. Advanced members are those with over 10,000 expert points and are awarded three, four, and five star honours. Technical advice from advanced grade members usually attracts attention, as such members are highly respected by their peers in the forum. CSDN also awards star membership to those who have made a special contribution to the community, such as, publish good technical articles and provide valuable suggestions for improving the quality of discussions in the community.

From the outset, the management of the forum follows a model of volunteerism based on self-organization. Besides several CSDN administrators, who are full-time staff of the service provider company, most of the daily maintenance work of the forum is done by volunteers. Each sub-forum has two or three board masters, who are selected from the most active members with advanced expert grade and high reputation account. The job of board master is unpaid. The board masters have powers to delete and move posts and replies, deduct or award the reputation points, force-out bad users, move posts to FAQ and elite boards, and so on. The forum also provides direct channels for members to complain (or praise) about board masters to CSDN administrators.

5.4. Business portfolio

CSDN has built up a diversified but integrated business portfolio around its virtual community with many free and fee-based services. The huge membership of the community provides many advantages to its business operations including both on- and offline services.

Free services

In CSDN many digital services to members are free of charge. On top of free participation in the technical forum, CSDN also provides free email accounts, private chat rooms and instant pop up message services to its members. Community members also freely submit and store their CV into the China Software Developer Database, which is the largest database about IT professionals in China. The company also regularly organizes free technical seminars and workshops for CSDN members in large cities throughout China. The CSDN website daily releases news, reports and technical articles covering a wide range of topics on computer based technologies.

Fee-based services and E-commerce

CSDN provides banner, pop up and rolling up advertisements for IT companies to market their technologies, products and services. Many large IT players, such as Microsoft, IBM, Sun, Cisco, BEA, rent long-term ad space in CSDN. Another segment for advertisement focuses on software training programs, courses and conferences. The international software technology accreditation and certification organizations also pay for ads in CSDN.

CSDN also provides human resource services to IT firms all over the country. In its main-page, ads space is available for recruitment announcements. Organizations pay to access the China Software Developer Database to search candidates. For some top technical positions in large companies, CSDN can help specialist 'head-hunters' to identify qualified candidates from its pool of experts.

CSDN has also an online IT focused bookshop, Dearbook.com, which sells a wide range of IT technical books, magazines, software, computer game, as well as, movie DVDs and music CDs. The bookshop has a friendly user interface, in which potential buyers can exchange ideas, read book reviews and comments posted by peers. The bookshop also provides free downloadable software technology, books and software.

Offline business

CSDN runs a publishing house, focusing on IT related books and magazines. It publishes two software technology magazines targeting different customer groups. '*Programmers*' is a professional magazine targeting software engineers in general. Besides technical topics and solutions, it also publishes articles about technology trends, interviews with IT gurus, market analysis, book reviews, and so on. It is the most popular software technology magazine in China, with a circulation of 80,000 copies per month. At the end of each year, CSDN also releases a bound edition of *Programmers* consisting of the 12 monthly issues plus some key special topics. The 2003 bound edition sold 180,000 copies.

CSDN Development Experts specifically focuses on technical issues in software development, providing technical solutions to complex software development problems. Besides the revenue from subscription, the magazines also brings revenue from the advertisements from the key IT technology providers and technology training program organizers who want to promote their technology and service to the software developers.

Based on its collaborative relationships with the key software technology providers, CSDN publishes annually a series of *Programmers' Encyclopaedia*, covering a broad range of fields such as Java, Visual C++, Delphi, web programming, games and PDA developing. The circulation of these encyclopaedia series added up to 160,000 copies in 2002. CSDN publishes annually a CD, releasing the best technical solutions from the CSDN forum. Last but not least, CSDN often collaborates with professional training institutes and certification organizations to provide in-company training courses.

6. EVALUATION AND CONCLUSIONS

From the analysis of findings above it is evident that CSDN has integrated its virtual community into its value chain for building up a business model with multiple revenue sources both online and offline. For CSDN members, the attraction of its virtual community comes from the huge volume of knowledge-rich contents it generates supporting members' daily work practices. The huge number of technical problems posted, discussed and solved in the forum establish a fertile ground for continuing success of its online community. The rapidly increasing membership further ensures a diverse knowledge base and positive feedbacks (Shapiro and Varian, 1999) resulting in a virtuous circle for solving problems efficiently and effectively. The ongoing online discussions are difficult to be replicated by competitors and switching costs are set too high, especially after members have accumulated many points for both expert and reputation accounts, got grades and stars. They reciprocally share knowledge and benefit from their membership in this particular community.

Besides technical support, CSDN also provides identity and social support to its members. People share their happiness and sadness, encourage and console peers, offer advice to those who need help in their private lives, share jokes and humorous stories. A sense of companionship and belonging grows as people spend time and interact with each other. They collectively make the CSDN technology forum an enjoyable social place rather than just a technical support centre. In an interview with an active CSDN member, when being asked why he always keeps online in CSDN, he mentioned: "I am used to spend sometime every day in CSDN to post messages and answer questions. I have so many net buddies there... There is nothing strange. If I don't go to CSDN, where should I go?" This statement may seem difficult for outsiders to understand, but the participants in the technical forums seem enjoying and getting a lot of emotional as well as practical support out of their participation in this virtual community.

The system design and organization model of the community are key factors for attracting and retaining its participants. The social process supporting components, i.e. the expert and reputation point accounts, and membership grade ranking system, make the interaction in the virtual community as 'real' as what happens in real world communities, such as communities of practice within software firms (Assimakopoulos and Yan, 2004). The self-organizing model based on unpaid volunteers - board masters – enables the participation of technical experts into the management of the community, not just reducing the running costs, but enhancing the quality of technical discussions. Moreover, many of the online services CSDN provides to its community members are free. This further strengthens the added value of CSDN to its members. As a professional occupation, IT software development has its special characteristics. Software developers have to update their techniques continuously throughout their careers to catch up with the relentless development of new technology. This is one of the key underlying reasons that engineers daily engage in CSDN forum sharing knowledge and experiences.

As we have seen, all the business activities of CSDN are organised and operate around its virtual community. Although the forum does not directly generate revenue and needs continuous investment in maintaining this free service, it provides value to the community operator by exposing a huge potential customer group to the mother company of CSDN. In its business portfolio, Unisun MDM Digital Technology Company has placed its virtual community as the hub of customer integration. The value of such virtual community is accrued by a set of diversified approaches both online and offline, taking advantage of the huge membership of the community. The e-commerce of online bookshop Dearbook.com; the offline publications of technical magazines and CDs; training programs, and publishing house are all directly targeting the community members. Moreover, as many CSDN members are among the senior technology management in their companies, they have influence to the decision making of their company in terms of new technology adoption. This attracts the IT technology providers such as Microsoft, SUN, Oracle, etc. to put investment in advertising in the community.

The implication of the CSDN case for company strategy is that a diversified virtual community business model which integrates the virtual community into the value chain of the company, benefits both community members and operator alike. The valuable contents of ongoing discussions are freely provided to the community, leading to the huge numbers in membership, which in turn generate revenues from other sources both online and offline for the mother company. The free service is the price the company is willing to pay for the great value of customer integration it gains from its virtual community. When a community operator receives good financial returns, it is able to further develop the portfolio of free services, which makes the forum more attractive and influential. This whole process generates a positive feedback cycle and further reinforces the leading position of CSDN as the China's leading software development community thanks to the Internet.

7. REFERENCES

1. Angehrn, A., Nabeth, B. and Subirana B. Designing Virtual Communities to support E-Commerce adoption, eBusiness and eWork Conference (E-2001), October 17-19, 2001, Venice, Italy.
2. Blanchard, A.L. and Markus, M.L. Sense of Virtual Community - Maintaining the Experience of Belonging, in the Proceeding of 35th hawaii International Conf. on System Sciences, 2001, Hawaii.
3. Bressler, S.E. and Grantham, C.E. *Communities of Commerce*, McGraw Hill, New York, 2000.
4. Brown, J.S. and Duguid, Knowledge and organization: a social-practice perspective, *Organization Science*, 2000, 12 (2), pp.198-213.
5. Brown, S.L., Tilton, A., and Woodside, D.M. The case for on-line communities, *McKinsey Quarterly*, 2000, [Available at: http://www.mckinseyquarterly.com/article_page.asp?ar=1143&L2=24&L3=45]
6. Bughin, J. and Hagel, J. The Operational Performance of Virtual Communities - Towards a Successful Business Model?, *Electronic Markets*, 2000, 10, pp.237-243.
7. Bughin, J. and Zeisser, M. The marketing scale effectiveness of virtual communities, in the Proceeding of the 7th Americas Conference on Information System, 2001, Boston, Massachusetts.
8. Butler, B., Sproull, L., Kiesler, S. and R. Kraut, Community Effort in Online Groups: Who Does the Work and Why?, in Atwater, L., *Leadership at a Distance* (Ed), Erlbaum, 2000
9. Dahan, E. and Hauser, J.R. The Virtual Customer, *Journal of Product Innovation Management*, 2002. 22, pp.332-353.
10. European Commission, European Initiative in Electronic Commerce, COM, 1997 (157). [Available at http://www.cordis.lu/esprit/src/ecomcom.htm]
11. Evans, P. and Wurster, T.S. *Blown to Bits: How the New Economics of Information Transfroms Strategy*, Boston, MA: Harvard Business School Press, 2000.
12. Franz, R. and Wolkinger, T. Customer integration with virtual communities, in Proceeding of Hawaii International Conference on System Science, January 2003, Big Island, Hawaii.
13. Hagel, J. and Armstrong, A. *Net Gain: Expanding Markets Through Virtual Communities*, Boston, MA: Harvard Business School Press, 1997.

14. Hara, N. Social construction of knowledge in professional communities of practice: tales in courtrooms. Unpublished doctoral dissertation, Bloomington: Indiana University, 2000.
15. Hewson, C., P. Yule, D. Laurent and C. Vogel, *Internet Research Methods : A Practical Guide for the Social and Behavioural Sciences*, London: SAGE Publications, 2002.
16. Hildreth, P. and Kimble, C. Communities of practice in the distributed international environment, *Journal of Knowledge Management*, 2000, 4 (1), pp.27-38.
17. Jones, Q. and Rafaeli, S. Time to split virtually: discourse architecture and community building create vibrant virtual publics, *Electronic Markets*, 2000, 10, pp.214-223.
18. Jones, S.G. Understanding Community in the Information Age, in Jones, S. G. (Ed.), *Cybersociety: Computer-Mediated Communication and Community*, pp.10-35, London: Sage, 1995.
19. Kenny, D. and Marshall, J.F. Contextual marketing: The real business of the Internet, *Harvard Business Review, 2000, 78*(6), pp.119-125.
20. Kling, R. Social Relationships in Electronic Forums, in *Computerization and Controversy: Value Conflicts and Social Choices*, San Diego: Academic Press, 1996, pp.426-454.
21. Koku, E. and Wellman, B. Scholarly Networks as Learning Communities: The Case of Technet, in Barab, B., Kling, R. and Gray, J., *Building Online Communities in the Service of Learning* (Ed), Cambridge University Press.
22. Kollock, P. The Economies of Online Cooperation: Gifts and Public Goods in Computer Communities. In *Communities in Cyberspace*, in Smith, M. and Kollock, P. (Eds.), *Communities in Cyberspace*, London: Routledge, 1998a.
23. Kollock, P. Design Principles for Online Communities, *PC Update*, 1998b, 15 (5), pp.58-60.
24. Kollock, P. The Production of Trust in Online Markets, *Advances in Group Processes*, 1999, 16 (1), pp.99-123.
25. Kollock, P. and Smith, M. Communities in cyberspace, in Smith, M. and Kollock, P. (Eds.), *Communities in Cyberspace*, London: Routledge, 1999.
26. Lakhani and von Hippel, How Open Source software works: Free user-to-user assistance, MIT Sloan School of Management Working Paper #4117, 2000, [available at http://web.mit.edu/evhippel/www/opensource.PDF]
27. Magretta, J. Why business models matter, *Harvard Business Review*, May, 2002.
28. McWilliam, G. Building stronger brands through online communities, *Sloan Management Review*, 2000, 41, pp.43-54.
29. O'Mahony, S. and Ferraro, F. Manage the boundary of an open project, Working paper NO. 537, 2004, IESE Business School, University of Navarra.
30. Resnick, P., Zeckhauser, R., Swanson, J. and Lockwood, K. The Value of Reputation on eBay: A Controlled Experiment, in the Proceeding of ESA conference, Boston, 2002.
31. Rheingold, H. *The Virtual Community: Homesteading on the Electronic Frontier*, Reading, MA: Addison-Wesley, 1993.
32. Rheingold, H. *The Virtual Community: Homesteading on the Electronic Frontier*, revised edition, Cambridge, MA: MIT Press, 2000.
33. Schubert, P. and Ginsburg, M. Virtual communities of transaction: the role of personalization in electronic commerce, *Electronic Markets*, 2000, 10 (1), pp.45-55.
34. Shapiro, C. and Varian, H.R. *Information Rules: A Strategic Guide to the Network Economy*, Harvard Business School Press, 1999.
35. Teigland, R. *Knowledge Networking: Structure and Performance in Network of Practice*, Stockholm School of Economics Press, 2003.
36. WAN *World Press Trends: 2002 edition*, World Report, World Association of Newspapers, 2002.
37. Wasko, M and Faraj, S. It is what one does: Why people participate and help others in electronic communities of practice, *Journal of Strategic Information System*, 2000, 9 (2-3), pp.155-173.
38. Wasko, M.M. and Teigland, R. The provision of online public goods: Examining social structure in an electronic network of practice, in the Proceedings of the 23rd International Conference on Information System, Barcelona, Spain, 2002.
39. Wellman, B. The community question, *American Journal of Sociology*, 1979, 84, pp.1201-1231.
40. Wellman, B. Computer networks as social networks, *Science*, 2001, 293, pp.2031-2034.
41. Wellman, B. and Gulia, M. Net Surfers Don't Ride Alone: Virtual Community as Community, in Wellman, B. *Networks in the Global Village* (Ed), pp.331-367, Boulder, CO: Westview Press, 1999.
42. Yan, J. and Assimakopoulos, D. Knowledge Sharing and Advice Seeking in a Software Engineering Community, in *Processes and Foundations for Virtual Organizations* (Eds, Camarinha-Matos L.M.and Afsarmanesh H.), Dordrecht: Kluwer Academic, 2003. pp.341-350.

44

A CONCEPTUAL FRAMEWORK FOR "PROFESSIONAL VIRTUAL COMMUNITIES"

Andrea Bifulco, Roberto Santoro
ESoCE-Net (abifulco@esoce.net, rsantoro@esoce.net), ITALY

Professional Virtual Communities (PVC) are emerging as human centred new organizational arrangements aimed at leveraging knowledge development, value creation and social welfare. This paper is aimed at defining a conceptual framework for the characterization of PVC, suitable for ascertaining the correlation among PVC constitutive elements and potential stakeholders' expected benefits. Such a theoretical approach leads to the identification of PVC typologies, which would optimally integrate themselves in business ecosystems, while ensuring member's motivation, commitment and welfare. The characterization of an emerging Professional Virtual Community, ESoCE-Net, is reported as a first attempt in characterizing a PVC with reference to the newly established conceptual framework. The results reported in this paper are also based on activities carried out within the ECOLEAD IP project, co-funded by the European Commission under the 6th framework programme.

1. INTRODUCTION

Virtual or online communities are important social structures emerging from an Internet-enabled society. These communities bring together people of similar interests in order to communicate, to share and exchange information, to have fun or just to fulfil the need of social belonging and empathy. Virtual communities are enabled and empowered by internet technologies such as e.g. bulletin boards, list servers, newsgroups, chat rooms, work spaces, etc. Such communities invent new social-relationships, resulting in new behavioural patterns and new ways of sharing and creating knowledge, which creates specific value from their activities.

On the other hand, Communities of Practice (Wenger, 1998) have been around for many years and are described as "groups of people informally bound together by shared expertise and passion for joint enterprise (that) share their experiences and knowledge in free-flowing, creative ways that foster new approaches to knowledge" (Wenger, Snyder, 2000). Leavitt et al. (2001) point out that Communities of Practice have become more prominent and formalized in recent years because they develop critical organizational knowledge assets. Most communities are "boundary-spanning units in organizations, responsible for finding and sharing best practices, stewarding knowledge, and helping members work better".

When communities of practice adopt computer networks and most of the practices and tools of virtual communities (Gongla et al., 2001) on one side, and pursue an explicit business mission on the other, they become Professional Virtual Communities (PVC).

2. THE PVC CONCEPT

In the current industrial context, the rapid evolution of technology has moved the focus from efficiency to creativity, for delivering suitable products and services to the economy. Furthermore, global challenges, such as environment, resources, competition, etc., are imposing new and harder constraints. With these challenges to face, the human capital is considered as an essential competitive advantage of business entities, being those both individuals, enterprises or communities.

Despite this situation, individual human potential is scarcely realized within current organizational business entities and within inter-organization business relationships. Among other causes, this situation is also activating a trend towards the increase of the percentage of Individual Professionals (self-employees, free-lancers etc.), which already constitute a considerable share of the total EU work force, as opposed to the Corporate Professionals' one.

A new organizational arrangement, referred to as Professional Virtual Community, is now emerging as the evolution of previous organizational schemes, to address, at the same time, the objectives of increasing the European Industrial competitiveness as well as the Knowledge workers' quality of life.

The innovativeness of the Professional Virtual Community concept stays in the comprehensive and appropriate inclusion of the three dimensions that are instrumental in increasing knowledge workers productivity and creativity:

- Knowledge
- Business
- Social & Ethics

According to this general definition, the PVC is intended to give to *individuals* motivation, a mean for economical sustainability and a feel of belonging, whilst addressing the objectives of the whole *society,* respectively in terms of knowledge-based work, economical growth and social welfare.

The characterization of the PVC concept is completed by the inclusion of appropriate ICT means, transversal to all the three dimensions, acting as necessary enablers for the PVC paradigm deployment.

The optimal harmonization of the three PVC elements can be seen, in a metaphoric sense, as the blending of the three basic colours (Blue for the Knowledge, Green for the Business, and Red for the Social dimension), resulting in one determined chromatic integration. This colour represents the inherent characteristics, as well as the delivered benefits, of a PVC typology which best fulfil the needs of a certain socio-economical context.

The following Figure 1 shows, as an example, the "colour" representation of a PVC which is mostly addressing the social aspects with respect to the Knowledge and Business ones, so positioning itself closer to the Social apex, within the triangular domain of all possible combinations.

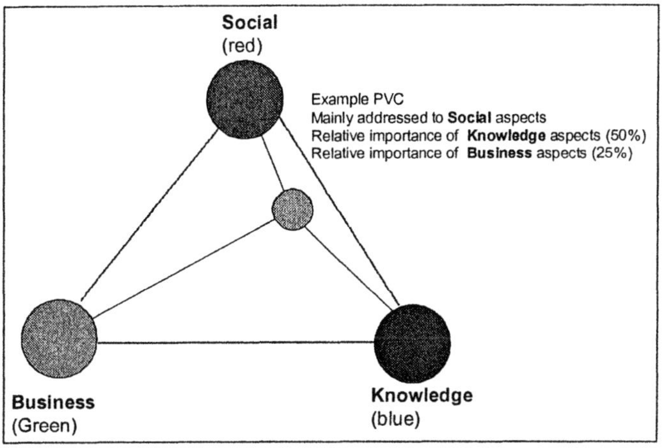

Figure 1 – The PVC colors' metaphor

This model represents the three necessary elements for a sustainable, motivated and durable community. As a matter of fact, the absence of the business dimension would result in a limited activity scope, putting at risk the PVC sustainability and members' viability to spend significant time in the community activities. The lack of the social element, ensuring trusted relationships among the members, would limit the readiness to approach business opportunities and impair the free share of knowledge among members. Not addressing the knowledge development element would limit the usefulness of the community for the build-up of the knowledge society, reduce motivation of the knowledge worker and impairs his aspiration to obtain higher recognition and even economical reward.

3. THE PVC CONCEPTUAL FRAMEWORK

The Conceptual Framework for the characterization of Professional Virtual Communities has been developed through the integrated definition of:

- a framework for the identification of needs and expectations of all the PVC potential stakeholders, particularized for all the most relevant aspects of the three PVC dimensions;
- a taxonomy for the characterization of constitutive elements and governance principles of a generic PVC, suitable also for the identification of specifically related ICT means;
- a rigorous logical process for determining the correlation existing among the stakeholder expectations and the PVC distinctive characteristics.

Such a theoretical framework leads to the identification of PVC typologies, which would optimally integrate themselves in business ecosystems, while ensuring member's motivation, commitment and welfare. The same framework can also be used for the characterization of existing communities in terms of delivered benefits to both individuals and society.

The following paragraphs explain in more details the single constituents of the PVC conceptual framework.

3.1 The PVC stakeholders' expectations

The PVC stakeholder expectations have been also derived on the base of interviews from a representative sample of PVC potential stakeholders.

The PVC potential stakeholders are defined as all the entities which may be affected, in some way, by the PVC operations, in particular including:

- Knowledge worker (Employee, Individual Professional)
- Enterprise (Micro Company, SME, Large Enterprise)
- Virtual Organisation
- Virtual Breeding Environment
- Institution (Local/Regional, National, International)

The other dimension for structuring the PVC stakeholder expectations is constituted by the three PVC characterizing fundamentals, in turn sub-structured in their major elements:

- Knowledge (Single Discipline, Multi-discipline, Unstructured)
- Business (Economic wealth, Growth & Development, Welfare)
- Social (Networking, Social Relationships, Global sustainability)

The combination of those two dimensions (PVC stakeholders and PVC main characterizing issues) provides a grid for the identification of specific expectations, such as, for instance:

- Expectation of "Corporate Knowledge workers" for the Knowledge (single discipline) issue: "*Continuous incremental enhancement of own core professional discipline Knowledge and Competence (K&C)*
- Expectation of "Large Enterprises" for the same issue: "*Company hired functional experts are trained and supported in their discipline K&C development by a dedicated PVC. The Enterprise accesses the K&C of a single discipline by getting the services from the related PVC (through its members temporarily allocated)*

3.2 The PVC distinctive characteristics

The reference framework for the PVC distinctive characteristics consists of the characterization elements of a generic PVC in its mature operational phase, along with the governance principles ruling both its regular functioning as well as the dynamic PVC lifecycle phases.

3.2.1 The PVC constitutive elements

The PVC constitutive elements are the *static* elements that characterize a PVC, in term of its ontological, business strategy and composition characteristics:

- Ontological elements
  - PVC Scope (field of knowledge / competence)
  - PVC Mission
  - PVC delivered Value (deliverables)

  - o PVC Shared ethical values (deontological code)
- Business strategic elements
  - o PVC strategic objectives
  - o PVC Business model
  - o PVC Market orientation
  - o PVC Lifecycle temporal horizon
- Composition characteristics
  - o PVC Organisational elements
  - o PVC dimension (Number of members)
  - o PVC geographical/cultural spread
  - o Members' characteristics (profiles)

As reported in the following Table 1, addressing the PVC specific requirements corresponding to a specific stakeholder expectations, each single element of the taxonomy is intended to identify both the PVC attributes and the related ICT enabling means.

Table 1 – Example of constitutive elements requirements and corresponding ICT means related to a specific stakeholder expectation

Stakeholder expectation		**PVC Constitutive elements: Ontological elements**			
		PVC Scope (field of knowledge / competence)	**PVC Mission**	**PVC delivered Value (deliverables)**	**PVC Shared ethical values (deontological code)**
E-K1 Employee – Knowledge (single discipline) **Continuous incremental enhancement of the core professional discipline knowledge and competence (K&C)**	PVC attributes	PVC scope precisely identified PVC scope coincident with the individual professional core discipline PVC Discipline Body of Knowledge	The PVC mission shall include the community increase of Knowledge & Competence on the PVC scope.	Community deliverables shall include documental formalisation of developed knowledge in terms of theory and practices relevant to the PVC professional core discipline The individual is also a client of the community deliverables	The strategic value of formalized knowledge is zero. The real strategic value is the capability of producing new knowledge. Hiding personal knowledge reduces that capability. Value=Knowledge sharing attitude
	ICT enablers	Structured Repository Ontology management	------	Document management Common repository	

3.2.2 The PVC governance principles

The PVC governance principles consists of the characterization elements of PVC management processes and governing rules, which have been grouped into the following clusters:

- Membership management (including, among others, the member qualification process, membership agreement, member profile management processes)
- Knowledge management (including all the processes aimed at supporting the Community Knowledge development)
- Business Process Management (including all the management principles and processes ruling the Community business activities)
- General Management and Support (including administration, PVC Management roles nomination and renewal processes, dispute resolution etc.)
- PVC lifecycle elements (i.e. the governing processes specifically aimed at ruling the PVC incubation, constitution, evolution, and dissolution phases).

As for the PVC constitutive elements described in the previous paragraph, also the PVC governing principle taxonomy can be used for both characterizing an existing PVC as well as identifying PVC requirements along with the corresponding ICT means.

3.3 The correlation process

The correlation existing among the stakeholder expectations and the PVC distinctive characteristics has been logically derived as follows:

- Identify specific stakeholder expectations
- For each stakeholder expectation:
  - Detail needs & expectation
  - Define Actual average situation
  - Ascertain the "reason why"
  - Determine how a PVC can provide a solution for reaching the stakeholder expectation by identifying the PVC constituent elements' and governance principles attributes. For each of them, define corresponding ICT enablers

Once determined, the established correlation among the stakeholder expectations and the PVC distinctive characteristics are used for identifying PVC typologies and characterize existing PVCs.

4. THE ESOCE-NET CASE

The characterization of an emerging Professional Virtual Community, ESoCE-Net, is reported as a first qualitative attempt in characterizing an actual Professional Virtual Community with reference to the newly established conceptual framework.

4.1 The Professional Virtual Community ESoCE-NET

The ESoCE-NET, European Society of Concurrent Enterprising Network, is a non-profit Association bringing together academics, researchers and industry practitioners to stimulate the exchange of ideas, views, practices and latest research and developments in the field of Concurrent Enterprising:

Concurrent Enterprising is the co-operation among Companies, possibly geographically dispersed, harmonising their processes and involving Customers and Suppliers for the design and manufacturing of products and services. Concurrent Enterprising conjugates the Virtual Enterprise concept and the Concurrent Engineering approach into a new business paradigm.

ESoCE-NET is offering to its Members the full potential of a Knowledge Community, to provide members with most useful support in their way to competitiveness through the Concurrent Enterprising paradigm, and with professional opportunities to exploit their expertise.

As a Community, ESoCE-NET has the mission of promoting and enacting the sharing and exchanging of latest developments in CE, as well as to act as catalyst of CE adoption in Industry, and to promote initiatives to widen the knowledge on CE and to complete the methodological focused framework for the industrial deployment of CE Concepts.

4.2 A first characterization per PVC dimensions

From the first characterization of the ESoCE-Net community, carried out with the limitations already indicated in the present chapter, the following qualitative outcomes yielded:

- As far as the **knowledge** dimension is concerned, the distinctive elements of ESoCE-Net are very well correlated only with a specific sub-dimension, the "multi discipline Knowledge", for the majority of the considered potential stakeholders. This confirm the specific intrinsic characteristic of ESoCE-Net as a Community whose knowledge scope can be defined a "multidisciplinary incipient discipline". This means that the knowledge dimension for this community is focused on the interaction of already established disciplines (such as engineering, economics, legal, social sciences, ICT) instead of the development of single disciplines. An identified gap consist of the lack of a theoretical foundation for the constitution of the CE body of knowledge. This point could also suggest the early identification of two PVC typologies, one dedicated to the development of an established discipline, the other dedicated to the tentative establishment of an incipient discipline as a composition of multidisciplinary knowledge.
- As far as the **business** dimension is concerned, it was observed that the distinctive elements of ESoCE-Net were very well correlated for the totality of the considered sub-dimensions, but only for some stakeholders, and in particular for the Individual Professionals.
- As for the **social** dimension, a well developed face-to-face interaction among members (e.g. ICE Conference and Industrial Forum) was not balanced by a virtually supported interaction.

In order to get an integral view of the ESoCE-Net characterisation, the position of this Community within the identified characterisation domain was also derived in a qualitative way. Figure 2 shows the graphical characterisation.

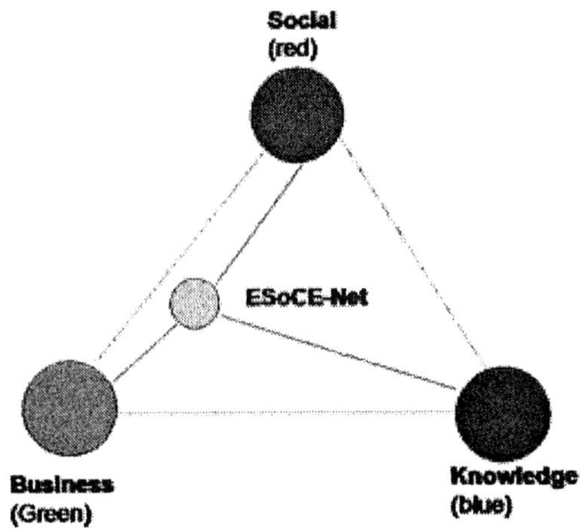

Figure 2 – The ESoCE-Net first qualitative characterisation

5. CONCLUSIONS

This paper presented the definition of a newly developed conceptual framework for the characterization of Professional Virtual Communities, suitable for ascertaining the correlation among PVC constitutive elements and potential stakeholders' expected benefits. Such a theoretical approach leads both to the identification of PVC typologies, which would optimally integrate themselves in business ecosystems, as well as to the characterisation of existing ones. In order to get the flavour of the possible outcomes of such a characterisation process, the ESoCE-Net case was considered, and the first qualitative results reported. The established conceptual framework will constitute the theoretical base for the identification of viable PVC business models as well as for the definition of PVC advanced collaboration platform requirements. The results showed in this paper are also based on activities carried out within the ECOLEAD IP project, co-funded by the European Commission under the 6th framework programme.

6. REFERENCES

1. Leavitt et al. – Building and sustaining Communities of Practice, http://old.apqc.org/ pubs/summaries/ CMKMCOP.pdf, 2001.
2. Wenger, E. C., and Snyder, W. M. - Communities of Practice: The Organizational Frontier, Harvard Business Review. January-February: 139-145. 2000.
3. Wenger, E. - Communities of Practice: Learning, Meaning and Identiy. Cambridge University Press. 1998.
4. Gongla, P. , and Rizzuto, R. – Evolving Communities of Practice: IBM Global Services experience, IBM Systems Journal, Vol 40, n.4, 2001.

45 MOBILE AND LOCATION-AWARE WORKPLACES AND GLOBAL VALUE NETWORKS: A STRATEGIC ROADMAP

Hans Schaffers
Telematica Instituut, hans.schaffers@telin.nl

Wolfgang Prinz
Fraunhofer FIT, wolfgang.prinz@fit.fraunhofer.de

Robert Slagter
Telematica Instituut, robert.slagter@telin.nl
THE NETHERLANDS

The introduction of new technologies and processes for communication, collaboration and knowledge exchange has changed considerably our work environment and the way we are organising our work. In this paper the implications of flexible mobile and collaborative workplaces for global value networks are explored through future scenarios and roadmapping. In particular we focus on the advances in mobile and location-aware workplaces and their role in organising and coordinating global business activities. The paper presents several mobile workplace scenarios and outlines a roadmap and a research agenda for strategic research and innovation.

1. INTRODUCTION

Due to the steadily introduction of new technologies and processes for communication, collaboration and knowledge exchange, our work environment and the way we are organising our work has changed considerably over the past 20 years. In this paper we explore the implications caused by the emergence of more flexible workplaces for global value networks. In particular we are looking at the advances in mobile and location-aware workplaces and their role in the organisation and coordination of global business activities. This paper is based on findings of the MOSAIC project[i], which has developed a set of generic and sector-specific scenarios, a roadmap, and a strategic research and innovation agenda for the area of mobile and collaborative workplaces.

In section 2 we are reviewing current trends towards networked organisation and networked workplaces. Section 3 presents the methodology for developing the scenarios and roadmap. The scenarios are discussed in more detail in section 4, whereas in section 5 we present the roadmap and research agenda.

2. NETWORKED WORKPLACES AND ORGANISATIONS

A networked organisation can be studied from different perspectives. Whereas the top-down oriented business transactions perspective is focusing on business processes within and across its constituting organisations and their result in terms of transactions, the bottom-up perspective is that of the human worker who is a member of temporary teams and projects. Both perspectives are valuable and complementary, but result in different approaches for developing process and organisational improvements and IT support. This paper approaches the networked organisation by emphasizing the people-centric "networked workplace" and the "we-centric" services that form the core of modern workplace support.

There is empirical evidence that innovations in collaborative workplaces may further contribute to creating value and increasing productivity. Measured over a period during the 1990s, it appears that ICT-endowed workplace innovations account for 30% of output growth in manufacturing, and 89% of multifactor productivity (Black and Lynch, 2003). Given the productivity gap between US and Europe in exploiting ICTs, one can assume that there is a real challenge for Europe in developing more innovative workplace support. In order to realise this apparent potential, a holistic concept of workplace innovation is needed, establishing a balance between the different viewpoints and instruments: workplace organisation, IT-support, business process management. In addition cooperation and workplace design must be understood as a socio-technical process that aims at the congruency of the different viewpoints (Prinz, et.al. 1998).

From a workplace confined to particular locations and fixed working times mostly, we now are accustomed to more flexible forms of working, allowing more flexibility in choice of where and when to work. However, current collaboration and teamwork applications have changed the way we carry out tasks. This leads to a flexible workplace model enabling a diversity of new forms of team collaboration that are more independent from location and time. The flexible workplace model is enabled by information technologies which - if combined with new organisational and management processes - affect the structuring of tasks and collaboration and their dependence on context parameters in a number of ways.

- *Context independence.* The balance between tasks that can be carried out independent or dependent of task context parameters (time, place) is changing. Tasks increasingly can be carried out independent of time and place. In the extreme, tasks are carried out "anywhere anytime".
- *Context awareness.* Tasks can be carried out context-independent and context-aware. This contributes strongly to opportunities for optimizing task execution. An example is the use of location information and personal profiles for mobile salespersons, or the use of presence information for organising real-time collaboration meetings.
- *Context switching.* Collaboration is supported in more diverse context settings, ranging from "same time and same place" to "different time and different place" settings, and even including unpredictable places and times (Grudin, 1994).

Figure 1 categorises different types of workplace support according to the dimensions of time and place. Working in networked organisations requires the possibility to switch between different contexts and different applications. It should be noted that applications intended for a certain context are often unexpectedly (mis-)used in other contexts. An example is the chat-like use of email for the frequent communication between local users.

Table 1: Workplace support categorisation (adapted from Grudin, 1994)

Place \ Time	Same	Different, predictable	Different, Unpredictable	Aware of Time
Same	Electronic meeting support	Newsgroups Electronic project room	Room infrastructure	Electronic project meeting
Distributed, predictable	Video/audio-conferencing; Co-authoring, Co-designing	Group scheduling E-mail Co-authoring	Shared workspace Virtual community	Co-authoring Shared workspace
Different, unpredictable	Presence-based audio-conferencing		Process coordination	
Aware of place	Mobile audio-Conferencing	Presence en instant messaging	Mobile document access	Context awareness services

As regards current work practice, still most work is being carried out at fixed locations and fixed working times, combined with traditional forms of teleworking and working on the move as is indicated with words like "nomad" and "yo-yo" (Lilischkis, 2003). Current mobile working applications are largely limited to supporting mobile individuals such as sales representatives and managers. The element of collaboration is still lacking as it is subsumed under the practice of mobile communication. Essentially these are solutions for mobile workers, supporting mobility by enabling new and mobile forms of communication in combination with presence and location awareness information.

Mobile work can be interpreted in an even more challenging way by applying the dimension of "mobility" to work and to the workplace. Following this view, a workplace could be envisaged allowing work to be carried out anywhere and anytime. Such a concept would include the use of context information beyond location and time, enabling new forms of cooperative interaction and workspace contextualization (Schaffers, Ribak and Tschammer, 2004). This concept also emphasizes emerging new structures of collaboration. The "virtual team" consists of a project team of geographically distributed members who temporarily cooperate to accomplish a common goal. Such global virtual teams provide an opportunity whose challenges require organizational skills and sophisticated ICT support. However, the "team" as the entity of work activity, as assumed by most CSCW (Computer Supported Cooperative Work) models, may decrease in importance giving rise to so-called 'intensional networks" (Nardi, Whittaker and Schwarz, 2002). In such a way, mobile and location-aware technologies together with broadband networks and groupware applications and embedded in new collaborative structures and processes provide much scope for exploiting the potential of decreasing cost of communication in enabling new forms of decentralization and networked organizations (Malone, 2004).

3. SCENARIO METHODOLOGY

Our approach to arrive at scenarios and roadmaps followed stages of vision development, analysis of current practice, trends and future scenarios, identification of gaps and challenges, development of a strategy for workplace innovation, and proposing a roadmap for research and technology development. The work was validated in workshops. We discuss some of these steps in more detail.

In order to explore the strategic research and innovation issues, we started with confronting current mobile working practice with a more future-oriented mobile workplace vision in order to explore the diversity of aspects in mobile work and workplace mobility. Three types of current workplaces were distinguished in terms of mobility support and work location changes (Figure 1): micro-mobility: supporting on-site mobility; multi-mobility: supporting ad-hoc and occasional mobility; and total mobility: supporting on the move working.

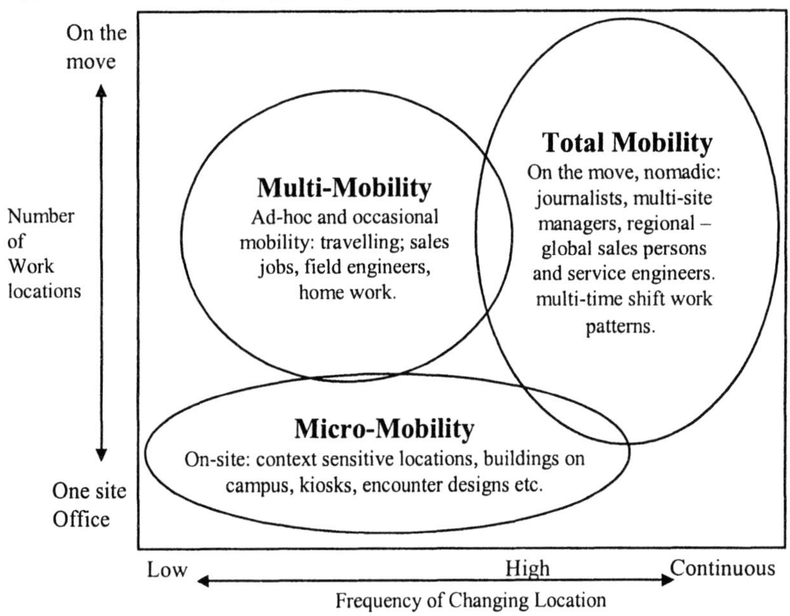

Figure 1: Mobile workplaces categorisation (Schaffers et al, 2005a)

The vision of "mobile and networked workplaces", emphasizing the concept of anywhere and anytime context-aware working, took its point of departure in the formulation of a strategy for workplace innovation at the European level. It was understood that modernisation of the work environment could contribute considerably to the objectives of growth, productivity and innovation. As the next step, the mobile workplace vision was made more concrete by developing a scenario framework of underlying driving forces.

Major forces driving future workplace designs were assumed to include technological transformation, globalisation and competition, demographic change, management style, European enlargement, and work-life balance needs. Two *uncertain* driving forces affecting future ways of working, "human identity" and "organisational development" were selected as key factors. This results into a scenario framework of distinct environments of future mobile and collaborative workplaces. The framework then was used to identify and analyse six different scenarios. These scenarios were conceived as strategies to cope with, and explore, the environments. Storylines were formulated and key aspects of the scenarios were assessed such as success factors and technology, behaviour, and organisational and societal requirements and challenges. Figure 2 depicts the scenarios.

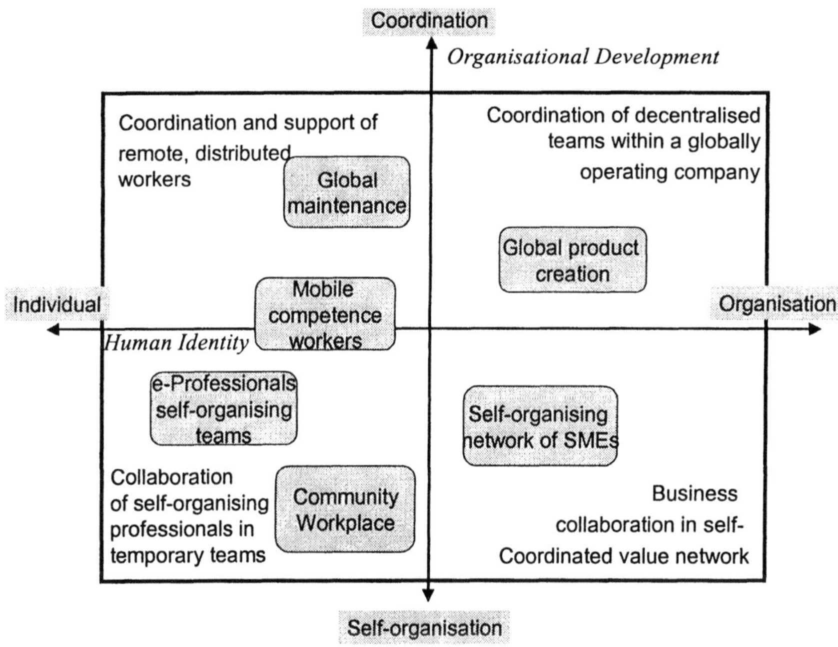

Figure 2: Workplace scenario driving forces framework (Schaffers et al, 2005a)

The objective of these scenarios is to challenge existing frames of mind in envisaging different types of workplaces than those already existing and to show plausible future directions for innovation. They highlight underlying forces and uncertainties, and enable us to anticipate change and to widen decision options. They are not meant to present business opportunities, but of course could embed such opportunities. In order to link the scenario process to the identification of new business opportunities, two levels of scenario development were distinguished. Apart from the generic scenarios, specific scenarios and deployment strategies for mobile workplaces have been developed for different sector domains such as aerospace, automotive, health, and building and construction as well as for working in rural and regional areas.

4. MOBILE WORKPLACE SCENARIOS

In focusing on the role of networked workplaces in global value networks, we present three scenarios of Figure 2, highlighting various aspects of the framework Schaffers et al. 2005b).

Scenario 1: Global product creation in a networked company

This scenario describes a global product creation environment of a company that has operations in several sites in different countries and in various time zones as well. Most of the product creation processes involve several partners, subcontractors and client sites in different countries. The company exploits a network of co-located sites in different time zones that optimally utilizes the available competencies of each different site. This requires effectively mobilizing both the work (tasks) and the worker, and has direct implications for work processes and the work environment needed to increase productivity. The rationale behind this scenario is the evolving global division of work and increasing speed of innovation and productivity requirements.

The scenario identifies three different patterns of mobility: the Mobile, Campus based and Desk-based worker. The Mobile worker typically works between many locations. He owns no dedicated workspace, needs remote access to most of his resources and may work from home for up to 2 days a week. The Campus mobile worker typically works in one location but is highly mobile and away from his desk for considerable amounts of time. This requires solutions for managing storage and personal material. The Desk-based worker uses a dedicated team workspace in a company location. Resources should be office based but preferably, desks should be cleared and made available to others when they are out. The technologies needed to support this scenario relate to hot-desking, context sensitive locations, instant privacy technologies, 'follow-me' printing services, security, authentication, interoperability issues and multi-access wireless technologies. The work tasks can be addressed by using multi-shift work patterns. This is also an area where exploitation of work mobility instead of worker mobility brings highest value and therefore different virtual workspace arrangements are common.

Scenario 2: Mobile competence workers in global supply chains

This scenario reflects ongoing trends in individual working habits of competence workers and in organizational structures of globally operating companies: the trend to mobile teleworking and mixed forms of teleworking; to more autonomy in the individual organization of working time and location; to blending in professional and private spheres; to more dynamic and flexible organizational structures and globalization with semi-autonomous decentralized bodies of subsidiaries.

The scenario shows how mobile technology can both improve work in a globally operating supply chain and how it can make life easier for competence workers. The work of a lead buyer of a globally operated and distributed trading company is described. The company is hierarchically structured with (almost) autonomous subsidiary companies in many countries throughout the world and in many time zones and languages, down to the actual markets for end customers. Purchasing is handled by decentralized purchase companies, one for each country, sometimes even for regions. The lead buyer works in a central purchasing unit and is responsible for strategic purchasing between the regional purchasing companies. She works in the central headquarters, but frequently has to travel around to coordinate purchasing with regional purchase managers in various countries or to negotiate with suppliers. Her work is characterized by a dependency on inhouse databases and information systems as well as a high degree of informal communication and document exchange with internal staff and external suppliers. The lead buyer frequently works at home or at other premises.

ICT in the company consists of standard inhouse applications which are networked (database systems, document management system, etc.). Security is an important issue, considering the amount of industrial espionage world-wide. The ICT system is quite regulated with a high degree of networking, but between subsidiaries, there is mainly informal communication and unstructured exchange of documents.

The scenario reflects a trend to more dynamic and flexible workplace organizational structures. Other trends focus on mixed forms of teleworking (as opposed to sedentary telework at home), more autonomy for the individual in the work organisation, excellent security for ubiquitous access to data and the blending of professional and private spheres. The scenario also identifies globally networked companies consisting of decentralized subsidiaries and support for an international multi-cultural workforce.

Scenario 3: Self-organising network of SMEs

This scenario represents the situation of SME managers collaborating in a self-coordinated network in order to jointly pursue business opportunities in design and manufacturing. The network expands internationally taking up new members and establishing local presence, and adding new services such as maintenance.

Whereas globalisation and outsourcing threaten the position of local suppliers, at the same time these forces provide new opportunities to participate in global supply chains. Research, design and production is migrating throughout the world, following local markets and enforcing optimization of supply chains. ICT and organisational innovations help SME suppliers to adapt to these forces enabling them to become part of international value systems. Collaborative workplaces and mobile working enable them to strengthen teamwork more independently of place.

Our SME initially collaborates within a regional SME network to jointly market products and share resources in design, accounting and marketing. Its members are independent and contribute to managing the network. An electronic market passes requests for supplies, and a collaboration platform is used to discuss project participation and sharing of resources. The network selects partners for collaboration with the contractor, using shared workspaces. New partners can be selected and negotiations supported. A design company in the network sets up design team and works with customer real-time and non-real time. The network gradually expands its international presence, allowing international partners to participate in the network. The network uses mobility support to enable communication and collaboration at varying places and times, access to documents and experts when needed.

Requirements and challenges to be met to make the scenario happen are many. Among them: business models for networked collaboration; new processes and tools for project oriented collaboration; integration of personal network presence and calendar functions into the network; near-life remote meeting support; competence and experience profiling of partners; trust and security management; collaboration between remote units and people; workspaces for co-design, co-engineering, project preparation and management; and supporting multi-dimensional work contexts such as working simultaneously for different companies.

5. ROADMAP AND STRATEGIC RESEARCH AGENDA

The scenarios learn us several lessons enabling us to sketch a plausible development path for future mobile and collaborative workplaces. To a large part, economic factors affecting mobility such as cost of transportation and ICT affect the future workplace. Technology factors such as the migration towards all-IP networks and the large-scale adoption of mobile technologies can also be considered as relatively certain trends. These trends are part of all scenarios. More interesting is the role of the uncertain factors that drive future ways of working. The scenarios are outcomes under a "what-if" question: what if individualism will grow, and organizations will tend to become more self-organising? What will be the problems and opportunities in that situation, and what are the instruments available? Such questions allow us to consider success and failure factors and situation-dependent strategies, even if such "if" situations will not be realised. In our opinion the most important lessons conveyed by the scenarios can be summarized as follows:

- Global division of work will be a major development, but work-life balance issues could hinder its full development and undermine current social models.
- Mobile workplaces can support the globalisation of supply chains, but require new forms of leadership, coordination and management.
- E-professionals in a self-organising community are a promising model, but will require new business models and legal arrangements.

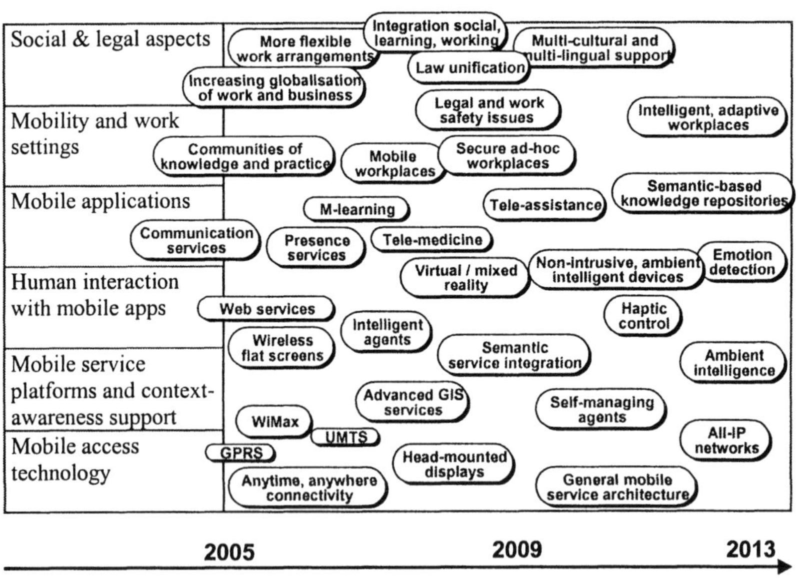

Figure 3: Initial roadmap for mobile work (Slagter and Schaffers et al, 2005)
Table 2: Mobile workplaces 2005 – 2013 (Slagter and Schaffers et al, 2005)

2005 – 2006
• Widespread use of combinations of PDA/mobile phone; mainly e-mail use; first mobile blogging approaches • Emphasis on limited forms of micro-mobility: on-site mobile working at context sensitive locations, kiosks, encounter designs etc • Standard groupware tools become more adapted to mobile settings • Context-sensitivity covers mainly location and time parameters • Emphasis on ad-hoc and occasional mobility: buildings on campus, traveling, sales jobs, field engineers, home work • Connectivity sufficient for document sharing and IP-based audio conferencing • Research on "workspace authoring" enabling on-demand workspace support for ad-hoc mobile teams
2007 – 2008
• Location-based personal services become dominant: where is my daughter? • Mobile community and content services; community based organisation structures • Complex forms of context sensitivity and better multi-user interfaces are realized, supporting mobile ad-hoc project teams • Increase of well-supported forms of micro-mobility and multi-mobility; decrease of forms of total mobility • Increasing support of mobile teamwork in engineering, maintenance, services industries; including solutions for mobile workplace knowledge access/ sharing • Pilots in on-demand mobile workplace support tools • Resistance to changing workplace settings is developing; is addressed by paying more attention to policies for workplace health and safety
2009 –2013
• Mobile phones migrate into clothes and other devices • Elementary forms of networked, "ambient" workplaces become reality with seamless transition between diversity of workplace styles • Applications of mobile working in globally dispersed engineering and service teams and in collaborative learning • New forms of networked organization, enabling high level of interaction between central and decentralised levels and accommodating flexible forms of mobile working become reality and are becoming part of EU business infrastructure • Negative impacts of workplace innovations on family conflict and work-life balance are not resolved, could create new divides

These aspects lead us to revisit the mobile workplace vision and develop a more concrete strategy for mobile workplace innovation and agenda for research. In Table 2 we propose a set of "stages" for mobile workplace evolution for the next decade. These stages represent advances including technical, social, behavioral and policy-related factors. These stages form the basis for a roadmap of technical and non-technical innovations represented in the roadmap in Figure 3. To structure this roadmap for collaborative mobile workplaces we have analyzed the emerging development pattern based on the following six RTD (Research Training and Development) and innovation areas: (1) Social and legal aspects; (2) Developments in mobility and work settings; (3) Implications for and developments in mobile applications; (4) Human interaction with mobile applications; (5) Mobile service design and service platforms; (6) Mobile access technology. In a next step these developments were positioned on a time-scale. The high-level roadmap shows the key challenges and milestones for realising mobile and collaborative work innovations.

Systemic innovation requires a multidisciplinary approach to joint RTD in Europe. Based on the MOSAIC scenarios and development pattern as well as on the scenarios of the Collaborative Work Experts Group[ii] we have identified key issues for joint RTD as summarized in the following as research clusters.

1) Business models for a networked and mobile society

The new opportunities and demands of mobile work require the development of new business models that reflect the change from application to service driven solutions. Workers will no longer work and cooperate with or through an application, but they will use a mobile collaboration service. Thus people will not focus in the procurement of devices or software but on the on demand use and payment of context available services.

2) Design and tailoring methods for mobile workplaces to address individual demand and needs for end-user tailoring

Local workplaces are often designed due to the organisational or group requirements and guidelines. However, mobile workplaces are more specific to the individual or the cooperating community. Therefore methods are needed that address the balance between the self-organisation of mobile and local work as well as the integration into the organisational procedures. This will lead to the development of community based workplaces vs. organisational departments, requiring flexible access to shared workspaces, from strictly private to publicly accessible.

3) Trust and security management in a mobile world

Big challenges for flexible, mobile and local cooperation are security issues. Security threats make it more and more difficult to establish ad hoc cooperation spaces between arbitrary partners. Organisations are very reluctant to open their cooperation environment to others. Thus users are often forced to use third party services for inter-organisational cooperation. This leads to inconsistencies and problems in intra- and inter-organisational cooperation due to inhomogeneous applications and systems. To overcome this problem we need new approaches to an easy to use and end-user configurable security management for inter-organisational community based cooperation.

4) Sharing multi-dimensional work contexts and telepresence

Community based and mobile workplace cooperation includes multi-dimensional work contexts such as working simultaneously for different companies, including their systems, processes, rules, cultures. This requires methods for easy switching between workspaces. This can be on a horizontal level: for co-design, co-engineering, project preparation and management; or on vertical levels: coordination of business processes at different levels (global data collection, local diagnostic centres, maintenance engineer). A particular demand derived from that is the need for awareness mechanisms that enable user to stay on top of their work processes and contexts.

5) Models for coordinating business work processes for mobile users

The coordination of business processes at different levels (global data collection, local diagnostic centres, maintenance engineer) integrating mobile users and processes requires new models to reflect the context (location, availability, service availability, etc.) of the users.

6) Tools and services enabling end-user configuration of community based workplaces in a mobile world
Beyond current services for shared workspaces we need tools for end-user creation of ad-hoc workspaces including services for ad-hoc contextualised collaboration as well as for finding people and knowledge.

7) Standardizing ubiquitous access to mobile workplaces and ambient intelligence environments: reference models for mobile workplaces and ambient environments
Mobile work in different environments demands ubiquitous access to Internet and to devices such as touch sensitive screens, keyboards and pens. This can be achieved only if standards exist. A prerequisite for this is the development of reference models for mobile workplaces and ambient environments that reflect adaptiveness, scalability and interoperability.

8) Field test for integrating the next generation mobile devices into real business
Special application domains must be identified to perform field tests or living labs in which the technologies as well as the impacts are investigated and understood.

9) Social impact of distributed working relations
The impact of mobile and distributed working relations in knowledge communities is not yet fully understood. Further research must be performed to understand the risks and opportunities and to develop methods for adequate training or tools (presence, awareness tools) that can support the transformation to these new work styles.

10) Adapting home and business environment
Mobile work involves working at different places including the home environment. This goes hand in hand with blurring the border between business and private life. As a consequence technologies are needed to adapt and to integrate the home and business environment as well as to find business and working models that support the integration of business and private life.

6. CONCLUSIONS

This paper contributes a scenario-based approach for the development of a roadmap and a research agenda for mobile and location-aware workplaces. Based on the identification of scenarios that represent different driving forces for future work situations, a roadmap has been presented that covers both ICT as well as social and organizational factors. Among the different research issues that have been identified we consider as the most important: design methods for mobile workplaces to address individual demand and needs for end-user tailoring such that a satisfactory work-life balance can be established. To overcome the increasing complexity of todays work-process easy methods for sharing multi-dimensional work contexts and task are needed. This must be combined with the development of tools that enable the end-user configuration of community-based workplaces to enable users to tailor their workplaces to the needs of the work task and processes instead of organizational constraints. Perhaps the most important but also most problematic issues is the standardizing of ambient intelligence environments to achieve reference models for mobile workplaces. Only such an effort can guarantee a local and global interplay. We hope that the thoughts presented in this paper can guide such a process.

7. ACKNOWLEDGMENTS

The work has partly been funded by the European Commission through the MOSAIC Specific Support Action (FP6-2003-IST-2). The authors express their gratitude and appreciation to MOSAIC project partners for their contributions to scenario building and roadmap construction. In particular we acknowledge Veli-Pekka Niitamo, Elke Hinrichs, Marc Pallot and Seamus Hickey for contributing to scenario development.

8. REFERENCES

1. Black SE, Lynch LM. What's driving the new economy? The benefits of workplace innovation. FRBSF Working paper 2003-23, 2003.
2. Grudin J. Computer-Supported Cooperative Work: Its History and Participation. IEEE Computer, 27, 5, pp19-26, 1994.
3. Lilischkis S. More Yo-yos, Pendulums and Nomads: Trends of Mobile and Multi-Location Work in the Information Society. STAR Project Issue report Nr. 36, Empirica, Bonn, 2003.
4. Malone TW. The Future of Work. Harvard Business School Press, 2004.
5. Nardi B, Whittaker S, Schwarz, H. NetWORKers and their activity in intensional networks. Journal of Computer-supported Cooperative Work, Vol 11, Issue 1-2, pp205-242, 2002.
6. Prinz W, Mark G, Pankoke-Babatz U. Designing Groupware for Congruency in Use. In Proceedings '98: ACM Conference on Computer Supported Cooperative Work, Seattle, ACM Press, pp373-382, 1998.
7. Schaffers H, Ribak A, Tschammer V. COCONET: A Roadmap for Context-Aware Cooperation Environments. In Processes and Foundations for Virtual Organizations, L.M. Camarinha-Matos and H. Afsarmanesh (eds), Kluwer Academic Publishers, pp47-64, 2004.
8. Schaffers H (ed), Carver L, Fernando T, Hickey S, Hinrichs E, Martland D, Niitamo VP, Pallot M, Prinz W, Vollmer S. Mobile working: vision, scenarios, challenges. MOSAIC FP6-2003-IST-2 Project Report D1.1 (Draft), 2005a.
9. Schaffers H (ed), Hickey S, Hinrichs E, Niitamo VP, Pallot M. The MOSAIC Mobile Workplace Scenarios. MOSAIC FP6-2003-IST-2 Project Report D1.1.2 (Draft), 2005b.
10. Slagter R and Schaffers H (Eds.), Brugnoli C, Hickey S, Lorusso I, Niitamo VP, Pallot M, Prinz W, Pulli P, Rissanen M, Tarchalska A, Turowiec A. Mobile workplaces roadmap report. MOSAIC FP6-2003-IST-2 Project Report D1.2 (Draft), 2005.

---

[i] MOSAIC is a Specific Support Action in the IST priority of the 6th Framework Programme of the European Commission, running 2004-2005. See: http://www.mosaic-network.org/.

[ii] http://europa.eu.int/information_society/activities/atwork/work_paradigms/experts_group/index_en.htm

PART 15

SERVICE ORIENTED ARCHITECTURES

46

OPEN MULTI-TECHNOLOGY SERVICE ORIENTED ARCHITECTUR FOR "ITS" BUSINESS MODELS: THE ITSIBus ETOLL SERVICES

A. Luís Osório[1], Carlos Gonçalves[1], Paulo Araújo[1], Manuel Barata[1]
J. Sales Gomes[2], Gastão Jacquet[2], Rui M Dias[2]
[1]ISEL, Instituto Superior de Engenharia de Lisboa, GIATSI research group, Portugal
{aosorio, cgoncalves, paraujo, mbarata}@deetc.isel.ipl.pt
[2]*BRISA, Auto-estradas de Portugal, DIT Innovation and Technology Department, Portugal*
{Jorge.Gomes, Gastao.Jacquet, Rui.Dias}@brisa.pt

The development of integrated solutions made of systems based on different technologies, adopting different implementation approaches and different versions is a complex challenge. The lack of standards or differences in implementations when they exist, are important obstacles to the construction of integrated, flexible and agile solutions. The incorporation of systems from different vendors and systems that evolve to answer innovation processes, suggests the advantage for a multi-technology systems strategy. This paper discusses the ITSIBus approach based on, a multi-technology service oriented infrastructure where specialized pluggable systems run services following a peer to peer architecture. The multi-technology approach is based on the discussed System Broker concept. The agility required by a crescent number of collaborative business process requires an advanced flexibility from the ICT technological infrastructure. The ITSIBus approach is also discussed as a grounding platform to support enterprise collaborative networks considering that services in different companies are based on different technologies.

1. INTRODUCTION

The integration of functions executed across networks of enterprises requires an advanced integration level for the internal enterprise processes. The emergent concept of enterprise collaborative networks (Camarinha-Matos, 2003) needs a long way to be adopted by existing de facto networked enterprise. These networks are deeply grounded on file transfer and are far to answer collaborative process requirements. There is an effective need for a tighter integration strategy among network members. This movement from a loose connection approach based on file transfer or even physical document transfer, to a transactional collaboration based on a tight integration approach, requires a new strategy from both technological and business process perspectives. However, before the discussion focused on enterprise network collaborative level, there is a need to establish at enterprise internal model (Camarinha-Matos, 1999) an infrastructure agile enough to cope with systems integration requirements. The integration among disparate systems developed on different technologies and supplied by different vendors is a main challenge for the agile collaborative enterprise network. This paper discusses the ITSIBus approach (Gomes et. al. 2003-b) (Osorio, et. al. 2004) considering its implementation on the

JINI (Flenner, 2002) platform with enhanced features aiming to interoperate with systems developed on other platforms like .NET (Rammer, 2005).

The ITSIBus was motivated by the extended ViaVerde toll payment business model (Osorio, et. al. 2003). The evaluated requirements have pointed out for the need to integrate a number of systems in different technological stages and versions – a strategy grounded on multi-vendor systems. The ITSIBus architecture proposes a set of standard services for specific functionalities like toll collection based on DSRC/RFID technology, vision based licence plate recognition and automatic toll collection based on card payment - ETOLL, among other systems. Beyond the specialized functionalities (generic services) the ITSIBus establishes a set of core services defined in WSDL and able to be bound to different platforms. The interoperability among services running on different technologies (platforms) is guaranteed by a special type of system, the SystemBroker. The SystemBroker provides inter-technology service interoperability. It offers a transparent access to services implemented in one technology, for instance on JINI, from services implemented in another technology, for instance on .NET.

The strategy aims to establish a technological infrastructure able to integrate services from concurrent providers (multi-vendor). Furthermore it considers that the services are plugged on a plug-and-play basis (Allard, 2003) and follow ITSIBus management specification. The adopted strategy is based on the assumption that holistic systems are made of heterogeneous components or systems independently of the underlying technologies. The strategy is quite different from the CORBA initiative where an object request broker and a binding mechanism for different languages were created for objects (or execution components) developed in different languages. The common denominator was the service definition language IDL (Interface Definition Language) with a set of standard bindings to different programming languages. The strategy proposed by ITSIBus considers a uniform service definition using the WSDL language as a common service definition language. Even if some extensions are needed to define concepts like event registration and subscription, the strategy is grounded on other efforts to use WSDL with or without extensions to be used as a reference service modelling language.

The paper discusses the System Broker strategy as a way to preserve development culture and at the same time offer a wide range of system developers the opportunity to integrate their solutions towards a holistic and open technological platform. The ETOLL System is discussed as a case study of such approach. The ETOLL system is an automatic tollbooth where car drivers can pay toll using payment cards, coins and other payment forms all done without the presence of an operator. This system was developed in C++ and based on Windows operating system. The challenge was to offer ETOLL development team an easy access to ITSIBus services and system concepts without too much interference on ongoing developments. For that a System Broker is being developed to accept ITSIBus service discovery, service registration, service calls, and call-back management mechanisms in order to interoperate with services implemented in other platforms than JINI (Osorio, et. al. 2004).

The paper discusses also a model based development approach to ITSIBus systems and services based on Eclipse platform (www.eclipse.org). A plug-in to Eclipse was developed to speed-up solutions development based on a set of wizards guiding code generation and providing a development framework where developers are focused on business logic and not on intrinsic of the underlying technology concepts.

Since the beginning of the ITSIBus project a special concern was dedicated to the "leaning curve" required to understand advanced systems and concepts like those proposed by ITSIBus and those associated to the underlying technologies. Even if JINI is not a complex platform it embeds a large number of new concepts and it is a huge framework requiring specialized knowledge do deal with. To facilitate service development, a plug-in for the Eclipse platform is being developed to guide toll management system developers to create systems, services and client applications. The client application aims to test ITSIBus systems and services during developments. The main goal for such a kind of workshop is to speed-up the development of new systems and services by focussing developers on service business logic. The objective is to offer experts on toll management an advanced tool where services and service integration on complex systems can be developed from models, reducing to a minimal the code needed to be written.

With ITSIBus development workshop a developer does not need to be an expert on JINI or in any other underlying technology selected to support ITSIBus concepts.

The ITSIBus is discussed as a grounding ICT infrastructure to support higher integration levels, namely that concerned with collaborative enterprise business processes. In fact the motorway management toll involves services to car drivers beyond the motorway management company (Osorio, et. al. 2004). In the case of the BRISA Company, the toll was extended for payments in car parking areas and gas stations. The ITSIBus infrastructure is also discussed as a grounding base for the supporting of some advanced challenges namely those related with the enterprise collaborative networks. It is a requirement of the toll technological infrastructure that collaborative companies access toll systems to audit toll collection processes. This requires an innovative approach to manage network level business processes. The ITSIBus is being considered as an underlying infrastructure to manage such cross company processes on a tight integration approach perspective.

2. THE MULTI-TECHNOLOGY APPROACH FOR ITSIBUS

The rapid evolution on ICT occurred during the last decades has put many challenges to ICT developing companies. Development teams have to deal with different equivalent technologies and with different frameworks and tools for each technology. There is a trend for some unification of key computational concepts but when implemented in different technologies it might originate interoperability problems. The utilization of Web Services is a way to get a common path but it is not a solution for all the challenges.

For ICT companies the challenge is how to deal with different equivalent technologies each one with its intrinsic and its corresponding learning curve. In fact, this is one of the bottlenecks when considering evolution of enterprise systems. When adopting new technologies companies need to make investments on training. Furthermore they have to support a lost of productivity until the development team gets ready with the new concepts and tools.

The ITSIBus strategy to cope with this multi-technology challenge is to establish a SystemBroker concept aiming to play a flexible bridge role connecting services developed in different technologies. In the area of network management systems

Grabowski (Grabowski, 1999) has also proposed an integration architecture of multi-technology management systems. The ITSIBus is a service-oriented architecture based on a community of peer systems. A system implements a set of basic services named core services (security, management and plug-and-play). The services are defined in WSDL and are a contribution from Brisa to standardize similar services exported by roadside systems (equipments). In the context of ITSIBus the services under standardization are the DSRC/RFID car identification service, car detection and classification (AVDC) service, car plate automatic recognition (ALPR) service, tollbooth system services and ETOLL semi-automatic toll system services. All these systems export services and generate events establishing this way a flexible infrastructure to interconnect peer services (through systems) providing synchronous or asynchronous association (Figure 1).

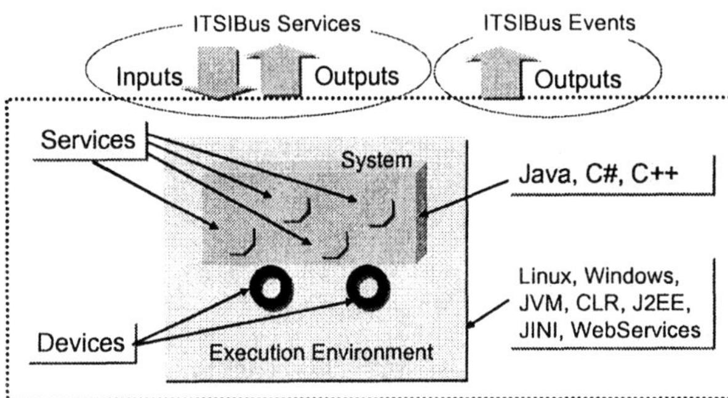

Figure 1 – Basic constructs of the ITSIBus infrastructure

Even if different underlying technologies where evaluated like Web Services and JXTA (Brendon, 2002), the JINI platform was the selected for the first reference implementation of ITSIBus. In fact, the productization process coordinated by Brisa and with the collaboration of WhatEverSoft, a Portuguese software development company, adopted JINI as the underlying technology to develop ITSIBus services. Nevertheless, some of the involved systems were integrated through adapters, i.e., service implementation is in the reality an adapter to establish the connection between ITSIBus infrastructure and the legated roadside system. This happen with the DSRC system already developed by Q-free and Kapsch companies as ITS (Intelligent Transport Systems) technology suppliers. Even if this was a successful strategy, the need for an adapter is a source for entropy mainly as far as evolution is concerned. In fact, the need for adapters is a common strategy to integrate disparate systems but it is also a source of problems. As already discussed, the experience with the added complexity reflected in a low quality of services and high costs of maintenance and evolution justifies the need for a different approach.

Considering that it is not advisable to impose a change in suppliers' technological culture the adopted strategy was to follow a multi-technology approach. The objective is to push for a common agreement at service definition level using standards like WSDL, UML and other more semantic oriented interoperability facilitators, considering the technological heterogeneity as a challenge for the ITSIBus platform. To promote technological interoperability based on multiple technologies the System Broker concept was proposed (Figure 2). The System Broker is a special ITSIBus System dedicated to offer platform level

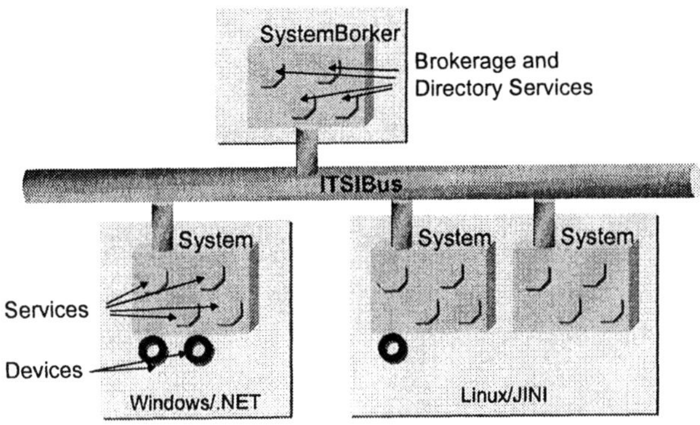

Figure 2 – Multi-technological peer-to-peer service oriented infrastructure

services like the Reggie Service required by JINI to implement system and service discovery and advertise mechanisms. It is assumed that systems developed in different technologies are grounded on the basic TCP/IP network protocols; this is the exclusive mandatory requirement for information exchange between heterogeneous systems. The System Broker is a multi facet system embedding components that know how to talk to services in all the accepted underlying technologies. Internally these components cooperate to dynamically exchange service calls and event routing among the heterogeneous systems/services. A deployed ITSIBus infrastructure must include at least one System Broker, however it can have more than one running, what might contribute to increase availability because the System Broker is a critical point of failure.

When a system is powered-on it registers itself on a System Broker and implicitly all its services are also registered. Depending on the underlying technology of each particular system it is necessary to guarantee the availability of discovery and advertising mechanisms enabling each system and service to known the other ones. As an example, if the underlying technology is JXTA all the Systems/services available in other underlying technologies must be represented by JXTA services embedded on a System Broker. When a JINI service looks for other services, it sees all of them independently of the technology in which they are implemented. When a JINI service accesses a service developed in JXTA the access goes through the System Broker and is the proxy service that bridges the call and replies to the JINI client service.

A first prototype involving services developed exclusively in JINI and implementing a System Broker is already implemented. To demonstrate the System Broker strategy a first prototype integrating ITSIBus services on JINI and services on .NET is being implemented. The selected scenario for this challenge is the ETOLL lane payment system based on a semi-automatic toll payment mechanism. In the next chapter, some details about ETOLL developments are presented.

3. THE ETOLL SYSTEM AND SERVICES EXAMPLE

The ETOLL system is another example of roadside equipment playing a tollbooth role without a person operating the tool payment. An existing system developed by Brisa initially implemented in C++ was the starting point. Considering the interest of its developing company, the evolution of this system was considered to plug to the ITSIBus resorting to the .NET technology rather then JINI. The decision taken was based on the existing ground culture within the company.

The ETOLL system incorporates a LMS system with a lane coordination service. This service manages other systems like DSRC, AVDC, LIT and a gate, responsible to interact with toll users (Figure 3). When using this kind of lane the driver selects the payment using a payment card through the LIT system or else using money (coins or paper) and in this case, the money input/change system is used. This type of lane includes also a gate to be opened when the payment succeeds, also implemented through a specialized service.

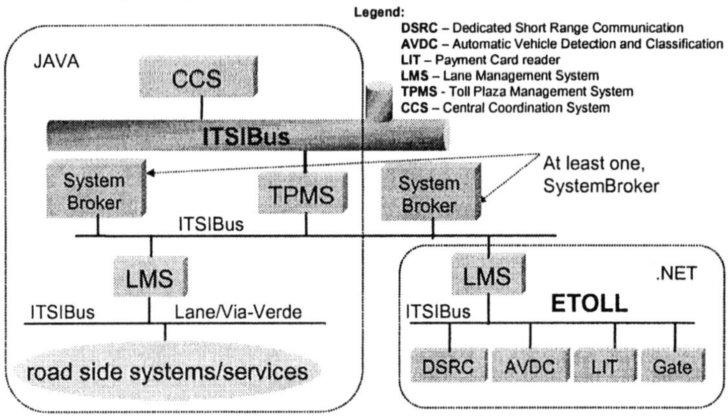

Figure 3 – Architecture of the toll technological infrastructure

What is important to the proposed discussion in this paper is not if the ETOLL subsystem follows the ITSIBus architecture but rather its integration to the toll management infrastructure. In fact, the prototype under development is considering the implementation of the ETOLL system following the ITSIBus architecture bound to the .NET technology suit. However, what is important is to promote interoperability according the adopted system/service granularity. In the case of the ETOLL system, the plugability is discussed at LMS level, i.e., the ETOLL system is a closed system (on .NET) that will integrate to TPMS and the other LMS systems developed on JINI.

All the systems/services are registered on a System Broker. The directory service needed to embed into System Broker depends on the adopted underlying technology. If the JINI platform is the adopted technology, the *Reggie* service needs to be running for services to be registered and discovered. The System Broker creates proxy services for each relation between services on different technologies. By now, only two underlying technologies were evaluated. When more than one underlying technology is considered the proxy needs to know how to bridge among different technologies. If JINI, .NET and JXTA are adopted a proxy service on a System Broker must route calls from any technology to implementations in any other technology (Xu, 2004). This is an open question under evaluation considering not only latency introduced by proxies but also dynamic adaptability to service definition changes. In order to facilitate developments on ITSIBus framework a set of tools based on Eclipse platform (Gallardo, 2003) are being developed. In (Figure 4) a partial view of the developed wizards to conduct developer on ITSIBus code generation is shown.

The first version of an ITSIBus tool suite (ITSIBus workshop) considers a guided (automatic) generation of Systems, Services and a Client application. The concept of client application was introduced to make developments easier by facilitate tests and debugging.

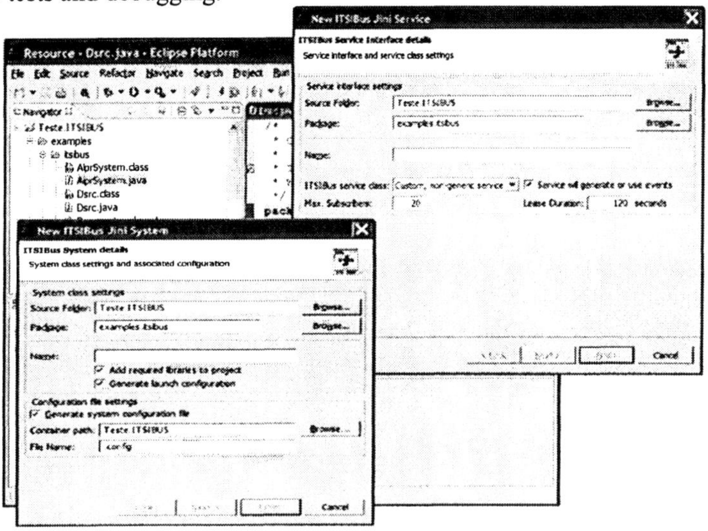

Figure 4 – Partial view of the ITSIBus Eclipse based development framework

The main objective of our research strategy is to contribute to reduce complexity when integrating systems based on different underlying technologies. Even if some technologies are being considered as a way to plug disparate systems like what is happening with Web Services, there is a generalized consensus that evolution will not happen under technology uniformity. Some specific requirements like those related with real-time systems, the reutilization of acquired knowledge and experience, cultural factors and other aspects, are some of the motivation contributing to accept the diversity of technologies beyond methodologies and tools. In fact the diversity contributes to an increased competition and to speed-up innovation processes. Therefore, systems evolution associated to an increased holistic approach are better supported by a multi-technology approach.

Considering enterprise collaborative challenges, it is mandatory to create such integrated systems at enterprise level in order to be prepared to collaborate on a service based considering process oriented transactions and not the already most used, file based collaboration.

4. CONCLUSIONS

The collaborative enterprise in the ICT era needs to achieve an added agility to cope with the dynamics of the collaborative processes. The ITSIBus technological infrastructure and the associated framework is a contribution towards a toll management system based on peer services. The services run on systems (as execution containers) connected on a plug-and-play basis. Furthermore, systems can be implemented on different technologies promoting this way an evolutionary strategy founded not only on existing knowledge but also on technology evolution (and competition). It is a reality that the standards and open reference implementations are facilitating the development of complex system by making easier the integration of heterogeneous components. Nevertheless, the adopted multi-technology strategy makes possible the inclusion of systems developed in different technologies increasing the systems integration potential. Furthermore, the ITSIBus specification is an open specification and there is a plan to transform the reference implementation in an open source initiative aiming to promote ITSIBus adoption by the ITS ICT industry.

The development of a framework where repetitive and complex tasks are automated through wizards helps the adoption of ITSIBus by ITS systems suppliers. The adoption of Eclipse follows a crescent consensus around the need for a common development platform extensible and used along the technological systems life cycle. The available tools present uniform concepts along the conception, design, development, deployment and operation cycles what might help to get a holistic perspective of enterprise ICT systems. This enterprise consistency is a key step for companies to get involved in collaborative networks on a wide service based collaborative infrastructure.

Acknowledgements. This work was partially supported by BRISA group, through the research and development ITSIBus project. The research groups GIATSI from ISEL-DEETC in collaboration with DIT, the Innovation and Technology Department of BRISA are developing the work. We also acknowledge the valuable contributions from Filipe Braz, Bruno Basílio, Joaquim Pereira, Rui Gonçalves and Rui Lopes. We also thank the valuable contributions from the WhatEverSoft team coordinated by José Rui Soares.

5. REFERENCES

Allard, J.; Chinta, V.; Gundala, S.; Richard, G.G., III - Jini meets UPnP: an architecture for Jini/UPnP interoperability, Applications and the Internet, 2003. Proceedings. Symposium on , 27-31 Jan.03.

Brendon, J. Wilson – JXTA, New Riders Publishing; ISBN: 0735712344, 1st edition, June 15, 2002.

Camarinha-Matos, L. M. - Infrastructures for virtual organizations – where we are, in Proceedings of ETFA'03 – 9th Int. Conf. On Emerging Technologies and Factory Automation, ISBN 0-7803-7937-3, pp 405-414, Lisboa, Portugal, 16-19 Sept 2003.

Camarinha-Matos, L.M.; Afsarmanesh, H. - The PRODNET architecture, , Proceedings of PRO-VE'99 - IFIP Int. Conf. on Infrastructures for Virtual Enterprises (L.M. Camarinha-Matos, H. Afsarmanesh– Eds.), Kluwer Academic Publishers, ISBN 0-7923-8639-6, pp. 109-126, Oct 99, Porto, Portugal.

Flenner, Robert - Jini and Javaspaces Application Development, Sams book Edition, 2002.

Gallardo, David; Burnette, Ed - Eclipse in Action: A Guide for the Java Developer, by, Robert McGovern, Manning Publications, ISBN: 1930110960, May 15, 2003.

Grabowski, C.; Bjerring, L.; Peykarimah, S.; Sorensen, L.B.; Bracht, R.; O'Hara, J.; Wade, V.P.; Karp, H. - Integration architecture of multi-technology management systems, Integrated Network Management, 1999. Distributed Management for the Networked Millennium. Proceedings of the Sixth IFIP/IEEE International Symposium on , 24-28 May 1999.

Osório A. L., Abrantes A. J., Gonçalves J. C., Araújo A.; Miguel J. M., Jacquet, G. C.; Gomes, J. S. - Flexible and Plugged Peer Systems Integration to ITS-IBUS: the case of EFC and LPR Systems, PROVE'03 – 4th IFIP Working Conference on Virtual Enterprises, published by Kluwer Academic Publishers, ISBN: 1-4020-7638-X, pages 221-230, 2003-b.

Osório, A. Luís; Barata, M. Martins; Abrantes, A. Joaquim; Gomes, J. Sales; Jacquet, G. Costa - Underlying ITS Business Processes with Flexible and Plugged Peer Systems: the Open ITS IBus approach, PROVE'03 – 4th IFIP Working Conference on Virtual Enterprises, published by Kluwer Academic Publishers, ISBN: 1-4020-7638-X, pages 221-230, 2003-a.

Osório, A. Luís; Osório; L., Barata, M.; Gonçalves, C.; Araújo, P.; Abrantes, A.; Jorge, P.; Gomes, J. Sales; Jacquet G.; Amador, A. - Interoperability among ITS Systems with ITS-IBus framework, BASYS 2004, Vienna, Austria 27-29 September 2004.

Rammer, Ingo; Szpuszta, Mario - Advanced .NET Remoting– Apress Editions, ISBN: 1590594177, 2005.

Xu, Jiangyun; Du, Weichang - Software brokers for quality of services in service-oriented distributed systems, Communication Networks and Services Research, 2004. Proceedings Second Annual Conference on, 19-21 May 2004.

47

ENHANCING SUPPLY CHAIN CO-ORDINATION BY MEANS OF A COLLABORATIVE PLATFORM BASED ON SERVICE ORIENTED ARCHITECTURE

Rubén Darío Franco, Angel Ortiz Bas, Rosa Navarro
Research Centre on Production Management and Engineering
Polytechnic University of Valencia
Camí de Vera S/N. Building 7D
Tel. (+34) 96.387.96.80/Fax: (+34) 96.387.76.89
{dfranco| aortiz_|_ronava}@cigip.upv.es

Every new technology promises to solve a lot of problems inside and between companies and, consequently, achieve unforeseen performance improvements. Nowadays, Service-Oriented Architectures begin to be promoted as a new field where companies may realize their visions and put all their new strategies in practice.
Although they initially were focused on intra-organizational integration efforts, now they begin to be used for inter-organizational business processes engineering support in networked organizations. But, when implementing these kinds of initiatives, successful histories are mostly linked to major companies, with considerable budgets allocated to the project.
By counterpart, the INPREX project (Spanish acronym for Interoperability in Extended Processes), here presented, falls out this category. By contrast, this is an undergoing initiative leaded by a Small and Medium Enterprise (SME) and founded by a local government in Spain. In this work, we will present main project's achievements where the IDIERE Platform is used to improve the co-ordination in a Networked Organization scenario. Five SMEs are involved in a project which main objective is to deploy a low cost and scalable platform that allows them to improve a Collaborative Production Planning business process.

1. MOTIVATION

Supply Chains (SC) are a very complex type of Collaborative Networked Organization (CNO, [2, 13]) established to transform raw materials into finished products that consumers are willing to buy [16]. Players involved exchange mainly two complementary flows within this network: material and information. The flow of information is used to signal the flow of material. For example, suppliers notify that requested parts are already in transit by sending some electronic communication to the Original Equipment Manufacturer (known as Advanced Shipping Notice).

How well managed such information flows are, along the whole supply chain, may restrict the overall performance. Poorly managed or distorted information may cause, for instance, poor inventory and production practices [1].

Several organizational models apply when dealing with this environment. Initially, Extended Enterprises [13] was used when a dominant player extended its boundaries for its operations.

In this context, it's very important to take into account that electronically supported networks, usually may present some relevant features that may affect the information sharing practices:

- Heterogeneity: Inside a SC, it's possible to find a set of legacy (or usually, proprietary) systems which are heterogeneous and not designed to be interactive. They are usually implemented using different technology, different languages and for different operating platforms.
- Scalability: Companies (or SC Players) usually must be able to integrate their new applications into the distributed system without affecting the other components of the system
- Adaptability: The interactions between players need to be changed as needed. Infrastructures and systems should be flexible and easy to accommodate to new requirements.
- Autonomy: Companies have their own IT/IS policies and must keep them besides well-established relationships. In most of cases, companies get involved in several supply chains (or clients) and additional efforts for information exchange practices are needed in each case.

In this work, we will present a case study that has been carried out under the INPREX Project (Spanish acronym for Interoperability in Extended Processes) and where a collaborative technological platform based on Service Oriented Architectures foundations has been used to enhance the co-operation when Collaborative Production Planning capabilities are required in a Supply Chain.

The paper is structured as follows: Section 2, introduces different models that historically have been used to solve this problem inside Networked Organizations; Section 3 is devoted to briefly show how Service Oriented Architectures are well positioned to automate the information sharing process and consequently reach inter-organizational business processes automation. Section 4, depicts the IDIERE platform main concepts which have been used to conduct the business case presented on Section 5. Finally, Section 6 states some conclusions of our work.

2. SERVICE ORIENTED ARCHITECTURES FOR INFORMATION SHARING AND INTER-ORGANIZATIONAL BUSINESS PROCESS INTEGRATION

It's argued that a Service Oriented Architecture (SOA) is many things [5]. Mainly, it can be conceived as a technological enabler or as a building block for new collaborative models.

Positioning companies under this paradigm implies not only adopting XML and web services related standards for process co-ordination [8] but also creating a new way of thinking about how information and knowledge must flow inside these breeding environments [2]. From this combined approach, it's possible to consider that SOA may be useful for enhancing Supply Chain co-ordination when engineering and deploying distributed business process, due these major reasons:

- The capability of closing the gap existing between the modelling and the operational phases of the business process engineering, because we are able of modelling them with Business Process Modelling Notation (BPMN), for instance, and getting one executable version of the process by using BPEL4WS.
- The emerging web-services technologies allow different levels of abstraction for business processes modelling and representation. Then, any CNO member in charge of executing some assigned activity of the process may locally explode it (preserving the public interface) by using their own BPEL4WS model as well.
- Also, always that one activity interface is preserved executors can be switched [12] depending on conditions under which process/criteria to be met.

Additionally, a complementary concept needs to be introduced here. According to Kraft (2002) web services concept must be refined by extending it in order to consider it as an object web service. An object web service has a set of methods that can be accessed by their interfaces (object oriented programming analogy).

3. A SERVICE ORIENTED PLATFORM FOR BUSINESS PROCESS MANAGEMENT

The INPREX project looks for innovative methods and tools for supporting whole business process life cycle. By doing so, a collaborative platform is being developed in order to achieve this goal.

Based on SOA principles, BPM and Web Service Objects the IDIERE Architecture has been defined as follows [7], in order to achieve Machine to Machine Automation of distributed business processes (see Section 2):

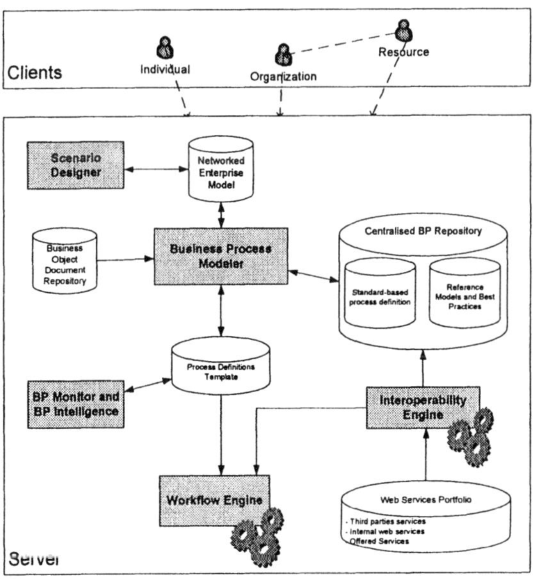

Figure 1 - The IDIERE Architecture

Although the system supports distributed business process enactment, the IDIERE Platform isn't P2P oriented. Instead of this, it is composed of two major components: a central server which stores process definitions and orchestrate activities execution and a set of clients which assume different roles along process life cycle.

More precisely, inside the platform it's possible to identify:

- The IDIERE Server: it supports two major phases: process engineering and execution. It allows defining collaborative business processes structure, storing them in a common repository, registering executors, assigning execution method and executors to individual activities or sub processes, monitoring delegated activities, deploying a set of indicators for performance measurement.
- Client-side: in terms of users, there would be a set of nodes which may be connected to the platform in order to notify each assignment status. Each node represents the instantiation of one executor for each process instance. Correspondingly, each deployed thin client, will act as Task Manager for the system (in workflow sense) but having some extended functionality.

Distributed business process may be conceived as a set of activities which are assigned to different roles to be accomplished. When modelling this kind of processes, is not always possible to keep the same abstraction level for each activity.

In fact, it depends on how much detail can be gathered. More, initial steps in process modelling always begin with a more or less clear picture but without so much detail.

Then, we prefer to define these related concepts:

*"**D1:** an Execution Unit is a work package that may be composed of a single activity or a whole process and that could be assigned to some executors which have the proper knowledge and capacity to accomplish the task"*

From the Information Management perspective, the execution unit can be seen as a computational function *ws* which maps some Data Inputs into Data Outputs trough some internal logic not accessible by others (in a black box way).

This led us to the concept of service and service provider. If each execution unit is wrapped under some interface that can be located and consumed by third parties, it is possible to consider it as a ***service*** that may be provided by some ***service provider***.

Then, service providers or **executors** can be defined as follows:

***D2:** executors are those service providers (organizations or their resources) that are capable of accomplish some execution unit for the global process by providing and consuming third-parties services.*

And relaying on SOA principles, it could be convenient to add:

"...by means of web services interface definitions and a supporting data model."

Then, **executors** have the following structure:

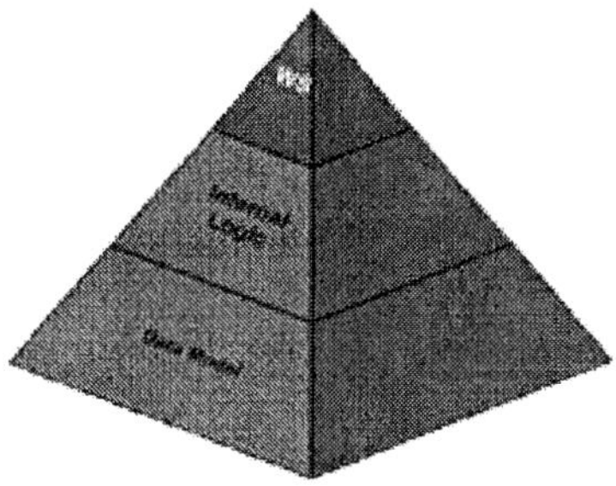

Figure 2 – Executor's architecture

Then, the IDIERE execution model is based on the orchestration of execution units' accomplishment that has been previously assigned to executors.

5. CASE STUDY

5.1 Business scenario

The SME is a first-tier supplier (design, procurement, production and hand-over), for a number of world-class manufacturers of the automobile industry.

The company's principal line of production consists of metal reinforcements for the main panels of a vast variety of cars of the above mentioned manufacturers, spare-wheel and their corresponding retainer, engine mountings, pedals, supports for the rear seats, and separate compartments, as well as other parts of the body.

Thus the SME becomes a Full Service Supplier (and high level sub-assembly supplier) for the Original Equipment Manufacturer (OEM) meaning that the company is a 1st-tier supplier that is responsible for its own logistics and independently chooses its own suppliers (2nd-tiers), the components of its products, etc.

The Supply Chain, as it is now, has a relatively low degree of synchronization and collaboration. Generally, although the production plans of the company that is directly connected with the demand are those who launch the supply chain's production, certain information that needs to be drawn upstream is held up and sequentially the cycles of planning and production decrease, and therefore the delivery time of the final item is significantly affected.

Currently, this information flow is relatively restricted. The SME receives OEM's demand planning and makes its production plans and attendant orders to 2nd-tiers according to it. But when small- scale changes and variation in demand coming from the OEM arrive, SME's production plans and order needs change, but the sub-tiers are not informed on time and thus do not have the time they may need to change their own planning, if this is possible.

This lack of collaboration (either for synchronization or visibility) results in a great number of problems arising from the uncertainty of information, whose impact is reflected throughout the supply chain.

5.2 Proposed solution

The networked enterprise involved in the solution directly includes the stamping firm (SME) and four more companies in the same scenario: a subsidiary stamping plant, a painting firm, a welding subcontractor and a second welding and assembly subcontractor. We have applied the IDIERE platform principles in order to achieve a successful reengineering of the Production Planning Process (PPP).
Inside this process, three kinds of executors were identified (see Fig 3):

1. Productive: they transform some inputs (raw material or components) into out-puts (components) by performing of some activity (stamping, painting, welding or similar).
2. Transport: it moves containers between productive executors.
3. Warehouse: they stores finished or semi-finished goods

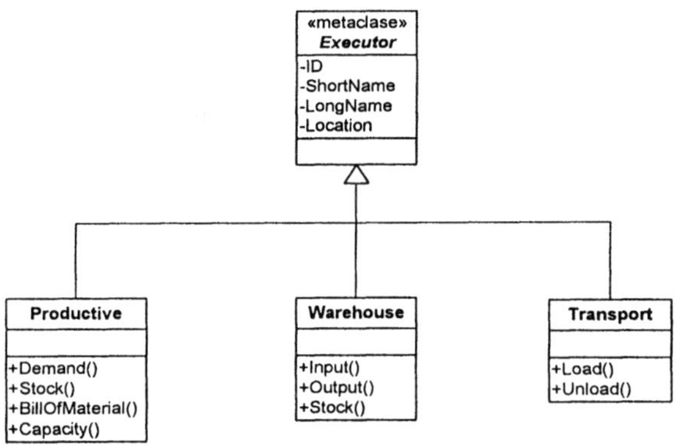

Figure 3 - Organizational resources have been modeled as executors

Once executors have been modelled, supporting services were developed for each kind of executor. Then, there is a set of services belonging to each one of them. For instance, productive executors are able of notify stocks, capacities, enact their Bill of Material, receive demand, put orders and so on.

Table 1 – Supported services (illustrative purposes only)

Executor	ServiceName	Description
Productive	NotifyDemand()	It allows to know which is the demand for some reference during the next days
	NotifyStock()	It returns stock of some reference
	BillOfMaterial()	It returns those references which compose other one
	Capacity()	Notify agreed capacity about some reference based on signed contracts
Warehouse	Input()	Register receptions of material
	Output()	Register material consuptions
	Stock()	Notify availability

After that, we modelled the production process of each reference (almost ninety) as a business process within which each activity (stamping, welding, and painting) is associated with the corresponding executor and its services by means of a contract that includes references, capacities, shipping units, etc. (see Fig. 4).

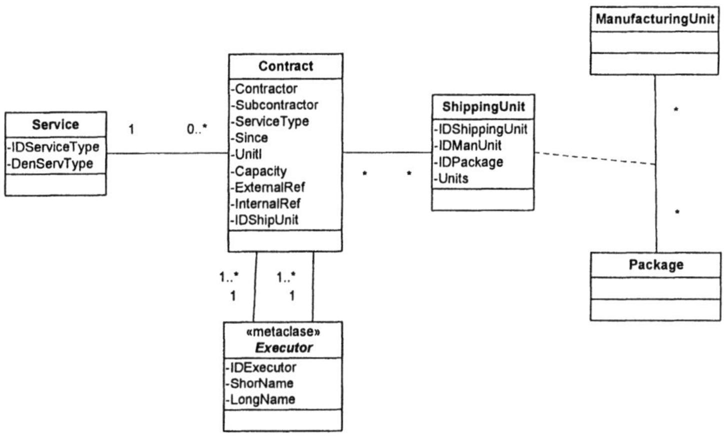

Figure 4 - Contracts establishes services to be provided between executors

Manufacturing some reference can be seen as an orchestration of those services that must be provided by all involved executors of the process. By establishing P2P contracts (or Service Level Agreements) it's possible to define the path from raw material to finished product (and consequently, the Bill of Material).

Once execution units and executors to accomplish them have been defined, an additional module that uses such capabilities and definitions has been developed: a *collaborative planner* which, based on process definitions and executors' services, allows checking SME's plans feasibility and needs.

6. CONCLUSIONS

In this work, we have tried to depict how Supply Chains are facing new challenges in reconfiguring themselves when looking for flexibility and adaptability.

The right way seems to be information sharing policies shifting by providing interoperability mechanisms that automate the information retrieval and sharing practices. By counterparts, Internet is fuelling Service Oriented Architectures deployment by supporting them not only as a new technology but also as a new way of business thinking.

We have tried to show how, by using SOA principles, manufacturing practices can be improved in a Supply Chain. We have created two building blocks, execution units and executors, which allow us to model a process as an orchestration of web services invocations.

The case presented here is a small example that shows how small and medium enterprises may also embrace this technology in order to improve the co-operation inside the network.

Acknowledgments

The INPREX (Interoperability in Extended Processes) project is an undergoing project founded by the Spanish government by means of its Office for Science and Technology.

6. REFERENCES

1. Brynjolfsson, E. and Smith, M. (2000) "Frictionless Commerce? A Comparison of Internet and Conventional Retailers". Management Science, April 2000 (volume 46, number 4), pages 563-585.

2. Camarinha-Matos, L. and Afsarmanesh, H. (2001). Dynamic Virtual Organizations, or Not So Dynamic? BASYS Proceedings pp 111-124

3. Camarinha Matos, L. and Afsarmanesh, H. (2004). "The Emerging Discipline of Collaborative Networks". In Virtual Enterprises and Collaborative Networks. Kluwer Academic Publishers. PRO-VE'04 Proceedings

4. Clarke, R. (2004). "Open source software and open content as models for eBusiness" Presented at 17th International eCommerce Conference, Slovenia, June 2004.

5. Erl, T. (2004). Service Oriented Architecrures: A Field Guide. Prentice Hall Ed. New Jersey

6. Fingar, P. and Smith, H. (2003). Business Process Management: The third wave. Meghan-Kiffer Press, Tampa, Florida

7. Franco, D., Ortiz Bas, A. and Anaya, V. "An Architecture for Managing Distributed Business Processes in Networked Organizations". International Workshop on Enterprise Integration, Interoperability and Networking (EI2N'2005). Proceedings to be published.

8. Hagel, J. and Brown, J.S. (2002). Orchestrating Business Processes – Harnessing the value of web services technology. Working Paper available at www.johnhagel.com

9. Handfield, R. and Nichols, E. (2002). Supply Chain Redesign. Transforming Value Chains into Integrated Value Systems. Ed. Prentice Hall. New Jersey.

10. Kraft, R. (2002). A Model for Network Services on the Web. International Conference on Internet Computing 2002: 536-541

11. Linthicum, D. (2004). Next generation application integration: from simple information to web services. Addison-Wesley Information Technology Series.

12. Mowshowitz, A. (1999). 'The switching principle in virtual organization', Virtual Organization Net eJOV, vol. 1, no. 1, pp. 6-17

13. Ortiz, A., Franco R.D. y Alba, M. "V-CHAIN: Migrating from Extended to Virtual Enterprise within an Automotive Supply Chain". PROVE'03 Proceedings. Processes and Foundations for Virtual Organizations.

14. Rappa M. (2003) 'Business Models on the Web', accessed on January, 2004 at http://digitalenterprise.org/models/models.html

15. Rust, R.T. and Kannan, P.K. (2002) E-Service: New Directions in Theory and Practice. ME Sharpe, Armonk, New York.

16. Shapiro, J. (2001). Modeling Supply Chain. Duxbury Press, 2001.

48 E-SERVICES INTEROPERABILITY ANALYSIS AND ROADMAP ACTIONS

Aphrodite Tsalgatidou, Eleni Koutrouli
Department of Informatics & Telecommunications, National & Kapodistrian University of Athens, Greece
{atsalga, ekou}@di.uoa.gr

e-Services are the building blocks for loosely-coupled, distributed applications based on the Service Oriented Architecture's principles. One of the major benefits they offer is interoperability both between components of Service Oriented systems and between different systems. Still, the variety and diversity of implementations and interpretations of SOA and the vast amount of emerging standards hinder interoperability. This paper examines the interoperability requirements and related issues for each one of the major e-Services categories: Web, Grid and P2P services. Our aim is to provide the basis for a roadmap towards improving interoperability of e-Services which will enable the successful formation of service-based distributed applications.

1. INTRODUCTION

Service Oriented Computing has revolutionized the way Information Technology is structured and has stimulated great expectation among the developers community. Service Oriented Architectures (SOA) emerged with the promise to support the loose coupling of system parts in a far better way than existing technologies and provide agility, flexibility and cost savings via reusability, efficiency and interoperability both between components of Service Oriented systems and between different systems.

However, the lack of agreement on what constitutes a SOA and the vast amount of emerging standards makes it difficult to understand and utilize the potentials of e-Services technologies. In this context, interoperability, which is one of the basic characteristics and benefits of SOA, needs to be further explored in order to find out the open issues and best practices.

In this paper we present the interoperability requirements and related issues in the e-Service area, considering interoperability both in terms of intra- and inter-paradigm integration. Our goal is to pinpoint the challenges and provide a roadmap of best practices for interoperability.

The rest of the paper is organised as follows: In section 2 we examine the major trends in Service Oriented technology which lie in the areas of Web, P2P and Grid services, with a focus on the standardization efforts in each area. We also provide the interoperability issues in each one of the three areas, synergies and integration efforts, and we present roadmap actions for intra- and inter- paradigm interoperability. In section 3 we provide our concluding remarks and a summary of the main interoperability issues, the current approaches and trends towards interoperability as well as roadmap actions for interoperability in a table that provides a general interoperability overview for the three areas of e-Services.

2. E-SERVICES AND INTEROPERABILITY

According to W3C (W3C, 2005), a Service Oriented Architecture (SOA) specifies a set of components whose interfaces can be described, published, discovered and invoked over a network. SOA is characterized by three basic service operations: publishing, discovery and invoking. Value added operations like composition and management can also be provided. Web Services (WS), Grid and P2P Services adhere to the SOA model and are all known as e-Services.

In the e-Services domain we view interoperability as the ability of systems, applications and services, to communicate, exchange data and files, work together or operate on behalf of one another. Standardization is one of the basic ways to achieve e-Services interoperability, therefore, in the following we briefly describe the three e-Services categories with a focus on standardization efforts in each area.

"A Web Service is a software application identified by a URI, whose interfaces and binding are capable of being defined, described, and discovered by XML artifacts, and supports direct interactions with other software applications using XML-based messages via Internet-based protocols" (W3C, 2002). What makes the Web Service vision attractive is the ability to discover the Web Services that fulfill users' needs, negotiate service contracts and have the services delivered where and when the users need them (Tsalgatidou, 2002). We are currently witnessing the rapid development and maturation of a stack of interrelated standards that are defining the Web Service infrastructure along with a great number of development tools that support the Web Service development. The key standards for describing, advertising, discovering and binding WSs are WSDL (WSDL, 2001) UDDI (UDDI, 2005) and SOAP (SOAP, 2001). Besides, there are ongoing standardization efforts in WS composition, orchestration, choreography, security and management, e.g. BPEL4WS (BPEL4WS, 2005), ebXML (ebXML, 2005), WS-Security (WS-Security, 2002), etc. An overview of the various WS standards that compose the current WS protocol stack, along with details regarding their standardization status can be found in (Wilkes, 2005).

The term Grid refers to "a system that is concerned with the integration, virtualization, and management of services and resources in a distributed, heterogeneous environment that supports collections of users and resources (virtual organizations) across traditional administrative and organizational domains (real organizations)" (OGSA Glossary, 2005). Significant effort led by the Global Grid Forum (GGF, 2005) has been channelled toward the standardization of protocols and interfaces. Such en effort is the Open Grid Services Architecture Grid Architecture (OGSA) (Foster, 2002) which integrates Grid and Web Services. OGSA was initially materialized by the Open Grid Services Infrastructure (OGSI) (OGSI, 2003), and more recently by the Web Services Resource Framework (WSRF) proposal (WSRF, 2004) which together with Web Services Notification specification (WS-Notification, 2004) have been submitted to OASIS (OASIS, 2005) for standardization. Many Grid communities use the open source Globus

Toolkit (Globus, 2005)(Foster, 1999) as a technology base. Currently, the efforts of the major industry players are also targeted to the support of Globus.

The term "Peer-to-Peer" (P2P) refers to a class of systems and applications that takes advantage of resources – storage, cycles, content, human presence – available at the edges of the Internet. P2P systems cover a large spectrum of application domains such as distributed computing, file sharing, collaboration, and platforms. Standards for P2P technologies have not yet been established. Efforts for defining specifications are made by the P2P Working Group (P2PWG, 2005) whereas two standardization initiatives relevant to P2P networking are Jabber (Jabber, 2002) and JXTA (JXTA, 2005). Jabber is an XML protocol for instant messaging applications that is currently being standardized under IETF (IETF, 2005). JXTA is an open-source framework for P2P systems, initiated by SUN that supports only a minimal underlying architecture as a base.

2.1 Intra-Paradigm Interoperability Roadmap

In each e-Service category interoperability has specific context. In the following we identify the specific requirements for interoperability in the areas of Web, Grid and P2P services and present the ways these interoperability concerns are being addressed by each category of e-Services. We also propose roadmap actions for intra-paradigm interoperability. Furthermore, we present synergies between different kinds of e-Services which also promote Service Oriented systems interoperability and present roadmap actions for inter- paradigm interoperability.

Web Services Interoperability

Web Services promise universal interoperability and integration by establishing commonly agreed protocols for mutually understanding what a service offers and for delivering this functionality in an implementation independent way. Interoperability of legacy applications is also enabled by allowing legacy applications to be exposed as WSs and, thus, facilitating a seamless integration between heterogeneous systems. Furthermore, new services can be created and dynamically published and discovered without disrupting the existing environment. Thus, WS technology provides a standard means of interoperating between different software applications, running on a variety of platforms and/or frameworks.

The issue of WS interoperability is addressed at a *conceptual level* by the W3C's Web Services Architecture (WSA) document (Booth, 2004), which identifies those global elements of the global Web Services network that are required in order to ensure interoperability between Web Services. The various WS standards and enabling technologies address *technical level* interoperability.

The common standards for the basic WS activities *description, publication* and *invocation* (WSDL, UDDI, SOAP) have effectively become de facto standards, and, thus, support basic technical interoperability. However, there is a need for enhanced interoperability both for basic WS activities, like *description*, as well as value added ones, like WS *management* and *composition* and also for non functional aspects like *security*. In the following, we describe the interoperability requirements concerning the aforementioned aspects.

Web Services *description* languages should support, beyond the functional characteristics of WSs, the description of semantic information that will enable the proper and meaningful interoperation between different WSs or applications. Semantic description is not supported by WSDL and is partially addressed by ebXML. WS description semantics can be offered by standardized ontology languages, such as OWL (OWL, 2004) and OWL-S (OWL-S, 2004), and a richer model of services, which incorporate ontologies of action to identify the effects of actions and concepts such as contracts, institutions, roles and regulations (Booth, 2004).

Web Service *management* which refers to monitoring, controlling, and reporting of WS qualities and WS usage, also requires semantics, management policies and management capabilities, which should be understood by the requester and provider entities (Booth, 2004).

In order to improve the *security* and *reliability* of WSs and to address more complex business scenarios that require WSs composition, a wide range of protocols have been proposed, the most prominent of which is BPEL4WS (BPEL4WS, 2004) while others like WS-Choreography (WS-Choreography, 2002) haven't completed yet the standardization process. Furthermore, different sets of vendors have been producing competing specifications in similar areas (e.g. WS-Coordination (WS-Coordination, 2004) and WS-CF (WS-CF, 2003)) making it difficult for widely accepted standards to emerge even where there is a clear need for standardization (e.g., *security*). Thus, developers can either build up services that do not use such capabilities or develop ad-hoc solutions that may lead to interoperability problems.

Enhancing interoperability between different implementations of WS technologies is the goal of the Web Services Interoperability (WS-I) organization (WS-I, 2005), which produces documents, like the WS-I Basic Profile and WS-I basic security profile that define how existing, stable and widely accepted WS standards should be used.

In order to address the aforementioned interoperability issues, we propose the following roadmap actions: (Similar work can be found in (Wilkes, 2005).)

1. Monitor progress of protocols through key standards bodies
2. Establish policy for compliance with standards
3. Use WS-I profiles wherever relevant. Create local profiles only where necessary, and plan to upgrade to WS-I as they are published
4. Coordinate use of protocols to ensure consistent implementation of versions and profiles. Publish best practices
5. Use ontologies and ontology languages, e.g. OWL, for provision of semantics concerning WSs activities, e.g. WS description and WS management
6. Use implementations of standards that have proven interoperability
7. Wherever possible wait for implementation of protocols in products
8. Keep up with the advancement of standards

Grid Services Interoperability

Grid services interoperability can be viewed along two different dimensions:

- interoperability between distributed resources in a Grid application, and
- interoperability between different Grid applications.

Interoperability between different distributed resources in a Grid application is a main goal of the various Grid projects despite the different infrastructures they use and the different aspects on which they focus. The OGSA/OGSI and WSRF models provide a framework for Service Oriented Grids aiming at supporting interoperability of distributed services and resources. Grid middleware implementations based on these models (e.g. Globus Toolkit (Globus, 2005), IGENE (Furmento, 2004)) provide services such as identification, authentication and authorization and promote interoperability by allowing interoperation of Grid components independently of the operating system and network topology. However, there are interoperability issues when different entities use the Grid for sharing purposes. Efforts are being undertaken to deal with the authorization of a community in a Grid environment like the Community Authorization Service (CAS) of Globus.

Significant effort has also been channelled toward enabling interoperability between different Grid applications. There is a number of different approaches that include the definition of a minimal set of Grid services which enable the interoperation of different Grid applications (Snelling, 2002), the integration of different Grid infrastructures (Wieder, 2002), the common Grid resources description (Brooke, 2003) and the Semantic Grid (Roure, 2005) which aims at providing interoperability across time as well as space both for anticipated and unanticipated reuse of services, information, and knowledge. Furthermore, the Enterprise Grid Alliance (EGA, 2005) has recently released a reference model for enterprise grids, laying the foundation for standardized solutions that will enable cross-departmental and cross-organizational interactions.

The above analysis of Grid services interoperability issues leads to the identification of the following roadmap actions:

1. Monitor progress of protocols through key standards bodies
2. Adapt standards that have gained broad acceptance (e.g. WS+I standards)
3. Conform to a reference model (e.g. EGA's reference model for enterprise grids)
4. Adapt semantic grid services vision
5. Use tools that have gained industry acceptance (e.g. Globus)

P2P Services Interoperability

P2P services interoperability, similarly to Grid Services, can be viewed either as:

- interoperability between different peers in a P2P network, or
- interoperability between different P2P applications.

Interoperability between different peers of P2P systems needs advanced interoperability techniques, since the various member nodes of a P2P network that have variety of operating systems, networking technologies and other platforms in business applications need to communicate, exchange content and aggregate their diverse resources, such as computing power or storage space. Most P2P systems use proprietary implementations and protocols for the peers interoperation and functionality. XML is expected to support peers interoperability in P2P systems, since it can be used for messaging, data storage, application deployment, resource description and distributed search (Buehling, 2001). A uniform resource description is commonly agreed to be a basic requirement that can be addressed by ontologies and standardized ontology languages, e.g. OWL, or local schema mappings (Aberer, 2004) and semantic routing which are the basis of several recent proposals for P2P data management, e.g. the Edutella project (Edutella, 2005) which facilitates the semantic discovery of resources based on RDF (RDF, 2005).

Interoperability between different P2P applications has not been addressed by the early P2P applications, which set up closed peer networks, accessible only to them. A user of a file sharing P2P system like Napster can not send an instant message to a fellow user without launching an Instant Messaging client to do so. Currently, only a few P2P systems are able to interoperate, such as Avaki with Sun's Grid, and Magi with JXTA (Milojicic, 2003). Efforts towards improved interoperability are made by the P2P Working Group (P2PWG, 2005). Early attempts on interoperability include Jabber and Groove Networks (Groove, 2005) which are mainly extensible attempts, and not fully interoperable systems. A common infrastructure that will contain the core services of a P2P application and can be shared by P2P applications, making them easier to develop and deploy, could be a more appropriate approach. Sun Microsystems' JXTA and Microsoft's .Net Framework (Microsoft .Net, 2005) are the most significant efforts to define the core elements of a P2P platform.

Based on the above, we propose the following roadmap actions for P2P services interoperability:

1. Agreement on the use of uniform P2P resources description, e.g. using ontologies, OWL and local schema mappings
2. Agreement on an underlying platform with core P2P elements for building P2P systems
3. Establishment of a collection of P2P standards that could launch P2P as a global way of doing business
4. Use of XML in P2P systems

2.2 Inter-Paradigm Interoperability Roadmap

Integration of heterogeneous e-Services allows the exploitation of the specific characteristics and benefits of each e-Services type by the other types of e-Services and the alleviation of their complexities. In the following we present synergies between Web, Grid and P2P services and propose roadmap actions for inter-paradigm interoperability that could lead to more flexible, efficient and interoperable Service-Oriented systems.

Convergence of Different Types of e-Services

As already discussed, Grid and WS technologies are in a convergence process, led by the OGSA/OGoSI and WSRF proposals. Grid developers can, thus, exploit the experience from the WS community and concentrate on building the higher-level services that are specific to the Grid application domain. There is a need, however, for Web Service specifications that could safely be used for building interoperable Web Service Grids, and for this reason a Web Service specification profile WS-I+ has been proposed in (Atkinson, 2004). Another proposal on how Grid applications could be built using existing WS specifications is found in (Parastatidis, 2005). An example of WSs and Grid services working together is found in the Web Security Services offered by McAffee.com which has implemented a security Grid with millions of sensors using a WS framework (Shread, 2002).

Recently we are watching a strong movement towards WSs and P2P services working in conjunction. Synergies between WS and P2P services include:

- WS or Semantic WS discovery using a P2P-based approach (Laoveerakul, 2001), (Thaden, 2003), (Schlosser, 2002), (Banaei-Kashani, 2004)
- Peer discovery in P2P systems using WS as registries (Prasad, 2003)
- WSs interconnection in heterogeneous networks (Schattkowsky, 2004)
- Search engines, such as Google, based on P2P and WSs (Bhusate, 2003)
- JXTA projects that incorporate WSs, e.g. Chinook (Chinook, 2005)

The technologies enabling this convergence are some of the leading P2P protocols such as Jabber and JXTA, whereas Microsoft .NET Framework provides a rich platform for building P2P applications and Intel is building P2P components and services on top of Microsoft's .NET platform (Intel Press Releases, 2001).

The techniques that the P2P and Grid models use to handle some of the main issues of distributing computing are discussed in (Talia, 2003) in order to find a common foundation that could alleviate the complexities of each other and fulfill the need for secure, scalable and decentralized collaboration. Another approach to combining aspects of Grid computing with P2P architectures is found in the proposal for a new architecture stack for Grids presented in the Next Generation Grids second Group´s report (NGG2, 2004).

The confluence of Web, P2P and Grid services provides the foundation for a common model —allowing applications to scale from proximity ad hoc networks to worldwide-scale distributed systems. Some approaches and research projects have started to appear towards supporting this convergence and reusability of the three categories of e-Services by providing appropriate models and platforms, e.g. for unified service discovery and composition (SODIUM, 2004) and Internet Distributed Computing (Milenkovic, 2003).

Based on the above, we propose the following roadmap actions for inter-paradigm interoperability:

1 Monitor progress of protocols in the e-Service area
2 Monitor integration efforts
3 Adapt interoperable protocols for synergies between different kinds of e-Services, e.g. JXTA and WS standards
4 Adapt integration paradigms between different e-Services to alleviate the complexities of each other

3. CONCLUDING SUMMARY

The advent of Service Oriented Computing has stimulated great expectation among the developers community. However, the heterogeneity and vast amount of protocols and standards of e-Services, which many times expose overlapping applicability, hinder interoperability which is one of the basic benefits of SOA.

In this paper we investigated the interoperability potential and challenges of Web, P2P and Grid services which are the building blocks of SOA and are known as e-Services. We also presented roadmap actions both for intra- and inter-paradigm interoperability. Our observations are summarized in Table 1.

We believe that the work presented in this paper and the suggested roadmap actions can enhance interoperability in the e-Services area and help developers to take advantage of the full potential and promised benefits of Service Oriented development.

Table 1. Interoperability approaches and roadmap actions for e-Services

		Web Services	P2P services	Grid services
Standardization Efforts	**Common Architecture**	Web Services Architecture (W3C)	Proposed architecture: JXTA	OGSA, EGA's Reference Model for enterprise grids
Standardization Efforts	**Standards for basic activities (description, publishing, invocation)**	WSDL / UDDI / SOAP initiative, ebXML	Standardization efforts: JXTA, Jabber for instant messaging systems, P2Pwg	OGSA/OGSI and WSRF models, no standardised Grid middleware implementations
Standardization Efforts	**Standards for value added activities**	Many standardization efforts (BPEL4WS, WS-security) but a few mature standards	No standards	OGSA security architectural components, no completely standardised implementations
Standardization Efforts	**Semantics support for basic and value-added activities**	Partially addressed (e.g. ebXML)	New approaches: Semantic routing (e.g. RDF-based routing algorithms, etc.)	Partially addressed-Semantic Grid vision
Other approaches & Roadmap Actions	**Approaches to intra-paradigm Inter/ty**	WS-I and WS-I+ profiles, integration of different standards (e.g. SOAP & ebXML)	Most different P2P systems do not interoperate, exceptions: Jabber with other IM systems, Magi with JXTA, different JXTA -built systems	Need for interoperability between different infrastructures, Grids middleware enable grid resources interoperability
Other approaches & Roadmap Actions	**Intra-paradigm Inter/ty Roadmap Actions**	1. Monitor progress of protocols 2. Establish policy for compliance with standards 3. Use WS-I profiles 4. Use interoperable standards and keep up with the advancement of standards 5. Provide semantics 6. Wherever possible wait for implementation of protocols in products	1. Agree on a uniform P2P resources description, eg. using ontologies, OWL, and local schema mappings 2. Agree on a common platform for building P2P systems 3. Establish a collection of P2P standards 4. Use XML in P2P systems development	1. Monitor progress of protocols 2. Adapt standards that have gained broad acceptance (eg WS+I standards) 3. Adapt semantic Grid Services vision 4. Use tools that have gained industry acceptance (eg. Globus)
Other approaches & Roadmap Actions	**Integration efforts for hetergeneous e-Services**	• P2P based WS discovery • Peer discovery in P2P systems using WS as registries • Search engines built using WS and P2P technology • WS Grids based on specific WS standards (WS-I+ profile) • Grid architecture based on P2P principles • Convergence of e-Services for unified service discovery		
Other approaches & Roadmap Actions	**Inter-paradigm Interop/ty Roadmap Actions**	1. Monitor progress of protocols in each e-Service area 2. Monitor integration efforts 3. Adapt interoperable protocols for synergies between different kinds of e-Services, e.g. JXTA and WS standards 4. Adapt integration paradigms between different e-Services to alleviate the complexities of each other		

4. ACKNOWLEDGEMENT

Part of this work has been supported by the IST Network of Excellence INTEROP (INTEROP, 2005) and the IST Project SODIUM (SODIUM, 2004). The authors would like to thank George Athanasopoulos and Vangelis Floros for their contribution in earlier drafts of this paper.

5. REFERENCES

1. Aberer, K., Cudr'e-Mauroux, P.,Ouksel, A.: Emergent Semantics Principles and Issues, Proc. of 1st Int Conference on Semantics of a Networked World (ICSNW04), Paris, France, 2004
2. Atkinson, M., DeRoure, D., Dunlop, A., Fox, G., Web Service Grids: An Evolutionary Approach, 2004, UK e-Science Technical Report July 13 2004 to be published in a special issue of Concurrency&Computation: Practice&Experience 2005
3. Banaei-Kashani, F., Ching-Chien Chen, C., Shahabi, C., WSPDS: Web Services Peer-to-peer Discovery Service, Proc. of Int Symposium on Web Services and Applications (ISWS'04), 2004
4. Bhusate, A., De Meer, H., Web Services Over Infrastructure-less Networks, Proc. of the London Communications Symposium, 2003
5. Booth, D., Web Services Architecture, W3C Working Group Note, 2004, http://www.w3.org/TR/2004/NOTE-ws-arch-20040211/
6. BPEL4WS 1.1, 2005, http://www-128.ibm.com/developerworks/library/specification/ws-bpel/
7. Brooke, J., Garwood, K., Goble, C.: Interoperability of Grid Resource Descriptions: A Semantic Approach, Proc. of the 1st GGF Semantic Grid Workshop, USA, 2003
8. Buehling, B.: P2P and XML in Business, published on XML.com, 2001, http://www.xml.com/pub/a/2001/07/11/xmlp2p.html
9. Chinook P2P Bioinformatics project, http://smweb.bcgsc.bc.ca/chinook.htm, last access 25/5/2005
10. ebXML, http://www.ebxml.org, last access 25/5/2005
11. Edutella project, http://edutella.jxta.org, last access 25/5/2005
12. EGA (Enterprise Grid Alliance), http://www.gridalliance.org/, last access 25/5/2005
13. Foster, I., Kesselman, C., Nick, J., Tuecke, S.: The Physiology of the Grid: An Open Grid Services Architecture for Distributed Systems Integration, Globus Project, 2002, http://www.globus.org/research/papers/ogsa.pdf
14. Foster, I., Kesselman, C.: The Globus Toolkit, In Ian Foster and Carl Kesselman, editors, The Grid: Blueprint for a New Computing Infrastructure, pp. 259-278. Morgan Kaufmann, San Francisco, CA, 1999, Chap. 11
15. Furmento, N., Hau, J., Lee, W., Newhouse, S., Darlington, J.: Implementations of a Service-Oriented Architecture on top of Jini, JXTA and OGSA, Proc. of the 2nd European AcrossGrids Conference, AxGrids 2004, Nicosia, Cyprus, 2004
16. GGF (Global Grid Forum), http://www.Gridforum.org/, last access 25/5/2005
17. Globus Alliance, http://www.globus.org/, last access 25/5/2005
18. Groove, http://www.groove.net, last access 25/5/2005
19. IETF (The Internet Engineering Task Force), http://www.ietf.org/, http://www.groove.net
20. Intel Press Releases: Intel Announces Technology Middleware To Accelerate Peer-To-Peer Capabilities, 2001, http://www.intel.com/pressroom/archive/releases/20010828tech.htm
21. INTEROP Network of Excellence, http://interop-noe.org/INTEROP/, last access 25/5/2005
22. Jabber Technology Overview, 2002, http://www.jabber.org/
23. JXTA project, http://www.jxta.org/, last access 25/5/2005
24. Laoveerakul, S., Laongwaree, K., Tongsima, S.: Decentralized UDDI based on P2P Protocol, Proc. of P2P/NSCD session, APAN Shanghai Meetings, 2002
25. Microsoft .NET, http://www.microsoft.com/services/net/default.asp
26. Milenkovic, M., Robinson, S., Knauerhase, R., Barkai, D., Garg, S., Tewari, V., Anderson, T., Bowman, M., Intel, Toward Internet Distributed Computing, published at Computer Society (IEEE), 2003, Vol. 36, No. 5, pp. 38-46
27. Milojicic, D., Kalogeraki, V., Lukose, R., Nagaraja, K., Pruyne, J., Richard, B., Rollins, S., Xu, Z., HP Laboratories Palo Alto: Peer-to-Peer Computing, HPL-2002-57, 2003

28. NGG2 (Next Generation Grids2nd Group) report, 2004, http://www.cordis.lu/ist/Grids
29. OASIS, www.oasis-open.org, last access 25/5/2005
30. OGSA Glossary of Terms, GGF document GGFD-I.044, J.Treadwell, ed., Jan. 25th, 2005, http://www.ggf.org/documents/GWD-I-E/GFD-I.044.pdf
31. OGSI (Open Grid Services Interface), http://www.Gridforum.org/Meetings/ggf7/drafts/draft-ggf-ogsi-Gridservice-23_2003-02-17.pdf
32. OWL Overview, 2004, http://www.w3.org/TR/owl-features/
33. OWL-S 1.1, 2004, http://www.daml.org/services/owl-s/1.1/
34. Parastatidis, S., Webber, J., Watson, P., Rischbeck, WS-GAF: A Framework for Building Grid Applications Using Web Services, Journal of Concurrency and Computation: Practice and Experience, 17(2-4), pp. 391-417, 2005
35. P2PWG (Peer to Peer Working Group), http://P2P.internet2.edu/, last access 25/5/2005
36. Prasad, V., Lee, Y.: A Scalable Infrastructure for Peer-to-Peer Networks Using Web Services as Registries and Intelligent Peer Locators, Proc. of the 3rd International Symposium on Cluster Computing and the Grid, 2003, Tokyo, Japan
37. RDF (Resource Description Framework), http://www.w3.org/RDF/, last access 25/5/2005
38. Roure, D., Jennings, N., Shadbolt, N., The Semantic Grid: Past, Present and Future, Preprint - to appear in IEEE Proceedings March 2005
39. Schattkowsky, T., Loeser, C., Müller, W., Peer-To-Peer Technology for Interconnecting Web Services in Heterogeneous Networks, Proc. of 18th Int Conference on Advanced Information Networking and Applications (AINA'04), 2004
40. Schlosser, M., Sintek, M., Decker, S., Nejdl, W.: HyperCuP - Hypercubes, Ontologies and Efficient Search on P2P Networks, Int Workshop on Agents and Peer-to-Peer Computing, Bologna, Italy, 2002
41. Shread, P., McAfee Taps Grid Power, Web Services To Boost Security, 2002, http://www.Gridcomputingplanet.com/news/article.php/3281_1010431
42. Snelling, D., van den Berghe, S., von Laszewski, G., Wieder, P., Breuer, D., MacLaren, J., Nicole, D. and Hoppe, H. C.: A Unicore Globus Interoperability Layer, Computing and Informatics 21, pp. 399-411, 2002
43. SOAP 1.1, 2001, http://www.w3.org/TR/SOAP
44. SODIUM project, 2004, http://www.atc.gr/sodium
45. Talia, D., Trunfio, P.:Toward a Synergy Between P2P and Grids, published in IEEE Internet Computing, July/August 2003, Vol. 7, No. 4, pp. 94-95, http://dsonline.computer.org/0307/d/wp4P2P.htm
46. Thaden, U., Siberski, W., Nejdl, W.: A Semantic Web based Peer-to-Peer Service Registry Network, Proc. of the 1st Workshop on Semantics in Peer-to-Peer and Grid Computing, at the 12th Int Wold Wide Web Conference, 2003
47. Tsalgatidou, A., Pilioura, T.: An Overview of Standards and Related Technologyin Web Services, Internation Journal of Distributed and Parallel Data Bases, Special Issue on E-Services 12(2), pp. 135-162, 2002
48. UDDI, http://www.uddi.org/, last access 25/5/2005
49. W3C (World Wide Web Consortium), http://www.w3.org/, last access 25/5/2005
50. W3C Web Services Architecture Requirements document, 2002, http://www.w3.org/2002/ws/arch/2/wd-wsawg-reqs-03262002
51. Wieder, P., Rambadt, M., UNICORE – Globus: Interoperability of Grid Infrastructures, Proc. of Cray User Group Summit 2002, Manchester
52. Wilkes, L., The Web Services Protocol Stack, 2005, http://roadmap.cbdiforum.com/reports/protocols/
53. WS-CF, OASIS, 2003, http://developers.sun.com/techtopics/webservices/wscaf/wscf.pdf
54. WS-Choreography, 2002, http://www.w3.org/2002/ws/chor/
55. WS-Coordination, 2004, ftp://www6.software.ibm.com/software/developer/library/WS-Coordination.pdf
56. WSDL 1.1, (Web Services Descriftp://www6.software.ibm.com/software/developer/library/WS-Coordination.pdfanguage), 2001,http://www.w3.org/TR/wsdl
57. WS-I (Web Services Interoperability Organization), http://www.ws-i.org/, last access 25/5/2005
58. WS-Notification 1.0, 2004, http://www-106.ibm.com/developerworks/library/ws-pubsub/WS-PubSub.pdf
59. WSRF (The WS-Resource Framework), March 2004, http://www.globus.org/wsrf/
60. WS-Security 1.0, 2002, http://www-106.ibm.com/developerworks/webservices/library/ws-secure/

PART 16

INTEROPERABILITY AND ICT INFRASTRUCTURES

49

FEATURE-BASED ANALYSIS FRAMEWORK FOR INTER-OPERABILITY IN NETWORKED ORGANISATIONS

Sobah Abbas Petersen
Dept. of Computer and Information Science, Norwegian University of Science and Technology Trondheim, Norway, Email: sap@idi.ntnu.no
Paolo Paganelli
Gruppo Formula SpA, Italy, Email: Paolo.Paganelli@formula.it
Burkhard Schallock
Fraunhofer IPK, Berlin, Germany, Email: Burkhard.Schallock@ipk.fraunhofer.de

Several forms of collaborative and networked organisations have emerged due to increased alliances, outsourcing, globalisation and improvements in distributed information systems. Interoperability demands and challenges are rising. There is a need to meet these interoperability challenges. This paper proposes a framework to assess how well a networked organisation supports interoperability. The framework is based on a set of features that describe the interoperability aspects of a networked organisation. By using such features, it is possible to identify business interoperability requirements for the networked organisation. This work has been conducted as a part of the EU project ATHENA, Workpackage B3.

1. INTRODUCTION

Several forms of collaborative and networked organisations have emerged due to increased alliances, outsourcing, globalisation and improvements in distributed information systems. Interoperability demands are rising, but a number of obstacles prevent fast solutions from spreading. The EU Integrated Project 507849 ATHENA, (Advanced Technologies for Interoperability of Heterogeneous Enterprise Networks and their Application), [1], will improve interoperability from the results of several research projects and community building activities, including development and application of some business concepts. The overall objective of ATHENA B3 is to lay down the foundation work for the long term research into interoperability, identify key business drivers and provide an impact assessment model to address interoperability systematically in a business context rather than a technical context.

A new way of assessing a network of organisations, and how it can be improved, is by analysing the partners' ability to interoperate at a business level. In such a case, the partners need to be able to share their strategies and business information and interoperate at the strategic level as well as the operational and data levels. We propose a framework for analysing networked organisations. The framework is based on a set of features, which indicate the level of interoperability in several aspects of collaboration. The framework will also help in detecting business interoperability requirements which can lead to improved interoperability and show the business value it creates. The framework will be illustrated using an example.

2. THE NEED FOR A FRAMEWORK

The subject of networked organisations and collaborating organisations has received enormous attention, both by the research community and industry, in the last decade. This area has also been the interest of a number of different disciplines, for example the manufacturing community, e.g. GLOBEMEN, [7], and the information technology community, e.g. COVE, [5]. This has resulted in a number of different concepts and numerous definitions of organisational forms, see [10] for an overview. However, each of these concepts and definitions are mostly influenced by the interest of the community, e.g. a concept proposed by the information technology community may focus on the distributed nature of the applications within a networked organisation while another community may focus on the collaborative nature or the lifecycle of the networked organisation. To illustrate the diversity of the concepts and definitions in the literature, a few definitions are presented below:

- A Virtual Enterprise, which is defined as "*an interoperable network of pre-existing enterprises that collaborate by means of specific information technology components towards the achievement of a common goal*", [6]. The use of information technology is explicitly stated in this definition.
- A Virtual Enterprise, which is defined as "*a composition of several companies, which enable them to make joint commitments to their common customers*", [8]. This definition is focussed on the joint commitments of the organisations within the network.
- An Extended Enterprise Network is defined as "*a network of companies that form Virtual Enterprises to deliver specific customer solutions*", [11]. This concept assumes that the network is formed by each company assigning a set of core competencies and that several Virtual Enterprises may be formed during the lifecycle of a network.

Previous attempts to analyse the different definitions and concepts have used the notion of characteristics of the networked organisations. Examples of such attempts are [3] and [10]. While these provide useful characteristics to describe and analyse a networked organisation, they do not provide an adequate set of characteristics and the flexibility to analyse a networked organisation in terms of interoperability. In order to be able to clearly identify interoperability issues and requirements, we need to have a flexible framework that takes into account all aspects of networked organisations. We believe that an open, flexible framework that helps to identify interoperability issues within a network must fulfil the following requirements:

- Incorporate very diverse aspects of networked organisations.

- Provide the possibility to adapt to the desired situation.
- Facilitate the extraction of interoperability requirements.

Such an approach is currently missing in the literature. We propose a "soft", feature-based interoperability analysis framework to address the above requirements. The rest of this paper is organised as follows: Section 3 describes the interoperability analysis framework; Section 4 explains in detail the kinds of features that can be used to describe networked organisations and Section 5 illustrates the use of the framework using an example.

3. ANALYSIS FRAMEWORK

A particular form of a networked organisation (e.g. a Virtual Enterprise) is called an *approach*. The central elements of the framework are *features* and they describe the various aspects of an approach. Features also relate an approach to *interoperability requirements,* described through further dimensions added on another plane of the framework. A conceptual view of the framework and how the features relate an approach to business interoperability requirements is shown in **Figure 1**.

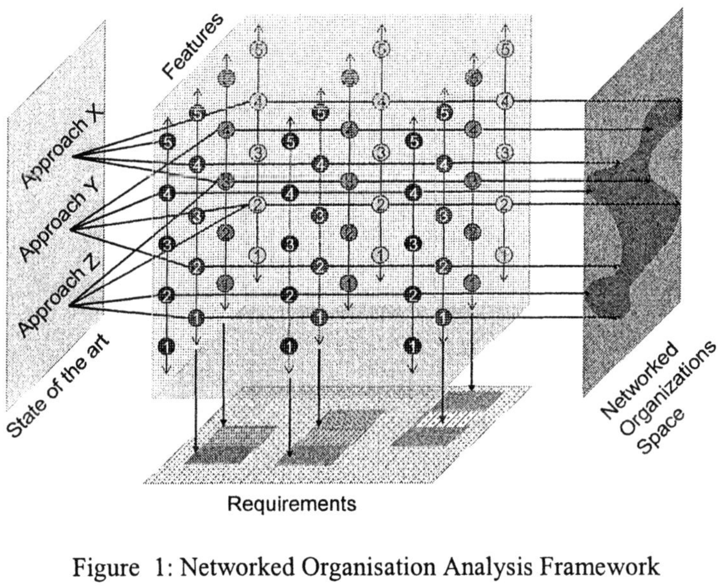

Figure 1: Networked Organisation Analysis Framework

A feature is not a fixed or discrete value; it is a range of values, with a minimum and a maximum. It allows the description of approaches when a certain organisational condition is partially fulfilled rather than either fulfilled or not. The range of values for the features indicates the degree to which a particular approach supports interoperability. This indication of the degree of interoperability facilitates the identification of requirements, which if fulfilled, will increase the degree of interoperability of that approach.

The combination of different approaches mapped through the set of features, sets the boundaries of the Networked Organisations Space. Within this space, we can look for similarities, redundancies and juxtapositions between the different approaches that are analysed. Outside the Networked Organisation Space, we can look for innovations to be pursued or unidentified requirements.

This analysis framework can be considered as a "soft" framework for the following reasons:

- It is tolerant of approximated or partial definitions of approaches, allowing the indication of a degree of fulfillment for a certain organisation condition through the value of the corresponding feature.
- It can be enhanced to include approaches that were not known or not completely specified at the time the framework was designed.
- It allows the inclusion of new features as the list of features to cover all possible approaches at all times will never be complete.

3.1 Features to Describe a Networked Organisation

An initial selection of features that can be used to describe and analyse different approaches are described in Table 1. The features are derived from our own experience as well as from literature, e.g. [3] and [10]. Each feature has a maximum and a minimum value and a value within this range can be used.

Feature	*Min*	*Max*
Extension The potential highest number of independent parties (companies, organisations, individuals) forming the Networked Organisation.	Pair	Open community
Duration The life time of the Networked Organisation.	Spot	Permanent
Involvement The level (and nature) of each partner involvement in the Networked Organisation.	Transaction	Strategic Alliance
Goal orientation The partners' degree of commitment to the Networked Organisation's common goal(s).	Individual purposes	Common mission
Interests Balance How much the individual partners' interests are represented in the Networked Organisation.	One dominant player	Democracy

Holistic Value-added The "virtual" value-added by establishing the Networked Organisation. (Assuming that the whole is greater than the sum of the parts.)	None	Virtual business
Subjective relevance (enterprise) The relevance of the collaboration initiative from the individual enterprise perspective.	Routine initiative	Strategic challenge
Association Cost How much individual partners have to invest to join the Networked Organisation.	Normal spending	Big Investment
Information sharing The relevance of information to be shared from an enterprise perspective.	Transaction data	Corporate Knowledge
Organisation evolution How much the networked organisation changes in terms of its partners, organisation, etc.	Stable	Continuous transformation
Trust level The level of trust among the partners.	Mistrust	Blind faith

Table 1: Initial set of Features

3.2 Business Interoperability Requirements

The features to describe the approaches are also considered as a means of identifying the business interoperability requirements of an approach to make that approach more interoperable. For example, if a particular feature is very low for an approach, there is likely to be a business interoperability requirement that must be met to raise the level of that feature. Interoperability requirements are mapped onto another plane of the analysis framework, where key issues are identified into three main areas: *Strategy, Organisation* and *Infrastructure.*

4. EXAMPLE

An example of a networked organisation approach is CPFR (Collaborative Planning, Forecasting and Replenishment), [4]. CPFR© is a standard approved by EAN.UCC[1] and promoted by the VICS Association[2] to "create collaborative relationships

[1] The EAN.UCC System (http://www.uc-council.org) standardizes identification numbers, Electronic Data Interchange transaction sets, Extensible Markup Language Standard schemas and other supply chain solutions, presiding over several standardization initiatives like, e.g., RosettaNet and U.P.C. Bar Codes.

[2] The VICS consortium (http://www.vics.org/) is the entity promoting and maintaining the CPFR standard.

between buyers and sellers through co-managed processes and shared information". The CPFR standard provides definitions and specifications for a set of collaborative processes between buyers and sellers in a consumer-oriented supply chain.

CPFR is analysed as an approach using the features in Table 2. The range of values for the features is from 1 to 5, where 1 is the lowest and 5 is the highest. The interpretations of the values of the features are also provided in the table. Using this framework, it is possible to obtain a very quick overview of the approach and identify areas where it can improve in interoperability.

Feature	*Value*	*Interpretation*
Extension	1	Bilateral relation.
Duration	4.5	Very long-term.
Involvement	4	Collaborates at the strategic level.
Goal orientation	1	Each partner follows individual goals.
Interests balance	3	The partners' interests are represented well in the approach, but it's not democratic.
Holistic Value-added	1	No new product or business is delivered through collaboration.
Subjective relevance	4	The initiative is perceived as strategic by each involved company.
Association cost	4	The partners have to make significant investments to join the network.
Information sharing	4	Corporate knowledge is shared (e.g., promotions, customer intelligence).
Organisation evolution	1	Little changes to the processes over time.
Trust level	4.5	Very high level of trust required between the partners.

Table 2: Analysis of an Example Approach

4.1 Extracting Requirements

By analysing the values of the features, it is possible to extract business interoperability requirements. Some examples of requirements are shown in Table 3. For example, the feature "involvement" has a value 4, which indicates that the agreements among the partners in a CPFR (who are retailers and manufacturers) are closer to the strategic level rather than the transaction level and have a strategic value. However, this can be further improved by improving the ability of the partners to share their process logic, thus improving their collaboration at the strategic level. The value for the feature "association cost" is high indicating a threshold for CPFR adoption that could be lowered by removing some technical difficulties. One of these is the need for product data consolidation, hence the requirements for shared catalogue services such as, e.g. UCC.NET provided by EAN:UCC.

Feature	*Value*	*Business Interoperability Requirement*	*Requirement level / Interoperability area*
Involvement	4	1. Shared Process Logic for collaboration.	Organisation / Processes
Interests balance	3	1. Shared Process Logic for collaboration.	Organisation / Processes
		2. Establish and share collaboration agreements.	Strategy / Objectives
Association cost	4	1. Consolidation of master item data through third-party service provider.	Infrastructure / Catalogue management

Table 3: Extracting Business Interoperability Requirements

4.2 Extending the Framework

Consider the approach a Virtual Enterprise. Different types of Virtual Enterprises have been described in the literature; for example, a Virtual Enterprise for one-of-a-kind manufacturing or for repetitive productions, [2]. To describe such Virtual Enterprises, we can add a new feature that describes the nature of the product: product orientation. The minimum value for this can be "once", which can be used to describe Virtual Enterprises for one-of-a-kind manufacturing. The maximum value can be "repetitive". Thus, a Virtual Enterprise that has the value closer to maximum (e.g. 4.5) for the feature product orientation and the value 4.5 for the feature duration is likely to be a long-term collaborative effort that delivers the same product over a long period of time.

5. CONCLUSION

The framework can be described as dynamic and inclusive as it allows the inclusion of new features, approaches and requirements at any time during its use. In general, the framework can be used for the following purposes:

- Capture similarities between apparently distant models, creating a unifying space where different approaches from different disciplines can be compared and combined.
- Map specific real organisations' situations, along with theoretical models and solutions, thanks to the "soft" quality of the framework.
- Relate approaches to Interoperability Requirements through Features. This enables the analysis of requirements from an organisational perspective, independent of the models and solutions addressing them.
- Facilitate the extraction of interoperability requirements

In addition to analysing and comparing existing approaches, the framework can also be used to design new approaches, either by combining features of existing approaches or by just focusing on specific features. Thus, this framework is aimed at supporting the design of new networked organistional approaches.

We plan to focus further on the features to make it a more comprehensive set as well as consider better ways to allocate values for the features. At present, features address specific aspects of the network that can be assigned a value to (e.g. extension) as well as aspects that indicate a relevance of that aspect to the network, (e.g. trust level). We plan to continue working on incorporating more flexibility into the framework to support different aspects of networked organisational approaches.

We also plan to use ideas of Active Knowledge Modelling, [9], to create a model of the framework and use the capabilities provided by the modelling environment to support the analyses. The results of this work presented as a model can be used by academia and industry for analysing networked organisations. Implementing the framework as a model will also make it easier for enhancing it in the future and to address business interoperability in a holistic manner.

6. ACKNOWLEDGMENTS

This work has been carried out as part of the ATHENA B3 workpackage. ATHENA Integrated Project is funded by the European Commission under the FP6 IST Programme. The authors would like to thank the members of the B3 workpackage, Guy Domeingts, Man-Sze Li, Peter Mayer, Nikos Pronios and the ATHENA consortium for the interesting discussions that have inspired this work and for their support.

7. REFERENCES

1. ATHENA 2004, Advanced Technologies for Interoperability of Heterogeneous Enterprise Networks and their Application, URL: http://www.athena-ip.org/
2. Bernus, P., Bertok, P. and Nemes, L., "Modelling Dynamic Management Features of Virtual Enterprises", in eds. Plonka and Olling, *Computer Applications in Production Engineering*, Chapman and Hall, London, 1997, pp. 643-655.
3. Camarinha-Matos, L. M., Afsarmanesh, H., Garcia, C. and Lima, C., "Towards an Architecture for Virtual Enterprises", in Proc. of the 2nd IMACS International Multiconference on Computational Engineering in Systems Applications (CESA'98), Nabeul-Hammamet, Tunisia.
4. Collaborative Planning, Forecasting & Replenishment (CPFR©), Version 2.0, June 2003, Voluntary Interindustry Commerce Standards (VICS) Association, URL http://www.cpfr.org.
5. COVE 2003, COllaboration infrastructure for Virtual Enterprises and electronic business, URL: http://www.uninova.pt/~cove/
6. Garita, C. and Afsarmanesh, H., "A Study of Information Management Approaches for Support Infrastructures", Cove *Newsletter*, (1), 2001.
7. GLOBEMEN 2002, Global Engineering and Manufacturing in Enterprise Networks, URL http://globemen.vtt.fi/
8. Jain, A. K., Aparicio IV, M. and Singh, M.. P., "Agents for Process Coherence in Virtual Enterprises", *Communications of the ACM*, Vol .42, No. 3, March 1999, pp. 62-69.
9. Lillehagen, F. "The Foundation of the AKM Technology", Concurrent Engineering: Enhanced Interoperable Systems, eds. Jardim-Goncalves, Cha and Steiger-Garcão, Balkema, The Netherlands, 2003, pp. 700-715.
10. Petersen, S. A., "Extended and Virtual Enterprises - A Review of the Concepts", Technical Report 02/02, Norwegian University of Science and Technology, 2000.
11. Vesterager, J., Larsen, L. B. and Gobbi, C., "Architecture and Methodology for Creating Virtual Enterprises" - Results from Globeman 21, Presented at the IMS Globeman 21 Open Day, Time24, Tokyo, Japan, March 1999.

50 E-BUSINESS SOFTWARE EVALUATION

Victor Fernandez P., Ricardo Chalmeta
Grupo Integración y Re-Ingeniería de Sistemas (IRIS)
Universitat Jaume I. Castellón. 12071. SPAIN.
Tel: 34-964-728343. Fax: 34-964-728435
E-mail: rchalmet@uji.es

E-business is a business strategy that is oriented toward the use of the new information and communication technologies, and mainly Internet, as a new way to communicate, to integrate business processes and to improve relationships with customers, suppliers and other enterprise collaborators.
This change towards an e-business strategy is leading to a strong demand by companies for e-business software solutions.
This paper provides guidelines for selecting e-business software according to the intended purpose of software use. The methodology and the basic criteria to be examined in the software evaluation process are listed together with the evaluation of the best commercial e-business software.

1. INTRODUCTION

An e-business company is an enterprise that integrates the capabilities offered by Information and Communication Technologies (ICT) with Internet in order to carry out their business in an efficient way.

Therefore, the term 'e-business company' arises when firms start to make use of the new possibilities offered by the Internet –in combination with the capabilities already developed in information technologies– to modify or to redesign their business processes so as to make both internal and external communication easier. It must be pointed out that, although conceptually an e-business company does not necessarily have to utilize Internet as a communication channel, the term e-business is intricately linked to the Internet. This is so because the advent of the World Wide Web made it possible to generate new forms of communication that either did not exist before or which could not be implemented due to the prohibitive costs and complexity involved.

This paper is organized as follows. Section 2 gives a brief description of an e-business technological infrastructure Section 3 shows the framework in which this research work has been carried out. Section 4 reviews the differences between commercial e-business software applications. In section 5 and 6, the main results obtained in the evaluation of commercial e-business software are presented, and finally, section 7 outlines main conclusions.

2. E-BUSINESS TECHNOLOGICAL INFRASTRUCTURE

This new model of enterprise incorporates the strategic use of Information and Communications Technologies (which includes, but is not restricted to, the Internet) to build a technological platform that allows interaction with customers, suppliers, employees, projects and partners through multiple communication flows and distribution channels (Damanpour, 2001). Therefore, to achieve the successful implementation of e-business, a suitable technological infrastructure is required in order to automate, improve and, if necessary, define new models of the business processes concerning the management of the relationships the firm have with all their collaborators (Kennerley, 2001), especially in the functional areas that characterize the new models of business processes found in e-business (Yen, 2001): BackSide, SellSide, BuySide & Supply Chain Management, Internal Relations and External Collaborations & GroupWare.

3. EVALUATION OF COMMERCIAL E-BUSINESS SOLUTIONS

The IRIS group at the Universitat Jaume I of Castellón, Spain, has been working on the project entitled "A methodology for the implementation of an e-business system" since 2003. The objective was to develop and validate a formal methodology that guides the process of developing and implementing an e-business system in a company.

One of the activities carried out as part of this project has been to evaluate the best commercial solutions for the development of a technological infrastructure for e-business. The procedure followed to evaluate these solutions is detailed below.

1. Selection of the best technological solutions for e-business.
2. Identification of the general, technical and functional criteria that a computer solution for e-business has to satisfy.
3. Analysis of the programs selected taking into account the general and technical criteria.
4. Evaluation of each of the computer applications selected based on the functional criteria that were taken into account.
5. Identification of the strong and weak points of each application, as well as a comparative study of the different applications.

Data for the study was collected by means of questionnaires and interviews with members of staff from the manufacturing and implementing companies, from publications and articles containing information about e-business software, online demonstrations provided by the distributors of the software packages that were evaluated, telephone conversations held with suppliers of the computer applications and visits to sites and forums on the Internet that are specialized in e-business.

4. SELECTION OF COMMERCIAL E-BUSINESS SOLUTIONS

The differences between commercial e-business software depend on the business area they are intended for. Hence, four types of applications can be observed:

1. **Software applications that offer specific solutions**, such as Enterprise Portals (EIS), E-business Portals (e-Commerce) and e-Shop Managers, Knowledge Managers, Collaborative Applications, customers and/or suppliers analysis, or contacts administration.
2. **E-business software applications**. These refer to software packages specialized in the management of the business transactions that take place among enterprise, customers and suppliers, and the financial institution used to complete the purchasing and selling processes.
3. **Software applications aimed at the customer service module**. This group includes software packages specialized in the automation, via the Internet, of the sales and marketing module, and in features such as telesales skills for managing advertising campaigns.
4. **E-business software applications that cover all the business areas of a company**. These are modular solutions that can be easily adapted to the characteristics of customers and can support large databases and different operating systems. Management of the relationships with customers, suppliers and employees is a highly automated process in the majority of these solutions. Most of the software packages that have been evaluated belong to this category.

The final list of commercial solutions to be evaluated (selected among the mainly e-business applications), was as follows:

Table 0 – Commercial e-business solutions to evaluate

• IBM WebSphere Portal – Express Multiplatform, v5.1 • Oracle e-Business Suite 11i.10 • Sun Microsystems ONE Portal 6,3.0 • BEA WebLogic Portal 8.1 • Siebel eBusiness 7.7 • PeopleSoft Portal Solutions (Enterprise & EnterpriseOne) • Vignette V7 eBusiness Portal	• e-Synergy Suite by Exact Software • Red Hat Portal Apps&Server 1.0 • mySAP eBusiness Suite • Cesser WebServices – Business Portal Solution – • ONYX Enterprise e-Business Portal 5.0 • MicrosoftSharePoint Portal 2003 • Livelink 9.2 by OpenText • Zope Plone 2.0/CPS

5. EVALUATION OF COMMERCIAL E-BUSINESS SOLUTIONS

The criteria taken into account in order to evaluate existing business solutions can be grouped in three large areas:

a) **General requirements**, which refer to different aspects of the enterprise that develops and distributes the e-business solution: Distribution Company; Location; Web Site; Years of experience; No. of Employees; No. of Customers; No. of Partners and Worldwide Presence; Market

Objective; Languages available; Training and Maintenance; Cost; Time needed in a company to implement the software.

b) **Technical requirements**, which analyze the technical characteristics of the solutions: Adaptation to the environment; Relational Management System /Database Manager; Hardware Requirements; Source Code Languages; Server application software; Integration with other systems that are already running; Software architecture; Robustness of the architecture; Software Connectivity; Configuration and Adaptation to the customer; Integration with BackSide (ERP); Security; Safety; Electronic trading contracts; Conformity with e-business frameworks; Customer Relations Management (Integration with CRM, eCRM); Supply Chain Management (Integration with SCM); e-Commerce Applications (Allard, 2001); Collaborative Applications and NetSourcing (Borghoff, 2000); Content Management; Integration with XML and Graphic tools for WorkFlow.

c) **Functional requirements**, which show the operational characteristics that a technological infrastructure for e-business must satisfy. The functional requirements have been organized into three modules: Analytic/Strategic (see Table 1), e-Business and Knowledge Management (see Table 2) and General Administration/Maintenance (see Table 3).

5.1 Analytic/Strategic Module Requirements

This module is responsible for, among other things, the control, integration and online creation of reports based on the data acquired from the operational information systems in the enterprise. The data are turned into information that is useful for running diagnoses of the management of the relationships with customers, suppliers, partners and employees, as well as for assessing their cost-effectiveness (in the case of customers and suppliers), their usability and the improvement in internal efficiency (in the case of in-house company staff), and for automatically defining (by means of alerts for the user involved in each case) opportunities for improvement (Chalmeta, 2005).

Table 1 – Analytic/Strategic Functional Requirements

Functional Requirement	Description
Access and Time Control. Generation of Reports	It allows to analyze the user's behavior and to create reports.
Graphic/Statistical and Planning/Forecasting Tools	Provide easy access to graphic tools in order to conduct statistical analyses of sales/income as well as planning/forecasting and lending support to the previous requirements.

5.2 E-Business and Knowledge Management Module Requirements

The purpose of this module is to provide customers, suppliers, business partners, employees etc. the access, by means of the Internet and/or a Web Service, to each of the functional areas that have been identified Backside, SellSide, BuySide & Supply Chain Management, Internal Relations and External Collaborations & GroupWare.

The functional requirements identified for each of the areas into which the e-business module is divided are detailed below:

Table 2 – E-Business and Knowledge Management Functional Requirements

Functional Requirement	Description
SellSide/BuySide Functional Common Requirements	
Capacity of the Portal and Individualized Customer/Supplier Service	Self-configuration updating the personalized information about the customer/supplier. Tools allowing private access to specific functions: records of orders, dispatch notes, invoices, offers, discounts, etc.
Facilitates email traffic	Handles the volume of email input and output. Enables automatic electronic responses.
Administration of interactivity with multimedia support	Personalized customer/supplier access to a chat with a representative from the enterprise in a 1:1 or 1:N session.
Order processing and administration of quotations	Feature allowing automatic processing of orders, including payment, taxes and transport management.
SellSide Function (Sales Management)	
Administration of Help Desk	Handles the entry of requests for help from knowledge bases, FAQ, etc.
Administration of Estimates and Orders & Life Cycle Tracking	Management and tracking feature including customer's ref., date, automation of estimate-order step, as well as the possibility of looking up status, validity, details, etc.
After-Sales Service	To solve customer problems by Internet.
BuySide Function (Purchase/Supply Chain Management – SCM)	
Catalogs and Delivery Dates Management	Management of supplier's products, catalogs, codes, prices, delivery dates, etc.
Auctions	Management of offers for an order made through the business portal.
Purchases Administration	To follow the workflow established for an order to be approved by the different people.
Management of dispatch notes and Self-Invoicing. Processing	E-business Re-Engineering of the processes involved in managing dispatch notes/invoices, approval, claims, digital signing and sending by EDI/XML for the dispatch note-invoice-payment stage, thus eliminating shortcomings found in SCM.
InSide/OutSide (Relations and Collaborations – CSCW) and Knowledge Management in the e-Business Company	
Document Management	Workflow document management as signing approval, revision, dispatching and/or corporative rejection.

Automated Workflow	Automation of business processes in a structured and collaborative environment, which ensures a predefined running order (Khoshafian, 1995).
Placeholder	Possibility of automatically sending personalized emails.
Alerts Management	Management of Alerts and Alarms for predefined events via the e-business solution.
Electronic Mail, Electronic Agenda and Conference Feasibility	Management of personalized and integrated e-business accounts for customers/ suppliers/ employees, as well as a private agenda/conference feature.
Decision Making Systems and Electronic Board Rooms	The aim here is to improve productivity in decision-making, whether it is achieved by speeding up the decision process or by increasing the quality of the decisions stemming from a virtual meeting.
Intranet/Extranet	Securing (certificates, authentication and non-repudiation service, among others) e-business accesses to the enterprise and associated measures to achieve integration of processes.
Control/Tracking of OutSourcing	Generation of Features allowing Outsourcing Management.

5.3 General Administration/ Maintenance Requirements

In addition to the functional requirements above, the system must also include other capabilities such as:

Table 3 – General Management/Maintenance Functional Requirements

Functional Requirement	Description
Main Administration	Content Management, Integration with WorkFlow/CSCW and General Configuration, thus allowing administration of the contents of the jobs and alerts module, among other associated features.
Administration of Users	Integrated Management of Roles, Profiles, according to corporative requirements, integrated with features for generation of the Map of the Organization. Associated Security Management. Records Management.
Management/Analysis of Customers, Suppliers, Business Partners and Employees	Segmentation, Profiles and Customer Potential, integrated via webService. Integrated Analysis of the lifetime and economic value of customers, suppliers and business partners of the enterprise.

6. COMPARATIVE STUDY

From the list of requirements taken into account for each of the computer applications under evaluation, the following should be highlighted:

a) Among the **general requirements**, one special point of interest is whether there is a firmly established distributor in the country or not, its experience in a particular sector or whether suitable maintenance and training are provided once the application has been implemented.
b) With respect to the **technical requirements**, the solutions studied here present very similar characteristics. In general terms, they have an open architecture of n layers that ensures it will be possible to expand the system in the long term and to use well-known servers such as Oracle, MSSQL Server, and so on. The main languages used in the development of the solutions include Java, JavaScript, HTML and XML, among others such as Phyton, DTML, PHP or ASP. Moreover, they can be closely integrated with ERPs, e-commerce applications, collaborative and teamwork tools, CRM software (especially e-CRM) and powerful content managers (CSM); furthermore, most of them run under the MS Windows 95/98/2000/NT and Windows XP operating systems and to a lesser extent on UNIX/Linux. On the other hand, the majority can be integrated with the different ERP and CRM that exist on the market, depending on each application, and most of them develop graphic workflow tools and integration with XML.
c) Lastly, with respect to **functional requirements**, the Fig.1 shows the score assigned after the analysis carried out on each commercial solution. Each of the subsections used to classify the functional requirements was given a value between 0 and 3, where: 0- not available, 1- acceptable, 2- good, 3- excellent.

Functional Requirements / Commercial sw solutions	Analytic/ Strategic	E-Business and Knowledge Management				Administration/ Maintenance
		SellSide	*BuySide*	*InSide/Out Side*	*Knowledge Management*	
IBM WebSphere Portal – Express Multiplatform, v5.1	1	3	3	3	3	2
Oracle e-Business Suite 11i.10	1	2	3	3	1	1
Sun Microsystems ONE Portal 6,3.0	1	3	1	3	2	3
BEA WebLogic Portal 8.1	1	3	1	3	1	3
Siebel eBusiness 7.7	2	3	0	0	3	3
PeopleSoft Portal Solutions (Enterprise & EnterpriseOne)	3	2,5	2,5	3	2	2
e-Synergy Suite de Exact Software	1	3	3	2	3	2
Vignette V7 eBusiness Portal	1	1	0	3	3	2
Red Hat Portal Apps & Server 1.0	2	0	0	3	2	3
mySAP eBusiness Suite	0,5	3	3	3	2	2
Cesser WebServices –Solución Portal de Negocio–	1	2	2	1	0	3
ONYX Enterprise e-Business Portal 5.0	0	3	1	2	2	2
Microsoft SharePoint Portal 2003	1	0,5	0,5	2	1,5	1
Livelink 9.2 de OpenText	1	3	2	2	2	2
Zope Plone 2.0/CPS	0	1	0,5	2	3	2

Figure 1 - Comparative Study of the functional requirements

7. CONCLUSION

The ICT and the Internet have meant that companies are changing the way they do business, so that today e-business is no longer an alternative but rather an imperative fact that each company, every organization must pursue and accomplish.

To implement an e-business system, it is necessary to develop a supporting computer infrastructure to automate and improve the business processes linked with managing the company's relationships with employees, customers, suppliers, creditors, and other collaborating partners.

In this article we have outlined the methodology followed to evaluate the commercial e-business solutions with the greatest presence on the market. As a result of the study conducted, it can be concluded that in general they all provide good management in the area of integration with corporative ERP and CRM. Nevertheless, the supplier relations (SRM) and value chain management (SCM) modules, as well as knowledge management and the analytic module, need to be more powerful as far as the generation of reports, planning and controlling goes.

Acknowledgments

This project has being funded by CICYT DPI2003-02515, FUE-UJI and different enterprises.

4. REFERENCES

1. Allard, S., W Holsapple, C. "Knowledge Management as a key for e-business competitiveness: From the Knowledge chain to KM audits". The Journal of Computer Information Systems, Stillwater, US, 2002; 42: 19-26
2. Borghoff, U., Schlichter, J. "Computer-Supported Cooperative Work: Introduction to Distributed Applications". Springer, 2000.
3. Chalmeta, R., Grangel, R. "Performance Measurement Systems for Virtual Enterprise Integration". Computer Integrated Manufacturing. 2005; 73-84
4. Damanpour F. "E-business e-commerce evolution: Perspective and strategy", Managerial Finance, Patrington 2001; 27: 16-18
5. Kennerley M., Neely A. "Enterprise resource planning: Analysing the impact. Integrated Manufacturing Systems", 2001; 12: 103-113,
6. Khoshafian, S., Buckiewicz, M. "Introduction to Groupware, Workflow, and Workgroup computing". Ed. John Wiley & Sons, Inc, 1995
7. Yen David C., Chou David C., Chang Jane. "A synergic analysis for web-based enterprise resources planning systems". Computer Standards & Interfaces, 2002; 24: 337-346

51 EXPERIMENTS ON GRID COMPUTING FOR VE-RELATED APPLICATIONS

Fábio R. Pinheiro; Ricardo J. Rabelo
Federal University of Santa Catarina
GSIGMA – Intelligent Manufacturing Systems Group
Florianópolis (SC), Brazil
{fjrp, rabelo}@das.ufsc.br

Companies have made invested increasingly in computing resources upgrades but this starts to be an obstacle to be supported by them and hence can hazard innovation activities. Most of computers are however underutilized at the companies so they could be used by external users if appropriate platforms could find them and manage them properly. This work aims at presenting some exploratory results of using Grid Computing as a supporting technology both to allow a company to use the computing resources of the other members of the Virtual Enterprise and to allow a flexible and smart selection of the most suitable resources to have access. A prototype has been developed and its results are discussed.

1. INTRODUCTION

Micro, Small and Medium-size Enterprises (MSMEs) have been facing enormous difficulties to acquire and to maintain enterprise systems, e.g. ERP and SCM/Virtual Enterprises (VE) management systems, regarding the required investment in technological, computing and human resources as well as in internal organization (Europe-EU, 05). This is particularly critical as around 99% of companies in Europe are formed by MSMEs and they are more and more dependent on investments in ICT to leverage their innovation and hence their competitiveness (Europe-EU, 05).

However, it is a paradox to see that, if from one hand enterprises have tried to increase their investments in ICT, from another hand the existing computing resources at the enterprises stay idle most of the time. According to IBM, desktop machines are busy less than 5% of the time (Berstis et al., 02).

A VE is defined as a dynamic, temporary and logical aggregation of autonomous enterprises that cooperate with each other as a strategic answer to attend a given opportunity or to cope with a specific need, and whose operation is achieved by a coordinated sharing of skills, resources and information, enabled by computer networks (Rabelo et al., 04). The VE paradigm has been seen as a strategic positioning of MSMEs in order to compete in the global market as stronger alliances.

The approach investigated in this work is based on the principle that that sharing of resources in a VE scenario has been so far exploited in a limited way. Actually, the fact of being a VE, i.e. a group of enterprises which are very much interested that every one can accomplish its business process in the most efficient way so that the whole team can make better profits, is underutilized. The proposed idea is to allow VE members to share the computing resources one of another and even applications one of another, so saving many investments and using the resources more rationally.

This corresponds to another level of cooperation, where other dimensions of virtualizations (e.g. equipments, software, people, etc.) can emerge and work concurrently with the business process execution. This cooperation is important as it strengthens partners' relationships and provides additional elements for the creation of trust building among VE's partners.

Grid computing (Foster, 01) seems to be a very promising and powerful technology to handle this scenario as it makes possible that interconnected and heterogeneous resources can be accessed, used and managed in a controlled and coordinated way seamlessly. Most of Grid applications has focused on high performance processing (Genoma, spatial applications, oil prospecting, etc.) requiring clusters of computers. This work, instead, focuses on the flexibility of resources allocation aiming at using idle computing resources.

This paper aims at discussing some experiments on Grid in the context of VE. It is organized as follows: Section 2 presents an overview about Grid Computing. Section 3 describes the proposal of this work. Section 4 shows some results of a software prototype. Section 5 discusses the results and points out next steps of this work.

2. GRID COMPUTING

The technology of Grid Computing offers a new approach for distributed systems, but with the difference of focus in large-scale resource sharing. A computational Grid is a hardware and software infrastructure – usually called as *platform* – that provides dependable, consistent, pervasive and inexpensive access to high-end computational capabilities (Foster, 01). This is not primarily concerned with file exchange but rather with direct access to computers, software, data, and other resources, as it is required by a range of collaborative problem-solving. This sharing is highly controlled, with resource providers and consumers defining clearly and carefully what is shared, who is allowed to share, and the conditions under which sharing occurs.

There is a good number of Grid platforms being developed over the world, with different levels of maturity, and that have been applied on several areas. Examples of stable platforms are: Globus Toolkit (Globus, 2004), Condor (Condor, 2004), Legion (Legion, 2004), Grip (Grip, 2004) and Alchemi (Alchemi, 2004). For this work, Globus was adopted as it is becoming the *de facto* standard for Grid Computing. Globus is a community-based, open-architecture, open-source set of services and software libraries that support Grid and Grid applications (Foster, 02).

Globus provides four basic types of components (Foster, 01):

- *Grid Resource Allocation Management* (GRAM): it is at the core of the Globus remote program execution infrastructure;
- *Information Service*: it provides information about Grid resources for use in resource discovery, selection, and optimization;
- *Data Management*: it supports access to and manipulation of distributed data that are stored in databases or files.
- *Authentication*: it supports some security access control upon resources.

However, considering the objective of this work, both Globus and the other current grid platforms present some drawbacks:

I. Grid platforms are not designed to be used by ordinary users:

   1. they are very complex to be deployed;
   2. they require IT specialists to use it;
   3. they are not transparent to the users.

II. Existing software systems are not designed to use grid computing:
   1. both traditional monolithic systems and even modern component-based systems don't use to be designed in/as separated parts that can run concurrently;

III. Lack of flexibility to define which computing resources are the most suitable ones to host a given processing:
   1. the user should know in advance the execution software's requirements;
   2. the user should know/specify in advance the computers where he wants to execute the software (or some of its parts).
   3. the user should know in advance which are the available computers.

Actually, the basic reason for these constraints is that Grid platforms are a new area and it has primary focused on high performance at the server side. In this work we are primary interested to focus on the client side, allowing a more rational and flexible resources utilization but transparently to the user as much as possible. Seeing in the literature, only two related works in that desired focus were found. However, they provided only an easier way of submitting jobs. The first one was performed as part of the Globus Project (Laszewski, 02). It introduced a Grid service that combines the ability of serving as an information service and as a job execution service, demonstrating a significant simplification of the architecture while treating job submissions and information queries. The second work was developed in the Gridway project (Gridway, 04) to provide an easier and more efficient execution of jobs in dynamic Grid environments. It automatically performs all the job scheduling steps, provides fault recovery mechanisms, and adapts job scheduling and execution to the changing Grid conditions. There are also other works being done that are independent of any particular grid platform that use the concepts of scheduler, meta-scheduler and workflow (Joseph et al., 04). This aims to offer some facilities at the server's side in terms of execution coordination as well as of inference about all grid providers in order to try to identify the best resources. However, this is done purely looking at software and hardware aspects, without any other complementary qualitative analysis.

3. PROPOSAL

Regarding those Grid drawbacks mentioned before, this work aims at contribution for the solution of the aspects I.2, I.3 and III. For that, this work proposes a smart, thin and transparent client architecture and software tool / "meta-interface" that makes possible to an ordinary end user to have access to several idle/available resources over the Internet in a transparently way. Figure 1 presents the proposed architecture.

The basic idea is that this tool can automatically evaluate when to use grid and which computers should be involved in the execution of a given application. This tool checks if there are enough resources to run an application locally as soon as it detects the application is to be executed. This is made checking the needed application's requirements against the existing computing resources in the local environment.

The architecture has two layers. Grid Independent layer is the one developed in this work and that contains supporting modules to help users to use Grid. Grid Dependent layer comprises modules that are specializations of Grid platform's implementation classes (APIs), i.e. that execute grid services themselves. At the server's side, Globus must be deployed in the companies that are going to share their resources. There must be one node in the net that should host the Information Service structure. Seen as a whole, these distributed resources from the members of a given VE create a (instance of a) Grid Resources Federation.

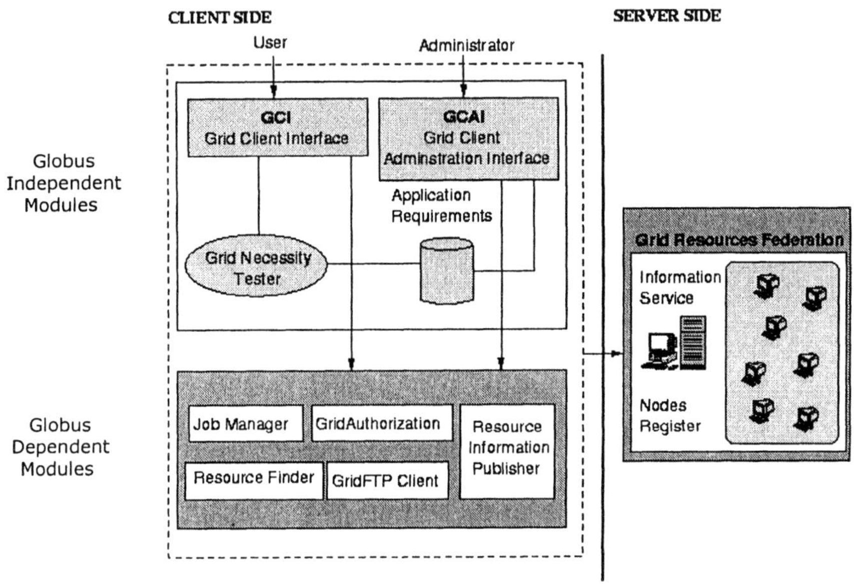

Figure 1 – Proposed Grid Thin Client Architecture

In general, the functioning of this tool runs as follows: i) every application that can make use of Grid must be registered in the platform by a local system administrator; ii) when the user executes a "gridable" application via the GCI module, GCI detects and compares the application's requisites with the current status (memory, hard disk, processor, operating system and architecture) of the local computer; iii) the need for the Grid is then evaluated by the Grid Necessity Tester (GNT) module; iv) if there is a need for Grid the user is authenticated via setting a login/password; v) the platform accesses the Globus' Index Service in order to find out the resources that can match the application's requirements. This service provides information about all the resources available in the VE members (or eventually in external and authorized providers), which were previously configured when the Grid platform was deployed. This information is stored in a structure called *Information Service*. The GNT module receives the list of resources and applies some selection criteria in order to elect the most suitable computer(s) to run the application; vi) the application and input data are sent to the computer(s); vii) the application, or part of it, is executed in the computer(s); viii) the result is returned to the Client / user after the execution of the application. It is important to mention that the user must require a certificate (signed by the Grid administrator) before executing applications.

3.1 Globus Independent Layer

3.1.1. Grid Client Interface to the Grid (GCI)
This module is responsible for creating the interface with the end user, and for abstracting the communication with the other modules. Its main features are:

- The user selects the application (s)he wants to execute, providing some essential input parameters/files for the execution.
- The user has a direct but transparent access to the modules that make use of Grid services.

3.1.2. Grid Client Administration Interface (GCAI)
This module has administrative purposes. It has two basic functions:

- Registering the applications that are candidates to use the Grid infrastructure. In order to accomplish this task, the user must have a minimum knowledge about the application requirements, such as executable, arguments, processor, architecture, operating system, amount of memory and hard disk;
- Publishing the resource's information in the case the user decides to turn his local machine a Grid resource. Thus, it is necessary to provide the information necessary to locate this resource, such as: architecture, operating system, amount of memory and hard disk available.

3.1.3. Grid Necessity Tester (GNT)
This module evaluates the current status of the local node and compares it with the application requirements. According to the results, it decides if Grid is necessary. This evaluation is immediately triggered when the user is going to launch an application. GNT acts only at the local machine. The parameters used for the comparison are:

- memoryFree: amount of free memory (megabytes) at the machine;
- freeHardDisk: amount of free hard disk space (megabytes) at the machine;
- freeProcessor: percentage of free processor.

Another main function of this module is to select the most suitable resource out of the Federation of Grid Providers. In the resource selection, if more than one node is selected, those attributes are also compared in order to choose the most effective one. For instance, if the application demands a large amount of data to be transferred, it could be preferred to choose a machine in the same LAN (Local Area Network).

3.1.4. Applications Requirements
The evaluation made by GNT module depends on the data (about the resource) provided. This data must be defined in a well structured and interoperable way. XML (eXtend Markup Language) (W3C, 2000) has become the standard for these purposes.

For each application (job) registered in the tool, two files are generated. The first one describes a job and it is used by the Globus container (Sandholm, 2003) to make a submission. For the job specification, it is used an XML based language, the RSL (Resource Specification Language) Schema (Globus, 2004a).

The second file describes the resources requirements. This file is used by the GNT module to perform the evaluation, as well as to search for resources. The initial idea was to use the same RSL file employed by the job submission since it provides some fields necessary to this function and a well defined structure. However, some additional information are needed. For this reason, an extension of this RSL file was created, adding the following elements: operating system, architecture, processor, clock, free hard disk, memory, band width (Figure 2).

These requirements are used in three different stages: in the job submission; in the Grid evaluation; and in the resource searching.

```
<gram:resource>
    <gram:operatingSystem><rsl:path>
        <rsl:stringElement value="Linux" />
    </rsl:path></gram:operatingSystem>
    <gram:memory><rsl:path>
        <rsl:integer value="256" />
    </rsl:path></gram:memory>
    <gram:freeHardDisk><rsl:path>
        <rsl:integer value="50" />
    </rsl:path></gram:memory>
</gram:resource>
```

Figure 2 - RSL Extension example

3.2. Globus Dependent Layer

3.2.1. Resource Information Publisher

Each node that integrates the VE must have a way to be found out. In the Globus Information Service component, it is possible to query any data that is registered in that component. The resources that will be available in the Grid must publish their own information in a way they can be found. In this sense, this module provides an easy way to get this information and to publish it in the Information Service. The publication is made through a Grid Service, in the Service Data (Tuecke, 2003), which has meta-information associated with the Grid Service. This Grid Service is deployed in the local machine, and after that, those data are aggregated in the central server where the Information Service is located.

3.2.2. Grid Authorization

In order to allow the user to submit jobs or transfer files to remote nodes, some kind of permission for this access is necessary. This access is obtained via a certificate required by the user, (creating a login/password), and then signed by the Certificate Authority (Tuecke, 2001). These operations are supported by this module.

3.2.3. Resource Finder

Once the need of a Grid has been detected, the next step is to find the resource(s) that supplies the application requirements. For that, this client provides access to the Information Service (Czajkowski, 01), where all nodes have their information published. When the resource is found, the Information Service returns the address of the selected to the client's node. This address is used by the Job Manager and GridFTP Client modules, which are described below.

3.2.4. Job Manager

This is the module that makes the job submission, in a direct connection with the Globus Container (Sandholm, 2003) of the selected nodes. This submission is made using the RSL file (described above), through the GRAM services.

3.2.5. GridFTP Client

It is a client of the GridFTP server, which makes the upload of the application and other essential files (e.g. input/output files) for the execution. The user's credential is also required to get permission to write files in a remote node.

4. PROTOTYPE

Globus Toolkit version 3.2 has been used in the prototype implementation. It provides a comprehensive Java API, which offers programming facilities to both server and client sides. Using Globus, servers should be Unix machines so applications should be written according to. At the client side, there is the CoG Kit (CoG), which makes easier some programming aspects related to the Grid services access. This led us to implement the prototype in Java. From the server point of view, Globus platform is obligatory to be installed in the machines that will act as grid resources, i.e. that will make available computing resources to the others. The client needs the CoG's APIs.

Only some attributes (memory, processor and hard disk) have been considered in as selection criteria out of the available resources. Other more "qualitative" attributes, such as trust levels, historical performance and use, costs safe and job's deadline, were not implemented in this first prototype. Other useful features, such as the possibility to set up precise values for the computing resources that every node is interested to make available, is so far not supported by any existing grid platform. In practice it means that a given computer stay either "totally" available for the others or it simply can't be accessed.

An application related to the partners' search and selection problem was developed to test the feasibility of the proposed approach. This application is a module of a wider VE management system called SC^2 (Rabelo, 2004) that supports some steps in the creation and operation phases of the VE life cycle. This module was designed having Grid philosophy in mind so it has parts that can run separately / concurrently. The part tested is the scheduling functionality, which is responsible for generating all the scheduling possibilities of VE for a given business and to select the best schedule. As it is CPU-bound, it is evaluated the situation where it is realized that the required computing resources are not available in the local machine and then external resources should be sought using Grid facilities. A given resource is further selected and the scheduling application and its data are sent to it and executed on it.

As said in the section 3.1.2, "gridable" applications must be previously registered and their requirements specified in order to make use of Grid platform's facilities. This is made by the system's administrator. Figure 3 shows this process for the case of that scheduling application.

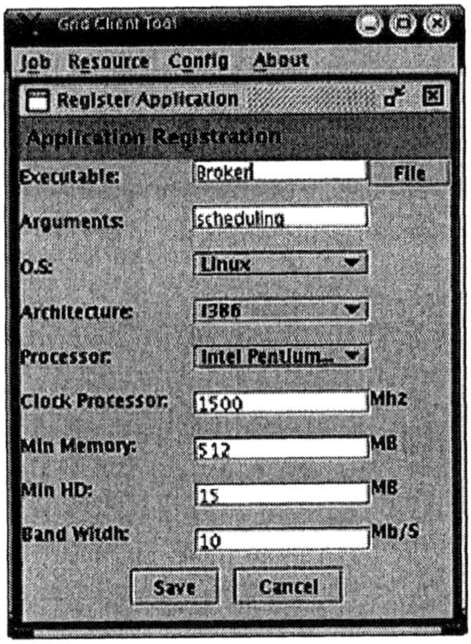

Figure 3 - Application Registration

Figure 4 shows another interface through which the user specifies the input data's file name that should be sent to the (previously) selected resource's URL. Thus, the job can be indeed submitted/executed.

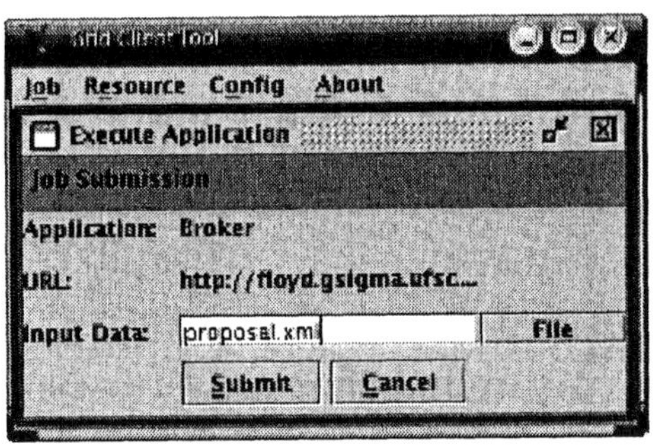

Figure 4 - Job Submission

Figure 5 shows the result of the VE scheduling algorithm/functionality. The result is generated as a XML file in this prototype as it is to be easily interoperable with other functionalities. However, for the user visualization, a more user friendly layout should be developed although it is a matter of how the functionality was implemented. This result shows the list of the selected enterprises (i.e. the VE), showing their identification, production cost and delivery date.

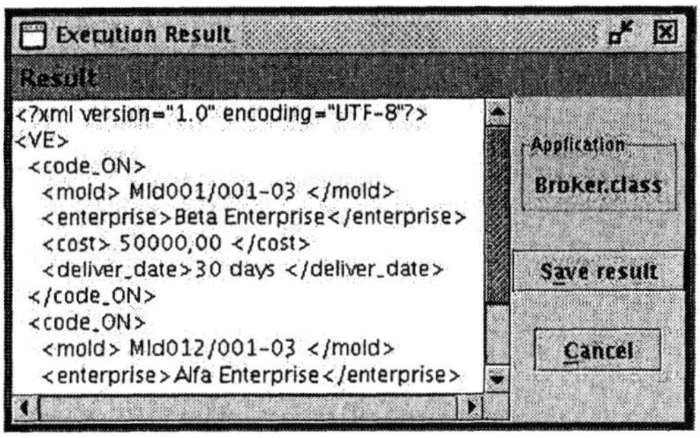

Figure 5 – Scheduling Result

5. CONCLUSION

This work proposed an approach to allow smart and flexible utilization of computing resources that are idle to overcome local software and hardware restrictions when executing applications. This execution is done remotely, seamlessly and by means of the support of a grid (Globus) platform and of a client interface to leave this transparent to the user as well as to make a more rational use of the resources.

It also realized that all VE members can benefit from making available their resources to the others and that richer qualitative metrics can be added in the future for smarter selection of computing resources.

The developed prototype has offered elements for preliminary conclusions that Grid computing is a feasible technology for dealing with the problem of the increasing complexity of enterprises' systems and that it can be useful to help MSME in their investments on IT.

The experiments involved several types of PCs, both powerful ones and old machines. In both cases the system worked out, with natural differences in terms of time processing.

However, some limitations could be observed. For example, so far applications can only run on Unix/Linux operating system, respecting the restrictions of current versions of existing Grid platforms. Besides that, only "pre-prepared" applications can benefit from Grid technology. Systems haven't been developed with the notion of concurrency among their submodules, which inhibits the achievement of most of grid advantages. A number of recommendations can be followed in this direction, as the ones proposed in (Ferreira, 04). More recent approaches for software development, like SOA (services oriented architecture) can naturally help this as it makes natural the "decomposition" of an application in several "parts" (services) that can run everywhere. There is also a reasonable difficulty in the resources matching. In a heterogeneous multi-institutional environment such as the Grid, it is difficult to impose common syntax and semantics for a resource description. An evolution on this can be implemented with the use of ontologies, as described in (Tangmunarunkit, 03).

Next steps of this work includes dealing with security (resources access policies; trust clients, etc.), extending the model to Microsoft OS as soon as Globus platform can support it. It is also important to better investigate "clever" meanings for "idle" resources. Another part of the intended research on this area comprises the possibility of a given company to offer its applications to the VE members, acting as an ASP (Application Service Provider) model once legal aspects related to software licenses are overcome.

ACKNOWLEDGMENTS

This work was partially supported by FAPEAL – Research Support Foundation of State of Alagoas (www.fapeal.br), and it has been developed in the scope of the Brazilian IFM project (www.ifm.org.br) and the European IST FP6 IP ECOLEAD project (www.ecolead.org).

6. REFERENCES

Alchemi .Net Grid Computing Framework, URL: http://www.alchemi.net, 2004.

Berstis, V., Fundamentals of Grid Computing, IBM Redbooks Paper, in http://www.redbooks.ibm.com/redpapers/pdfs/redp3613.pdf, 2002.

Condor High Throughput Computing, http://www.cs.wisc.edu/condor, 2004.

Czajkowski, K., Fitzgerald, S., Foster, I. and Kesselman, C., 2001, Grid Information Services for Distributed Resource Sharing, Proceedings of the Tenth IEEE International Symposium on High-Performance Distributed Computing (HPDC-10), IEEE Press.

Europe-EU, http://www.eubusiness.com/topics/SMEs, accessed in 21/05/2005.

Ferreira, L., Thakore, A., Brown, M., Lucchese, F., RuoBo, H., Lin, L., Manesco, P., Momtaheni, N., Hernandez, O., Grid Service Programming and Application Enablement, IBM Redbooks, 2004.

Foster, I., Kesselman, C. and Tuecke, S., 2001, The Anatomy of the Grid: Enabling Scalable Virtual Organizations, Int. Journal of High Performance Computing Applications, 200-222.

Foster, I., Kesselman, C., Nick, J. and Tuecke, S., 2002, The Physiology of the Grid: An Open Grid Services Architecture for Distributed Systems Integration.

Globus, 2004, The Globus Alliance, URL: http://www.globus.org.

Globus, 2004, Managed Job Service - Resource Specification Language (RSL), URL: http://www-unix.globus.org/toolkit/docs/3.2/gram/ws/developer/mjs_rsl_schema.html.

Grip: Grid Interoperability Project, 2004, http://www.grid-interoperability.org.

Gridway, 2004, http://www.gridway.org.

Joseph, J., Fellenstein, C., Grid Computing, Prentice Hall, IBM Press, 2004.

Laszewski, G. Von., Foster, I., Gawor, J., Schreiber, A., Pena, C., InfoGram: A Grid Service that Supports Both Information Queries and Job Execution, Proceedings of the 11th IEEE International Symposium on High-Performance Distributed Computing, 2002.

Legion: A Worldwide Virtual Computer, 2004, URL: http://www.cs.virginia.edu/~legion.

Rabelo, R. J.; Pereira-Klen, A. A.; Klen, E. R.; Effective Management of Dynamic and Multiple Supply Chains. In: Int. J. of Networking and Virtual Organizations, V 2 N 3, p. 193-208, 2004.

Sandholm, T., Gawor, J., Globus Toolkit 3 Core – A Grid Service Container Framework.

Tangmunarunkit, H., Decker, S., Kesselman. C., Ontology-based Resource Matching in the Grid - The Grid meets the Semantic Web, Proc. of the Second Int. Semantic Web Conference, 2003.

Tuecke, S., Czajkowski, K., Foster, I., Frey, J., Graham, S., Kesselman, C, Maguire T., Sandholm, T., Snelling, D., Open Grid Services Infrastructure (OGSI) Version 1.0, Global Grid Forum, 2003.

Tuecke, S., Engert, D., Foster, I., Thompson, M., Pearlman, L. and Kesselman, C. Internet X.509 Public Key Infrastructure Proxy Certificate Profile, IETF, 2001.

W3C, Extensible Markup Language (XML) 1.0 (Second Edition). W3C Recommendation, URL: http://www.w3.org/TR/REC-xml, 2000.

52 TECHNOLOGY INFRASTRUCTURE FOR VIRTUAL ORGANISATION OF TOOLMAKERS

John Mo
Commonwealth Scientific and Industrial Research Organisation, John.Mo@csiro.au
AUSTRALIA
Ron Beckett
Reinvention Network, rcb@reinvent.net.au
AUSTRALIA
Laszlo Nemes
Commonwealth Scientific and Industrial Research Organisation, Laszlo.Nemes@csiro.au
AUSTRALIA

Globalisation has forced companies to work together in a new arrangement known as virtual enterprise. An Australian initiative called RELINK aims to demonstrate the methodologies and systems, that will enable small firms in the tooling and automotive industry to participate with medium and large firms in turnkey projects as part of a broader supply chain. The initiative draws on this body of knowledge in conjunction with research and university partners and concentrates on the practicality of the formation of virtual enterprises in the tooling and automotive industries competing with larger toolmaking companies globally. This paper explores a 5 layer open communication framework for virtual enterprise to establish a continuity of functionality in the communication process that enables B2B operations within a virtual enterprise with varying levels of communication capabilities. The framework identifies options for bridging gaps in communication functionality between the desired application level and the varying situations of the participants.

1. INTRODUCTION

Globalisation has forced companies to work together in a new arrangement known as virtual enterprise. This is characterised to be flexible, dynamic with minimal or sometimes no contractual agreements among the partners. A virtual enterprise can be created and disbanded in very short time frames. Interactions at organizational, technical, social and commercial levels give rise to emergent properties that have specific technical, communications and infra-structural issues. These issues have been investigated in many research projects in the last decade and a vast volume of information can be found in literature (Williams *et al*, 1994, Callaham, 1996, Bernus *et al*, 1997). The Australian "RELINK" initiative aims to demonstrate the methodologies and systems that will enable small firms in the tooling and automotive industry to participate with medium and large firms in turnkey projects as part of a complex supply network. It draws on the body of knowledge of virtual enterprise in research and university partners and concentrates on the practicality of the formation of virtual enterprises in the Australian tooling and automotive industries competing with larger toolmaking companies elsewhere.

In a typical virtual enterprise, a large amount of data transfer and real-time coordination is necessary to ensure fast turn around time of activities. Achieving this outcome involves sharing sophisticated applications across offices irrespective of whether they are in the neighbourhoods, far away cities or sometimes continents. The use of ICT to carry large amount of data is a critical factor making the virtual enterprise a success. Therefore, one of the focal points of study in RELINK is on the application of ICT tools among members of the toolmaking virtual enterprise and the effectiveness of these ICT tools on collaboration and enhancing business opportunities. This paper explores the issues and considerations that will be evolving in the project.

2. COMPATIBLE COMMUNICATION MODEL

It is observed, in various roadmapping studies, that communication technology level in SMEs varies greatly between companies (Beckett *et al*, 2003, Barradas *et al*, 2004). However, technology level affects the effectiveness of communication between two parties. Communication by fax is obviously inefficient as compared to electronic data transfer or emails. Likewise, a highly automated internet communication channel will be a good choice for some but not other toolmakers. Some of the computer technologies such as CAD-CAM, CSCW, multimedia, data exchange standards and PDM systems are affordable only in medium sized companies. The RELINK project objective of linking tooling/component manufacturer teams of medium sized companies in mobilizing the capabilities of a large number of small companies linked with the medium sized ones will have particular difficulty in overcoming the communication issue.

To develop the conceptual framework, we make reference to the international standard Open Systems Interconnection (OSI) model (ISO, 1983). The OSI model is a framework for communication between computers. The model establishes the elements in the communication framework to handle complex situations such as noise in connection, error processing, detection, request for re-send, language and conversation synchronization. The fundamental principle of OSI is to divide the functionality of the communication system into smaller sections so that the problems can be confined to specific issues when the communication modules are developed. The sections are known as layers, which have defined functions to be fulfilled by any system claiming to comply with the standard.

Another important characteristic of OSI is its peer-to-peer communication process. OSI evolves from the concept of distributed communication services. Each layer has a defined set of rules that governs successful communication procedures and formats between communicating entities located at the same layer in two different systems. The set of rules is referred to as a communication protocol. Hence, two entities at different layers cannot communicate but will be able to do so through their compatible layer components in the system. There are three consequences:

- Both sides must have all 7 layers in order to communicate properly between applications;

- If one side does not have full 7 layer functionality in the system, it will receive information at its highest layer. A separate process is required to process the information at that layer to the application layer.
- If both sides do not have the full 7 layer functionality, the two systems will communicate at the lower of the highest layer available in the two systems. The two systems will have separate internal processes to convert information at that layer to their application layer.

It is necessary to point out that the functional modules can either be software, hardware or a combination of both. All levels (except the physical connection) can be implemented in software and equally, all levels can be implemented in hardware. Hardware modules tend to be used for lower level applications in the OSI model due to the simpler functionality. However, as many hardware devices are now made programmable, the distinction between hardware and software modules is not important in computer network elements nowadays.

3. THE VIRTUAL ENTERPRISE REFERENCE ARCHITECTURE

The modelling of virtual enterprise has been studied in a number of international projects (Hsu *et al*, 1994, Pan *et al*, 1991). The most well-known project is the IMS project GLOBEMEN which defines the Virtual Enterprise Reference Architecture (VERA) (Zwegers *et al*, 2003). VERA, which originates from Generalised Enterprise Reference Architecture and Methodology (GERAM) (Bernus *et al*, 1997), illustrates the logical, recursive relationships between the network entity, the VE entity and the product entity. Each of these three entities is represented by a life cycle describing possible phases an entity can be in throughout its life span from identification to decommission. VERA illustrates that the network can create VEs in its operational phase and, correspondingly, that a VE can create products and/or services in its operational phase.

The important characteristic of VERA is the changes of architecture requirements in different phases of the virtual enterprise. Conceptually, there are 3 architectures: Information Systems, Manufacturing Equipment and Human and Organisational architectures. Information systems and manufacturing equipment architectures represent automation of information and materials flows. Human and Organisational architecture sits between the two architectures and serves as the operating centre of the virtual enterprise. It is essential that a balance is required to ensure all three architectures are running in supporting each other rather than one moving too far (or behind). Individual companies may vary the balancing point (known as "extent of automation") but in a virtual enterprise, collaborative partners must find a common acceptable extent of automation. In essence, the "extent of automation" defines the ICT level at which the virtual enterprise is to operate.

4. THE RELINK COMMUNICATION FRAMEWORK

We use the OSI and VERA concept to consider the communication process between two toolmakers or a toolmaker and his/her customer. A 5 layer model can be used to describe the functionalities required to carry out the tasks transmitting information from one end to another. This model is designated as RELINK Communication Framework (RCF) as shown in Figure 1. Note that the case of customer to customer is not in the scope of this study.

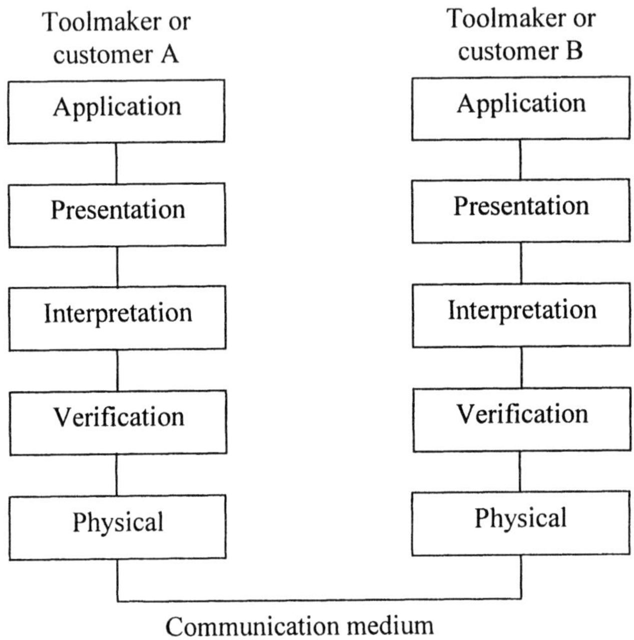

Figure 1 – The RELINK Communication Framework

The application layer describes the functions that a toolmaker needs to use the information for their work. For example, the toolmaker may use the information as a basis to design a new part, or he/she will use the information to schedule the machines for the next 24 hours. Two toolmakers, or the customer and the toolmaker must communicate at this level in order that the VE can fulfil its mission.

The presentation layer is the interface between application layer and interpretation layer. It contains the functions to convert the information to a format suitable to be used by the application that the toolmaker wants to run. For example, a toolmaker may receive a faxed drawing. Someone will perform the presentation layer function to convert this information into a computer model. There is no fundamental change of the content of the information. Communication between two communicating parties at this layer requires evaluation and perhaps, confirmation of the accuracy in the content of information being transmitted.

The interpretation layer performs the function of diverting information into relevant streams. In a communication process, there are many types of information transmitted. For example, a parcel consisting of some drawings, a project plan and a product specification is received. Different people in the company will process each of this information and hence a normal handling procedure is to divert parts of this information to different departments for processing. Communication between two communicating parties at this layer involves the identification of corresponding functional departments of the partners and gathering of information pertinent to (not necessarily exactly the information the other party desires to have) the communication parties.

The verification layer performs the function of ensuring the information transferred is actually the data that the sender wants to transmit. This includes tasks such as receipt certification, content acknowledgement, re-transmit request when errors occur, incomplete delivery handling, master copy filing, etc. In the toolmakers' VE environment, these functions will sometimes be performed by a number of parties, including outsourced entities. For communications using electronic media, this layer will probably be handled automatically.

The physical layer represents the transmission media that will be used in the communication process. The choices depend on the sophistication of technologies available to the partners in the VE.

5. AN EXAMPLE RCF SCENARIO

We attempt to illustrate the RCF concept by an example scenario. Communication scenarios can occur with toolmaker to toolmaker, or customer to toolmaker, or vice versa. The aim is to model the complete end-to-end activities in a process map, which can then be combined with other process maps to enable abstraction of functions to RCF. Note that the processes described are examples of activities that are likely to occur in this scenario. Different companies may have slightly different set of activities and work sequences. The processes are captured by software called VSMap.

The example scenario is to "design new tool from part model". A customer requests a toolmaker to design a new tool for his new part. The customer sends his part model in a CAD system to the toolmaker. The toolmaker has an alternative CAD system and will design the new tool based on product information supplied. Figure 3 shows the process map of the scenario.

The customer has already designed the product in his CAD-a system. He runs the CAD-a system and extracts the part model from the overall product model into a STEP file. The STEP file is too big to be transmitted through email so it will be sent as a CD. The customer also plots the drawings of the part model for inclusion into the information that the toolmaker can use to verify correctness of the part model. The customer also compiles supplementary product information that the toolmaker may need to design the tool. He then writes a covering letter explaining the actions required and the information packaged in this transmission. The CD, drawings, supplementary information and covering letter are packed into postpak and sent by mail.

Upon receiving the postpak the toolmaker unpacks it and verifies that the items are intact. Confirmation of receipt of postpak may be required but in this model, it is assumed that it is not a registered post. The transmitted information is divided into 2 parts: part STEP file and drawings (mainly part geometry), and product information (usage, appearance, application considerations, part weight, part size, materials, texture, etc.). The toolmaker tries to read the part geometry information into his CAD-b system. Most of the data are accepted except some critical sections, which the toolmaker has to compare with the drawings supplied and makes necessary corrections (or if the CAD-b system cannot handle such feature, an alternative CAD modelling method is applied). The outcome of this work is to produce a CAD-b model that represents the original CAD-a model. The toolmaker then takes this model together with other product information and develops a specification, which consists of the concept and geometrical formulation of the tool required to manufacture the product. This information is produced either through a thinking process or in a team working environment. When the tool is conceptualised, the tooling specification is compared with the available manufacturing processes to make the tool. Decisions will be made on process adaptation, partners' contribution, outsourcing (jobs to be done outside of the tooling VE) and other factors. The tool is finally designed in the CAD-b system and its database. The process model is overlaid with the RCF layers as shown in Figure 4.

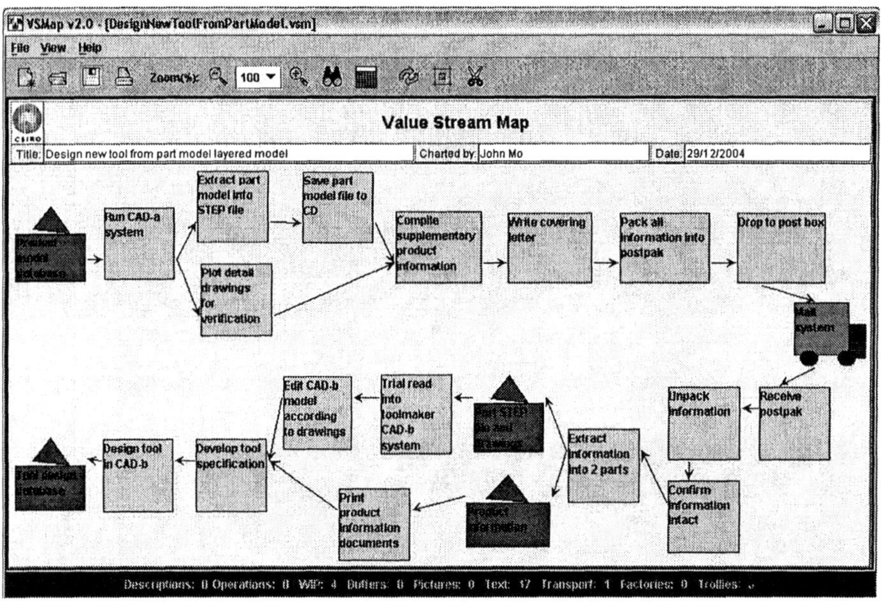

Figure 3 – Process map for exchanging CAD information

In Figure 4, activities "drop to post box", "mail system" and "receive postpak" are classified as physical layer functions. These activities serve as moving the information from one physical location to another. The content may be damaged in the activities. Traceability of where the parcel was during transmission may be included and in this case, acknowledgement through the mail system is necessary. The return path of acknowledgement is not modelled here.

The customer verifies the data to be transmitted through the activity "pack all information into postpak" while the toolmaker verifies the data received by "unpack information" and "confirm information intact". These activities are primarily to ensure that the parcel has no apparent distortion and is in its original form, as packed at the customer's location. Request for resend may be required if damage is found unrepairable.

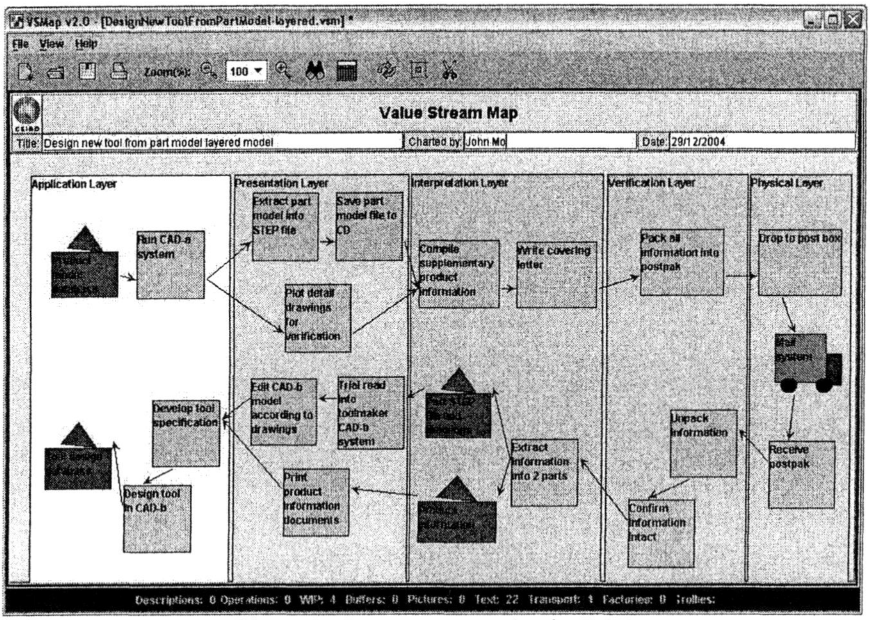

Figure 4 – Layer segmentation by RCF

The customer provides an interpretation of the information to be sent by activity "write covering letter". The letter not only provides meaning to the information but also lists the information that will be transmitted and how they are linked. In a normal transmission, some description of the product is required and such data may come from several departments (activity "compile supplementary product information"). The toolmaker's engineers interpret the customer supplied information in activity "extract information into 2 parts". The two streams of information are separated into appropriate files/directories: part STEP file and drawings, production information.

Following on the toolmaker's process, the STEP file is read into CAD-b for presenting to the engineers in 3D form. It is well known that STEP files do not usually transfer 3D model completely. Hence, an additional activity "edit CAD-b model according to drawings" is required to present the information in a form that is compatible with the same view as the customer had. Product information is normally represented conceptually and hence is printed. Back to the customer side, the customer's view of the part is extracted from the CAD-a model and presented as a STEP file generated from CAD-a system. To ensure complete presentation of the part model, a set of drawings of the part is also created to accompany the electronic STEP file.

The application layer consists of the customer accessing the CAD-a product model from his design database. At the toolmaker side, having the same view of the customer's part model (3D and product information), design of the tool can be started. The outcome of the function is a tool design that is stored in the CAD-b database.

The ICT used in this scenario are:

- **Information** – CAD systems, STEP Level 1 exchange mechanism, document repository
- **Communication** – postage, and possibly telephone confirmation

6. CONCLUSION

The RCF shows that communication within a tooling VE is a chained process. Activities that are planned according to the framework will be effective and efficient. Activities that need to break the chain can be done but the costs of communication will be significantly higher.

To develop the RCF further, studies of the existing communication processes that actually occur in the tooling industry will be vital to the success of modelling RCF and projecting how RCF migrates to describe the future scenarios.

7. REFERENCES

1. Williams T.J., Bernus P., Brosvic J., Chen D., Doumeingts G., Nemes L., Nevins J.L., Vallespir B., Vlietstra J., Zoetekouw D., Architectures for integration manufacturing activities and enterprises, *Computers in Industry*, Vol.24, 1994, pp.111-139

2. Callaham J.R., Preface of special issue, WET ICE'95 Fourth IEEE Workshop on Enabling Technologies: Infrastructure for Collaborative Enterprises, *Computers in Industry*, Vol.29, 1996, pp.1-3

3. Bernus P., Nemes L., Requirements of the Generic Enterprise Reference Architecture and Methodology, *A. Rev. Control*, Vol.21, 1997, pp.125-136

4. Beckett, R.C; Hyland, P and Sloan, T (2003) "Mapping Collaborative Transactions in Networks that Yield Business Benefits" *Proc 19th Annual IMP Conference,* University of Lugano, Switzerland, 4-6 September (ISBN 82-7042-576-1)

5. Barradas L.C.S., Pinto-Ferreira J.J., "P2P Infrastructure for tourism electronic marketplace", Paper 49, 18th IFIP World Computer Congress, Toulouse, France, 22-27 August, 2004

6. ISO, (1983), Open Systems Interconnection – Basic Reference Model, ISO 7498

7. Hsu C., Rubenstein A., Enterprise Information Management for Global Manufacturers, 4th International Conference on Computer Integrated Manufacturing and Automation Technology, 10-12 October, 1994, Conference Proceedings, IEEE, Troy, N.Y., U.S.A., pp.364-371

8. Pan J.Y.C., Tenenbaum J.M., An Intelligent Agent Framework for Enterprise Integration, *IEEE Transactions on Systems, Man, and Cybernetics*, Vol.21, No.6, November/December issue, 1991, IEEE, U.S.A., pp.1391-1408

9. Zwegers A., Tolle M., Vesterager J., (2003). "Virtual Enterprise Reference Architecture and Methodology", *Global Engineering and Manufacturing in Enterprise Networks*, VTT Symposium 224, 9-10 December, Helsinki, pp.17-38

10. Bernus P., Nemes L., The Contribution of the Generalised Enterprise Reference Architecture to Consensus in the Area of Enterprise Integration, ICEIMT GERAM, 21 August, 1997

PART 17

LEGAL ISSUES AND ENTITIES

53 LEGAL SECURITY AND CREDIBILITY IN AGENT BASED VIRTUAL ENTERPRISES

Francisco Andrade[1], José Neves[2], Paulo Novais[2], José Machado[2] and António Abelha[2]

[1]*Escola de Direito, Universidade do Minho, Braga, Portugal*

[2]*Departamento de Informática, Universidade do Minho, Braga, Portugal*

fandrade@direito.uminho.pt, {jneves, pjon, jmac, abelha}@di.uminho.pt

Recent trends in the field of Artificial Intelligence, brought along new ways of formalizing and expressing wills and declarations. Its application to Virtual Enterprises requires an analysis of the interactions among agents, frameworks and users, as well as technical and legal analysis, in order to discover the rules to be applied, to solve a particular problem under a prospective scenario. Credibility, trust and security issues must be taken under consideration, especially concerning authenticity, confidentiality, integrity and non-repudiation. In order to increase the use of agents in Virtual Enterprises, besides the analysis and research of legal solutions in the commercial arena, it is essential to assure that agents will meet requirements of credibility and trust, insuring a transparent and secure way for their commercial acting, now capable of generating legal relations. This paper shows how to construct a dynamic virtual world of complex and interacting entities or agents, in which fitness is judged by a quality of information criterion.

1. INTRODUCTION

The use of multi-agent systems in Virtual Enterprises (VE) scenarios pleads in favour of the answers to different and simultaneous user demands, under a secure and error free way. Agents must be able to manage knowledge in terms of beliefs, desires, intentions, expectations, goals and values, but also to plan, receive information, commands or instructions, reacting to environment stimulus, communicating and cooperating with other agents. On the other hand, the agent's knowledge is generally incomplete, contradictory or error sensitive, being desirable the use of formal tools to deal with incomplete, contradictory, imperfect, wrong, nebulous or missing information.

New developments concerning the roles an agent may play in such environments are arising but, still nowadays, agents are seen as mediators, playing generally passive roles, being used as searching or filtering devices. However, buyer or selling robotic devices are eager for the most advanced computational functionalities that may contribute to abide new users. Under this realm, new agents, working as brokers, initiators of commercial relations and/or generating agreements without human participation, are emerging [17]. These agents will perform an active/participative role in the trading process, and must be taken into consideration.

In order to increase the use of agents in VE, besides the analysis and research of legal solutions in the commercial arena, it is essential to assure that agents will meet requirements of trust and credibility, insuring a transparent and secure way for their commercial acting, now capable of generating legal relations, established by the inner states of an agent and its capability to determine, acquire and express beliefs, desires and intentions, constraining through direct or indirect ways, trust, reputation and credibility [16].

2. LEGAL SECURITY IN E-CONTRACTS

Actually, to speak about contracts there must be two or more declarations of will, containing a consensual agreement, consisting of an offer and of an acceptance. But agents operate in VE without any direct intervention of humans, and they have a control on their own actions and on their own inner states [1]. So, legal difficulties obviously arise in such situations of contracting through the only intervention and interaction of autonomous intelligent systems, capable of acting, learning, modifying instructions and taking decisions [2]. Traditional legal principles have some difficulty to deal with the fact of agents celebrating contracts on their own. We must keep in mind that the used devices can act in such an autonomous way that it may have severe implications in the process of contract formation as we know it. Because intelligent artefacts will not only act according to their built-in knowledge and rules [3] but they also will be able to learn from experience, and to modify its own behaviour, according to cognitive, reactive and pro-active processes quite similar to human acting [1]. So, as Emily Weitzenboeck puts it, "agreements will therefore no longer be generated through machines but by them, without any intervention or supervision of an individual" [3]. And since the program changes overtime, without any human intervention, it would be very difficult to characterize it as the embodiment or expression of human intention" [2].

This leads us to an imperious need of analysing the question of expression of consent in transactions performed by agents. And two main possibilities have been suggested: the possibility of considering these as mere machines or tools, used by its owner, and the daring possibility of considering the agent as a legal person. The first perspective would be simpler to adopt and it seems in accordance with legislation already enacted in the United States and Canada: The US Uniform Electronic Transactions Act (UETA), the Uniform Computer Information Transactions Act (UCITA) and Canada's Uniform Electronic Commerce Act, which already expressly recognize that a contract may be formed by the interaction of electronic agents. The second possibility, although presenting some practical difficulties, may appear quite fascinating and must be considered. But, for the moment being it is not yet possible to think of the "electronic agents" as legal persons. Should we accept the fiction of considering them as mere tools the humans are using, even knowing humans may not be able to control them? Or is there another solution? Considering that European jurisdictions have not yet decided what regime to adopt concerning electronic agents, it might be wiser to accept the suggestion of Giovanni Sartor, of "...creating companies for on-line trading, which would use agents in doing their business. Such agents would act in the name of a company, their will would count as the will of the company, their legally relevant location would be the company's domicile, and creditors could sue the company for obligations contracted by those agents. The counterparties of an agent could then be warranted by the company capital, and the legal remedies available towards defaulting commercial companies" [4].

But, even considering this, there must also be a link between the commercial act and the agents. Each agent must be identified; i.e., the agent must have access to a signature (e.g., an electronic signature, certified by a trusted third party), allowing an electronic performance of the traditional functions of a signature, such as the identification of the signer, and the manifestation of a will [5], in terms of assuring intention, authenticity and non-repudiation, and also of establishing integrity and certainty of the contents of the issued messages or declarations [6]. The question here is that the agent is not yet a person. Can it therefore use an electronic signature of its own? For the moment being the point is doubtful [7]. In order to avoid difficulties in law interpretation, it would be advisable that law clearly establishes the possibility for agents to use qualified electronic signatures, in order to enhance the use of agents in electronic commerce in a trustable and secure way.

Another important issue is certainly the one related to the proof value of such dematerialized informatics documents. May these documents be admitted to prove a contract before the Court, and if they may what will be its value? Under Portuguese law, the function of evidence is to create a firm belief in the reality of a fact. We know that contracts may be concluded by any means, except in certain situations when law requires a specific form or instrument. But, the general rule in Portuguese law is: if the contract is not subject to a written form, also the proof may be done by any means. Documentary evidence is stated in article 362 of the Civil Code, which defines document as "any material object created by man capable of representing a fact, event, thing or person". Under Portuguese law, electronic documents satisfy the requirement of written form when its contents are capable of being represented as a written declaration (art. 3 nr. 1 Decree 62/2003) and when signed with a qualified electronic signature certified by an accredited certification authority they will have the proof value of a private signed document (art. 3 nr. 2 Decree 62/2003). This kind of signature has the consequence of establishing a legal presumption that not only the signature was used with the intention of signing and that the document was not altered since then, but also that the person who used the signature is the holder of the signature or the legal representative of the company that holds the signature (art. 7 nr. 1 Decree 62/2003). Once again, according to this article, it is quite doubtful that an agent would be considered as entitled to sign on behalf, for instance, of the company that owns the agent. In order to enhance the use of agents, law should be revised accordingly.

Yet, it is possible for parties using electronic agents to agree on a convention in order to establish the acceptance, in their relations, of the electronic documents as proofs of their transactions. The Portuguese Civil Code (art. 345) admits this kind of conventions, with some exceptions [8]. Indeed, as it happens very often, and as it is suggested by Chris Reed, "many of the potential problems, once they are properly identified, can be overcome quite simply through the mechanism of properly drafted contracts" [9]. It is the will of the parties replacing law whenever law just ignores the reality and/or the actual needs of the commercial practice.

Related to the proof value of electronic documents appears the role, each day more and more important, of electronic evidence, in its broader sense, strongly related to the notion of traceability: As Michael Overly refers, "Electronic documents may include word-processing files, spreadsheets, e-mail, records of instant messaging (IM) exchanges, Web pages, online order forms, databases, and digitised pictures, video and audio files" [10]. The idea is that electronic evidence will perform a more and more important role in the subject of proof of electronic contracts.

Also quite relevant for electronic contracting will be to establish the precise time when electronic communications really occurred. Time stamp services, determining the date and hour of an electronic operation [11], will be of utmost importance.

Having the above stated in mind, it is essential to consider that all intervenients and processes in VE also should be seen as secure, trustable, reliable and credible [13, 14, 15, 16].

3. CREDIBILITY

Credibility is a synonym of believability and is not observable in an agent, a person or information, i.e. credibility must be evaluated in a subjective way through the perception of multiple ambiguous dimensions. The majority of researchers identify two key components of credibility: trustworthiness and expertise [12]. In evaluating credibility, a person makes an assessment of both trustworthiness and expertise to arrive at an overall credibility evaluation. To formalize the trustworthiness of an agent, a person or information, one must estimate if it is well-intentioned, truthful, unbiased, honest and good. To formalize expertise, one must estimate if it is experienced, intelligent, powerful, competent and knowledgeable. It is helpful to distinguish four types of credibility [12] even though these distinctions are not considered in the psychology literature and are based upon the information sources for credibility: presumed (based on a mind state), reputed (based on third parties reports), surfaced (based on a simple inspection) or experienced (based on first-hand experience). Credibility is obviously related to legal security.

4. KNOWLEDGE REPRESENTATION

Knowledge representation techniques as a way to describe the real world, based on mechanical, logical or other means, will be, always, a function of the systems ability to describe the existing world. Therefore, in the conception of a knowledge representation system, it must be object of attention [19]:

- Existent Information: it may not be known in all its extension.
- Observed Information: it is acquired by the experience, and obtained by contact or observation.
- Represented Information: with respect to a certain situation, it may be relevant to represent a given set of information. In spite of all the limitations, it is possible that observations made by different individuals, with distinct education and motivations, show the same set of fundamental data, function of its utility.

Prior to the characterization of the agent's structure in terms of Extended Logic Programming (ELP) productions, the agent's knowledge base has to be addressed. It will be built around a set of logical clauses subject to proof.

Definition. *The knowledge available in each agent's KB is made of logic clauses of the form* $P_{i+j+1} \leftarrow P_1 \wedge P_2 \wedge \ldots \wedge P_{i-1} \wedge not\ P_i \wedge \ldots \wedge P_{i+j}$, *where I, j, k* $\in N_0$, $P_1, \ldots, P_{i+j}$

are literals, i.e. formula of the form p or $\neg p$*, where p is atom, and where* r_k*, not,* P_{i+j+1}*, and* $P_1 \wedge P_2 \wedge \ldots \wedge P_{i-1} \wedge not\ P_i \wedge \ldots \wedge P_{i+j}$ *stand, respectively, for the clause's identifier, the* ***negation-as-failure*** *operator, the rule's consequent, and the rule's antecedent. If i=j=0 the clause is called a* ***fact*** *and is represented as* P_1*.*

i.e., with respect to the computational model it were considered extended logic programs with two kinds of negation, classical negation ¬ and default negation not. Intuitively, not p is true whenever there is no reason to believe p, whereas ¬p requires a proof of the negated literal. An extended logic program (program, for short) is a finite collection of rules r of the form:

$$p \leftarrow p_1, \ldots, p_n, not\ q_1, \ldots, not\ q_m$$

where the pi, qj, and p are classical ground literals, i.e. either positive atoms or atoms preceded by the classical negation sign ¬.

The knowledge base of an agent is taken from an ordered theory OT=(T,(S, <)), where T, S and < stand, respectively, for an agent's knowledge base in clausal form, a set of priority rules, and a non-circular ordering relation over such rules. An argument (i.e. a proof, or series of reasons in support or refutation of a proposition) or arguments have their genesis on mental states seen as a consequence of the proof processes that go on unceasingly at the agent's own knowledge about its states of awareness, consciousness or erudition. On the other hand the mental states that have been referred to above are by themselves a product of the reasoning processes over incomplete or unknown information; an argument may not only be evaluated in terms of true or false, but it may be quantified over the interval [0, 1] (e.g. agent is able to deal product with agent using the set of conditions C1; however it is not known if it can do the same thing with a set C2 -leading to further confrontation) [15].

This work is supported by the developments in [19] where the representation of incomplete information and the reasoning based on partial assumptions is studied, using the representation of null values to characterize abnormal or exceptional situations. The identification of null values emerges as a strategy for the enumeration of cases, for which one intends to distinguish between situations where the answers are known (true or false) or unknown [18, 19]. The representation of null values will be scoped by the ELP. In this work, it will be considered two types of null values: the former will allow the representation of unknown values, not necessarily taken from a given set of values, and the later will represent unknown values, taken from a given set of possible values. Consider the following as a case study to show some examples of how null values can be used to represent unknown situations. In what follows it will be considered the extensions of the predicates that denote some of the properties inherited by an agent, aiming at a measure of its credibility:

```
truthful: Entities × Value
good: Entities × Value
honest: Entities × Value
intelligent: Entities × Value
competent: Entities × Value
```

where the first argument denotes the agent and the second represents the value of the property (e.g. truthful(paul, 100) denotes that the truthfulness of the agent paul has the value 100).

```
truthful( paul,100 )
¬truthful( E,V ) ←
        not truthful( E,V )
```

Program 1: Extension of the predicate that describes the truthfulness of an agent.

In Program 1, the symbol ¬ denotes the strong negation, denoting what should be interpreted as false, and the term not designates negation-by-failure. Following the example given by Program 1, one can admit that the truthfulness of the agent cesar has not been established. This situation will be represented by a null value, of the type unknown, that should allow one to get the conclusion that the truthfulness exists, but to which it is not possible to be affirmative with respect to its value (Program 2).

```
truthful( paul,100 )
truthful ( cesar, ⊥ )
¬ truthful ( E,V ) ←
      not truthful ( E,V ),
       not exception(truthful ( E,V ) )
exception(truthful ( E,V ) ) ←
      truthful ( E, ⊥ )
```

Program 2: Information about the truthfulness of the agent cesar, with an unknown value.

Symbol ⊥ represents a null value of an undefined type, in the sense that it is a representation that assumes that any value is a potential solution but without being given the clue to conclude about which value one is speaking about. Computationally, it is not possible to determine, from the positive information, the value of the truthfulness of the agent cesar; under the description of the exception situation (fourth clause from Program 2, the closure of predicate truthfulness), it is discarded the possibility to be assumed as false any question on the specific value of truthfulness of the agent cesar.

Consider now the example in which the value of the truthfulness of an agent josé is foreseen to 65, with a margin of some mistake (15). It is not possible to be affirmative regarding the truthfulness value. However, it is false that the agent has value of truthfulness of 85 or 100. This example suggests that the lack of knowledge may only be associated to an enumerated set of possible values. On the other hand, consider the truthfulness of the agent francisco that it is unknown, but we know that it is specifically 25 or 50.

```
truthful ( paul,100 )
truthful ( cesar, ⊥ )
¬ truthful ( E,V ) ←
       not truthful ( E,V ),
        not exception(truthful (E,V ))
exception(truthful ( E,V ) ) ←
       truthful ( E, ⊥ )

exception (truthful ( josé, V ) ) ←
       V ≥ 50 ∧ V ≤ 80

exception (truthful ( francisco, 25 ) )

exception (truthful ( francisco, 50 ) )
```

Program 3: Representation of the truthfulness of the agents josé and francisco

To reason about the body of knowledge presented in a particular knowledge, set on the base of the formalism referred to above, let us consider a procedure given in terms of the extension of a predicate called demo, using ELP as the logic programming language. Given a question it returns a solution based on a set of assumptions. This meta predicate will be defined as:

demo: Question × Answer

where Question denotes a theorem to be proved and Answer denotes a truth value: true (T), false (F) or unknown (U) (Program 3).

```
demo( Q, T ) ← Q
demo( Q, F ) ← ¬Q
demo( Q, U) ← not Q ∧ not ¬Q
```

Program 4: Extension of meta-predicate demo

The first clause of Program 4 sets that a question it is to be answered with appeal to the knowledge base positive information; the second clause denotes that the question is proved to be false with appeal to the negative information presented at the knowledge base level; the third clause stands for itself.

Indeed, in the search for an answer, we are looking into the Case Based Reasoning (CBR) methodology for problem solving [21], and postulate that each case is to be given in terms of a logic theory, built upon the extensions and the exceptions of the predicates that make their realm, i.e. for all cases in the case's memory and for each property inherited by an agent, that is selected, and their relevance to the answer evaluated, in terms of a measure of the quality of the information it carries. The CBR life cycle is therefore defined as follows, in terms of the algorithm:

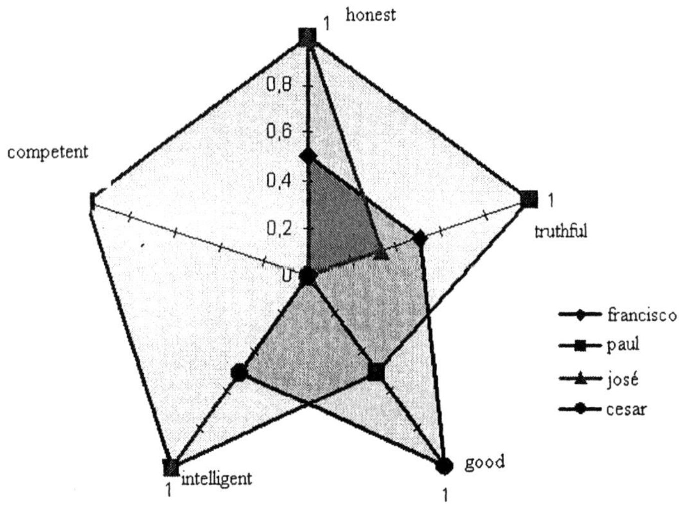

Figure 1 – A measure of the quality-of-information for the individual agents *francisco, paul, josé,* and *cesar (here presented in terms of different areas and colors)*

- A new case is set in terms of the agent's data, and given as the extension of a set of predicates and the exceptions to these extensions;
- The new case is re-defined in terms of the extension of an unary predicate $L_P/1$ that evaluates the agent's quality of information with respect to a particular property (here given in terms of the subscript);
- Using L_P , a mapping into an hyperspace is built, where the axes stand for the agent's state of knowledge, and the area delimited gives a measure of the quality of information carried out by each case under consideration (Figure 1).

i.e. using L_P and the extension of predicates *honest, competent, truthful, good* and *intelligent*, a mapping into an hyperspace is built, and the area delimited by the arcs gives a measure of the quality of information carried out by each case under consideration [20]. In the example of the Program 3, and to predicate *truthful,* this situation corresponds to a case where a measure of the quality of the information it carries is given by:

$L_{\text{truthful}}(\text{paul}, V) = 1$

$$L_{\text{truthful}}(\text{cesar}, V) = \lim_{x \to \infty} \frac{1}{x} = 0$$

$L_{\text{truthful}}(\text{jose}, V) = 1 - (75\text{-}55 + 1) / 100 = 0.29$

$L_{\text{truthful}}(\text{francisco}, V) = 1 / 2 = 0.5$

Similar calculi are to be made for the predicates *honest*, *competent*, *intelligent* and *good.*

5. IMPLEMENTATION

Using JADE a prototype has been developed in order to evaluate *credibility* and *trust* using the formalisms mentioned to above, in VE scenarios. Some print-screens are shown in Figure 2.

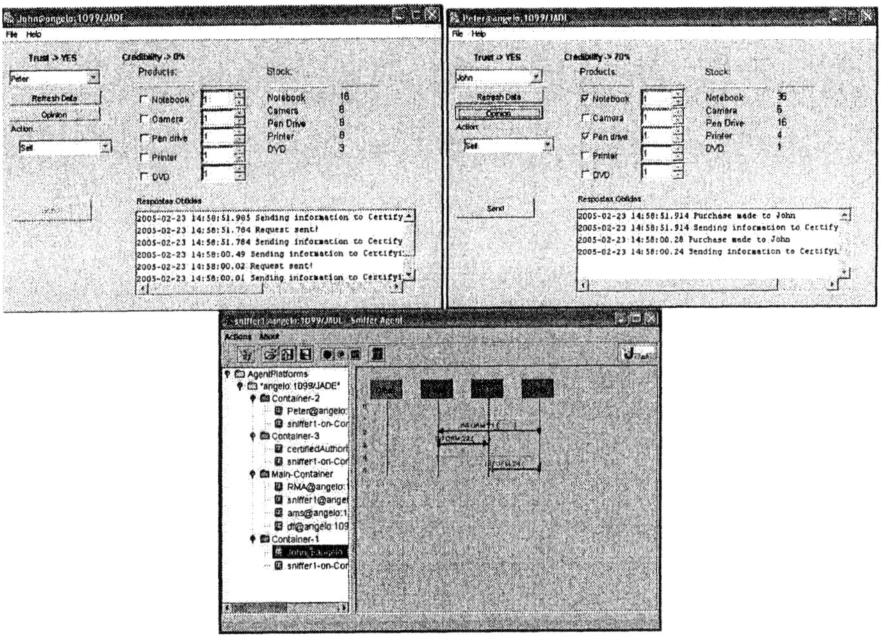

Figure 2 – Given a measure of the agent credibility and trust

6. CONCLUSIONS

This paper shows how to construct a dynamic virtual world of complex and interacting entities or agents, in which fitness is judged by one criterion alone: quality of information. The architecture underlying this system is versatile, creative and powerful enough to engender a practically infinite variety of data processing and analysis capabilities, adaptable to almost any conceivable intellectual tasks. This virtual world could witness the emergence of a learning, thinking machine, and foray into a vast, untapped technological market.

In order to obtain a solution to a particular problem, one looks at a repository, in order to evaluate cases, based on a measure that is given in terms of the information quality carried out by each case. Usually important is that the logical system have associated with it a meta-theory, which would address questions such as whether the system in question is sound, complete, decidable, and so on. Such meta-properties are determined by bringing mathematical tools to bear on the system in question. In this work such a meta-theory was defined in terms of the extension of an unary predicate L_P that evaluates the credibility of each agent, in terms of the quality of information it carries and its contribution to the problem's solution.

7. REFERENCES

1. Ruggiero E., Il contratto telematico, Edizioni Simone, 2003.
2. Allen T, Widdison R., Can Computer Make Contracts?, Harvard Journal of Law and Technology, Volume 9, Number 1, Winter 1996.
3. Weitzenboeck E., Electronic Agents and the formation of contracts, http://www.eclip.org/documentsII/elecagents/contract_formation.pdf, visited 2003/9/8.
4. Sartor G. Agents in Cyberlaw, point 4 in http://www.cirfid.unibo.it/~lea-02/pp/Sartor.pdf , visited 2003/9/8.
5. Antoine M., Robert D., Pistes de réflexion pour une législation relative à la signature digitale et au régime des autorités de certification, in "Revue Générale de Droit Civil", septembre 1998, n° 4, pp. 285 a 310 e em http://www.droit.fundp.ac.be/textes/signaturergdc.pdf (visited in 30-7-2003).
6. Murray J., Public Key Infrastructure Digital Signatures and Systematic Risk, in The Journal of Information, Law and Technology 2003 Issue 1 and http://elj.warwick.ac.uk/jilt/03-1/murray.html visited in 9/10/2003 (página 3)
7. Lourenço Martins A., Garcia Marques J.A., Dias P., Cyberlaw em Portugal, CentroAtlantico.pt, 2004.
8. Rodriguez M., Derecho Informático, Aranzadi Editorial, 1993, pages 202-203.
9. Reed C., Advising Clients on EDI contracts, Computer Law and Practice, volume 10, nr. E, 1994.
10. Overly M., Overly on Electronic Evidence in California, Thomson-West, 2003.
11. Van den Eynde S., Wat archiveren en hoe? Op zoek naar de rol van PKI voor digitale archieven, in http://www.antwerpen.be/david/website/teksten/ Rapporten/Rapport6.pdf (visited 28th February 2005).
12. Fogg BJ, Persuasive Technology - Using Computers to Change What We Think and Do, Morgan Kaufmann, ISBN: 1558606432, 2002.
13. Sabater J. and Sierra C., Reputation and social network analysis in multi-agent systems. Proceedings of the first International Joint Conference on Autonomous Agents and Multiagent systems, Italy, pp. 475-482, 2002.
14. Sabater J. and Sierra C., Social ReGreT, a reputation model based on social relations. SIGecom Ex-changes. ACM, Vol 3.1, pp 44-56, 2002.
15. Novais P, Analide C, Machado J, Neves J. Reputation and Trust in the context of Logic-based argumentation. ICKEDS'2004 – International Conference on Knowledge Engineering and Decision Support, Porto, 2004.
16. Andrade F., Neves J., Novais P., Machado J:, Software Agents as Legal Persons, in Virtual Enterprises and Collaborative Networks, Camarinha-Matos L. (Ed), Kluwer Academic Publishers, ISBN 1-4020-8138-3, pp 123-132, 2004.
17. Novais P., Brito L., Neves J., Experience-Based Mediator Agents as the basis of an Electronic Commerce System, em Proceedings of the Workshop Agent-Based Simulation - 2000, Passau, Germany, 2000.
18. Traylor, B., Gelfond, M.: Representing Null Values in Logic Programming. Proceedings of the ILPS'93 Workshop on Logic Programming with Incomplete Information, pp. 35-47, Vancouver, Canada, 1993.
19. Analide C., Antropopatia em Entidades Virtuais, Ph.D. Thesis, Engineering School, University of Minho, Portugal, 2004 (in Portuguese).
20. Abelha, A., Sistemas Multiagente de Apoio ao Trabalho Cooperativo em Unidades Hospitalares, Ph.D. Thesis, Engineering School, University of Minho, Portugal, 2004 (in Portuguese).
21. Aamodt A., Plaza E., Case-Based Reasoning: Foundational Issues, Methodological Variations, and System Approaches, in AI Communications, Vol. 7, N° 1, pages 39-59, 1994.

54

LEGAL RISK ANALYSIS WITH RESPECT TO IPR IN A COLLABORATIVE ENGINEERING VIRTUAL ORGANIZATION

Tobias Mahler
Norwegian Research Center for Computers and Law (NRCCL), University of Oslo, tobias.mahler@jus.uio.no
Fredrik Vraalsen
SINTEF Information and Communication Technology, Fredrik.Vraalsen@sintef.no
NORWAY

Establishing and operating a virtual organization implies a number of challenges from many different perspectives, including socio-economic, organizational, legal and computational issues. This paper focuses on the legal aspects with a particular view on legal risks with respect to intellectual property rights. A risk analysis with respect to legal issues can either be based on abstract legal reasoning or it can focus on the business reality and the specific characterizations of the virtual organization. This paper follows the latter approach; it presents selected findings of a legal risk analysis of a business scenario in the collaborative engineering field. The legal risk analysis was performed in collaboration between lawyers and other professionals in order to highlight how different legal and non-legal aspects relate to each other. Graphical models of risks and treatments were utilized in order to reduce communicational barriers between experts in this multidisciplinary setting.

1. INTRODUCTION

A virtual organization (VO) can be understood as a temporary or permanent coalition of geographically dispersed individuals, groups, organizational units or entire organizations that pool resources, capabilities and information to achieve common objectives (Dimitrakos et al 2004).

From a legal point of view, it is advisable to base the establishment and operation of a VO on a clear contractual basis, which outlines rights and duties of the VO participants. An example of such a contract is outlined e.g. in (ALIVE 2002a). The ALIVE template provides a good starting point for negotiating contracts for VOs where the partners will collaborate on a medium-term to long-term basis, similar to a joint venture.

There is no general European legal framework for the establishment and operation of virtual organizations, thus legal issues in relation to VOs are still a topic for research. A recently published *strategic roadmap for advanced virtual organizations* points out that the analysis of legal risks arising in operating VOs and the development of legal strategies to overcome them is an important research task in order to support collaborate networked organizations (Camarinha-Matos et al.

2004, p. 296). One area where VO participants face a number of legal risks is the protection of intellectual property rights (IPR), which is the focus of this paper.

Others have addressed risk management for projects (e.g. Baccarini & Archer 1999, Raz & Michael 1999), focusing on general risks for the project as such. Compared to these approaches, this paper focuses not on general risks but only on risks that can be related to legal issues; in this sense it is more specific. The legal risk analysis presented in this paper utilized some of the UML-based graphical models for risk analysis developed by the CORAS IST project to facilitate documentation and communication of risk analysis results (den Braber et. al. 2005). The goal of the analysis was twofold; 1) to identify legal risks and treatments related to IPR in the selected VO scenario, with the aim to create a set of reusable results for use in future analyses, e.g. in the form of templates and checklists, and 2) to evaluate the suitability of risk analysis, in particular the CORAS model-based risk analysis (MBRA) methods and graphical language, with respect to supporting the analysis of legal issues in relation to contract formation in VOs.

The remainder of this paper is structured as follows: Section 2 describes how legal risk analysis can be performed utilizing graphical models; section 3 introduces the collaborative engineering scenario which is the basis for the analysis; section 4 outlines the role of IPR issues in VO-related contracts; section 5 presents selected results of the legal risk analysis performed on the basis of the scenario. Finally, section 6 draws the main conclusions.

2. LEGAL RISK ANALYSIS

The establishment of a VO often occurs under the pressure of time in order to avoid losing the business opportunity which is the primary driver for the collaboration. On the other hand, the parties need to define a contract that sets out the internal functioning of the VO; the contract is a key mechanism for the VO management.

In such cases it is advisory to base the contract on an existing template. However, such contractual templates can not be used "off the shelf"; they need to be adapted to the needs of the specific VO. This implies an adjustment of the contractual rules, taking into account the specific aim of the collaboration, how the partners want to organize the internal management of the VO, whether the VO structure is more static or more dynamic, and what kinds of specific risks have to be taken into account.

Legal risk analysis (LRA) can be applied to the process of adjusting a contract template to the specific risks of the VO. The VO needs to avoid two situations: First, the contract should not overlook relevant risks that should have been addressed in the contract. Second, the contract should avoid addressing issues that are of little business relevance and where the related contractual terms would themselves present a barrier for a successful collaboration, e.g. by providing very bureaucratic rules for cooperation.

For the purpose of this paper, we define LRA as a risk analysis that focuses on the one hand on risks that stem from the legal domain (e.g. loss of a legal right) and on the other hand on non-legal risks that can be treated with legal means. The advantage of this rather broad understanding is that it provides an integrated approach, where legal risks also can be treated by non-legal means and non-legal risks may be addressed with typically legal approaches, e.g. a contractual rule.

2.1 Model-based Risk Analysis

Risk analysis requires a clear understanding of the system to be analysed. Normally, this understanding can be obtained only through the involvement of different stakeholders, e.g. legal experts, security experts, system developers and users. In fact, most methods for risk identification make use of structured brainstorming sessions of one kind or another, e.g. Hazard and Operability (HazOp) analysis (Redmill et. al. 1999), involving 5-7 stakeholders and domain experts with different backgrounds. The effectiveness of such sessions depends on the extent to which the participants are able to communicate with and understand each other. The CORAS language for threat modelling (den Braber et. al. 2005) has been designed to mitigate this problem within the security domain. Recent work has focused on application of the CORAS language and methodology to the analysis of legal issues (Vraalsen et. al. 2005).

The CORAS language covers notions like asset, threat, risk and treatment, and supports communication among participants with different backgrounds through the definition of easy-to-understand icons (symbols) associated with the modelling elements of the language. The CORAS language is an extension of the UML 2.0 (OMG 2004a) specification language, the de facto standard modelling language for information systems. It is defined as a UML profile (Lund et. al. 2003), and has recently become part of an OMG standard (OMG 2004b).

3. COLLABORATIVE ENGINEERING SCENARIO

This section presents the scenario which is being used in the remainder of the paper. It is a simplified version of a collaborative engineering scenario from the aerospace industry which is being used in the TrustCoM IST project (www.eu-trustcom.com) as part of a test bed. It is being analyzed from different perspectives, including computational aspects, socio-economic aspects and legal aspects. A similar version of this scenario is described in (Wesner et al., 2004), who focus more on computational aspects.

The scenario addresses a collaborative engineering project typical of the aerospace industry, where a lead contractor collaborates with a large number of subcontractors and peer organizations on the development of an airplane or similar product over a 15 year time period, followed by a 20-40 year deployment period. The TrustCoM collaborative engineering scenario consists of three VOs:

- An airliner VO, (Air VO) consisting of the carrier, support and maintenance teams;
- A Collaborative Engineering VO, (CE VO) which has the technical expertise to specify, design and integrate systems into complex products, and which may also manufacture the solution for the customer. This VO's business goal is to win a contract with the Air VO regarding the upgrade of a particular aircraft type with a new feature. One of the partners of the CE

VO, the Systems Integrator (SI), is specialized in the integration of different aircraft systems.
- A number of engineering analysis consultancies that form a VO to support design activities within engineering companies. The Analysis VO (AVO) supports general analysis work across engineering and scientific sectors.

The themes covered by TrustCoM in this scenario include:
- Design and analysis data security; protection of intellectual property;
- Enforcement of Trust and Security policies through the interpretation of contracts and by reacting to notable business 'events';
- Contract negotiation between clients and service providers to support collaborative agreements and service level agreements.

Whilst the main focus of this paper is the protection of IPR in a contractual context, we also attempt to relate the legal issues to the trust and security issues addressed by other parts of the TrustCoM project.

4. INTELLECTUAL PROPERTY RIGHTS IN VO CONTRACTS

A number of different contracts will govern the internal and external relations in the scenario. These will include at least the following types of contracts: (1) VO-internal consortium agreements, which establish consortia of organizations with respective VO goals. All CE VO members will be parties to a consortium agreement. (2) Contracts about the provision of a service or the purchase of a good, without establishing a consortium. This type of contract will be in place between the CE VO (possibly represented by a lead contractor) and the two other VOs, AVO and Air VO. Both types of contracts should also cover IPR issues.

Intellectual and industrial property (IP) rights consist of a variety of rights, including copyright, database protection, patent protection, trademark and design protection and the protection of confidential information (i.e. know-how and trade secrets). The legal framework for these rights shows some variations, taking into account the nature of the protected intellectual property. The law is regulated in slightly different ways in the various member states of the European Union, despite a harmonization of selected IPR issues in European law.

For a VO, the protection of copyrights is closely related to the question of legal personality. In principle, only an entity with legal personality can hold legal rights. Therefore, if the VO has legal personality, it can hold most intellectual property rights. VOs that lack legal personality must refer to their members as holders of all legal rights. A general analysis of IPR issues in a VO context was carried out by the ALIVE project (ALIVE 2002b).

Relevant IPR issues that are likely to be encountered in the formation and operation of a VO can, for the sake of simplicity, be split into two principal categories: Internal issues arise among the various members of a VO, whereas external issues arise between the VO and/or its members, on the one hand, and parties outside the VO on the other hand. We should also make a distinction between pre-existing IP, which is brought into the VO by the partners, and the IP developed during the co-operative process.

5. SELECTED RESULTS OF THE LEGAL RISK ANALYIS

This section presents selected results of the legal risk analysis, which was performed according to the CORAS risk analysis process. The initial step of this process consists of describing the context of the analysis, i.e. the target of analysis and relevant stakeholders and assets. The target for the risk analysis was the scenario presented in section 3, with a focus on the analysis of IPR, as detailed in section 4, in particular know-how and trade secrets (confidential information). The analysis was performed from the viewpoint of the airplane Systems Integrator (SI) partner of the CE VO.

The risk identification was performed during a number of HazOp brainstorming sessions involving participants with backgrounds in law, engineering, economics, computer science and philosophy. Risks were assigned consequence and frequency values and prioritised, and treatments were then identified for the major risks through another brainstorming session. Some examples of identified risks and treatments are presented below.

5.1 *Example of Identified Risks*

The identified risks relate to different IPR issues, including the protection of confidential information (i.e. know-how and trade secrets), the ownership of IP and liability for IPR infringements by other VO partners. It would be outside the scope of this paper to present all identified risks. We will therefore concentrate on risks related to the loss of confidential information, which was identified as a major risk category. The internal collaboration in the CE VO and its cooperation with the AVO and the Air VO, respectively, may imply that confidential information is shared or otherwise disclosed to VO partners or to external parties. This involves a risk that such confidential information is disclosed to third parties or used by VO members for purposes that are not related to the VO.

Figure 1 shows a CORAS UML diagram describing some ways in which confidential information can be disclosed and potential consequences this disclosure may have. In the CORAS language for risk analysis a threat is described using a *threat agent*, e.g. a disloyal employee or a computer virus, typically represented in the diagram by a stick figure. The threat agent initiates a *threat scenario*, which is a sequence of events or activities leading to an *unwanted incident*, i.e. an event resulting in a reduction in the value of the target *asset*. Furthermore, an unwanted incident may initiate or lead to other unwanted incidents, forming chains of events. For example, an unfaithful employee working for one of the CE VO partners may have access to confidential information which he/she could disclose to a third party. This disclosure could lead to the information reaching the public domain and thereby losing its legal protection and value as a trade secret. A similar but opposite scenario is that an employee of our stakeholder (SI) is unfaithful and discloses the client's confidential information. This again could lead to the CE VO or the SI being sued for breach of the non-disclosure agreement with the Air VO. The latter unwanted incident may not only have consequences for the SI's revenue, it may also lead to further consequences, like negative publicity.

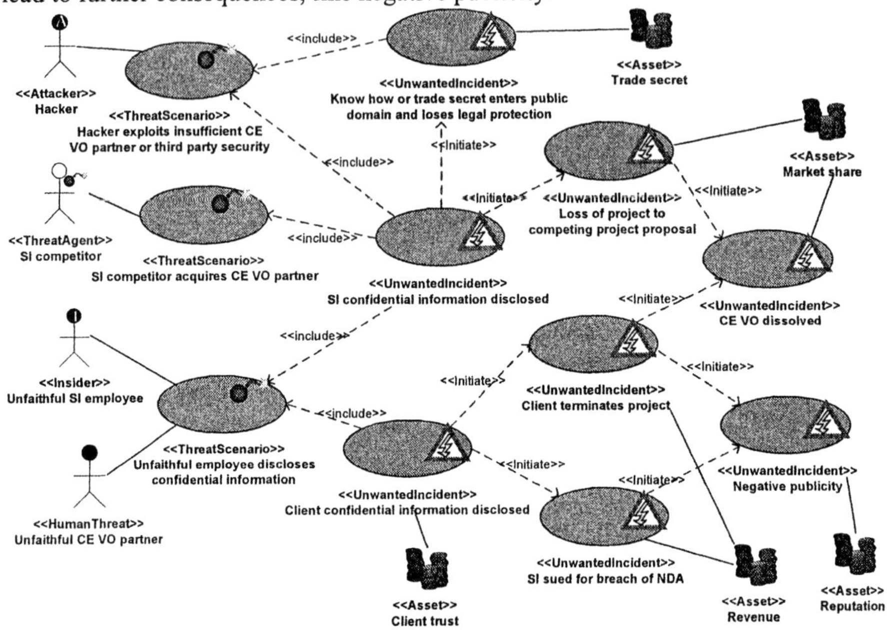

Figure 1 Confidential information loses legal protection

5.2 *Example of Identified Treatments*

For each of the risks, we have explored potential treatments related to three main areas of the TrustCoM project, namely trust, security and contracts. Our aim was to develop an integrated set of treatments, where legal and other measures are integrated. In this context we focused on law as a proactive mechanism, which tries to solve legal issues before they arise; legal reactions *ex post* were not addressed.

Treatments may have different effects on risks, they may e.g. reduce the consequence or frequency of the unwanted incident occurring, or transfer the risk to another party, e.g. through insurance. A selection of treatments to the risks described above is shown in the CORAS treatment diagram in Figure 2. Two of these treatments are clearly within the legal domain: First, a contract clause could avoid the disclosure of confidential information in case of a merger or acquisition, by allowing a re-negotiation of the general VO agreement in this event. Second, specific contractual rules in the VO agreement should address the VO members' liability towards third parties. The remaining treatments involve legal and non-legal elements: Information security mechanisms like limitations to storage time and the deletion of data after an analysis are of key importance. Such mechanisms can be made obligatory via contractual clauses in the agreement between the CE VO and the AVO. If the technology was available, a VO-internal enterprise Digital Rights Management (DRM) system could also reduce the likelihood of confidential information being disclosed, particularly if some of the contractual obligations could be enforced through technology.

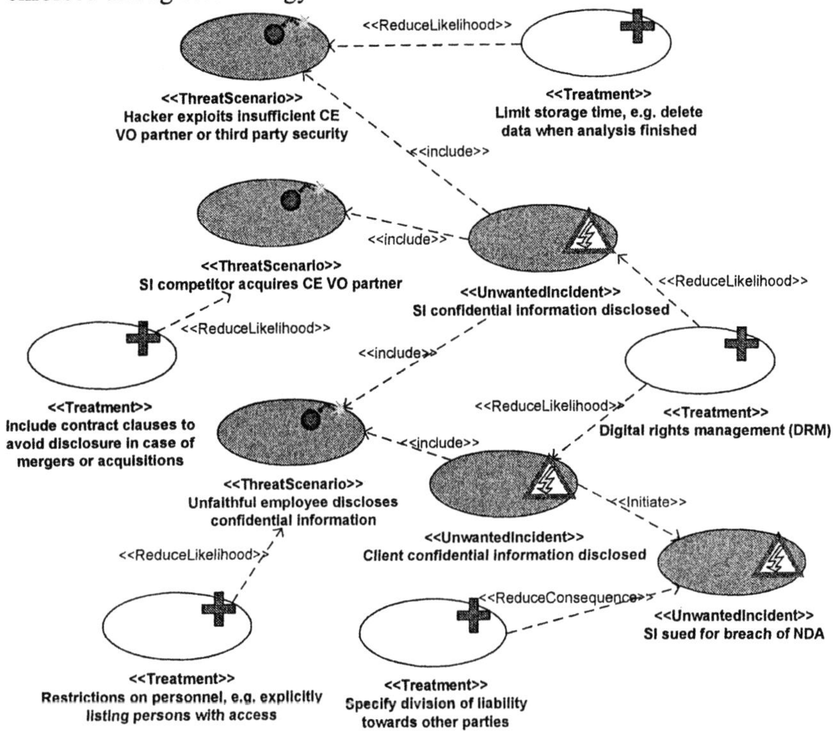

Figure 2 Risk treatments

6. CONCLUDING REMARKS

We have presented results from the analysis of a collaborative engineering VO scenario, where a number of legal risks and treatments were identified. Our risk analysis results indicate how legal risks, such as the loss of protection of confidential information, can be treated by an integrated solution, including contractual elements, trust management and security management. Interestingly, many of the relevant contractual treatments were also included in a general manner in the ALIVE contract template for VOs (ALIVE 2002a). The performed legal risk analysis provided indications about how these rules can be adapted to the specific scenario. Since the graphical representation implies a simplification, a lawyer would have to integrate analysis results into the contractual document in an appropriate way, taking into account the terminology and the system of the contractual template.

The analysis results were generated during a number of brainstorming sessions involving participants with varied backgrounds, including law, computer science, engineering, economics and philosophy. Based on our experiences, the graphical models can indeed facilitate the communication and understanding with respect to legal issues in a multidisciplinary context. Ongoing work is focusing on further adapting the CORAS methodology and graphical language to better suit legal risk analysis (Vraalsen et. al. 2005), as well as on creating reusable elements in the form of e.g. checklists based on the results of this analysis in order to facilitate future analyses.

7. ACKNOWLEGEMENTS

The results presented here are partly financed by the European Commission under contract IST-2003-01945 through the project TrustCoM and partly financed under the Research Council of Norway through the project ENFORCE.

We would like to acknowledge the work done by David Goldby from BAE Systems, who has defined the collaborative engineering scenario for TrustCoM. We would also like to thank David Goldby, Mass Soldal Lund, Xavier Parent and Claudia Keser for participating in the risk analysis sessions.

8. REFERENCES

ALIVE IST Project (2002a). Report D 17 a, VE Model Contracts, available at http://www.vive-ig.net/projects/alive/docs.html.

ALIVE IST Project (2002b) *Report D 13, ALIVE Project, Intellectual & Industrial Property Rights Legal Issue Subgroup*. http://www.vive-ig.net/projects/alive/docs.html.

Baccarini, D. and Archer, R. *The risk ranking of projects: a methodology*. International Journal of Project Management 19 (2001) 139-145.

Folker den Braber, Mass Soldal Lund, Ketil Stølen, Fredrik Vraalsen. The CORAS methodology: Model based security analysis using UML and UP. Encyclopedia of Information Science and Technology. Information Resources Management Association, USA (2005)

Camarinha-Matos, L., Afsarmanesh, H., Löh, H., Sturm, F., Ollus, M. A strategic roadmap for advanced virtual organizations. In collaborative networked oganizations: a research agenda for emerging business models. Camarinha-Matos, L and Afsarmanesh, ed. New York: Springer 2004.

Dimitrakos T, Goldby D and Kearney P. Towards a trust and contract management framework for dynamic virtual organizations. In E-Adoption and the knowledge economy: eChallenges 2004, IOS press 2004.

Lund, M.S., Hogganvik, I., Seehusen, F., Stølen, K.: UML profile for security assessment. Technical Report STF40 A03066, SINTEF Telecom and informatics (2003).

OMG: UML 2.0 Superstructure Specification. (2004a) OMG Document: ptc/2004-10-02.

OMG: UML Profile for Modeling Quality of Service and Fault Tolerance Characteristics and Mechanisms, Draft Adopted Specification (2004b) OMG Document: ptc/2004-06-01.

Raz T and Michael E. Use and benefits of tools for project risk management. International Journal of Project Management 19 (1999) 9-17.

Redmill, F., Chudleigh, M., Catmur, J.: HazOp and software HazOp. Wiley (1999)

Vraalsen, F., Lund, M.S., Mahler, T., Parent, X. and Stølen, K. Specifying Legal Risk Scenarios Using the CORAS Threat Modelling Language – Experiences and the Way Forward. In Proceedings of the 3rd International Conference on Trust Management (iTrust '05). Paris, France, May 2005. Springer LNCS 3477.

Wesner S, Schubert L, Dimitrakos T. *Dynamic Virtual Organizations in Engineering*. Forthcoming, the Proceedings of the Second German-Russian Workshop. Notes on Numerical Fluid Mechanics and Multidisciplinary Design (NNFM). Springer.

55 INSTITUTIONAL SERVICES FOR DYNAMIC VIRTUAL ORGANIZATIONS

Henrique L. Cardoso, Andreia Malucelli, Ana P. Rocha, Eugénio Oliveira
LIACC – NIAD&R, Faculty of Engineering, University of Porto
R. Dr. Roberto Frias, 4200-465 Porto, Portugal
hlc@ipb.pt, malu@fe.up.pt, arocha@fe.up.pt, eco@fe.up.pt

Electronic Institutions are comprehensive frameworks that may effectively help in the collaborative work of virtual organization activities. This paper focuses on an effort to create e-contracting and ontology-based services in the context of Electronic Institutions. The e-contracting services provide automatic specification of business agreements by formalizing them through e-contracts, plus the procedures for enforcing them. Moreover, ontology-based services enable the interoperability between agents representing organizations using different ontologies. Ontology services provide useful advices on how to negotiate specific items, leading to appropriate conversations and making agreements possible. We believe that the rendering of these services will provide a level of trust and normative behavior allowing the creation, through electronic institutions, of dynamic virtual organizations and their operation.

1. INTRODUCTION

Virtual organizations (VOs) are a major trend in cooperative business. Some of the key aspects of modern businesses include specialization and flexibility. The temporary nature of VOs requires that they should be formed quickly, allowing them to start operating as soon as possible. Technological support towards VO formation is a strong research topic. Some approaches include the multi-agent systems (MAS) paradigm, which aim at automating the process of creation and operation of dynamic VOs. A related topic within the MAS community is how to develop means to allow the interoperation of agents in open environments (that is, with no centralized approach).

Electronic institutions are frameworks that provide and enforce rules and norms of behavior, offering services to assist both interaction and operation monitoring of computational business entities. In (Rocha *et al.*, 2005) we presented a sketch of an electronic institution, relating it to the virtual enterprise lifecycle. Moreover, we detailed an advanced negotiation protocol, and delved into the state-of-the-art on e-contracting automation. In this paper, we present an integration of services that allow for the establishment and execution of contracts. We then describe our approach towards handling e-contracts within an institutional environment, and on developing services that provide automatic monitoring and enforcement of business agreements. We also present ontology-based services that enable interoperability between agents representing organizations using different ontologies.

The paper addresses the aforementioned concepts as follows. Section 2 introduces the electronic institution and its services. Section 3 details the issue of contracts and norms, together with related institutional services, and section 4 presents ontology-based services. We conclude in section 5, referring also to some related work.

2. ELECTRONIC INSTITUTIONS

Human societies are governed by institutions providing services or regulating the way citizens interact. The same approach has been proposed, in the last years, as a means to regulate the interaction among software agents. The *electronic institution* (EI, for short) concept represents the virtual counterpart of real-world institutions.

According to (Dignum and Dignum, 2001), the benefit of an EI resides in its potential to assure legitimacy and security to its members, through the establishment of norms. Besides enforcing norms, institutional services should be provided to assist the coordination efforts between agents which, representing different real-world entities, interact towards the establishment of business relationships.

In our perspective, an EI is thus a comprehensive framework that provides a set of institutional services, while assuring norm enforcement through the imposition of sanctions and reputation mechanisms. The EI provides an environment where regulated agent interactions can take place. One of the main roles of such an environment is to provide the necessary level of trust that enables agents from different sources to safely engage in business interactions.

As the establishment of business engagements is central to our purposes, we consider an evolving normative environment, including formalizations of "handshakes" by means of contracts that the EI monitors and enforces.

2.1 Institutional Services

We may summarize the main goals of an EI as follows: (1) to support agent interaction as a coordination framework, making the establishment of business agreements more efficient; and (2) to provide a level of trust by offering an enforceable normative environment. These two issues are closely related to the lifecycle of contractual relationships, namely information discovery, contract negotiation and execution. In the particular case of a virtual organization's lifecycle, (Rocha *et al.*, 2005) dissects institutional modules assisting the formation, operation and dissolution stages, and focuses on advanced features for the first stage.

We identify institutional services addressing both identified main goals, as depicted in Figure 1, where we omitted typical e-market facilities, such as registration and brokering.

Towards assisting the establishment of contracts, we emphasize on negotiation mediation, based on appropriate negotiation protocols and contract templates, which is complemented with ontology-based services. These are necessary if we aim at automating the whole process while keeping an open environment, since different domain-dependent vocabulary may be used by different business entities. However, a common institutional ontology must be used regarding general contract-related terms. The validation and registration of contracts allows for their "legal" existence. This may happen as a result of a successful mediated negotiation; however, contracts can be created by other (external) means, still being possibly registered within the EI.

An enforceable normative environment is established by rendering a contract monitoring and enforcement service, which registers transactions and verifies norm applicability, as well as the fulfillment of signed contracts.

Every agent intending to use an institutional service must be registered as a member. Agents have, inside the EI's boundaries, a record of reputation concerning their observance to past contractual relationships.

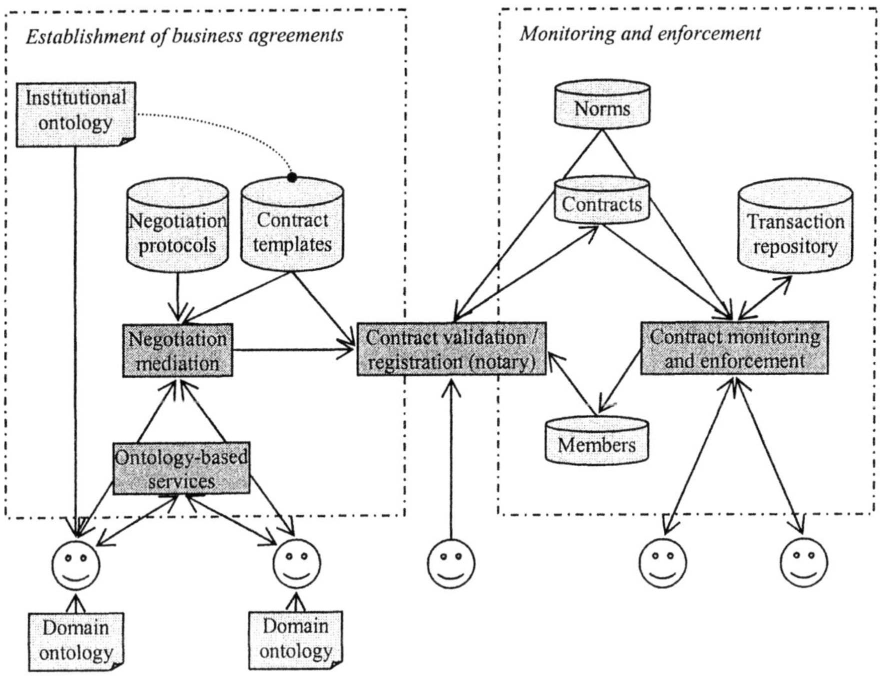

Figure 1 – Services of an electronic institution

The identified services are quite challenging, from an agent-based automation point of view. While advanced features (such as adaptive aspects) included in a negotiation mediation service are dealt with elsewhere (Rocha *et al.*, 2005), in this paper we give particular emphasis to ontology-based services and to the normative framework that allows for contract monitoring and enforcement.

3. CONTRACTS AND NORMS

Contract monitoring and enforcement is achieved by considering the EI as a normative framework. E-contracts are achieved inside this controlled environment, which establishes certain rules of behavior to be followed by members. The EI imposes a set of institutional norms by ensuring that norm violation is penalized.

We approach contract representation using norms, which will complement the institutional normative background. Contract creation may be greatly simplified with templates, which provide a structure for negotiation. Agents negotiate contract details by instantiating template parameters into a mutually agreeable contract, reusing domain-independent interaction schemes.

The temporary nature of VOs requires a quick set-up phase, allowing them to start operating as soon as possible. Templates and automated negotiation tools serve this purpose. Different templates for diverse VO settings may be provided.

In fact, the VO/VE spectrum covers a wide range of organizational structures (Camarinha-Matos and Afsarmanesh, 1999). We consider an open environment, with agents representing the interests of different entities (organizations or business units). Agents negotiate to establish dynamic virtual organizations, which stipulate cooperation terms, may exist for a period of time and have a variable topology. There will typically be a dominant participant, embodying the final destination of products (as far as the consortium is concerned). This entity can be regarded as a customer (Oliveira and Rocha, 2000), or participate in the production process.

Considering these properties, we aim at automating the monitoring of well-defined contractual agreements that establish multi-lateral business relationships between self-interested entities, which may not have worked together in the past.

3.1 A Structured Normative Framework

Considering the ongoing nature of virtual organizations, and taking into account that these are created inside our EI environment, we conceive a structured normative framework (see Figure 2) that considers both institutional as well as contractual norms (Lopes Cardoso and Oliveira, 2004).

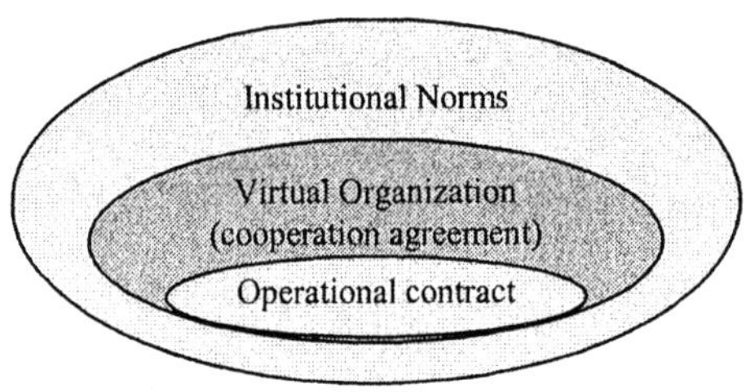

Figure 2 – Normative framework

Institutional norms and rules include default contract clauses, allowing contracts to be underspecified, thus further facilitating their creation. General regulations concerning the nature of consortiums may also be defined. Agents can rely on these regulations as a ground basis to raise VO contractual formalizations.

Rules recognizing violation or fulfillment conditions are also defined at this level, as these are contract-independent concepts. Specific policies may be defined towards institutional penalizing of violations (e.g. through reputation mechanisms).

Virtual organization constitutional norms describe the terms of cooperation that parties adhere to. Our first approach considers that each partner states workloads and prices for its contribution, and that a general business process outline is specified. This umbrella agreement represents a set of norms parties commit to, and which set up the ground for the VO operation phase. Specific contracts indicating actions to be performed make up the third normative layer. Operational contracts are proposed and signed within the context of VO contractual agreements, and their creation and execution are subject to enforcement and monitoring procedures.

3.2 Contract Monitoring and Enforcement

Taking into account the described normative framework, our contract monitoring and enforcement infrastructure is illustrated in Figure 3.

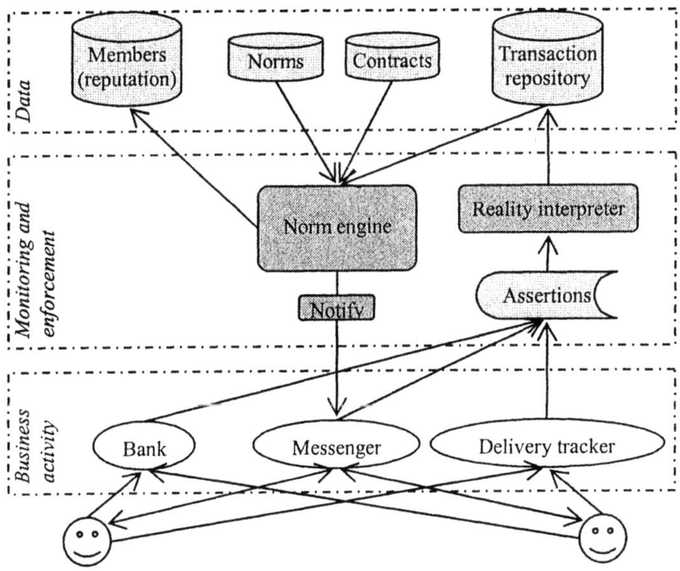

Figure 3 – Contract monitoring and enforcement

In order to fulfill their contractual promises, agents have a set of institutional facilities (roles performed by institutionally certified agents) related to different kinds of operations. Namely, we consider actions that involve information exchanges, monetary value transfers, and product delivery. These services allow for acknowledging what is going on in the real world. The reality interpreter establishes authoritative relations between institutional roles and the assertions of agents enacting those roles: these are interpreted to check which contractual transactions are being accomplished.

Transactions feed a rule-based engine applying both institutional and contractual norms; some, prescribing penalties in case of contract violation, are applied as enforcement measures. Violations may also imply updates concerning the reputation of prevaricators. Notifications are sent to contractual parties concerning the state of their contracts, in the event of obligation fulfillment, violation, or arising.

4. ONTOLOGY-BASED SERVICES

An ontology is required to help in the collaborative work and ensure that enterprises (represented by software agents in the context of our work) are negotiating about the very same good/product/service. Agents may use different ontologies to represent their view of a domain. Each domain may be specified in many different ways, and this ontology mismatch is a question under intensive research.

As cited in subsection 2.1, one of the main goals of an EI is to make the establishment of business transactions more efficient. The enterprises involved in the same transaction are interested in products in the same application domain. However, both use their own private domain ontology.

We provide an institutional ontology defining a business vocabulary to be used for all registered agents. This ontology contains terms which are used during the negotiation process, ensuring a meaningful communication since all agents will uniformly interpret the messages exchanged. Moreover, the contract templates are based on this ontology and new terms may be added according to contractual needs.

The institutional ontology (see Figure 4) defines *Concepts* (for example "Price"), *AgentActions* (for example "Buy") and *Predicates* (for example "IsPurchasable"), which describe the basic concepts and relationships used when any information in a business context is expressed in natural language. The institutional ontology may be applied for any domain.

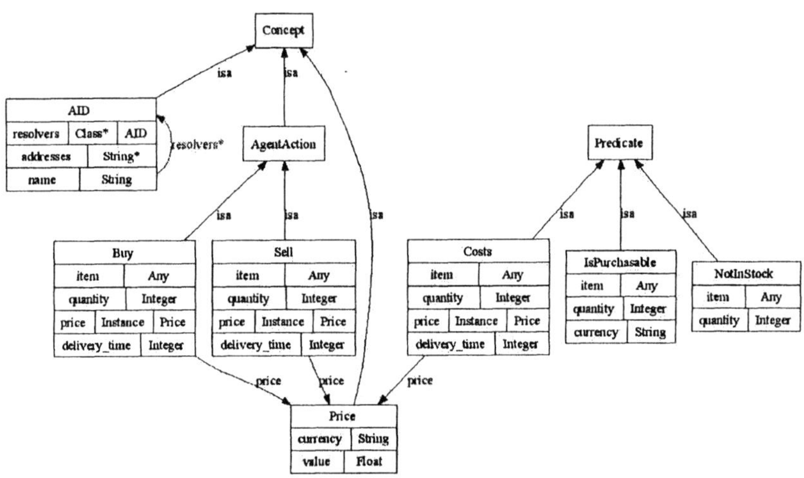

Figure 4 – Institutional ontology

Besides this shared Institutional ontology, each agent has its own private domain ontology, designed and built by some developer with some tool and, later, the agent will access the generated file/database. The characteristics of the institutional ontology do not allow identifying the right requested products/services because this is based on the domain ontology and people use different terms to represent the same concept. One of the main goals of the Ontology-based services is to provide a meaningful negotiation, to ensure that agents are negotiating about the same product/service.

The Foundation for Physical Intelligent Agents (FIPA) has analyzed the interoperability problems in heterogeneous multi-agent systems and has proposed an Ontology Agent (OA) for multi-agent platforms. FIPA proposes the following responsibilities (FIPA OSS): (i) The OA maintains ontology by defining, modifying or removing terms and definitions contained in the ontology. (ii) The OA responds to queries about the terms in an ontology or relationship between ontologies. (iii) The OA may provide the translation service of expressions between different ontologies or different content languages by itself, possibly as a wrapper to an ontology server.

A system implementing an OA should at least provide one of these functionalities. We have created an Ontology-based Services Agent (OSAg) (Malucelli and Oliveira, 2004), which is responsible for providing services to other agents in order to ensure an effective, meaningful negotiation. The OSAg provides the following services: (i) Matching terms service. (ii) Currency conversion service. (iii) Measurement conversion service.

The Matching terms service is required when some agent does not understand the content of a message, i.e., the item under negotiation. This service is the most complex one and it is implemented based on lexical and semantic similarity measures. Our approach aims at creating a methodology that assesses lexical and semantic similarity among concepts represented in different ontologies without the need to build an a priori shared ontology. The lexical measures are used to compare attributes, relations between concepts and descriptions of the concepts. We have classified attributes according to their data value types and considered the relation *has-part*. For the final validation, we are using the Leacock & Chodorow (LCH) method (Budanitsky and Hirst, 2001) based on WordNet (Miller, 1995) between concept names.

Moreover, a currency conversion service may be useful in the calculation of prices when agents are dealing with different currencies. The currency conversion service is implemented as a Web Service. Similarly, the measurement conversion service may be useful when agents are dealing with different measure units.

In addition, the ontology editor Protégé (Gennari *et al.*, 2002) is integrated in the framework to facilitate the creation and maintenance of ontologies.

5. CONCLUSIONS AND RELATED WORK

We presented a comprehensive infrastructure – an electronic institution – providing several services towards assisting the establishment of business contracts and further their execution. In (Rocha *et al.*, 2005) we presented a negotiation protocol devoted to the creation of virtual enterprises, and discussed the importance of making the outcome of a negotiation verifiable, by using e-contracts. Considering our developments presented in this paper, integration efforts are being conducted in order to achieve a computational environment that includes negotiation, ontology-based and contracting services. We believe that the rendering of these services will provide a level of trust and normative behavior necessary for the creation of dynamic virtual organizations and their operation.

The EI concept (and normative multi-agent systems in general), is being addressed by several researchers. Previous approaches towards regulating agent behavior through EIs include (Rodríguez-Aguilar, 2001). However, this model formally defines an institution using a rigid structure that implements a well-defined protocol. It is thus not amenable to contract handling, as contracts typically alter the normative structure. As to norm organization, (Dignum and Dignum, 2001) presents a two-level approach, considering norms at institutional and operational levels.

Several approaches concerning e-contracts would also be worth mentioning. In (Milosevic *et al.*, 2004), a business contract architecture having some similarities with our monitoring infrastructure can be found, although not using a normative perspective.

An implementation of (FIPA OSS) is presented in (Suguri *et al.*, 2001), a sample application of an ontology shopping service that integrates multiple database schemata to verify and demonstrate the specification. However, there is no possible way to match terms between ontologies.

6. REFERENCES

1. Budanitsky, A., Hirst, G. "Semantic distance in WordNet: An experimental, application-oriented evaluation of five measures". In Proceedings of the Workshop on WordNet and Other Lexical Resources, Second Meeting of the North American Chapter of the Association for Computational Linguistics, Pittsburgh, USA, 2001.
2. Camarinha-Matos, L.M., Afsarmanesh, H. "The Virtual Enterprise Concept". In L.M. Camarinha-Matos, H. Afsarmanesh (eds.), Infrastructures for Virtual Enterprises: Networking Industrial Enterprises, Kluwer Academic Publishers, pp. 3-14, 1999.
3. Dignum, V., Dignum, F. "Modelling agent societies: co-ordination frameworks and institutions". In P. Brazdil, A. Jorge (eds.), Progress in Artificial Intelligence: Knowledge Extraction, Multi-agent Systems, Logic Programming, and Constraint Solving, LNAI 2258, Springer, pp. 191-204, 2001.
4. FIPA – The Foundation for Intelligent Physical Agents, http://www.fipa.org
5. FIPA OSS – Ontology Service Specification, http://www.fipa.org/specs/fipa00086/XC00086D.html
6. Gennari, J., Musen, M.A., Fergerson, R.W., Grosso, W.E., Crubézy, M., Eriksson, H., Noy, N.F., Tu, S.W., "The Evolution of Protégé: An Environment for Knowledge-Based Systems Development", Technical Report. SMI Report Number: SMI-2002-0943, 2002.
7. Lopes Cardoso, H., Oliveira, E. "Virtual Enterprise Normative Framework within Electronic Institutions". In Proceedings of the Fifth International Workshop Engineering Societies in the Agents World (ESAW'04), Toulouse, France, 20-22 October 2004.
8. Malucelli, A., Oliveira, E. "Ontology-Services Agent to Help in the Structural and Semantic Heterogeneity". In Virtual Enterprises and Collaborative Networks, L. M. Camarinha-Matos (ed.), Kluwer Academic Publishers, pp. 175-182, 2004.
9. Miller, G. "WordNet: A Lexical Database for English". Communication of ACM, 38(11), pp. 39-41, 1995.
10. Milosevic, Z., Linington, P.F., Gibson, S., Kulkarni, S., Cole, J. "Inter-organisational collaborations supported by e-contracts". In I3E: Fourth IFIP Conference on e-Commerce, e-Business, and e-Government, Toulouse, France, August 2004.
11. Oliveira, E., Rocha, A.P. "Agents Advanced Features for Negotiation in Electronic Commerce and Virtual Organisations Formation Process". In F. Dignum, C. Sierra (eds.), Agent Mediated Electronic Commerce: The European AgentLink Perspective, LNAI 1991, Springer, pp. 78-97, 2000.
12. Rocha, A.P., Lopes Cardoso, H., Oliveira, E. "Contributions to an Electronic Institution Supporting Virtual Enterprises' Life Cycle". In G. Putnik, M. M. Cunha (eds.), Virtual Enterprise Integration: Technological and Organizational Perspectives, Idea Group, Inc., 2005.
13. Rodríguez-Aguilar, J.A. On the design and construction of Agent-mediated Electronic Institutions, Ph.D. Thesis, Universitat Autònoma de Barcelona, 2001.
14. Suguri, H., Kodama, E., Miyazaki, M., Nunokawa, H., Noguchi, S. "Implementation of FIPA Ontology Service". In Proceedings of the Workshop on Ontologies in Agent Systems, 5th International Conference on Autonomous Agents. Montreal. Canada. 2001.

PART 18

LEARNING AND KNOWLEDGE CREATION

56 A DIFFERENT VIEW OF LEARNING AND KNOWLEDGE CREATION IN COLLABORATIVE NETWORKS

Frans M. van Eijnatten
Dept. of Technology Management, Eindhoven University of Technology, The Netherlands
F.M.v.Eijnatten@tm.tue.nl

Goran D. Putnik
University of Minho, School of Engineering, Guimarães, Portugal [i]
putnikgd@dps.uminho.pt

This conceptual paper considers in some detail Nonaka's Dynamic Theory of Knowledge Creation. Especially the concept of Ba or Basho is explored to figure out its applicability as an alternative view of learning in Collaborative Networked Organisations (CNOs). To that end its grounding in East-Asian thinking is further analysed, and some similarities and differences with Chaordic Systems Thinking (CST) – are described. It is concluded that Nonaka's theory can support learning in CNOs, and that it might be regarded an early, alternative view of CST.

1. INTRODUCTION

Chaordic Systems Thinking (CST) is a qualitative approach to both organisation and management, which is grounded in the Chaos and Complexity (C&C) lens (Van Eijnatten, 2003). CST is all but new in the absolute sense of the word. It rather 'integrates' existing concepts, methods, and approaches from several authors to provide a consistent C&C framework for learning (Van Eijnatten & Putnik, eds., 2004), that may be used as a toolkit for both the design and explanation of the functioning of Collaborative Networked Organisations (CNOs).

Collaborative Networks (CNs) as complex, dynamical networks of Virtual Enterprises (VEs) might provide new challenges for flexibility, quality and speed in 21st-century business ecosystems (Miles & Snow, 1984/ 86; Camarinha-Matos, 2004; Putnik et al., 2005). Theoretically, CNs might gain from a C&C approach. In an earlier paper CST for CNOs was introduced, and some basic C&C concepts were presented: Discontinuous, fractal growth; and the emergence of real novelty (Van Eijnatten, 2005). In that paper we have proposed a chaordic view of CNOs, in which the basic reconfiguration process of a dynamic virtual organisation or CNO network is seen as routine, continuous change, and in which creative processes taking place within the virtual organisations' Market of Resources (MR) – or 'breeding environment' as MR- like environment (Cunha & Putnik, 2005) – are seen as incidences of nonroutine, discontinuous, leap-like changes (Van Eijnatten, 2005). It was suggested that in an effective organisational approach to CNOs both routine and nonroutine developments might be smoothly balanced with one another in order to keep flexibility, creativity, and competitiveness at acceptable high levels, not only occasionally but constantly.

In this paper a well-developed Japanese approach is presented – Nonaka's (1994) 'Dynamic Theory of Organisational Knowledge Creation', and its revision by Nonaka & Toyama (2003) – with the explicit goal to research its applicability as an alternative view of learning in CNOs. Taking into account the specific oriental context, similarities and differences between Nonaka's theory and CST are distinguished.

2. THE CONCEPT OF BA OR BASHO

Nonaka's 'Dynamic Theory of Knowledge Creation' is solidly based in Japanese Thinking. According to Robert Chia (1998: p. 2) Eastern thought stresses the inherent inadequacies of language and rational analysis for describing natural and social phenomena. Instead, direct knowing is highly recommended, see *Box 1*.

Box 1 – Some basic characteristics of East-Asian thinking

Sources: Nonaka &Takeuchi (1995), pp. 27-32; Chia (2002), pp. 4-24; Yuasa (1987), p. 68

The following nine aspects are some fundamental characteristics of Oriental Thinking:

1. Holistic approach (unity of humanity and nature; no separation of self and nature; perception is orientation towards objects that are subtle, but, at the same time visible and concrete).
2. Non-separability of body and mind (Non-Dualism; no Cartesian Split; entire personality).
3. Co-emergence of self and other (collective and organic view of human relationships; you and I are two sides of the same coin; individual self is a secondary phenomenon, not a primary unity of reality; goal in life is existing among others harmoniously as a collective self).
4. Primacy of pure experience (knowledge, feeling and volition remain undifferentiated; direct unmediated understanding through the ongoing perfecting of action; immediacy of lived experience).
5. Primacy of acting instead of cognising (acting intuition; emphasing performative action as bodily experience).
6. Correlative instead of linear-causal thinking (iterative movement, change, and transformation instead of stasis, form and permanence; urging the harmonising of internal wills through concrete-existential engagement rather than external causal relations).
7. Language and written documentation are secondary (knowing is achieved directly through the immediate engagement of tasks rather than through the acquisition of linguistic signs and symbols; perform instead of explain; words are used only as pointers; actions speak louder than words; perfect truth cannot be expressed in words).
8. Progenerative emptiness/ absolute nothingness/ concrescence (Concrete Existentialism; grasping the absolute in a primitive state of pure unself-conscious experiencing; pure experience is prior to consciousness and words; fact from pure experience).
9. Flexible view of time and space (time is seen as a continuous flow of a permanently updated 'present'; ultimate reality is confined to 'here and now'; space is free from a fixed perspective; no fixed view- or standpoint).

Ikujiro Nonaka stresses interaction as a primary condition for knowledge creation (Nonaka, 1991). He interprets knowledge creation as a dynamic, iterative, spiraling process from, what Michael Polanyi (1967) has called, 'tacit' into explicit knowledge, and back again. The core concept in Nonaka's theory is a central time and place where information is interpreted through interacting individuals in order to become knowledge, which he indicates with the Japanese term 'Ba'. This concept was originally proposed by Kitarō Nishida, Japan's foremost theoretical philosopher of the twentieth century, and co-founder of the Kyoto school, in 1911 (Nishida, 1921; Shimizu, 1995). Based on Zen learning, he developed the Buddhist notion of 'Pure Experience' or 'Absolute Nothingness' which is both active and prior to awareness (Chia, 1998, p. 14). The individual self is secondary. According to Nishida, facts can only be acquired from direct, on-the-spot, personal experience. Nishida (1970: pp. 61-41, 68, 80-84) distinguished three concentric fields or 'Bashos' in his 'logic of judgment' (as summarized by Chia, 1998: pp. 14-15). The following summing-up was further edited by the authors of this paper:

- Basho of Being: Empirical judgments are made unreflectively (i.e., the observing self is ignored).
- Basho of Relative Nothingness: Existential judgments (self-consciousness of the self; self as acting intuition).
- Basho of Absolute Nothingness (or Tao): Purified experience (direct knowing by pure experience of the complexity of the ultimate reality, in which all distinctions – like subject/ object – converge). Progenerative field of primordial knowing, prior to consciousness and words.

Nonaka adapted Nishida's notion of Basho to fit his Dynamic Theory of Knowledge Creation. Nonaka and associates define Ba as a "fertile ground" (Nonaka & Nishiguchi, 2001: p. 3), as a spontaneous or man-built "context that harbors meaning" (Nonaka et al., 2001: p. 19), as a background for learning, as a "platform where knowledge is created, shared, and exploited" (Nonaka et al., 2001: p. 19). Ba is "a shared context in cognition and action" (Nonaka et al., 2000b: p. 8); "Ba is fluid, and can be born and disappear quickly" (Nonaka et al., 2000b: p. 8); "Ba has a 'here and now' quality" (Nonaka et al., 2000a: p. 15). According to Nonaka & Nishigushi (2001: p. 4): "Ba is a shared time and space for emerging relationships – either physical, virtual, or mental – shared by two or more individuals or organisations." Ba (Basho) is defined as a holonic concept:

> *"Ba exists at many levels and these levels may be connected to form a greater Ba (known as Basho). The self is embraced by the collective when an individual enters the Ba of teams. Just as the Ba for individuals is the team, the organisation in turn is the Ba for the teams. Finally, the market environment is the Ba for the organisation. Ba is of fundamen-tal importance for knowledge creation, and this creative process is amplified when these Ba conjoin to form a Basho."*
>
> Nonaka & Konno (1998: p. 41)

A firm is a dynamic configuration of 'Ba' (Nonaka et al., 2000b: p. 8). Nonaka and associates distinguish between four types of Ba (Nonaka & Konno, 1998: p. 46; Nonaka et al., 2000b: p. 10; Nonaka et al., 2001: pp. 20-21):

- Originating or Primary Ba: Subjective, ontological, existential field. Physical world, time and space of day-to-day social interaction where individuals share feelings, emotions, experiences, and mental models (tacit knowledge). Central characteristics: Physical, individual (face- to- face), context for socialisation, empathising.
- Dialoguing or Interacting Ba: Collective, reflective field. Physical world, conscious-ly constructed time and space of interaction where mental models (tacit knowledge) are shared, and analyzed. The space is man-made, for instance by careful selection of

heterogeneous team members. Basic characteristics: Physical, collective (peer-to-peer), context for externalisation, articulating.

- Systematising or Cyber Ba: Collective, interactive field. Virtual world, cyber space where combination of new and existing explicit knowledge take place in collabora-tive networks. Essential characteristics: Virtual, collective (group-to-group), context for combination, connecting.
- Exercising Ba: Subjective, synthetic field. Physical world, consciously constructed time and space of interaction where explicit knowledge is internalized by on-the-job training and participation. Main characteristics: Physical, individual (on-the-site), explicit, context for internalisation, embodying.

Recently, Ba was reconceptualized as "a shared context in motion, which can transcend time, space, and organisational boundaries to create knowledge" (Nonaka & Toyama, 2003: p. 2). "Ba should be understood as a multiple interacting mechanism explaining tendencies for interactions that occur at a specific time and space" (Nonaka & Toyama, 2003: p. 6). "Thus Ba is a continuously created generative mechanism that explains the potentialities and tendencies that either hinder or stimulate knowledge creative activities" (Nonaka & Toyama, 2003: p. 6). Nonaka and Konno (1998) define learning in a rather indirect way:

> *"To participate in a Ba means to get involved and transcend one's own limited perspective or boundary. This exploration is necessary in order to profit from the 'magic synthesis' of rationality and intuition that produces creativity. Within an organisation, then, one can both experience transcendence in Ba and yet remain analytically rational, achieving the best of both worlds."*
>
> Nonaka & Konno (1998: p. 41)

This quotation illustrates how well Nonaka's approach fits a C&C approach: Self-transcendence is a key issue. Nevertheless, its source is rather different, and is deeply rooted in Oriental thinking, see *Box 1*. Robert Chia (1998: p.1) remarks: "Theory is available in the rich tradition of Eastern thought where Complexity is understood as 'nothingness', absence, decentredness, and 'unspeakability' and where the language is elliptical, allusory, implicit and immanent."

3. BA/ BASHO AS PLATFORMS FOR LEARNING AND KNOWLEDGE CREATION IN A CNO

We propose the use of Nonaka's theory for the design and explanation of the functioning of CNOs, especially with respect to Ba/ Basho for learning and knowledge creation. These environments are shown in *Figure 1*, in an ad-hoc representation of a CNO – as conceptualised by ECOLEAD (2004) – i.e., Mono-Disciplinary Professional Virtual Communities (PVCs) together with a Multi-Disciplinary Virtual Organisation Breeding Environment (VBO), and a number of Dynamic Virtual Organisations (DVOs). Such a CNO may provide "a common platform where knowledge is created, shared, and exploited" (Nonaka et al., 2001: p. 19), which is the definition of a 'Ba' or 'Basho'. People who are interacting in the CNO's Basho get involved and transcend their own limited perspectives or boundaries. For an illustration of the CNO's Basho, see the concentric circles in *Figure 1*.

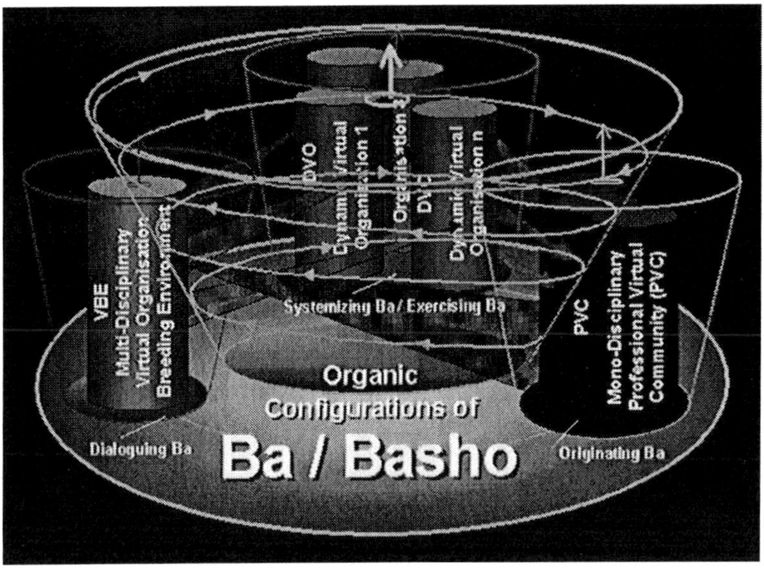

Figure 1 – Environments for learning and knowledge creation, illustrated in an ad-hoc CNO Model (ECOLEAD, ed., 2004)

Legend: = Information as flow = Spiraling process of knowledge creation

= Time (Ba/ Basho) = Space (Ba/ Basho)

We assume that in the PVCs interactions take place in a process called 'socialisation' (conversion from tacit into tacit knowledge). The ideal type of environment is an Originating Ba, or *physical* place, where individuals can share feelings, emotions, experiences, and mental models. Conferences, colloquia, and workshops might provide such a space. In a VBE we assume interactions will result in 'externalisation' (the conversion from tacit into explicit knowledge). The ideal environment for this is a Dialoguing Ba or consciously constructed physical space where mental models (tacit knowledge) are shared, and analyzed. In the DVOs we assume interaction of people will trigger processes of 'combination' and 'internalisation' (conversions from explicit into explicit, and explicit into tacit knowledge). The accompanying ideal types of environments are Systematising and Exercising Ba, partly virtual spaces in collaborative networks, and partly physical spaces, where knowledge is integrated and competencies are trained.

Also at the level of PVC, VBE, and DVO, within the three individual CNO pillars, learning and knowledge creation might take place, see the cones in *Figure 1.* Individual learning is taking place by self-organising, communicative interaction of the people who participate within the three individual, by ECOLEAD (2004) defined, CNO pillars (PVC, VBE, and DVO); organisational learning seems to be happening in the DVOs only; interorganisational learning is likely to occur at the CNO, seen as a whole or holon.

4. CONCLUSIONS AND DISCUSSION

4.1 An alternative view of learning in CNOs

In this paper we have suggested Nonaka's interaction fields as ideal-types of environments for learning in CNOs. But we have to take into account that the basic idea of Ba or Basho stems from a complete different world context, as was shown in *Box 1*. However, a closer inspection of that Box learns that the Eastern mindset shows striking similarities with a C&C approach. For instance, the holistic, non-dualistic method, the correlative thinking, and the flexible view of time and space are also characteristics of CST. Therefore, we think Nonaka's concepts – especially the distinction between physical versus virtual Basho – might be helpful for a better holonic understanding of the complex interplay between individual, organisational and inter-organisational learning in CNOs, and might be regarded as an early, orientally-based view of CST.

4.2 Learning versus knowledge creation: Different viewpoints of the same communicative interactions

As we have seen in the previous paragraphs, Nonaka's theory focuses on knowledge creation (c.f., Nonaka, 1991; Nonaka & Takeuchi, 1995). In CST, learning is put more central (c.f., Van Eijnatten & Putnik, 2004). We think that learning and knowledge creation can be viewed as indications of one and the same communicative interaction process, seen from different angles or perspectives. We second Stacey in defining the process of learning as "the activity of interdependent people, which can only be understood in terms of self-organising communicative interaction and power relating in which identities are potentially transformed" (Stacey, 2003: p. 325). This process of self-organising communicative interaction and power relating might result in both knowledge creation and knowledge destruction as a CNO goes through the different stages of its life cycle.

4.3 The possibility of 'real novelty'

Stacey et al. (2000) claim that conventional Systems Thinking basically is unable to create novelty, because – in line with Formative Teleology – the system's ultimate goal already is known in advance (c.f., *Table 1*). Although we concur with Stacey and associates that previous system approaches indeed suffered from a Kantian split, we think that the term 'system' as such is not fully obsolete yet, as long as it is seen as a whole-part or holon. Therefore, a methodological migration was suggested from Open Systems Thinking into Chaordic Systems Thinking (Van Eijnatten, 2000; Van Eijnatten & Hoogerwerf, 2000). We claim that CST will prevent any split between different frameworks of causality. By the identification of the five chaordic properties – conciousness, connectivity, indeterminacy, dissipation, and emergence – we propagate in line with Stacey et al. (2000) the use of a Transformative Teleology. In that sense we speak of organisational renewal or organisational novelty as transformation instead of reformation, the latter we have called improvement, see *Table 1*.

Although Nonaka and Konna (1998: p. 41) also are talking about "transcending one's own limited perspective or boundary", which might be interpreted as a process leading to novelty, Nishida (1970: p. 80-84) seems to seriously question whether novelty can be 'created' (Tanaka, undated), or that it is just a matter of "pure experiencing the unfolding of a complex reality". Although both path and goal might be unknown in advance, learning takes place by immediate perception or intuition. This issue might be interesting enough to deal with in more detail, in another paper.

Table 1 – Real novelty as contrasted with improvement and renewal

Adapted from Stacey et al. (2000)
Van Eijnatten (2005), further refined on the basis of Van Eijnatten (2003)

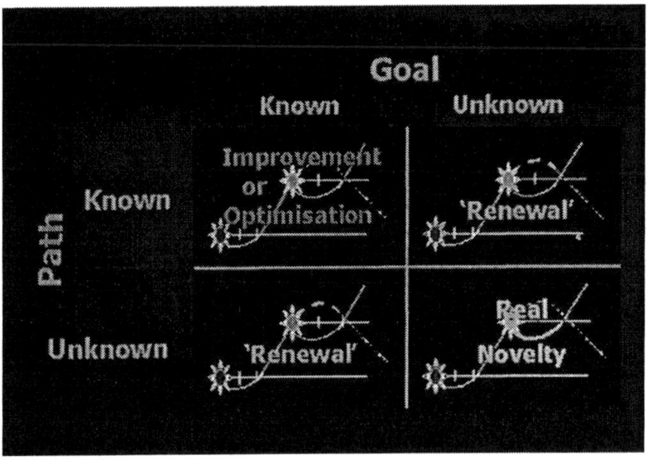

REFERENCES

1. Camarinha-Matos, L. M.; Afsarmanesh, H.; Ollus, M. – ECOLEAD: A holistic approach to creation and management of dynamic virtual organizations, in Collaborative Networks and their Breeding Environments, Springer, Sept 2005.
2. Chia, Robert. Complex Thinking in 'Eastern Thought': Non-Presence, Decenteredness and the Unspeakable. Paper presented at the CSTT/ ESRC workshop 'Language and Complexity', Centre for Culture, Social Theory & Technology, Keele University, Keele, Staffordshire, UK, 1998.
3. Chia, Robert. From Knowledge-Creation to the Perfecting of Action: Tao, Basho and Pure Experience as the Ultimate Ground of Performance. School of Business and Economics, Exeter University, Exeter, Devon, UK, Paper 02/ 04, 2002.
4. Cunha, MM, Putnik GD. "Market of Resources as an Environment and Enabler for Agile/ Virtual Enterprise Dynamic Integration and Business Alignment". In: Encyclopedia of Information Science and Technology. Hershey, PA: Idea Group Publishing, forthcoming in 2005.
5. ECOLEAD, ed. Creating Necessary Foundations and Mechanisms for Establishing an Advanced Collaborative and Network-Based Industry Society in Europe. ECOLEAD: European Collaborative Networked Organisations Leadership Initiative. Brussels, Information Society Technology Programme, Sixth Framework Program, Integrated Project IP 506958, 2004.
6. Eijnatten, Frans M. van. From Intensive to Sustainable Work Systems: The Quest for a New Paradigm of Work. Keynote Speech at the TUTB/ SALTSA Conference "Working Without Limits: Re-Organising Work and Reconsidering Workers' Health". Brussels: 25 September 2000.
7. Eijnatten, FM van. "Chaordic Systems Thinking: Chaos and Complexity to Explain Human Performance Management". In: Business Excellence 1: Performance Measures, Benchmarking and Best Practices in New Economy, G.P. Putnik, A. Gunasekaran, eds. Braga/ Guimarães, Portugal, School of Engineering: University of Minho Press, 2003: 3-18.
8. Eijnatten, Frans M. van. A Chaordic View of Collaborative Networked Organisations. Yokohama, Japan: Yokohama National University. Unpublished paper, 2005.

9. Eijnatten, FM van, Hoogerwerf, EC. "Searching for New Grounds: Beyond Open Systems Thinking". In: The New Sociotech: Graphity on the Long Wall, E. Coakes, R. Lloyd-Jones, D. Willis, eds. London: Springer-Verlag, 2000: 39-50
10. Eijnatten FM van, Putnik GD. Chaos, complexity, learning, and the learning organisation: Towards a chaordic enterprise. The Learning Organisation 2004; 11 (6): 418-429.
11. Miles RE, Snow CC. Fit, Failure and the Hall of Fame. California Management Review 1984; 26 (3) Spring: 10-28.
12. Miles RE, Snow CC. Organisations: New Concepts for New Forms. California Management Review 1986; 28 (3) Spring: 62-73.
13. Miles RE, Snow CC. Fit, Failure and the Hall of Fame. How Companies Succeed or Fail. New York, NY: The Free Press, 1994.
14. Nishida, Kitarō. An Inquiry into the Good (Zen No Kenkyuu: 1921). New Haven, CT: Yale University Press. English translation by Masao Abe, and Christopher Ives in 1990; earlier edition in 1960: A Study of Good. Tokyo, Japan: Japanese Government Printing Office, translated by Valdo H. Viglielmo; also published in 1988, Westport, CT: Greenwood Press.
15. Nishida, Kitarō. Fundamental Problems of Philosophy (Tetsugaku No Kompon Mondai: 1933/ 34): Volume I, The World of Action; and Volume II, The Dialectical World. Tokyo, Japan: Sophia University, English translation by David A. Dilworth in 1970.
16. Nonaka, I. A Dynamic Theory of Organisational Knowledge Creation. Organisation Science 1994; 5 (1), 14-37.
17. Nonaka I, Konno N. The Concept of 'Ba': Building a Foundation for Knowledge Creation. California Management Review 1998; 40 (3) Spring: 1-15.
18. Nonaka, Ikujiro, Nishiguchi, Toshihiro. Introduction: Knowledge Emergence. In: Knowledge Emergence: Social, Technical, and Evolutionary Dimensions of Knowledge Creation, I. Nonaka, T. Nishiguchi, eds. New York, NY: Oxford University Press, 2001: 3-9.
19. Nonaka, Ikujiro, Takeuchi, Hirotaka. The Knowledge- Creating Company: How Japanese Companies Create the Dynamics of Innovation. New York, NY: Oxford University Press, 1995.
20. Nonaka I, Toyama R. The Knowledge-Creating Theory Revisited: Knowledge Creation as a Synthesising Process. Knowledge Management Research and Practice 2003; 1 (1): 2-10.
21. Nonaka I, Toyama R, Konno N. SECI, Ba and Leadership: Unified Model of Dynamic Knowledge Creation. Long Range Planning 2000a; 33 (1): 5-34.
22. Nonaka I, Toyama R, Nagata A. A Firm as a Knowledge-Creating Entity: A New Perspective on the Theory of the Firm. Industrial and Corporate Change 2000b; 9 (1): 1-20.
23. Nonaka, Ikujiro, Konno, Noboru, Toyama, Ryoko. Emergence of 'Ba'. In: Knowledge Emergence: Social, Technical, and Evolutionary Dimensions of Knowledge Creation, I. Nonaka, T. Nishi-guchi, eds. New York, NY: Oxford University Press, 2001: 13-29.
24. Polanyi, Michael. The Tacit Dimension. New York, NY: Anchor Books, 1967.
25. Putnik GD, Cunha MM, Sousa R, Ávila P. Virtual Enterprise Integration: Challenges of a New Paradigm. In: Virtual Enterprise Integration: Technological and Organisational Perspectives. G.D. Putnik, M.M. Cunha, M.M., eds. Hershey, PA: Idea Group Publishing, forthcoming in 2005.
26. Shimizu, Hiroshi. Ba- Principle: New Logic for the Real- Time Emergence of Information. Holonics 1995; 5 (1): 67-79.
27. Stacey RD. Learning as an Activity of Interdependent People. The Learning Organisation 2003; 10 (6): 325-331.
28. Stacey, Ralph, Griffin, Douglas, Shaw, Patricia. Complexity and Management: Fad or Radical Challenge to Systems Thinking? London: Routledge, 2000.
29. Tanaka, Yutaka. The Topos of Nothingness and the World Process: An Essay on Process Cosmology in Science and Religion. Tokyo, Japan: Sophia University, Department of Philosophy, undated.
30. Yuasa, Yasuhito. The Body: Toward an Eastern Mind-Body Theory. Albany, NY: State University of New York (SUNY) Press, translation by S. Nagatomo, & T.P. Kasulis, 1987.

---

[i] The University of Minho is the partner of the EU FP6 Network of Excellence I*PROMS – Innovative Production Machines and Systems.

57 A NEW APPROACH FOR E-LEARNING IN COLLABORATIVE NETWORKS

Dan Gârlaşu, Ioan Dumitrache, Aurelian Mihai Stanescu
Politehnica University Bucharest
313, Splaiul Independentei, 060042 Bucharest, ROMANIA
{dgarlasu@yahoo.com; dumi@ics.pub.ro; ams@cpru.pub.ro}

The paper proposes a new holistic model - the E-Learning Cube – with the aim to enable better understanding and characterization of the basic principles and mechanisms of E-Learning, for efficient use of the underlying infrastructure and a successful implementation strategy within Collaborative Networks. A short case study is presented in order to demonstrate how the new model was used for the implementation of an e-Learning system in a Collaborative Environment. Eventually the authors conclude with guidelines towards an ontology-based approach for e-Learning.

1. INTRODUCTION

Knowledge Economy (KE) refers to the new paradigm that has changed in the past fifteen years the functionality and economic rules at global level. The essence of these changes refer to the fact that ideas and knowledge become essential for the new economy as compared to the industrial model based on material resources. The key for the creation of new working places and the increase of the quality of life are the innovation and the technology embedded in services and products. As a consequence, the future belongs to the accumulation and execution based on knowledge. The Virtual Enterprise (VE) is the representation of the basic entity that operates in the knowledge economy. Knowledge is not only learning and information - these are in fact the raw materials of the new economy. Knowledge represents the added value of providing services and products. When converging, learning and technology enable individuals and teams to provide value for their customers and competitive advantage for the team or their organization. The discovery of new information is the key of the knowledge economy. Also, the desire to develop the self and the others – learnativity, is a term that states the dependence of the individual and organizational efficiency of a better, faster, more intelligent assimilation of information through a consistent application of instruction combined with creativity and flexibility (Hodgins, 2000). Also the Web enables people to build enduring communities of practice when they can come together to share knowledge and insight long after the training has taken place. This can be a tremendous motivator for organizational learning. Key for this process is the efficient absorption of information that makes possible the knowledge transfer within the appropriate time interval, to the right person, at the right moment and in a form suitable to what the receptor. When such a process takes place, the student can act promptly and efficiently. Traditional Instructor led training cannot scale to meet the new learning challenges. Or exactly here the authors see the role of E-learning – to provide the tools able to create, deliver and facilitate the training of the knowledge workers, anytime and anywhere.

2. THE E-LEARNING CUBE MODEL

There is much controversy around the e-Learning topic today. Be it from material (infrastructure reasons) or immaterial (lack of strategy, poor content, lack of interactivity and pedagogical skills, etc.) e-Learning did not succeed everywhere. That is the reason why the present paper introduces a new model, the E-Learning Cube, as a tool able to facilitate the understanding and faster identification of the root causes for various problems and ensure a successful implementation process (Figure 1).

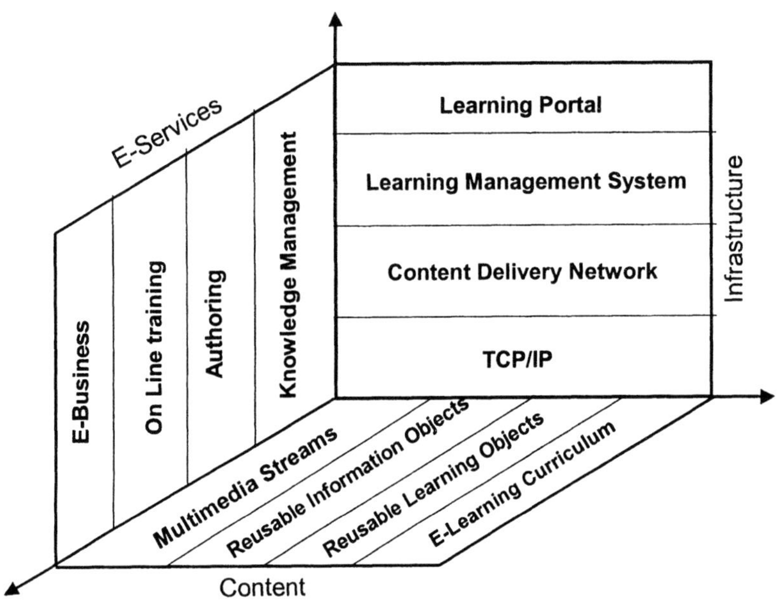

Figure 1 – E-Learning Cube

The available literature provides various one-dimensional models that capture part of the problem, be it about infrastructure or services (Dumke, 2003) or about the content involved during the knowledge transfer (IBM, 2001). Intuitively a multidimensional approach may represent better the complexity of the domain. Since a Cartesian frame provides orthogonal dimensions, independent views were searched in order to provide independent paradigms. The initial CIMOSA (ISO/TC

184/SC 5) with its 4x3x3 graphical representation provided a framework for information systems infrastructure (http://cimosa.cnt.pl/). This is in fact how the e-Learning cube was evolved from the extended CIM-OSA , eCube' (Stanescu, 2002) with three dimensions (Infrastructure, Content and eServices) and their related components as described in the next paragraph.

2.1 The Infrastructure Dimension

The infrastructure – technological capabilities to deliver and manage E-learning - is key for a successful deployment. From the last mile access to the learning management system and the learning portal, lacking of a good infrastructure can jeopardize an e-Learning initiative. The goal however is to leverage on the mission and functions of a Collaborative Network (CN) as described in Figure 2.

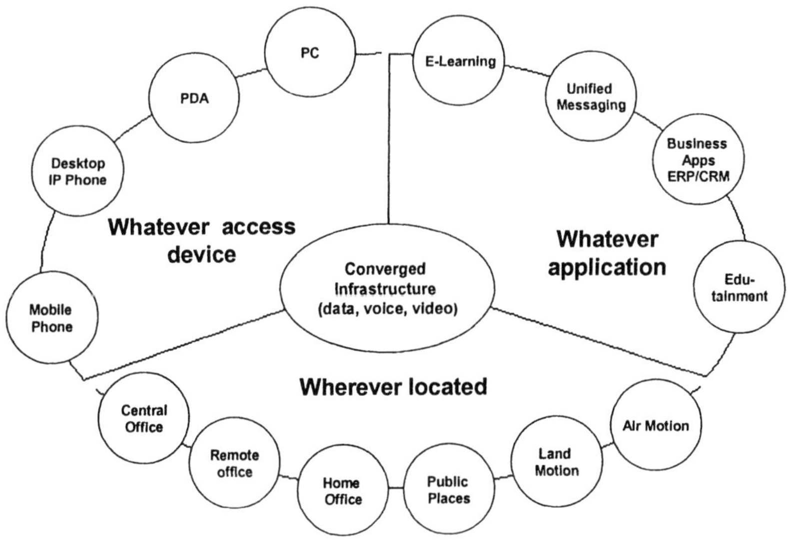

Figure 2 - Collaborative Networks Ubiquitous Access

A certain number of elements characterize the *infrastructure dimension*:

- **TCI/IP** is the underlying protocol for a communication infrastructure able to deliver real convergence of data, voice and video for scalable, secure and highly available applications. This objective is achieved through intelligent network services able to provide QoS (Quality of Service) for the constraints of the real time media streams, policing for differentiating between classes of services, network management, multicast, etc. The multimedia traffic dominant in e-Learning applications may use multicast with predilection as it has different characteristics than HTTP or FTP traffic. A number of protocols have been developed that increase the efficiency of the Internet architecture and improve the support for audio, video and interactive multimedia conference streams. As a consequence multicast and real time multimedia flows are associated with protocols built on top of UDP such as RTP, RTCP, RSVP and RTSP. CORBA based middleware applications, enable implementation of mechanisms and services such as request-reply, naming, events notification, persistence, security, etc. independent of the underlying transport be it TCP or UDP (Coulouris 2001).

- **Content Delivery Networks** represent the infrastructure layer that enables content optimization. This layer provides mechanisms such as Web-browser TV used to broadcast live video to a big number of users at the same time, or VoD (Video on Demand) to allow the presentation of the content directly to the learner on demand, or Interactive multi-media that combines self-paced web-based training, online communities and instructor-led forums creating a complete way to transfer the knowledge and finally virtual class rooms that allows collaboration of geographically dispersed audience with interactive presentation capabilities, virtual hands-on labs, etc. Linking users with common interests to each other allows them to share views on the usefulness of information provided and to share experience and continuously enhance their knowledge thus building Communities of Practice (CoPs) (Skyrme 2001).
- **Learning Management System** is the application platform covering the e-Learning solution that provides functionalities for content management, delivery, learning management and other VE business services. It uses the Internet technologies to manage the interaction between users and learning resources. An e-Learning deployment starts with an assessment of current learning modes and new educational objectives for the trainees. These objectives should be in line with the VE business objectives.
- **Learning Portal** is a Web based, single point of access that serves as gateway to a variety of e-Learning resources for employees, partners and customers using various forms of CNs. It aggregates information based on VE communities with common needs/interests: Field, Manufacturing, Leadership Development, Partner Development, etc. Besides a navigational role, the portal can serve as launching point for business applications, content search, discussions and collaboration, workflow tools and other resources and services. The learning portal can be used also to reinforce CoPs: threaded discussions, online chat, news groups, online conferencing, instant messaging and personal web pages (Rosenberg, 2001).

2.2 The Content Dimension

It is very often that e-Learning initiatives get stuck with content issues such as availability and quality. The best strategy here is to create e-Learning content that relates directly to the learning objectives and is reusable in order to optimize efforts and resources – a shift from creating and delivering monolithic courses to fine-grained content that can be reused in many contexts. A number of organizations that promote standards such as ADL (Advanced Distributed Learning) with its well known initiative SCORM (Sharable Content Object Reference Model), www.adlnet.org), IMS (Instructional Management System), www.imsproject.org), AICC (Airline Industry CBT Committee), www.aicc.org), ARIADNE (Advanced Distributed Learning), www.ariadne.unil.ch) and IEEE LTSC (IEEE Learning Technology Standards Committee, www.ltscl.org) play a major role by enabling interoperability, reusability and scalability. The *content dimension* comprises the following entities:

- **Multimedia Streams** are entities that pack the content with ingredients such as voice, data and video in order to enliven a course page and add visual variety to the learning experience. Because of constraints related to the real time specifics of these structures, their delivery quality is directly impacted by the quality of the infrastructure, specifically bandwidth and QoS. Streaming solutions available today come from Microsoft (WMT – Windows Media Technology), Real Networks (Real Video/Audio) and Apple (QT – Quick Time). ISMA (Internet Streaming Medial Alliance) is the organization whose purpose is to accelerate the adoption and deployment of open standards for streaming rich media content such as video, audio, and associated data, over Internet protocols.
- **Reusable Information Objects** (RIO) are self-contained chunks of information built around a single learning objective, as defined by (Clark, 1989): a concept, fact, procedure or principle. Each RIO is tagged with metadata that describes its characteristics, purpose and relationship with other objects. The term „reusable" is used to emphasize the advantage of authoring smaller pieces of learning that enable content repurposing. Thus, learning objects are created that form a useful database for content that may be recombined to fit specific needs.
- **Reusable Learning Objects** (RLO) are the lessons. As in the traditional lessons, RLO give learners the needed learning context, the knowledge and skills they need to perform towards a given objective and a method to assess mastery. According to (Cisco, 2001) a RLO can be created by combining an overview, summary, assessment and five to nine RIOs. A RLO is based on a single objective derived from a specific job task. Each RIO is built upon an objective that supports the RLO objective. The RLO approach has benefited the research and best practices found in (Merrill, 1983) and (Bloom, 1994) and has resulted in successful implementations (Clark, 2002) and (Rosenberg, 2001).
- **E-Learning Curriculum** joins together RLOs into a larger hierarchy depending on the author, business requirements and the packaging of the offering in the learning management system. The curriculum can also be expressed as an employee development roadmap or part of a performance support system that is customized to the learner. A sample structure of curriculum is as follows: Curriculum, Unit, Module, Lesson (RLO) and Section (RIO).

2.3 The eServices Dimension

This dimension includes the generic services available through the Web portal. There is still a large perception that learning is related to classroom teaching. That is why many people continue to see the web as an online replica of the classroom experience. However, online training is only a part of e-Learning. Access to the information is also essential for learning as instruction. From business performance to employee services, intranet-based knowledge management can create a communication and collaboration network that links every individual in the organization. The following components form the *eServices dimension*:

- **Knowledge Management (KM)** is the area that deals with the means to supply information that people can use and rely on. It supports the creation, archiving and sharing valued information, expertise and insight within and across communities of interest. Currently most businesses use Internet and the web and have abandoned the silo model of preserving information in favor of various forms of CNs (corporate intranets and extranets) that facilitate secured access to information for employees, partners, customers and suppliers. This trend reflects a knowledge management strategy – providing a common approach and a common architecture for managing information. KM differentiates from the information-laden Web sites by its focus on collaboration and community, allowing new ideas and insights to be shared in a more open environment, enabling trusted groups of professionals united by a common concern or purpose to reach new insights and enhance performance in a particular domain.

- **Online Training** – there is a strong opinion that simply providing information is an inefficient way to learn – that is why instruction is needed. An essential part of an e-Learning strategy, the Computer Based Training (CBT) has received the *online* ingredient in order to eliminate well known disappointments of CBT (unfit content, unauthentic learning, form-over-substance, etc.). Online training must provide simulation and interactivity in order to increase the authenticity and motivate the learner. The knowledge acquisition element of online training may come also from story telling. With primary learning on the Web, the instructors are free to become true coaches and consultants to the trainees focusing more on facilitating the transfer of knowledge, converting themselves into e-moderators (Salmon, 2005).
- **Authoring** is an essential part of the E-learning system because only building an infrastructure and just placing a lot of content on a server is not enough. The reusable learning objects, content, sources and formats must be combined through authoring into sound instruction or information. The material is delivered through the learning portal via synchronous or asynchronous learning. Asynchronous delivery refers to programs that are independent of time („prerecorded", as VoD). Synchronous programs are time dependent and take place in real time. The simplest forms of synchronous learning consist of classroom training but also some Web applications such as chat rooms, IP/TV live multicast, etc. While asynchronous programs require much deeper understanding of instructional design and are more costly to develop, synchronous programs also take into account important design considerations but focus more on delivery. Depending on the needs of the learner that result upon a competency assessment the right curriculum and other resources are delivered to the desktop. A new direction – „Edutainment" emerged from the combination of „education" and „entertainment" that encompasses various aspects of pure information transfers as well as complex entertainment applications such as game-based learning environments (Encarnacao, 2004).
- **EBusiness** refer the set of Internet enabled business tools for electronic commerce, workforce optimization, ERP, customer support, supply-chain automation and of course E-learning. We have included e-Business on the eServices dimension of the e-Learning cube because we see a trend for convergence of e-Learning and e-Business towards the *knowledge commerce* – the ability to leverage an organization's intellectual assets to improve its competitive advantage. More and more e-Learning companies will convert

themselves to Business-to-Business (B2B) or Business-to-Consumer (B2C) entities with e-Learning as a defining characteristic of their services offering. New models such as Business-to-Employee (B2E) and Employee-to-Employee (E2E) are placing e-Learning in the focus of the efforts to create more collaborative, knowledge-sharing work environments such as virtual communities. Knowledge products and services, Knowledge markets/distribution together with the e-commerce and the underlying Internet result in a new business, for marketing and sale of knowledge over the Internet, referred as K-Business.

3. USABILITY OF THE MODEL – CASE STUDY

Once the e-Learning cube was conceived it became essential to check upon its usability. The first opportunity was offered by a GSM company that provides mobile voice and data services on all territory of Romania. Operating from multiple locations across the country it also belongs to a global telecom organization thus presenting all characteristics of a VE. The company had recently acquired an e-Learning application and was faced with the challenging task to successfully implement and get it fully adopted. By using the e-Learning cube model the HR and the training departments have succeeded to pass a very clear and consistent message about the implementation strategy to all the other departments within the organization and to deploy the first phase of e-Learning services. Among those, electronic training and assessment for work protection and accident prevention, as well as a GSM technologies curriculum for new employees. The first application was particularly appreciated because it took a lot of burden away from the HR department that was supposed to monitor the work protection activities in accordance with the law, stage periodic training sessions adapted to the specifics of the activity of more than 1000 employees scattered across the country as well as maintain accurate files. The lesson learned from this project was that the cube model was a valuable tool for positioning an e-Learning system in a collaborative environment mostly when it came to roles of various stakeholders, strategy and rollout planning. For example the IT department understood that they only needed to provide the intranet infrastructure and host the e-learning system (they were doing this anyway for many other applications across the CE), the content generation was outsourced to a third party, and the functional departments (such as Operation and Maintenance, Network Planning, Sales, etc.) provided SMEs (Subject Matter Experts) for the validation of the content and the Training department started to convert the instructors into e-moderators. Eventually the HR department, traditionally composed of nontechnical personnel was able to manage a complex application in a technology driven virtual organization.

A second project in developed was proposed and is currently under evaluation with the EMeL (Experimental Mobile eLearning) initiative at IST Framework 6.

4. CLOSING REMARKS AND FURTHER WORK

(Senge, 1990) defines the learning organizations as entities that continuously expand their capacity to create their future. In the KE one approach is to create an environment and a culture that encourages knowledge generation and sharing, supports learning by doing and ensures that learning is incorporated into future activities, decisions and initiatives of the company. Further efforts are focused towards ontology based E-Learning. This idea became obvious after understanding how the e-Learning cube was useful to the GSM operator. Ontology was defined (Gruber, 1993) as a formal, explicit specification of shared conceptualization. For the purpose of this paper „conceptualization" refers to the abstract model of the E-Learning Cube. The term „Explicit" means that the type of concepts used and the constraints on their use are explicitly defined. „Formal" refers to the fact that the ontology should be machine understandable. There has been considerable effort put into the Meta languages to model VE processes and structures (Atanasiou, 2001). The term „Shared" reflects the trend of ontology as being able to capture consensual knowledge. Efforts are going both in the scientific direction as well as towards real world implementations of E-Learning solutions for Collaborative Networks.

5. REFERENCES

1. Stanescu, A.M., Dumitrache, I., Curaj, A., Caramihai, S.I. and Chircor, M. Supervisory Control and Data Acquisition for Virtual Enterprise, in Int. Prod. Res., 2002, Vol. 40, No 15, 3545 – 3559.
2. Hodgins, Wayne. Into the Future: A Vision Paper, www.learnativity.com, February 2000.
3. Clark, R. Putting Learning Standards into Practice, "ASTD E-Learning Handbook", McGraw Hill 2002.
4. Clark, R. Developing Technical Training: A Structured Approach, Perform Technology Press, 1989.
5. Cisco Systems. Reusable Learning Object Strategy, Version 4.0, November 2001.
6. Bloom, Benjamin S. and Krathwohl, David R. Taxonomy of Educational Objectives, Handbook 1: Cognitive Domain. Addison-Wesley Publishing Company, 1994.
7. Merrill, M.D. Component Display Theory, in Instructional Design Theories and Models. Edited by C.M. Reigeluth, Hillsdale, New Jersey, 1983.
8. Rosenberg, J. Mark. E-Learning, McGraw Hill 2001.
9. Senge, M. Peter. The Fifth Discipline: The Art and Practice of Learning Organization, New York, Doubleday, 1990.
10. Coulouris G., Dollimore J., Kindberg T. Distributed Systems, Concepts and Design, Addison Wesley 2001.
11. Skyrme, David J. Capitalizing on Knowledge: from e-business to k-business, Butterworth Heinemann 2001.
12. Encarnacao, Jose L. Edutainment – The colorful world of Computer - generated images, Europaischer Wirtschafts Verlag GmbH. 2004.
13. Gruber, T.R. „Towards Principles for Design of Ontologies used for Knowledge Sharing", in Proceedings of International Workshop on Formal Ontology, Padova, Italy, 1993. Ed. N. Guarino.
14. Atanasiou, Maria. UEML State of the Art – Summary, IST-2001-37368, www.ueml.org, 2001.
15. E-learning: Implementing the 4-Tier Blended Learning Model from IBM, White Paper, November 2001.
16. Dumke, Horst. Introduction to Content Delivery Protocols and Technologies, Cisco Systems 2003.
17. Camarinha-Matos, Luis, Afsarmanesh, Hamideh. Infrastructures for Virtual Enterprise, Kluver Academic Publishers, 1999.
18. PRO-VE 2004, IFIP Prodnet Working Conference for Virtual Enterprise, Zurich, Sept. 2004.
19. Garlasu, D., Stanescu, A.M. - A New Approach For E-Learning In Robotics, 14-Th International Workshop on Robotics in Alpe-Adria-Danube Region RAAD'05 Bucharest, Romania: May 2005.

58

A SIMULATION GAME APPROACH TO SUPPORT LEARNING AND COLLABORATION IN VIRTUAL ORGANISATIONS

Max Schwesig, Klaus-Dieter Thoben, Jens Eschenbächer
BIBA at the University of Bremen, GERMANY
max@biba.uni-bremen.de, tho@biba.uni-bremen.de, esc@biba.uni-bremen.de

As products are getting more complex, it often requires various enterprises with certain key competencies to produce a product in collaboration in e.g. a virtual organization. The resulting specialization leads to an increased demand for knowledge. Thus, especially interorganisational learning gains importance. As a consequence of the stated developments, the way of working and thus the educational requirements have changed as well. Performance skills about the processes and challenges within interorganisational product development and -learning are becoming vital to efficiently participate in future working scenarios. This paper describes the research approach, development and evaluation of a web based group simulation game that has been built to address these new educational demands.

1. INTRODUCTION

In recent discussions there is a growing trend to consider products and services more as a customer benefit or a solution to a customer problem, which has been described by the term extended product. Such complex extended products and services cannot be created by single enterprises but from enterprise networks such as virtual organisations (Thoben et al. 2001). The resulting specialization within companies accelerates innovation speed and thus increases the demand for knowledge. As half time of knowledge continuously decreases, the organizational capacity for learning is being identified as one of the key abilities for organizations to survive. As a consequence of the stated developments, the way of working and thus the educational requirements that engineers face have changed as well. Communication skills, collaborative skills as well as performance skills about the processes and challenges within organizational and interorganisational learning and -product development are becoming vital. Appropriate tools to mediate such skills are simulation games.

Existing games in the field of organisational learning and the closely related knowledge management (Büchel, Probst 2000) as the simulation game "KM Quest" (KITS 2003) and "Wissensmanagement Planspiel für soziale Organisationen" (BBJ 2002) emphasize on the mediation of basic principles of knowledge management as well as the implementation and intervention related aspects.

Existing simulation games in the field of product development like "COSIGA" (Pawar et al. 1995) "City Car Simulation" (Goffin, Mitchell 2002) and "GLOTRAIN" (Windhoff 2001) focus on the mediation of certain approaches or emphasize on important success factors in product development or even distributed production. So far, (inter)organisational learning, company collaboration in a virtual organisation and product development have not been considered in a single gaming approach. In order to address the mentioned educational requirements, we proposed a web enabled group simulation game simulating processes and challenges in interorganisational working and learning in a virtual organisation.

2. RESEARCH APPROACH

As the initial evaluation and validation of the COSIGA simulation have been very encouraging (Riedel et al. 2001), this four step product development and manufacturing process will be used as a basis for the design of the new simulation. Since this new game emphasizes the active experience of intraorganizational and interorganisational learning, it is necessary to identify key processes and challenges within intraorganizational and interorganizational learning. In order to simulate interorganisational manufacturing, it is important to identify organisational principles of distributed manufacturing as well as the life cycle of a manufacturing network of companies. Together, these design elements will then be used to shape the simulation game.

2.1 Processes and challenges of organizational learning

After having regarded the existing simulation game for Concurrent Engineering-"Cosiga", which serves as a conceptual basis for the new game, we identify processes and challenges within organisational and interorganisational learning. Together, these game elements will form the SHARE gaming approach.

"Cosiga" is a multimedia computer based simulation game being played by five individuals in the same room (co-located) or in a distributed group (virtual) interacting in a product development scenario and using the Internet and telecommunications. As initial evaluation and validation with target users have been very encouraging (Riedel et al. 2001), this four step product development process will be used as a basis for the design of the SHARE game. Since this new game emphasizes the active experience of organizational and interorganisational learning, it is necessary to identify key processes and challenges within organizational and interorganizational learning. Organisational learning is interpreted from a multi level perspective, comprising of the individual, group, organizational and inter-organizational level (Nonaka 1994), since this point of view enables us to regard main levels of action within an enterprise. According to this perspective, the following working definitions of the different learning levels have been created:

Individual level learning focuses on individual knowledge acquisition without further social interaction. Group level learning happens, if more that one individual consciously or unconsciously acquires knowledge interactively. Organisational level learning focuses on perspective taking between groups in a company (Sumner et al. 1999). As organisations are typically composed of multiple interacting communities, each with highly specialized knowledge, skills and technologies, knowledge intensive firms require these diverse communities to bridge their difference to create a new shared perspective Interorganisational learning happens in two ways: either through the transfer of existing knowledge from one organization to another, or through the creation of new knowledge (Larsson et al.1998). Group level learning ,organizational level learning and interorganisational learning are affected by "people barriers" like proprietary thinking and skepticism towards the sharing of knowledge and various fears (Barson et al. 2000). Additionally, interorganisational learning is affected by organisational boundaries like space, time, (cultural) diversity, structure and distribution of knowledge and results (Bosch-Sijtsema 2001).

Especially organizational level learning is difficult to simulate as it requires the professional and technical identification of the players with their departments specialized background. As this effect cannot be reached in a multiple hour simulation game, we mainly consider individual- group- and interorganisational level learning in the simulation game. Together with the mentioned barriers and boundaries, these game elements form a gaming approach will be implemented in two game scenarios..

2.2 PRINCIPLES OF DISTRIBUTED MANUFACTURING IN A VIRTUAL ORGANISATION

According to Windhoff (Windhof 2001, p. 31) game relevant characteristics of distributed manufacturing are cooperation, interconnectedness, symbiosis and probability. As key competencies and knowledge are distributed, companies have to cooperate to combine them in order to be successful. Due to this cooperation, the different systems are interconnected, so that especially interorganisational business processes and the related material – and information flows have to be considered in a simulation. As the companies are standing in symbiosis to other companies, the success of an individual company depends on the performance of the other partners. On the other handed side, the optimisation of one company does not automatically lead to the optimisation of the network. Additionally, the behaviour of the overall system cannot be predicted precisely, which might lead to complex nontransparent working situations. Figure 1 illustrates the mentioned characteristics of distributed manufacturing and their implementation.

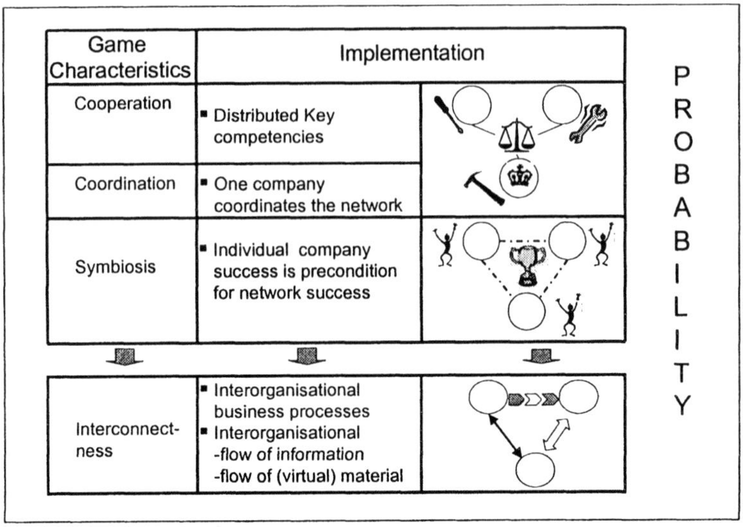

Figure 1: Characteristics of distributed manufacturing and their implementation

2.3 THE LIFE CYCLE OF A MANUFACTURING NETWORK

As manufacturing networks are dynamic and constantly changing, temporary consortia of enterprises that strategically join skills and resources to better respond to business opportunities are gaining importance. The life cycle of such virtual manufacturing organisations consists of four phases: creation, operation, evolution and dissolution (Camarinha-Matos, Afsarmanesh 1999). As the simulation model is rigid and the inclusion of additional partnering organizations would increase the models complexity, the evolutionary aspect of virtual organizations is not considered in the simulation. Since the simulation does not aim on simulating the complete life cycle of a virtual organization, the dissolution of the virtual organization is not considered, either. Thus, the simulation considers the creation and operation of the virtual organisation. Figure 2 illustrates the life cycle of such a virtual organisation.

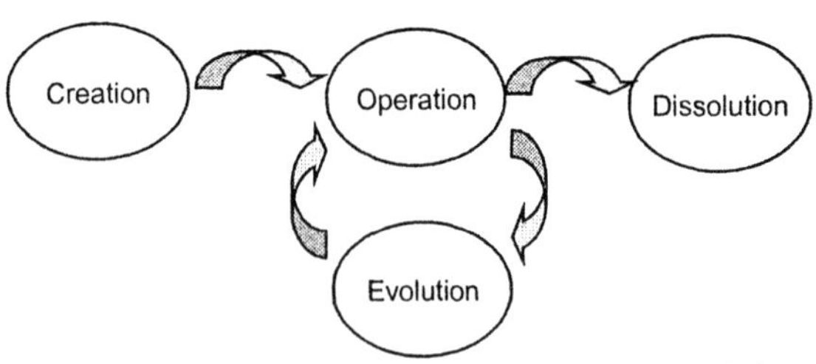

Figure 2. The life cycle of a virtual organization (Camarinha-Matos and Afsamarnesh 1999, S. 17)

3. The simulation game approach

551

The following descriptions discuss the main Game levels with a specific focus of the developed functionality. Additionally the web-solution is presented and explained.

3.1 Level 1 of the SHARE game

In the first level, nine players have to specify, design and produce a jetski in one company. They act as employees of an organisation that covers the basic economical functions. Each department is responsible for the successful completion of at least one step within the product development process. The game engine measures time, the expenditures as well as the product quality in order to create a competitive situation that increases the motivation of the players. The players are divided into three groups resembling the departments of the company. These three groups are distributed in disperse locations in order to enable the players to experience working in distributed environments. Each player uses an individual web interface to accomplish his given tasks within the simulated product development process. They have the opportunity to communicate using the built in chat function as well as the telephone.

In order to simulate organisational knowledge exchange realistically, essential information that is required to accomplish the product development process is distributed unequally, so that the players have to cooperate and to communicate to be successful. Following their role descriptions, some players act non collaborative to form "people barriers". The information seeking players have to convince their non collaborative colleagues to share their knowledge. In order to support this process, they can apply "trust enhancing measures" like inviting their opposite for dinner or for a sports trip. Off course, these illustrated symbolic measures only present a limited variety of measures that can be applied in real life. However, we aim on mediating that relationship building can be accelerated by special attention and symbols of good will. By letting the players experience the destructive effect of non collaborative behaviour, we want them to understand the benefits of knowledge sharing. The layout of the first level is illustrated in Figure 3.

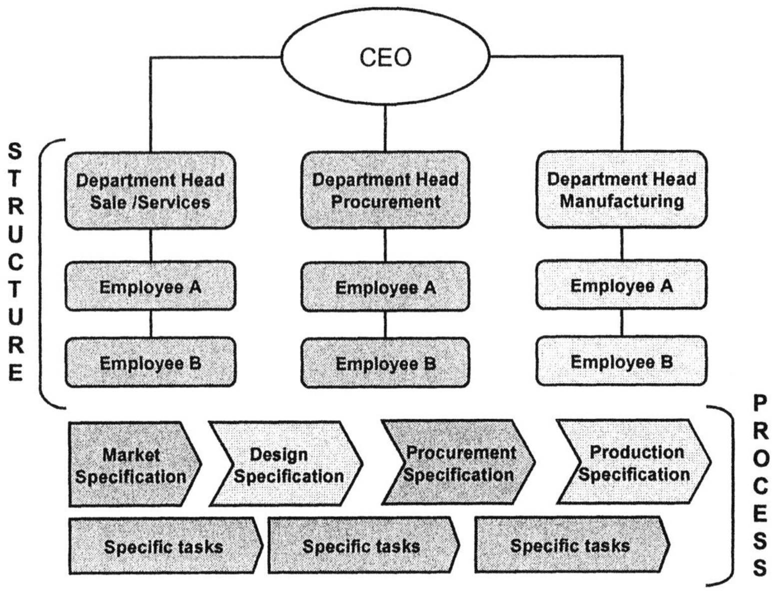

Figure 3. Structure and process in level 1

After the game, the players come together physically in order to reflect on what has happened and why certain events took place. Within this debriefing phase, they identify problems and initiating events that occurred in the areas of communication, collaboration and of course trust. Together, they develop problem solutions in order to improve their communicative- and cooperative skills.

3.2 Level 2 of the SHARE game

Within the second level, the players use the acquired knowledge and skills in the interorganisational contract negotiations in order to then specify, design and produce an extended product interorganisationally: a cell phone enriched by certain services. While the simulated service company takes consortial leadership and develops services, the two simulated manufacturing companies develop and produce the cell phone in a generic approach. Again, the players are divided into three groups resembling the particular companies in the production network. These three groups are distributed in disperse locations in order to enable the players to experience working in distributed environments. As consortia responsibilities are distributed unequally, the partners have to cooperate to enable constant flow of information that will then lead to a constant flow of material. In order to develop and produce this extended product, the overall success depends on every partners successful contribution. In order to simulate interorganisational learning related challenges realistically, this constant flow of information is affected by the simulated organisational boundaries space, time, diversity and structure. In order to successfully accomplish the overall scenario, the players are required to find appropriate solutions in order to overcome the barriers. The layout of the second level is illustrated in Figure 4

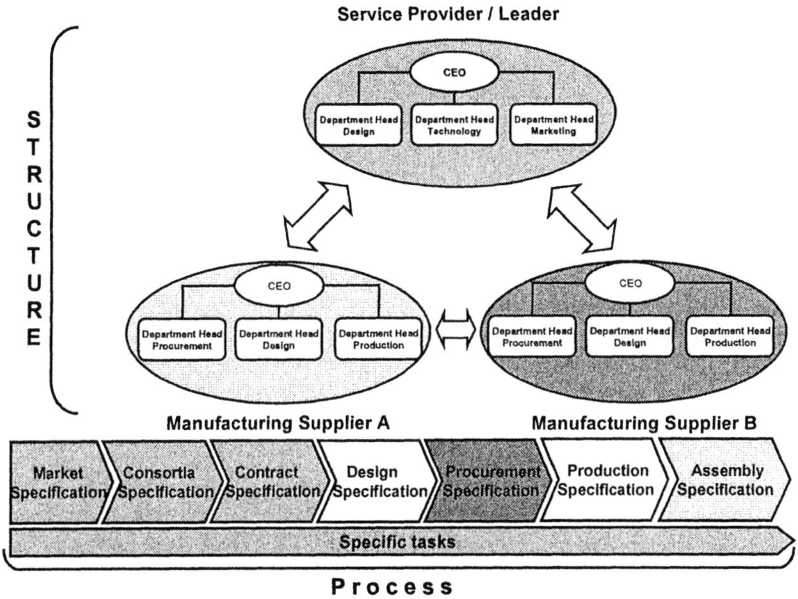

Figure 4. Structure and process in level 2

After the game session, the players come together physically again in order to reflect on what has happened and why certain events took place. Within this debriefing phase, they identify problems and initiating events that occurred in the areas of interorganisational knowledge exchange and related boundaries. Together, they develop strategies how to overcome such boundaries in order to acquire performance skills in interorganisational working and – learning.

3.3 The web interface

The described structures are implemented in a web interface. This web interface displays the main game features to each player. After having logged into the web interface by using individually assigned login data, the players enter their individual game interface. While the left handed side contains links to information about the company structure and the different players, the items on the right handed side are linked to templates representing the product development process that has to be completed. Additionally, the player can access information about the scenario, the final product and the particular individual task including information about the responsibilities within the company as well as role descriptions at the upper part pf the screen. This information has proved to be essential to provide basic orientation to the players during the game. Status information is displayed at the lower part pf the screen. Apart from that, the players can apply the described trust enhancing measures to other players in order to build up a trustful working relation. In order to communicate with each other, the players can use the built in chat function at the screen bottom.

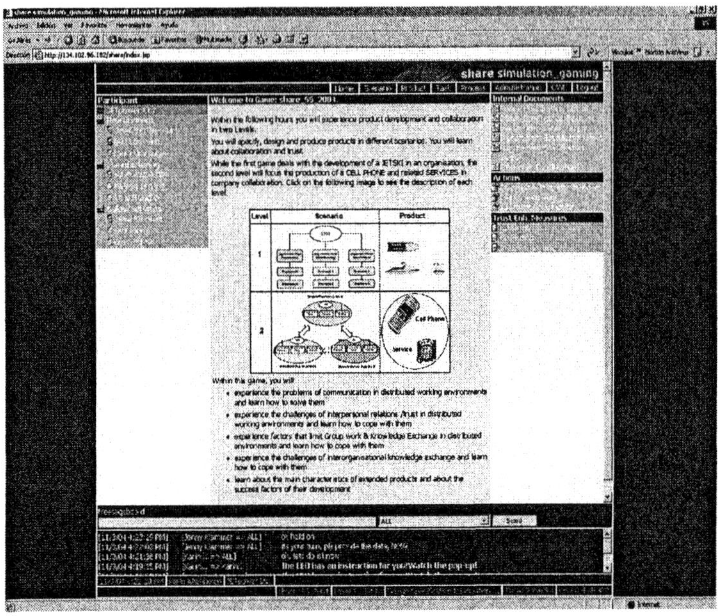

Figure 5. The SHARE Web interface

4. CONCLUSION

We have created a web based group simulation game focussing on the learners experience of (interorganisational) product development as well as organisational and interorganisational learning processes and challenges. Therefore we have combined a gaming approach used in the simulation game "COSIGA" with identified processes and challenges in (inter)organisational learning. An initial version of the game has been evaluated and validated in four gaming sessions with 36 students and industry representatives. Each gaming session consisted of two levels being played in two complete consecutive days.

In order to evaluate the suitability of the implemented game characteristics and the individual learning outcome, two questionnaires have been created. We felt that this form of evaluation was most appropriate, since it enabled us to get a rough idea about he game characteristics and its effects at a reasonable evaluation effort.

This initial evaluation of the first level showed that the players rated an improvement in their communication skills in distributed environments. Additionally, the value of interpersonal relations and trust was experienced as the precondition for successful collaboration. Occasionally, the players felt overstrained by the initial complexity of the gaming model. This will be improved by detailing the introduction to the game and its features. As a consequence of the sequential product development process, some players suffered from limited involvement in the game at certain times. This will be addressed by implementing additional supporting tasks that have to be completed by idle departments and by the enrichment of the department heads responsibilities to assure equal workload among the employees of a department.

This evaluation of the second level showed that the players appreciated the realistic simulation of interorganisational product development and – collaboration in a virtual organisation. They suffered from the implemented organisational boundaries and recognized their challenging effects, as they especially enjoyed the simulation of diverse cultures and different time zones. At the beginning, the players felt overstrained by the initial complexity of the simulated interrelations between companies. This will be improved by detailing the introduction to the game and explaining the particular company interrelations.

During this initial testing phases, the web based simulation game suffered from minor system instabilities, so that the learning outcome was not optimal for every player. This is optimised by extensive testing using simulated game sessions to identify and solve the occurred server problems. Additionally, the games usability is currently optimised by enhancing the graphic user interface.

Furthermore, it is planned to develop an adjustable game that is able to simulate different kinds of vertical and horizontal collaborations. An accordant system architecture is in development. Apart from that, modern wireless technologies will be integrated to enable an easy implementation in working and learning environments and to realistically present of future ubiquitous learning environments for engineers. This is partly addressed within the upcoming EU-NMP research project PRIME (Providing Real Integration in Multi-disciplinary Environments)

4.2 Acknowledgments

The paper is mainly based on work performed in the project GEM funded by the European Community under the Framework programme 5 (IST-2001-32059) and comprises a minor contribution form the IP ECOLEAD (IFP6-IP 506958).

5. REFERENCES

1. Barson, R.; Foster, G.; Struck, T.; Ratchev, S., Pawar, K.; Weber, F.; Wunram, M. (2000): Inter- and Intra-Organisational Barriers to Sharing Knowledge in the Extended Supply-Chain. Proceedings of the eBusiness and eWork 2000. The Key Action II Annual Conference. Madrid

2. BBJ Consult AG (Eds.).(2002): Wissensmanagement-Planspiel für soziale Organisationen: Abschlussdokumentation. München

3. Bosch-Sijtsema, P. (2001): Knowledge development in a Virtual organisation: an Information Processing Perspective, Licentiate dissertation from Lund University, KFS AB Lund, Sweden

4. Büchel, B.;Probst, G.(2002): From Organizational Learning to Knowledge Management. Genf. 2000. www-

Seite:http://hec.info.unige.ch/recherches_publications/OL%20Article%20for%20Encyclopedia%20for%20Life%20Support%20Systems1.pdf. 16.11.

5. Camarinha-Matos, M.; Afsarmanesh, H., 1999. The virtual enterprise concept In: L.M. Camarinha-Matos and H. Afsarmanesh, Editors, Infrastructures for Virtual Enterprises—Networking Industrial Enterprises, Kluwer Academic Publishers, pp. 3–14

6. Goffin, K.; Mitchell, R.(2002): "Teaching Innovation and New Product Development using the "City Car" Simulation" 13th Annual Meeting of the Production and Operations Management Society, San Francisco 5th-8th April

7. KITS: Webpages of the KITS Project describing the simulation game KM-Quest. WWW-page. www.kmquest.nl/index.html. 03.01.03

8. Larsson, R.; Bengtsson, L.; Henriksson, K.; Sparks, J. (1998): The Interorganizational Learning Dilemma: Collective Knowledge Development in Strategic Alliances. In: Special issue: Managing Partnerships and Strategic Alliances, in Organization Science Vol. 9, pp: 285-306

9. Nonaka, I. (1994):A dynamic Theory of Organizational Knowledge Creation, in: Organization Science, Vol 5

10. Pawar, K.S., Thoben, K-D. and Oehlmann, R. (1995). Developing concurrent engineering conceptual model and knowledge platform. In: Proceedings of the second conference on Concurrent Engineering, Research and Application (CERA). USA: Washington DC. 23–25 August. pp. 487–497

11. Riedel, J.; Pawar, K. S.; Barson, R.(2001): Academic and Industrial User Needs for a Concurrent Engineering Simulation Game. In: Concurrent Engineering: Research and Applications. 11.

12. Sumner, T., Domingue, J., Zdrahal, Z., Millican, A., Murray, J.(1999): Moving from On-the-Job Training towards Organisational Learning. Proceedings of the 12th Banff Knowledge Acquisition Workshop, Banff, Alberta, Canada, October, 16-22

13. Thoben, K.-D., Jagdev, H. and Eschenbaecher, J. (1999): Extended Products: Evolving Traditional Product concepts. Proceedings of the 7th International Conference on Concurrent Enterprising: Engineering the Knowledge Economy through Co-operation. Bremen Germany 27-29th June 2001, pp. 429-439.

14. Windhoff, G. (2001): Planspiele für die verteilte Produktion. Entwicklung und Einsatz von Trainingsmodulen für das aktive Erleben charakteristischer Arbeitssituationen in arbeitsteiligen, verteilten Produktionssystemen auf Basis der Planspielmethodik. Dissertation Bremen

PART 19

COLLABORATIVE NETWORKS IN TRANSPORTATION SYSTEMS

59 A COLLABORATIVE NETWORK CASE STUDY: THE EXTENDED "ViaVerde" TOLL PAYMENT SYSTEM

A. Luís Osório[1] ; Luis M. Camarinha-Matos[2]; J. S. Gomes[3]
[1]ISEL, Instituto Superior de Engenharia de Lisboa, Portugal
aosorio@deetc.isel.ipl.pt
[2]New University of Lisbon, Portugal, *cam@uninova.pt*
[3]*BRISA, Auto-estradas de Portugal, Portugal, Jorge.Gomes@brisa.pt*

The extended ViaVerde business model is presented and discussed as a case study of an enterprise collaborative network in the domain of toll payment systems. In order to offer ViaVerde clients the possibility to use the installed RFID transponder to automatically pay services in car parking areas and gas stations, a complex collaborative enterprise network comprising a diversity of business models, was established. Besides banks and clearing house, there are other players involved. The car parking area owners, co-located shops, and companies offering employees parking facilities are examples of such players. The life cycle management of the underlying distributed business process requires a new framework able to deal with the distribution of contributing actors and the need to guarantee interoperability among the various heterogeneous systems. The paper focuses on the requirements for a technological platform to deal with such complex enterprise network. A service oriented infrastructure developed for toll management systems is taken as the baseline for supporting the new enterprise collaborative processes.

1. INTRODUCTION

The collaborative networks paradigm (Camarinha-Matos, 2004), represents an appropriate approach to a new business scenario where a group or companies contribute to offer car drivers a transparent and smooth payment of services involving a wide number of companies. The considered services include toll payment in highways (ViaVerde system) as well as payment in car parking areas and in gas stations using a uniform payment system based on DSRC technology (Jordan, 2001), a kind of car RFID. Car drivers do not need to have any direct relationship with the involved companies; but rather a unique contract with a single entity. For the customers these companies are "invisible"; in fact they only see an integrated payment system presented to them under the ViaVerde brand.

The enterprise collaborative network paradigm or networked organizations (Bacquet, 2004) is emerging in different contexts and it corresponds to a strategy to model collaborative systems involving a number of companies that appear to customers or service consumers as a single (apparent) unit. Such units offer services or products making transparent the complex interactions performed in the background.

The ViaVerde tolling system is based on the free-flow of cars equipped with an RF identifier. When cars cross a ViaVerde toll, without stopping, a transaction is automatically generated and processed. The ViaVerde system uses a technology similar to the emergent RFID. In fact the DSRC is a kind of RFID where an active tag (transponder) installed in the car, communicates with a toll antenna through a 5.8 GHz wireless link (the road side equipment reads and writes information to the tag). Recently, the ViaVerde automatic payment system has been extended by BRISA to offer car drivers the possibility to access car parking and gas station areas equipped with DSRC system. With this extension, the car drivers receive on their billing report a list of transactions from different places that are controlled by different companies operating under different business models. The car drivers establish a contract with the ViaVerde Portugal company (VVP), which is a physical enterprise but with a trend to move towards a more agile organization focussed on the management of cross enterprise business processes.

This paper analyses the underlying business model associated to this virtual toll and fee payment system and discusses it in the context of the enterprise collaborative networks paradigm (Camarinha-Matos, 2003). The first objective of this work is to establish the technological infrastructure requirements taking as reference the ITSIBus project (Gomes et. al. 2003) (Osorio, et. al. 2004) and a set of basic conceptual constructs contributing to establish such distributed business model targeting the enterprise collaborative network (Camarinha-Matos, 2004). In the proposed enterprise network there are two coordinating companies. One is BAER (BRISA Access Electrónica Rodoviária), a company from the BRISA group responsible to manage the technological infrastructure. The BAER company is facing a complex challenge considering the number of technological business agreements it has to manage. The other company is ViaVerde Portugal, also a company from the BRISA group responsible to manage the ViaVerde payment related services, and as mentioned above, it is responsible to make transparent to clients (ViaVerde clients) fee payments in a number of contexts (motorway toll, parking areas, gas stations, etc.).

In this context different business models are being implemented to offer access to car parking areas, be them private or public, to ViaVerde customers. Situations exist where parking fee discounts are given to customers when they shop in some stores served by a car parking. In other situations credits are accumulated in association or not to some brand fidelity card and used to pay car parking. All these services result in different contractual situations that need to be properly structured and also require an integrated infrastructure able to manage such processes. In fact, there is a challenge on how to model such complex and evolving network relationships and on what would be the best information and communication infrastructure to cope with the involved companies.

A systematic approach is necessary to address business models management involving different companies under different contractual agreements and in this case offering ViaVerde clients a number of new services making transparent for them the underlying complexity. Another vector of this challenge is the need for a structured framework to represent and manage the collaborative business models and link them to the executing information and communication technology (ICT) infrastructure. It shall be noted that in this domain there is a trend to a fast and unpredictable evolution of business models integrating additional services with the corresponding need for agility to better adapt to new business strategies. This evolution requires a structured approach to model the development and deployment of the virtual systems that support the collaborative business processes.

The proposed approach departs from the ITSIBus initiative, a service based architecture that is being defined to promote interoperability among diverse technological systems by defining a multi-technology platform where unification is achieved at the service definition level based on WSDL. The ITSIBus initiative is being extended to include a development framework able to address virtual systems development following a model driven approach.

2. DISCUSSION OF THE COLLABORATIVE NETWORK

The business model under discussion involves a number of players each one responsible for specific roles. The ViaVerde company plays a central role considering that it is the entity that manages the relations between car drivers (ViaVerde Clients) and the ViaVerde virtual business model. This business model aims to facilitate the life of customers by giving them access to various services without requiring them to stop to pay service fees. As an example, when DSRC/RFID is installed in a car parking gate, a car with an OBU (On Board Unit, according to TC 278 terminology) can enter without the need to get a ticket or present any card. When exiting the parking lot the exit gates will open when a ViaVerde client approaches the exit lane. This new payment mechanism on car parking areas "inherits" other business mechanisms used to promote other businesses like discounts when shopping in some co-located stores or agreements with other companies to offer car parking facilities to their employees or customers.

To clarify the collaborative network shown in Figure 1 let's identify the role of each one of the business and technological players. A central role is played by the motorway user that adhered to the ViaVerde toll payment system available in all the Portuguese motorways and in many other countries in Europe and outside Europe. The ViaVerde company manages the business model by maintaining contractual relationships with the Portuguese payment clearing company (SIBS), with the car parking owners, and other companies that need to offer car parking access to their customers or employees. As a matter of fact, there is no limit for the contractual relationships related to the fee payment being it car parking, gas station services, or access to city historical areas, a situation already managed by ViaVerde in the city of Lisbon.

In summary, the roles of each main player are the following:

- ViaVerde company – manages the integrated (virtual) business model, maintaining the relationships with clients, including billing, and the relationships with SIBS and any other company (parking, store, employer, municipality) to manage other related services when clients access car parking areas, gas stations, city historical areas or any other place which access requires DSRC/RFID technology.

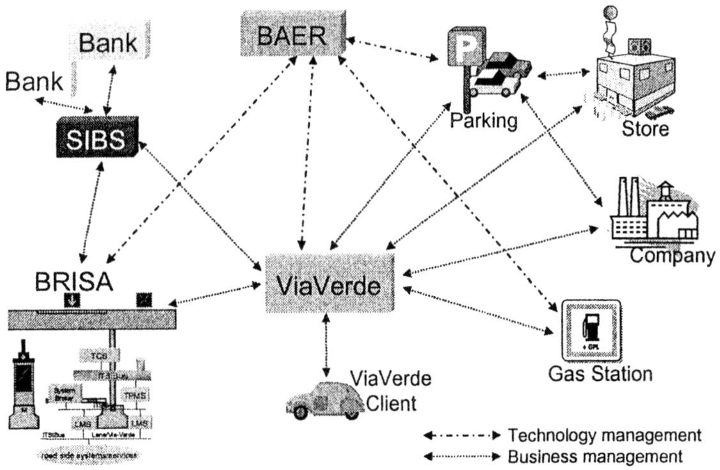

Figure 1 – Extended ViaVerde business scenario actors

- BAER, Brisa Access Electrónica Rodoviária – manages the underlying technological infrastructure to support the ViaVerde business model, including its extended form (parks, gas stations and city access beyond motorways);
- SIBS company – it is the Portuguese bank clearing company responsible to manage the Multibanco payment network involving ATM and POS systems. All the electronic payments flow is processed via SIBS that guarantees the bridge between card holders and banks;
- Car parking companies – companies that manage car parking areas with DSRC/RFID access installed. The ViaVerde clients are automatically recognized in this parking areas and the payment is done through ViaVerde. The ViaVerde company has to manage payments under some special business models like those involving the relations between ViaVerde clients and store discounts or employers;
- Gas stations – the ViaVerde client fills the car tank after it is automatically detected by the DSRC/RFID system and as soon as a PIN is introduced the payment is automatically processed by ViaVerde;
- Store companies – some stores offer discounts on neighbour car parking areas in order to attract or facilitate the access to clients. For clients holding the DSRC/RFID system the discounts have to be processed on an agreement basis between the shop owner and ViaVerde;
- Company – there are companies that make agreements with car parking areas to facilitate access to their employees. When they hold the DSRC/RFID system the access can be facilitated without the need for any other mechanism and it is managed automatically by the ViaVerde company;
- BRISA – the motorway management company that offers non-stop toll infrastructures based on the DSRC/RFID technology. The ViaVerde brand was initially associated to toll payment.

The challenge created by this scenario is complex considering that the involved companies are different, possess heterogeneous information systems, have different communication infrastructures and above all, there is some lack of trust regarding the introduction of new technological solutions. This lack of trust is understandable considering that the business model involves a huge number of transactions, involves a critical set of processes and it requires the trustiness also from ViaVerde clients, those that are the users of the virtual payment system. It is mandatory for the technological infrastructure to be failure free and also in the case some exception occurs the recovery mechanism must allow a clear and efficient resolution. Another important requirement is security considering that the business model deals with payments and even if small amounts per transaction are the majority of the cases, any security flaw would compromise the business model.

In order to better deal with this business scenario two main management domains were considered: business management, and technology management domains. The business management domain is related to the ViaVerde business model and deals with service related issues like contractual relationships with the ViaVerde clients and contractual relationships between ViaVerde and companies that are associated to the DSRC/RFID facility. The technology management domain is related to the supporting infrastructure and involves the BAER company. In order to materialize this system, there is a need to install new systems like DSRC/RFID antennas and their integration with the existing technological systems (systems integration). To some extent, the BAER company is responsible for the operational aspects of the collaborative network and beyond the mentioned partners, this company has to collaborate with the ICT development and services provider companies.

There is an extended scenario related to the interoperation of the ViaVerde business model with similar solutions implemented in other European countries. By contributing to the Pan-European ETC network, BRISA expects to offer ViaVerde clients the possibility to pay toll, car parking and other services in other European countries using the same DSRC/RFID technology (Figure 2).

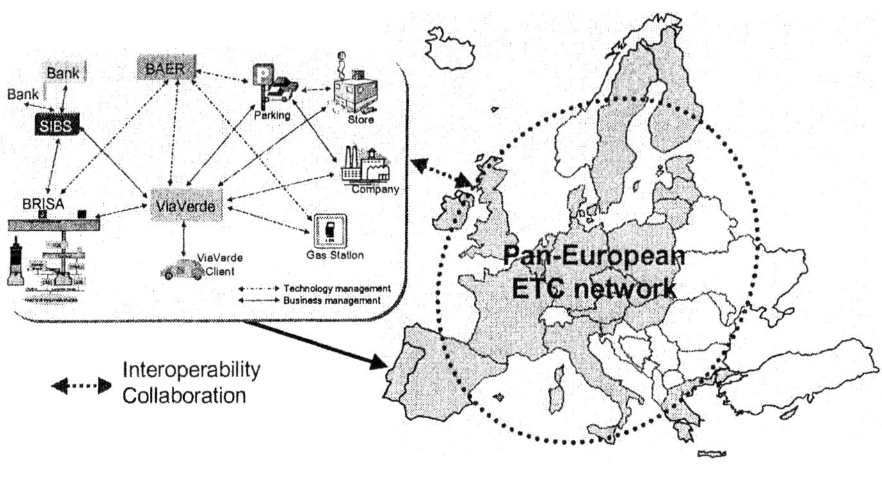

Figure 2 – Interoperability challenge for Pan-European ETC network

The objective is to offer a ViaVerde client the possibility to park in Madrid or Paris without the need to use another system than the DSRC/RFID tag installed in his/her car. This extended scenario towards a Pan-European ETC or electronic fee collection (EFC) network requires collaboration among European motorway companies to get true interoperability among their technological infrastructures. This European wide facility extends the enterprise collaborative network beyond country borders, what requires the establishment of an interoperability framework able to run the underlying enterprise collaborative business processes.

3. ITSIBUS TOWARDS A FEDERATION OF SERVICES

The electronic toll collection (ETC) infrastructure developed by BRISA follows a service based approach (Osório, 2004). The toll systems are built around standard services and implemented on a diversity of technologies (Osório, 2005). Nevertheless, there is already a strong file transfer pattern behind most of the collaborative processes. As an example, the list of valid DSRC/RFID identifiers is transferred in a file from the ViaVerde company to the BRISA toll management infrastructure. When a ViaVerde client changes the associated bank card or needs to perform a simple update operation the change requires some days to be effective. Even if the solution performs well, there is an extra effort that can be avoided if more operations are automated and if what today involves file transference evolves to service level interactions. Similarly to the IBM initiative named Autonomic Computing (Ganek, 2003), the suggested approach is based on the recognition for the need of an added intelligence associated to the management of the technological systems supporting the integrated or holistic enterprise. As a matter of fact a technological infrastructure to support enterprise collaborative processes will be developed around evolving autonomous heterogeneous systems responsible for specialized services. The execution of a number of distributed enterprise collaborative processes depends on the quality of the participating systems which range from storage, transaction management, security, fault tolerance, backup, to human interaction, to mention only a few of the panoply of systems underlying the services that contribute to the execution of the envisaged collaborative processes.

The ITSIBus infrastructure proposes for the Electronic Toll Collection (ETC) systems an architecture based on a set of autonomous systems implementing a set of core services aiming to contribute to infrastructure management and the specialized services targeted to implement specific functionalities (Osório, 2004). There is already a long way to run considering that the increasing "intelligence" associated to each system or enterprise technological component is contributing to an increased management complexity thus requiring advanced skills, not only during development but also during the operations phase. The adoption of open standards is contributing to facilitate the collaboration among heterogeneous systems. As an example, initiatives from the Distributed Management Task Force (DTMF) and Application Response Measurement (ARM) of Open Group, addressing software instrumentation of autonomous systems, are key contributions to an agile management of enterprise heterogeneous systems. In (Turner, 2002) the ARM standard is applied on a framework for identifying, monitoring and accessing to performance data of critical transactions implemented by web services. These concerns are as well addressed by the ITSIBus through the monitoring and plug-and-play core services aiming at contributing to provide system's autonomy and manageability. The ITSIBus system as a container of a set of services, the core ones common to all the other systems and the specific services implementing specialized functionalities, constitute a federation of systems/services able to be organized according to the enterprise process needs (Figure 3).

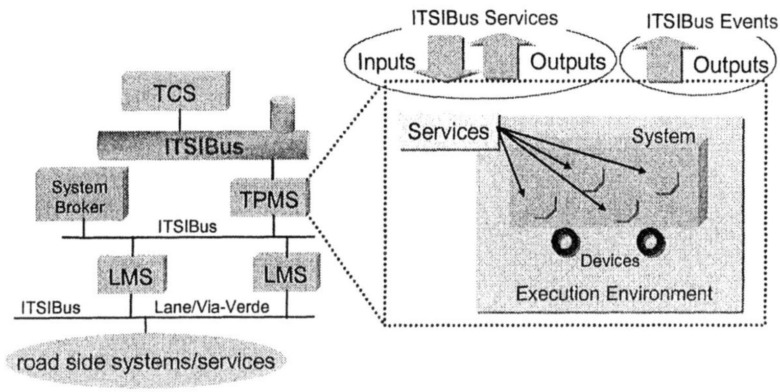

Figure 3 – Toll technological infrastructure based on a federation of services

Each system/set of services of the ETC infrastructure contributes to the execution of the ETC process which is responsible to manage toll information transactions and technology operations management. Each ETC system has an underlying process that is being transposed from a hard-coded approach to a model driven development and operations management approach (Osório, 2005). As shown in (Figure 4) the new generation of the ITC management system is based on a federation of services and the design and development of strategic services like the Toll Coordination Service (TCS), the Toll Plaza Management Service (TPMS) and the Lane Management Service (LMS) are being developed following a model driven approach through process definition in a procedural language (XPDL/BPEL) and its execution based on an orchestration engine.

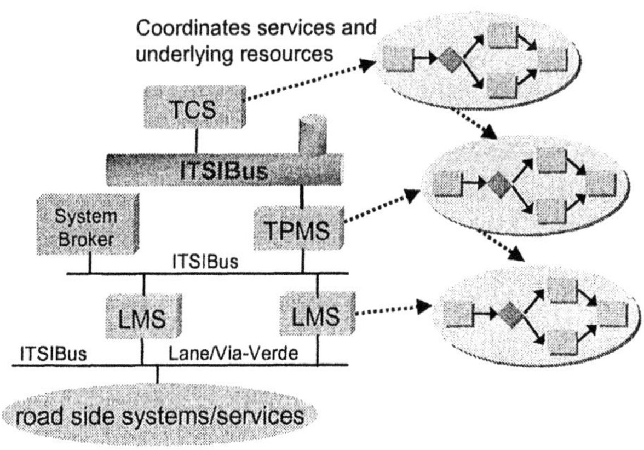

Figure 4 – The ETC management system/services based on service orchestration

Considering the challenges proposed by the extended ViaVerde business scenario, the strategy under evaluation is to extend ITSIBus to the enterprise collaborative space, following an initial proposal discussed in (Gomes, 2003). At the moment, collaboration is deeply grounded on ad hoc information exchange, which is difficult to develop, deploy and manage and not agile enough to cope with new business dynamics and unpredictability imposed by a fast evolution of the business models.

The adoption of the enterprise collaborative network paradigm is seen through a set of collaborative enterprise processes (CEP) designed to cope with specific collaborative business models. Considering the example of the extended ViaVerde business model, an underlying CEP needs to be defined as choreography of a number of services required to implement specific functionalities on each enterprise network member (Figure 5). The proposed approach requires a service definition framework able to deal with the enterprise systems requirements like:

- Distributed transaction management in order to guaranteeing system consistency against failures;
- Service location transparency and an efficient service discovery and advertisement mechanisms. Transposition of enterprise borders is a challenge considering security requirements;
- Distributed information management for high data volumes considering performance and availability;
- Security considering resource access policy management, user authentication, information privacy, integrity and non refutation are some of the related security issues;
- Integration with legacy enterprise systems.

The definition of such integrated view for the enterprise collaborative processes requires a number of consensuses, both regarding process definition and the distributed execution environment. The emergent grid initiative promoted by the Globus Alliance and its initiative on the Open Grid Services Architecture (OGSA) in collaboration with W3C, IETF and OASIS after adopting Web Services as the reference implementation technology are being analyzed as potential contributions to such required distributed service execution environment. OGSA addresses the creation (factory) of services global naming, Grid Service Handle (GSH) and references Grid Service Reference (GSR), lifetime management, registration and discovery, authorization, notification, concurrency and manageability (Foster, 2004).

Even if the OGSA initiative is important to the development of collaborative distributed computational environments, it shall be noted that the strategy adopted by ITSIBus is a multi-technology approach (Osório, 2005). The strategy is to develop a platform and a framework able to deal with complementary strategic and technological approaches. The first productized version of the ITSIBus was based on the JINI platform whilst the reference implementation has services bound to Web Services and JXTA technology. As a matter of fact enterprise systems evolve more than revolve; any framework has to deal with different cultures and systems at different development stages. This means that some companies of the collaborative network are not able to definitely adopt new system but rather accept a kind of adapters making the bridge between legated systems and the required facilities to integrate the new collaborative networks.

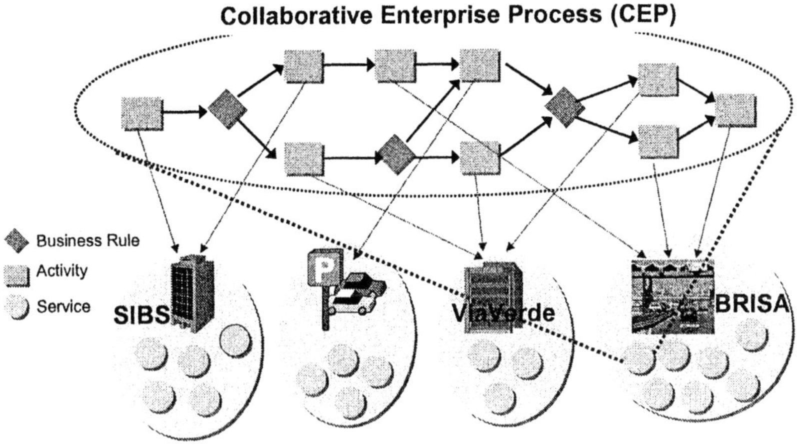

Figure 5 – Enterprise network based on a federation of collaborative services

Another line of the research under discussion is to contribute to the model driven development like it is proposed by MDA initiative of OMG considering a model-driven approach for process integration (Koehler, 2005). The adoption of a declarative approach through the process definition language BPEL and complementary UML graphical representation for activities and constraint rules like Object Constraint Language (OCL) is a way to offer process experts the right tools to generate complex enterprise collaborative systems. Developing at model level, the guidelines proposed by OMG through the MDA initiative can be more easily considered, in particular the Platform Independent Model (PIM) construction and its (semi)automatic mapping to different Platform Specific Models (PIM). This is however a complex research topic that requires further contributions in order to achieve an effective MDA approach, at least considering a completely automatic process to map PIM to PSM.

4. CONCLUSIONS

The presented case study aims at contributing to establish a technological framework for enterprise collaborative networks in the ITS industry. A new structured approach for the challenges faced by the BRISA company to extend its toll infrastructure to payments in car parking and in gas stations was presented. The discussion was centered on the requirements and a first approach was discussed considering two main aspects for the collaborative network. One important aspect addresses the management of the collaborative business processes. The other complementary aspect addresses the management of the technological infrastructure considering as a main concern the interoperability among technological systems of the network members. The discussion is grounded on the ITSIBus as a multi-technology infrastructure based on services to manage motorway toll systems. Furthermore there is a concern in the described work to promote a model-driven approach as a way to cope with the underlying complexity and to be able to map (bind) models on different technological infrastructures. This approach aims to contribute to develop a new generation of technologies, methodologies and tools able to cope with the complexity associated to the life cycle management of these collaborative networks.

ACKNOWLEDGMENTS

This work was partially supported by the BRISA group, through the research and development projects ITSIBus and PReCE and by the European Commission through the ECOLEAD integrated project.

5. REFERENCES

Bacquet, Joël; Fatelnig, Peter; Villasante, Jesus; Zwegers, Arian - An Outlook of Future Research Needs On Networked Organizations, PROVE'04 – IFIP 18th World Computer Congress, TC5 / WG5.5 – 5th Working Conference on Virtual Enterprises, 22–27 August 2004, Toulouse, France, published by Kluwer Academic Publishers, ISBN 1-4020-8138-3, pages 17-24, 2004.

Camarinha-Matos, L. M. - Infrastructures for virtual organizations – where we are, in Proceedings of ETFA'03 – 9th Int. Conf. On Emerging Technologies and Factory Automation, ISBN 0-7803-7937-3, pp 405-414, Lisboa, Portugal, 16-19 Sept 2003.

Camarinha-Matos, Luis M.; Afsarmanesh, Hamideh - The Emerging Discipline of Collaborative Networks, PROVE'04 – IFIP 18th World Computer Congress, TC5 / WG5.5 – 5th Working Conference on Virtual Enterprises, 22–27 August 2004, Toulouse, France, published by Kluwer Academic Publishers, ISBN 1-4020-8138-3, pages 3-16, 2004.

Foster, Ian - The Grid: Blueprint for a New Computing Infrastructure, 2nd Edition, Morgan Kaufmann. ISBN: 1-55860-933-4, 2004.

Ganek, A. G.; Corbi, T. A. - The dawning of the autonomic computing era, IBM SYSTEMS JOURNAL, VOL 42, NO 1, 2003.

Gomes J. Sales, Jacquet G., Machado M, Osório A. Luís, Gonçalves C., Barata M. - An Open Integration Bus for EFC: The ITS IBus, in ASECAP2003, 18 - 21 May 2003 in Portoroz, Slovenia

Jordan, J.G.; Soriano, F.; Graullera, D.; Martin, G. - A comparison of different technologies for EFC and other ITS applications, Intelligent Transportation Systems, 2001. Proceedings. 2001 IEEE , 25-29 Aug. 2001

Koehler J.; Hauser R.; Sendall S.; Wahler M. - Declarative techniques for model-driven business process integration, IBM SYSTEMS JOURNAL, VOL 44, NO 1, 2005.

Osório A. L., Abrantes A. J., Gonçalves J. C., Araújo A.; Miguel J. M., Jacquet, G. C.; Gomes, J. S. - Flexible and Plugged Peer Systems Integration to ITS-IBUS: the case of EFC and LPR Systems, PROVE'03 – 4th IFIP Working Conference on Virtual Enterprises, published by Kluwer Academic Publishers, ISBN: 1-4020-7638-X, pages 221-230, 2003-b.

Osório, A. Luís; Barata, M. Martins; Abrantes, A. Joaquim; Gomes, J. Sales; Jacquet, G. Costa - Underlying ITS Business Processes with Flexible and Plugged Peer Systems: the Open ITS IBus approach, PROVE'03 – 4th IFIP Working Conference on Virtual Enterprises, published by Kluwer Academic Publishers, ISBN: 1-4020-7638-X, pages 221-230, 2003-a.

Osório, A. Luís; Gonçalves, Carlos; Araújo, Paulo; Barata, Manuel; Gomes, J. Sales; Jacquet, Gastão; Dias, Rui M - Open Multi-Technology Service Oriented Architecture for ITS Business Models: the ITSIBUS eToll services, submitted to PRO-VE'05 Valencia – Spain, 26 -28 September 2005.

Turner, J. D.; Bacigalupo, D. A.; Jarvis, S. A.; Dillenberger, D. N.; Nudd, G. R.. - Application Response Measurement of Distributed Web Services. CMG International Journal of Computer Resource Management, 108:45-55, 2002.

60 TOWARDS A VIRTUAL ENTERPRISE FOR PASSENGER TRANSPORTATION USING AGENTS

Claudio Cubillos[1], Franco Guidi-Polanco[2] and Claudio Demartini[3]
[1]*Politecnico di Torino, C.so Duca degli Abruzzi 24, 10129 Torino, Italy, e-mail: claudio.cubillos@polito.it*
[2]*Pontificia Universidad Católica de Valparaíso, Av. Brazil 2241, Valparaíso, Chile, e-mail: fguidi@ucv.cl*
[3]*Politecnico di Torino, C.so Duca degli Abruzzi 24, 10129 Torino, Italy, e-mail: claudio.demartini@polito.it*

This work presents a framework for developing a virtual enterprise for passenger transportation using the agent paradigm as baseline. The framework provides a set of base agents and behaviours that give the basic service functionality. The agent architecture allows the integration of different fleet operators and vehicle providers on one side, and users with their different groups and requirements on the other. A Service Ontology uniforms the semantics for building customized transport descriptions and for formalizing the interaction among the different actors and agents. An implementation focused in the centralized planification of the trips requests has been done using Jade and their results are presented.

1. INTRODUCTION

Nowadays flexible passenger transportation systems, also known as demand responsive transport (DRT), promise a greater flexibility for the user, a wider range of destinations and an increased opportunity for mode shift as potential benefits.

However, these benefits can get lost due to lack of integration. The spatial and administrative distribution of the different transport providers operating on specific areas (whether metropolitan or rural) often determines a fragmented coverage of the user needs. This results in poor customer service provision and in negative feedbacks for the authorities. Therefore, DRT transportation solutions need to be efficiently coordinated between them and with the other transport solutions. As a result, the trend is to move from a group of individual DRT systems towards a single virtual transport provision enterprise, a Virtual Mobility Agency.

On the other hand, the agent technology has been successfully applied to the transport domain and to system-integration scenarios (Zhang et al, 2003). Therefore, this work extends our research (Cubillos et al, 2004) on a single operator transportation framework to a virtual enterprise scenario that integrates different vehicle providers, using the agent paradigm as baseline.

2. TRANSPORTATION REQUIREMENTS

In a complex service system like passenger transportation, there are many actors that have a direct interest in the commercial, social and infrastructural impacts of the services. Four main Actor Categories can be identified, each of which with several subgroups. The categories are:

End Users: Are the direct or potential customers of the provided transport service. They can also be described as the "passenger" or "consumer". Commonly DRT services are considered most important among the following End User groups: the elderly, the disabled, healthcare patients (trips to health centers), school children and students, shoppers/visitors and persons with no access to a car.

Transport Operators: The Operator is directly involved in the provision of the transport service to the End User by providing some or all of the service elements such as the vehicle, driver, dispatch and support services.

Active Destinations: Certain destinations may play an active role in arranging transportation for their customers. For example, they may supply information to the operator about trips to the destination or they may order them for their customers; they may assist the operator in planning the services, or they may co-operate with the operator to provide a reasonable price for the trips. For example, hospitals, shopping centers and several civil service departments are typically this kind.

These actors usually have different and sometimes conflicting needs. Users commonly specify transport requests with different characteristics (pick-up/delivery place/time, low floor, WC, Air Conditioning, etc). On the other hand, single vehicle providers and fleet operators offer different transportation alternatives such as busses, minivans, vehicles for disabled people and taxis among others, each of them with diverse characteristics. Therefore, the flexible transport system we are treating consists of requests coming from a set of clients which should be satisfied by such an heterogeneous fleet.

From a mathematical point of view the problem corresponds to the dynamic version of the Dial-a-ride Problem (D-DARP) in a multi-depot scenario. This dynamicity means that the vehicle progress is monitored; clients can modify or cancel their trip requests, vehicle delays can occur, clients may not show up at the pickup place and vehicles can breakdown among others, involving the re-scheduling of the trips and their management.

3. THE VIRTUAL TRANSPORTATION ENTERPRISE

The framework provides a set of base agents and behaviours that provide the basic service functionality. As Figure 1 shows, an agent architecture allows the integration of the different transportation operators and vehicle providers on one side, and users with their different groups and requirements on the other. In addition, an Enterprise Service Ontology uniforms the semantics for building customized transport descriptions and for formalizing the interaction among the different actors and agents (service provision). The architecture relies over the Jade agent platform (Bellifemine, 1999) that provides a distributed environment with the basic communication and management services for the agents to interact.

First are explained the single vehicle and user parties, while in a next section is explained the integration of operators and user associations.

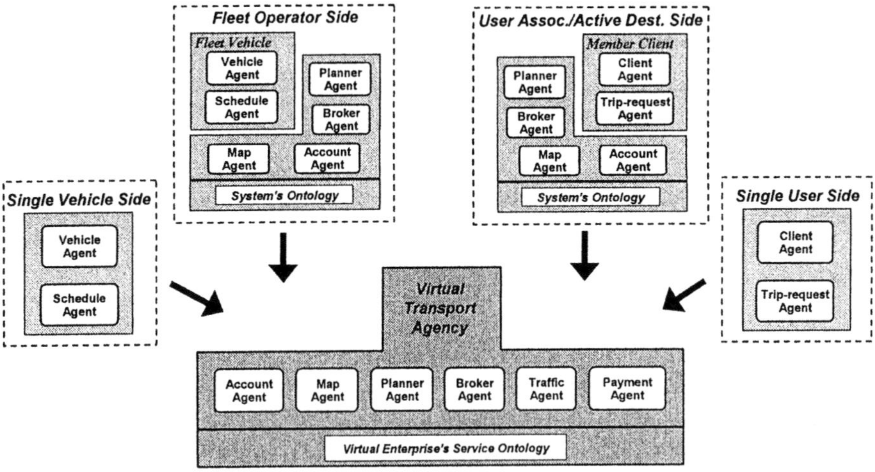

Figure 1 – Virtual Transportation Enterprise model.

3.1 Single User Side

Individual clients and their requirements are captured by Client and Trip-request agents. Together they provide full communication and interoperability of the real end user with the transportation system. The Client agent is in charge of providing a personalized user interface while the Trip-request manages the process of requesting the servicc, its characteristics and the decision making required.

The interface provided by Client agents should be adaptable to the different devices that can be used by clients for establishing the communication. Client agents can reside on different devices such as cell phones, PDAs or PCs, allowing offering the end user a pervasive interaction with the transport service. In addition, the Client agent is responsible for capturing all the client's requirements not only concerning the desired type of transport service but also his preferences upon contingency situations (e.g. delays, traffic jams, deviations, etc). The Trip-request takes these requirements and preferences to act on behalf of the real client during the whole process. Depending on the degree of autonomy provided by the client, the Trip-request can act as a personal trip assistant or simply as a mere proxy of the client decisions.

3.2 Single Vehicle Side

Each real vehicle is represented by an agent couple, the Vehicle and the Schedule agents. They provide interoperability between the vehicle they represent and the transportation system to which they belong to. The Vehicle agent plays an interface role, providing the vehicle and its driver with a communication channel with the rest of the transportation system. Through it, the driver is able to communicate along the journey about any contingency that could arise. From the other side, the driver receives through the Vehicle agent any information regarding changes on the original planification such as new client to transport, client cancellations and relevant traffic conditions changes among others. The Schedule agent is in charge of managing the vehicle's route and processing any new request for client transportation.

The Vehicle agent is also responsible for monitoring and informing about the vehicle state and progress of the service along the day. In a complementary way, the Schedule agent is responsible for any adjustments needed on the vehicle's route or schedule of their trips, motivated by any change or eventuality.

Both agent couples, Vehicle – Schedule and Client – Trip-request, can be developed independently by each involved party. The agent architecture defines the base roles for these agents to implement together with providing a common platform for enabling the communication. The Service Ontology defines without ambiguity the terms and concepts required for the agent understanding. In addition, this common ontology provides the formalization of the interaction protocols required by agents to communicate. In this way, any of the above agents can be constructed externally by implementing the functionalities required for its roles following the semantics and interaction specifications provided.

3.3 Transportation Enterprise Side

The transportation service role is mainly carried out by the Planner agent acting as a front face to the clients. Besides it there is a whole set of service agents collaborating to give support to the different required functions, such as the matching of request to vehicles (Broker Agent), the geographical data access (Map Agent), the accountability of the transactions (Account Agent) and the service payment (Payment Agent) among others.

From them, the most critical ones from the planning and control point of view are the Broker and the Map agents. The Broker is the one in charge of carrying out the matching of transport requests with available vehicles. For that is able to manage service descriptions coming from both sides, understand their semantics and perform the search.

The Map agent represents the geographic area giving information about localization of addresses and stops, street names and distances between localizations among others. For this purpose, the Map can perfectly act as a wrapper of a Geographical Information System (GIS). An important feature is the possibility of complement the information provided by the GIS with current traffic data. This can be done by a Traffic agent that is connected to different traffic information services and is able to inform about relevant events occurring in the streets and highways being covered. In this way, the system can consider those eventualities and re-plan the initial scheduling of vehicles to best adapt to the new situation.

Other complementary services can be "agentified" within the system. A service that can be put under this category is the collection and management of the information related to the fares, timetables, schedules and service characteristics of each of the involved vehicles. In this way, this information can be given to the interested users and organizations.

These supporting services can be externalized, that is, other third parties can interact with the enterprise in order to provide those services from the outside. In this sense an important thing to highlight is that as the enterprise's Service Ontology defines the valid interactions among agents and hence formalizes the way of providing any support service. Then, any party wishing to supply a service within the framework has to implement the respective agent adopting the specification given by the ontology. For example, a party that wants to offer the service of vehicle-request matching within the organization has to implement a Broker agent able of processing the specific query messages and of registering the available vehicles as defined by the ontology. Refer to (Cubillos et al, 2004) for further details on the ontology.

In this way, B2B relations are established among transport operators and support-service providers. For example, the geographical and traffic information services are used internally by the planning agents and the accountability services are required by the Planner to register the transactions that are carried out. In contrast, some of the services imply a direct request and benefit of the client. In these cases, B2C relations are created. For example, the information on traffic, timetables and fares provided to the clients goes under the B2C service category.

4. FLEET OPERATORS AND USER GROUPS INTEGRATION

Up to now have been identified the three main actors. In addition to them there are other parties associated to the problem that would be important to consider. These are the user associations, the active destinations and fleet providers or operators.

Each fleet operators needs an own planning and control system for working. As Figure 1 shows at the up-left, each transport operator's system can be modeled within our architecture in a recursive way. In other words, each operator can have his system conformed by agents for their vehicles monitoring, integrated planning and supporting services. All this sustained by a local ontology that provides common service concepts and interaction formalizations. In this way, the operator's agents are capable of interoperation with the virtual enterprise by using their local ontology for the internal communication, while using the common enterprise ontology for the external communication with the virtual enterprise or a third party.

An analogous situation happens with the integration of the different client associations and active destinations. As Figure 1 shows on the up-right, they can also be modeled following a similar model as the one used for the operators. Clients pertaining to an association or active destination are able to access the virtual transportation system by passing through their local systems. In this way, the preferential terms agreed with the association can be used by their members. This mechanism enforces the adaptation of the service offer to the different client demands. Again in this case, the association's system uses a local ontology used by their agents for the internal coordination and communication while the common enterprise ontology is used for the external interactions.

4.1 Wrapper Agents

Assuming the similar agent architecture for the different parties (operators, user associations and active destinations) enforces a straightforward integration of them within the virtual enterprise. However, this assumption is rather strict as many of them will have their own (and perhaps legacy) systems already working. In these cases, their integration through wrapper agents is the right move to follow.

Each party's system can be easily integrated into the common architecture by using agents for wrapping their functionalities and enabling the interoperation with our virtual enterprise model. In this way, each wrap agent plays the role of translating some functionality from the party's local system (with a particular way of working, processing and interact) to the common enterprise framework defined by its service ontology. From that point on, the way of interaction between the wrapper agents and the enterprise ones is similar to the previous case with local agent systems.

4.2 Hierarchical Interaction

The interaction of the Planner and Service agents across the different sides (Fleet Operators, User Associations, Transport enterprise) is ruled by the formalized interactions (Service Ontology) and follows a hierarchical/federated model.

In particular, the interaction between the fleet operator (or user associations / active destinations) agents and the virtual enterprise ones follows a one-to-one relation between agents of each side, that is, planner with planner, broker with broker and so on, in such a way to conform a hierarchical/federated structure. For example let's analyze the Planner agents' interaction. The enterprise Planner will receive a transportation request from a client and in order to answer it needs to check the possibilities available. Therefore, it will query all the Planners of the registered fleet operators, collecting the alternatives and prepare a proposal.

5. BASE IMPLEMENTATION

Up to now have been described a transportation framework and its underlying agent architecture. In this section is described the basic planning functionalities and the default implementation provided to the different agents involved in the model considering the single vehicle and user sides. Similar extensions can be made to the fleet operator, user associations and active destination sides.

The underlying planning problem is treated in a distributed way following a two-phased model. The former is an optimization phase, aimed to the identification of trip solutions that maximize the operator's utility, subject to the (client) request restrictions. This involves the Planner and Schedule agents. The latter is a negotiation phase that pursues an agreement between the transportation proposals and the client's interests. This is done by the Planner and the Trip-request agent.

5.1 Generic Planning Sequence

The dynamics of the generic planning sequence is shown at Figure 2: In step 1 (Schedule-me), for each transportation request from a Client a Trip-request agent asks the Planner to process it. The Planner processes the request (step 2) first by obtaining from the Broker the vehicles that match the required profile, and then (step 3) by making a call for trip-proposals to all the corresponding Schedule agents.

They send back their proposals and then the Planner (step 4) selects the most suitable alternatives among the received trip proposals by applying filtering policies and starts a negotiation process with the client (through its Trip-request agent). After arriving to agreement the Planner (step 5) tells the Schedule agent that won the proposal to add the trip to its actual schedule and tells the others their proposal rejection.

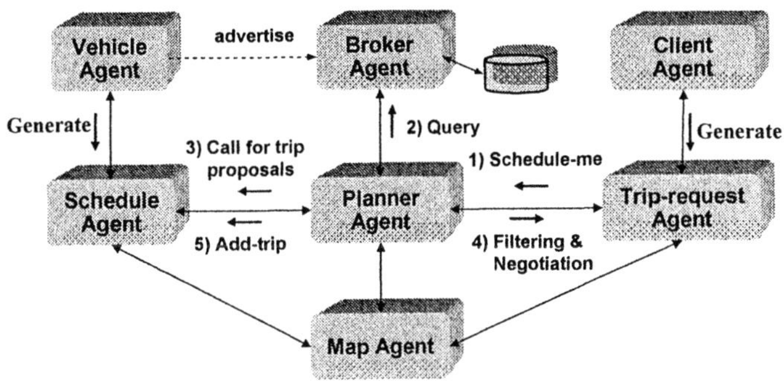

Figure 2 – The planning sequence

In the real world, clients can miss, cancel or modify the ride at last minute. The agents are able to deal with these situations and re-plan. As already mentioned, the route progress of each real vehicle is monitored by its Vehicle and Schedule agent. Upon differences in the planification (due to breakdowns, traffic jam, etc) the Schedule agent re-plans. In the case of having an infeasible trip request (mainly due to the time-window restrictions), it informs the Planner agent about the situation.

The Planner makes a call for trip-proposals to try reallocating the request in other available vehicle. In any case, the result is informed to the corresponding Trip-request agent, which depending on its degree of autonomy will process the alternatives and take a decision or will inform the client about the change. This change may imply a different vehicle processing the trip only or also a delay or an anticipation of the pickup and delivery times defined previously.

5.2 Tests

In order to check the correctness of the framework, a concrete system was built to provide a centralized scheme of planification. This centralized model was confronted with ADARTW (Jaw et al, 1986), a traditional centralized greedy insertion heuristic. Both systems minimize the number of used vehicles and were set with the same parameters.

The following operational decisions were adopted for both models: 1) the same utility function and scheduling algorithm were used for all the vehicles, 2) all the clients share the same utility function, 3) the available fleet is of 30 identical vehicles with capacity 20, 4) one depot is used for all the vehicles and 5) in all cases the effectiveness measures (utility variables) were weighted with value 1.

All the tests considered the same geographical net and 20 demand scenarios with 50 trip requests each, distributed uniformly in a two-hour horizon. For each demand scenario 25 runs were done. The Table 1 shows that the mean values for the different effectiveness measures are similar on both cases. Therefore, our centralized planification model extended from the transport framework performs in a similar way to ADARTW system.

Table 1 – Centralized v/s ADARTW

	Serv. Users	Used. Veh	Cost	Wait Time [min]	Excess Time [min]	Bus Travel Time [min]	Slack Time [min]
Centralized							
Mean	50	27	1.687	23	9	1.655	72
Desv.Est	0	2	115	6	5	117	27
Min	47	21	1.412	6	0	1.383	20
Max	50	30	2.008	41	22	1.984	157
ADARTW							
Mean	50	27	1.688	23	9	1.585	72
Desv.Est	0	2	113	6	6	119	28
Min	48	20	1.394	4	0	1.280	19
Max	50	30	2.001	41	28	1.912	170

The main difference between both systems is in the processing time. ADARTW takes 1 second in processing the run with 50 requests, while our agent-based model takes 20 seconds running on 1 machine. This allows to have an idea of the overhead introduced by two things: 1) the agent platform (Jade), and 2) the agent architecture.

A following step is to implement different planification models and provide a test bed for distributed execution.

6. CONCLUSIONS

The present work has described a transportation architecture that has been developed thinking in the independent implementation (externalization) of all the roles and functionalities involved, by providing a common framework that formalizes and enables the relations between the different parties. It is able to broaden along the whole transportation chain and is flexible enough to incorporate new actors.

In this way a true virtual transportation agency is provided, capable of putting together different groups and types of transport providers, end users and support-service providers interested in using (or being part of) an integrated gateway for flexible people mobility.

7. REFERENCES

1. Bellifemine, F. et al.. "JADE - A FIPA Compliant Agent Framework". CSELT Internal Technical Report, 1999. Available at: http://jade.cselt.it/
2. Cubillos, C.; Guidi-Polanco, F.; Demartini, C. "Multi-Agent Infrastructure for Distributed Planning of Demand-Responsive Passenger Transportation Service". IEEE Int. Conf. on SMC, 2004, pp. 2013 – 2017.
3. Jaw, J.; Odoni, A.R.; Psaraftis H.N.; Wilson, N.H.M. "A Heuristic Algorithm for the Multi-Vehicle Advance-Request Dial-a-Ride Problem with Time Windows". Transportation Research B, Vol. 20B, No. 3, 1986, pp. 243-257.
4. Zhang Jin; Wang Hui; Li Ping; "Towards the applications of multi-agent techniques in intelligent transportation systems". Proc. IEEE Int. Conf. on ITS, Oct. 2003, Vol. 2, pp. 1750 – 1754.

61

THE GLOBAL AUTOMATION PLATFORM: AN AGENT-BASED FRAMEWORK FOR VIRTUAL ORGANIZATIONS

Franco Guidi-Polanco[1]
Claudio Cubillos[2]
Giuseppe Menga[2]
[1]*Pontificia Universidad Católica de Valparaíso, Chile*
franco.guidi@ucv.cl
[2]*Politecnico di Torino, Italy*
{claudio.cubillos, menga}@polito.it

This work presents our agent-based architecture for the development of Global Automation Systems. These systems consist of software applications that manage all the processes in a network of enterprises, in distributed, decentralized and autonomous way.

1. INTRODUCTION

Global automation is a new concept that transfers and extends classical process control and factory automation ideas to a large scale distributed environment. It exploits the current trends of information and telecommunication technology, especially embedding on the Internet data acquisition and control devices.

Global automation systems consist of software tools and applications that process, handle, and control the business, logistic, production (and today the surrounding environment) activities of a network of enterprises. They can be considered as the nerve system of a world-wide organization. They facilitate the exchange of information among customer offices, business units, departments, production cells, and distribution centers. They allow a variety of functionalities to be automated, that otherwise would require the direct intervention of human operators. Global automation systems are built on complex concurrent, distributed, and autonomous modules that integrate functionalities drawn from a variety of application areas (e.g., telecommunication, databases, virtual reality, artificial intelligence).

The need for an architectural reference model to implement global automation systems has been envisioned. Such model has been identified as an agent-based framework that offers a communication infrastructure and a uniform system architecture. We call this infrastructure the "Global Automation Platform" (GAP). The GAP is a framework sufficiently flexible to be used at multiple levels in a global automation system, ranging from the monitoring and control system for a single production cell (the virtual SCADA), to the integration of the supply chain of a multi-national corporation (the virtual factory), up to the construction of a global organization.

Concretely, this work proposes an agent-based framework for the development of global automation systems. Such a framework is responsible to support three aspects of these systems: (1) the definition of base elements from which global automation components will be extended; (2) the support for the interactions among participants; and (3) the basic services required in global automation systems.

2. BACKGROUND: THE GLOBAL AUTOMATION

In the era of Computer Integrated Manufacturing (CIM), an automation system was conceived as a strong and rigid hierarchy of control layers: Facility, Shop, Cell, Workstation and Equipment. According to the USA-NBS CIM reference model (Maclean et al., 1983), each layer is populated with a set of control modules (the device controller, the workcell controller, the cell controller, etc.) with precise responsibilities. In particular, a higher layer control module coordinates the control modules below it. The flexibility of such systems is limited to the possibility of reconfiguring the production process off-line by re-programming each control module. A local area network or a hard-wired field-bus represents the communication medium between the different factories' sub-systems. The inter-factory communication is usually handled via telephone, fax, or e-mail. An example of this old style architecture is described in our past research (Brugali et al., 1999).

In the era of Internet, global automation systems are conceived as flat interconnections of autonomous and decentralized decision making/control modules dominated by the two concepts of "heterarchy" and "proactivity": the former means that no hierarchy in decision making is enforced, the latter that each partner takes the initiative to reach a decision (e.g. planning production) and the global behavior of the system is an "emerging behavior" (Bemelman et al., 1999). Control modules have decision-making capabilities and coordinate their activities by exchanging data and events according to a peer architectural model and common protocols.

Thus, creating global automation systems requires the adoption of an organizational model that recognizes autonomous and cooperating entities as system's elementary building blocks. These entities have the ability to determine their actions and to develop cooperating societies.

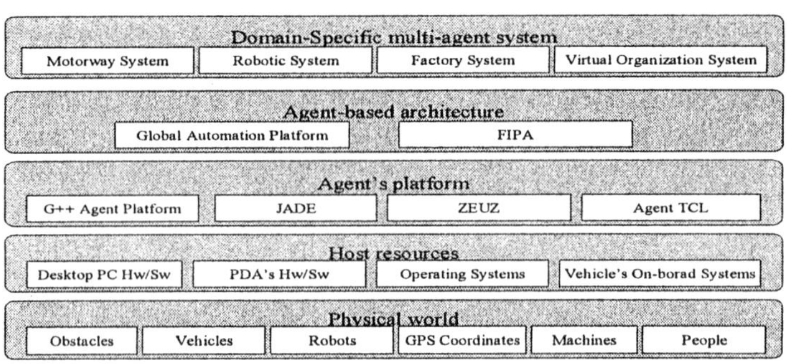

Fig. 1. The Abstract Architecture for MAS.

3. THE ABSTRACT MODEL FOR AGENT-BASED ORGANIZATIONS

In general terms we envision the use of agents as a way of representing software architectures. This vision is constructed as the abstract model depicted in Figure 1. The abstract model is composed by the following layers:

- *Physical world*: it is composed by things pertaining or observed in the real world (e.g. objects in mobile robot's environment, wired or wireless communication networks, computational systems, humans, traffic lights, etc.), and concepts conventionally adopted for its characterization (e.g. geographical coordinates obtained from a GPS service, temperatures, data transmission latency, water flows measurements, etc.). The physical world is conceptualized as a multidimensional space surrounding agents accomplishing physical-related tasks.
- *Host resources*: represent a computing system in terms of CPU, runtime memory, data storage, data communication, operating system, and peripheral devices (e.g. thermometers, valves, engines, etc.) where the agent software is executed. The hosts can be seen from two perspectives: (1) internally, they offer the runtime environment for the agent platform, so hosts must satisfy a set of minimum hardware/software requirements imposed by the platform's software (or in an opposite point of view, the agent platforms must be designed to be executed in specific categories of devices); and (2) externally, the host resources offer the "physical body" for agents, that is, the means for agents to perceive the physical world, and/or to influence it with their actions. Examples of common environments are desktop computers, vehicles' on-board units, PDAs, and mobile robots.
- *Agent platform*: corresponds to the software that offers the base classes to build agents, and to virtualize environment-dependent services (e.g. interfaces to peripheral devices, motors, databases, network communication, etc.). It also offers the execution environment that controls the entire agent's life-cycle, and regulates its interactions with other agents, and other resources. As it was stated above, agent platforms must be designed for their execution in devices with different hardware (e.g. PDAs, mobile phones, desktop computers) and software capabilities (in terms of operating systems and programming languages). Examples of agent platforms are JADE (Bellifemine et al., 1999), and AgentSheets (AgentSheets, 2004) (a comprehensive list of agent platforms can be found in (AgentLink, 2004)).
- *Agent-based architecture*: represent a reusable architecture to support the development of different kind of agent-based systems. The architecture specifies a set of common services (e.g. directory facilitator, yellow pages, etc.), and a framework of communication/content languages (e.g. ACL (Genesereth and Ketchpel, 1994), KQML (Finin et al., 1993), etc.) and interaction protocols (e.g. FIPA Request Interaction Protocol (FIPA, 2002), the Contract Net protocol (FIPA, 2002b), etc.), necessary to achieve interoperability among agents. The services offered by the architecture can be implemented by service agents (such as a yellow-pages agent), or as environment-dependent service (e.g access to

some kind of physical device). An example of a particular agent-based architecture is specified by FIPA standards (FIPA, 2002c), which was conceived to obtain interoperability between different and generic agent systems.
- *Domain-specific multi agent system (DSMAS)*: corresponds to a concrete instance of a multi-agent system, where domain-dependent agents are designed to represent real-world services and systems, and interactions among them are well defined. In most cases agents at this level are abstractions of real entities pertaining to the application domain. DSMAS architectures can be reused within the scope of the context they were created for. A reusable DSMAS architecture constitutes an agent-based framework for the development of systems within its domain. DSMAS architectures are supported by the services offered by the agent-based architecture.

The model proposed above has three main characteristics:

- *Decouples design responsibilities*: the model presents the different aspects related to a multi-agent architecture in a separated way. Therefore, the design responsibilities can be clearly identified and assigned to different development projects or teams.
- *Promotes high cohesion within each layer*: components within each layer are closely related from the functional and communicational point of view, in such a way that their interactions are optimized.
- *Clearly emphasizes the environment*: traditional agent architectures consider the environment implicitly, in most cases just as a mere communication supplier. In our model, the environment is distinguished as a physical and a virtual one.

4. AGENT TECHNOLOGIES IN GLOBAL AUTOMATION

The adoption of agent systems as enabling technologies for the development of distributed organizations' infrastructures is currently matter of research. In particular, the agent technology seems not only to satisfy the demand for high flexibility requested by enterprise-wide integration (Rimassa, 2004), but also to provide approaches to support autonomous self-configuration and self-adaptability of their activities in their operational environment (Gou et al., 2003), (Niessen, 2001).

Historically, the research behind agent systems addressed the agent microarchitecture, that is, the internal structure that describes the underlying intelligence model. This was especially motivated by trends coming from distributed artificial intelligence (DAI). More recent platform implementations are aware to accomplish the FIPA standard, which is focused in achieving interoperability among heterogeneous agent systems. Now that agent internals and interoperability challenges have been achieved, the next step is to provide a more enhanced environment, able to empower the relationships not only among agents, but also between agents and their physical environment.

In this context, the GAP corresponds to a high-level reusable software infrastructure designed to implement Global Automation Systems. It is an agent-based framework, which is made up of a communication infrastructure, logically structured as an information bus, which is embedded in a uniform system architecture. Agent properties that we have specially considered while developing the GAP were autonomy, social ability, reactivity, pro-activity and mobility

4.1 The physical environment

The GAP provides the agent-based architecture to interface the physical environment (*host resources* and *physical world* in the model of Section 3) with the domain-specific agents in a distributed system. The components of the physical environment depend directly on the domain that the system pertains to.

4.2 The G++ Agent Platform

Several agent platforms are currently offered for the development of multiagent systems. However, to build the GAP we have developed our own agent platform, that we call the G++ Agent Platform (Guidi-Polanco et al., 2004). The G++ Agent platform is a Java framework for the development of agent-based systems, focusing in architectural aspects related to components distribution and communication. Our work was motivated by the need for creating and integrating autonomous systems through geographical scale cooperation networks. Under such a scenario, the possibility of leaving the agent with all the responsibility for its integration with the environment (and consequently other peers) implied the agent overload and the replication of a series of complex functionalities. Due to this, was noticed that existing platforms were not suitable to accomplish these requirements.

Inspired in communication models from telecommunication systems, the platform provides a strong and reliable communication infrastructure that supports wireless communication among agents hosted in physically mobile devices.

Another distinguishable feature of the G++ Agent Platform is the possibility to integrate within the system other non-agent systems (e.g. legacy applications) by using the provided API.

4.3 The Agent-Based Architecture

The Global Automation Platform (GAP) is the agent-based architecture which offers a collection of components and services specially intended for the development of global automation systems. Specifically it offers *communication standards* and a set of supporting *services*. The former defines the languages that will be used for exchange of information between entities participating in global automation systems. The latter, the set of services made available to support distributed integration and collaboration. Three services are offered at this level:

- *Messaging*: it provides persistence and reliability in direct messaging between senders and well-defined receivers.
- *Event distribution*: it implements the asynchronous publish/subscribe communication model.
- *Service brokering*: it supports dynamic reconfiguration of the relationships between service providers and consumers.
- *Gateways*: allows interactions through systems pertaining to different domains

5. CASE OF STUDY: A MOTORWAY CONTROL SYSTEM

Generally the motorway network of a country is split into a number of sub-networks under the responsibility of several motorway administrations (see Figure 2). Each administration is in charge for the management (technical and financial) of its domain, and it maintains a relationship with the other administrations and with the national bodies (Ministry of Transport, Firemen, Civil Protection, Police). The functions of each administration are at two levels: (1) *Low level*: toll collection, on-road data acquisition, and traffic control; and (2) *High level*: maintaining the network database, monitoring of the whole network information flow, planning the network load (high level traffic planning), supporting centralized network facilities (data base of traffic events related to network sections within their own responsibility, call center for traffic information), managing emergencies, maintaining relationships with the other administrations.

Traffic control is the activity of regulating access to the highway, and settings on-road signals in order to avoid traffic saturation and optimize transit times. Traffic control is achieved -at cell level- by regulating incoming traffic at the toll plazas. Inputs for the traffic control process are forecasts of this incoming flow and forecasts of the traffic conditions of neighbor cells. These forecasts make it possible to determine the optimal traffic flow (the one that actually should enter the motorway) that minimizes the global transit times. If the current incoming flow exceeds the computed prevision, traffic control will introduce a delay at toll plazas. Priority Schedulers of each cell can negotiate among these outcomes in order to distribute the access priorities given to different cell traffic controllers during the day, with the objective of achieving a globally optimum compromise.

Our model for traffic monitoring and control subdivides administrations into disjoint *motorway cells*. A motorway cell is an autonomous control module that performs low-level monitoring and control of local traffic and exchanges traffic status data and events with neighbor cells. The graph of motorway cells conforms to a cellular interconnection architecture that supports decentralized control. The short-term traffic control of the whole motorway network emerges as an intrinsic property

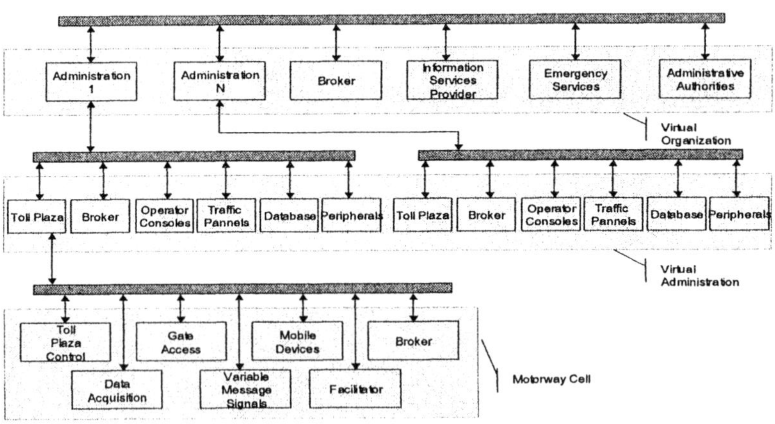

Fig. 2. The motorway system

of the cellular cooperative structure. In the following subsections, the traffic and control motorway system is described using the abstract model of Section 3.

5.1 *Physical environment* (level 1) and *host resources* (level 2)

A cell's *physical world* is mainly composed by:

- *Operative Toll-Plazas*: perform classical toll-plaza activities (e.g. collecting tolls, collection of data to transfer to the higher decisions level) including traffic access regulation at gates under the control of a Major Toll-Plaza.
- *Major Toll-Plaza*: extends the standard function of a toll-plaza with the responsibility of cell's traffic monitoring and control. It also performs traffic access regulation at their own access gates following its own traffic decisions.
- *Fixed Devices*: are the set of sensors, traffic signals and other traffic control facilities assigned to fixed places along the motorway.
- *Wireless Mobile Devices*: are sensors, signals, and other intelligent units mounted on users' and maintenance vehicles moving along the motorway.

In the motorway system, the *host resources* correspond to every kind of computing device available for the execution of agents. These devices can be fixed computing systems such as toll-plaza's desktop computers, or wireless mobile computers mounted on signals and vehicles.

5.2 The *agent platform* (level 3)

The base environment for the traffic monitoring system is made-up by the *G++ Agent platform* and the set of services defined for global automation systems (message and event distribution, and gateway agents).

5.3 The *GAP agents and services* (level 4)

The GAP services are used to achieve interoperability among different participants (internal and external to an organization). For example the *Brokering service* is responsible for maintaining the address of agents pertaining to each administration domain, in such a way that they could be automatically identifiable by other agents interested in interacting with them. The *Gateway service* enables agents to be reachable by other agents pertaining to different organizations. The *Messaging service* is used to support reliable communication mainly with wireless devices. The *Event service* is used by monitoring agents of toll-plazas to subscribe to relevant events occurred within their domain, in such a way to opportunely react in case of accident or traffic jams.

5.4 *Domain agents* (level 5)

The traffic monitoring system is made up of two main components that are implemented by specializing the GAP framework agents: the General Administration Agent (GA-Agent) and the Motorway Cell Agent (MC-Agent).

- *GA-Agent*: it performs high-level monitoring and control of motorway traffic, and is also responsible for dealing with special events (e.g. emergencies). It accesses a database that stores information about high-level daily traffic measurements, reported events and toll data, which is the result of interactions either with MC-Agents within the administration, or external organizations.
- *MC-Agent*: is an element of a cellular decentralized distributed control system. The MC-Agent resides in the major toll plaza of the respective cell. It

encapsulates its own forecasting function and is able to control the traffic in its section. The cell has a state represented by *density*, *queue length* and *speed (flow)* as a time function of its internal traffic, which are the results of real-time processing of data collected by on-road sensors (e.g. vehicle detectors, video-cameras) and the forecasted incoming traffic. Each MC-Agent communicates directly with local devices, and through *Gateways* agents with its peers.

- *Device Wrappers:* they are agents that interface road traffic devices, such sensors or gates. In the case of gate access systems, they perform their operations under priority access cycles determined by the scheduling process.

6. CONCLUSION

A layered model for the implementation of global automation systems has been introduced. This model allows the development of agent-based software infrastructure in distributed domains, ranging from intra-factory applications to wide-range virtual enterprise organizations.

4. REFERENCES

1. AgentLink "Software Products for Multi-Agent Systems". Technical report. Europe's Network of Exccellence for Agent-Based Computing , 2004.
2. AgentSheets "Getting Started with AgentSheets". Available at http://agentsheets.com, last visited: January 20, 2004.
3. Bellifemine F., Poggi A., and Rimassa G. "JADE - A FIPA-Compleant Agent Framework". CSELT Internal Technical Report, 1999 .
4. Bemelman R., Tharumarajah A., Welgama P., and Wells A.J. "Application of a Behaviour-Based Scheduling Approach for Distributed Scheduling of an Assembly Shop". Production Planning and Control, vol. 10, n.3, 1999; 266-275.
5. Brugali D., Menga G., and Aarsten A. "A Case Study for Flexible Manufacturing System". Domain-Specific Application Frameworks (Fayad, Johnson, Schmidt eds.). John Wiley & Co. 1999 .
6. Edwards W.K. "Core Jini". Prentice-Hall, Inc. Upper Saddle River, New Jersey, 2001.
7. Finin T., McKay D., Fritzson R., and McEntire R. "KQML: An Information and Knowledge Exchange Protocol". In Proc. of the International Conference on Building and Sharing of Very Large-Scale Knowledge Bases (December 1993) .
8. FIPA. "FIPA Request Interaction Protocol Specification". Standard N. SC00026H .December 3, 2002.
9. FIPA. "FIPA Iterated Contract Net Interaction Protocol Specification". Standard N. SC00030H December 3, 2002.
10. Genesereth M.R., and Ketchpel S.P. "Software Agents". Communications of the ACM, vol. 37, n. 7 1994; 48-53.
11. Gou H., Biqing H., Liu W., Li X. "A Framework for Virtual Enterprise Operation Management". Computers in Industry 2003; 50: 333-52.
12. Guidi-Polanco F, Cubillos C, Menga G. The Agent-Based GAP: A Framework for Global Automation Systems, Proceedings of the Thirteenth IEEE Internatonal Workshops on Enabling Technologies: Infrastructure for Collaborative Enterprises (WET ICE), Modena (Italy), 2004; 3.
13. Maclean C et al. A Computer Architecture for Small-Batch Manufacturing. IEEE Spectrum, vol. 20, 1983;5 .
14. Niessen, M.E. Agent-based Supply Chain Integration. Information Technology and Management 2001; 2:289-312.
15. Rimassa G. Applying Agent Technology for Enterprise-Wide Solutions. Proceedings of the Thirteenth IEEE Internatonal Workshops on Enabling Technologies: Infrastructure for Collaborative Enterprises (WET ICE), Modena (Italy), 2004; 3.

PART 20

OTHER CASE STUDIES

62 BUILDING AN INTEGRATED PAN-EUROPEAN NEWS DISTRIBUTION NETWORK

Markus Schranz
Research & Development, pressetext Nachrichtenagentur GmbH, Vienna, Austria
schranz@pressetext.at

Schahram Dustdar
Vienna University of Technology, Institute of Information Systems
Distributed Systems Group, Vienna, Austria
dustdar@infosys.tuwien.ac.at

Christian Platzer
Vienna University of Technology, Institute of Information Systems
Distributed Systems Group, Vienna, Austria
cplatzer@infosys.tuwien.ac.at

News Agencies, like any other provider of electronic services, start to make heavy use of modern Internet technologies to provide fast, reliable and user-oriented services for their customers. To meet today's requirements it is becomes necessary to not only improve these services but also enhance the quality of the underlying methods to create, modify and distribute news articles all over the world. In this paper we discuss an approach to integrate services from already existing news agencies, and build a platform that enables international news agencies to take advantage of the extended functionality and information. Furthermore, we discuss the Web Service-based peer-to-peer network NEDINE, which will act as a case study for the presented approach.

1. INTRODUCTION

State-of-the-art Internet technologies are nowadays used to reach billions of people all around the world. Especially in the media-domain, these technologies pose a valuable tool to establish e-businesses which are able to keep pace with the emerging need for global information.

Electronic publishing has introduced a wide application range within the information management field, including the digitisation of ancient archives, the manageability and availability of enormous amounts of data or the visualization and provision of contents to the research world and the open public[Paepen, 2002; Schranz, 2004]. Based on research in areas like information retrieval, eLearing, security, privacy and especially the Semantic Web, information management systems take advantage of results and enrich their functionality to create modern solutions [Berners Lee, 1998].

Beside the large variety of scientific approaches, serious business impacts have been provided by Internet technologies. Distributed computing algorithms, the use of modern Internet protocols, and adequate content types have created complex and powerful web-based services [Kirda, 2001]. Utilizing such results, online information like news have been spread with a new class of speed and range all over the world, making news available to virtually everyone within a very short time.

Recent research work within the EU-funded project NEDINE[Nedine, 2004] focuses on the creation and the conception of an intelligent news publishing and distribution network consisting of existing local news agencies that use modern Internet and distributed computing technologies to build up a new kind of multinational and multilingual news distribution service. Research fields such as network communication [Yu, 2004; Birman, 2003] have been involved to create a scaleable peer-to-peer architecture, artificial intelligence is utilized to identify the most relevant related articles within the entire multinational network that can add to the quality of the business news currently in focus. The vector space model [Salton, 1983; Wong, 1985] has been utilized to provide easy access to related and most relevant business news articles within a multilingual and multinational context.

This paper is focused on the integration of modern Internet technologies such as Web Services [Haas, 2002] and peer to peer architectures [Birman, 2003] to create a scalable and high traffic information exchange and distribution network. A brief introduction to the investigated domain is presented in section 2. Requirements analysis and the systems architecture developed within the research work of this project is described in section 3. As proof of concept the prototype implementation and innovative features are presented in section 4. A short summary and an outlook to further developments, practical and commercial use concludes the article.

2. INTEGRATING EXISTING SERVICES TO A PAN-EUROPEAN NETWORK

Throughout an entire decade, modern Internet technologies have brought unmanageable amounts of information to the average user's fingertips. The information business has gone through dramatic changes in the last century and with the potential range of more than 800 million users [Internet World Stats, 2005] the management of mass information dissemination has become a challenging social and economical task.

The application domain we are focusing on has built a business on top of the technological features and basic services available on the Internet: Several PR-companies and news agencies in Europe have utilized modern synchronous and asynchronous Internet technologies such as web-based information access frontends for business news archives or email-based mass news distribution or content provision for next generation user devices. A media industry has emerged that uses complex and technologically challenging Internet services to create, aggregate, exchange, publish and distribute current business news.

European business today is highly segmented and widely unrecognised beyond national borders. Business news mostly bear national relevance but hold the potential to spread cooperation opportunities and business changes towards an economically and socially integrated Europe.

The discussed project is initiated to build a network to integrate multiple European national information sources consisting of participating news agencies, PR agencies and independent journalists into an international information service for news professionals and decision makers. Existing services are based on modern

Internet technologies like Web application servers holding the business logic in the services middleware [Cvitkovich, 2005] and maintaining a local network of content providing editors and commercial customers as well as thousands of subscribers and readers. Each business news service provides a set of features to these specific user groups (see table 1) that need to be normalized and shared within the integrated network of media partners.

Table 1. User groups and services within the application domain.

Users	**Services**	**Interface Technology**	**Scale**
Journalists and opinion leaders	Free business news	Access via modern web archives, XML-based mobile devices and standard electronic mail	Hundreds of thousands
Editors	Business news creation and aggregation	Modern web forms and interactive web content management systems	hundreds
Distribution customers	Business news dissemination	Customer-oriented web content management interfaces	thousands
News agencies	Business news exchange, aggregation and dissemination	XML-based application interfaces, Web Services	dozens

In several European countries Internet-based businesses following this model have emerged recently. Technologically, the implemented services lack homogenous implementation models, data structures and communication protocols. With modern Internet technologies like Web Services for the information exchange and peer to peer architectures to manage a scalable integration of several local service providers a meta-network has been designed within the scope of the project NEDINE.

The project aims at providing a network of news exchange and distribution that supports mutual awareness of relevant topics and information areas within all European countries. With its main focus on widespread availability and affordability for all partners it addresses news providers to transport national and international information to the relevant target group, regardless of the origin, nationality and financial capability of the information provider.

The network discussed within this paper is targeting at a multinational and multilingual integration of such business cases, thus allowing the news agencies of different European countries to share their contents and exchange their business news towards an integrated network for news aggregation, creation and dissemination. Aside from the obvious business benefits of such a service integration, there are necessary steps to be taken to technically and organizationally bring the services and the systems of the existing news agencies to an integrated network. Beyond this, the project consortium is currently developing a demonstrator and initial business service that shall attract additional agency partners throughout Europe to join the network in order to have access to relevant business news at an international level and to offer a distribution and dissemination interface for their customers that provide news to the network.

3. SYSTEM ANALYSIS AND DESIGN

Internet technologies in the area of business news distribution involves technical features to manage scalability and performance in mass information provision (millions of page impressions per month) and mass distribution (millions of electronic mails sent per day). Since scalability is managed by integrating local strength into a powerful network, modern networking features and capabilities are within the focus of the technical architecture.

The goal is to set up a sophisticated news platform and a high performing distribution network based on convenient digital news exchange technologies, not only targeted at newsrooms but aimed at reaching as many individual business leaders and decision makers as possible directly and personalized at their desktop. Experiences from local providers give figures of hundreds of thousands of electronic mails per day and about the same amount of visits to the online business news archives (Web presentations).

Besides the challenging distribution scale, the network shall also integrate independent journalism work and company-oriented business news to form a comprehensive international information service for business leaders. Basic online content management software shall be extended with features for multilinguality, XML-conforming standard formats and personalized distribution. Current distribution technologies have been extended to reach information professionals at multiple end user devices in most current formats. NEDINE has been preparing for different submission channels by using standardized data formats like XML news applications (NewsML[IPTC, 2003], NITF[IPTC, 2000]).

3.1. Requirements Analysis

In order to build a pan-European network of business news brokers, we have been concentrating on common features and identified technological concepts shared by the participating news agencies within the NEDINE project consortium. The agencies have developed a strong national news network and have been recently developing digital electronic platforms to manage the news provided by own staff or integrated from remote resources. The subscribed content customers utilize their business connection to the agencies to be able to retrieve contents from the digital platforms.

The news agencies manage their content platforms by providing news of different areas of interest via typical Internet protocols and interfaces. All partners utilize Web servers as part of their service, so the integration could be started from this point. External resources like national and international content providers are used by the agencies to enrich the contents for the national platforms.

The integration work was started in the requirements analysis by identifying and describing the existing platforms and services in order to come up with a feasibly information exchange interface and an integrated network service. As a result we have identified the existing services worth being maintained and integrated into an international network of strong local partners.

The integrated news distribution network includes several services that originate from different sources: some are provided by the existing local services and others are provided by the integrated network capabilities and features. An important precondition to facilitate both technical feasibility and business initialisation was to not reinvent existing solutions. In order to fulfil the multilingual and multinational requirements of the integrated news distribution network, existing solutions needed to be adapted and new software had to be designed and implemented. In order to keep costs manageable and the network attractive for future partners to join, the consortium followed the approach to request as few adaptations to existing services as possible and as much adaptations as necessary.

The requirements focused at the features of the existing services and the necessities of the integrated multinational network. Table 2 briefly shows an overview on the tasks already managed in existing systems and those that have been designed for the integrated network.

Table 2. Requirements analysis – Services locally and in the integrated network

Local system services	**Data Design and Processing**
News creation and management	Handled in relational database schemata, manipulated by web-based content management engines
News aggregation	Aggregation of third party information (b2b news exchange); Upload of business news by customers; Handled by local protocols, web-based applications
News distribution	Handled by email services to individually managed profiles of readers and subscribers
News presentation	XML-based, mainly web-oriented interfaces to provide free access to business news via Web browsers
Integrated network services	
Multinational distribution	Aggregate business news from other partners and use local distribution mechanisms
International enrichment	Provide most relevant semantically related business news for each article; focus on local strength and specific enrichments per partner
Multilingual news distribution	Provide business news for all subscribers and opinion leaders in targeted business languages
Multinational and multilingual news service	Offering multilingual and international business news tailored to the individual needs of the subscriber for asynchronous or synchronous media access

Technologically, the legacy applications at the existing systems provide only a subset of the required functionality of the designed multinational and multilingual news distribution service and therefore need to be extended with the following unified features: a unified access to local articles, the standardized distribution of foreign articles and a unified presentation of network articles.

3.1.1 Unified Access to own articles

The integration design requires a unified interface to the existing system in order to access a single business news article dedicated to dissemination via the NEDINE network. The defined requirements include (1) the definition/existence of a unique ID of such articles, (2) a URL to retrieve an entire article for NEDINE activities (enrichment, distribution), (3) a unique standardized format for the article content and meta information (XML NewsML resp. NITF).

3.1.2 Standardized distribution of foreign articles

Each integrated network partner is obliged to offer a distribution service to send all information that is sent to the partner on a distribution request by NEDINE to all interested local subscribers and present the information on the local archive (website or other electronic publishing services). The defined requirements include (1) the interface partners are obliged to accept electronic data from other network partners in order to integrate it with his local distribution service. The interface is based on SOAP and defined in WSDL[W3C, 2001], (2) the data format accepted by existing services is defined to be NewsML resp. NITF; (3) a common branding of NEDINE articles is designed

3.1.3 Unified presentation of network articles

Multinational and multilingual aspects of the integrated network require additional features from local services in presenting contents to their subscribers and readers: (1) multinational semantic enrichment: the local partner needs to present the automatically created links to related news on its presentation platform by adequate visualisation; (2) local articles need to be provided at foreign news archives. Whenever a subscribers requests one of the related news from the above mentioned enrichment, the article needs to be provided at the site of the requestor, independent of the site of the originator; (3) the interface partners are obliged to accept electronic data from in order to integrate it with his local distribution service is based on SOAP and defined in WSDL.

3.1.4 Specific multinational and multilingual network features

The integration of multiple local services to a news distribution network involves administrative features that create a integrated service that offers more than just the sum of the individual partner's products. To integrate common services, the system has been designed to be able to (1) register all potentially reached subscribers (in terms of language, topics of interest and quantities) within the local service to a logically centralized component of the NEDINE network; (2) present the range of all reachable subscribers with a single article submission, according to the customer-selected topic areas and distribution languages; (3) offer Multilanguage translation of relevant business news through the local competences of the participating network partners in order to optimally serve the customer.

3.2 Architectural details

The requirements analysis has shown the need for a scaleable integration of exiting systems with little intervention and adaptation to the heterogeneous software components. The final decision taken in the project is based on a peer to peer network which is a unique way to create a network for news exchange between European news agencies. Properly developed state machines and interaction models define the entry point for the implementation that was started to create a first prototype. New technologies like NewsML, Web Services via SOAP or XML in general, have been used to create this decentralized system and connect it to all participants.

With the implementation of the methods described briefly in the requirements analysis, we have established a reliable network which is easy to use and easy to integrate into the target systems. The core architectural concepts handle data management, the publishing interface (main focus on web technologies using modern web application servers) and the interface connections. The interfaces between the communicating peers and the interfaces between a peer and an existing local system are defined in detail by Web Service descriptions. The WSDL details are out of scope of this paper. Every news agency only sees the SOAP interface of the peer that is assigned to it as shown in Figure 1. Therefore, NEDINE functions as a black box environment for them.

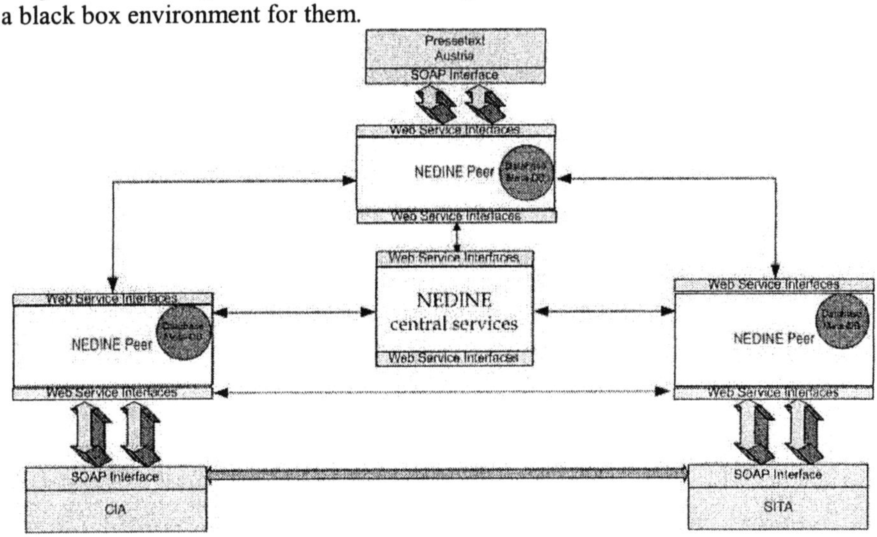

Figure 1: NEDINE P2P architecture – existing agencies and peer components

Existing services use modern web services to retrieve remote business news information to be published by Internet technologies for the local service and/or distributed business news via local channels and the network for remote distribution. Figure 1 shows the existing service as a circle and the newly introduced peer component as an attachment.

The peer to peer concept was chosen since technically all current and future network partners can be equipped with the same software. The network communication can be handled within the peer logic, only the interface between the peer and the existing service needs to be implemented by the joining partner.

All activities within the multinational and multilingual network are triggered by the actions of one of the participating partners, which are represented in the architecture as an existing agency. The communication types within the system are structured in service registration, information upload, news distribution, and news enrichment calls.

3.3 Use Cases

Based on the requirements, the technical architecture and the communication types the created NEDINE network architecture can be explained in different use cases and possible scenarios during service utilization. To demonstrate Web services and peer to peer communication in action we chose a specific scenario on delivering a business news item multinationally in multiple languages.
The originating network partner (in Figure 2 named CIA) sends several messages to its peer, one per language (Czech and English, in this specific case), each with a request for enrichment containing an enrichment flag with a non-existing country and the article in the corresponding language.

The answer to this message will contain a set of articles, those related to the one in the message both locally and in the countries supporting the language of the article, in the same language. That means, after several enrichment processes for each language and each country, the result dataset has to be merged to one final result set.

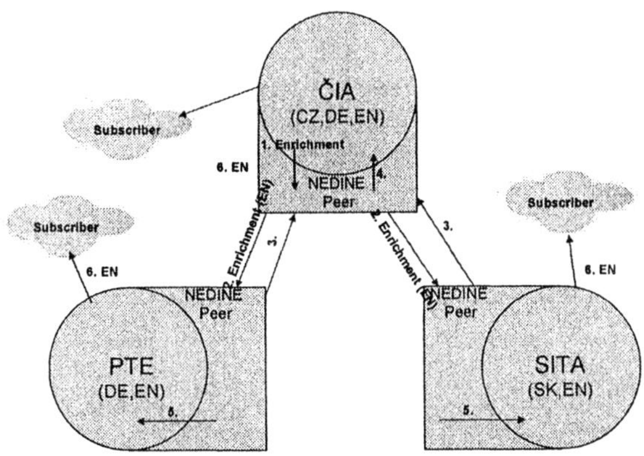

Figure 2: Scenario multilingual and multinational news distribution

The originating network partner sends a message to its peer with a push request containing a push set with all the articles in the different languages and a push flag with the same contents as before (Lang). The answer to this message indicates whether the article has been effectively pushed into the countries supporting at least one language of the article (but in all the languages supported that match with the languages of the article).

The receiving network partners (in the graphic PTE and SITA) send a message to their peer with a polling request and receive pairs of an article (the article in the initial push request, in the use case) and a set of articles, those related to the other article in the pair either locally or in the originating country (in the use case, CZ), in one language. Note that intermixing related articles of different languages is not desired by the news agencies, because of usability reasons.

4. SEMANTIC ENRICHMENT OF BUSINESS CONTENTS

Business news reach a specific audience: researchers that observe markets for specific branches or to analyze modern trends as well as competitors and commercial organizations observing tendencies to optimise their business. Publishers hold the power to bias the market by filtering or targeting the business news towards their own needs. With sophisticated methods of the area of artificial intelligence, automatic content relation management has been applied to the discussed business news publishing and distribution service in order to provide a fair and informative enhancement to existing solutions. The most relevant semantically related business news applied to the current news item in focus are retrieved and provided via the network service.

For this purpose the practical prototype as a proof of concept for the technical architecture and the semantic coupling of contents uses a search mechanism common in modern information retrieval systems: the Vector Space Model [Wong, 1985]. This approach is mainly used for search engines, based on natural language. Google for example utilizes this method to search their repository of Web pages. The underlying concept is quite simple. Any document is split up in keywords. Each of these keywords constitutes a dimension in a n-dimensional vector space. Therefore a document can be seen as a vector within this "term space". The position of this vector to other vectors within the same vector space describes their similarity to each other. The mathematical method to evaluate how similar two documents are to each other varies. A simple method is to calculate a cosine value for them and express the result as a percentage rating. This method produces very good results for natural language but it is not limited to this field alone.

Virtually any document collection can be mapped to a vector space to create an efficient search environment. In the case of business news publishing and distribution, specific weighting can be applied according to the data formats used within the information network. It is possible to apply phonetic algorithms to methods name. As a result, methods with an equal "sound" produce a high relevance rating. Furthermore, keywords like the business news category or the document title are used to categorize news items according to the assumed behaviour.

Since the Vector Space Model creates high ranking results whenever more terms in the observed article set match, the model provides a neutral and automatically created semantic neighbourhood to the article in focus. Especially in business the most relevant related articles are of high value to the subscribers, since they often want to have a comprehensive overview of a specific market niche or a business area identified or addressed by a single article.

5. SUMMARY AND FUTURE WORK

What we presented in this paper, is a business-oriented network to publish and distribute news over a peer-to-peer network. The Web Service-based architecture guarantees a high interoperability-level with minimum of necessary changes to legacy systems and on the other hand a future-proof and easy method to expand the network to numerous participants when needed. Internet technologies and AI-methods for information retrieval have been investigated and the most feasible approaches have been shown to prove the power of modern research results and to use them to build a successful multilingual and multinational business news platform in Europe.

Apart from the technological challenge, the industrial and commercial sector is an ample motivator, as the described project is funded by the European Commission as an eContent project with strong market orientation. One of the goals is, to apply modern technologies in successful business environments.

Supported by the research experience from project partners, the creation of the final service architecture and interaction model was possible. The result is more than just a junction of networks and services. It is an aggregation of independent journalists who can present national relevant articles and at the same time, internationally operating companies can use the network to present their information in both, national and international context. The AI technologies used to create the connections between the published articles enrich the content and therefore provide an additional feature for every single participant.

For the future, the existing prototypes will be integrated to a stable network to create an affordable solution for all interested partners in all participating countries. On the business side, the NEDINE project will create a valuable service for news distribution which opens up new markets of existing news providers.

ACKNOWLEDGEMENTS

This work was partially funded by the EU eContent project NEDINE (News Distribution Network, EDC-22225).

REFERENCES

1. Birman P., K. IEEE Internet Computing: Peer To Peer - The League of SuperNets. IEEE Distributed Systems Online 4(10): (2003).
2. Berners-Lee, T. Semantic Web Road map, 1998, http://www.w3.org/DesignIssues/Semantic.html
3. Cvitkovich, A. & Schranz, M. (2005) Applied Middleware: Object-Oriented Content Management Components with Mason, IADIS International Conference on Applied Computing 2005, Algarve, Portugal, Feb 22-25, 2005.
4. Haas H. World Wide Web Consortium - Web Services, http://www.w3.org/2002/ws/.
5. Internet World Stats – Usage and Population Statistics (2005), http://www.internetworldstats.com/
6. Kirda, E. et.al. Experiences in Engineering Flexible Web Services, in IEEE Multimedia, V8(1), January 2001.
7. NEDINE – Intelligent News Distibution Network for multinational business news exchange and dissemination, EC eContent project EDC 22225, http://www.nedine.org/
8. NewsML, IPTC-NewsML Standard, http://www.newsml.org, 2003.
9. NITF, IPTC News Industry Text Format Standard, http://www.nitf.org/ or http://www.xmlnews.org/NITF, 2000.
10. Paepen, B. et.al. OmniPaper: Modern Approaches for an Intelligent European News Archive, Proceedings of the IADIS WWW/Internet2002 Conference, Lisbon, Portugal, November 13-15, 2002.
11. Schranz, M. & Paepen, B. Architecture design and application for an Intelligent Distributed News Archive, Proceedings of the ICCC 8th International Conference on Electronic Publishing – ELPUB2004, Brasilia, Brazil, June 23-26, 2004.
12. Salton, G. Introduction to Modern Information Retrieval, volume 1. McGraw-Hill, Inc., 1983.
13. Wong, W.Z. & Wong, P. and Patrick Wong. Generalized vector space model in information retrieval. ACM, 1985.
14. World Wide Web Consortium (W3C). Web Services Description Language (WSDL) 1.1, http://www.w3.org/TR/wsdl/, 2001.
15. Yu, S., Liu, J. & Le, J. Decentralized Web Service Organization Combining Semantic Web and Peer to Peer Computing. ECOWS 2004: 116-127.

63 SUCCESS AND FAILURE FACTORS OF COLLABORATIVE NETWORKS OF SME

Michel Pouly*, Francis Monnier**, Daniel Bertschi***
(*) MTO Research Network, Lausanne, e-mail: michel.pouly@epfl.ch
(**) President of Swiss Microtech Network, Corcelles, e-mail : f.monnier@ravine.ch
(***) Founding member of the USCO network, Préverenges, e-mail : info@dynatec.ch

The enterprises active in the industrial subcontracting branch are in a very competitive market and support large pressures on their prices and delivery schedules. The arrival on the market of suppliers from low-cost countries like Eastern Europe or the Far East increases the pressure and drives towards delocalization. One possible answer to these demanding challenges is to cooperate within collaborative networks. Even if this concept is now rather well known, few SME are actually involved in such alliances and their success rate after a couple of years seems low. This paper presents a study of the success and failure factors resulting from the analysis of two collaborative networks of SME in the Swiss subcontracting industry.

1. INTRODUCTION

Available estimates indicate that SME are the main generators of employment in Europe, representing 66% of all jobs. It is also estimated that industrial subcontractors represent roughly 20% of all industrial jobs (Liikanen, 2000). In 2000 and for fifteen EU member states only, 7 million jobs existed in the 277'000 subcontracting enterprises and the turnover of this industrial branch reached 350 billions Euros (Coué, 2000). These figures show the importance of the subcontracting industry for the European economy and employment level.

The enterprises active in this industrial branch are in a very competitive market and support large pressures on their prices and delivery schedules. The arrival on the market of suppliers from low-cost countries like Eastern Europe or the Far East increases the pressure and drives towards delocalization. The subcontractors in the developed countries must adapt themselves to this new environment if they want survive and have to:

- reduce their production costs
- shorten their delivery schedules and increase their flexibility
- provide complete solutions
- add new services like engineering of parts, logistics, etc.

One possible answer to these demanding challenges is to cooperate within collaborative networks. Even if this concept is now rather well known, few SME are actually involved in such alliances and their success rate after a couple of years seems low. This paper presents a study of the success and failure factors resulting from the analysis of two collaborative networks of SME in the Swiss subcontracting industry.

2. FIRST CASE STUDY : SWISS MICROTECH

Swiss Microtech (SMT) is a network of 8 independent SME active in the screw machining industry. They produce parts for the automotive, medical, space and telecommunication branches and export 90% of their production.

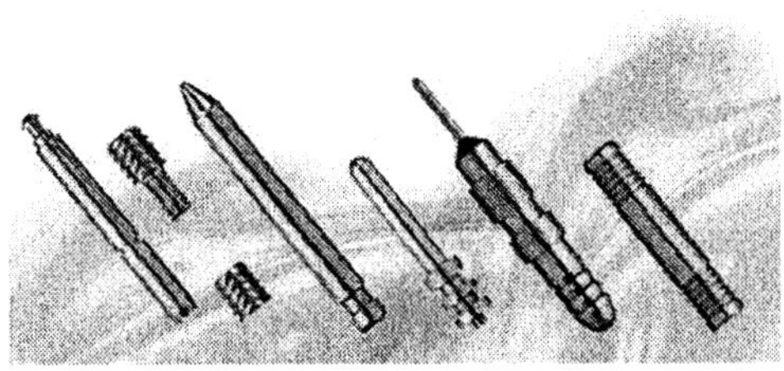

Figure 1 – Some screw-machined parts

2.1 Reasons for creation

A study conducted in the late 90's (Bigoni et. al, 1998) showed that these companies are too small to do business with large customers of the automotive, electronics and medical branches which drastically reduced the number of their suppliers to those able to provide a complete solution including engineering, machining, thermal treatments and sometimes assembly. Most SME of this branch are technically up-to-date, but their commercial services are lacking and their delivery schedules are too long and not reliable enough. As Switzerland is a high-cost country (like all industrialized nations), more and more orders are lost to competitors from the Far East or Eastern Europe. Following the recommendations of this study, a group of 10 enterprises belonging to the same professional association decided to join an applied research project aiming to define a competitor based strategic industrial network in order to improve their position on the market and to address their weaknesses. Swiss Microtech was created by the four founding members at the end of June 2001 as the result of this project (Pouly et al., 2002) and now counts eight members. The four new ones are SME bringing complementary activities like thermal treatments or plastic parts.

2.2 Members typology

The members of SMT have the following typology : four screw machining enterprises that are competitors in some market segments but also have a certain degree of complementarity, one specialist of thermal and metallic treatments, one specialist of square parts, one general machining SME and one specialist of plastic technical parts. They have between 15 and max. 80 employees and are all ISO 9000 certified.

2.3 Organization of the SMT network

The legal framework of Swiss Microtech is an association with lucrative goals and the chosen structure is based on *roles* (Katzy et. al, 1996, Schuh et. al, 1998). A role is a function that must be fulfilled by one or more persons. Four main roles have been defined (see figure 2) :

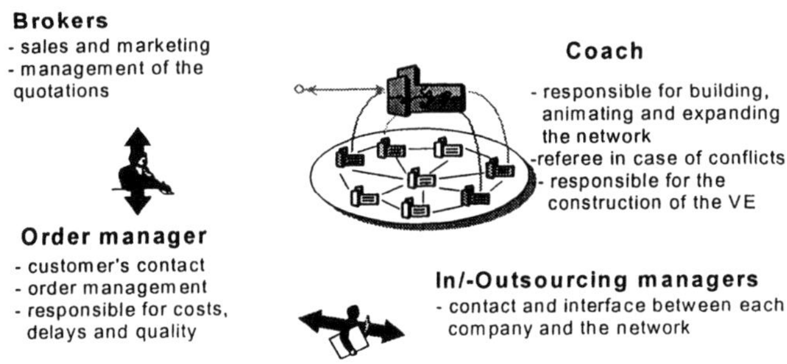

Figure 2 – Roles within the network

Like any association, a committee formed by a President and a Vice-President elected by the general assembly, which is the highest steering authority, governs Swiss Microtech. The President is assisted by the coach, an externally recognised expert of this particular branch of industry who looks after for the "housekeeping" activities as well as the network strategy (selection of new members for instance). A face-to-face network meeting is held each month.

In addition to the roles, *work groups* have been created to address particular problems in a smaller circle and propose solutions for the whole network. They are also very useful for integrating and implicating the network members and to have common activities at this level. The following work groups have been created so far:

- *"Common purchases"* was the first established group responsible for negotiating better prices with the suppliers of raw materials, commodities, consumable goods, machines and equipments etc. The network member having the biggest volume with a supplier negotiates new conditions for the whole network and recommends (or not) adding this supplier to the SMT preferential suppliers list.
- *"Marketing"* addresses the visibility of the network by preparing common SMT booths for the most important technical fairs and studying new ways of doing business like e-commerce. This group is also engaged with its academic partners in a new research project that will explore the possibility of creating and operating an international collaborative network with a network of Chinese screw machining companies.

- *"Energy"* is mainly dedicated to the purchase of electricity as the protectionist barriers are actually falling in Switzerland and the market is becoming a real jungle where the amount of consumed megawatts dictates the conditions. The "Energy" group will also offer services to reduce the consumption in collaboration with a specialized engineering and brokerage company.

2.4 Results and benefits

The principal results and benefits for the participating companies can be summarized as follows:

- A reduction of the production costs (~10%) has been reached through the common purchases and a better occupation of the production tool: some repetitive orders lost because of too high prices have been recovered
- A reduction of the investments has been reached by the "outsourcing" of some production processes within the network and the sharing of non critical production machines
- Better delivery schedules have been reached with the aggregated production means and this has allowed winning new orders
- A reduction of the dependence from large customers has also been reached by sharing orders within the network and freeing capacity for the other clients
- Few new products have been developed by two or more network members, this must be improved in the future
- Common booths at commercial fairs presenting the partners as members of a collaborative network were always a success. Their visibility compared with their competitors was considerably increased and the visiting clients confirmed their interest in an alliance
- The exchange of technical and commercial knowledge and experience within the network was and is still very active and each network member learns a lot from the others. In a sense, a collaborative network can be seen as a true learning organization.
- A certain sentiment of security has been developed within the network as each member thinks now that he could rely on the others in case of severe difficulties like an accident or an illness of the owner and general manager

3. SECOND CASE STUDY : USCO

USCO is a network of 11 independent complementary SME active as suppliers to the machine industry. They produce parts and services mainly to local machine manufacturers.

3.1 Reasons for creation

In 1995, a major local machine manufacturer announced its new purchasing strategy to its suppliers: they would have to reduce their prices by at least 10% and deliver complete subassemblies instead of parts otherwise they would be dropped from the list of agreed suppliers. This was an impossible challenge for most of these local SME if they remained alone and they could not afford to loose their biggest client. They also realized the danger of being too dependent on one large customer and also looked for diversification. Two SME took the initiative to talk with other companies to form a network able to address this new situation. The result of this initiative was the creation of USCO in 1995 with 10 complementary companies. The network now counts 11 members.

3.2 Members typology

The members of USCO have the following typology : one specialist of laser and water jet cutting, one specialist of sheet metal working, three general machining SME, one specialist of plastic technical parts, one specialist of plate handling, one plastic injection specialist, a mechanical, an electronics and a software engineering company. They have between 2 and max. 30 employees and are all ISO 9000 certified.

3.3 Organization of the USCO network

The legal framework of USCO is an independent limited liability company; each network member has one share and is member of the Board. One of the network members acts as CEO of this company, which has actually no employees. At the beginning, meetings with all members have been regularly organized but a Direction Board of four members has been created, as the participation of the members was deceptive.

3.4 Results and benefits

The principal results and benefits for the participating companies can be summarized as follows:

- The network was able to deliver the requested subassemblies and machine parts and the members could retain their most important customer
- New customers were found as USCO could deliver complete machines integrated into their final products
- A new measuring machine developed by an Engineering School has been industrialized and produced within the network
- A reduction of the dependence from a few large customers has also been reached by the development of new activities
- A certain sentiment of security has been developed within the network as each member now thinks that he could rely on the others in case of severe difficulties like an accident or a an illness of the owner and general manager.

4. SUCCESS AND FAILURE FACTORS

Participating in a collaborative network means investing time and money, both resources that are scarce for an SME. The motivation to continue to actively participate clearly depends on the balance reached between efforts and benefits. The analysis of these two networks shows that success and failure factors may be common or dependent on the type of network.

4.1 Common success and failure factors

- the network must be customer oriented and must bring more advantages to the customer than any individual company alone
- the network members must be carefully selected during the construction phase to create added value for all of them. If a small core of companies are always participating in new business, frustration will increase for others, they will stop investing time and money into the network and finally leave it
- the size of the network plays an important role: smaller networks may be more lively as all partners know each other and decisions can be taken together, larger networks have more impact and resources and can be more attractive for very big customers
- even if the creation of such an alliance is a bottom up process initiated by the industrial partners themselves, the presence of an independent coach like a research institute during the creation phase will speed up its birth
- the partners of such an alliance should have a similar size. Partners that are too small do not have the resources to really participate or invest and a gap between the "rich" and the "poor" will arise. They should also have a similar level of quality (for instance ISO certification) and IT integration
- the partners must consider the network as a company strategic goal; the commitment of the top management is essential
- the partners must share a common view of doing business with partners, customers and employees and be ready to give before receiving during a certain time as new business will not profit all companies immediately. A compensation scheme (a certain amount being levied on each new business to cover the network housekeeping costs) could be introduced
- transparency is a key success factor, opportunistic and selfish behaviour will kill the collaboration very quickly. As the virtual enterprises created for new orders or projects must group the companies that best fit the requirements, the network must work in a very transparent way. The consequence for the partners is that they will have to share their cost structures and load situation already during the quotation phase and this is really not obvious as many companies consider such figures as state secrets!
- as in any association, there is a need for "motors", i.e. charismatic partners who motivate and also keep the network alive and agree to take some responsibilities to act as President or member of the Board even if they are not rewarded for these extra tasks

- an acceptable balance between the time invested in the collaboration and the time needed by each partner for its own enterprise must be reached
- successes are very important to keep motivation high. Cost reductions are helpful at the beginning of a collaboration but value-added transactions and new business opportunities are necessary for the long term

4.2 Success and failure factors depending of the type of networks

Common activities for all members are easier to find for *networks that are active in the same industrial branch or are even competitors* like Swiss Microtech:

- common purchase of raw material, machines, equipments, consumables, commodities or services as well as the reduction of production costs may alone bring enough benefits to motivate a long term participation
- common marketing (participation in technical fairs) or sales activities such as using the agents or sales forces of one member to promote the whole group
- the exchange of experiences about market trends, technical subjects or even customer behaviour is also very profitable. Such a network becomes a real learning organization, which is considered as a key competitive advantage for the future (Flanagan et al., 2003)
- the level of fear is very high at the beginning of the collaboration, when some companies may be direct competitors: they think that sharing sensible data like price structures or even the names of their clients would have losing customers as a direct consequence. The future partners must commit themselves not to use the alliance to "steal" customers or make any non-loyal competition (underbidding for instance)
- trust is an absolute necessity when members could be competitors or also work for competitors, which is the case for members bringing complementary activities. With time, however, the network members will realize that really faithful customers are very rare as they also look everywhere for better conditions

New business opportunities are indispensable *for networks of complementary enterprises* wishing to develop new products or services as common activities are reduced:

- during the first years of activity, a few companies may really profit from the network as new business opportunities depend on the market and are not easily predictable. Frustration could arise for the less lucky members
- common purchases are less evident and fruitful, as the members do not necessarily need the same goods. Buying together commodities like office or IT equipment, energy or services are nevertheless possible
- common activities like training or participation in research projects should be found whenever possible to bind all members and keep motivation high
- the level of fear and the risks of conflicts are considerably lower

5. CONCLUSIONS

Collaborative networks can really help SME to survive as the trend towards further reduction of suppliers to those able to provide complete solutions will certainly continue (Guide européen des alliances, 1998). A deeper penetration into the value adding chain of the customers is a good way to become an important partner instead of remaining just a supplier among many others. Nevertheless, few collaborative networks of SME have been created and are still working after a couple of years. This could indicate that the collaboration spirit is not broadly shared among entrepreneurs who have a strong character and are probably rather individualistic. Even if rational facts like increase of market share, new business or cost reductions are key factors in evaluating the interest of a collaboration, the pleasure meeting others and sharing common activities, problems and interests should not be underestimated as the human factor is, and will remain, a central element in any enterprise.

If the economical benefits can be measured, further research is still needed to measure the "soft" factors like the exchange of experience and knowledge or the increased sentiment of security achieved by the collaboration.

6. ACKNOWLEDGMENTS

The authors would like to thank the enterprises members of the Swiss Microtech and USCO networks for their commitment and support as well as the Commission for Technology and Innovation of the Swiss Federal Government, which funded this work.

7. REFERENCES

1 Bigoni P, Glardon R, Pouly M, Décolletage dans l'arc jurassien, Rappport final CTI, 1998
2.Coué, D. Etude sur la sous-traitance européenne, MIDEST 2000
3.Flanagan K, Green L, Malik K, Miles I, Leitner K-H, Dachs B, Wagner P, Weber M, The Future of Manufacturing in Europe, 2015-2020, Industrial approaches, Final Report, March 2003
4.Flanagan K, Green L, Malik K, Miles I, Leitner K-H, Dachs B, Wagner P, Weber M, The Future of Manufacturing in Europe, 2015-2020, The challenge for sustanainability, Final Report, March 2003
5.Guide européen des alliances entre PME de la sous-traitance, Office des Publications des Communautés Européennes, Luxembourg, 1998
6.Katzy B, Schuh G, Millarg K, Die virtuelle Fabrik – Produzieren im Netwerk – neue Märkte erschliessen durch dynamische Netzwerke, in Technische Rundschau 43/1996, pp 30-34
7.Liikanen E, Commissioner for Enterprise and Information Society, Keynote speech at the RIOST Conference "European Enterprise Policy : inter-enterprise relations and Subcontracting", Milano, 2000
8. Pouly M, Glardon R, Huber C, Competitor based strategic networks of SME, in Knowledge and Technology Integration in production and Services, pp149-156, edited by V.Marik, L. Camarinha-Matos, H. Afsarmanesh, Kluwer Academic Publishers, 2002
9.Schuh G, Millarg K, Göransson A, Virtuelle Fabrik, neue Marktchancen durch dynamische Netwerke, Carl Huber Verlag, Munich, 1998

AUTHOR INDEX